PALESTINE: THE REALITY

Palestine: The Reality
Joseph Mary Nagle Jeffries
Originally published by Longmans, Green and Co.
London—Madras—Boston—Toronto, 1939

By the same author:
The Palestine Deception—Daily Mail, 1923
Front Everywhere (WW1 reminiscences)—Hutchinson & Co., 1935
London and Better (travel in Britain)—Hutchinson & Co., 1936

palestine
THE REALITY

THE INSIDE STORY OF THE BALFOUR DECLARATION 1917–1938

J.M.N. JEFFRIES

FOREWORD BY GHADA KARMI

An imprint of Interlink Publishing Group, Inc.
www.interlinkbooks.com

This edition first published in 2026 in the USA by

OLIVE BRANCH PRESS
An imprint of Interlink Publishing Group, Inc.
46 Crosby Street, Northampton, MA 01060
www.interlinkbooks.com

Originally published in 1939 by Longmans, Green and Co., London

Cover photograph courtesy of the Library of Congress [LC-DIG-matpc-15731]

The publisher and copyright owners wish to the thank the Jeffries family and their representative for their kind permission to reissue this edition.

ISBN 978-1-62371-558-8

Library of Congress Cataloging-in-Publication Data
Names: Jeffries, J. M. N. (Joseph Mary Nagle), 1880- author. | Karmi, Ghada, writer of foreword.
Title: Palestine : the reality : the inside story of the Balfour Declaration 1917-1983 / Joseph Mary Nagle Jeffries ; foreword by Ghada Karmi.
Description: Northampton, MA : Olive Branch Press, an imprint of Interlink Publishing Group, Inc., 2017. | "Published in 1939 by Longmans, Green and Co., London." | Includes bibliographical references and index.
Identifiers: LCCN 2017011031 | ISBN 9781566560245 | ISBN 9781623715588
Subjects: LCSH: Palestine--History--1917-1948. | Jewish-Arab relations--History--1917-1948. | Zionism. | Balfour Declaration.
Classification: LCC DS126 .J37 2017 | DDC 956.94/04--dc23
LC record available at https://lccn.loc.gov/2017011031

Printed and bound in China

Contents

To my colleagues at The Arab Centre.

★ 39 October 4–8, 1914

DOOM OVER ANTWERP

I Witness a Nation's Exodus

by J. M. N. Jeffries

'Daily Mail' Correspondent, 1914–1933

THE utterly harrowing scenes which accompany the flight of a civilian population have never been more poignantly described than by Mr. Jeffries, who was representing his paper in Antwerp during the city's last hours. In the words of a master journalist he tells of the final attacks of the Germans, of Mr. Winston Churchill's effort to save the city, and of the despairing trek to refuge of the remnants of a nation

EYE-WITNESS AT ANTWERP
When war broke out the younger correspondents of newspapers were sent to the countries where fighting was not expected to be heavy. Mr. Jeffries, then a new member of the staff of the "Daily Mail," arrived in Brussels on August 3, 1914, and went back with the retreating Belgian Army to Antwerp.

other, with the prospect of enemy shells landing at any moment in the midst of the disorder, and no one to direct, no one to disentangle the jumble which grew worse every minute.

No one, that is to say, till a man jumped from a car and, hoisting himself to vantage upon some unseen pedestal or other, began to cry out at the mob in Anglo-French, and to point with

danger of being outflanked and so of being cut off, owing to the weakening of resistance on its left. Resistance, indeed, was ebbing most definitely. As I crossed the fields again, I was aware of troops dropping back, dropping back. Uncertain of my own situation, and obliged to keep away from the roads which were no places to linger near, I skulked about close to the railway-line

THE PALESTINE DECEPTION.

THERE IS NO MANDATE.

From MR. J. M. N. JEFFRIES.

To the Editor of "The Daily Mail."

Sir,—A. W. L. in to-day's issue draws attention to a *reply* of Mr. Ormsby-Gore in the House of Commons upon Palestine.

I should like to draw attention to a more important reply of the Colonial Under-Secretary to a question put recently by Mr. Oswald Mosley. In his reply he confessed that the supposed Mandate for Palestine had only been approved by the League subject to an agreement being reached by the Powers concerned *about a certain clause*, and that on that clause agreement had not yet been reached.

Therefore, as one cannot too often repeat, in Palestine *there is no Mandate*. When will the public realise this cardinal fact and refuse to lose British honour, prestige, and money for the sake of what does not exist even?

Mr. Ormsby-Gore tried to cover everything up by saying that the above situation made no difference to the Government of Palestine because the president of the Council of the League of Nations meanwhile had asked the Palestine Government to carry on *in the spirit of the Mandate*. What absurdity! What value on earth has the pious aspiration of the president of the Council of the League of Nations as the charter of a Government?

How can the "Government" of Palestine hold elections in which it gives votes to Russian and Rumanian subjects, take illegitimate advances upon unfloated loans, and so on, all on no legal right, save a "carry on" from a Chilian gentleman in Geneva?

In a reply in the House of Lords (to Lord Sydenham, I think) the Duke of Devonshire gave an Order in Council as the legal authority for the holding of elections in Palestine. But is Palestine part of the British Empire, so that Orders in Council apply there? It is not British territory.

I am astonished that some of the legal members of the House of Commons do not push this question from point to point. It is no good asking one question; the Colonial Office must be driven into the corner by repeated questions.

March 23. J. M. N. JEFFRIES.

"From the *Daily Mail*, 24 March 1923."

How Britain 'flirted' in Palestine

Daily Express Staff Reporter

Documents showing how Britain made promises about Palestine and Syria to the Arabs, the Jews and the French, all mutually contradictory, are published today in "Palestine—the Reality," by J. M. N. Jeffries (Longmans, 25s.).

Mr. Jeffries has spent five years collecting material on the Palestine case, having become interested in it through first-hand experience He takes the Arab cause to heart without reservation.

He tells the full story of the McMahon Treaty of 1915, by which we agreed to grant Arab independence in all Arab countries if the Arabs revolted against the Turks. They did.

He produces much hitherto unpublished material showing how Britain had been flirting with Arab Nationalism long before the war.

'RECKLESS'

But while we were negotiating with the Arabs we were at the same time negotiating with the Zionists for a Jewish home in Palestine, and with the French for a French protectorate in Arab Syria.

Mr. Jeffries argues that the British Government has behaved dishonestly throughout, and makes severe accusations against Mr. Lloyd George and Lord Balfour.

He writes: "The real question is how far anybody in Whitehall knew what everybody else was doing. . . . The various policies were continued recklessly by their authors."

Mr. Jeffries's case is for an independent Arab Palestine because the Arabs were there before the Jews, the Arabs fought magnificently for the allies and are as capable of running the country as the Jews.

"A rare review of the book, in the *Daily Express*, 1939."

The Arab Centre

554 Grand Buildings – Trafalgar Square
London W.C.2

April 26th, 1939

Dear Sir,

May I, on behalf of the Arab Centre, draw your kind attention to a book of considerable importance. The Arab Centre, I should explain, exists to represent in GB the interest of the Arab Peoples. It was founded three years ago by a body of British friends, but in 1937 was transformed into a purely Arab organisation under Arab Control. It is the in the closest touch with the authorities and to leaders of opinion in the Arab countries, and acts as a vehicle for various public announcements. During the recent Conference at S. James's Place, for example, it was so used for several statements.

The Arab Centre would wish to draw your attention then, to the book entitled "Palestine : The Reality," by J.M.N. Jeffries, (Longmans, Green & Co., 25/) which was published towards the end of March. We should highly appreciate it if you would see your way to placing it on the shelves of the library under your control. We ask this because Mr Jeffries' book, which is a detailed history of the 'Palestine Question' from the period of the Great War till now, fulfils a notable want.

We believe that you will agree, whatever be said of the unhappy state of things which has endured so long in Palestine, that every party to this question should be able to put its case before the British public. It scarcely is necessary to point out how deeply concerned the British public is in the matter, and how false is a position in which that must form its opinion and must support or reject governmental policy without ever learning the contentions of a primarily interested party, the Arabs.

But unfortunately, for reasons it would be too long to recount here, the entire, fully-documented Arab case has never come before the British People. Consequently, as we hold, conceptions of the Palestine Question have been formed generally in Britain which have no relation whatsoever to true fact. These misconceptions are corrected and the gaps of information are filled with equal completeness in the book on behalf of which we now appeal to you.

As so many happenings, spread over two decades, have had to be covered in detail in Mr. Jeffries's work, it is a book of some length. It has had to be issued therefore at a price which makes it more of a library book than one for the average private purchaser.

One of the reasons which have induced this letter is that there appears to be little desire to review a book which makes unpalatable revelations, however well proved by documentary evidence.

How far it is just to establish a boycott of this sort, which keeps the book from public knowledge, we must leave to others to say. But there have been exceptions to the general silence, and in 'Truth' of March 17th last, Sir Arnold Wilson, MP, closed a more than favourable review with the words :

> "It is the most important study yet published; as such it deserves to be in the hands of every man who cares for justice and peace."

On the Twentieth of March, the Western Morning News wrote :

> "Mr Jeffries's book will no doubt evoke criticism, but it puts the Arab side in a fair and exhaustive manner, and is mainly composed of actual facts, very often with the indisputable evidence to support them. We have heard the one side often enough, and it is time we heard the other and were presented with some adequate reason for the very lamentable state of affairs in that country (Palestine) and the persistence of the Arabs in their long struggle."

We trust that you will be so good as to heed our appeal, and to take the necessary measures to have this book placed in your library. It would be a further kindness if you would invite your local public to read it.

I beg to remain,
Yours faithfully,

George Mansur
For the Arab Centre

Preface

The back story of the back story

The Balfour Declaration and JMN Jeffries' years of sleuthing resulted in this untimely 1939 book. Published at over 700 pages in the months before the breakout of the then-expected Second World War, such a tome didn't have much of a chance for influence.

Joseph Mary Nagle Jeffries risked his life during the Great War, reporting for the *Daily Mail,* and for years thence served as the newspaper's presence in the Middle East. In 1922, he accompanied the then-ailing press baron Lord Northcliffe (Alfred Harmsworth, who owned both *The Times* and *The Daily Mail*), on a tour of the Middle East. Subsequent reporting on Palestine, urged on by the *Mail*'s editor Thomas Marlowe "to go fully into the question," was not suppressed by Westminster, although the McMahon-Hussein correspondence was not allowed to go public until the Palestine Conference in London, in 1939. And so, Jeffries regular reportage during the crucial years of the 1920s was disseminated in what then was Britain's largest-selling newspaper. But by the 1930s, he was no longer a major journalist and his few subsequent books caused no booksellers' tills to ring with regularity.

The original publishers, Longmans & Co., had had a fleeting interest in Palestine, having published *Dr. Liddon's Tour in Egypt and Palestine in 1886. Being Letters Descriptive of the Tour Written by his Sister, Mrs. King* (1997); M. Rider Haggard's *A Winter Pilgrimage: Being an Account of Travels through Palestine, Italy and the Island of Cyprus, Accomplished in the year 1900* (1901); George Robinson Lees' *Village Life in Palestine* (1905); Jacob Stoyanovsky's *The Mandate for Palestine: A Contribution to the Theory and Practice of International Mandates* (1928); and William Bernard Ziff's *The Rape of Palestine* (1938). This last title was challenging indeed; not only did the author claim that the late 1930s Arab uprisings were *paid for* by the French, but that "Arab megalomania developed like a well-watered weed."

Palestine: The Reality was well reviewed in the weekly Catholic journal, *The Tablet,* for which Jeffries himself wrote. At the time of publication, he even reported on the failure of the March 1939 Palestine Conference. And GR Driver gave it a nod in *The Spectator*, lamenting its length.

But the mainstream press mainly ignored his book and it appears that the publisher Longmans' warehouse was soon after bombed in the Blitz. As such an important work has been unavailable in the used book market and there are fewer than two dozen copies in British libraries, it was time for republication, especially given the centenary of the Balfour Declaration and that Jeffries sought to elevate the Palestinian Arabs' contemporary viewpoints as they were being shut out of the Mandate process.

Jeffries' inventiveness with English vocabulary is most entertaining and he'd be pleased that we're leaving his eccentricities just as we found them. These lettered confections aside, he uses legitimate but arcane words too, and one must pity the typographer back in 1938–39, who had to sit at a Monotype type-setting machine the size of a church organ and make all 350,000 words sing. Some words were made up in the manner of a newspaper reporter: *pamphletic*, *disconfess*, *unbosom*, *keennesses*, *Sharifial*, *mathematico-geographical* ... and on. Jeffries was writing in a time when conventional English spellings of Middle Eastern locales weren't yet set. So, he wrote *Irak* for Iraq, *Koweit* for Kuwait, *Druses* for Druze, *Akaba* for Aqaba, *wakfs* for waqfs, and *jehad* for Jihad. Istanbul was, of course, Constantinople, back in the day. And Jewish surnames weren't yet standardised in English, so Nahum Sokolow is spelled "*Sokolov*".

Given the length of the book, he must have worked tirelessly to uncover roomfuls of governmental correspondence and the back-channel communications of other social actors. To put it in a way he might have done, he's opened the doors to vintage back room clandestinity. As such, most of what the author wrote herein has not been published elsewhere. But beyond the factual gems in this scoop-of-a-book, there is JMNJ's pointed analysis, such as:

> "Perhaps a record was set up for aggressive bluff when Mr. Churchill on the eve of his departure informed a Moslem deputation that they were 'partisans.' To call inhabitants who were defending their right to their native soil 'partisans' was far beyond the range of the average politician."

Mr. Jeffries' pursuance of justice for Palestinian Arabs was clearly humanitarian and he harboured no bigotry towards Jews. In his earlier book, *Front Everywhere* (Hutchinson, 1935), he wrote, "The Jewish colonies in Palestine had been treated with shameful injustice by the Turks

(p. 231)." Despite most of his sources having been European actors, he admirably used the more limited Arab leadership for reference too.

In fact, in 1959, Rabbi Elmer Berger's Manhattan-based American Council for Judaism enquired to Longmans, Green & Co., about republishing *Palestine: The Reality.* The publisher's reply was that they "would have formally returned the rights to the author if we had been able to make contact with him," that they did "not want to be associated further" with it, and that original copies were "probably destroyed in the Blitz." Further, Longmans had no contact for the author, who'd been living in Spain for fourteen years by that point.

In 1969, the Institute for Palestine Studies (Beirut) published a 20-page version of Chapter 11. And in 1976, Hyperion Press, of Westport, Connecticut, republished the whole book, of which there are three known copies in UK libraries.

According to Palestinian-British author Karl Sabbagh, copies of such a rare book haven't been on for sale for many years, due no doubt to the aerial bombardment of London during the Second World War. Some library copies have gone missing and the original publisher Longmans' own archives, held at the University of Reading, include an empty folder about the author (MS 1393 2/290/12).

This trove of information challenges many of the myths of the past century, many of them in equally weighty volumes that are still holding open the doors to the Zionist interpretation of this saga. Some "doorstopper" tomes have been gatekeepers to the region's past. So it is our hope that JMN Jeffries, all these many bloody years later, will set the record straight in understanding the history of Palestine, and Great Britain's disreputable role in it.

—Andy Simons

New Introduction

On 17 March 1939, Sir Arnold Wilson MP wrote: "[*Palestine: the Reality*] is the most important study [of Palestine] yet published. As such it deserves to be in the hands of every man who cares for justice and peace". In the same year and to mark the book's publication, Jemal Husseini, President of the Palestine Arab Delegation, said this: "We request everyone in England who can to read this book. It tells the facts about our country."

These statements, the first by a decent member of the British political establishment who thought Britain's policy in Palestine in pursuance of the Balfour Declaration dishonest, and the second by an impassioned native of that "small, wronged country", sums up the significance of JMN Jeffries' epic work, *Palestine: the Reality.* It was his third and most important work, and the culmination of more than 12 years' study of what was called at the time, "The Palestine Question", drawing on his first-hand experience as a Middle East correspondent for *The Daily Mail* and the source material he collected, much of it never published before. From 1922 when he accompanied the paper's owner, Lord Northcliffe, on a tour of the Middle East, Jeffries reported regularly on the situation in Palestine, urged by Thomas Marlowe, the *Mail*'s editor of the time, "to go fully into it." This Jeffries did with enthusiasm, sending in his despatches until 1933 when his assignment for the paper ended. In the process he acquired a deep knowledge of and feeling for the situation on the ground.

Joseph Mary Nagle Jeffries was born in 1880 of an Irish family. Little is known of his personal life beyond the fact of his having two siblings, a brother and a sister. It seems that, like this sister, he never married, and following the publication in 1939 of *Palestine: the Reality,* which was written at Easthays, Cullompton, Devon, the address he gives at the end of it, he spent some 16 years in Spain. He died in 1960. He was chiefly known as a major war correspondent for the *Daily Mail,* reporting on the First World War from 1914 to 1918, in which time he set a record by sending important despatches from 17 countries, including Egypt, Albania and in the end, Russia. He took great personal risks in doing this, and was especially courageous reporting from France at the outset of the war expressly against British government strictures.

After the end of his work for the *Mail* ended in 1933, he seems to have devoted the subsequent time to writing. *Front Everywhere*, his reminiscences of the First World War, was published in 1935, and *London and Better*, his travels in England, in 1936, both by Hutchinson & Co. But his major book was without doubt, *Palestine: the Reality* (Longman Green & Co, 1939). It is a very big book at 758 pages, unavoidably so, he said, because of the large number of documents and facts covering the years from 1918 to 1938 in Palestine's history that he wanted taken out of obscurity. Writing such a book, he maintained, required the author to have spent time in the country in order to find and evaluate the evidence. The writing of it had taken a great deal of time and resources he could ill afford, having no access to the great wealth the Zionists could lay their hands on, and those who like him wished to set the historical record straight were forced to work at their own expense, a situation all too familiar to this day.

What emerges in *Palestine: the Reality* is an invaluable contemporary record of events in Palestine from an observer who did not belong to either the Arab or the Zionist camp, and could fairly be said to be neutral. What Jeffries saw during his time in the country made him, as the *Daily Express* put it, "take the Arab cause to heart", and determine to lift the silence on the great injustices perpetrated against the Palestinians—what he termed the hidden history of Palestine—over the two decades following the end of the Great War. This seminal period in Middle Eastern history encompassed the 1916 Sykes-Picot Agreement and the early years of the British Mandate over Palestine, crucially important antecedents to the development of the unstable and turbulent Middle East we see today. It was a story he believed had been deliberately obfuscated or withheld by British politicians engaged in a great deception. And he saw it as his mission to reveal the truth behind the deception, an urge instantly recognisable by all those frustrated, or more often enraged, by the enormity of the injustices perpetrated against the Palestinians and the obstacles in the way of their redress.

The centrepiece of Jeffries' book is the 1917 Balfour Declaration, whose centenary falls on 2 November 2017, and its consequences. For Jeffries, by then fully apprised of the circumstances in which the Declaration was drawn up and of its true authors and their real motivation, it was "unlawful in issue, arbitrary in purpose, and deceitful in wording. The Balfour Declaration is the most discreditable document to which a British Government has set its hand within memory." That indictment has lost none of its force today, and the passage of time has not dimmed the perfidy of those who created it.

For Palestinians like me who were among the direct victims of the Balfour Declaration it was a license for the unleashing of a pernicious, unstoppable process that inexorably led to our eviction, dispossession and life-long exile. Because of it my family was forced out of Jerusalem, the city of my birth, in 1948 and onto a journey of displacement and dislocation that has continued ever since. The majority of Palestine's expelled Arabs at the time went into refugee camps, all still in existence, and the rest, such as we, struggled to find new lives in other countries. We were never permitted to return by the Jewish state that the Balfour Declaration had helped create to take our place.

Nor could it have been otherwise once an alien people was safeguarded the right to establish itself as a "nation" in a country not its own. It was inevitable that the new "nation" would exclude "non-nationals", that is, the indigenous people like us, and ensure they never returned. The Balfour Declaration, approved without thought for the consequences by a British government during a war it feared to lose as a bribe to the Zionist to further its own interests, became a catastrophe without end for its victims. The casual insouciance with which the government was prepared to offer Palestine to the Zionists is exemplified in Sir Mark Sykes' (of the Sykes-Picot Agreement) flippant exclamation when the cabinet passed the Balfour Declaration on 2 November. "It's a boy!" he cried joyfully to the Zionist leaders waiting anxiously for the cabinet's vote outside the meeting.

In one short page, a 67-word letter from Arthur Balfour, the then Foreign Secretary, to Lord Rothschild, a leading British Zionist figure of the time, it committed the British government to supporting the establishment in Palestine of a "National Home for the Jewish people", and from that moment set the stage for the unending strife and conflict that has blighted the country and the Middle East region ever since, and whose ramifications have long since spread far beyond. It is doubtful that the British cabinet of 1917 anticipated any of the long term consequences the Balfour Declaration set in train when it was passed, and perhaps did not give the matter much consideration.

Yet the Declaration was in every sense a strange document, neither legal pledge nor formal contract between the British government and the Zionists, ambiguously worded and so left open to interpretation by the interested parties. Its exact status should have been questioned from the outset. Jeffries' detailed analysis of its content reveals the deliberate vacuousness of some of its parts and the duplicity of others. What, for example, does the sentence, "His Majesty's government *views with favour* the establishment of a national home for the Jewish people" precisely mean (emphasis added)? And what was a "national home"? No such entity existed anywhere, even in concept, at the time. And who exactly were the "existing non-Jewish communities" in Palestine?

Beneath its deceptively vague phraseology the main thrust of the Balfour Declaration was the centrality it accorded to the Zionists and the primacy of their claim to Palestine over any other. The insertion of the word "national" betrays its real purpose: the eventual emergence of a Jewish state from the "national home". Jeffries shows how the text's every word had been pored over repeatedly, and discussed and amended to reflect this fact. Many readers of the present book may be surprised to learn that the real authors of the Balfour Declaration were not British government officials, nor the man who gave it his name, but a committee of some 20 Zionist leaders working in unison on both sides of the Atlantic. Chaim Weitzman, the prominent chemist and ardent Zionist leader at the centre of influence over Balfour and other top British officials, coordinated its transatlantic composition after having been assigned responsibility for the drafting of the declaration by Balfour.

In 1915 the Zionists were influential at many levels of government in both Britain and the US, and included in their ranks top financial and professional figures. They were well placed to push the issue through the administrations of both countries, and did so with considerable success. When Balfour's British delegation visited America in the spring of 1917, they found an administration that was, in Jeffries' phrase, thoroughly "zionized". The Balfour Declaration was two years in the making, its successive drafts shuttling between Britain and America to gain the approval of both governments, which acted as nothing more than facilitators and enablers of the Zionist project. The drafts written before November 1917 were little more than Zionist wish lists, giving the Zionists complete autonomy in Palestine and unlimited Jewish immigration into it. According to Jeffries, it seems that Britain was initially prepared to turn over the whole of Palestine to them for the establishment of the Jewish national home. But for the strong objections of a small group of British Jewish leaders opposed to Zionism, the Balfour Declaration might have been even more partisan than it already was.

When it was finally issued in November 1917 it was a Zionist document almost entirely, and the Zionists unsurprisingly seized on it as if it had been a contract set in stone giving them the unquestionable right to put into effect their plan to establish a state for Jews in Palestine. From then on the contortions and tussles between the immigrant Zionist community and the British authorities ruling Palestine all stemmed from that initial Zionist assumption: that they had an unarguable right to the country, and that it was Britain's obligation to assist them in its takeover. And that essentially has been the position of the heir to the "Jewish National Home", Israel, in the world to this day: its absolute right of claim to what had once been Palestine, and the international community's obligation to protect that right on Israel's behalf.

In the scheming, machinations and bargaining over the drafting of the Balfour Declaration, the Arabs were totally forgotten, as if they did not exist. To credit this extraordinary situation, one would have to enter the colonial mindset of men who saw subject peoples as savages and natives of no account. But even with that, Britain's cavalier disregard for the effect the Zionist plan would have on Palestine's indigenous people was inordinately callous. It was the more heinous for taking advantage of their backward situation at the time.

The majority of Palestinians in 1917 were peasants and farmers without education. They were in no position to resist or even comprehend the complex ideology of Zionism, linked as it was to a European Jewish history they were ignorant of. And Palestine's middle class of old families, religious leaders and professionals, was too small to be effective and the task too hard. My grandfather was a landowner, and also a noted religious authority and sharia judge, but he could no more have fought the Zionists than any of his illiterate peasants.

In these circumstances, imposing a well-organised politically experienced and ideologically driven Zionist movement, backed by a major imperial power, onto an Arab population so ill-prepared and helpless was an act of the most cynical exploitation. Neither people had anything in common, the one agrarian and uncomplicated, struggling to reconstitute itself after centuries of Ottoman rule; and the other, urban, complex, and imbued with a fervid sense of entitlement to what it saw as its exclusive patrimony. The disparity of education and political and cultural development between the parties meant that the result was a foregone conclusion.

For Jeffries British policy in Palestine always involved "fraud and perfidy". It was not the result of an honest mistake or made in ignorance of the facts. Britain's decision makers knew exactly what they were doing when they withdrew from the Arabs of Palestine their natural right to their land and substituted for it a bogus "right" of a foreign community with no claim to it other than that given by a spurious "declaration" of uncertain legal status and ambiguous meaning. The only way such a shaky construct could ever have succeeded was to impose it by coercion and brute force, both of which the British employed in Palestine throughout the Mandate years.

What outraged our author most was the deception the government practised to cover this shameful reality. It presented the Balfour Declaration as its own production, when it was not, and the tawdry details of how the supposed recipients of Balfour's letter to Lord Rothschild were in fact its authors were kept hidden.

From the start British policy was aimed at privileging the Jews in Palestine. They were appointed at senior level in all sections of the Mandate government; at the department of education, where my father worked, for example, Jews were given higher rank posts to Arabs of equal or greater competence, and, to his and his colleagues' chagrin, were left free to run their own education system, unlike Arabs; the Hebrew university was established in Jerusalem as far back as 1922 when the Mandate government was barely in operation, but nothing comparable was ever allowed for the Arabs. At no time was any attempt made to consult them or seek their permission for what was happening to their country. And the Balfour Declaration was not, as unctuously claimed by the government, an expression of its sympathy for the Jewish longing to "return" to Palestine, but a shoddy private agreement to use the spoils of war as payment to the Zionists for their help in the war.

Most importantly, the British knew all along that the Jewish National Home they were helping to establish in Palestine would lead eventually to the creation of a Jewish state, as the Zionists always meant it to. Without Britain, Jeffries says of his mission, there would never have been a "Palestine Question". Nor, he might have added, a State of Israel.

Palestine: the Reality is a mine of information, containing, as mentioned above, material not in the public domain at the time. It covers an extensive list of topics relevant to understanding the genesis of the Palestine problem, from the early years of the Zionist movement, through to the 1937 Peel Commission set up by the British government to find a way out of the quagmire Britain's support for Zionism had created. Such a book, virtually unique in its time, should have been in the front rank of source works on the modern history of Palestine. Instead, it was marginal, only a few papers reviewed it, and it was not widely disseminated. Not long after, the bulk of the original print run was destroyed in the bombing of Longman's warehouse during the blitz.

When in 1959 Rabbi Elmer Berger's American Council for Judaism was considering a republication of *Palestine: the Reality,* and contacted Longman's about the book, they were informed that Longman's would by then have formally returned the rights to the author, who was said to be living in Spain at the time. But they had no contact details for him, and, curiously, they added that they did "not want to be associated further" with it. In 1969, the Institute for Palestine Studies in Beirut published a 20-page version of Chapter 11, "The analysis of the Balfour Declaration, its sham character and deceptive phraseology". Finally in 1976, Hyperion Press, of Westport Connecticut, republished the whole book, of which there are only three known copies in UK libraries.

By the time of the present edition, copies of the book had become very rare. No more than 20 or so remained in various libraries, and some of them had gone missing. Longmans' own archives at the University of Reading library included a folder about the author (MS 1393 2/290/12), but its contents had also gone missing. One is almost tempted to wonder if there is something sinister in this, that a well-documented, contemporary exposé of a particularly ignoble period in Britain's recent history whose disastrous results live on to this day might not have been worth suppressing, or at least making inaccessible. Perhaps what the *Western Morning News* of 30 March 1939 said in its review of the book: it "puts the Arab case in a fair and exhaustive manner…We have heard the other side often enough, and it is time we heard the other," was not welcome in a situation where ensuring the success of the Zionist project was paramount government policy.

Jeffries had already observed how the Zionist case was always given preference, and those who tried to put the Palestinian one across never "obtained in the newspapers or upon the platform one thousandth part of the space or of the time which they needed to say all that they had to say." The effect of this bias was to leave the other side free to present its own version of the facts with little opposition, and for the British public to hear only from sympathetic ministers and from Zionists and their supporters, and nothing at all from the Arabs. It was already the case, Jeffries points out, that the Zionist point of view was well represented to the public through the variety of influential positions held by pro-Zionist Jews in parliament, the press, and in commerce.

Growing up in the Britain of the 1950s as I did, that was the situation I faced. It was virtually impossible to put forth the Palestinian side of the story. Even the name, "Palestine", had gone out of popular usage, and when asked where I came from and I answered, "Palestine", people would respond, "did you say Pakistan"? Astonishingly, the name of a new state only created in 1947, Pakistan, was better known by 1955 than that of Palestine, the country of the bible, of pilgrimage, and the historical destination of scores of pious Christian travellers. Everywhere the concept of my country as the land of the Jews, in which non-Jews were more like squatters than natives, was rife. As a child, I found it the most frightening deletion of my identity, history and memory imaginable, further compounded by so profound a British dismissal of our side of the story as to make me doubt the reality of my own living experience.

It has taken years for the public to be allowed to hear "from the other side". There is now in Britain and in Europe a far greater awareness of the Palestinian case than ever before, and a public airing of the facts to a much larger extent than previously, though it is still more selective than exhaustive. Palestinian spokespeople have more of a media presence today, where it had been the norm to hear only from so-called "neutral" western commentators. But it is still a race to keep up with the Zionist narrative, which uses every event to update and recreate its message. As the conflict has gone on and new developments have appeared, the Zionists have seized on each one to cloud the main issue which had been clear at the beginning.

The truth of this observation is manifest today in the simplistic media reporting of the Israeli–Palestinian conflict that uses the present as its starting point without reference to previous history or context. The result of such uninformative reporting is either to confuse and exhaust—the "plague on both their houses" response—or to entrench the Zionist version of reality still further. As Jeffries put it, through the sheer passage of time the build-up of questionable facts, bias and misinformation produced by the other side could reach a point where it would be impossible to overturn.

Like so many of Jeffries' observations, this has already come to pass. Who now insists that the origin of the conflict was the Zionist-driven mass expulsions and dispossession of 1948 and not the war of 1967? And hence any solution must include the right of return of all those expelled and the restitution of their property? That story has been steadily eroded and submerged, and attention diverted onto Israel's occupation of the 1967 territories and the creation of two-states as the best solution for the conflict.

JMN Jeffries' monumental work is here deservedly re-published after decades of obscurity, which will make it accessible to all who seek the truth behind one of the most disgraceful episodes in Britain's colonial history. Jeffries put the blame for the Balfour Declaration squarely on the shoulders of Arthur Balfour himself. But he also decried the failure of successive British governments to do anything about it. "It is a pity that it cannot be lost from sight," he wrote, "and a greater pity that it has not yet been removed from our public records."

If 2017 turns out to be the year when Britain did indeed decide to rescind the Balfour Declaration and remove it from the public record, it would have cleared its name of a hundred years of dishonour. And if it were to happen, then *Palestine: the Reality* may well have been a major catalyst, and the principled, honest man who was its author could rest content that his mission had been fulfilled.

Ghada Karmi
September 2016

Original Introduction

Though the world of today, in these last months of 1938, has much for which to be ashamed, there is nothing in it so shameful as the condition of Palestine. From end to end the Holy Land has been running with blood. Evening after evening the voice of the wireless announcer has brought news of another combat, another ambush, another assassination perhaps, on the soil once pressed by the feet of Christ.

Yet the more we are grieved by these events, the more it is incumbent upon us to examine into the causes which have produced them. Political murder, in particular, is a product of the extreme degrees of exasperation. Though nothing condones it, yet ere it becomes common in any State something must have been thoroughly wrong with that State, and wrong for a considerable time, and all reasonable means of procuring redress of what was wrong must have been found worthless.

Unhappily that is what has occurred in Palestine. The Arabs, the people of that country, are suffering from a supreme injustice. We have abstracted from them the control of their own destinies and by force of arms have imposed upon them a multitude of undesired immigrants and an alien system of life. For twenty years now they have essayed every form of pacific appeal to have this injustice remedied. Interviews and petitions, mass-meetings, public pronouncements, protests to the League of Nations, repeated embassies to England, all have been tried. All of them have failed. Not only have the Arabs' petitions not been granted, but of what was fundamental in them consideration itself has been refused. They have never been allowed to place their full case before any national or international Court in the world, with a right to win a verdict upon the facts.

A principal reason for this is that in the first instance the Arabs' case has remained unheard before the court of public opinion. If they had won their suit there, a just settlement would have been imposed elsewhere. But the Arabs have never been able to make their full case known to the public, especially in Great Britain, where it was so important that it should have been known.

The aim of the present book is to give this case as amply as possible. It is a history of what really happened in Palestine and of what was done concerning Palestine from the days of the War till now. That the book comes after such a long time, at what seems such a late stage of the conflict, is not because of any accident or any remissness. It is because of the primary handicap upon the Arabs and their defenders.

The Arabs of Palestine are a small body, living far from this country and having perforce—since they are Arabs—none of their race in positions of influence in Great Britain.

On the other hand, their opponents in the matter have been constituted by a series of British Governments themselves and by the extremely influential members of the Zionist organizations, who either live in this country or are constantly visiting it. These Zionists and their British backers hold prominent positions in Parliament, in the Press, in the social and in the professional and commercial spheres of our national life. So that from voices which are familiar in their varying degrees and respected in their varying degrees the public has heard over and over everything that is to be said for political Zionism, for the theory, that is, which establishes Jews by main force, not as a religious but as a political entity, in the Holy Land.

From the Arabs the British public has heard little, despite all the endeavours the Arabs themselves have made to present their cause. How could it be otherwise? The lonely groups of men, whom their countrymen have sent so often to our shores to plead for them, have never obtained in the newspapers or upon the platform one thousandth part of the space or of the time which they needed to say all that they had to say. They had a great deal to say, because as time went on what is called the "Palestine Question" became increasingly intricate.

Any first-class political question grows intricate if it is left without an effort to solve it for a number of years. It grows particularly intricate when one of the parties to the affair finds refuge in this passage of the years, taking advantage of all the secondary issues naturally or artificially produced during them to cloud the main issue that was clear at the beginning. There becomes so much to speak about, so much to controvert and so many falsely raised issues to pursue that a vast deal of time and of space presently would be needed by the other party to accomplish this. But time and space on such a scale have been quite unprocurable. To give the full Arab case the newspapers of Britain would have had to turn themselves into political documents dealing with the Levant. Anybody can see that was impossible.

So that the Arab delegates who came to England never had a chance in reality to do anything but encounter the stone wall of ministerial obstinacy, to address a few drawing-room and Rotary Club meetings and to have inadequate pamphlets distributed here and there. The situation the British public was bound to hear a good argument on the Palestine Question from Ministers and Zionists and their supporters, it heard, to all intents, nothing from the Arabs.

Now we come to those from whom the public should have heard, in principle, something at some length upon the Arabs' behalf, that is to say we come to British sympathizers with the Arabs. But here it is that the handicap upon the Arab cause is perceived even more distinctly.

We who sympathize actively with the Arabs are a small group, a pitifully small group. We are bound to be a small group because knowledge of the Arab case, knowledge of the true facts concerning Palestine, was never to be acquired easily and ordinarily in England.

It required special knowledge to be a champion of the Arab cause. This knowledge in general was only to be gained in Palestine itself, or by close acquaintance with others who had been in Palestine, or through the study of evidence which practically remained private, so that we who were cognizant of the facts were necessarily few in numbers. We were a few ex-soldiers, some former officers and functionaries of the Administration in Palestine, a fact which had its significance to some dwellers in that country, some missionaries and teachers there, one or two journalists whose eyes had been opened there. Against us stood the Government of Great Britain and the Zionist societies with their ramifications throughout the universe. Against us stood the wealth used to spread the Governmental and the Zionist case. In comparison with this the Arabs were paupers, and we few who knew the justice of the Arab cause had to suffer all the impediments and heaped obstacles of their and of our own poverty in trying to reveal it.

In consequence, though this book is as full as I can make it, it is not quite as full as it might be and as it should be. There is for example a great deal which should be divulged about the way in which political Zionism came to be espoused and the Arab case came to be put aside by the Government of the United States at the time of the Peace Conference. I was offered opportunities for investigation into this, what appeared to be singular opportunities, but I could not avail myself of them because I had not the money to go to the United States and to stay there the length of time which would have been necessary. For the same reasons I could not even return to Palestine before I began writing and then go on to Irak, though it can be imagined how much there is in that quarter still waiting to be investigated and to be read.

It is not usual perhaps to mention personal affairs of this sort, but here they must be mentioned because of their political importance. We who are on the side of the Arabs are a group with a good deal of special knowledge, but without the funds to use it and to diffuse it as we should wish. In that we differ from our opponents, who when the spreading of their gospel is concerned, can talk in tens of thousands of pounds and in hundreds of thousands of dollars.

By a natural sequence too we who should have wished to plead the cause of the Arabs have been as much without time to do so as we have been without funds. We have had no leisure: we have had our livings to make. That is why this book, which has demanded an entire seclusion in the subject and the abandonment of every other interest, has not appeared before. It was produced as soon as the bare possibility of producing it existed.

Some other points need to be prefaced here. Readers will see that I have not dealt tenderly with certain statesmen and certain Governments of ours. There is no reason, to my mind, for euphemism, for saying that these men and these Cabinets were mistaken or ill-advised or pursued mere erroneous policy in Palestine, or foolishly accepted an unworkable Mandate. They did nothing of the kind. They pursued a policy involving fraud and perfidy. They tyrannously withdrew from the Arabs the Arabs' natural and inherent rights over their native land. They broke Britain's word to the Arabs. To suit their aims in Palestine they gerrymandered as far as they could the Covenant of the League of Nations, and where they could gerrymander it no further they broke it. They falsified the Mandate.

Later Governments have been less guilty. But they have committed their own sins of omission by not reconsidering the acts of their predecessors, and by continuing with a policy into the antecedents of which they have not inquired.

These charges have to be made. The evidence which justifies them accompanies them. But it is painful to be obliged to make them, in particular under the actual circumstances of the world. It would be very short-sighted, however, at the present juncture to reason that this was not the moment to weaken our national prestige by disclosing the misdeeds of some of our rulers.

The position is just the reverse. If in this hour free institutions are indeed imperiled, then there is nothing better than to give evidence of what free institutions allow and autocratic institutions forbid, that is, the right of the individual to arraign any Government for its improper employment of power. However distasteful too in one respect it may be to speak out, in every other respect, and in the overriding respect, not to speak out would be to miss a capital opportunity. Something more than an opportunity indeed is offered. It is a privilege of ours today, which we share with few, that in a Europe muzzled with self-conceit we in England still can tell the truth about ourselves. Only as long as we tell it are we free. It is the proof itself of liberty. When we leave the telling of it to the foreigner our day will be over.

Besides, this Palestine question tarnishes every effort of Britain for good in other directions. The British public is not aware how much our doings in Palestine are discussed in other lands, and what a savour of hypocrisy they convey to our most genuine impulses. How can we raise our voice in protest at the concentration-camps of Prussia when in Palestine we maintain our own? How can we denounce the expulsion of Jews by Germans when with equal arbitrariness we impose Jews upon Arabs? How can we cavil at men being kept in prison without trial, when we too have exiled, imprisoned and proscribed without trial?

The excuse that in our case it is different, that we do what we do regretfully, in the interests of the Mandate which it is our duty to the world to carry out, is a sham excuse. We ourselves arranged for our Mandate, we and our friends gave it to ourselves, we and our accomplices in the Zionist policy composed its very terms, with the sole aim of enforcing this policy thereby.

How that was done the reader will learn in this book. It is quite possible I may be called an anti-Semite for writing it. I must put up with that. But I have never had any truck with anti-Semitism, and I find the persecution of the Jews in Central Europe as crying a disgrace to humanity as their imposition upon the Arabs has been. There is nothing too which gives such a handle to the oppressors of the Jews elsewhere as the oppression by them and for them in Palestine.

As regards the subject-matter of the book, there are some points to make. It is a very long book, but it has to be long. Since the real history of Palestine for two decades has been kept hidden from the public, it is in a sense necessary here to recreate those lost twenty years, in as much of their detail as possible and with a little at least of the repetition of facts which occurred during those twenty years themselves. Half the facts I have to give have never been mentioned at all, many of the documents have never been quoted. I have therefore thought it necessary, for the sake of readers coming fresh to the subject, to make the more important points more than once. When it is remembered how the Arabs have suffered from silence upon everything, occasional repetition of some points can hardly be grudged, and really is desirable.

The history of Palestine from the days of the War till now is sometimes, as I have said earlier, intricate. It ought not to be intricate, because it is only the so-called "Palestine Question" which makes it intricate, and the Palestine Question ought not to be in existence. There was no Palestine Question, nor ever would have been one, if certain statesmen had not created it. Since it was thus unnaturally created, however, it tends at times to intricacy. The meaning of phrases has to be considered closely then, or the map has to be closely regarded.

The men who created the Question, however, should not be able to escape being held to account by their agility in complicating our national books. If political personages can toy with treaties or wriggle out of pledges simply because the public will neither examine treaties nor analyse pledges, then the public has abdicated its control over government.

The book deals principally with the story of how Palestine was placed under Mandatory government in order to establish the "Jewish National Home," which later—it was intended—should become a Jewish State. It has been completed while the future policy of the Chamberlain Government in Palestine remains undefined. At the moment of revising it the Partition scheme inherited from the previous Government has been dropped. But it covers any other scheme which may replace Partition. Any such scheme, which does not recognize that we disregarded the rights of the Arabs and defaulted from our own engagements, and does not affirm that these rights henceforth shall be recognized and these engagements kept, will find its own condemnation in the history detailed herein.

Even were the present Cabinet to perceive the virtue of confession, to reverse policy, and to start again in Palestine as we should have started twenty years ago, even then this publication of the real story of those past years would be essential. Only thus could three things which call for demonstration be demonstrated; the need for reversal of policy; the justice of the Arabs' demands; the guilt of those who have kept Palestine in misery for so long.

Especially must the Arabs have the justice of their cause made clear. There must be no imputation lying upon them, should a proper settlement be reached, that they achieved it merely by resorting to insurrection, and that it was granted to them only for peace's sake.

I think it is right that the public should know the names of some of those who have kept the cause of the Arabs alive in Great Britain in the teeth of overwhelming opposition. Two motives have maintained their courage, when hope seemed farthest away. One was that a small country should never be downtrodden if they could help it. The other was that their own country should be true to her vows and to herself.

Some of the men spoke forth in Parliament. Lord Islington, Lord Sydenham, Lord Buckmaster, Lord Brentford, Lord Lamington, Lord Templetown—those are names the Arabs will never forget. Nor will they forget Sir Ernest Bennett, Mr. Somers Cocks, Sir Frank Sanderson, Colonel Howard Bury, Colonel Clifton Brown, Lord Winterton, Sir Arnold Wilson, and among younger members of the Commons in more recent days, Mr. Anthony Crossley. These peers and members of Parliament did not all advocate just the same policy in Palestine: there were differences of application amongst them. But they all strove to present the Arab standpoint. The names of Lord Islington and Lord Sydenham will be particularly remembered for the force and the ability with which they combated Governmental policy. Neither was in his youth then: both were already retired from posts of high honour in overseas dominions and, in Lord Islington's case, in a Cabinet. But in defending the forlorn Arab cause they re-found their prime. They fought for Palestine and for England's honour like crusaders, and indeed the ranks they led are engaged in the last Crusade.

A tribute to Lord Northcliffe is paid in the text of this book. But there are others whose names are not likely to come before the public, who have taken a great part in the defence of the Arabs. Every soul in Palestine knows what Miss Frances Newton has accomplished on behalf of the land in which she had made her home for so many years. Everyone who has engaged in the defence of the Arab cause has owed something to her knowledge and to her inspiration. I am deeply in her debt. In Palestine her house upon Mount Carmel is, in the eyes of the Arabs, the true Residence of old British tradition.

In London the Arabs' defenders know the great work, the cardinal work done for many years by the late Miss Broadhurst and by Miss Farquharson, of the "National League." In their eyrie over St. James's Street Arabs and their British friends met and took counsel, learned of any a plan and an intrigue of their opponents which had not escaped the ever-vigilant eyes of their hostesses, and concerted resistance. It was the Arab fort and Arab embassy in one. Like others I always found there help, information, and enthusiasm, and great cause for gratitude.

Another name I mention with respect and gratitude is that of Mrs. Steuart Erskine, one of the first to come to the rescue of our common cause with her book Palestine of the Arabs. Its title was a lesson in itself in the days when it was written. As Secretary of the "Arab Centre" in Victoria Street, Mrs. Erskine has worked unremittingly. Coupled with her are Mrs. Fox-Strangways, Mrs. Cecil Brooks, Miss Blyth and Mrs. Swinburne.

In Palestine Mr. Nevill Barbour has used a very valuable pen, and I am indebted for a quotation from him in this very Introduction. Mr. Ernest Richmond and Mr. CR Ashbee, both of whom served under Administrations in Palestine, have written about that country in that particular direct and unsparing fashion which characterizes those who have had the closest inner acquaintance with the question. Professor Garstang, of Liverpool University, who has conducted remarkable archaeological excavations in Palestine, has compiled, along with the Bishop of Chichester, a very telling pamphlet.

Above all there is Lawrence's old companion, Colonel SF Newcombe, whose courteous and conciliatory manner, expressed in plans of his own for a settlement, has never hidden his firm espousal of justice for the Arabs.

A final point calls for introductory mention. It is one which in a sense lies outside the whole sphere of the present discussion, which treats of political matters. It is a religious consideration. Since many persons however judge the subject of Zionism solely from this standpoint, it is proper that it should be considered.

Those who take this view are moved by the fact that the return of the Jews to the Holy Land is an accomplishment of the prophecies of the Bible. Because of this they feel that no opposition of any sort should be made to this return. They do not like to criticize or to hear it criticized in any fashion.

Most earnestly I beg of any who entertain such opinions to consider more carefully than they have done the attitude of those who defend the Arabs. Hardly any of us, certainly not I, oppose the return of Jews to Palestine. What we resist is a very different thing, the manner of their return and the extent of their return. The manner has been illegal and arrogant, the extent excessive.

In any event, the reinstallation of Jews in Palestine cannot be said to be impeded or jeopardized by our actions, since the Jews have returned there. Everything calls for criticism in the whereabouts and style of their return, but that is their responsibility, not their critics'. As far as numbers go, at the close of the Great War there were some sixty-thousand of them in residence, who had lived for the most part on terms of reasonable understanding, if not amity, with the native population. Most of them were recent comers, who had entered the country in the proper way, under its common law, as pilgrims or as settlers, demanding no special status for themselves at the expense of that native population. Since then their totals have increased sevenfold.

The additional three hundred and forty thousand and more, who have entered under our noses, have been brought in arbitrarily. To all intents the Arabs have been tied by Great Britain to their doorposts while the Jews streamed past. Despite this, the Arabs—so regularly traduced as unreasonable—are willing so far to accept a compromise concerning them. It would be well, incidentally, not to strain over-strained Arab patience any further, and to take advantage of the willingness to compromise while it exists. Further obduracy in meeting the just claims of the Arabs will only drive the direction of their national movement into uncompromising hands.

At present, however, they are willing to regard the great bulk of the immigrants as innocent and ignorant agents, who have come to Palestine thinking it was theirs, and they do not seek to expel them. The terms of the immigrants' residence remain to be settled, but as long as they are content with the common rights of inhabitants and do not demand extravagant privileges such as territoriality and extra-territoriality at once, they should be able to stay. That means that 400,000, probably over 400,000, Jews are in Palestine and are not likely to leave it unless of their own free will.

This fact is of great significance if considered in conjunction with the prophecies of the Bible. These prophecies are very numerous, spread through many of the books of the Old Testament. It will be enough to cite a couple of characteristic passages. In the eleventh chapter of the Book of Isaiah we read, "And it shall come to pass in that day that the Lord shall set His hand the second time to possess the remnant of His people, which shall be left from the Assyrians and from Egypt, and from Phetros and from Ethiopia and from Elam and from Senaar and from Emath and from the islands of the sea. And He shall set up a standard to the nations and shall assemble the fugitives of Israel and shall gather together the dispersed of Judah from the four quarters of the earth."

In the thirtieth chapter of Deuteronomy is found, "The Lord thy God will bring back again thy captivity (reverse the situation of thy captivity) and will have mercy on thee and gather thee again out of all the nations into which He scattered thee before. If thou be driven as far as the poles of Heaven the Lord thy God will fetch thee back from thence. And will take thee unto Himself and bring thee into the land which thy fathers possessed, and thou shalt possess it, and blessing thee He will make thee more numerous than were thy fathers."

These prophecies today are accomplished. The four hundred thousand inmates of the Holy Land form a full remnant of the Jews in the world, whose numbers are very variously estimated from fourteen to sixteen millions. Only a remnant of these millions can return to Palestine. Till the second coming of Christ brings in the era of miracles and the limitations of our present human earth melt away, the settlement of all the Jews in that small and often sterile land would be quite impossible. Nor is there the slightest desire on the part of these millions to return. Out of three hundred thousand Jews, say, in Great Britain, less than two thousand have gone back to Palestine. Those who have returned there are preeminently the "fugitives of Israel" and the "dispersed of Judah" who have fled from those parts of Europe where they are depressed or persecuted.

In addition to promise of restoration, the prophecy of Deuteronomy declares that the restored Jews shall possess the land more numerously than their fathers. That too is accomplished, an accomplishment to which no attention at all has been drawn.

The size of the Jewish population when it was in possession of parts of Palestine—for it was never in possession of the whole of Palestine—cannot of course be computed exactly. Biblical critics unite in discrediting some of the poetic totals which have been bequeathed to us by the remote Past. They speak of the numbers given as incredibly vast, of the "boundless extravagance" of the figures even of Josephus.

Sir George Adam Smith, whose *Historical Geography of the Holy Land* remains the classic work upon that country and has reached twenty-five editions, has applied himself however to the question of Jewish population in Old Testament days. In another authoritative book of his, *Palestine*, after deducing from the bas-reliefs of the Assyrians that the Jews deported to Babylon were at the most 70,000 in number, after reminding his readers that some scores of thousands did not go into exile, and that during the long and prosperous reign of Manasseh the losses suffered under Sennacherib must have been made good, he draws this final conclusion. "We cannot therefore be far from the truth in estimating the Jewish nation at the end of the seventh century (before Christ) as comprising at least 250,000 souls." This gives a reasonable average population upon which to calculate.

If, in deference to Adam Smith's qualification "at least," even 100,000 be added, which from the context is an exaggeration of this qualification, none the less even then in all reasonableness the Jews today in Palestine are "more numerous than their fathers," and what was announced in Holy Writ has been accomplished. There can be no question of the Arabs or of those who sustain the Arabs' rights impeding the fulfilment of a prophecy, since already it has been fulfilled.

As Mr. Nevill Barbour points out:

> "There exists in Palestine today, as the result of fifty years of Zionist enterprise, a Jewish National Home, containing some three hundred and fifty thousand souls [written in 1936], which fulfils the purpose of a spiritual centre for Jewry. It is now possible for a Jew to be born in Palestine and pass through an all-Jewish kindergarten, school and university without ever speaking anything but Hebrew; to work on a Jewish farm or in a Jewish factory; to live in an all-Jewish city of 150,000 inhabitants; to read a Hebrew daily newspaper; to visit a Hebrew theatre and to go for a holiday-cruise on a steamer flying the Jewish flag."

This may, I think, fairly be described as a full and sufficient Jewish return to Palestine in accordance with the prophecies of the Scriptures. What the Arabs are resisting now is nothing but the demand of divers politically-minded secular Zionists that Jewish totals in Palestine should be extended by further additions. These increments to population vary with appetites from a few more hundred thousand to several millions. Dr.

Weizmann proposes bringing another million and a half into the country during the next twenty years. All this stuffing of repletion is justified by nothing in the Scriptures.

So much for those who deprecate defence of the Arabs' rights because of its supposed "interference" with the prophecies. There is this too which they must remember. Under no circumstances can it be sustained that because of the prophecies of the Old Testament the Jews have a permit to return to Palestine arbitrarily and wrongfully, after the manner in which their own peccant leaders and certain British statesmen have forced entry for them. The standards of moral conduct cannot be set aside. Those who would use the authority of the Bible in order to perpetuate injustice in the Holy Land would provide an example never before seen of Scripture being quoted for the devil's purpose.

In fine, to suggest that the rights and the wrongs of the question between the Arabs and the Zionists must not be taken into consideration because the Jews are predestined to return to Palestine is equivalent to suspending right and wrong themselves. It is to imagine an impossible issue, to which, in order to fulfil the promises of God, the commandments of God do not apply. It is to make sin the means of salvation and to controvert Christianity. Therefore it is a doctrine which no Christian for a moment should permit himself to entertain.

I have thought it more convenient to refer throughout to persons by their more recently known designation when they have undergone a change of name, for example, I have spoken of "Lord Balfour" from the beginning, even when he was Mr. A. J. Balfour. On the other hand, extremely recent changes of name have been disregarded, for example, I have spoken of "Sir Herbert Samuel," not Lord Samuel. Convenience has been studied: I have not followed any one rule. In quotations I have left names as they were given.

Names in brackets following quotations identify the writers. Z.O.R. stands for *Zionist Organization Report*.

J.M.N.J.

Easthayes,
Cullompton,
Devon.

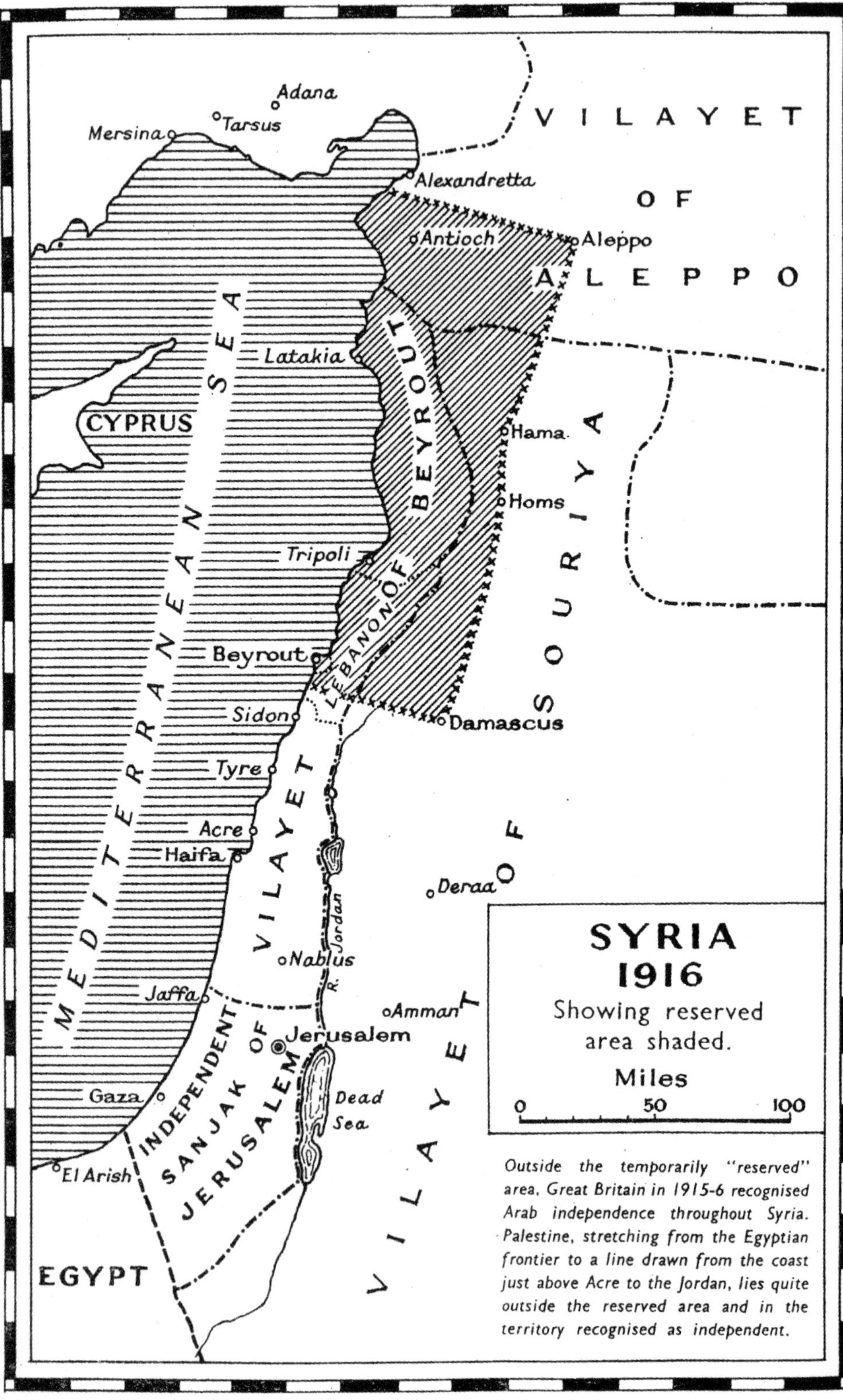

Outside the temporarily "reserved" area, Great Britain in 1915-6 recognised Arab independence throughout Syria. Palestine, stretching from the Egyptian frontier to a line drawn from the coast just above Acre to the Jordan, lies quite outside the reserved area and in the territory recognised as independent.

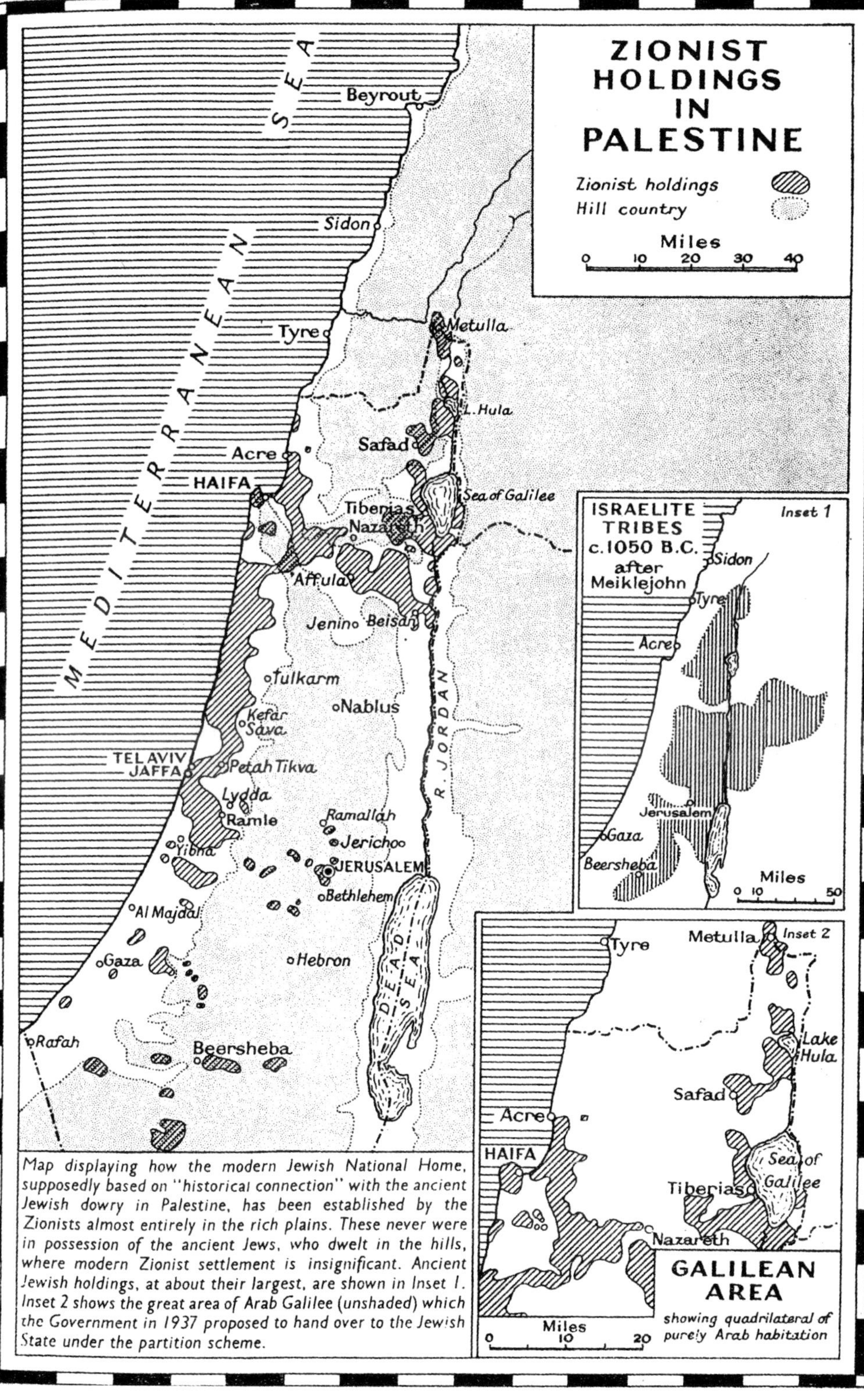

Map displaying how the modern Jewish National Home, supposedly based on "historical connection" with the ancient Jewish dowry in Palestine, has been established by the Zionists almost entirely in the rich plains. These never were in possession of the ancient Jews, who dwelt in the hills, where modern Zionist settlement is insignificant. Ancient Jewish holdings, at about their largest, are shown in Inset 1. Inset 2 shows the great area of Arab Galilee (unshaded) which the Government in 1937 proposed to hand over to the Jewish State under the partition scheme.

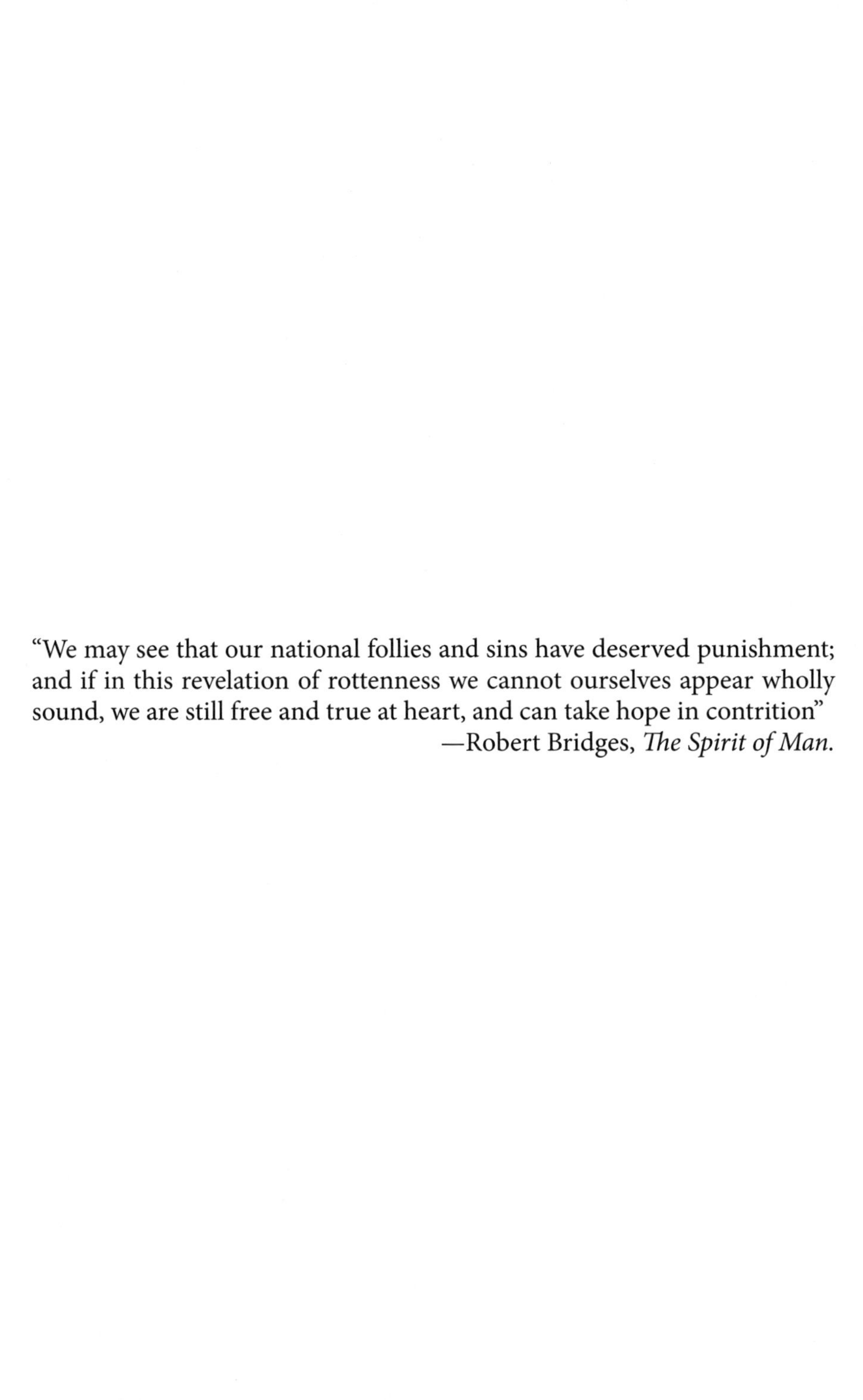

"We may see that our national follies and sins have deserved punishment; and if in this revelation of rottenness we cannot ourselves appear wholly sound, we are still free and true at heart, and can take hope in contrition"

—Robert Bridges, *The Spirit of Man.*

Chapter 1

"For what have you to do with me, O Tyre and Sidon, and all the coasts of the Philistines?"—Joel iii. 4.

In 1922 Lord Northcliffe, visiting Palestine and perceiving the results of our government there, declared that we were making a second Ireland of that country. What happened in succeeding years, and even more what has been happening of late, in 1937 and 1938, show that he spoke only too truly. All the mistakes and misdeeds which fed eternal discontent in Ireland and culminated in so much vain bloodshed and destruction there have been reproduced in Palestine. It is almost as though the Irish precedent, far from being kept in mind as a warning, had been remembered as a valuable example of success, and was being copied sedulously in every detail.

But if this imitation of the worst policy is mentioned here, it is but to emphasize the fact that Palestine has less room in it for bad policy than even Ireland had. It is a very small place.

There is a natural tendency to transmute the spiritual greatness of the Holy Land into physical largeness, and to ascribe wide acres to the locality where the horizons of the human race were opened by the Redeemer's birth. Christianity, however, like its Founder, was born in a narrow dwelling. Palestine is closer in size to a county than to a country. Take a couple of Yorkshires and you would have the acreage of Palestine. Of its famous subdivisions Judaea is about the same size as Northumberland: neither Galilee nor Samaria is quite as big as Somerset. These comparisons too are made without reference to the number of persons living in these districts. Were settled areas only to be considered, traditional Palestine shrinks still further in comparison with the populous counties of England. In the epoch of its independence half of Judaea was desert: inhabited Judaea was not as big as Wiltshire.

The length of Palestine, from Dan to Beersheba, is about 180 miles, about as far, say, as from London to Exeter, or to Hull. Its extreme breadth is seventy miles across, but for about half its span the breadth is rarely more than fifty miles from the Jordan to the sea, much the same distance as from Berwick to Edinburgh, not as distant as is Liverpool from Sheffield. Dean Stanley notes that "from almost every high point in the country its whole breadth is visible, from the long walls of the Moab hills on the east to the Mediterranean on the west."

In the terms of the atlas, indeed, Palestine is little more than a stitch on the front of the vast mantle of Asia. Its exiguous size of course is not the measure of its importance. Yet when we read its history in the Old Testament, read of its kings and their kingdoms, we are reading local chronicles. And it must be remembered that local chronicles always expand automatically the territory with which they deal. They are like reading-glasses or microscopes which magnify things out of their actual dimensions.

The reason for thus emphasizing this aggrandisement of the tiny area of Palestine is that there has been so much loose talk of settling therein great numbers of immigrants. Millions even have been proposed, a settlement which could only be achieved if the country was turned into something like one of those unnatural boxes in which expert nurserymen pack together seedlings for sale, and if every man were as artificially planted as his soil would be artificially tilled.

Not only though is Palestine a tiny area, but it has never been a true administrative unit. Its uncertain boundaries are a proof of this. Its present northern boundary is one contrived in 1921, as a sequel to an Anglo French convention, of which railway-routes formed the chief concern. This artificial frontier, separating the territory under British mandate from the territory under French mandate, for the first time enabled calculations to be made of the total superficies of Palestine, or rather of the Palestine thus constituted.

Previously, to the north and to some extent to the east, no one could say where it began or ended. The creators and protagonists of the "National Home" themselves were not sure of the perimeter of the land in which it was to be established. There is an organ of theirs, a pamphletic publication named Palestine, which is an acknowledged herald of their cause in Britain. Mr. Sidebotham, the noted publicist, was its founder and he and other chief Zionist supporters among the Gentiles are fond of contributing to it. When the question of boundaries first arose, Palestine was quite clear about Palestine. It said that "Palestine has never, except for very brief periods, been a political unity, and hardly any definition of its geographical boundaries would agree in detail."

In the official Report of the Shaw Commission, issued in 1929, it was stated that "viewed in the light of the history of at least the last six centuries, Palestine is an artificial conception."

More explicit still was the declaration of the main authority in the realm upon boundaries and all other territorial qualities of States—the Foreign Office. In its pre-War handbook for the guidance of consular and diplomatic officials, the Historical Department of the Foreign Office enunciated that "in modern usage the expression 'Palestine' has no precise meaning, but is taken as equivalent to Southern Syria."

These pronouncements should be remembered tenaciously by the reader. The reason for this is that a practice has been developed since the War of giving the name of "Syria" to the northern part alone of the country. That is to say, the French Mandated region from Tyre to the Turkish border is termed "Syria," as though Palestine were not included in it.

This is a mere deception, and a raw one at that, introduced to consecrate the scission of Syria into two at the end of the late war, and arbitrarily carried out in the interests of the two Mandatory Powers concerned, at the time of the Treaty of Versailles.

Ere then, and from the days of remotest antiquity Syria had been regarded as a natural unit embracing Palestine. In the fourth century before Christ Herodotus wrote, "this part of Syria is known by the name of Palestine." Two thousand years ago "Joseph went up from Galilee out of the city of Nazareth into Judaea to the city of David which is called Bethlehem … to be enrolled with Mary his espoused wife, who was with child," in obedience to the local decree of "Cyrinus, the Governor of Syria." Thus through the succeeding centuries was Syria cited as the country containing the whole littoral at the eastern end of the Mediterranean, down to modern times. One has but to look into any standard history or geography of pre-War date to see it so recorded:

> Syria [for example says Meiklejohn] is a long strip of high mountain country which stretches in an almost straight line from the Peninsula of Sinai to the Gulf of Scanderoon. A small district in the south is called Palestine or the Holy Land."
>
> Its well-defined boundaries, [says George Adam Smith] "the sea on the west, the desert south and east, the Taurus mountains on the north, give it a certain unity and separate it from the rest of the world. If it has not become a single country yet, it is obviously waiting to be one.

When you look at the map, for preference a pre-War map before the treaty-tinkering began, you will see that Syria in shape is a sort of throat under the projecting chin of Asia Minor, and that it closes the eastern end of the Mediterranean. The birth, or spring, of the throat rises out of the desert borders of Egypt, some 120 miles away from the Suez Canal.

The name "Syria" has been thought to be a corruption of "Assyria," but scholars reject this derivation, and say that it comes from the more ancient Babylonian "Suri," a word used three thousand years before the advent of Christ. It entered modern languages through Latin and originally it was not to be found in Arabic, though afterwards it made its way in. The reason for this is most instructive. In classic Arabic Syria is called "Ash Sham," which means "The Left," and the significance of this name is emphasized by its being given in addition to the capital city of the country. Damascus (as we term it) also is designated by its inhabitants Ash Sham." Arabic speakers today, especially in Egypt, often call Syria "Barasham," or "the Land of the Left."

The corresponding word in Arabic for "right" is Yemen (as we spell it) the word we use in English to indicate the south-western tip of Arabia. But the Arabic world also uses it in a more extensive sense, arriving it in a general way to the whole peninsula. Traditionally the Arabs call the Arabian peninsula their right and the Syrian frontage to the Mediterranean their left, showing thereby that from of old the two lands have been the two integral wings of the Arab body.

So therefore in the Arabic name of the country itself—and the Turks call it "Arabistan"—we find implanted a refutation of the character which some of our politicians for their own purposes have sought to apply to it. They have amputated it: they belittle it. They would like Syria to be thought an enigmatic, scarce christened, ill-defined species of no-man's-land, hardly worth a mention, subordinate to Palestine. For them, not surprisingly, the part is greater than the whole.

They have not scrupled even to justify such distortion of geography by invoking the sanctity of Palestine to eke out their pleas. By a quasi-clever confusing of moral with physical and political values, they have said Palestine was "no mere Arab province" but the greatest site in the world, overshadowing all around it. A specious piece of advocacy indeed, for that Bethlehem should be in a humble, "mere Arab province," is a situation consonant with the spirit of Bethlehem. The sacred value of Palestine precludes the political value these same politicians would attribute to it. "My kingdom is not of this world."

No, it is Syria, not Palestine, which is the true unit deserving consideration, and Syria with Palestine in its breast, is Arab territory, inhabited by Arabs for thirteen centuries through good and through ill; "Ash Sham," the left side of their body, the very half of themselves.

That however is not the whole truth. This vast period of thirteen centuries is but the recent period of their immemorial habitation. They have held it thus long as "Arabs." It is exactly thirteen hundred years since their forefathers won a great victory on the banks of the Yarmook against the Byzantine Empire, which had followed the Roman in the overlordship of the country. But the hosts who flowed in then welded with the ancient inhabitants, so that the Arabs of today do not represent a mere conquering race, but are the descendants of the peoples who lived in Palestine before the Israelites. We call them "Arabs," but in that great concourse of their race which stretches from Alexandretta to Mecca and beyond there are many strains to be found, and their roots in the land are those from which history itself springs.

It will no doubt be a great surprise to the average reader to learn that the Arabs preceded the Jews in Syria. Indeed ignorance of this fact, which is altogether too common, is a plank in the platform of the political Zionists. But the very name of the country discloses its un-Jewish character. "Palestine," a word we have taken through Greek and Latin, is a variant of the Arabic "Filisteen," which means the "abode of the Philistines." In the Old Testament the prophets here and there use the word in varying forms. "Rejoice not thou, whole Philistia, that the rod of him that struck thee is broken in pieces.... Howl, o gate; cry, o city! all Philistia is thrown down." (Isaiah, xiv. 29, 31.) "Nations rose up and were angry: sorrows took hold on the inhabitants of Philistiim. Then were the princes of Edom troubled; trembling seized on the stout men of Moab; all the inhabitants of Canaan were made stiff." (Exodus, xv. 14, 15.)

In the quotation from Exodus the word Canaan occurs. As Professor T.H. Robinson, a very great authority, says in his History of Israel, the name "Canaanite is sometimes used as a generic term for pre-Israelite inhabitants of Palestine.... It seems to include the Phoenicians." The name which preceded "Palestine" in its various forms, or the principal of preceding names, was in this way "Canaan." The word still survives as a surname amidst the un-Moslemized inhabitants of the country. It is an extraordinary boomerang-stroke of history, what the French call a *retour des choses*, that one of the ablest of the Arabs today writing in defence of his people's rights should be Dr. T. Canaan.

"The limits of Canaan", says Genesis, "were from Sidon as one comes to Gerara, even to Gaza"—the fruitful coastal plain in fact stretching south from Tyre and Sidon by Haifa and Carmel to the marches of Egypt, different branches of the Canaanite inhabitants were fixed in the inland hilly regions. Amongst these were the Jebusites, who occupied Jerusalem, the site of their city lying outside the walls of the present city.

> It is the opinion of competent judges [declares a great scholar, Sir James Frazer] that the Arabic speaking peasants of Palestine are the descendants of the pagan tribes which dwelt there before the Israelite invasion, and have clung to the soil ever since, being submerged but never destroyed by each successive wave of conquest which has swept over the land.
>
> They are the veritable descendants of the Canaanites described in the bible, of the Jebusites and of the Amorites. [says Sir Richard Temple]. Originally they must have had a decided character of their own and a settled form of society. Their system may have been broken up by the Jewish conquest; but, as the students of Bible history will remember, they

> never yielded to Jewish influence. On the contrary, they often made their influence disastrously felt by the Jewish nationality. They were probably not converted in any large numbers in the early days of Christianity. In short they preserved their ancient idolatry up to the days of Mahomet. Then they were converted by the Arab soldiery to the faith of Islam about twelve hundred years ago. In that faith they have remained this day. They cultivate the soil, chiefly as peasant proprietors, directly under the Turkish official who collects the land-tax. [Written in 1888.] They have extensive rights of grazing and of pasturage, on all which they pay their dues to the Turks. They are called Fellaheen, the same name as their fellow-subjects in Egypt. They till their fields and pay taxes to the Turk patiently, just as they did to the Saracen, to the Arab to the Roman, to the Greek, to the Persian, to the Assyrian— probably also as they did to the Jew. After the Jewish conquest they must often have become tenants of their lands under the Jew as landlord. They probably performed the labour in the fields, even if the Jews worked in the vineyard and in the orchard.

The Canaanites, Jebusites and Amorites of whom Sir Richard Temple speaks were three out of seven indigenous races who, "according to tradition dating back at least to the latter half of the seventh century before Christ" (Robinson), occupied the land before the Jews came. But, as has just been explained, Canaanite is considered more of a generic term for them all than anything else. Of the others the Amorites and the Hittites were the more important, particularly the Amorites, who mainly occupied the country south of the plain of Esdraelon. The Hittites were to the north. Professor Robinson opines that the Amorites emerged, not later than the beginning of the third period of a thousand years before Christ, from the Arabian Peninsula. They "mingled so completely with their predecessors that their identity was lost in most districts." They formed the true Semitic type, and have transmitted their features to their descendants the Arabs.

Such a tenure it is, held in a simple, faithful, laborious way since man emerged from the mists of the unknown, probably the simplest and longest tenure in the world, that we are now finding the means to disintegrate. The Israelites, for the sake of one thirty-fifth of whose descendants we are engaged on this scurvy business, entered the lands of the indigenous peoples at a date which cannot be determined exactly. "The general tendency of the dates at our disposal is in favour of a Fourteenth Century (before Christ) date for the Conquest, but the margin of probability is very small." (Robinson).

On this basis the Israelites came one thousand five hundred years or so after the Amorites. The Philistine cities of the coastal plain had been established somewhere about a century to a century and a half before then.

At first the Israelites entered the hills peacefully in small numbers. Then they took up arms and the warfare began which is chronicled in the Old Testament.

These are very ancient affairs, but it is necessary to deal with them in some measure before turning to modern events. The reason for this is that the Zionists of today have been introduced into Palestine under colour of their ancestors' possession of that land. It is convenient to examine this plea, in some part at least, while the first data of the country are being supplied. The relevant section of the Palestine Mandate declares that, through the institution of the Mandate itself and the special character which it bears:

> ...recognition has thereby been given to the historical connection of the Jewish people with Palestine and to the grounds for reconstituting their national home in that country.

"Historical connection"—that is what is used to justify the establishment of the "National Home" and all that has resulted from it. There are two points from which it can be considered: (1) Why should remote historical connection confer any right to territory some eighteen and a half centuries after Jewish power ended; and (2) If remote historical connection is to be regarded as conferring rights, what sort of historical connection was there with the land in which this national home was to be reconstituted?

The second point really contains the first, since any value there might be in this plea of Palestine being the historic patrimony of the Jews must be considerably affected by the character of their occupation when they were there. Yet nothing contrasts so much with the free hand given to the Zionists in the Holy Land as the entire disregard of this point by those who were responsible for giving them this free hand. Everything to go with the "National Home" was left purposely in the most obscure state by the politicians who engineered its creation.

No word was uttered by them to disclose which phase of the very varied Jewish past in Palestine the Zionists were to reconstitute. The probability of course is that "The Principal Allied Powers," the junta which, seated round a table at the San Remo Conference of 1920, introduced the establishment of the "National Home" as an obligation of the Mandate, knew and cared nothing about any such phases. I should not credit the Principal Allied Powers, as far as they found form in flesh and blood at San Remo, with much or any reading of the Scriptures, except indeed the important section of the Principal Allied Powers which came from Criccieth in North Wales. That body politic has stated in a speech, "I was brought up in a school where I was taught far more about the history of the Jews than about the history of my own land. I could tell you all the kings of Israel but I doubt whether I could have named half a dozen of the kings of England... We were thoroughly imbued with the history of the Hebrew race in the days of its greatest glory."

Mr. Lloyd George seems to have been imbued rather too much with greatest glory for any of his impregnation to have filtered into geographical definition of the "National Home" by himself or by his compeers. Yet there would seem to have been the most obvious need of such definition because between the days of Joshua and the final victory of the Romans under Titus the Jewish holdings in Palestine expanded, and then contracted like a concertina in play. For a good period they slipped from Jewish grip altogether. So that in order to reconstruct them, it would have appeared the essential first step to discover and to delineate them.

It was decided otherwise, though, at San Remo or, more probably, in the manner of the Principal Allied Powers, attention discreetly was not directed to the matter. The Zionists were left to reconstruct wheresoever they liked west of the Jordan. It is a significant testimony to the genuine ness of the transaction.

This renders it needful, however, for anyone trying to treat the whole business seriously to pay some attention to the extent and to the duration of Jewish territorial possession of Palestine. It may seem to be challenging all traditions to say that it was ephemeral, but that is what it was. It was ephemeral and inextensive. Only during the reigns of David and Solomon did anything like Jewish possession of what we call Palestine exist. Eight hundred years afterwards the Maccabees re-established the Jewish power which had faded with Solomon, but only for a short spasm did it perhaps reach again the dimensions of David's and Solomon's days.

Before David the settlement of the twelve tribes by Joshua was purely nominal. "Joshua assigned territory to tribes which they could not fill." (Belloc, in *The Battle-Ground.*) Biblical research discredits the power and the hegemony of the tribes. "In Judges V," says Professor Robinson, "there are significant omissions. Of the four senior Leah tribes Reuben only is mentioned. Our evidence suggests that Simeon and Levi disappeared at an early period," and again "Verse 19 of Judges I. ('And the Lord was with Judah and he possessed the hill-country, but was not able to destroy the inhabitants of the valley, because they had many chariots armed with scythes') tells us that the lower land was not taken." The tribe of Judah itself is not included amidst the victorious tribes in the canticle of Deborah in the later fifth chapter of Judges. "We can only suppose that it was not yet fully recognized as an Israelitish tribe." "The early history of the tribe of Judah is even more obscure than that of most of the others, and we have to wait till the time of David before we have unmistakable evidence of its existence and of its self-consciousness."

The tribes named as by the sea were there in a situation of dependence and there is no proof of their being in any numbers. The coastal cities held sway over the plain of Esdraelon.

> Sometimes the guardianship was so effective and close that Israel was denied the use of the main roads altogether, and the tribesmen had to creep by unfrequented by-ways and crooked paths from one place to another if they wished to cross the forbidden land. (Robinson.)

When Saul established his kingdom, he never obtained possession of the plain of Esdraelon, and he was indeed so little master in his own hills that the Philistines had a fortress looking down on the Jordan Valley. There is no evidence that David himself conquered the Esdraelon plain, no direct evidence. The nearest is supplied by recent archaeological excavation which has found traces that the strong place of Bethshean was destroyed by fire round about the year 1,000 B.C. Inferentially it is clear though that the plain must have been open to David, since it formed the turn-table of routes to his outlying possessions. He may have held it in some sort of condominium with the Philistine cities. At the apogee of his rule after fighting them he had grown to such terms with the Philistines that his own personal forces or life-guards were drawn from a sort of Foreign Legion of the Arabs' ancestors.

> In addition to his national levy, David had at least the nucleus of a standing army. It is interesting to observe that its main strength was drawn from foreign sources, for the Cherethites and the Pelethites were almost certainly Philistines, and they not only formed the mainstay of David's personal force, but their presence in the ranks of Solomon went far to secure his accession. They were to David what the Praetorian Guard were to Roman Emperors. (Robinson.)

Since King David forms a pedestal of Zionist claims, he being considered as it were an ancestor of modern Zionists, equal connection between that far yesterday and today must be granted to the Arabs. The pedestal of Zionist claims reigned by support of Arab troopers. Arabs in large part gave his throne to Solomon.

The effect of these considerations need not be emphasized. But, without pursuing them, granting for argument's sake that David won power over Esdraelon, to which his son succeeded, to what a tiny span this reduces the Israelite possession of Palestine. David reigned for about forty years, from somewhere round 1016 B.C. Solomon succeeded him and reigned as long. After these two all collapsed. It will have taken David a good part of the earlier half of his reign to reach the maximum of his power, and Solomon well before the end of his reign had begun to sell or lose art of his possessions. Let ten years be deducted, and that is as little as can be deducted reasonably, from the total David-Solomon period of rule. Then seventy years remain.

It was only during those meagre seventy years that the Jews held something like two-thirds of Palestine, and there is doubt enough of that. "It is probable," says Wade in his *Old Testament History*, "that only in the neighbourhood of Joppa (the modern Jaffa) did David's empire touch the sea. North of this the Phoenician towns of Tyre and of Sidon were left unmolested, while in the south-east the Philistines, though crippled, maintained their independence."

Dean Stanley crystallizes the position when he says, "Palestine reverses the usual situation wherein the aborigines are driven into the hills. The Jews conquered the hills but failed to take the plains."

In this seventy-year empire there was little territorial basis or unity. David within his small limits—"120 miles at longest and 60 at widest and often much less" are the limits Mr. Belloc assigns to the Jewish State at its most prideful—was something of an Austro-Hungarian monarch occupying the throne while Austria and Hungary fought each other.

Even David on two critical occasions seems to have saved his throne by playing off the one (the North or Israel and the South or Judah) against the other, and it is noticeable that when Judah rose against him he received the support of the other tribes and vice-versa. It is clear that the ideal unity was far from being achieved in his lifetime, and the policy of Solomon, so far from cementing more firmly the two parties, tended rather to emphasize the distinction between them and to widen the original breach. It is then hardly surprising that, when the North found the burden of the House of David intolerable, the South should have taken the opposite side and maintained its allegiance to Rehoboam.

From that time onward, though there was a certain sense of unity as against the rest of the world, that feeling never found expression in a single political organization. There were periods in the history of the divided kingdom when the two sections worked together in harmony, though North was the dominant partner, and we may suspect that the co-operation of the South was not wholly voluntary. But down to the time when the kingdom of Israel came to an end and the Samaritan territory was incorporated as a province of the Assyrian Empire, there does not seem to have been a single point at which the possibility of a formal reunion entered men's minds. [There was a sense of kinship, of oneness, but] the fundamental basis of this sense of oneness lay less in the common descent than in the common religion. The Judaean had always stood apart from the Ephraimite.

Reviewing David's reign, Professor Robinson continues:

> David, as it were, collected and laid in place the material for a noble kingdom which might have been expanded into an empire. But it inevitably lacked that cement of habituation which time alone could supply, and for its endurance it needed a succession of rulers who would maintain his spirit and carry on his traditions. But the two kings who immediately allowed him were cast in another mould, with the result that first the outlying portion fell, and then, at the touch of a real test, the whole fabric crumbled away.... The bubble was pricked and the house of David was left with territories scanty and infertile in themselves, suffering from the ravages of despotism and of war.

How far these territories shrank is well shown by another historical authority, Dr. Foakes Jackson of Cambridge University, in his Josephus and the Jews. Commenting upon the silence of Herodotus, "the most persistent and inquisitive of globe-trotters," concerning the Jews, he says:

> The silence of Herodotus is still a problem to some, but its solution is perfectly simple. Judaea was so small a district and its inhabitants were so insignificant that the most intelligent traveller in the fifth century B.C. (the date of Herodotus) might even visit what was then called Syria Palestine, or Syria of the Philistines, and never hear of the Jews. In the time of Nehemiah (a contemporary of Herodotus) Jerusalem must have been a very insignificant city in which the inhabitants of the neighbouring villages were only with difficulty persuaded to dwell; and no place mentioned in his Book as Jewish was much more than ten miles away. As the prophet says, it was "the day of small things". What is more remarkable than the insignificance of the Jews in Palestine in the days of Nehemiah (445–432 BC) is that their territory remained restricted, nor do they seem to have multiplied in the country for nearly three centuries. The Temple at Jerusalem increased in splendour and probably the city in population, but the Jews did not become a power in the land till nearly the middle of the second century before Christ. [The Maccabee period.] They were no doubt numerous in Babylonia and Egypt, but in Palestine they were well nigh negligible.

In his *The Battle-Ground* Mr. Belloc says of the tiny plot of Judah, "How small it was can best be seen in this; that a man walking out from Jerusalem eastward or northward or westward would have reached its boundaries in a morning. It was not a dozen miles in any direction before he was out of the district which the chieftain, the petty so-called 'king' of Jerusalem claimed to govern." "It was a poor handkerchief of a realm."

It would be easy enough to emphasize this point with further quotations from further sources, old and new, but the truth of the matter is sufficiently clear. Jewish tenure of Palestine, in any real sense of the word "Palestine," was never complete and it only lasted continuously, within its limits, for seventy years. It lasted, this vaunted possession, for no longer than the lifetime of one man, and that was three thousand years ago. Under the Maccabees it was a still shorter possession, some fifty years at the most between Simon and Alexander Jannaeus. But the Maccabees really ruled as High Priests, and the essential quality of Judaism, that it was religious and not territorial, was emphasized under them by the action of Eleazar. He called on the Maccabee John Hyrcanus to divest himself of his priesthood, his true quality at the head of the Jews, because of Hyrcanus's very absorption in the unbecoming secular conquest of lands and cities.

If we turn, then, bearing all this in mind, to compare the Arab historic situation in Palestine with the Jewish historic situation there, what a contrast between the two there is. The Arab possession began five thousand years ago and has never ceased. It has been the most thoroughgoing possession of all possessions, one which had its own share of conquest and its lengthy dominion where the Israelite power came and glittered and buzzed for a gnat's span and was gone, but it has been above all possession by uncounted generations of peasants. The passing centuries have given them different names, as one strain after another was absorbed into them, but Amorite, Canaanite, Philistine, Arab, it has been the labouring stock of each and of all which has held the soil, and by that tenure their present representatives, the Arabs, claim Palestine today.

Peasants as they were, and pagans for so long, it is not to be assumed that in every aspect the Arabs' ancestors represented barbarism in contrast to Israelite civilization. The Phoenicians were the traders and the voyagers of the ancient world, who reached Britain itself. The Philistines "possessed an advanced and ancient culture." (Robinson.) "It is," he adds, "a curious irony of fate that the term Philistine should have come to mean barbaric." This usage of course sprang up through the history of their day coming to us through the Israelites, who had no brief for their foes. "If the Gentile accounts," says Dean Stanley, "are insensible to the cruel idol-worship of this race" (speaking of "the Canaanites") "the Israelite versions mostly take no heed of the noble aspect which this great people presented to the Western world."

"The Old Testament is the only document illuminating the life of the country." (Belloc.) Or again, in Stanley, "the detested and accursed race of Canaanites, as it appears in the Books of Joshua and of Judges, is the same as that to which from Greece we look back as to the parent of letters, of commerce, of civilization."

So much for "historical connection." To resurrect that which the Jews had in order to impose them upon the Arabs of Palestine does not bear consideration. That a possession of Palestine so ephemeral and so broken as the Israelite should give them a valid right to oust the Arabs in any degree, eighteen centuries after the last shadow of the Israelite flicker of power faded, is a thesis too fantastic to be taken seriously. If, though, the historic connections of far-vanished eras are to be used as a charter today, then at least let it be historic connection. If extravagant claims drawn upon dim antiquity provide title-deeds in Palestine, then it is the Arabs who have the really extravagant and wholly ancient claim, and their right to these strange title-deeds is as unquestionable as their right to the true deeds, proceeding from their current thirteen centuries of occupation.

Now for the codicil to this. The Jews, in their territorially exiguous stay in a comer of Palestine, were, but for the passing few years above mentioned, confined to its hill recesses. Josephus himself, the historian of the Jews, who described the fall of Jerusalem, underlines this fact:

> As for ourselves, [he declares] we therefore neither inhabit a maritime country nor do we delight in merchandise, nor in such a mixture with other men as arises from it. But the cities we dwell in are remote from the sea, and having a fruitful country for our habitation, we take pains in cultivating that only.

What follows from this? When the "National Home" was established under British patronage—we are leaving aside now the question of the "National Home's" legitimacy—the assumption surely was that the new Zionist colonies would have been established in the old eyries of the Jewish interior. A certain number, it is true, were so founded eventually. But from the start the Zionist authorities preferred to seek land in the plains. The acreage they own in the plains now far and away surpasses their acreage in the hills. If the figures of the Peel Commission be taken the total of Zionist holdings in Palestine is 1,332,000 dunams, or 333,000 acres. In the hills they hold about 80,000 acres. "It is not the hills, but the plains, the Maritime Plain and the Plain of Esdraelon—which are the centres of Jewish colonization," observes Mr. Leonard Stein in the course of an argument that the Zionists are not responsible for Arabs being crowded into the heights.

This means that the Zionists have preferred to buy where the land was level, or convenient for transport, or suitable for reclaiming, or rich, rather than to buy where the land was Zion. No pressure was put on them to purchase the particular sites which they chose. All their apologists have gone out of their way, indeed, to maintain that till fairly recently Arabs made no difficulty about selling to Jews anywhere. The recent difficulties, they never tire of repeating, are due to the artificial anti-Semitic agitation organized by the politicians in the towns.

Well and good. This is an argument to be considered and to be met when the question of the relations between Arab leaders and the Arab population comes under examination. But if in that issue the Zionists can employ it, just as decidedly it is an argument against them in this issue and one which they themselves must admit, since it was they who produced it. When they were free, then, to buy where they liked, which was pretty well all the time, they bought (and they have continued to buy) principally in the plains.

Without any doubt the motives of the Zionist leaders in making these lowland settlements were extremely practical. Here were the accessible sites for the industrial transformation of Palestine which they planned. As far as agriculture was concerned, they were determined that their colonies should possess the finest land obtainable. They fixed their farms and their orchards, their experimental stations and dairies where a good return from them seemed likely, so that they might be self-dependent. They did not want their colonies and their colonists to be maintained by the bounty of Jews in other parts of the world, which bounty had been in general the uneconomic mainstay of the pre-War Jewish population and the pre-War Jewish colonies.

They took into consideration the agricultural future of the region and came to the conclusion that the finest prospects in the country lay in citrus-planting, a generic term for the growing of fruit of the orange family. There was perhaps not so much difficulty in arriving at this conclusion, since Arab fruit-growers had long established the Jaffa orange on the markets of the world. The Zionists decided to follow in their lead, and determined to specialize in orange-groves and in plantations of like nature. They also engaged, as is known, in forestry and in the drainage of marshes, work of primary value in a country neglected by the Turks.

In fine, their agricultural policy was good and sensible, with the sole proviso that for trading reasons they might be in danger of over-production of citrus-fruit. There would be nothing to say about it but to commend it, were it not for one reason. That reason, however, is all-important.

The Zionists did not come to Palestine to practise colonization. The Mandate did not summon them thither because of their historic connection with oranges. They are practicing Zionism. They have obtained their warranty for entry into the land—such as it is from such as gave it to them—and they have been set down there in a situation of privilege beyond the dreams of colonists in any other part of the world, for what cause? Precisely upon the grounds that they are not ordinary colonists seeking for good land or for advantageous concessions. Precisely upon the grounds that they are not planting trees or draining marshes or sowing vegetables like other pioneers in other lands, but are engaged in a spiritual act, in the rebuilding of its vanished sanctuary for the errant Jewish soul. Precisely because they are returning like pilgrims, austerely, to their ancient home, be it ever so humble—and ever so profitless.

The extraordinary licence which they have received, to be injected into Palestine against the will of its inhabitants, is based purely upon their coming to regain the soil which they lost, "to reconstitute their national home," to reconstruct the walls of Zion which have fallen down. I say nothing now of the full motives of those who gave them this licence. Whatever these men had in their hearts, it was under the terms of "reconstituting their national home in that country" that they summoned the Zionists to Palestine. But what regard for that did the Zionists show?

What sort of connection is there between reconstituting this home and the planting of 30,000 acres of orange-groves in the maritime plain which even David could not make Jewish, in the plains of the Canaanites and the Philistines and of their descendants, the Arabs? How does historical connection square with the Jewish National Fund's holdings, three years ago, of some 8,000 acres in the fruitful Phoenician plains of Acre and Haifa, confronted with a single thousand in stony Galilee? How do the 80,000 acres occupied in the hills, a vision of Zionism, blot out from sight the 250,000 substantial acres in the plains? What are the 150,000 town dwellers of Tel-Aviv doing by the Mediterranean? Are they reconstructing the tents of Saul, or perhaps the pillars of Samson? Of the 400,000 souls who constitute to date the Jewish National Home, how many are tilling in the hills? Four thousand one hundred. If ever figures spoke, these do.

It might be objected that the Zionists could not have got in Judaea the extent of land they obtained in Phoenicia. It might be objected that they could not acquire what was not existent, or not available, and that they only were taking what they could get where they could get it. But that was exactly what they must never do. It was a question of principle. If Zionist motives were to stand examination Zionists must refuse to consider land, however fertile, which had no part in the reconstruction of Zion. The situation would have been different if they had been entering the country as ordinary colonists under the regulations laid down by a native government or by a government in consultation with the natives, with no Mandatory clearing a way for them.

Under such circumstances they could have entered Palestine wherever it was convenient and have bought wherever they wished, and have won the usual rewards of increased wealth.

But when they entered as they did, ringed by bayonets, against the will of the native population, on the ground that they were to reconstruct something out of the past which they alone could reconstruct, and that its transcendent character gave them a right to such privilege, then by the Lord Harry they had to reconstruct it only, nor ever stir from its site. "For what have you to do with me, O Tyre and Sidon and all the coasts of the Philistines?", it is written in the Book of Joel.

Suppose, however, that amidst their many holdings a few had been scattered round the retreating borders of ancient Israel's ever-shrinking realm. It would have been perhaps academic to quibble about the situation of these. But, as things were and are today, we are not dealing with a few accidental border-holdings of this type. We are dealing with a policy which is content, nay, anxious, to "re-establish" the Jewish National Home as a State where previously it had not been established. Under the guidance of their leaders the Zionists return—to whence they have never come forth. British statesmen, or men at least occupied in affairs of state, incite them on, authorize their arrival because of their "historical connection" with Palestine, and in virtue of that encourage them to take over territory with which at no time, since history began, have they had any true, durable, historic connection whatsoever.

Now, as these pages are being revised, the National Home may be transmuted (as was intended always) into a Zionist State or "autonomous enclave" or "self-governing canton" or whatever other pseudonym is preferred. If this be so, it will be established in the plains, by the Mediterranean and amid the orchards, a travesty of the Israelite past, a Temple to the design of the money-changers, a Zion for Sadducees.

But the admonitions of that rejected past wait upon the modern Zionists and visit their imposture with prophetic rebuke. "Because thou hast forgotten the God of thy salvation and hast not been mindful of the God of thy strength, therefore shalt thou plant pleasant plants, and shalt set it with strange slips." "O God, the heathens are come into thy inheritance; they have defiled thy holy Temple; they have made Jerusalem as a place to keep fruit."

Chapter 2

The great Arab race.
The possession of Palestine necessary for its expansion.

In the previous chapter it has been shown that Palestine is but a section of the larger natural unit of Syria; that Syria itself is an integral portion of the great Arab inheritance; that the plea under which the Zionists have been introduced into Palestine, their "historical connection" with the land, cannot be properly used to override the ownership of the Arab inhabitants who have an infinitely more ancient historical connection; and finally, that the Zionists themselves have betrayed their inner estimation of this "historical connection" by "reconstructing" their National Home where for the most part the Jewish race has never had a home.

I now return to deal with the Arabs, the Arabs strictly so-called, of the last thirteen centuries in Palestine. Strange to say, the name they bear is a marked disadvantage to them. Relatively few people know anything of the Arabs' great past. We Europeans owe more to them than we credit. For nearly three hundred years they led the world in civilization. We drew from them most of our mathematical system. The figures or numerals we use are "Arabic numerals." Algebra is a corruption of "Al-jebr," the first words of the title of a ninth-century work by an Arab scholar. The Arabs also developed the practice of medicine, founded universities, brought farming and gardening to a high level.

Today the extraordinary achievements of the Arabs are forgotten and the destruction of their civilization by the Turks passes as a consequence of its own decay. No other race has had such a hard lot in history as to be identified with its own oppressors and to be found guilty of the crimes by which it was slain. But this false and absurd verdict has been accepted in popular belief through the centuries. In our time the barrenness of any plot of Arab ground is attributed to the shiftlessness of the Arab, who in reality is as good a husbandman as his forefathers, and never to the pestilent Ottoman yoke. That yoke forced parts of the Arab race out into the desert, and it seems to be these Arabs of the desert alone who typify the race to the Western publics.

The average Briton thinks of the Arab as a bearded man in flowing robes who gallops about firing rifles at nothing (except perhaps latterly in

Palestine). He lives in a tent and is ruled by sheikhs with burning eyes and a tendency to abduction.

This concept is nonsensical. Still, it is widely held. One of the Arab delegates who have come so regularly, and so vainly, to England for so many years, to plead the cause of their people with successive occupants of Whitehall, told me of an incident which shows this well. He and his fellow-delegates were paying a visit to the House of Commons.

They waited in the lobby for a Member to come out and see them. Presently he emerged, cast his eyes over them and over others waiting, and then looked round at a loss. He did not conceive that the quiet men dressed in clothes like his own could be an Arab delegation. His gaze searched the lobbies for banditti in burnouses, girt by dangling scimitars, with cords binding their head-dresses.

The grave disadvantage of this preconception is that it makes those who entertain it fall in only too readily with the notion, so valuable to Zionists, that the Arabs are a semi-barbaric block of Easterns, who need direction at all points from educated Western governors.

Whereas the Arabs, like the peoples of Europe, are an assemblage of all ranges of men. They have of course their great peasantry of shepherds and husbandmen wearing the old traditional garments that were worn by the first Christians. But they possess an educated, professional, commercial class in as large proportion to their numbers as we possess ourselves, possibly in a larger proportion. The educated youth of Syria has long frequented schools and universities of French and United States' foundation. A number of them have come to England to study law or medicine, or to engage in commerce. In Manchester there is a considerable colony of Arab business-men, but as it happens there and elsewhere these Arabs escape notice because they are known by their truer name of Syrians.

There are Syrian clergy of all the principal confessions. There are numbers of Syrian bank-clerks, Syrian chemists, Syrian journalists.

It may stir some readers to know that there are Syrians who are millionaires. A good many others, without becoming millionaires, have gained various degrees of wealth and of comfort in South America. In a humbler stage of activity, droves of them traverse as pedlars the republics of Latin America. In the United States they have large colonies. There are plenty of them in Africa.

Wherever the Syrians live they show themselves exceedingly competent business-men. In fact, they are sometimes thought too competent, too versed in the tricks of business. Perhaps they are so on occasions, but at least this is a proof that they need none of the schooling from the Zionists of which one reads so much.

Altogether they possess a full complement of educated persons, and if education goes for anything have as much right to look after themselves and to be masters in their own land as we have.

I might have added to my little catalogue of their capacities that the Arabs are good linguists. This is not surprising, because they are a diverse people in themselves. The Arabs of Syria have, as we have just seen, a good many strains in them. Their country has been held by a series of overlords, and has been at different times both a place of battle and a place of refuge. Pursuers and pursued alike have left their traces.

In the *Seven Pillars of Wisdom* Lawrence of Arabia enumerates at least sixteen sub-divisions of the population between the Turkish and the Egyptian borders. But it would take a Lawrence to perceive these sub-divisions, just as it takes foreign specialists to distinguish between the provinces and counties of the British Isles, and he himself put the general position admirably when he said that "the appearances and customs of the present Arabic-speaking peoples of Asia, while as varied as a field full of poppies, had an equal and essential likeness."

To take a different kind of metaphor, it might be said that the Arabs are like a great wall in which there are bricks of many shapes and hues, but all mortared together. Their junction perhaps, is more elastic, looser, more insecure even, than that of bricks laid upon each other, but the resemblance is near enough to give a fair idea of their national formation.

The Arabs' mortar is largely compounded of religious faith. Whether in Irak or in Syria or in Sinai they mostly are Moslem. But in Syria there is a big Christian minority, a minority of Christians too who have a lineage of belief from the days of Christ in Palestine. (Yet of the "historical connection" of Arab Christians with the land of Christ what have we heard from British Government or from League of Nations?) And there are small bodies amongst them with other beliefs.

Therefore while religious faith is a powerful bond it is not the supreme bond. This bond is the Arabic language. The Arabic language binds all the sections of Arabs together. Their common use of it, and the common ways of thought which this entails, have made them one of the great national units of the world. Indeed they have attained before others that type of national unity to which mankind is moving, the unity of those who speak a single tongue.

They have an evident affinity with the British Commonwealth in the sense that (if they get a proper chance) they are likely to form a group of Arab countries, each independent of the other, but with some common link, as the King is for our various self-ruling states.

Their nearness to each other ought to prove helpful towards this ideal. They are bunched together in the south-western corner of Asia. There is however another point of view from which their geographical position has to be considered, and it is one which has an important bearing upon the particular affairs of Palestine.

If you look off-handedly at a map of Asia, the Arabs, with Syria. Irak and the great peninsula of Arabia proper, appear to hold a huge extent of territory. The friends of political Zionism are always drawing attention to this. They wave their hands in wide circles at the Arab territories and then ask rhetorically whether with all this in their possession the Arabs cannot spare them a morsel in Palestine. Lord Balfour himself, in an unusual apologetic moment, made this plea in a speech once.

But if you look at the map carefully you see that most of the great Arab expanse is uninhabitable. Limitless stretches of naked desert occupy nearly the whole surface of it. In Syria there is an inhabited western fringe; in Irak a broader eastern fringe watered by the Tigris and the Euphrates. The peninsula of Arabia has a mere band of cultivation and of habitation round its extreme hilly edges, a few oases inland. Desert, desert and desert; gravel, lava and sand; that is the story of the Arabs' country in the main.

So for them, their most precious holdings are their rare cultivable tracts, on the east in Irak and on the west in Syria. Therefore Palestine is not a superfluity of theirs but a necessity. Lord Balfour's appeal should have run, "Can the Arabs not spare for the Jews the small cornfield out of their vast desolation? Can the Arabs not spare for the Jews the iron ration out of their famine?"

There is another consideration, too, and an even greater one. For the Arabs, Syria represents their outlook upon the Mediterranean Sea, their contact with the West. It is their forward gate, and it is in so far as they hold it and keep it and make it thoroughly their own that they will mingle their lives and their destinies, in their own way, with Europe. It is not by rickety back-doors on the Persian Gulf, by the hot oven-lids of Muscat or Koweit, that the Arabs are going to find their way into the world's centre. Now they are cooped up amidst the arid lands and the baking seas which lie between Persia and Egypt. But this has never been their desire. It is a situation which has been forced upon them. Their natural outlook is the European Mediterranean. "The Arabs," says Lawrence, "looked always to the Mediterranean, not to the Indian Ocean, for their cultural sympathies, for their enterprises, and particularly for their expansions, since the migration problem was the greatest and the most complex force in Arabia, and was general to it, however it might vary in the different Arabic districts."

"The new Arabia," writes Professor W. E. Hocking of Harvard University, in his standard work, *The Spirit of World Politics*, "reached the Mediterranean through Palestine. The progress of the Zionist colonization thus becomes for the Arab national outlook a culminating stroke in a prolonged series of breaches of faith."

These breaches of faith will be exposed in the course of this book. What is to be noted at the present point is—who speaks at Geneva or in Whitehall of the Arab migration problem? There has been infinite, endless talk there about Jewish exiles, though indeed not much hint of settling them in our own lands, for all our professed sympathy. But about the plight of the Arabs, continually driven north by their increasing numbers, or driven into the desert because of their inability to reach the more fertile northern or eastern fringes, is there a word spoken?

Lawrence tells of these currents of tribal movement and shows how they have not at all been due to hazard—what we might call Bedouin errancy—but instead have been the result of economic want. "Nor then," says he, "did the pressure cease: the inexorable trend northward continued. The tribes found themselves driven to the very edge of cultivation in Syria or Mesopotamia. Opportunity and their bellies persuaded them of the advantage of possessing goats, and then of possessing sheep; and lastly they began to sow, if only a little barley for their animals. They were now no longer Bedouin, and began to suffer like the villagers from the ravages of the nomads behind. Insensibly they made common cause with the peasants already on the soil, and found out that they, too, were peasantry. So we see clans, born in the highlands of Yemen, thrust by stronger clans into the desert, where, unwillingly, they became nomad to keep themselves alive."

The race which has this unceasing dilemma of settlement before it is very prolific. Its progeny almost springs as we look at it. To where shall it expand? It is not oases in the desert which will increase to suit it. Irak can take a moiety, no doubt, but no more. It is true that the narrow fertile belts of Palestine and of Northern Syria can indeed receive themselves but few newcomers. Yet what is to be said of the statesmanship which is determined to go on filling with persons from foreign lands the little space that is available therein? What sort of statesmanship is it which places across the narrow Arab upward and westward path the bar of Jewish occupation? What right and what sense is there in denying to the Arabs their natural opening to the Mediterranean, or, to put it better, since they already possess it, in taking it from them and in placing strangers at their gates?

On that Mediterranean shore, so near the highway to India, we especially have deep concern. We shall have to seek accommodation for our interests there. The more these interests are pondered, the more wildly foolish does our present policy appear. Into a plain issue between the Arabs and ourselves, which might have been determined by motives of friendship, we insert a foreign factor. We banish friendship, we introduce the

Zionists and go on introducing them, we levy an army and call reservists to the colours and ship troops and lose our soldiers' lives so that Zionists may continue to be introduced. We, as it were, plant brambles everywhere, and defend with rifle and gun the international tangle which ensues. The problems of the future which should have been simple enough become ravelled and complex and even perhaps beyond our untwisting.

Chapter 3

The Zionist movement an intrusion upon a previous Arab movement. The modern Arab renaissance. The Arab preparations to overthrow Turkish rule in Syria and to re-establish the old Arab State.

One of the axioms upon which the Palestine Question too often is based is that there has been in that country of late but a single political movement, which is Zionism. Zionism, according to this theory, impinged upon a population which mentally was motionless, and any vigour, or political activity which that population may have showed since has been nothing but a reaction to the intense Jewish effort.

This is a wicked perversion of fact. The Zionist movement, as far as it took shape within Palestine in these later years, followed upon an Arab movement, so genuine and so strong that in the end men were to lay down their lives for it. The Zionist movement sprang, as will be seen, from outside the country: the Arab movement was a native one comparable to the irredentist cause in the parts of Italy which were under Austrian rule, or in Alsace-Lorraine or in Poland. Like these causes, it aimed at the restoration or completion of an old sovereignty, and would without doubt have developed as they have done into fully restored nationhood if it had not been for the unexpected establishment of the Mandatory system.

Therefore Zionism, which as a political reality was only created by the terms of the Mandate, far from being the sole force which has stirred Palestine, was a secondary force arbitrarily introduced from outside which did nothing but retard the native, previous and primary force of Arabism.

The great difference between the two movements will become apparent as I detail them. *Seniores priores:* let me take the Arab action first.

The Arab empire in Syria, which underwent many vicissitudes, and was nearly destroyed by the Crusades, ended in the sixteenth century. The Turks then became masters of the country, but the Arab population continued to hold the land under their suzerainty. This situation lasted till the Napoleonic wars, when the French established themselves in the south. But how Sir Sidney Smith defended Acre against them is one of the doughty records of our history.

There followed an interlude of Egyptian overlordship and then, through European intervention, the Turks were re-established and ruled over Palestine and the other parts of Syria (the Lebanon canton, predominantly Christian, having a measure of autonomy) till their power broke for good before the armies of Allenby in 1918.

It may be noted that I have used phrases such as "suzerainty" and "overlordship" to describe the Turkish dominion in Syria. This is because the Turks conquered lands, but did not colonize them. Once their rule was established, thenceforward they confined themselves to milking the territories under their control for taxes and, amongst Moslems, for conscripts for their army. The Sultans held sway over many non-Turkish peoples, and the Sultan himself was little other than a supreme landlord possessing a vast number of tenants. Provided they paid exorbitant rents and did not question his ownership, the Sultan and his pashas left the tenants, strangers to him, to look after themselves.

This has a notable bearing upon Syria. The people of Palestine in one respect remained their own masters under Turkish rule. When the Turkish officials were not exerting themselves harshly the Arabs were free and entirely amongst each other. In the course of time, too, they came to have compatriots set over them, Arabs who acted indeed as Turkish officials and had to identify themselves with Turkish rule, but none the less were Arabs. Musa Kazim Pasha, who led till his recent death the Arab delegations to London, had been governor of the Jaffa district under the Turks.

Therefore the Arabs are not unaccustomed to governing. The Turkish system which they administered was a bad one, and nobody could shine in office, but at least they had experience of governmental routine. Dispatches and files and so forth are not the mysteries to the Arabs which is suggested by the latter's description in Article 22 of the Covenant of the League of Nations. Therein they are catalogued along with other mandated peoples as "not yet being able to stand by themselves under the strenuous conditions of the modern world."

This phrase of the Covenant, it may be as well to interpolate here, is part of the chicanery developed for the benefit of Palestine. In Palestine until 1918 there were no strenuous conditions. Existence went along on traditional lines in general. Clearly, there would have been some gradual and quiet development after 1918, with British help, if the Arabs had been left to themselves. But there would have been no sudden appearance of strenuous modern conditions, because the Arabs had no desire to install them.

As soon though as we could, as soon as the then British Government could, it imported the Zionists into Palestine and ipso facto created, as it intended to create, "strenuous modern conditions" in that unhappy country. The next step, of course, was to take charge of the natives to protect them from the strenuousness. The situation of Palestine, in fact, became that of a man whom a benefactor knocks down with a motor-car, so that he may not be able "to stand by himself." Whereon the benefactor leaving the car, rushes to uphold the victim and to guide his faltering steps

However the point is that before being thus succoured, the Arabs were not thrust out by the Turks of all control in and over Palestine. The educated classes had some part in their own government, and the Arab masses even had a say in a more extensive field of affairs. "Under the Ottoman regime," says the official report of the 1929 Shaw Commission, "no doubt the more important activities of provincial and even perhaps of municipal bodies were controlled either directly or indirectly by the central Government. But the fact remains that even the peasant, provided that he paid so small a sum as ten shillings per annum in direct taxation, could feel that through the exercise of his voting powers he had a voice in the control of his village, and indirectly, through the system of secondary elections, in the control of the affairs of the larger administrative units, up to the Ottoman Empire itself."

These are the words of a British Commission, which in its next few sentences, after allowance has been made for the material benefits and for the better administration of our rule, recognizes that a case exists for those who contrast Arab self-government under the Turks with their situation under our regime. The Arabs, sums up the Commission, were indeed given opportunities of self-government in 1922, but their leaders refused them on the ground that they would not amount to as much as they had under Turkey. The Commission records this fact without attempting to controvert it.

Still, that share in local self-government and that small say in the first class affairs of Turkey which the Arabs held, if they do show to advantage compared with the Arabs' present abject political status, were in themselves nothing so much. They were only enjoyed at the price of the surrender of national feeling. Men who exercised them had to drop Arab nationalism and act as Turkish subjects.

But Arab nationalism, or rather the feeling that Arabs had of individuality and of insulation from their rulers, which later was to take the usual guise of nationalism, always existed amongst them. It had dormant periods, but like so many nationalisms began to emerge vigorously into life in the mid-nineteenth century. It was stronger in Syria than in any other part of the Arab lands. Syria was in contact with Europe. The Christians of the Lebanon, benefiting by their special rights, led the way.

The Syrians began the national renaissance with what may be called an intellectual rising. They made the printing press busy. They published an Arabic encyclopaedia They translated Homer and Virgil and other classics, and then the works of more modern poets and essayists out of the various European languages. There was more than research in these discoveries of the literature of the West. Reading great Western books, the youth of the country responded to the sentiments of liberty they found in the poets, and to the themes of the essayists which were based implicitly on liberty of thought. They made parallels between Homer's heroes and the traditional heroes of their own race. Each book, though born long before Turkey was born, deepened their discontent with their Turkish environment.

In what is read lies the germ of what is to be written, and presently Arabic newspapers appeared, dealing rather with the news of ideas than the news of happenings. In 1860 Boutros al Boustani founded one that had considerable influence, the *Nafeer Souriyya or Syrian Trumpet*, a name sufficiently explicative of the paper's mission. Another journal of the kind was *Al Jinan, The Garden*. Beyrout, where were the foreign schools, became the chief centre of nationalist journalism, though the other towns of Palestine and North Syria had their share. Women began to take a part in the rising movement: several of them helped to edit sheets and pamphlets which became more patriotic and more clandestine as Turkish attention by degrees was aroused.

The movement went underground also. Secret societies were formed. It also went abroad, for the Turks began to banish the more prominent nationalists. Some of these fled to Egypt and became the leaders of the anti-Turkish activities there. Others went to France which provided them not only with a refuge but with a natural forcing-ground for the growth of national feeling by reason of its own stir and agitation.

Ideas of freedom filled the air and moved Constantinople itself. The Sultan granted a Constitution in 1876, which stayed dormant however till 1896, when under renewed pressure from liberal elements a Parliament met. It was short-lived, but presently the "Young Turkish" Party arose, and in 1908 the Sultan Abdul Hamid opened yet another Parliament. It served the Arab cause, for Syria elected representatives along with the other countries of the Turkish Empire, and they all were nationalists.

This Parliament was dissolved in 1912. Most of the Arab members went into exile, but they had gained their status and now formed an authoritative Arab nucleus abroad, in secret touch with the homeland. The Arabs in France had organized themselves. A "National Committee" had been founded in Paris by an Arab of Egypt, Mustapha Pasha Kamel.

In 1895 this Committee issued a document of high importance. It was the prospective charter of Arab Independence, which was never to be lost from sight and to re-appear, some twenty years later, under the pen of the Shereef Hussein, in Mecca itself. The essential parts of its explanatory preamble ran, "The Arabs are awakened to their historical, national and ethnographical homogeneousness and aim at separating themselves from the Ottoman body and forming an independent State… Its boundaries will be from the Tigris and the Euphrates to the Suez Canal and from the Mediterranean to the Gulf of Oman (the continuation of the Persian Gulf). It will be governed by an Arab sultan as a liberal constitutional monarchy."

Everybody in 1895 was liberal and constitutional in the Gladstonian fashion, and it is a question whether Arabia could produce then, or now, for that matter, Gladstones cut to the exact Hawarden pattern or Gladstonian constituents of the Midlothian breed. But this does not matter. In the manifesto of the National Committee the project for an Arab state was publicly filed, its dimensions and boundaries were publicly declared, and the principle of a non-despotic government was laid down for it.

Arab leaders in Syria of course could not openly espouse the Paris proposals. They sought for a measure of autonomy under the Turkish rule, and formed a "Decentralization Committee," as it was called. This committee published a scheme under which governing officials should only be appointed with the consent of local authorities, and also they demanded the creation of provincial diets.

By the beginning of the new century, official Arab claims had grown bolder. A still more representative committee numbering eighty-four members, of whom half were Christian and half Moslem, was established, of which the object was to secure a "General Provincial Council for Syria," Home Rule for Syria in fact.

The movement abroad and underground, aiming at complete independence, gathered impetus meanwhile. The Paris National Committee expanded into the "League of the Arab Motherland" and set forth as its aim the return to the Arabs of all Arab countries.

Some hesitations upon policy came when the Young Turk movement gained strength. Various personalities amid the Arabs were affiliated to this at first, thinking that as it was a general advance towards emancipation, it might be a step also towards the Arabs' goal. An Arab, Shawki Pasha, was prominent in the group which dethroned the Sultan, Abdul Hamid. Under his successor, Mohammed V, Arabs held Cabinet posts and in general higher positions than had been their lot previously.

But the Young Turk movement soon became more a pan Turk movement, introducing the idea of Turkish nationalism at the expense of the previous Ottoman dynastic regime. This meant the suppression of all non-Turk elements in the life of the country, and the Arabs, seeing they had nothing to look forward to but subordination, soon began to break, openly or in secret, their connections with Enver and his companions.

Arab hopes now centred in the secret and semi-secret national societies The most powerful of these perhaps was the *"Hizb al Ahd,"* sometimes called "Ahad" for short, or "Party of the Oath." It was the most dangerous to Turkey because its members were all officers in the Turkish army, who swore, as Lawrence puts it, "to acquire the military knowledge of their masters, and to turn it against them, in the service of the Arab people, when the moment of rebellion came."

A larger secret society, in some way the civil counterpart of the Hizb Al Ahd, was the so-called "*Fatah*" It was, says Lawrence, the "society of freedom in Syria. The land-owners, the writers, the doctors, the great public servants, linked themselves in this society with a common oath, passwords, signs, and a central treasury, to ruin the Turkish Empire." The full title of this society was "*Al Arabiyah al Fatah*" which means "Arab Youth." Its members were the Young Arabs, in fact, who thus faced the Young Turks. It was founded in Paris, amidst Arab students there and some residents. Three of its founders hailed from Palestine and one of them was to become well known later on as Auni Bey Abd-el Hadi, signatory of the Versailles Peace Treaty, and years after internee of the Sarafend Concentration Camp. [Author's note: Auni Bey Abd-el Hadi is one of the Arab delegates at the Conference convened by the Government at St. James's Palace, being held in February 1939, as these pages go to press.]

The widest-spread society of all was the Literary Club—"*Al Muntada al Adabi*"—which was founded at Constantinople in 1912, but like the other societies had its main membership and organization in Syria. Ostensibly the Literary Club had no political interests, but was concerned with social and literary pursuits. It could enjoy, therefore, a public existence. It produced a widely read magazine, the joint editors of which were an Arab man of letters from Baghdad and Asem Bey Bseso, who came from Gaza. Its founder, Jameel Bey al Husseini, was from Jerusalem. The Literary Club of course, under cover of its innocuous public meetings and conversaziones, was a focus of national action.

There were several other smaller societies, but these three were the principal. The reader will observe that the Arabs of Palestine, far from being inert, uninterested and obscure, were extremely prominent amidst the organizers of the movement.

Lawrence, who did not care for townsmen and, despite his own gifts of manipulation, did not care for intrigue on behalf of any cause, speaks contemptuously of the Fatah. He would have wished its members to have sought freedom "through sacrifice," that is, by risking a revolt. But he grants that it became a formidable organization. It is possible that the Arab societies at the time knew best what advanced their cause.

An Arab National Conference was held in Paris three years later, but the Balkan and Tripoli wars gained for the Turks some respite from the Arab strain. The more advanced Arab irredentists became nervous of the advance of European arms against Turkey. It was not that they cared a whit for the preservation of the Turkish Empire, but that State did not present such an obstacle to their hopes as did this European advance. The Turkish yoke was something which sooner or later they felt they could slip, but they were very doubtful about their own prospects on soil which in the interval Europe might have garnered from the Turks. These apprehensions have not proved so ill-founded.

However, after the close of the Tripoli and Balkan conflicts, Arab pressure on Turkey grew, and the approach of the Great War found Syria close to a formal demand for autonomy. But as the events which ushered in the Great War, and afterwards followed it, are of more importance than anything else in the history of the Palestine Question, it will be better to return to them at full length later. Some account must first be given and some comment made upon the origins and the rise of the other force mentioned at the beginning of this chapter, Zionism.

Chapter 4

The Jews in Palestine.—Misuse of the term "exile." Did they survive in Palestine?—The two Zionisms. Early Zionists.—Herzl and political Zionism. Refusal to be aware of the Arabs.

Few causes have owed so much to ignorance as the cause of Zionism. This does not mean that Zionists themselves are ignorant. Far from it.

What is meant by the debt of Zionism to ignorance is that the measure of success which Zionism has won in British circles, above all its enrolment amidst British political causes, is in great part due to the ignorance of the general public. The cabinet ministers who adopted Zionism during the latter years of the war were able to force it upon Palestine largely because no one at home knew anything about the more recent past of Palestine. Things were done there which would not have been ventured if the electorate of the United Kingdom had been informed and alert.

No doubt some of the British politicians who were responsible may not have had so much knowledge themselves of the history of the land they intended to govern. In this case, they might have read something of it and like other apprentices have taken a course in the subject which they intended to profess. But most of them, I fear, had no interest in dissipating public ignorance. One of them, Lord Balfour, went further. Lord Balfour kept himself determinedly innocent of everything concerning Palestine, and then exploited his own innocence. It was a state of mind which appealed to his peculiar cast of character.

One piece of general ignorance which helped enormously, and without doubt still helps the Zionist cause is the popular notion that all Jews were driven into world exile when the Romans took Jerusalem and destroyed the Temple in A.D. 70. As a matter of fact the Jews remained still strong enough in Palestine after the fall of Jerusalem to launch a final revolt sixty years later.

But that is a very minor point. The primal point is that most Jews were never driven into world-wide exile at all. They left Palestine, long before Roman days, because they wanted to go. Under pressure of hard times or in hope of bettering themselves they quitted the homeland and settled down all over the ancient universe. They were not exiled: they emigrated. They and theirs, when they had the means, liked to come back for visits to Palestine, but they had not the least intention of returning to live there.

Their own writers today, as in bygone days, quite recognize the situation:

> The children of Israel, [says Mr. Norman Bentwich] were scattered far and wide in all the countries of Hellenistic civilization, in Persia and Babylon Egypt and Cyprus, the isles of Greece and the coasts of Asia Minor "Earth and sea are full of them," said the Sibylline oracle. And at Alexandria, the intellectual capital of the world [in the pre-Christian era] they were gathered in hundreds of thousands and occupied two of the five quarters of the city. By their numbers and their commercial prominence they held a position there, at the centre of the Orient, analogous to that which the Jews hold in the metropolis of the New World today.
>
> At the time of the debacle [(the fall of Jerusalem) writes Mr. Leonard Stein] Palestine did not contain more than a fraction of the Jewish race. Flourishing Jewish communities had long existed in Egypt and in Cyrenaica, in Syria [north Syria, that is] and in Mesopotamia, in Italy and Greece. The Jews were dispersed long before the collapse of the Jewish State. Indeed at the opening of the Christian era there are said to have been only about 700,000 Jews in Palestine out of something like 4,000,000 in the Roman Empire alone.

The plain fact is that the vast majority of Jews for more than two thousand years has been satisfied to live outside Palestine. They remained attached to Palestine, at least those who remained attached to it were very attached. But they were not and never have been exiles for an enduring space in any true sense of exile, as the comings and goings to Palestine of those who returned to visit it showed.

Unfortunately this fact is not widely known. Our own politicians have been the last men to disclose it. They preferred their constituents to think that the Jews had been driven en masse from their home and had been impeded en masse from returning thither, and that these conditions always prevailed.

However, let us trace the course of the Jews *in* Palestine. After the final insurrection, the land was laid waste. They were butchered in great numbers and were enslaved. Many of the Palestine Jews endured genuine exile for a while, such as the Arab leaders have suffered in the Seychelles. Under the emperors who followed Hadrian however they were allowed to return, though there was little then to induce them to return. Jerusalem had been made into a Roman city, entitled Aelia Capitolina, and this particular area, their own capital, was forbidden to them. They chose in the main to stay in Alexandria and in the other cities in which they had taken refuge.

A group of their priests and teachers however never were expelled from Palestine, though driven from this place to that. Eventually they came to rest, chiefly in Galilee, where they established rabbinical schools. They were men of strong faith, who when their visible sanctuaries were destroyed, made sanctuaries of their minds and kept alight in them the holy lamp of Jehovah. They gained reverential repute throughout the Diaspora, the Greek word generally used to designate the mass of Jewish settlements scattered about the world.

But with the passage of time their schools declined, and Jewish representation in Palestine grew more and more tenuous. Whether for a period it survived or vanished altogether is a moot point. No one can be quite sure about what happened in the middle of the Dark Ages. Laurence Oliphant, the traveller, about eighty years ago, paid a special visit to Bukera, or El-Bukhera, a village west of Safad in Northern Galilee, situated "in a savage mountain wilderness of desolation," because of a few Jews living there who were reputed to be the only Jewish community which had kept on the soil since the time of Christ. Such a tradition might well be accepted.

After the battle of the Yarmook, to which reference has already been made, in the first part of the seventh century, the Arab Caliphs who followed certainly ruled over a number of Jews, for there is record that they treated them very tolerantly. The Jews existed in the chief towns and survived the convulsions of the next centuries. But the Crusaders slaughtered a considerable number when they captured Jerusalem.

When Saladin regained the realm he was kindly to the Jews, who by now again were very few. A scarcely known and curious episode of history was his reception in the year 1211 of three hundred rabbis of England and France, who sought to investigate the prospects for Jewish immigration. They deserve surely to be called the first Zionists, and they show an example to their successors of the twentieth century, who, before entering Palestine, did everything but "investigate prospects" amid Arabs.

Their mission however cannot have had any results, for some fifty years later, in 1267, there were only two Jews, brothers, living in Jerusalem. In 1327 a small community was established there, who were dyers for the most part. At the beginning of the fifteenth century there was a synagogue in the Holy City, but its congregation was oppressed and a hundred families, which must have been about the sum total of believers, emigrated.

During the fifteenth and sixteenth century the Jews in Jerusalem seem to have varied in number from 250 to 1,500 souls. The expulsion of the Jews in 1492 from the Spanish peninsula accounted for the larger total. Most of the expelled Jews however who came to the Orient went not to Palestine but to Salonica, where they have remained ever since.

The Moslem population of Jerusalem varied also at that time. It was 10,000 in 1481, by the account of travellers. But plague reduced it by a half within a few years, and the Jewish nucleus with it.

Mr. Bentwich mentions a curious episode of the sixteenth century. A member of a Jewish family exiled from Portugal, Dorn Joseph Nasi, "who had become the most trusted diplomatist of the Ottoman Empire and had been created Duke of Naxos, after entertaining and then abandoning the idea of establishing a Jewish colony in an island of the Greek archipelago, obtained from the Sultan Selim II the grant of a large tract in Galilee, with the permission to rebuild the town of Tiberias and to populate it exclusively with Jews." This Selim was the Sultan whose fleets threatened Christendom but were destroyed at Lepanto by Don John of Austria. The Tiberias enterprise never apparently was put into operation, but Mr. Bentwich, unaware probably of the embassy of the three hundred rabbis to Saladin, says of it that it was the anticipation of the modern movement for the return of the Jews to their ancestral soil, the first vague expression of the reviving national consciousness, and that some of the Jewish settlements in villages of Northern Galilee are effects of it.

In the first half of the next century 2000 Jews are reported in Jerusalem. Their numbers fell to a thousand in 1730. Outside Jerusalem there were groups only, for the most part in Safad and in Tiberias.

With the arrival of the nineteenth century comes the period of larger numbers. A species of census made by Ludwig Franklin in 1856 counted nearly 5,000 in Jerusalem, and there will have been rather more in the other parts of the country. There was an estimated population of 20,000 Jews in the whole of Palestine in the [eighteen-]eighties, which increased under modern conditions of government and with the first foundation of Jewish colonies to 85,000 or so before the war of 1914.

So much for the numbers of the Jews in Palestine. The figures I have quoted, and other such evidence as there is, go to show that they may have kept a minute thread, a mere filament of residence in a nook of Galilee from the time of Christ. In Jerusalem there was a break in their residency as the Roman era merged into the Dark Ages, and most probably one also after the Crusades. Still, Jerusalem has been the real centre when they have lodged in Palestine amid the Arabs since Henry III ruled in England, six hundred and fifty years ago. During these centuries they maintained, though with what continuity it is not possible to say, the ceremony of "Wailing at the Wall" in pious memory of their destroyed Temple.

There is nothing in all this to disturb any defender of the Arab cause in Palestine today. If modern Jewish immigration, in continuance of the old connection, had been properly begun and conducted and had been reasonable in volume, there would have been (as I have said) probably no Palestine Question and no Arab cause to defend. It is only because this old connection is interpreted after a fashion which challenges the Arab ownership of the country that trouble has arisen and has become endemic.

That Arab right of ownership should not have had to meet a challenge so groundless. It is a right which—it must be repeated again and again—devolves upon the Arabs because they are the present representatives of races who possessed the land when the Jews were not even yet a people. It devolves also upon the Arabs because they have been and are today the occupiers of the soil for one thousand three hundred years without a break, a period of time conveying such evident and absolute ownership that anywhere else in the civilized world a kindred title would only be questioned by lunatics and disregarded by rogues. However, since this challenge was made, the question is, how did it come to be made? How did modern Zionism arise? It is a modern movement, whatever some of its protagonists may say about the age-long desire of the Jews to repossess Palestine.

Mr. Leonard Stein, a conscientious writer, has some instructive paragraphs on the attitude of Jews throughout the ages. He says that

> Jews might have lived for generations in Poland or Russia, in Italy, Spain or the Rhineland: but Palestine was still the Land of Israel.... Through good and evil days alike, Palestine remained the desire of their hearts. In the ease and security of Andalusia, hardly less than in the gloomy recesses of the Ghetto, they stretched out their hands to Palestine—sang of it, prayed for it, wept for its fallen majesty, and patiently awaited the hour of redemption.
>
> The Palestine of which they dreamed had for most of them long ceased to be the Palestine of concrete reality. Of its geographical position or of its physical form they knew little or nothing. They were not bound to it by ties of personal affection, nor haunted by memories of its sights and sounds. It was not indeed a mere abstraction. The return of the exiles [Mr. Stein would call them the "exiles"] assuredly would be a return in the most literal sense. But it would not come as the result of human effort. It would come in God's good time with the appearance of the Messiah.

The whole matter of the thing is in this paragraph. Till recent days, till the start of the nineteenth century, say, the cry of the Jewish race for Palestine has been a religious one. That has made it, to begin with, only nominally the cry of the Jewish race, since out of the millions of Jews how many have been bound by the horizons of commerce and of humanitarian ism, and have seen no further? Those of them who did look beyond, dwindling into a smaller and smaller minority as the centuries went past, never thought they would occupy Palestine till a time had come when Time would be no more. The Messiah would bring them back to a Palestine transfigured, a stepping-stone to the next world. It was not for a territory, not so much for earth that they prayed as for Heaven. It has been left to an entirely different set of men, not at all their heirs, the Zionists of today, to insinuate that they did dream of a delimited country, and to produce atlases to measure their ancestors' transfiguration.

There were some rather fanciful beginnings to modern Zionism just after the French Revolution. An anonymous letter to the Jews of France, published by one of them in 1798, suggested the creation by the Jews of the world of a Jewish Council, which should treat with the French Government for the restoration of Palestine to "its traditional people." "The country *we propose to occupy*," said the characteristic text, "shall include—subject to such arrangements as shall be agreeable to France—Lower Egypt, with the addition of a district which shall have for its limits a line running from Acre to the Dead Sea and from the south point of that lake to the Red Sea." The writer went on to expound the economic advantages to everyone of this calmly proposed occupation.

Some very uncertain evidence makes Napoleon toy with a species of Zionist scheme. On the 22nd of May in 1799 a message appeared in the *Moniteur*, the official organ of the then French Government, dated from Constantinople, which ran, "*Bonaparte a fait publier une proclamation, dans laquelle il invita tous les juifs de l'Asie et de l'Afrique à venir se ranger sous ses drapeaux pour rétablir l'ancienne Jérusalem. II en a dejà armé un grand nombre, et leurs bataillons menacent Alep.*" That is, "Bonaparte has caused a proclamation to be issued, in which he calls upon the Jews of Asia and of Africa to join his colours in order to reconstitute ancient Jerusalem. He already has armed a considerable number of them, and their battalions are threatening Aleppo."

Some weeks later the *Moniteur*, for reasons which alas! remain unknown, proceeded to exculpate itself. "*Ce n'est pas seulement*," it explained, "*pour rendre aux juifs leur Jerusalem que Bonaparte a conquis la Syrie. Il avait de plus vastes desseins...de marcher sur Constantinople, pour jeter de là l'épouvante dans Vienne et dans Pétersbourg.*" "It is not merely to restore to the Jews their Jerusalem that Bonaparte has conquered Syria," says the *Moniteur*. "He nourished vaster plans...of marching from there upon Constantinople, to cast terror into Vienna and St. Petersburg."

These extracts from the French organ have been studied and have been followed up by Mr. Philip Guedalla, whose lively mind plays amid them and inquiring sense is unsatisfied altogether about them. He can find no trace of the proclamation amidst the archives of the Egyptian expedition, nor any trace of other documents confirming or even referring to it. No Jewish battalions ever threatened Aleppo. No one threatened Aleppo, not even Napoleon, who never came near it.

Asking himself in consequence whether the restoration of a Jewish State in Palestine was any part of Bonaparte's plan, Mr. Guedalla replies that "The answer is not free from doubt." He adjudges however that there is some bare chance of an idea of the kind having floated through that great soldier's mind, and he recognizes as a possibility that "for a few weeks in the spring of 1799 Napoleon was a momentary Zionist." The adjective is well chosen: it is about the space of time during which Napoleon would have been a Zionist.

This odd little episode indeed might have been scarcely worth recording here, were it not for a singular sequel to it. Mr. Guedalla's researches into the matter were made public by him in the form of a lecture which he delivered on the 25th of May in 1925 to the Jewish Historical Society of University College, London. As it happened, Mr. Lloyd George was a guest of the Society on that occasion, and after the lecture he proposed the usual vote of thanks to the lecturer. In this address he was franker and more expansive upon the circumstances under which Zionism was adopted by the War-cabinet, and especially by himself, than he has been at any time since. At the proper juncture I shall cite his remarks. It is a strange combination of circumstances indeed: a semi-apocryphal declaration of the French Empire: an esoteric lecture upon it a hundred and twenty-five years later: Mr. Lloyd George blurting out thereon why he adopted a policy which is proving a disaster for the British Empire.

Returning to the history of Zionism, it was only in the latter part of the last century that it either took on any importance or took a political aspect. In 1827, the Jewish philanthropist Sir Moses Montefiore, who was the first Jew ever to be a Sheriff of London, visited Palestine, and conceived the hope of settling, as he said, "thousands of our brethren in the land of Israel." He intended to form a company for the purpose and applied to Mehemet Ali, the Egyptian Pasha who then held Syria. But Mehemet Ali was driven back to Egypt and the plan of Sir Moses fell through.

Various writers during the next few decades gave birth to schemes for the resettlement of Jews or nurtured the idea that they should be resettled. Some of these were Gentiles, Laurence Oliphant being the most conspicuous. His, and most of the plans suggested, began to be political in character. There is unsuspected humour in the title of the book sent to Queen Victoria in 1846 by a Colonel George Gawler, *The Tranquillization of Syria and the East by the Establishment of Jewish Colonies in Palestine.* A Mr. Hollingsworth, a frank political ancestor of Mr. Ormsby Gore, suggested that a Jewish State should be set up in Palestine under British suzerainty in order to protect the road to India.

A few colonies were founded beginning in 1870, by a society called "*Choveve Zion*" or "Lovers of Zion." The senior of these, Mikveh Israel, founded south of Jaffa, still exists.

It was persecution, in two very different forms, which really brought modern Zionism into being. In the year 1881, in the reaction from the assassination of the liberal Tsar Alexander II, a wave of tyranny rose in Russia. One of the too frequent pogroms against the Jews followed as a matter of course, and the legislation which succeeded this was so despotic and injurious to them that great numbers fled the country. The majority made for the United States, where within thirty-five years the Jewish population increased from 250,000 to 3,000,000, and made of New York with its million of these the chief Jewish residence in the world.

A certain number however turned to Palestine. "Three thousand Jews," says Mr. Stein, "landed at Jaffa within twelve months of the enactment of the Russian 'May Laws' of 1881." He points out that they were a new type of colonist, men who by implication preferred Palestine to the United States or to any other place of refuge. Previous colonists when they went to Palestine had had no choice between going there and going anywhere else. "Nor," adds Mr. Stein, "were they moved by the old-world sentiment which craved for the pious consolations of the Holy Cities."

The fact is notable, and so is the phraseology used to describe it. In so far as there had been a link between Palestine and scattered Jewry, it was this same "old-world sentiment," the strength of which Mr. Stein himself stresses, since he asseverates a Jewish continuity based upon it, in the paragraphs of his quoted a page or two back. But the new colonists would have nothing to do with old-world sentiment. Yet, while they repudiated it, they made use of it, acting as though it still were there. This employment of bridges into Palestine after blowing them up was indeed to become a commonplace of the singular modern Zionist movement.

The second act of persecution which had so much influence in determining the rise of this movement was exerted against a single man, not a multitude. It was the condemnation and the transportation to Guiana of Captain Dreyfus. The well-known *Neue Freie Presse* newspaper of Vienna, sent as its correspondent to Paris in 1891 a young Jew of Budapest named Theodor Herzl. Three years later Herzl had to chronicle the Dreyfus trial and all the attendant anti-Semitism which it aroused. What he saw and heard made such a deep impression upon him that he grew conscious of his own people and of their difficult situation in the world. Hitherto he had thought of himself as an Austro-Hungarian subject and no more. Now he thought of himself as a Jew and nothing else. Where his fellow-Jews had emigrated physically from Russia, he emigrated mentally from Austria.

Herzl reviewed the condition of the Jews. In Eastern Europe they were oppressed. In Western Europe they were tolerated at the best, as it seemed to him, and in some countries toleration was wearing thin. Wherever Jews lived, the more their very capacities advanced them and increased their influence in that country, the more was its Gentile population irked by them and made increasingly hostile to them.

Herzl brooded on this indeed terrible dilemma, and he came to the conclusion that the sole solution for it was for the Jews to have a State of their own. He did not intend by this a State to which all Jews should repair, but one to which those should go whose position in Russia or elsewhere had grown intolerable. His was a stop-gap idea, destined really to deal with the existing situation of the depressed Jews, and did not peer much into the future. In 1896 he published his theories in a book entitled *Der Judenstaat, The Jewish State*. This made a great sensation and was read in translations in all parts of the world.

Herzl at very first did not advocate the establishment of the Jewish State in Palestine. His cry was for a State, here, there, anywhere, as long as it was a Jewish State. He received indeed, some years later, an offer from the British Government, through the medium of the by now established "Zionist Organization." This offer was of six thousand square miles of uninhabited land in the highlands of British East Africa. Herzl would have closed with this offer of 1903, prompted by the interest which Mr. Balfour, the Prime Minister, had long taken in Jewish affairs. It was, thought Herzl, a step to the goal. A night-refuge, a "*nachtasyl*" he called it, for such as then were homeless. But by that time there were too many others in the Zionist movement whose thoughts were riveted on Palestine, and they brought about a refusal, albeit a grateful and a polite one, of the African offer.

Herzl's own attitude towards Palestine was that while it was not indispensable, it was the location which he would prefer for the Jewish State. His writings had awakened and had coalesced a good deal of Jewish feeling, and representatives of the race from many lands gathered in 1897 at Basle in Switzerland to hold the first Zionist Congress. The Sultan of Turkey had been approached in the meantime, and there seemed some chance of his granting a charter of occupation in Palestine to the newly formed Zionist Organization. The aim was a Chartered Company, with "John Company" privileges and headquarters in London. In his presidential address Herzl was guided by this and proclaimed that "the aim of Zionism is to create in Palestine for the Jewish people a publicly recognized homeland under legal guarantees." As a matter of fact the Chartered project fell through. Abdul Hamid himself had been not so disinclined to dispose of Palestine and its people for a return in cash, but the sum which he had asked, ten million pounds, was beyond attainment. He became aware, too, as negotiation went on and grew known, that there was more and much stronger Moslem sentiment against the plan than he had expected, and his willingness for the bargain lessened correspondingly. He indeed gave a promise, in answer to remonstrations from Palestine, that he would impose a check on Jewish immigration, though he did not do much to fulfil it. On the fall of his throne, the Zionists placed some hopes in the Young Turks, who had a strong Jewish tinge themselves ("the Committee of Union and Progress was largely under Dônmé, crypto-Jew, influence" says Sir Ronald Storrs), but the Zionists soon enough were disillusioned. The Young Turks were a local cabal, to which Russian-inspired Jewish nationalism made no sort of appeal. To have identified themselves with political Zionism would have been to disidentify themselves with their doctrine of Turkish nationalism.

There is no occasion here to go at length into all the ensuing details of the rise of pre-War Zionism. The 1897 Congress was the first of a long series held in various cities and countries. "Appropriately nomad Parliaments" a French writer has called these Congresses. The Eleventh was held in Vienna in the year before the War. Herzl himself died prematurely, from overwork, in 1904. The Zionist Organization was founded to embody the movement, to arrange the Congresses, and generally to form a representative body for purposes of negotiation. Its membership rose at one time to 200,000, but declined to 130,000 at the outbreak of the War.

In comparison with the number of Jews in the world then, somewhere about thirteen million, 130,000 was not a large proportion, particularly when this proportion was obliged by its own tenets to offer itself as representing the whole of Jewry. It did not of course do so at all. Some of the impoverished and down-trodden Jews and a group of "intellectual" secularized young Jews in Russia and in a number of other countries adopted Herzl's doctrine of the Jewish State. The average commercial Jew, the bulk of orthodox rabbis and their congregations, the Jew settled in one of his many modern Alexandrias, nine-tenths of the race that is to say, fought shy of it.

As usual however, the small group which wanted to go somewhere and to do something had its own way very much. The 130,000 Zionist cavalry charged into the Chancelleries of Europe and America and created an excitement and an impression of overwhelming unity, unaltered by the pedestrian Jewish millions living peaceably at home. The existence of the non-Zionist multitude, though, is a point which, to say the least of it, deserves to be remembered, now and at all times. Whenever a political Zionist declares that Zionism as begun in Palestine was the cause of the

Jews, he can always be gently corrected. It was not the cause of the Jews, it was a cause of Jews.

The chief result of the passage of the sixteen years between the First and the Eleventh Zionist Congresses was that the doctrine expounded at them changed definitely from Herzl's scheme for housing the depressed Jews in a territory of their own. It changed into the modern Zionist doctrine of making Palestine a Jewish country, in order to regenerate the status of the Jew outside it, and to provide a spiritual sanctuary for his national feelings or national sanctuary for his spiritual feelings, whichever he preferred.

That closes the story of pre-War Zionism so far as it need be told for present purposes. There are, though, some matters in connection with it which have a marked bearing on the problems of today. These particular points have been noted little and still less driven home.

In the first place the quotation from Dr. Herzl's presidential address to the First Zionist Congress, which I have already given, is worth studying again. "The aim of Zionism," he said, "is to create in Palestine for the Jewish people a publicly recognized homeland under legal guarantee." Along with this may be quoted the words of his precursor, Dr. Pinsker, who in 1881 wrote that the Jews "must be amalgamated *as a nation among nations*, by the acquisition of a *home* of their own." [italics mine.]

The interest of these assertions is that they demonstrate how the "National Home" phrase found in the Balfour Declaration had been devised by Zionist leaders decades before it was proclaimed as the watchword of Britain's own policy. Moreover, the word "Home" was to be used by its British borrowers as a periphrasis, or more properly as a pseudonym for a Jewish State while in its period of incubation, but there never was any concealment about its meaning when it was invented by the first Zionist leaders. When Herzl spoke of a "homeland" he meant a sovereign State, for it was the only conception which he admitted. Pinsker wrote of the "home" as a "nation among nations."

This establishes what so many interested parties do not care to have established, that Zionism from the start, wherever it was to be installed, stood for sovereignty. The pretences of partnership and of blended authority in Palestine—themselves indefensible—with which, till in 1937 Partition was frankly proposed, it had been thought to delude the Arabs, never were the aim of the movement. This always was what Herzl said it was—sovereignty. The other formula was only put forward while it was believed that the Arabs might be deceived by a system under which they would only lose their natural authority by degrees.

The point of essential sovereignty is not the only one which emerges from Dr. Herzl's declarations. Reading them, the reader may be conscious of a remarkable anomaly in them. If Herzl's fundamental thesis was that persecuted or unenfranchised Jews should get away from their false environment and found a State where they would be by themselves and so be the equals of any men, if this was what Herzl meant, how then could he come to consider Palestine as a spot where such a State could be founded? It was a territory where the Jews could not be self-secure, for the Arabs were already living there in hundreds of thousands. How could Herzl fix his eyes on Palestine then, where the conditions for his Sinn-Fein "ourselves-alone" State were unobtainable?

The question may well be asked. But it would be difficult for Zionism to provide an answer to it. Nothing is more significant of the character of the Zionist movement than the fact that in those crucial days of last century it never paid the least attention to the Arabs who peopled the country upon which all its efforts were directed. Not a lift of a Zionist eyebrow seems to have been wasted upon an Arab form.

The sincere Mr. Stein is one of the few Zionist writers who seems conscious of this shortcoming. He does what he can to rectify it. "When Herzl," he explains, "had spoken of a Charter [from the Sultan] he had not, needless to say, contemplated any eviction of the Arabs of Palestine in favour of the Jews. He was, to judge from his Congress addresses, hardly aware that Palestine had settled inhabitants, and he had, in perfect good faith, omitted the Arabs from his calculations."

Was there ever anything more extraordinary than this? Vast plans are made engaging the destinies of a multitude of people, yet the man who engenders these plans never takes the essential first step of surveying the land where he proposes to carry them out. Nor apparently do any of his associates suggest it to him. There might be no Arabs in the world for all the difference it makes to him or to his associates.

Year by year Zionist congresses are summoned, and from their platforms and in the corridors of the assembly speakers discourse incessantly about themselves, about champions and about opponents of the cause within the ranks of Jewry, about the dovetailing of ill-fitting factors in their programme, about their hopes and their fears of Gentile help, about their own culture and their own need for spiritual expansion. Without doubt these were reasonable and respectable topics. When however were they put aside to consider the existence of inhabitants in the land which the Congress members proposed to acquire? When indeed? Was a single day's session of a single Congress devoted to the discussion of the understanding which must be reached with the people of Palestine? Not one.

Herzl's own situation is the most extraordinary of all. He justly becomes celebrated. He goes about the world spreading his gospel. He interviews monarchs and chiefs-of-government. Strange interviews they must have been, for he is closeted with the Sultan, the ruler of Palestine, yet comes away without news that Palestine has a population. He interviews the Pope and talks with him of the custody of the Holy Places, but never learns of the Christian inhabitants who frequent them. He even visits Palestine, but seems to find nobody there but his fellow-Jews. Arabs apparently vanish before him as in their own Arabian Nights. The Arabic tongue at the moment of utterance is transmuted magically into Hebrew or Yiddish or German!

But it is when we turn from Herzl to his associate leaders, and still more when we consider the action of the chiefs of Zionism who immediately succeeded him, that this plea of not having perceived the Arabs cannot be entertained. We are given to understand that this blankness of view persisted for some six or seven years. Mr. Stein, writing of the period round 1905, says that "it was now coming to be realized that Palestine was not empty." Herzl had died after the Sixth Congress, in 1904, and his death makes a point of demarcation.

I cannot see how it can be held that for six years a great number of admittedly intelligent educated men remained ignorant of the presence of the Arabs. If they did remain so ignorant, theirs was as bad a case of culpable ignorance as can be imagined, and they cannot be allowed to profit by it. But I do not believe in this ignorance, and I maintain that the half-and-half prolongation of it which was kept up till the War, and to all intents was resumed afterwards (as will be seen when the Balfour Declaration is analysed) altogether discredits the leaders of the Zionist cause as well as their friends in our own Cabinet.

There were nineteen Jewish colonies established in Palestine before the year 1900. The colonies of Rishon-le-Zion, Zichron Jacob and Rosh Pinah had been founded in the early 'eighties, and housed thousands of Jews who had fled from Russia. The international Jewish Colonization Association, founded by Baron Hirsch in 1891, was busy in 1900 reorganizing these colonies, which had been over-subsidized by Baron Edmond de Rothschild. The "*Choveve Zion*" or "Lovers of Zion" organization, established in Russia, but with committees in Vienna, Berlin, New York, Paris and London, had been engaged in Jewish settlement for six years. The "Jewish Colonial Trust" had been founded and registered in England to collect funds for use in Palestine and had received a quarter of a million pounds in its first year. The Jewish "National Fund," created to acquire land in Palestine, was founded in 1901. In Jerusalem there were many thousands of Jews, and also in Jaffa.

All these trusts and colonies and the people who inhabited them were in regular continuous communication with Jewish bodies and persons throughout Europe and America. Many of the Jews of Jerusalem were subsidized by pious co-religionists, so that they alone were responsible for a network of correspondence between Palestine and innumerable synagogues and congregations everywhere. The "*Choveve Zion*" and the secular associations necessarily were drawn into association with the Zionist Organization and with the Zionist Congresses. At Basle and at the succeeding Congresses there was infinite discussion about the colonies.

In a hundred ways the conditions prevailing in Palestine and the existence of the Arabs and the varying ways in which the Arabs reacted to existing colonies and to the promise of more colonies must have been known to all active Zionists.

The only conclusion then, and it is a conclusion forced upon the observer, is that if Zionism was unaware of the Arabs it was because most Zionists perceived an obstacle in the Arabs and did not want to be aware of them. The Zionist leaders, and the more prominent of their followers, obsessed with the absurd notion that Palestine had always been the patrimony of the Jews, did not intend to be aware of anything which conflicted with this. To have made approaches to the Arab population, and to have discussed at any length the bar which that population presented or might present to the accomplishment of their plans, would have to disconfess the plea upon which those plans were based. It would have disclosed to most of the non-Jewish world, and indeed to a good part of the Jewish world, that there was a factor in existence which upset the whole formula of Jewish ownership.

I do not say that all of the leading Zionists viewed the matter quite in this fashion. Some of them will have thought about the Arabs in a careless, indifferent way. They will have considered them as nobodies who would disappear presently, decamping from the soil after a little money had been spent or by some other almost natural sequence. They would vanish like the mist before the sun of Zion.

Those who thought like this wasted no time in discussing persons of such little import as the Arabs. As far as they themselves were concerned the Sultan of Turkey was the temporary population of Palestine. Of him they did talk, and with him they dealt, if unsuccessfully.

But most of the principal figures of Zionism must lie under the imputation of not having desired to perceive the Arabs. Their attention had been called to them by one man at least who belonged to their own number, Achad Ha'am. Achad Ha'am was the pen-name of Asher Ginsberg, whose essays and treatises became the literary focus of all Jews who opposed the establishment of a Jewish State. His patent disinterestedness and his altruism marked him out amidst his contemporaries. He declared that the political Zionists, that is to say those who worked for a Jewish State, were ruining the cause. "Judaism," wrote he in 1897, "needs at present but little. It needs, not an independent State, but only the creation in its native land of conditions favourable to its development ; a good-sized settlement of Jews working without hindrance in every branch of culture, from agriculture and handicrafts to science and literature."

Achad Ha'am protested even some years before the Basle Conference against the Zionist wilful or casual exclusion of the Arabs. It was folly, he said, to treat them as wild men of the desert who could not see what was going on around them. At the Basle Conference he sat "solitary amid his friends, like a mourner at a wedding-feast," and wrote afterwards of "the complete absurdity of Herzl's statesmanship, aimed inexorably at a Jewish State in Palestine."

Twenty-three years later, in 1920, he wrote, "From the very beginning we have always ignored the Arab people."

That is the truth. The Zionist movement, as it took shape, aimed at superseding, or expected to supersede, the Arabs on their own soil. It is vain for the defenders of the system which has developed in Palestine from these beginnings to try and deny their real character now. If, as they assert, the Zionist goal was always friendship with the Arabs, then not alone would such warnings as Achad Ha'am's have been heeded. There would have been no necessity for their utterance. From the first moment the Arabs would have been sought out quite automatically, and would have been canvassed by those who proposed to suggest themselves as their partners.

This never was done. No contacts were made either with the mass of peasants in the countryside or with the professional men and the other dwellers in the towns. No public meetings were arranged to enlist the sympathies of the rising generation of nationalist Arab youth. No speeches were heard then, and no letters were written then to *The Times*, about Jews and Arabs hand in hand working out the future of Palestine.

With these points in mind, the reader will understand better now why the Arabs make no response to the protestations of friendliness with which they are assailed at intervals.

Chapter 5

The Powers and the Arab National Movement. The Headship of the Movement shifts to Mecca. The Shereef Hussein.—The Emir Abdullah's visit to Kitchener. War between Britain and Turkey. British negotiations for Arab support begin.

In the third chapter the progress of the Arabs towards emancipation from their Turkish rulers was traced to a period within sight of the Great War. The secret or semi-secret societies which worked for Arab independence, or, as a first step, for Arab autonomy, had grown very powerful. The names of several have been given. The more notable by now, each working to the common end in its own way, were "*Al Fatah*"; "*Al Aha-ul-Arabi*," the "Arab Brothers"; "*Al Muntada-Adibi*," the "Literary Club"; the "*Khatanyeh*" Club; the "*Hisb al Ahd*," the "Society of the Oath"; "*Al Thevriyet-ul-Arabieh*," the "Arab Revolt"; "*Nahdat ul-Lubanyeh*," the "Awakening of the Lebanese"; the "*Islahyeh*" or "Reformist" group; and "*Al-Lamarkazieh*" the (to give its full title) "Ottoman Decentralization League." Of these the Lebanese group was entirely Christian. The "Decentralization League" somewhat sardonically revived an old title, as it aimed at complete independence from Turkey, possibly though through local autonomy.

The "*Hisb al Ahd*" composed of officers in the Turkish Army, was of its very nature more secret and did not entertain the half-way goal of home rule. It looked forward to mutiny on a great scale and secretly prepared it. Its members were men with the temperament of their calling, without much contact with the West, and they were suspicious of any prospective Western aid. It was strongest amidst Mesopotamians, born remote from the sea, and its adherents were scattered amidst many Turkish garrisons.

On the other hand the civil societies were inspired by Western examples, were full of men who had had Western educations, and some of these societies had begun upon foreign soil. They were strongest in Syria which was in perpetual contact with the West through its Mediterranean seaboard. It was inevitable that they should look for some sort of help from the West, and they did their best to establish contacts with the Powers chiefly concerned,

Great Britain, France, and in a lesser degree, Russia. Nor did the Powers concerned, however circumspectly they behaved, evade these contacts. The break-up of Turkey had long been in prospect and it was but rational to keep in touch with those who at any time might succeed her.

Britain and France at least displayed a watchful interest in the progress of the Syrian or Arab national movement. In fact they showed something more than interest. They extended, not perhaps both in the same degree and in the same manner, for each had its own fashions, an altitude towards the Syrians which is difficult to define but is a recognized diplomatic attitude. In its then stage, it might be called encouragement without encouragement. Those to whom it was extended felt themselves to be encouraged, while those who extended it felt that they had not encouraged them.

The recipe for this attitude, as may be imagined, is a delicate one. Its very ingredients can hardly be listed. It goes without saying that they do not include official negotiations, for no respectable Power's ambassadors or ministers will engage in negotiations with conspirators plotting to overturn the rule of the government to which they themselves are accredited. But unofficial persons who have unofficial relations with official persons can always form a link. Consuls have to make reports about more than surface conditions in their districts, and they must gain knowledge in some discreet way.

Unofficial persons, it is true, will negotiate perhaps with prospective rebels no more openly than do consuls and diplomatists. Their business is to gather information concerning conditions where they are stationed or sent. But information can only be gained by conversation and the closer this is with the persons about whose activities inquiry is being made the more reliable and the more worth sending it is. Such conversation means an understanding of the interlocutor's point of view, and understanding of this easily shades into sympathetic consideration, and sympathetic consideration into amicable relations. Between friends there is no limit to the theoretic horizons which may be discussed and to the prospects which may be envisaged.

They were being envisaged, with a gradually broadening outlook upon "Arab autonomy," in 1913, in Syria and even more out of Syria. The hazards of the war, which were to include unexpected fates for various documents, fortunately allow some of their general trend to be followed now. In the January of 1913 the French Ambassador in Constantinople, M. Bompard, sent an account to M. Poincaré, then Minister of Foreign Affairs, of a talk which he had had with Shefik Bey el Mouayid, an Arab notable and deputy. The latter with what must have been disconcerting openness asked the Ambassador, in the course of conversation, whether France, if Turkish forces were sent to Syria to keep it under Turkish rule, would send an army-corps to Aleppo to intervene. There had been a precedent for French military intervention in 1861, when French troops had been dispatched to Syria after a massacre of Christian Syrians. This intervention might have become French occupation, if the great Lord Dufferin, sent out from England, had not skilfully settled the matter with the Turks before the French forces arrived, so that there was no excuse for them to stay and they made a rather lame return to France.

M. Bompard in 1913 could not listen of course to such proposals. He told his visitor that the best thing the Arabs could do was to be faithful to the Sultan, and by evident fidelity to win from Turkey the right to have their own Syrian officials in charge of the Syrian administration. Thus, he said, *"ils auraient réalisé toutes les réformes réalisables aujourd'hui et desquelles pourraient par la suite sortir toutes les autres."*

The Ambassador, who had the experience of his rank, added for M. Poincare's information that the Bey was leaving for Cairo, "where doubtless he will make the same appeal to the British, and will compare their answers with mine." "*Je souhaite,*" added M. Bompard, "*qu'elles soient aussi correctes.*" The Ambassador does not seem to have been quite so sure of British correctness as he might have been, for he used the word "*souhaiter*" which, in the special notation of diplomatists, is always employed to express a hope rather than to hope.

It is extremely unlikely that Mouayid Bey got any change out of Cairo, our own people always being twenty times more correct and careful than their colleagues of any other country, though remaining obstinately well informed. Meanwhile however there had been an abortive rising in the Yemen, and the news of this, in which Syrians had had a hand, had been much exaggerated in Syria. The French Consul-General in Damascus, M. Ottavi, sent, in February, a minute to M. Bompard, telling him that the rumour was that a former deputy of Basra, Seyyid Taleb, had raised the standard of revolt and had declared that Mesopotamia and the Koweit district were henceforth an Arab State under British protection. M. Ottavi said he did not believe all this; there had been a lot of smoke but little fire. "In my opinion," he wrote, "we are merely confronted by an Anglo-Egyptian manoeuvre designed to evoke before the Arabs the glittering mirage of the reconstitution of the Empire of Haroun al Rashid under the aegis of Great Britain." In his original draft the good Consul-General had written first *"nous nous trouvons simplement en face d'une manoeuvre des agents de Lord Kitchener,"* but on second thought had crossed out the phrase referring to Lord Kitchener's agents and had substituted cautiously *"une manoeuvre anglo-égyptienne."* The shadow of Fashoda still hung over Egypt then.

A month before M. Ottavi's note was dispatched there had been an important move in the Arab campaign for autonomy. A public meeting had been held in Beyrout with the agreement of the liberal Vali, or Governor, under the auspices of a newly formed Syrian "Committee to Examine Administrative Reform." This was composed of twelve Moslems, twelve Christians and, it is interesting to observe, one Jew. But the friendly Kiamil Pasha fell from power in Turkey, and the "Union and Progress" Government at once dissolved the Beyrout Committee and warned the people of the town that a court-martial would deal with any more such illegal manifestations.

This forced the administrative section of the Arab movement abroad once more. The Decentralization League held a meeting in Cairo in March, at which a Syrian, M. Tueni, "auxiliary dragoman of the French Consulate-General in Beyrout", was present "in his private capacity as a member of the Syrian Committee of the League." The reader will perceive in M. Tueni a precious item in the construction of the diplomatic attitude just now described. The meeting passed a resolution, as M. Tueni informed his superiors, in favour of Syria being created an autonomous principality under the rule of a Moslem prince and the protection of France. M. Tueni was instructed to inform the French Minister in Cairo, M. Defrance, of this, for which the French Minister thanked him, and agreed "at M. Tueni's request" to inform the Quai d'Orsay of what had occurred, *"mais à simple titre d'indication et en lui conseillant de maintenir l'action du comité dans la voie de la prudence et de la légalité."* The rules of the game were being scrupulously observed. The message was thought important enough for M. Paléologue, then at the head of the Quai d'Orsay, to send it to the Consuls-General in Damascus and in Beyrout, though it cannot have conveyed much news to the latter.

But about a week later M. Defrance was writing a dispatch to M. Pichon. now Minister of Foreign Affairs, which ran, "Judging by supplementary information which I have been able to gather since the event, it appears that the resolutions of the (Decentralization) Committee were neither as decisive nor as unanimous as they seemed to M. Tueni, who, only acting besides as a private individual, in his quality as a Syrian notable, and in nowise because of the official situation which he occupies at Beyrout, gives evidence of a certain excess of zeal on behalf of an immediate and radical solution of the Syrian question." The fact was, as M. Defrance communicated to M. Pichon, that M. Tueni had been too "optimistic about the Moslems," who wished for protection not by France but by England.

A stiff if covert struggle for the contingent patronage of the movement undoubtedly set in then. The two Powers stood at proper diplomatic distance but knew that their respective adherents were battling for them. The Congress which should have been held in Beyrout was transferred to Paris, where it took on the likeness of a Syrian Parliament and drew the remonstrances of the Turkish Ambassador. Beside the delegates already mentioned some two hundred Syrians were present, from all parts of the globe. Resolutions were passed demanding autonomy and drawing up plans for it, with a central government at Damascus or Beyrout, but there was a good deal of dissension in the Congress. Many of those present wanted resolutions of entire independence to be passed. The autonomists aimed at independence but thought it wiser to put up with autonomy for the present.

But the cleavage on the question of the Power to which the national movement should turn for help was perhaps a more evident cause of disagreement. The Moslem elements lobbied very successfully for Great Britain, so much so that M. Pichon sent a circular letter to the French consuls in Syria in which, without naming names, he said that the Reformist movement, which had been so favourable to France, now was veering away. The Consuls were recommended to be helpful to the Reformists, that is, the members of the various national societies, and to stem the Arab current straying from Francophilism.

A more definite move was made on behalf of the Foreign Minister by M. de Margerie, who sent from the Quai d'Orsay to M. Ottavi a singular note which had been received from the Resident-General in Tunis.

> There has been communicated [it ran] to the Tunisian Government a certain quantity of correspondence sent by Tunisians living in Constantinople, Beyrout and Medina, according to which representatives of the British Government have got into touch with certain personages and religious leaders of the Moslems (*avec certains personnages et chefs religieux musulmans*) both in Mecca and in Medina with the aim of forming bonds of sympathy and of common interests between the religious capitals of Islam and the British Government.
>
> According to some of this correspondence, addressed from Beyrout, British agents in Syria are vying with each other in the endeavour to bring about the triumph of British influence at Beyrout, Smyrna and Damascus. It would seem that certain members of Parliament have decided to visit Asia Minor during the coming summer and to study the country and its inhabitants at first hand. It is upon the advice of these politicians that the Moslem-Christian Association has apparently been established in Paris, the object of this body supposedly being to restore the Arab Caliphate instead of the Sultan's in Constantinople.

The note went on to say that "British diplomacy and the British Press" had decided to summon an Arab Congress to this end. The note had been written in Tunis on the 28th of May, before the Congress did come to being in Paris in June. The odd collaboration of British diplomacy and British Press "summoning" the Congress, though, was a characteristic piece of hyperbole by the French intelligence-agent who drafted the note— for it was not the work of the Resident himself. It was the Syrians who had determined on the Congress, Paris was the consecrated place for it, and one of the most active conveners was M. Chukri Ganem, a Syrian who had spent most of his life in France, was far more French than Arab, and had the definite task of keeping the national movement infeodated to France. That is not to say that there were no supporters of British influence facing him. But in our way, they had been given no definite task of opposition. The thing was implicit. They were Anglophile for this reason or the other and could be trusted to manifest their sentiments.

The information from Constantinople, Beyrout and Medina came from native agents of the French Intelligence Service. They exaggerated in describing the unnamed visitors to the three cities as "representatives of the British Government," but there was a basis of fact in their news. If Great Britain had stood entirely aloof from the rising Arab movement it would have been stupid. It was perfectly reasonable and proper that she should maintain sympathies, as a great Moslem Power, in all centres of Moslem influence.

The course of events in Turkey pointed to the rapid downfall of the Sultan, whose religious influence as Caliph was a barrier to complete domination of Turkey by the modernist "Union and Progress" coterie. It would have been madness for Great Britain not to have prepared for such an eventuality. The Caliphate originally had been Arab and had been centred in the Red Sea. If it were to perish in Turkey, Mecca would be the natural place in which to restore it. For Great Britain to lend her help or her patronage to this, should the need for it arise, was but one of those exhibitions of divine common sense which had inspired her policies so often, though her rivals, as in the actual case, presented her action as artificially composed and labyrinthine.

This policy of favouring Arab development, a development which was now inevitable, was one which had always particularly appealed to Lord Kitchener, then in full power at the Residency in Cairo. His own early days as a soldier had been passed a good deal in Syria, which he had helped to map, and there have always been two meanings to surveying the ground when it has been carried out by European officers in the Near East.

It is likely enough that the "representatives of the British Government" whose acts disturbed the dreams of the Intelligence-bureau in Tunis were really some members of the "Decentralization League," who did go down into Arabia, particularly to reach some kind of understanding with "Moslem leaders." Sheikh Reshid Riza, who had a largish acquaintance in Cairo, visited the Emirs of Muscat and Mohammerah. Other delegates visited the Imam Yehia, and Seyyid Taleb the Emirs Ibn Saud and Idris. Sheikh Reshid Riza went on then to India, to perform the important work of canvassing Moslem opinion there upon the Caliphate question, and no doubt to inform Indian Moslems of the character and progress of the Arab National cause.

Exactly what were the relations between Cairo and the delegates of the Decentralization League would not be easy to say. Most likely they were very far from being as defined as the French imagined, but none the less they served their purpose, and were a preliminary stage in the prospective development of Anglo-Arab relations should Turkey dissolve or be helped to dissolve by her Arab subjects.

There was then a good deal of difference between British attitude and French attitude towards Syria. France had long taken the closest interest in Syria, since the days of her kings, and had traditionally acted in Syria as the protector of the Latin Christians under the Turkish regime. This was not a legal situation: it was a custom which had grown up which conferred a special standing on French consuls rather than a status. No doubt the French would have liked to transfer this situation into something closer to a protectorate, but this was not possible of course while Turkey was there, though in 1861 the French, as we have seen, missed an opportunity of installing troops and building up a protectorate in the best nineteenth-century manner.

France, however, maintained her hankerings for the country, and had much closer connections with it in general than Britain had. French missionaries and schools, as we have seen, were very important there. It was for this reason that the French followed the National movement in Syria so closely.

British interest in Syria itself was less. While it remained in Turkish hands there was no particular problem concerning the approaches of the Suez Canal to consider. In 1912 the British Government had assured the French that in Syria "it had no action in view, no aims, no political designs of any sort," and had by the mouth of Sir Edward Grey accepted that France had "special interests in Syria."

In 1913 the situation began to change with the manifest dissolving of the Ottoman regime and the manifest rise of the Syrian national system. The new factor was that the Syrian movement did not now appear as a Syrian movement alone, but as part of the national renaissance of all the Arabs, and in a general Arab movement, involving too the Caliphate question, Britain was vitally concerned as a Moslem-ruling Power and because of the strategic importance of the Arab territories on the road to India and at the gate of Egypt.

So that Britain no longer could disinterest herself as much as she had done in Syrian affairs. They touched her vitally as Arab affairs, and she had now to consider the advantages of friendliness towards the Syrians as Arabs. The natural pendant to this was that a large section of the Syrians began to consider the greater advantage to their cause of closer friendship with Britain as a more powerful and probably less acquisitive Power, on this occasion, than France. They were headed by the capable Syrian colony in Cairo, always closely allied with British interests in Egypt, and very prominent in the National movement. Cairo too became more and more the centre of Syrian political activity in the whole Levant because of its geographical and social advantages, and this naturally increased the volume of Syro-British conversations of one kind or another.

As the summer of 1913 passed into autumn, the situation grew more tense in Syria and, because of their nervousness at the growth of the pro British strain in the National movement, the French grew less diplomatic in their own relations with it, and passed to pure support of the Arab societies. In October the Ambassador in Constantinople had asked whether a newspaper in French interests could be produced in Damascus, and the answer he received from M. Ottavi makes the development of relations very plain. M. Ottavi wrote:

> The Arabic newspaper mentioned in your Excellency's telegram of the 21st, which I hope soon to be able to answer, can only exert a cautious influence—which is more desirable in itself—or else it will be at once suppressed. In my opinion, therefore, recourse will have to be had to pamphlets, secretly printed and distributed. This would mean an outlay of 150 to 200 francs a month, and I should be obliged if your Excellency would telegraph this sum to me, if your Excellency approves of my opinion.
>
> (*Le journal arabe dont il est question dans le télégramme de Votre Excellence du 21 de ce mois, auquel j'espère être en mésure de répondre incessamment, ne pourra exercer qu'une action discrète—et cela est préférable—pour ne pas être aussitôt supprimé. Aussi faudrait-il, à mon avis, recourir aux pamphlets imprimés et distribués sécrètement, ce qui exigerait des frais s'élevant à une somme de 150 à 200 francs par mois, que je serais reconnaissant à Votre Excellence de m'accorder par le télégraphe, si Votre Excellence approuve ma maniere de voir.*)

It is clear that towards the end of 1913 the French were thoroughly involved with the Arabs in Syria. With the approach of the fateful year,

1914, we may shift the scene to Mecca, the sacred city and heart of the Islamic world. It was there that British interests were more closely focused. Mecca was conspicuous not alone because of its character as a sanctuary and because of the purity of the Arab stock in the Hedjaz, as the district surrounding Mecca was called. It was the part of the Arab world where the Arabs had more power, and much more appearance of it.

Since the days of Mohammed, Mecca had remained in some degree under the sway of his descendants. This sway extended, less definitely perhaps, to the other holy city of Medina, to the port of Jeddah, and to the rest of the Hedjaz, a coastal section of territory, some 500 miles long by 150 in breadth.

The Arab ruler of this nucleus in 1914 was not so much an official ruler as the Controller of the Holy Places, and he held his position because he was or was assumed to be the senior of the Prophet's descendants. The Hedjaz was not a State. In theory it was a province of the Turkish Empire and Turkey exercised suzerainty over it and its semi-ruler, who was termed the Shereef of Mecca. Shereef is a title given to descendants of the Prophet: the Shereef of Mecca was the Shereef of Shereefs, and sometimes was called the Grand Shereef.

Lawrence records the situation of the Shereefs as Turkish power increased over the Hedjaz in the nineteenth century. "As the Sultan grew stronger there he ventured to assert himself more and more alongside the Shereef, even in Mecca itself, and upon occasion ventured to depose a Shereef too magnificent for his views, and to appoint a successor from a rival family of the clan [of the Prophet's descendants] in hopes of winning the usual advantages from dissension."

However, under one Shereef or another, the Hedjaz had kept a greater measure of independence than any Arab district of any size and importance, while the Shereef, as the custodian of the Holy Places, enjoyed the highest prestige amongst the Arabs. He became more and more the chief dignitary of their race, and when modern times set in the eyes of the leaders of the Arab movement turned to him.

At that date the Shereef of Mecca was Hussein ibn Ali. He had always been impatient of Turkish suzerainty and, as a younger man but already important in Mecca by reason of his birth, he had been deported by order of the Sultan to Constantinople, where he was kept for sixteen years under polite supervision. The Turks always injured their own cause by exiling Arabs. Just as the Arabs driven to Egypt and to France sowed the seeds of the secret societies, so did the Arab Hussein profit by his exile. His sons received a modern education in semi-European Constantinople. There were four of them, Ali, Zeid, Abdullah and Feisal.

On the fall of Abdul Hamid, the Young Turks made the grave mistake of sending Hussein back to Mecca as Shereef. This was during their pan-Islamic period, before they turned to the policy of "Turks only for Turkey," and probably they believed they had won the sympathies of the Hussein family during his long residence in the capital. His son Feisal was deputy for Jeddah in the last transient Turk Parliament and Feisal's elder brother, Abdullah, even held a post equivalent to Deputy-Speaker of that assembly.

Hussein, outwardly complaisant, from the day of his return began to restore and to extend his power as Shereef. And as it grew quietly, the connection between Mecca and the secret societies in Syria grew closer and closer. The project of a principality under a Francophile Egyptian prince hung fire. Those who were working for Arab independence began to look to the Arab Shereef, who had semi-independence already and the headship of the Holy Cities, as a prospective titular leader and mouthpiece of something wider than a local principality. In the spread of this idea British attitude certainly played a part.

The Turkish authorities, as their interior policy began to change and, without doubt, as they got some inkling of what was going on, became more repressive. In Syria they closed some of the smaller "social clubs," but the larger ones eluded them, and underground action went on unabated. Down in the Hedjaz, they appointed a new Vali of the province, who was known for his anti-Arab feeling. His first act was to order the surrender of a hundred rifles belonging to the Shereef's bodyguard. This was a stupid thing to do, since the rifles were old and of no great use, while the seizure of them was a piece of disrespect to the Custodian of the Holy Places, which much inflamed local opinion. It was believed to be a prelude to a campaign for the Turkification of Mecca and Medina.

It showed Hussein that he had grown suspect to the Young Turks, or lay in the way upon their new road. He set himself all the more determinedly to consider how he might counteract their plans. Shortly after this, in February of 1914, he dispatched his second son, the Emir Abdullah, to Egypt. This was a definite move towards the strengthening of the relations which so far had been loosely knit. The ostensible reason for the Emir's journey was to pay a visit to the Khedive Abbas Hilmi. But the Turks, who had their suspicions of what was going on in the Hedjaz, were not satisfied with his story. When the Emir had an audience of Lord Kitchener they were still less satisfied, and from Constantinople they conveyed a message of this dissatisfaction. Lord Kitchener therefore did not see Abdullah again. Abdullah at the time had a mysterious plot of his own for involving Turkey with the chief Moslem Powers through some religious "frontier-incident," but whether he embarked on explanations of this when he saw Lord Kitchener cannot be said. K. of K. kept his own counsel on that point.

But Abdullah must have made the general drift of his ideas evident, for when he asked, as he next did, to see in place of Lord Kitchener Mr. (now Sir) Ronald Storrs, who then was Oriental Secretary at the Cairo Residency, Kitchener instructed Storrs to avoid any encouragement of the Emir's plans, personal or other. Kitchener's own account of the episode is given by Sir Ronald Storrs in his highly interesting book, Orientations. He quotes a note of Kitchener's to Sir William Tyrrell concerning his (Kitchener's) talk with Abdullah.

> The Emir sent for Storrs who, under my instructions told him the Arabs of the Hedjaz could expect no encouragement from us and that our only interest in Arabia was the safety and comfort of Indian pilgrims.... The Shereef(according to his son) seemed to be disappointed with the Jesuit of his visit to Constantinople and with the determination of the Turkish Government to push the railway on to Mecca, which he saw would mean the economic death of the camel-owning population of Arabia.... It will be interesting to see developments, as the Arabs seem to be much excited.

Sir Ronald Storrs thus recounts his own interview:

> The Emir Abdullah showed a mind filled with Arabic poetry.... Travelling by a series of delicately inclined planes, from a warrior past I found myself in the defenceless Arab present, being asked categorically whether Great Britain would present the Grand Shereef with a dozen or even half a dozen machine-guns.
>
> When I inquired what possibly could be their purpose, he replied (like all re-armers) "for defence," and, pressed further, replied that the defence would be against attack from the Turks. I needed no special instructions to inform him that we could never entertain the idea of supplying arms to be used against a Friendly Power. Abdullah can have expected no other reply, and we parted on the best of terms.

Sir Ronald Storrs in fact was as correct towards Abdullah as M. Bompard had been fourteen months before towards Shefik Bey el Mouayid. As long as Turkey remained a friendly power, it was useless for the Arabs in the Hedjaz to expect help from Great Britain, nor was it to be expected that British standards of neutrality would become less definite in any way, whatever other nations were doing.

But if there was a surer note in these British conversations, and if it must have been clear to Abdullah that what was said to him really was meant, it is equally certain that he went off with a conviction of an entente with Britain, if any sort of political convulsion were to disintegrate the established order of things in the Turkish dominions. Sir Ronald Storrs, it is true, seems to suggest that the Emir did not unbosom himself to Lord Kitchener, prior to his own interview with Abdullah, writing that "He appeared to have something to say, but somehow did not reach the point of saying it." But the very instructions given to the Oriental Secretary presuppose that Abdullah had either talked of war with Turkey to Kitchener, or of something so akin to it that both knew how the land lay. Abdullah had brought to the Residency the news of his father's inquiries in Constantinople upon probable Turkish action in the Hedjaz. Hussein would have had exceptional opportunities for learning the "inside story," as it is called, in Constantinople, and knew of the great part Germany had in the intention to press on with what, after all, was a branch of her *Bagdadbahn*. Kitchener had listened to talk about the railway, and the contingencies from the extension of it were pretty clear.

Captain Liddell Hart in his life of T.E. Lawrence cannot be assumed to have been speaking without data when he writes of the Kitchener-Abdullah interview that "Abdullah had found in Kitchener a sympathetic listener who himself had long cherished the idea of founding an independent Arab State in Arabia and Syria." There is too the further testimony of D. G. Hogarth, Lawrence's Oxford mentor, who was to play a prominent part himself in Anglo-Arab negotiations before very long, that "Lord Kitchener was already contemplating the possibility of an autonomous Arabia, between Teutonized Turkey on the one hand, and Egypt and India on the other, before war was ever so much as dreamed of."

To imagine that Abdullah came to Kitchener without any previous connections at all between Cairo on the one hand and Mecca and Syria on the other, however contingent and verbally correct these connections may have been, and however indirect, is not reasonable. Such connections had to be made as a mere form of insurance in the event of a break-up of Turkey, and they were made.

However in February and April of 1914, there was no immediate prospect of a revolt, though the Arab menace was increasing fast. In Europe there was disquiet, but the Archduke Francis Ferdinand of Austria was still alive and well.

In August the War, like a great engine out of the skies, crashed to earth and the countries of the West burst into flame. Kitchener left Egypt for London. But the bearings of the conflict on the lands which were so close to his heart were not eradicated from his mind. In Syria the Arab nationalists were deeply stirred. At first it was but by a general sentiment that out of such a universal situation as was developing their chance ought to come somehow. Then as German diplomacy began to capture the Young Turks, and the possibility of Turkey becoming a belligerent became greater, that chance looked more precise.

There was a certain strangeness in the prospective situation which the entry of Turkey into the War would create. The Shereef and his people would become enemy subjects, should Britain fight Turkey. But how far the Arabs contemplated this status as likely to endure was shown by a reminder which, as Liddell Hart states, came to Lord Kitchener in London from the depths of Arabia. It was "a cryptic message sent by a circuitous route" and it ran thus—"Following for Lord Kitchener. Remember our conversation. The day has come." It is not difficult to imagine who sent it, nor what it meant.

But this message was sent in August, while Turkey was still neutral. A month passed. The attitude of Turkey became more and more suspect. Kitchener, however, in London, was involved now in the intense preoccupations of the War in France. The French Government had evacuated Paris: our Expeditionary Force was retiring from the Marne. In Cairo, even, the Arabs were rather forgotten.

But Sir Ronald Storrs, who has never received sufficient credit for his important action in this juncture, remembered the Emir Abdullah's visit, and thought of the difference to a hostile Turkish force the legion of camels of the Hedjaz would make, either to speed, to weaken by abstention, or to threaten on the flank a Turkish advance in the Sinai deserts. He submitted, as he records, "a short note suggesting that by timely conversation with Mecca we might secure not only the neutrality but the alliance of Arabia in the event of Ottoman aggression."

While he was doing this, the most active arrangements were being made between the French and the Arabs of Syria for common action there against Turkey should she declare war. But they can be detailed later.

Storrs' note did not elicit a response at the Agency in Cairo till he turned to Captain Clayton (afterwards Sir Gilbert Clayton), who was the representative in Cairo of the Soudan Government, in whose military sphere of influence Palestine and the Sinai lay, and also Director of Intelligence of the Egyptian Army. Clayton "actively condoned my proposed irregularity of urging it (consultation with the Arabs) upon Lord Kitchener in a private letter."

In a week, on the 24th September, the answer to this letter came in the form of a coded cable to "His Majesty's Representative in Cairo," as follows:

> "Following from Lord Kitchener. Tell Storrs to send secret and carefully chosen messenger from me to Shereef Abdullah to ascertain whether, should the present armed German influence in Constantinople coerce Sultan against his will and Sublime Porte to acts of aggression and

war against Great Britain, he and his father and Arabs of Hedjaz would be with us or against us."

Sir Ronald Storrs chose for this task an agent named Ruhi, a Persian, in whom he could place confidence. In *Orientations* the reader will find a fascinating account of Ruhi's mission. He reached Mecca on the 9th of October. The Grand Shereef was not there however, but at a little village in the neighbourhood called Al Taif, where he often went in the summer. There was a special reason for his presence there now. As Ameen Rihani tells in his valuable *Around the Coasts of Arabia*, Hussein was now aware that the Turkish Government was likely to throw its lot in with the Central Powers in the War. He had warned Enver Pasha against this, but in vain, and Enver had made clear that he would demand the participation in the War of the Arabs of the Hedjaz. The Shereef had left Mecca in anger, declaring that he intended to retire from all dealings with politics. His presence in Taif was symbolic of his unwillingness to follow the Turks.

But he came back to Mecca to meet the British agent. Hussein, after inviting the latter to a meal with him and his four sons, saw him alone, and spoke of the letter to Abdullah which Sir Ronald Storrs had written. "My son," he said, *(Orientations, p. 174)* "though I am as one uninvited in this matter I will yet speak." He walked up and down and said, "The Ottoman Empire has rights over us, and we have rights upon her. She has made war on our rights and I am not responsible before God if she has made war upon our rights; nor am I responsible before God if therefore I have made war upon hers."

The meaning here was that as overlord of the Arabs the Turkish Sultan was within his rights to demand that the Shereef should not oppose Turkey in the coming war. Hussein first had agreed that he would maintain his relations with Turkey on condition that the Turkish Government granted instant autonomy to Syria and to Mesopotamia and released the Arab political prisoners whom it held. In short, he demanded that Turkey should recognize the Arabs' right to be free of Turkey and to be under the nominal suzerainty only of the Sultan. This had been refused, and the Turkish leaders even had declared they would force conscription on the Arabs of the Hedjaz, so Hussein now felt he was at leisure to oppose Turkey, passively or even actively.

"Drawing back the long sleeve of his garment, he said (to Ruhi), 'My heart is open to Storrs even as this,' and with a gesture, 'stretch forth to us a helping hand and we shall never at all help these oppressors. On the contrary we shall help those who do good.'" In addition to this message, a letter was delivered to the agent which he was to hand over to Sir Ronald Storrs.

It is important to realize what lay in Hussein's promise of helping those who did good. He was in a key situation. The great menace of Turkey's entry into war against the Allies was in the possible effect of this upon the Moslem subjects of Great Britain and of France if the Turks proclaimed a "*jehad*" or "Holy War." What result it might have was not at all clear. The Moslems of India indeed had been gallantly prompt in their reply to the Empire's call to arms against Germany. But a war against Turkey was a different matter. It was generally hoped that it would not affect the allegiance of British Moslems nor make the Moslem world at large inimical to us, but there was no certainty of this. The issue was a critical one.

Mecca was the saving point. If the probable Turkish proclamation stayed Turkish and did not become really Islamic, the danger might pass. It would be all very well for the Sultan or for the tame Sheik-ul-Islam to announce a *jehad*, but a summons to battle against infidel Britain and France did not ring very true from the allies of infidel Germany and Austria. The only peril lay in the *jehad* being countersigned by Mecca. If the Shereef accepted it and gave it forth, it would be a cry as from the tomb of the Prophet and would work who knew what havoc for France and for ourselves.

Hussein's letter arrived in Cairo on the day before Turkey entered the War. He had much to consider and very reasonably wanted proper assurances before he risked braving the suzerain who had garrisons in his very towns. "He did not forget," as Liddell Hart puts it, "that it was the policy of the Turks to keep alternative Shereefs in stock" at Constantinople. He himself had been taken out of stock to replace a cousin. So he answered that he would not take any measure in Turkish interests voluntarily, and left it to Kitchener or to other spokesmen of Great Britain to extract what this meant.

That was not difficult, of course, and as Turkey became a belligerent next day, it became possible for us to speak to him more openly. On the 31st October Lord Kitchener cabled:

> "Salaams to Shereef Abdullah. Germany has now bought the Turkish Government with gold, notwithstanding that England, France and Russia guaranteed the integrity of the Ottoman Empire if Turkey remained neutral in the war. Against the will of the Sultan the Turkish Government has committed acts of aggression by invading the frontiers of Egypt with bands of Turkish soldiers. If the Arab nation assist England in this war England will guarantee that no intervention takes place in Arabia, and will give the Arabs every assistance against external foreign aggression. It may be that an Arab of true race will assume the Caliphate at Mecca or Medina, and so good come by the help of God out of the evil that now is occurring."

This held out a great prospect to the Shereef of Mecca, to whom alone the hypothesis of the Arab Caliphate could apply, and is also of the highest importance because of the use in it of the words "the Arab nation." It did not merely accept the Shereef as the spokesman of the Arabs, it implicitly placed him in that situation and began negotiations with him on the plane that they meant negotiations with all the Arabs.

Years later, after the need of finding arguments to escape from our bond to King Hussein became stringent amidst Government and Zionist advocates, endeavours have been made to decry Hussein's situation. It has been asserted for example that he "did not represent the Arabs" because the Emir Ibn Saud gave him no fealty and indeed was always at variance with him and preparing to overturn him. The other Arab princes too of the coastal fringe had in nowise accepted him as their representative and the Lebanese had not accepted him, and so on.

These autumnal arguments only have the red vigour of October's leaves. In the first place, considering that we negotiated with King Hussein as spokesman of all the Arabs, we certainly cannot withdraw from him now the very situation which we ourselves extended to him. To accept him as representing the Arabs, and then, after having drawn all the advantage possible to us from this acceptance, to evade our part of the bargain with him on the plea that all the time he had not represented the Arabs—that would be a piece of scandalous sharp practice.

In the second place, these arguments conceal an outrageous assumption, that the future King Ibn Saud and the other Arab potentates stood apart from the restoration of the Arab race. Their differences with Hussein were personal, not national. King Ibn Saud, after ousting Hussein, took up exactly the same Arab attitude which Hussein had held, in so far as the restoration of the Arab race was concerned. To present jealousy and even conflict for the leadership between Arabs as disagreement with Arab independence is to misinterpret everything.

It is to be noted that the agreement with King Hussein made by Great Britain was precise upon the point that there could be no question of his situation as negotiator being held in any way to affect the individual situations of the other Arab princes. In a letter which will be quoted shortly, which on the British side was the basis of the Anglo-Arab treaty, the High Commissioner said that he accepted King Hussein's terms "without prejudice to our existing treaties with Arab chiefs." King Hussein when replying said that he respected "your agreements with the Sheikhs of these districts." It was specially arranged therefore that the treaty position of Hussein should have no bearing on the existing status of Arab princes, nor altering effect on their relations between each other. By a necessary converse their interrelations and existing status al no time had any bearing nor altering effect on Hussein's treaty-position.

Still less can dissensions between the Arab princes be put forth as, by implication, support of Zionist pretensions. King Ibn Saud and his people are as desirous to overthrow political Zionism as they were to overthrow King Hussein, probably more so. No Arabs favour Zionism except a few unwittingly well-described "thoughtful Arabs…whose economic interests are not in conflict with the economic interests of the Jews." *(Peel Report, p. 5)* Such Arabs keep their thoughts in their pockets.

I return to Lord Kitchener's dispatch. If it recognized that the Shereef of Mecca spoke on behalf of the Arab nation, it was not very explicit about the future condition of the Arabs. After all that was the Arabs' matter. The dispatch however was accompanied by an assurance of our support of the Shereef's dynastic independence, and of our readiness to assist in the liberation of the Arabs, subject in his case and theirs to active participation in the War on our behalf.

This assurance to the Shereef was by word of mouth. But written or spoken it was the first clear promise of independence in any form we made to an Arab leader, and deserves to be remembered as such.

About this time, as Lawrence records, Lord Kitchener made overtures to another prominent Arab, a soldier, Aziz el Masri, who was in exile in Egypt, with the aim "of winning to our side the Turkish Mesopotamian forces," largely composed of Arab conscripts under the influence of the "Hisb al Ahd." Lawrence goes on to recount how the opportunity was lost through India Office opposition, and it is a bitter little story. The interest of it here is that it confirms how Kitchener was appealing to the Arabs to come to our aid.

Hussein's reply to the British "assurance" and letter was sent to Cairo. It was "an unequivocal promise that he would abstain from helping our enemies." (Hogarth.) He promised neutrality, and would endorse no *jehad*, therefore, if it were proclaimed.

The *jehad*, though, was proclaimed, early in 1915, and Hussein was invited or rather ordered, says Lawrence, by the Turkish Government to echo its cry. He refused. His refusal was not altogether a manoeuvre. He was not only Shereef of Mecca but a sincere Shereef of Mecca, true to his beliefs, and it did seem to him unlawful to proclaim the Holy War when Islam had not been attacked (for Turkey took the first steps in fighting) and when Germany was Turkey's ally.

By his refusal he laid himself open to the Turks' anger and this was quick to follow. They dammed the flow of pilgrims, from whom Mecca drew most of its income, and the food-supplies which went there by rail.

The Hedjaz was very dependent upon outside sources for its food, for the country shelved into the desert. We, on our part, now tried to balance this by allowing food-ships from India into Jeddah with a certain regularity.

The Arabs of the Hedjaz therefore, in return for Hussein's action, were not treated by us as enemy subjects. It would indeed have been singularly impolitic to have shown any form of hostility towards the enclave of the Moslem Holy Cities, whatever had been the attitude of the Shereef. The maintenance of the food-ships was, however, a tangible proof of our appreciation of his help to our cause.

Without mistake, it was great help. "The Shereef rendered Britain a service greater than any that could be expected in the material realm," is the comment of Liddell Hart. "He drew the sting of the *jehad*. Outside Turkey now it would have little meaning, despite the assiduous efforts of Turkish and of German missionaries. Britain had a war with Turkey on her hands, but to all intents she was saved the back-breaking burden of a Holy War."

I cite these comments to emphasize the great obligations under which we lie to the Arabs, obligations too easily and too conveniently forgotten nowadays. Nor did Hussein merely help us: he took supreme risks for himself. He might quite well have played an easier hand, knowing that had he endorsed the *jehad* we could do little beyond blockading his coasts. We might not even have been in a position to enforce a blockade, because of the odium which might have resulted for us throughout the East if we had tried to starve Mecca.

Whereas by refusing to endorse the *jehad* he made the Turks furious. He settled his fate at their hands if they came out of the War as victors or reached a stage of it when they were sufficiently victorious elsewhere to be able to pay attention to him. They were otherwise occupied at the moment and had no troops to spare, but as soon as they had time and troops he might expect to be plucked from the divan upon which they had placed him.

Hussein knew this, and in his mind was pretty well determined now to go to full lengths and to espouse the cause of the Allies in the open. If he were to join them he would have internal support and vastly enhanced prestige amidst his own race. He would join them not as the half-sovereign of the Hedjaz, but as the leader of all the Arabs. His position as such was becoming defined. Directly the War broke out the secret societies of Syria had got into touch with him. A secret Nationalist committee had been formed in Damascus, composed of Arabs from Syria, from Mesopotamia and from Arabia proper. This committee formulated a programme for the independence of the Arab regions and for co-operation with the Allies.

This was sent on to the Shereef, to whom it was left, if he acquiesced in the programme, to negotiate with Great Britain for help in its carrying-out, in return for Arab support in the field against the Turks. The leaders in Syria were aware of the negotiations which had preceded between the Emir Abdullah and Lord Kitchener. They now brought their adherence to them and suggested lines for developing the negotiations into a pact.

In the first weeks of 1915 the Shereef received various appeals calling on him to take action in accordance with this Damascus programme. "The Committees of the Ahad and the Fatah," says Lawrence, "were calling on him as the Father of the Arabs, the Moslem of Moslems, their oldest notable."

But for a month or two Hussein bided his time, watching the situation in general. A new High Commissioner, in the place of the absent Kitchener had arrived in Egypt from India, Sir Henry McMahon. He had instructions from the Foreign Office to "foster the Shereef's friendship."

Egypt had its own preoccupation, for the Turks had attacked the Suez Canal in February. This attack had been ineffectual and had been beaten off without much difficulty, but the Turkish force had not been pursued, and its commander, Djemaal Pasha, was officially understood to be refitting for a second effort. This was considered in Egypt to be a piece of bluff only, but it had to be watched. In April too came the graver preoccupation of the beginning of the Gallipoli expedition.

Hussein's son, Feisal, in his capacity as a Turkish officer went to the Dardanelles, and sent secret messages home about the difficult advance of the attacking force but the considerable losses of the Turks. The latter's measure of success in resistance however and these same losses combined to make the Turkish Command talk of instituting the threatened conscription in the Hedjaz. The Shereef evaded this by raising a contingent of volunteers for Djemaal Pasha's "resumed attack upon Egypt." Since it was Turkish policy to pretend this attack was in preparation, Hussein's policy was to pretend he believed the pretence, and to furnish men for an army which he expected would never take form. Even if some of them had to join the Turkish colours, the greater evil of conscription for all his people would be escaped.

Meanwhile the Turkish High Command had removed its Arab troops from Syria, and dispersed them amidst German and Austrian troops upon south-eastern European fronts. The leaders of the "Ahad" had planned a mutiny of these troops, while there was but one Turkish division in Syria to their own five. The "Decentralization Society" was preparing plans for a rebellion of the populace at the same time, and circularized all its Syrian depots from Cairo to obtain an estimate of the numbers which might be recruited for this, and to inquire where certain leaders who would take charge might be hidden in security till the moment for rising had come. A promise of subsidies, of 20,000 rifles and of the dispatch of three warships to cover Beyrout and the coasts during the insurrection, had been obtained from the French, French officers were to lead the insurrection, of which the centre was to be Zahle in the Bekaa, at the foot of the Lebanon slopes.

Unfortunately these plans, which if effected promptly, might have altered the whole Eastern campaign, were never realized. The Ahad and the "Decentralization" societies worked independently, the French promises were given by officials in the Levant, not directly from France. The French military and naval chiefs had other things than Syria to occupy them at the time, and the promised help lingered. While everyone was waiting for everyone else the Turks moved the Arab divisions piecemeal under German supervision, and the opportunity was lost.

Hussein had been asked at first to raise the Hedjaz when the insurrection would break out in Syria, but was not very satisfied with what he heard of the preparations, and demanded some sort of screen of Allies or of revolted regulars between himself and Constantinople. The dispersal of the Arab divisions ended this prospect.

The emissaries of the Syrian Societies, though, who now were represented by a group of councillors in Mecca, still were for action, and the Shereef presently came to share this view. It is true that Feisal had advocated more prudence because of the growing in success of the Dardanelles expedition. But Hussein feared that this might be the very reason for an extension of Turkish activity into the Hedjaz.

So he set all other considerations aside and made a bold and definite offer of revolt if his conditions based on the Damascus programme were met by Great Britain. This offer took the form of a letter which reached the High Commissioner in Egypt early in August. It is a letter memorable for the Arab race, because it was in its way their Magna Charta, the foundation of their independence. For the Arabs of Palestine it is one of the great salient events in the history of the question with which we are here concerned, and therefore it merits to be considered in a fresh chapter.

Chapter 6

The Treaty between Great Britain and the Arabs. Arab independence to be recognized and supported within frontiers including Palestine.

The Shereef of Mecca's letter to the High Commissioner in Egypt was dated the 2nd of Ramadan in the year 1333 of the Moslem calendar, that is the 14th July, 1915, so it took well over a fortnight to arrive at its destination. Fifteen years ago I published the essential passages of this and of the succeeding letters or dispatches which passed between the Shereef and Sir Henry McMahon, in the series of articles I wrote in the *Daily Mail,* but I think it as well to give their entire text now. This text, there is no harm in saying today, I received chiefly through the goodwill of the late King Feisal, when I was in the Near East in 1922. It was not proffered to me: I set about obtaining it myself, as it seemed so wrong that—as was being done at the time and has been done since— these papers should be kept unpublished while the pledges contained in them were being denied. The text is the official text, that is to say the English version of it, from the Shereefial archives. It is the accepted first translation from the Arabic, taken very literally from the original. The grammar, occasionally faulty, I have left unaltered. Phrases within brackets, unless italicized, are part of the text.

The letter of the 15th July, then, ran:

> "To His Honour,
>
> Whereas the whole of the Arab nation without any exception have decided in these last years to live, and to accomplish their freedom and grasp the reins of their Administration both in theory and in practice: and whereas they have found and felt that it is to the interest of the Government of Great Britain to support them and aid them to the attainment of their firm and lawful intentions (which are based upon the honour and dignity of their life) without any ulterior motives whatsoever unconnected with this object:
>
> And whereas it is to their interest also to prefer the assistance of the Government of Great Britain in consideration of their geographical position and economic interests, and also of the attitude of the above

mentioned Government, which is known to both nations and need not therefore be emphasized:

For these reasons the Arab nation sees fit to limit themselves, as time is short, to asking the Government of Great Britain, if it should think fit, for the approval, through her deputy or representative, of the following fundamental propositions, leaving out all things considered secondary in comparison with these, so that it may prepare all means necessary for attaining this noble purpose, until such time as it finds occasion for making the actual negotiations:

Firstly. England to acknowledge the independence of the Arab countries, bounded on the north by Mersina-Adana up to the 37° of latitude, on which degree falls Birijik, Urfa, Mardin, Midiat, Amadia Island, up to the border of Persia; on the east by the borders of Persia up to the Gulf of Basra; on the south by the Indian Ocean, with the exception of the position of Aden to remain as it is; on the west by the Red Sea, the Mediterranean Sea up to Mersina. England to approve of the proclamation of an Arab Khalifate of Islam.

Secondly. The Arab Government of the Shereef to acknowledge that England shall have the preference in all economic enterprises in the Arab countries whenever conditions of enterprise are otherwise equal.

Thirdly. For the security of this Arab independence and the certainty of such preference of economic enterprises, both high contracting parties to offer mutual assistance to the best ability of their military and naval forces, to face any foreign Power which may attack either party. Peace not to be decided without agreement of both parties.

Fourthly. If one of the parties enters upon an aggressive conflict, the other party to assume a neutral attitude, and in the case of such party wishing the other to join forces, both to meet and discuss the conditions.

Fifthly. England to acknowledge the abolition of foreign privileges in the Arab countries, and to assist the Government of the Shereef in an international convention for confirming such abolition.

Sixthly. Articles 3 and 4 of this Treaty to remain in vigour for 15 years, and if either wishes it to be renewed, one year's notice before lapse of Treaty to be given.

Consequently, and as the whole of the Arab nation have (praise be to God) agreed and united for the attainment, at all costs and finally of this noble object, they beg the Government of Great Britain to answer them positively or negatively in a period of thirty days after receiving this intimation; and if this period should lapse before they receive an answer, they reserve to themselves complete freedom of action. Moreover, we [Shereef's family] will consider ourselves free in word and deed from the bonds of our previous declaration which we made through Ali Effendi."

For a number of reasons this was a remarkable document. To begin with, it was couched in the name of the Arab Nation, which thus was formally proclaimed in it as a political entity again in the world after centuries, never of eclipse, but of subordination. This proclamation cannot have come as a surprise to the recipients of the letter, for in his cable of the previous October Lord Kitchener himself had been the first to give back their old status to the "Arab Nation." His use of the title betokened that even then there was an understanding between him and Mecca that the nation was to be revived as such. But now it was definitely, not incidentally, declared. It was as the spokesman of the Arab nation that the Shereef penned his letter. His personal Government was not mentioned till the second clause, and again in the fifth, where it was given the role of negotiating on behalf of the "Arab countries."

In respect of these countries the Shereef adopted the role of *primus inter pares*. But how far he sank his own identity and the fortunes of the Hedjaz in the general cause of the Arabs is evident from the final sentence, in which it is stated that failing a reply within a month the Shereefial family would consider itself freed from all previous declarations. The declarations in question were of course those made in answer to Lord Kitchener, Ali Effendi being the confidential messenger who brought in December the second of the previous communications from Mecca.

In his message just after war had broken out with Turkey, Kitchener had assured Hussein that Great Britain would support his own "dynastic independence" and "assist in the liberation of the Arabs." The first promise to Hussein himself was concrete, the second as concerned the Arabs at large was vague. The Shereef therefore sacrificed something by merging his claims in the claim on behalf of the Arab nation. In the light of later events it is desirable to underline this.

No doubt the requirement that Britain should approve the proclamation of an Arab Caliphate may appear to be a sufficient recompense for anything Hussein might have lost in prospect, for he of course would be the new Arab Caliph. But the Caliphate demand was not a fresh demand: it had been canvassed before with Kitchener, who had agreed support.

There was a second very noteworthy point in the document which came to the High Commissioner. Not alone did the Arab nation reappear in it as a conscious and vocal unit again, but the boundaries proposed within which Arab independence was to be restored were based upon those which had been postulated twenty years before by the "National Committee" in the proclamation which it had published in Paris. The preamble of Hussein's declaration was an adaptation of the Paris preamble, the heavy Gallicized formula—"The Arabs are awakened to their historical, national and ethnographical homogeneousness"—being turned into the simpler Arabian, "Whereas the whole of the Arab nation without any exception have decided in these last years to live."

As for the boundaries, the Paris declaration did not mention the northern boundary, for the reason perhaps that it was not always so well defined where the Arab and Turkish races ran into each other along the edges of Asia Minor, from Alexandretta to the Persian border. Of the other three boundaries, Hussein's declaration extended the Paris claim on the east from the great rivers to the Persian frontier. The southern and western boundaries, which latter concerns us particularly, were the same as in the 1895 proclamation.

Hussein's document particularized the more general terms of the Paris one, assured to Great Britain the retention of Aden, and found a real mathematico-geographical solution for the northern boundary. In both sets of boundaries the Mediterranean coast, the Syrian coast from the junction with Turkey to the junction with Egypt, inevitably was postulated, and Palestine thereby was included in the Arab dominions. It could not have been otherwise. Of all the boundaries of the Arab people the Mediterranean boundary is the most definite and most natural.

These two things, the emergence of the Arab nation as a negotiating body and the continuity of its action from exile in west Europe in 1905 to Mecca in 1915, deserve continuous emphasis. In the interests of the Zionist thesis the Shereef's demands have been treated sometimes as the wanderings of an old Oriental potentate putting his imagination impulsively on to paper. They were nothing of the sort. They were the reiteration of a programme long conceived by all branches of Arabs and now adopted by the Shereef in conjunction with them. (Mr. Antonius [In his recently published *The Arab Awakening*] records that the leaders of the Arab societies in Damascus drew up a document enshrining the conditions under which they would be prepared to cooperate with Britain against Turkey. It provided almost word for word the first of King Hussein's "fundamental propositions" in his letter just quoted, and the others were developments of it. It was in fact sent to him so that he might make it the basis of his negotiations, and he did so. Feisal conveyed it to him, along with the tidings that the Arab leaders in Syria had sworn oaths of allegiance to him as spokesman of the Arab race should he accept it.)

His document, when it reached Cairo, caused some "searching of hearts." Commander Hogarth, who records this fact, explains that there were various reasons for it. The ill-success of our arms in the Dardanelles and "a new doubt for the safety of the Red Sea route" were largely responsible for a relatively lukewarm reception. The prevalent attitude, except amid a few wiser men, was not so much to see in the promised Arab revolt a new help as a new commitment, in an area where we already had more than we had bargained for on our hands. Besides, the unequivocal character of the demand for general Arab independence had to be faced by various non-Kitcheners. Cairo was in an uncertain, worried mood, reflecting dilatoriness in London, and a reply was delayed till the last day but one of August. After saluting the Shereef with the customary compliments, the High Commissioner wrote:

> "We have the honour to thank you for your frank expressions of sincerity of your feeling towards England. We rejoice moreover that your Highness and your people are of one opinion, that Arab interests are English interests and English Arab. To this intent we confirm to you the terms of Lord Kitchener's message, which reached you by the hands of Ali Effendi, and in which was stated clearly our desire for the independence of Arabia and its inhabitants, together with our approval of the Arab Caliphate when it should be proclaimed. We declare once more that His Majesty's Government would welcome the resumption of the Caliphate by an Arab of true race. With regard to the questions of limits, frontiers and boundaries, it would appear to be premature to consume our time in discussing such details in the heat of war, and while, in many portions of them, the Turk is up to now in effective occupation; especially as we have learnt, with surprise and regret, that some of the Arabs in these very parts, far from assisting us, are neglecting this, their supreme opportunity, and are lending their arms to the German and the Turk, to the new despoiler and the old oppressor.
>
> Nevertheless we are ready to send to Your Highness for the Holy Cities and the noble Arabs the charitable offerings of Egypt so soon as Your Highness shall inform us how and where they should be delivered. We are moreover arranging for this your messenger to be admitted and helped on any journey he may make to ourselves."
>
> Friendly assurances.
>
> Salutations.
>
> A.H. McMahon

This was a thoroughly diplomatic response, and there is a certain humorous idiosyncrasy about diplomatic responses, which may be noted without losing sight of their serious import. A letter such as the Shereef's may make some cardinal proposition, and you would imagine therefore that the reply to it must either accept or refuse this proposition or say that a verdict upon its acceptability will be given later. Not at all. The diplomatic response ignores the cardinal proposition. The diplomatic response is given to an imaginary proposition, which not only is not cardinal, but is not even to be found in the letter which is being answered. The recipient of the letter in question blandly assures its sender that he will give every consideration to what the sender has nowhere put forward. In the case in point the Shereef had demanded independence for the whole group of Arab countries, but Sir Henry McMahon warmly confirms the independence of Arabia, which peninsula the Shereef had never mentioned.

The Shereef did obtain the reaffirmation of British approval for his prospective Caliphate. But after that, in the Cairo response, came the artistic waiving of details. The pertinent question of boundaries was given an altogether different air by the introduction (from nowhere) of two additional, cognate words, "limits" and "frontiers." By introducing the extra words and by stringing the three together the impression was conveyed that the Shereef wanted limits and boundaries and frontiers *and* Heaven knows what else. His one plain enumeration of boundaries was turned into a fantastic miscellany of requirements which the realist…High Commissioner could but dismiss, nor waste further time upon in the "heat of war."

Next followed surprise and regret at the presence of Arab troops amidst the fighting forces of Turkey. Regret, yes; but only in a diplomatic letter from Cairo would it have been possible to feign surprise at their presence.

However, the High Commissioner's diplomatic recitative ended with this last show of surprise, and he went on to an appreciated item of news in conversational tone. The Shereef, who had inquired anxiously, by separate letter, about the subsidies for the Holy Places contributed by Moslems in Egypt, learnt that he was to receive the alms which helped to keep his barren little State alive. It was the crumb of comfort at the end of a letter which left his proposals unanswered.

The matter, of course, did not stop there. Hussein and his councillors took Sir Henry McMahon's reply on the rebound. The Shereef sent an answer to it on the 9th of September (29th Shawal, 1333) by return of secret agent, so to speak. It is a longer document than his first.

> "To His Excellency the Most Exalted, the Most Eminent, the British High Commissioner in Egypt—may God grant him success!
>
> With great cheerfulness and delight I received your letter, dated the 19th Shawal 1333 (30th August 1915) and have given it great consideration and regard, in spite of the impression I received from it of ambiguity and its tone of coldness and hesitation with regard to our essential point.
>
> It is necessary to make clear to Your Excellency our sincerity towards the illustrious British Empire, and our confession of preference for it in all cases and matters and under all forms and circumstances. The real interests of the followers of our religion necessitate this.
>
> Nevertheless Your Excellency will pardon me and permit me to say clearly that the coldness and the hesitation which you have displayed in the question of the limits and boundaries by saying that the discussion of these at present is of no use and is a loss of time, and that they are still in

> the hands of the Government which is ruling them, etc., might be taken to infer an estrangement or something of the sort.
>
> As these limits and boundaries demanded are not those of one person whom we could satisfy and with whom we should discuss them after the War is over, but our peoples have seen that the life of their new proposal is bound at least by these limits, and their word is united in this.
>
> And therefore they saw the discussion in it first the place of their confidence and trust the axis of final appeal now, and that is the illustrious British Empire: the feelings of its inhabitants to know how to base their future and life for not to meet her or one of its allies in front of their resolution when the thing comes to a contrary result, which God forbid."

I break off the transcript of the text here because of the obscurity in the two foregoing paragraphs, particularly of the second. The first is only clumsily put together in the English translation, for the meaning is clear enough, viz., "this is not an individual matter, I am not discussing on behalf of any single Arab potentate with whom the rectification of a boundary-line could be discussed in confidence after the War, but on behalf of all the Arab peoples, who perceive that their existence is bound up in the frontiers they demand." You are not dealing with me only,...nor am I acting for myself only, says Hussein in an Oriental way.

The second paragraph, literally translated above, is more obscure, and the official Arab translator has appended to it an explanatory version which goes as follows:

> Therefore they have found it necessary to first discuss this point with the Power in whom they now have their confidence and trust as a final appeal, viz., the illustrious British Empire. Their reason for this union and confidence is mutual interest, the necessity of regulating territorial divisions and the feeling of their inhabitants, so that they may know how to base their future and life, so not to meet her [England?] or any of her allies in opposition to their resolution which would produce a contrary issue, which God forbid!

The translator has not been entirely successful in his own explanatory version towards the end, which might be bettered as: "Their reason for confidence in and desire for union with Britain is mutual interest, coupled with the need felt by the Arab peoples for laying the basis of their future in a way which will not bring either Britain or any of her allies across the path of their intent. God forbid any such antagonism! "

This paragraph, in any case, is not of importance save as an explanation of motive. I continue the text:

> "For the object is, honourable Minister, the truth which is established on a basis which guarantees the essential sources of life in future.

> Yet within these limits they [the Arabs] have not included places inhabited by a foreign race. It is a vain show of words and titles [i.e., to include such places would be a vain show of nominal claims]. May God have mercy on the Caliphate and comfort Moslems within it.
>
> I am confident that Your Excellency will not doubt that it is not I personally who am demanding of [sic] these limits which include only our race, but that they are all proposals of the people who, in short, believe that they are necessary for economic life.
>
> Is this not right, Your Excellency the Minister?
>
> In a word, Your High Excellency, we are firm in our sincerity and declaring our preference for loyalty towards you, whether you are satisfied with us as has been said, or angry.
>
> With reference to your remark in your letter above-mentioned, that some of our people are still doing their utmost in promoting the interest of Turkey, your Perfectness would not permit you to make this an excuse for the tone of coldness and hesitation with regard to our demands, demands which I cannot admit that you, as a man of sound opinion, will deny to be necessary for our existence. Nay, they are the essential essence of our life, material and moral.
>
> Up to the present moment I am myself with all my might carrying out in my country all things in conformity with the Islamic law, all things which tend to benefit the rest of the kingdom, and I shall continue to do so till it pleases God to order otherwise.
>
> In order to reassure Your Excellency, I can declare that the whole country, together with those who you say are submitting themselves to Turco-German orders, are all waiting the result of these negotiations, which are dependent only on your refusal or acceptance of the question of the limits [i.e., boundariesj, and on your declaration of safeguarding their religion first and then the rest of rights from any harm or danger.
>
> Whatever the illustrious Government of Great Britain finds conformable to its policy in this subject, communicate it to us and specify the course we should follow.
>
> In all cases it is only God's will which shall be executed and it is God who is the real factor in everything."

The Shereef's letter concluded with some technical details about how the Egyptian alms for the Holy Places and grain for the Hedjaz population were to be sent. But in the Shereef's own words, "The said grain has nothing to do with politics," and there is no cause to lengthen Hussein's already sufficiently long letter by adding this finale.

It is a long-winded letter, but for all that very much to the point and carrying some sly hits in it. In his own phraseology the Shereef told Sir Henry McMahon that the latter's message was seen to be a piece of temporization. The High Commissioner's air of not observing the Shereef's demands in nowise deceived that dignitary.

He reiterated his situation: he was not speaking for himself: that must be understood once and for all. He was speaking now and henceforth for all Arabs, who knew of his demands, and had entrusted him with the making of them. This was as true of the Arabs serving at present under the Turkish colours as for anybody, and the part that Arabs took now in the War would depend upon the High Commissioner's acceptance or rejection of the terms formulated in the Shereef's first letter. Hussein stood by these terms, i.e., the independence of all the Arab peoples within their natural boundaries. The boundaries he had postulated contained no foreign inhabitants, but were truly Arab. It was to Britain the Arabs now made their final appeal, as they believed that Britain could serve them best and they best serve Britain. God forbid that Britain should refuse this appeal, and that they should have to turn to the foe for help in securing their aims.

The hint that the Arabs might be driven to come to an arrangement with the Turks was a timely one. Though a good bargaining move, it was no mere bargaining move. The Dardanelles expedition was now evidently no longer likely to succeed, and with the Turks victorious at the Dardanelles, the position of Hussein would become perilous. His only resource might be to patch up relations with the Turks. He did not care for this, because his heart was set on the British alliance, and all that would be obtained from Turkey would be a promise of autonomy for the Arab countries as provinces of Turkey. Whether this promise too in the event of Turkish victory would ever be fulfilled and he himself be left in Mecca was very doubtful. But he might be forced to compound upon those lines, if the present opportunity of acting along with the Allies was lost, and he and his people became isolated.

It is to be noted that the Arabs, whom he represented, sought to join forces with the Allies at a juncture when things were not looking at all favourable for the latter. There was no question of the Arabs flying to the help of the conqueror: Hussein himself was fully informed of the setback at Gallipoli. Not long after his second document reached Cairo, indeed, the possibility of an evacuation from the Straits began to be considered. On the 11th of October Lord Kitchener cabled from London to Sir Ian Hamilton to ask what losses he foresaw if this operation were undertaken.

Our authorities in Egypt, as may be imagined, were careworn now. In addition to the great Gallipoli peril, other dangers had manifested themselves which, if small in comparison, were disturbing and might extend. To this day some of these lesser troubles remain unknown by the general public, though they have been chronicled. "On every hand," says the *Official History of the War*, "German and Turkish agents were at work to make trouble, seeking out weak spots, blowing the smouldering coals of religious hatred." On the western frontier of Egypt the Senussi tribe was in communication with Constantinople. Enver's half-brother, Nuri Bey, and a stiffening of German and Turkish officers was with the chief of the tribe, Sayed Ahmed, who had been urged (as Cairo learned from intercepted letters) by the Sultan to proclaim the *jehad* against the Allies.

> This threat in the western desert continued to grow till it culminated in the autumn in war.... In the Soudan also there were sporadic disturbances. These were due in part to the uneasiness which Great Britain's war with the Caliphate (i.e. with Mohammed V, the existing Turkish Caliph) aroused among the Moslem population, but still more to the propaganda of Turkish emissaries. (*Official History.*)

On the west of the Soudan too, the Sultan of Darfur was rousing anxiety which was to be justified. He was planning in fact an attack on the Soudan which it was his role to deliver at the same time that the Senussi struck at Egypt. He did not keep this appointment, but was crushed six months later in the most ignored, the smallest and one of the most enterprising actions of the War.

At one time, however, the military and civil chiefs in Cairo, between him and his compeers, had about eighteen hundred miles of complications to deal with on the flank of Egypt and of the Soudan, in addition to the major operation at Gallipoli. At the gates of the Red Sea, too, at Perim and at Aden, attacks had been launched by the enemy. Therefore the Shereef's renewed offer to Sir Henry McMahon of an Arab alliance was something that could no longer receive a temporizing answer. The High Commissioner, who had been anxious himself from the first for Anglo-Arab co-operation and had not put Hussein off very voluntarily, pressed upon the Home Government the necessity of a definite step to win over the Arabs.

Aubrey Herbert, who was engaged on politico-military missions then in the Near East, after being wounded when serving with the Irish Guards in France, arrived in Egypt that October. His record of the situation there shows how things stood, and his record can be trusted. Few men had had such intimate contact with the Moslem world as he, and few have enjoyed such qualities of head and of heart. He was that greatest of all rarities, a chivalrous expert. When he arrived in Cairo, he says, "the Arab question had reached a crisis. I saw the General (Sir John Maxwell, G.O.C. in Egypt), Clayton (the Chief of Intelligence), Cheatham (Sir Milne Cheatham, the Foreign Office representative), and the High Commissioner (Sir Henry McMahon). They all agreed that it was of *almost supreme importance*" (the italics are mine) "to get the Arabs in with us, that the opportunity would be lost if this was not done soon."

Herbert, who knew the Turks so well, thought that they would before long come round to that offer of autonomy to the Arabs which they had before refused to make. "Three years ago Talaat Bey," he said, "told me that the Committee of [Union and Progress; the Young Turk ruling group] had learnt its lesson in Albania and were ready to offer the Arabs practically any form of autonomy that they might choose to demand. He thought that these concessions, accompanied by flattery and the petting at Constantinople of the Sheikhs would dispose of the Arab question. The Germans have even more dazzling gifts to offer, and fiercer penalties to threaten, and the Arabs feel that the moment for making their decision is at hand."

The Arab attitude and Arab hopes were explained to Herbert by Aziz Bey el Masri. Aziz Bey, whom Lawrence calls an "idol of the Arab officers," was unofficial Arab legate in Cairo at the time. Through him, as has been stated, Lord Kitchener had inquired, more than a year before, whether the Arab battalions in Mesopotamia might not desert to the British flag.

Aziz was well qualified to expound his countrymen therefore and he told Herbert what the reader has already learned, that the strength of the Arab movement lay in its young men. The Committees of the Arab youth, the men of the secret societies, wherever they were placed, however, were wise enough to work through the Shereef of Mecca. They did not make the mistake of the Young Turks in despising reverence and tradition. Under the Ottoman regime many of them had aimed at winning autonomy, but the Young Turks so far had made that impossible. If England would help the Arabs they would accept from her a portion of what they were promised by the Germans. The Germans had made sweeping offers in British Africa. But if England remained cold they would have to make the best terms they could and that, in all probability, very soon. The way in which the War was going for us in the East made the Arabs fear for their freedom. Aziz, in fact, corroborated that what Hussein had said was indeed the genuine demand of all the Arabs, and he confirmed the need of speedy action.

After communicating with the Government in England, Sir Henry McMahon was empowered to take this action. This he did despite certain complications which now beset him. They arose from the French aspirations in Syria. A French diplomatist, M. Picot (not too well chosen, for reasons which will transpire) was then engaged in what was described as "a mission of inquiry and consultation" in the Near East, which looked like the prelude to some official move or other by France. The nature of this had been forecast in Egypt to Sir Mark Sykes, a British knight-errant, under direct orders from Kitchener to make a report on conditions in the same area as Picot, though his commission antedated Picot's. In July a French official had told him that "France must have Damascus."

The truth was that the French at that moment were anxious to part the lion's skin as soon as war with the Turkish lion began. They had a tentative arrangement, concluded in the spring of 1915, with Britain and Russia by which the spheres of influence of the three countries in the Turkish dominions were generally indicated, Russia to be granted the Straits and Constantinople. The spheres of influence of course were intended to become spheres of annexation, in the minds of two of the parties concerned, France and Russia, though nothing was defined and as far as France was concerned her aims in Syria might have been reached through a vassal principality. It was arranged that the agreement should take definite form later.

It is important to understand that this agreement had nothing to do with rights. None of the parties concerned had any rights in the Turkish dominions. The ornamental religious protection given to Latin Christians in Syria by France, Russia's similar protection of Greek Christians, gave them no territorial claims whatever on Turkish soil. The tripartite agreement was simply one for convenience in view of the division of possible future spoils, so that quarrelling and disputes about them might not set in at once, following success of Allied arms at the Dardanelles or elsewhere.

That this was so—that there was no question of any "rights" belonging to any of the Allies preventing Sir Henry McMahon's action—can be established from diplomatic documents of the period. They will be quoted in due course, in a later (the twenty-fifth) chapter of this book. It would complicate the subject-matter of the present chapter to introduce them textually here. It will do to say that in March the British Government had not accepted a declaration of the French Government that France would annex Syria in the event of Turkish defeat, and had declared formally that it was precipitate to divide the Turkish dominions at the present stage. The British memorandum which conveyed His Majesty's Government's views had gone on to declare that what had to be kept in mind was not division of this kind but the creation of an independent Moslem Power, into which Arabia would probably enter, to replace the (assumed) disappearance of the Turks from Constantinople.

This Moslem State, the British Government said, it considered absolutely necessary. The French had to put up with this, but insisted on maintaining their contingent "sphere of influence." The "sphere of influence" provided therefore a complication, but not an impediment in the negotiations with the Shereef. For these reasons McMahon, when he resumed correspondence, made allowance for it. It does not appear that he knew of the exchange of notes in Europe between France and Britain and Russia, but he had received general directives from London upon the subject of the French sphere.

It was on the 25th of October that the High Commissioner, then, replied to the Shereef of Mecca. The document which he sent to him was an acceptance of the Arab terms, with a modification in the interests of France, as follows:

"To the Shereef of Mecca [with titles].

I have received your letter of the 29th of Shawal [9th of September] with much pleasure, and your expression of friendliness and sincerity have given me the greatest satisfaction.

I regret that you should have received from my last letter the impression that I regarded the question of the limits and boundaries with coldness and hesitation. Such was not the case, but it appeared to me that the moment had not yet arrived when they could be most profitably discussed.

I have realized however from your last letter that you regard this question as one of vital and urgent importance. I have therefore lost no time in informing the Government of Great Britain of the contents of your letter, and it is with great pleasure that I communicate to you on their behalf the following statement, which I am confident you will receive with satisfaction.

The districts of Mersina and Alexandretta and portions of Syria lying to the west of the districts of Damascus, Hama, Horns and Aleppo cannot be said to be purely Arab, and should be excluded from the proposed limits and boundaries. With the above modification, and without prejudice to our existing treaties with Arab chiefs, we accept these limits and boundaries, and in regard to those portions of the territories therein in which Great Britain is free to act without detriment to the interests of her ally, France, I am empowered in the name of the Government of Great Britain to give the following assurances and to make the following reply to your letter:

Subject to the above modifications, Great Britain is prepared to recognize and support the independence of the Arabs within the territories included in the limits and boundaries proposed by the Shereef of Mecca.

Great Britain will guarantee the Holy Places against all external aggression and will recognize their individuality.

When the situation admits, Great Britain will give to the Arabs her advice, and will assist them to establish what may appear to be the most suitable forms of government in these various territories.

On the other hand it is understood that the Arabs have decided to seek the advice and guidance of Great Britain only, and that such European advisers and officials as may be required for a sound form of administration will be British.

With regard to the vilayets of Baghdad and Basra, the Arabs will recognize that the established position and interests of Great Britain necessitate special measures of administrative control, in order to secure these territories from foreign aggression, to promote the welfare of the local population, and to safeguard our mutual economic interests.

I am convinced that this declaration will assure you beyond all possible doubt of the sympathy of Great Britain towards the aspirations of her traditional friends, the Arabs, and will result in a firm and lasting alliance, the immediate result of which will be the expulsion of the Turks from the Arab countries and the freeing of the Arab peoples from the Turkish yoke, which for so many years has pressed heavily upon them.

I have confined myself in this letter to the more vital and important questions, and if there are any other matters dealt with in your letters which I have omitted to mention, we may discuss them at some convenient date in the future.

It was with very great relief and satisfaction that I heard of the safe arrival of the Holy Carpet and the accompanying offerings, which thanks to the clearness of your directions and the excellence of your arrangements, were landed without trouble or mishap, in spite of the dangers and difficulties occasioned by the present sad war. May God soon bring a lasting peace and freedom to all peoples.

I am sending this letter by the hand of your trusted and excellent messenger, Sheikh Mohammed Ibn Arif Arayfan, and he will inform you of various matters of interest, but of less vital importance, which I have not mentioned in this letter. [*Here follow the usual compliments.*]"

A. Henry McMahon.

That was the crucial document. The Shereef had presented his terms and in it they were accepted formally, under the hand of the High Commissioner for Egypt, the appointed representative of His Majesty's Government, who declared himself empowered to act upon that Government's behalf. The whole is as solemn and binding an engagement as any into which Great Britain has entered. It accepts the Shereef of Mecca as the accredited spokesman of the Arab peoples and accepts them as a negotiating body, inasmuch as it stipulates in several paragraphs of what nature the relations between them and Great Britain are to be.

Its terms are as plain as its character. It undertakes to recognize and to support the independence of the Arabs within the frontiers designated by the Shereef. But it makes a couple of provisos to this undertaking. It rejects the Arab claim to Mersina and to Alexandretta, in the northern boundary; and in the western boundary, which in the Shereef's draft was to be constituted by the coasts of the Red Sea and of the Mediterranean in succession, it makes a proviso concerning the extreme northern portion of this. "Portions of Syria lying to the west of the districts of Damascus, Hama, Homs and Aleppo cannot be said to be purely Arab and should be excluded from the proposed limits and boundaries."

The Arabic word here translated as "district" is equivalent to a town and its adjacencies, what we call nowadays "urban district." The four towns or cities specified lie, as a glance at the map shows, pretty much in a straight line, one below the other, in the order from the north of Aleppo, Hama, Homs and Damascus. The country lying to the west of them roughly corresponds to the coastal territory of the present French Mandatory sphere. At the time the document was indited it corresponded to the sphere of influence which she claimed.

But if there was this reservation placed upon the northern coastal district of Syria, there was no reservation whatsoever mentioned of the southern sphere of the Arab territories, Palestine. For this reason, today, more than twenty years after this Anglo-Arab treaty was concluded, the treaty remains of momentous importance to Palestine. It is not indeed the basis of the primal claim which the Arabs make to Palestine, for that is based on their primordial right to their own country, and upon the illegitimacy of any Powers or of the League of Nations or of any governments or institutions disposing of territory that does not belong to them.

But after that claim, this one comes next, that in this document of the 25th of October, 1915, Great Britain pledged herself to grant an independent Arab Government to Palestine. That this is a just claim cannot be denied. The reservation made by Sir Henry McMahon that the territory to the west of the four cities of Damascus, Horns, Hama and Aleppo must be excluded does not affect Palestine which lies, not west of these cities, but well south of them. In Syria, as it happens, the coastline is so straight that "west" is all but an absolute term there. There are no jutting peninsulas, nor capes to be called "south-west." Palestine is no more west of the French section of Syria than the lower half of this page which the reader has under his eyes is west of its upper half.

Apart too from the inclusion of Palestine being self-evident upon the map, the very phrases of the treaty, as it were, asseverate its inclusion. Where we were free to act without detriment to French interests, that is where we accepted the Arab boundaries without question. In the Persian Gulf hinterland there are stipulations about administrative control, and about the acceptance of British advisers or helpers in the new Arab States, but about fundamental Arab independence being reserved anywhere in the section left to Britain, about the Arab flag not flying anywhere in the British section or about any part of the British section not being purely Arab, there is no sentence, no word, no comma.

Palestine, in fact, is as firmly committed to self-government, under our tutelage, in so far as it might be required, as was the Hedjaz itself. I do not propose, therefore, to enlarge much further upon this point, important as it is, at this stage. We shall return to it, and to full examination of it, when we come unhappily to the endeavour of British statesmen to escape from the Anglo-Arab Treaty, in the interests of Zionism.

All that need be emphasized for the moment is that in October, 1915, there was no thought in responsible quarters of anything in Palestine but of an Arab State under British guidance. There was no question of Palestine being considered a Jewish or part-Jewish country which required a special regime. Palestine was not yet invested with political singularity nor was there any show of inability to treat it, because of a supposed historic Jewish lien upon it, exactly as the other parts of the Arab territories were treated. In October, 1915, the official doctrine of dual ownership of Palestine had not yet been concocted.

All the phrases and descriptions and formulas indeed which appertain to this doctrine, to which we have grown accustomed since upon the lips of our pro-Zionist Cabinet-ministers and other adherents of the Zionist doctrine, are all catchwords of yesterday, nothing but figments and pretences imagined in order to screen a theory which cannot bear the light and to give a long-descended air to a policy without antecedents.

That required to be stated plainly. We can now pass on again to the documents exchanged by the Shereef of Mecca and the High Commissioner. Hussein had been urged, in the last quoted of these, to take up arms against the Turks without delay. In its text the hope was expressed that the immediate results of the new alliance would be the expulsion of the Turks from the Arab countries.

The Shereef however had some stipulations yet to make. He could not leave the Arab attitude towards the modifications and amendments of Sir Henry McMahon unstated.

He replied quickly enough, on the Moslem date of the 27th Zul Hijj, 1333 (5th November, 1915):

> "In the Name of God, the Merciful, the Compassionate.
>
> To His Excellency the Most Exalted and Eminent Minister who is endowed with the highest authority and soundness of opinion. May God guide him to do His will!
>
> I received with great pleasure your honoured letter, dated 15th Zul Hijj [24th October], to which I beg to answer as follows:
>
> 1. In order to facilitate an agreement and to render a service to Islam, and at the same time to avoid all that may cause Islam troubles and hardships—seeing moreover that we have great consideration for the distinguished qualities and dispositions of the Government of Great Britain—we renounce our insistence on the inclusion of the Vilayets of Mersina and Adana in the Arab kingdom. But the provinces of Aleppo and Beyrout and their sea-coasts are purely Arab provinces, and there is no difference between a Moslem and a Christian Arab: they are both descendants of one forefather.

We Moslems will follow the footsteps of the Commander of the Faithful, Omar Ibn Khattab, and other Caliphs succeeding him, who ordained in the laws of the Moslem faith that Moslems should treat the Christians as they treat themselves. "No," Omar declared with reference to Christians, "they will have the same privileges and submit to the same duties as ourselves." They will thus enjoy their civic rights in as much as it accords with the general interest of the whole nation.

2. As the provinces of the Irak are parts of the pure Arab kingdom and were, in fact, the seat of its Governments in the time of Ali Ibn Abu Talib, and in the time of all Caliphs who succeeded him; and as in them began the civilization of the Arabs, and as their towns in those provinces are the first towns built in Islam where the Arab power became so great: therefore, these provinces are greatly valued by all Arabs far and near and their traditions cannot be forgotten by them. Consequently, we cannot satisfy the Arab nations or make them submit to give up such a title to nobility.

But in order to render an accord easy, and to take into consideration the assurances mentioned in the fifth article of your letter, to keep and guard our mutual interests in that country, as they are one and the same, for all these reasons we might agree to leave under the British administration for a short time those districts now occupied by the British troops, without the rights of either party being prejudiced thereby (especially those of the Arab nation, which interests are to it economic and vital), and against a suitable sum paid as compensation to the other kingdom for the period of occupation, in order to meet expenses which every new kingdom is bound to support, at the same time respecting your Agreements with the Sheikhs of those districts, and especially those which are essential.

3. In your desire to hasten the movement, we see not only advantages but grounds of apprehension. The first of these grounds is the fear of the blame of the Moslems of the opposite party, as has already happened in the past, who would declare that we have revolted against Islam and ruined its forces. The second is that, standing in the face of Turkey, which is supported by all the forces of Germany, we do not know what Great Britain and her allies would do if one of the Entente Powers were weakened and obliged to make peace. We fear that the Arab nation will then be left alone in the face of Turkey, together with her allies, but we would not at all mind if we were to face the Turks alone. Therefore, it is necessary to take these points into consideration, in order to avoid a peace being concluded in which the parties concerned may decide the fate of our people as if we had taken part in the War without making good our claims to official consideration.

4. The Arab nation has a strong belief that after this war is over the Turks, under German influence, will direct their efforts to provoke the Arabs and violate their rights, both material and moral, to wipe out their

nobility and honour, and reduce them to utter submission, as they are determined to ruin them entirely. The reasons for the slowness shown in our action have already been stated.

5. When the Arabs know that the Government of Great Britain is their ally, who will not leave them to themselves at the conclusion of peace in the face of Turkey and Germany, and that she will support and effectively defend them, then to enter the War at once will, no doubt, be in conformity with the general interests of the Arabs.

6. Our letter dated the 29th Shawal, 1333 [9 9th of September 1915] saves us the trouble of repeating our opinions as to Articles 3 and 4 of your honoured last letter regarding administration, Government advisers and officials, especially as you have declared, O exalted Minister, that you will not interfere with internal affairs.

7. The arrival of a clear and definite answer as soon as possible to the above proposals is expected. We have done our utmost in making concessions in order to come to an agreement satisfying both parties. We know that our lot in this war will be either a success which will guarantee to the Arabs a life becoming their past history, or destruction in the attempt to attain their objects. Had it not been for the determination which I see in the Arabs for the attainment of their objects, I would have preferred to seclude myself on one of the heights of a mountain, but they, the Arabs, have insisted that I should guide the movement to this end.

May God keep you safe and victorious, as we devoutly hope and desire."

In this communication the Shereef Hussein takes the very proper precaution of demanding a guarantee that peace shall not be concluded by his future Allies without their giving official support to the Arab claims. He accepts, in some ways more definitely than had been asked, British control in Irak—for a time and against a suitable consideration.

But what concerns us most here is his first article. Renouncing Mersina and Adana, he still lays claim to the provinces of Aleppo and of Beyrout and their coasts rather than to the urban districts only of Homs, Hama, Aleppo and Damascus. He had been told of the French contention founded upon France's protection of the Christian Arabs in Syria, but gave no heed to it.

Sir Henry McMahon did not reply till mid-December. Much had happened in the interval. Lord Kitchener himself had come out to survey the situation in Gallipoli and in all the Levant. Plans for evacuation of Gallipoli were now in preparation, and a proposal for a landing at Alexandretta by the Allies in force (an army of 100,000 men was suggested) had been debated. Lord Kitchener examined into it on the day of his arrival at Mudros, the 10th of November.

The Arabs could no longer take part in this scheme as they could have done earlier in the year, for the Turks, we know, had sent away from Syria the Arab divisions, sent them, says Lawrence, "anywhere, so long as they were put quickly into the firing-line, or withdrawn far from the sight and help of their compatriots." There could be no mutiny now to accompany the landing at Alexandretta.

The Alexandretta plan was disapproved, as it happened, on strategic grounds, independently of this consideration, by both the Admiralty and the General Staff of the Army. But the chance in early November that it might be adopted led to an important occurrence. The French Military Attache in London presented to the Chief of the Imperial General Staff a short note of which these are the first two paragraphs:

> "Should the British Government be considering a disembarkation of troops in the gulf of Alexandretta in order to cut the railway to Palestine, they will have to take into consideration not only the economic interests but also the moral and political interests of France in these countries.
>
> French public opinion could not be indifferent to any operations attempted in a country which it considers as destined to form part of the future Syrian state; and it would require of the French Government not only that no military operations should be undertaken in this particular country without previous agreement between the Allies, but also that, should such action be taken, the greater part of the task should be entrusted to French troops and to the French generals commanding them."

This was an odd announcement, for the French at the time could not have produced the troops to whom they demanded that the greater part of the task should be entrusted. The note in reality was a veto upon an Alexandretta expedition, and after a day of conference the Prime Minister cabled to Kitchener that our Government had decided against it.

The chief consequence of the note, however, was to bring to a head the business of the French sphere in Syria—the preposition "in" under the circumstances having an unwontedly expansive sense. It was evident that Great Britain must know where she stood in this matter by getting the French to define their demands. Lord Kitchener had returned to England at the end of November, and in December his emissary Sir Mark Sykes, who had gone meanwhile to India to talk to the Viceroy upon the future of Mesopotamia, returned home too.

Almost at once Sir Mark Sykes was commissioned by the Foreign Office to meet M. Picot, the French diplomatist who had been on mission in Egypt, and with him to put on paper a scheme for the definition and delimitation of French and British interests in the Turkish Near East. These were not their very terms of reference, but to this they amounted. The agreement when reached was to remain confidential, as the negotiations between the two men were to be. The reason adduced for this was that since it was a division of the lion's skin, it had better not be published while the lion lived. It would of course be submitted to Russia, as whatever delimitations Sykes and Picot drew up would be the expected definite form of the earlier "spheres of influence" agreement.

The French Government, through M. Picot, who in preparation for his mission had gone to confer with the Foreign Office in London, had been informed of the Anglo-Arab Treaty after Sir Henry McMahon had sent the crucial letter of agreement to the Shereef of Mecca. M. Picot, told on the 23rd of November, had returned on the 21st of December to signify French agreement to the situation on the lines of the McMahon reservations. The French would administer the coastal area, while Arab government of the four towns of Homs, Hama, Damascus and Aleppo would be "under French influence."

On the other hand Sir Henry McMahon was never informed of the Sykes-Picot negotiations. The Shereef Hussein consequently was kept in the dark about them also. The Arab bureau in Cairo, founded by Gilbert Clayton, to which Lawrence had gone, and Hogarth, and Newcombe—the gunner who disguised as a Bedouin had mapped the Sinai peninsula—and others who were to make considerable names, that too was kept in the dark. So that its business of controlling relations with the Arabs was vitiated unknown to it.

It was in this ignorance, therefore, that the High Commissioner now sent his third reply to the Shereef. Things were as bad as they could be at the time in respect of the War in the Near East. The evacuation of Gallipoli was at hand: it started just after his missive was sent. Sollum had been evacuated too, and hostilities against the Senussi had become necessary. German submarine warfare was beginning to impede Mediterranean communications. In Mesopotamia the British force under General Townshend was besieged in Kut-el-Amara, with no prospect of relief. It was more than ever imperative for us to gain the help of the Arabs.

Sir Henry McMahon wrote, on the 14th of December:

> To Shereef Hussein.
>
> [After customary greetings and acknowledgment of previous letter]
>
> "I am gratified to observe that you agree to the exclusion of the vilayets [provinces] of Mersina and Adana from the boundaries of the Arabs' territories.
>
> I also note with great pleasure and satisfaction your assurances that the Arabs are determined to act in conformity with the precepts laid down by Omar Ibn Khattab and the early Caliphs, which secure the rights and privileges of all religions alike.
>
> In stating that the Arabs are ready to recognize and respect all our treaties with Arab chiefs, it is of course understood that this will apply to

all territories included in the Arab kingdom, as the Government of Great Britain cannot repudiate engagements which already exist.

With regard to the vilayets of Aleppo and Beyrout, the Government of Great Britain had taken careful note of your observations, but, as the interests of our ally, France, are involved, the question will require careful consideration, and a further communication on the subject will be addressed to you in due course.

The Government of Great Britain, as I have already informed you, are ready to give all guarantees of assistance and support within their power to the Arab kingdom, but their interests demand, as you yourself have recognized, a friendly and stable administration in the vilayet of Baghdad, and the adequate safeguarding of these interests calls for a much fuller and more detailed consideration than the present situation and the urgency of these negotiations permits.

We fully appreciate your desire for caution, and we have no wish to urge you to hasty action, which might jeopardize the eventual success of your projects, but in the meantime it is most essential that you should spare no efforts to attach all the Arab people to our united cause and urge them to afford no assistance to our enemies.

It is on the success of these efforts and on the more active measures which the Arabs may take hereafter in support of our cause, when the time for action comes, that the permanence and strength of our agreement must depend.

Under these circumstances I am further directed by the Government of Great Britain to inform you that you may rest assured that Great Britain has no intention of concluding any peace on terms of which the freedom of the Arab peoples from German and Turkish domination does not form an essential condition.

As an earnest of our intentions, and in order to aid you in your efforts in our joint cause, I am sending by your trustworthy messenger a sum of £20,000."

[Customary greetings.] A. H. McMahon.

By this document, the Shereef received the guarantee he had asked that no separate peace would be concluded by the British Government, and that the liberation of the Arabs would be an essential part of any peace treaty. The Arabs in fact were made members of the comity of the Allies by it, and with Great Britain in particular it might be called a wedding. The prosecution of the War was now "our joint cause": Britain and the Arabs were one. Even the gold wedding-ring was clasped on, in the final paragraph.

The High Commissioner was not in a position to give Hussein a definite answer upon the territory between the coast and Aleppo and Beyrout. He supposed no doubt that the Home Government would come to a decision upon French claims someday, and that whenever this occurred he himself would be informed and would have to tell the Shereef. But he dated this announcement at the Whitehall Kalends, "in due course," unaware that the Sykes-Picot negotiations had begun.

He sent a private letter to the Shereef along with the official one, in which there is reason to suppose he warned him that it was no good holding everything up by insistence upon the North Syrian territory, as in this matter the British Government's hands were bound, and the War must be over before they were unbound. Also any idea of monetary compensation in Irak had best be left for future discussion.

His advice, by letter or word of mouth, was taken, and on New Year's Day of 1916, the Shereef sent his final reply:

> "In the name of God, the Merciful, the Compassionate.
> To His Excellency the eminent, energetic, and magnanimous Minister.
>
> [*16th December, 1915. Note. There is some confusion of dates here. The date of Sir Henry McMahon's letter is given as the 14th. His private letter may have been dated the 16th and the two were dispatched together. Or the translator may have made a slip. It is of no consequence, as the last communication from Cairo, whether of the 14th or 16th is the subject of reply. I now repeat the first phrase for clarity's sake.*]
>
> We received from the bearer your two letters, dated 9th Safar 1334, with great respect and honour, and I have understood their contents, which caused me the greatest pleasure and satisfaction, as they removed that which had made me uneasy.
>
> Your Honour will have realized, after the arrival of Mohammed (Faroki) Shereefand his interview with you, that all our procedure up to the present was of no personal inclination or the like, which would have been wholly unintelligible, but that everything was the result of the conditions and desires of our peoples, and that we are but transmitters and executants of such decisions and desires in the position they (our people) have pressed upon us.
>
> These truths are in my opinion very important, and deserve your Honour's special attention and consideration.
>
> With regard to what has been stated in your honoured communication concerning El Irak, as to the matter of compensation for the period of occupation, we, in order to strengthen the confidence of Great Britain in our attitude and in our words and actions, really and veritably, and in order to give her evidence of our certainty and assurance in trusting her glorious Government, leave the determination of the amount to the perception of her wisdom and justice.
>
> As regards the northern parts and their coasts, we have already stated in our previous letter what were the utmost possible modifications. And all this was only done so as to fulfil those aspirations whose attainment is designed by the will of the Blessed and Supreme God. It is this same

feeling and desire which impelled us to avoid what may possibly injure the alliance of Great Britain and France and the agreement made between them during the present war and calamities; yet we find it our duty that the eminent Minister should be sure that, at the first opportunity after this war is finished, we shall ask you (what we avert our eyes from today) for what we now leave to France in Beyrout and its coasts.

I do not find it necessary to draw your attention to the fact that our plan is of greater security to the interests and presumption of the rights of Great Britain than it is to us; and will necessarily be so, whatever may happen, so that Great Britain may finally see all her own peoples in that contentment and advancement which she is endeavouring to establish for them now, especially as her allies being neighbours to us will be the germ of difficulties and discussions with which there will be no peace of mind. In addition to which the people of Beyrout decidedly will never accept such isolations, and they may oblige us to undertake new measures which may exercise Great Britain, certainly not less than her present troubles, because of our belief and certainty in the reciprocity of our interests, which is the only cause that caused us never to care to negotiate with any Power but you. Consequently, it is impossible to allow any derogation that gives France, or any other Power, a span of land in those regions."

On receipt of this Sir Henry McMahon cabled home for final instructions. The Shereef had shown himself accommodating by his willingness to adjourn a settlement in North Syria with the French till the close of the War. He did not accept an iota of the French claims, though. To obtain an adjournment and to leave the issue open, however, fitted in temporarily, if it did nothing else, with the Foreign Office's plans for the coming Sykes-Picot arrangement with France. All really would depend in the upshot upon how far this arrangement conformed to the Treaty with Hussein. What would happen if the Shereef and the Arabs were confronted eventually with an arrangement which did not so conform, no one apparently stopped to consider.

So the High Commissioner was told to close with the terms as now finally adjusted. There was some satisfaction indeed that the Shereef had not stuck out for more. We needed the Arabs very, very badly, and the High Commissioner actually had in his desk a permit to abandon all claim to British control in the provinces of Basra and Baghdad if something more were needful to bring the Arabs in.

Sir Henry wrote to the Shereef a short final letter on the 30th January, announcing:

"I have received orders from my Government to inform you that all your demands are accepted, and that all that you ask for will be sent."

What had been requested was munitions and funds, and the rest of the letter dealt with technical details. The Shereef acknowledged it from Mecca on the 14th Rabi el Ahar *(Rabi II)* 1334 *(16th of February, 1916)* in a short final letter, saying:

> "I have received with joy and happiness your last letter, dated 24th Rabi I, 1334 [30th January, 1916] and I have taken thorough understanding of what it contained. I shall—God willing—work to write the word of the Arabs and to begin with God's permission the activities soon [i.e., shall strive to put on record how the Arabs keep their word and shall with God's will start our hostilities soon]."

The rest of the text of this final letter was lost in Mecca at the fall of the Hashimite dynasty. But it was not of consequence. The McMahon Hussein Correspondence, as it is generally called, closed as a political instrument with Great Britain's acceptance of the Shereef of Mecca's final terms. It is a correspondence only in so far as the papers which compose it, owing to the distance between the negotiators, had to be exchanged in the form of letters. But in fact it was as much of a correspondence in the ordinary sense of that word as were the notes which the negotiators of Versailles occasionally pushed across the table to each other.

It constitutes the negotiations of a treaty and the conclusion of a treaty. The pertinent portions of its text enunciate and then ratify the terms. It is a treaty. The Shereef of Mecca described it in his first document as a treaty, and the terms thus enunciated were accepted. Mr. Lloyd George himself as Prime Minister acknowledged, and indeed insisted to the French Government, that it had treaty-force.

It forms a lengthy set of documents, particularly if read with the explanations made necessary to describe its course as negotiations went along, and on some counts I should have preferred to quote its salient passages only. But I have decided to give it in full because it has never been published in Britain, [1] nor, as far as I know, been published at all anywhere, save in Arabic works.

[Author's note: Since this book has been completed Mr. George Antonius has included the McMahon-Hussein Correspondence in his The *Arab Awakening*. Equally a scholar in English and Arabic, he has made his own translation of the text, and the reader will find interest in comparing it with literal version given to me in 1922. Mr. Antonius writes a full account of the rise of the Arab societies, which should be read to supplement my brief summary. The same may be said of his account of the Arab revolt. I have had the benefit of Mr. Antonius's wide knowledge and erudition when preparing Chapter 15 of the present work, and the reader will find elucidation and confirmation of various details in that and in adjoining chapters in Mr. Antonius's admirable book.]

Reading the full text the reader too is made aware better of the attitude of the persons concerned in the negotiations. Some things stand out. Under all the occasionally involved phraseology of the Shereef, he is seen to be a shrewd, yet straightforward negotiator. He is seen to be anxious for alliance with us, and to repose full trust in our promise.

On our part, the essential pledges we made were clearly and definitely phrased. "Great Britain is prepared to recognize and support the independence of the Arabs within the territories included in the limits and boundaries proposed by the Shereef of Mecca."

These boundaries enclosed Palestine. There was no mention of its exclusion. We gave our word that on its soil the Arabs should be free of all foreign control save such as they chose of their own will.

Furthermore, we gave our word to the Shereef Hussein, not as Shereef of Mecca, but as the representative of the Arab peoples, amongst whom are the Arabs of Palestine, so that we are directly indentured to them.

The terms which he stipulated were drawn up by him in concert with members of national societies which had their roots in Palestine. They reproduced boundaries which had long been the fundamental programme of these societies, comprising all the land facing the Mediterranean from Asia Minor to the Egyptian borders.

Chapter 7

The Progress of Zionism.
Weizmann, Balfour, Sir Herbert Samuel appear.
Zionist approaches to Asquith, Lloyd George and Grey.
Another Manchester School.—The first false step.
The Grey Memorandum.

While the Arabs had moved on to recognition of their independence and to alliance with Britain, what had happened amidst the Zionists?

At the outbreak of the War there were fifty-nine Jewish colonies in Palestine, nurturing a population of some twelve thousand inhabitants. Some seventy thousand more were congregated in the towns, mostly in Jerusalem. Of the eighty thousand odd in Palestine the great majority, between fifty-five thousand and sixty thousand, had come into the country during the last thirty years.

Most of the colonies were subsidized by wealthy Jews, especially by the philanthropic Baron Edmond de Rothschild, of the French branch of the great family. In Jerusalem the Jews maintained themselves in great part by the help of pious offerings from co-religionists of all classes throughout the world.

Latter-day Zionists have not much good to say for the pre-War Zionists because they were so largely maintained by others. Their establishments have been called almshouses. But they practiced a Zionism which did not seek to oust the Arabs. They came back to the country in the one guise which, intolerable to their recent successors, yet consorts with the aim of seeking Zion—in the guise of pilgrims. Moved by their faith, they entered the country without making demands of any sort, and having learnt, it would seem, from what numbers of them had endured in Russia not to act arbitrarily towards another race in false reaction from their own sufferings.

In 1914 a scheme of intenser colonization was being studied as a result of the resolutions of the Eleventh Zionist Congress of the previous year. There was a plan being mooted already for a Jewish university in Jerusalem and Baron Edmond de Rothschild was about to make big purchases of land to establish fresh colonies.

August saw all this activity suddenly brought to a stop. Zionism, an international cult, was split by the War. It was strongest in Russia, but it had an organization of importance in Germany. Its central offices were in Berlin, but its funds were mainly concentrated in British banks, though in England, according to Zionist testimony, "the least significant group of Zionists" was to be found. As for Palestine itself, German Zionist organizations were prominent there.

At first the leaders of Zionism opened a centre in Copenhagen, hoping to keep the international organization together upon neutral soil. This proved impracticable, and presently they changed their attitude. The entry of Turkey into the War was responsible for this. Now that she had become a belligerent she ran the risks of defeat, and if she were defeated the Allies ought to be in a position to dictate the future lot of much, perhaps of all Turkish territory. This might include Palestine, and therefore if Zionism were to attach itself to the Allied cause, the way to a Jewish Palestine might lie open at last.

The Zionist leaders lost no time in making their attempt, and they chose England as the country in which to make it. "Hopes from the outset," says Mr. Stein, "were centred mainly on Britain. ...Great Britain's genius for colonial administration, her reputation as a liberal power, the generous instincts with which the Jews in particular had every reason to credit her," her successive offers of land for Jewish settlement in East Africa and in the Sinai Peninsula—all these had marked her out as the Power first to approach.

Mr. Stein says nothing of the influence which could be exerted in Britain by the Jewish body, and some might think this an omission on his part. But it is not so. What is generally meant by "Jewish influence" had little to do with the launching of the political Zionist campaign in this country. For some reason "Jewish influence" is always taken to mean financial influence behind the scenes. I shall not delay to speak of this particular form of influence except to say that as a rule it is not very reasonably treated, Jewish writers denying its existence and anti-Jewish writers declaring that it is omnipotent.

In 1914, at any rate, political Zionism had made no headway in the Jewish circles which are called influential. Such personalities in Anglo Jewry as were enshrined in the *Directory of Directors* were altogether uninterested in it and generally ignorant of its very existence. But there is another kind of Jewish influence at work in England, and it was to this that political Zionism now trusted itself.

The men who were to spread its doctrines were not far to seek. Two of the chiefs of Zionism in the Russian dominions, M. Tschlenow of Moscow and M. Nahum Sokolov of Warsaw, journeyed to London. They were joined in their work by a man whose name was to become best known among the names of all political Zionists, Dr. Chaim Weizmann.

Dr. Weizmann had been born in Grodno in Poland just about forty years before. He had emigrated to England, after some time passed in Switzerland, (where he had known Trotsky and had often publicly combated his opinions), and had become a lecturer in Chemistry at Manchester University. He had been naturalized as a British subject. As a chemist he was extremely able, and to his professional parts he added eloquence and marked individuality. Mr. Horace Samuel speaks of Dr. Weizmann's "Mephistophelian face and subtle, sinister charm." He gives a picture of him addressing a Jewish battalion of the Royal Fusiliers in Cairo during the War. "I well remember how he addressed them. Lolling at a table with his hands deep in his trouser-pockets, he just spoke to them easily and racily and familiarly, in their own and his own native Yiddish, getting his points well away with that idiomatic shrug and gesture which constitute one of the most intimate parts of the language.

"The audience responded to a man. They were all his, body and soul, ready to leap into his pocket at the first word of command. As he walked across the camp the men just followed him like rats after the Pied Piper." But Dr. Weizmann has always been able to pipe his Pan-like summons to the intellectual as to the private soldier, and men have fallen in behind him in drawing-rooms as they have in camps. One who was present has told me of the irresistible potency with which he saw him once draw Lord Balfour aside after a dinner in Lady Astor's house, as he remembers, and how the two sat together on a sofa for an hour or more, oblivious of all present. It was in the course of hours like this that the foundations of political Zionism in England were laid.

The foundation-stone itself may be said to have been laid ten or eleven years before the date of the conversation just mentioned. Appropriately enough this event was enshrouded by the mists of Manchester. Balfour was electioneering (he was still AJ Balfour then) in that city, which has always been an important focus of Jewry. His chairman was a Jew, a Mr. Dreyfus, and he took occasion of this to inquire through him why the Zionist Organization had rejected the offer of territory in East Africa which had been made to that body in 1903 under his own Premiership.

The rejection of this offer had roused in Balfour, says his niece and biographer Mrs. Dugdale, "a curiosity which he found no means to satisfy." He told Mr. Dreyfus that he wanted to "fathom the reasons for it." It was a matter which had lain in his mind, for he was interested in the Jews. The future of Jewry as a subject was one of his favourite distractions. Of

Zionism he had been aware for a considerable while in that sidelong way of his, when his mind seemed to enter and to retreat from a subject at once.

That he needed really to "fathom" the reasons of Zionist refusal of the East African offer is unlikely. The reasons, if only out of common politeness, must have been given to him as Prime Minister, when the offer was not accepted. They also had been fully discussed at the sittings of the Sixth Zionist Congress. But Balfour characteristically had recoiled from overt knowledge of a matter in which he had played a prime part, and his artificial ignorance now had to be enlightened.

For this purpose Mr. Dreyfus sent Dr. Weizmann, whom he knew as an ardent Zionist, to Balfour's hotel, and the young lecturer in chemistry and the statesman met thus for the first time. Mrs. Dugdale recounts the interview which followed. Sympathy was engendered immediately between the two men so differently circumstanced. Dr. Weizmann, however, was not quite fluent in the English tongue then, and found some difficulty in making his points. Finally, though, he found a way:

> I began to sweat blood to make my meaning clear through my English. At the end I made an effort: I had an idea. I said, "Mr. Balfour, if you were offered Paris instead of London, would you take it? Would you take Paris instead of London?" He looked surprised and said, "But London is our own." I said, "Jerusalem was our own when London was a marsh." "That's true," was his reply.

Balfour seems to have been dumbfounded by Dr. Weizmann's remark. The interview ended under the impact of it. "It was from this talk with Weizmann," he said in later years to Mrs. Dugdale, "that I saw that the Jewish form of patriotism was unique." Balfour, she continues, "pursued the train of reflection then started for the next few years, intermittently no doubt, but with the ardour reserved for his speculative moments."

One accepts, of course, the accuracy of the biographer's record of this interview, which was to have such important bearings. But there is no obligation to accept Mr. Balfour's attitude as real. Was this very erudite person to be struck all-of-a-heap, like a charwoman told a commonplace, when he was informed that Jerusalem had been Jewish long ago? Was this ardent student of the Jewish situation to be amazed at claims which had been current for a decade? It is not to be credited.

This rhetorical ingenuousness gave a clue to the manner in which Mr. Balfour might lead himself or be led to envisage the future of Palestine. When he and Weizmann next met, eight years had passed and the War had been in progress for four months. In the interval Dr. Weizmann's status had altered no little. His professional attainments soon brought him to notice in Manchester. He made the acquaintance of a number of its prominent citizens, and amongst these was Mr. C. P. Scott, the widely known editor of the *Manchester Guardian*. Scott, under his influence, became an adherent of Zionism, which cause thereby gained an invaluable entry to the columns of a great English newspaper. But that the *Guardian* should espouse Zionism was indeed almost a natural event. It was the protagonist of a school of thought which always found many of the Jewish intelligentsia in its ranks, and the newspaper itself had several of them amongst its staff abroad. So when Weizmann indoctrinated Scott and the *Guardian*, it was like the sowing of grass-seed upon a lawn.

Dr. Weizmann's reunion with Lord Balfour took place in mid-December. He "found the conversation of eight years back fresh in Balfour's mind." They continued this conversation "on abstract lines." But before they parted Lord Balfour asked if he could help Dr. Weizmann in any way. "Not while the guns are roaring," said Weizmann; "when the military situation becomes clearer I shall come again." "Mind you come again," said Balfour; "it is a great cause you are working for. I should like you to come again and again." (Dugdale.)

As soon as Turkey entered the War, Weizmann started to elaborate his political ideas and produced "definite proposals for the establishment in Palestine of a national home for the Jews under a British Protectorate." (Stein.) The next step was to bring these to the notice of men in power in London. The centre seems to have shifted away for a little while from Balfour: he was not a Cabinet Minister at the time, though on the War Council. Scott gave Weizmann and his two Russian colleagues letters of introduction to a pair of Cabinet Ministers, Mr. Lloyd George and Sir Herbert Samuel.

What happened thereon Sir Herbert Samuel himself has explained, with characteristic carefulness and conscientiousness, in the course of a lecture he delivered to a private auditory in 1935. Speaking before the Jewish Historical Society, he explained that he was much impressed by Dr. Weizmann. Furthermore, as the first member of the Jewish community ever to sit in a British Cabinet—Disraeli having left that community—he felt it was incumbent upon him to examine into the Zionist movement. Up till then he had had no connection with it. Now, besides conferring with Dr. Weizmann, he held conversations with M. Sokolov and with other exponents of the Zionist gospel.

"I soon arrived," says he, "at the definite conclusion that if, as we all anticipated, the War ended in the victory of the Allies, Palestine ought undoubtedly to be separated from the Turkish Empire; that the opportunity should be taken to facilitate the establishment of a great autonomous Jewish community there; and that this ought to be done under some form of British [note: original text mistakenly reads 'Jewish'] protectorate." He spoke in November of 1914 (which shows that Dr. Weizmann had approached him even before the former took up his post at the Admiralty) to Sir Edward Grey. To Grey he said, "Perhaps there might be an opportunity for the fulfilment of the ancient aspiration of the Jewish people and the restoration there [in Palestine] of a Jewish State." "That was at the time," adds Sir Herbert Samuel, "the Zionist proposal."

It is well to have this fact, clear though it has been from the outset, thus categorically and authoritatively stated. Sir Herbert went on to speak to the Foreign Secretary upon how a Jewish State in Palestine might become the centre of a new culture, how the sight of men of their own blood achieving great things in Palestine would raise the character and influence the outlook of the millions of Jews scattered in other parts of the world, how the proximity to Egypt of his Jewish State *"would render its goodwill to England a matter of importance to the British Empire."* The final words merit italicizing.

The next sentence—the speaker had transcribed from his original notes of his interview with Sir Edward Grey—is very interesting. It shows that Sir Herbert Samuel at least was aware of the existence of the Arabs. "The building-up of the new State from the foundations," he acknowledged, "was, of course, an undertaking of the most formidable character, especially in view of the elements which were to be found in the present population of Palestine." A remarkable twisting of realities, which treated the Arabs, 91 percent of the population, as an "element" in it, but it was an advance upon contemporary Zionist thought and long to remain an advance upon all Zionist thought.

Sir Herbert Samuel went on to suggest that the economic resources of Palestine could be developed if the right population were admitted and a "community of petty traders" avoided. As things have turned out, a community of petty traders is exactly what has been established since then in the town of Tel Aviv, with its 150,000 population out of 400,000 Jews in Palestine, but let that pass now. Sir Herbert Samuel ended by suggesting that the Russian Government might be sounded before long about the project, if military conditions seemed favourable. This, no doubt, was because of the concentration of potential Jewish immigrants in Russia.

Sir Edward Grey said in reply that "the idea had always had a strong sentimental attraction for him. The historical appeal was very strong. He was quite favourable to the proposal and would be ready to work for it if the opportunity arose. If any proposals were put forward by France or any other Power with regard to Syria, it would be important not to acquiesce in any plan which would be inconsistent with the creation of a Jewish State in Palestine. He asked whether I thought that Syria must necessarily go with

Palestine." ("Syria" here is being used in the false restricted sense.) "I said, 'No, but on the contrary it would be inadvisable to include such places as Beyrout and Damascus, since they contained a large non-Jewish population which could not be assimilated.'"

Here is a lesson upon the deficiencies of statesmen. Lord Grey, reckoned as one of the most altruistic, listened to Sir Herbert Samuel yet never observed to him that what was true of the north of Syria was true of the south also. The population of Palestine was not merely non-Jewish in the main: it was and had been for centuries overwhelmingly non-Jewish. As it was before the War, the Jews, half of them foreign subjects, were but 83,000 out of a total population of some 757,000. But Sir Herbert Samuel, while shrinking from the assimilation of a "large population" in the north, proposed by inference the "assimilation" of 91 percent of the population in the south. The Foreign Secretary, whose particular business it was to have at least a general knowledge of the Turkish Empire's constituent factors, let this proposal pass.

Worse than that, he himself ushered in the said proposal by asking Sir Herbert Samuel whether he thought that "Syria must necessarily go with Palestine." That is to say the Foreign Secretary did not for one moment remember that Syria was a country inhabited by the Arab people, or by any sort of people at all. He spoke as though it were inhabited by draughtsmen or halma-pieces, a land which could be cut in half or in quarters or could have the pieces upon it shifted about to suit his designs. But it was never his business to ask Sir Herbert Samuel whether Syria must necessarily go with Palestine, a matter with which Sir Herbert had no concern whatsoever. Grey's real duty was to ask himself what justified his cutting the land in half in order that he might work out some scheme of his and his friends in the lower half.

Sir Herbert Samuel went on to tell the Foreign Secretary that it was essential that the Jewish Palestine State should be neutralized, since it would not be large enough to defend itself. Christian pilgrims to the Holy Land should be guaranteed free access. If the remainder of Syria could be annexed by France it would be a great advantage, as it would be far better for the Jewish State to have European neighbours than Turkish. Sir Herbert Samuel, in after years more mindful, in this early recommendation took no more account of the Arabs than if they were the furniture of Palestine.

That closed his interview with Sir Edward Grey, but he added that he saw Mr. Lloyd George the same day. His record of this visit ran: "I had an opportunity today of a brief talk with Lloyd George on the subject. He had referred in the Cabinet to the ultimate destiny of Palestine, and said to me that he was very keen to see a Jewish State established there."

To be keen on anything was a cant phrase of the date, and its employment was more a daily exercise of vocabulary than a guarantee of feelings. A couple of months later, on the 17th of January, 1915, which was Mr. Lloyd George's birthday, Lord Riddell dined with him. He wrote in his diary afterwards, "Ll. G. says there is a movement on foot to take the Jews back to Palestine—some new scheme—and that much to his surprise Herbert Samuel is very keen on it."

I think that this extract gives the measure of the respective keennesses then of the two Cabinet Ministers. Mr. Lloyd George so far had but played transiently with some halcyon Cambro-Hebraical vision of Judah re-enthroned in Palestine. Sir Herbert Samuel was considering the matter seriously. He was considering it so seriously that, even if a little late in reaching it, he did come to the conclusion presently that "an autonomous Jewish State was impracticable. In the conditions that prevailed, five sixths of the population of Palestine being Arabs" (nine-tenths would have been nearer their proportion), "such a solution could not be adopted."

Note that Sir Herbert Samuel, though, did not find a Jewish State illegitimate: he only found it impracticable. The solution to which now he turned was "the establishment of British control, together with the fostering of Jewish immigration, and the conferment upon the new Jewish community in Palestine of the broadest autonomy that the practical conditions would allow." This amounted to establishing a state of things in Palestine out of which the Jewish State gradually would come to life. The conferring of autonomy, also, would take the Jewish immigrants out of control of the people of the country. So while Sir Herbert Samuel did not propose a Jewish State immediately, what he proposed made an Arab State not possible at any time.

He prepared a memorandum on these lines which was circulated in the Cabinet. He says that he prepared the memorandum in January but did not circulate it till March. It would seem, however, that he must have sent a draft of it at least to some of his colleagues, for on the 28th of that month of January, 1915, Mr. Asquith wrote in his diary:

> I have just received from Herbert Samuel a memorandum headed "The Future of Palestine." He goes on to argue at considerable length and with some vehemence, in favour of the British annexation of Palestine, a country the size of Wales, much of it barren mountains and part of it waterless. He thinks we might plant in this not very promising territory about three or four million European Jews, and that this would have a good effect upon those who are left behind. It reads almost like a new edition of Tancred brought up to date. I confess I am not attracted by this proposed addition to our responsibilities. But it is a curious illustration of Dizzy's favourite maxim that "race is everything" to find this almost

> lyrical outburst proceeding from the well-ordered and methodical brain of H.S.

Mr. Asquith judged the memorandum in his characteristic level-headed way, and his remark "he thinks this would have a good effect upon those who are left behind" shows that he did not believe much in the regenerative effect upon an individual of a tonic administered to his cousin. The most important thing in his comment, though, is the evidence that the Samuel project aimed at settling (no doubt eventually) three or four million Jews in Palestine. Such numbers, of course, would make a Jewish State practicable.

There is no evidence that any of the Zionist leaders proper dropped the idea of an immediate Jewish State at the time for Sir Herbert Samuel's deferred Jewish State. Indeed there is evidence to the contrary. Dr. Weizmann had gone to Paris in January, to sound opinion in French Governmental circles. Lord Bertie, the British Ambassador, recorded his visit on the 25th. In his diary he wrote:

> Edmond de Rothschild came this morning, and afterwards sent a Russian co-religionist established in Manchester to "talk" about what I think is an absurd scheme, though they say that it has the approval of Grey, Lloyd George, Samuel and Crewe. They did not mention Lord Reading.
>
> It contemplates the formation of Palestine into an Israelite State under the protectorate of England, France, or Russia, preferably of England. They did not think that Russia or France would raise objections...The scheme-maker would be ready to leave the custody of the Holy Places and even of old Jerusalem to an international body. They would build a new one nearby.... My Russian visitor says that such a solution must come within the next hundred years, perhaps in forty years. He hopes that I don't think him a dreamer! The Jews are the only people capable of reclaiming Palestine by intensive culture!

Lord Bertie, an ambassador, whose whole business in life had been to speak of political affairs in accurate terms, would not have written that an Israelite State was in contemplation unless his "Russian visitor" had spoken unambiguously of such a State. The succeeding phrases confirm this too. A new Jerusalem is to be built as the Jewish capital. The ancient Holy City is to be "left," conceded that is, by the Zionists out of their territory, for international administration.

There is a curious sequel to this intention of building a new Jerusalem as the Jewish capital which is worth interpolating here. In later years, when the Zionists were active in building their "garden-suburb," as it was rather insufficiently termed, on the Bethlehem side of Jerusalem, round a prominent hill or swell of the ground, the general plans had to be sent in to the Palestine Government.

Mr. C. R. Ashbee, the distinguished architect and man-of-letters, was in charge of the town-planning scheme. When he examined these plans he found a disproportionately large building prospected for the crowning site on the summit of the hill. He asked the designer, Mr. Richard Kauffmann, for what purpose this was intended. Mr. Kauffmann was the architect of the Zionist Organization, and his plans were drawn up to its requirements, of course. His answer to Mr. Ashbee, very seriously given, was, "Das ist unser Parliamentsgebaude" ("That's our House of Parliament"). The High Commissioner, to whom this was reported, found the attribution provocative, or possibly found it premature. He gave orders in consequence and the "House of Parliament" became the "Gallery of Fine Arts." There was a certain subtlety about the new title.

I return to the memorandums and projects of early 1915. Sir Herbert Samuel, having distributed his memorandum, left it to take effect in the minds of its recipients. "It attracted," he says, "a considerable body of support among Ministers." The campaign was now so well launched in England that the Zionist leaders could give more attention to other countries for a while. Undeterred by the frigidity of Lord Bertie, Dr. Weizmann with his colleagues MM. Sokolov and Tschlenow went back to Paris. Presently, "full of great hopes," M. Tschlenow returned to Russia to act as liaison-agent there.

Back in England, Weizmann and Sokolov spent most of 1915 in quiet but effective spade-work. With charming naiveté Mrs. Dugdale records that "the Zionists had not as yet access even to the corridors of the Government Offices." But in compensation "occasionally they met various Ministers in their homes."

Mrs. Dugdale adds something to our knowledge of Sir Edward Grey's mind at the time. "He was in full sympathy with the Zionist ideal, but was afraid lest mention of a British Protectorate over Palestine might offend the French, and offend also some English Liberal opinion. The Liberal Cabinet would not be likely to commit themselves to any responsibility for Palestine. At the same time they did not want to see it in the hands of any other Great Power. They might favour the organization of a Jewish Commonwealth there as an independent political unit. These views were not officially expressed, but the Zionists sensed them." The Zionists were not without means of "sensing," during home-chat with Ministers around their hearths.

Mrs. Dugdale goes on to say that whenever a chance occurred the Zionists pressed the arguments for a British Protectorate. It must have been when one of these chances did occur, though she does not specify when or how it came about, that Dr. Weizmann put his argument upon paper:

> "If Great Britain [he wrote] does not wish anybody else to have Palestine, this means that she will have to watch it and stop any penetration of another Power. Such a course involved as much responsibility as would be involved by a British Protectorate over Palestine, with the sole difference that watching is a much less efficient preventative than an actual Protectorate. I therefore thought that the middle course could be adopted: viz., the Jews take over the country. The whole burden of organization falls on them, but for the next ten or fifteen years they work under a temporary British Protectorate."

This was a pretty accurate forecast for 1915 of what has happened since in Palestine. But of course Dr. Weizmann has always been in the position of a Jupiter forecasting the weather that he was about to manufacture himself.

His excursions abroad or to London could not be many, however, because of his work in Manchester. So most of the chances of which Mrs. Dugdale speaks must have occurred in that city. Indeed, between Weizmann and Scott, and the recruits who soon joined them, Manchester now was turned into a regular Zionist base. "A large group of Zionist writers joined the leaders, conspicuous among whom was Major Norman Bentwich," later to be Attorney-General for Palestine. Not all these recruits worked in Manchester but they were mentally provisioned from there. As for the *Manchester Guardian* itself, several members of its staff became active propagandists of the cause. Notable amongst them were Mr. Harry Sacher and Mr. Herbert Sidebotham. Mr. Sacher, a barrister, was to be notary for the Rutenberg contracts in Palestine and also became known, at least to a certain circle, as "For-Ever Sacher." Giving evidence before one of the Commissions which have so often visited Palestine, and being asked how long he thought the British Mandate should last, his answer was, "For ever."

Mr. Sidebotham organized the establishment of a "British Palestine Committee" to spread the Zionist theories in the United Kingdom, and founded a publication ad hoc (already mentioned) entitled Palestine, which still exists, though I fancy that for a year or two there was a break in its continuity. He has proved the most prolific defender of political Zionism, and in many pamphlets has shown himself the leader of the idealist-realist school. This professes the idealism of the return to Zion and of the Mandate side by side with the realism of the possession of the approaches to the Suez Canal.While Zionism was thus consolidating itself in Manchester, major political events took place which were to affect its future considerably. Mr. Asquith formed a Coalition Cabinet and in May Lord Balfour, who though attending the War Council had been in Opposition, became First Civil Lord of the Admiralty. Dr. Weizmann had been experimenting very successfully meanwhile in the manufacture of explosives. "He brought before

Scott," says Mr. JL Hammond in his biography of the great editor, "his plan for manufacturing chemicals needed for munitions. Scott paid several visits to London to urge on Mr. Lloyd George, Mr. McKenna, Lord Balfour and others, the importance of Weizmann's experiments. Mr. Lloyd George promised in the summer to consider the question as soon as the issue of conscription had been settled."The probability of Dr. Weizmann (the Dr. is Doctor of Science) being called to London, where he would have more regular opportunities of contact with members of the Government, was thus postponed a while. But M. Sokolov and others were busy in the fostering ante-chambers of the English political world. They made converts, and the converts made their converts, and Zionism by degrees became a topic amidst the persons and the groups that count in that world, and in its social centre. The thesis which Asquith had found extravagant as a novel of Disraeli's became through repetition not so extravagant to other statesmen, and then became an idea present in the air, and soon was a possible line of conduct. In December Scott took Weizmann to breakfast with Lloyd George to discuss the former's experiments, which dealt with the provision of acetone for cordite. Subject to the success of some final trials, Dr. Weizmann's transfer to London to work in a Government munitions laboratory was decided. He went back awhile to Manchester, just about when McMahon in Egypt was inditing the conclusion of the compact of Arab independence for which Kitchener had led the way.

Dr. Weizmann's trials were altogether successful. In February 1916 he was appointed to the Admiralty. Lord Balfour became his chief. To do Dr. Weizmann justice he does not seem to have intruded the Zionist side of his life into his office. But Lord Balfour took the initiative. One day Weizmann "came to his room on official business. As the interview ended Balfour introduced the other subject. 'You know, Dr. Weizmann, if the Allies win the war you may get your Jerusalem.' He bade him call again, he wanted to discuss the Russian and the English Jews." (Dugdale.)

Mrs. Dugdale says that in the course of 1916 Balfour and Weizmann only met "once or twice." Whether with him or with others, though, the spade-work of the Zionist leaders continued unabated through the first half of the year. M. Sokolov and Dr. Weizmann turned their attention a good deal to spreading the doctrine amidst English Jews. The two knew nothing about the Arab alliance which had ushered in the year. Besides, what were Arabs in their schemes at any time?

However, for the statesmen who had dealings with the Zionist pleaders the new-made alliance should have marked a great difference. To date they had been able to toy with the Zionist project with some show of legitimacy, but now to consider a Zionist State, which was what they were asked to consider, whether it were created immediately or by degrees, upon territory where we were engaged to support Arab independence, ceased to be legitimate. In diplomatic language what they began to do was undesirable; in plain language it was dishonest.

But a subterfuge can generally be found by those who wish to find one, and the method now adopted to evade our obligations was this. The actual character of Zionist aspirations was left in a haze, and the Government—for by February some portions or persons of the Governmental body were engaged in the business—could therefore begin to patronize the movement on the plea that a resettlement of Jews in Palestine was a worthy object in itself, and need not be envisaged as leading to this or to that particular conclusion.

They were rather helped in this evasion by the existence of a group of British Jews who were interesting themselves by then in the opening opportunities for Zionism. Their plans, as far as they were formulated, did not bespeak a Jewish State at any time, and were wholly free of political taint. These moderate men were consulted and canvassed alongside with Messrs. Weizmann and Sokolov. Though their propositions were only read to be dropped, the mere fact that parallel communications were made with them gave the requisite air of open-mindedness to the tentative negotiations, or whatever they were to be called, in which the section of the Government responsible for them was engaged.

Obviously the straightforward action would have been to inform the political Zionist leaders of our engagements to the Arabs, bidding them curb their plans in accordance with these engagements. Or if it were impossible to acquaint them of the engagements, as most likely in fact it was till the Arab revolt should have started, then no steps at all should have been taken to encourage the Zionists.

No one however seems to have been stopped by any such considerations in Whitehall. The real question is how far anybody in Whitehall knew what everybody else was doing. At that period of the War, Ministries, and even individuals in Ministries, seem to have conducted policies without communicating them to each other, or without communicating them in any adequate degree. The argument used for justifying this seems to have been that while negotiations were only feelers they were a departmental business. Time enough to tell ministers all about them, and time enough for ministers to tell the Cabinet all about them, when the moment arrived for turning them into national policy itself.

No other explanation for what occurred is possible. That all the members of the Cabinet, including the Prime Minister, were aware fully how far we were engaged to the Arabs is highly improbable. There were plenty of indications in the dispatches which had reached Egypt before the conclusion of the Alliance that the matter was being treated confusedly and being studied insufficiently at home. Captain Liddell Hart, drawing his information from Lawrence, who was in the thick of things, says that the High Commissioner himself cabled from Cairo to warn the Foreign Office upon "the danger of underrating the possible development of the Arab movement." He urged (how significant, this) "the need for unity of control over all negotiations."

It made no difference, in any case. The various policies were continued recklessly by their authors. The situation in February, so far as it can be disentangled, was that we had a genuine treaty with the Arabs, an "arrangement" pending with the French, and an "affair" developing with the Zionists. Some people knew of some of these and a few may have known of all of them, though nobody with much clarity. The French "arrangement" was being kept secret from the Arabs and the Zionists, the Arab treaty was being kept secret from the Zionists, and the French only had general notions of it, which into the bargain a few officials of the Quai d'Orsay seem to have kept to themselves. There was no reason of course why a line of anything confidential should have been communicated to the Zionists, as they had no standing, but since they are involved in the business it is worth noting that the secrecy extended to them.

Needless to say, there must be secrecy in war-time: no one is going to be so foolish as to question that. But there is all the difference in the world between keeping engagements secret from the enemy and from neutrals, and keeping engagements secret from those whose intimate affairs are covered by these very engagements.

In due secrecy Sir Mark Sykes and M. Picot now completed their "Arrangement" on behalf of their respective countries. Sykes left for Russia before the end of the month, to submit it to the Russian Government, which was to be associated as third party to the pact.

In March, the memorandums and conversations of Sir Herbert Samuel, of Messrs. Weizmann and Sokolov and of the other friends of the Zionist cause, bore their first fruit. This was a document owing its origin supposedly to Sir Edward Grey. For a piece of evidence of its importance it is still not very well known. As far as I am aware it has only been quoted in this country by Mr. Leonard Stein in his Zionism. In the United States Mrs. Andrews, the author of a very considerable, much documented, standard work, *Palestine under the Mandate* [Author's note: Produced later in Great Britain by Messrs. George Allen and Unwin], has published a version which differs somewhat from Mr. Stein's.

The document is one sent to our Ambassador in Petrograd, bidding him sound the Russian Government upon its attitude towards "Jewish Colonization in Palestine." It would never have seen the light but for the Russian revolution. After this had taken place, the new Soviet Government published a number of secret dispatches from the files of the Imperial Ministry of Foreign Affairs, and the dispatch in question was included in a volume entitled (in Russian) *The Partition of Asiatic Turkey,* which appeared in 1924.

It is dated the 13th of that month of March, and was presented apparently in English to M. Sazonoff, then Russian Foreign Minister. The dispatch in the Petrograd archives at least is in the English tongue, though it was translated into Russian for the work which the Soviet authorities edited.

For convenience I give Mr. Stein's version of the text, his convenient book in which it is reproduced being more accessible to average readers than Mrs. Andrews's pair of tomes. It runs as follows:

> "Aide-Memoire presented by the British Embassy in Petrograd to the Foreign Minister, M. Sazonoff.
>
> A telegram has been received from Sir Edward Grey stating that the attention of His Majesty's Government had recently been drawn to the question of Jewish colonization in Palestine.
>
> Although, as is known, many Jews are indifferent to the idea of Zionism, a numerous and most influential section of them in all countries would highly appreciate the proposal of an agreement concerning Palestine, which would fully satisfy Jewish aspirations.
>
> If the point of view set forth above is correct, it will be clear that by means of utilizing the Zionist idea, important political results might be achieved. One of these would be the conversion to the side of the Allies of Jewish elements in the East, in the U.S.A., and other places, whose present attitude towards the cause of the Allies is, to a considerable extent, hostile.
>
> Mr. Lucien Wolf has defined Jewish aspirations in Palestine in the following manner: 'If as a result of the war, Palestine should fall within the sphere of French and British interests, the French and British Governments will not fail to take into consideration the historic interests of Jewry in this country. Both Governments would assure to the Jewish population equal political rights with other inhabitants, religious and civil freedom, such municipal privileges in colonies and towns as would appear necessary, as well as reasonable facilities for colonization and immigration.'
>
> Sir Edward Grey has no objection to the formula quoted above, but in reply he simply informed Mr. Wolf that he must discuss this question with the Allied Governments, and that this matter will be sympathetically considered by His Majesty's Government.
>
> The only object of His Majesty's Government is to devise some agreement which will be sufficiently attractive to the majority of Jews to

> facilitate the conclusion of a transaction securing Jewish support. Having this consideration in view, it appears to His Majesty's Government that if the scheme provided for enabling the Jews, when their colonies in Palestine are sufficiently strong to be able to compete with the Arab population, to take in hand the administration of the internal affairs of this region (excluding Jerusalem and the Holy Places), then the agreement would be much more attractive for the majority of Jews. His Majesty's Government would not wish to express a preference for this or another solution of the question. However, it is informed that an international protectorate would meet with opposition on behalf of influential Jewish circles.
>
> Communicating all this telegraphically, Sir Edward Grey instructs Sir George Buchanan to solicit from the Russian Government a serious consideration of this question and to favour him at the earliest possible date with the communication of the Russian point of view."

What a document! It is scarcely credible that within ten weeks of pledging Arab independence "in every sense of the word independence" to the Shereef of Mecca, the Foreign Minister was thus preparing coldly to hand over the administration of Palestine to the Zionists. The only sort of palliative for it, and practically the only explanation of it is to be found in the perilous situation of the country then and in the consequent disorder of the Cabinet. One hundred and fifty thousand tons of merchant shipping were being sunk every month by enemy submarines; the Turks were triumphant at Gallipoli; the War was costing a sum which now approached six million pounds a day, and there seemed no issue from it, let alone any sign of a victorious exit. The Cabinet itself was distracted, discredited and moribund: the disunion of the whole Governmental machine began within the body of men who should have held it together.

Lord Curzon, referring a couple of years later to the conduct of the country's business at the period under discussion testified that the old Cabinet system was "quite impossible in times of war." "The meetings of the Cabinet were most irregular. There were no agenda, there was no order of business. No record whatever was kept of the proceedings, except the private letter written to the King by the Prime Minister, the contents of which were never seen by anybody else. The Cabinet often had the very haziest notion as to what its decisions were.... It was always congested with business." There were two dozen Cabinet Ministers, a situation which led Mr. Lloyd George to declare, "You cannot run a war with a Sanhedrim."

No doubt it was out of such peril, such disorder and such absence of supervision that the memorandum sent to Petrograd sprang. It slipped through in the confusion. Even so, with every allowance for the circumstances which attended its appearance, it is inexcusable. The question at once rises to the mind; who wrote it; who was responsible for it? Who were aware of its contents before it was dispatched to Russia? Was Lord Kitchener, who had been the prime mover in approaching the Arabs? On that presumption alone, it is hardly likely. Apart from this his relations at the time were growing steadily more and more restricted with the other members of the Cabinet. He did not give them much of his confidence. That close-placed observer, F. S. Oliver, wrote of the Government that it was in a kind of dusk with regard to military operations. If it was in a dusk about Flanders, in what sort of night will it not have been about operations and commitments to the Hedjaz? While, on the other hand, by a natural reaction the members of the Cabinet who suffered from Kitchener's taciturnity did not treat him to their own plans. Was the Petrograd memorandum ever communicated to him? Was it ever even treated *in extenso* at any Cabinet meeting or any governmental gathering at which he was present? Every presumption is that it was not, nor ever treated *in extenso* at any such meeting at all.

Had the very Prime Minister seen it? When the Zionist proposals in Sir Herbert Samuel's memorandum were first sent to Mr. Asquith he had spoken of them pretty contemptuously, and he never changed his mind about them. In the House of Commons, six years after, he was calling them still "a staircase of fragile, precarious, stumbling hypotheses," adding that it was a very large hypothesis to assume that "by judicious administration and by pacific penetration and in other ways the Jews and the Arabs were going to live side by side."

In 1924, on the soil of Palestine itself, as the guest of Sir Herbert Samuel, now High Commissioner, when, if ever, he was going to be converted, he wrote instead "the talk of making Palestine into a Jewish National Home seems to me as fantastic as it always has done." Was a man of his temper one to induce the Russians to take any share in what he found fantastic? Was Asquith the man to propose to anybody a policy in which he himself altogether disbelieved?

No, the only conclusion is that the memorandum had not been submitted to him, or that no sufficient version of it had been submitted to him, before it was dispatched, and he was not cognizant of what was going on.

As for our engagements to the Arabs, I do not believe that these had been communicated to the Prime Minister sufficiently, if at all. In 1923, on returning from Palestine, I went myself to see him, in the House of Commons, upon this subject. Carmelite House had just brought out in pamphlet form my *Daily Mail* articles, wherein I had given the crucial portions of the Hussein-McMahon treaty. It was the first time they had been disclosed to the public. I visited Mr. Asquith, now out of office, specially to beg him to examine them, so that he might judge of the strength of the pledges which bound us to support Arab independence in Palestine.

His whole attitude was of one being informed. Indeed the interview between us had been mooted by a common friend and accepted by Mr. Asquith on the principle of engaging his interest in these newly produced documents. If Asquith had known of them, there would have been no meaning in our interview. When I said to him, "I want particularly to show you the extracts from these papers, sir, I am convinced that they will impress you," he did not say to me that he knew them. He did not say that he had examined them when he was in power but had forgotten them, or that he had only seen them cursorily.

He acted absolutely as though he had had no kind of acquaintance with them before. What he said was, "Certainly. Let me see them." Afterwards he said, "Leave this with me. I'll go through it. I'll look into it all." I was not "interviewing" him in the technical sense. During such interviews statesmen are often on the defensive and make show at times of false ignorance. This was a personal meeting, of which none but the three people involved ever knew till today, and in the course of it he was perfectly blunt and unambiguous, though he said little, the whole thing having been arranged so that I might appeal to him rather than he say anything to me.

The mystery does not stop with him, however, nor with Lord Kitchener. This Petrograd memorandum, violating our engagements to the Arabs, does not fit in with the character even of the man in whose name it was dispatched. Was Lord Grey another victim of departmental secrecy? Before he set his hand to the Petrograd memorandum, had he ever studied thoroughly the text of the Anglo-Arab pact? He was under a crushing burden of work at the time, when the tendency would have been for him to demand only outlines of all but major documents. The decision upon what were major documents would rest with permanent officials, especially as regards documents dealing with outlying sections of the vast field of foreign affairs in war-time. In the din of the conflict on the Western Front the Foreign Secretary perhaps heard only abstractedly some general account of an understanding with the Hedjaz.

It may seem at first sight extravagant to suggest indeed that a Foreign Secretary remained unacquainted or was insufficiently acquainted with a matter which engaged the full responsibility of the Government. Yet his own words, when this question first came up for discussion in the House of Lords towards the end of the succeeding month of March, confirm such a suggestion. This 1923 debate was initiated and led by Lord Islington, the most gallant, unceasing, and intelligent fighter for justice to the Arabs since the question first arose. He quoted my extracts from the McMahon-Hussein documents and made evident how we were committed by them. Lord Grey's speech was awaited with the interest that may be imagined. He had been the responsible Minister at the time the commitments were made. Whatever he had to say, the House expected that his contribution to the debate would be authoritative.

Yet that was the one quality it lacked. He said that he did not propose to go into any detail over the points which had been traversed by Lord Islington and by Lord Sydenham (who had spoken on kindred lines to Lord Islington's). Detail was the very point the House expected from him of course, but it was soon clear that he could not give it. He spoke in his characteristic, sincere, gentlemanly way, but he seemed to have no knowledge. He was roundabout and vague about facts. He said that secret engagements were inevitable during a war. If all our war-time engagements were considered as a whole there might well be what he called "inconsistencies" between them. "I think it exceedingly probable that there are inconsistencies," he said. He did not think that there were any referable to his period of office. But he did not know. He confessed he had not "refreshed his memory" upon what secret engagements had been made during that period. (It is a very noteworthy fact that having refreshed his memory later, he never afterwards sought an occasion to deny our obligations in Palestine to the Arabs.)

He actually, in this Lords speech, asked for information, asked that the Government should publish all papers, so that our honour might be cleared. Texts were becoming public "through other sources," he said. He agreed that the situation was, as he put it, a difficult one. "An exceedingly difficult one," he said, "when it (the Balfour Declaration) is compared with the pledges which undoubtedly were given to the Arabs."

In making this admission, Lord Grey spoke as though he were a high-minded stranger to whom the pledges were a revelation. Under these circumstances how is it possible to assume that he compiled the Petrograd memorandum in full knowledge of the Anglo-Arab treaty? Did he compile it himself, indeed?

This lends a greater interest and a greater importance to the analysis of this memorandum, the first official step along the path which led to the dishonouring of Great Britain's obligations. I ask the reader to reconsider its text therefore.

There is one paragraph in it to which no exception can be taken, Mr. Lucien Wolf's excellent formula. There is nothing else in the memorandum which is recommendable. Two phrases call for attention particularly. The first is "an agreement concerning Palestine which would fully satisfy Jewish aspirations." The second is the awkwardly phrased statement that "if the scheme provided for enabling the Jews, when their colonies in Palestine are sufficiently strong to be able to compete with the Arab population, to take in hand the administration of the internal affairs of this region, then the agreement would be much more attractive for the majority of Jews." The English of this is very cumbersome and unreal. The word "for" should be read with "enabling" and "provided" is not a past participle but the past tense. It means "If the scheme made it possible for the Jews, when their colonies, etc."

I do not believe that this formula, ostensibly phrased by the Foreign Secretary, was his work at all. To every appearance it was taken, and inserted as it stood, from some unacknowledged text of the political Zionists' own, and was not first written in English. The reference which follows the formula goes to show that this was what happened. This runs "His Majesty's Government would not wish to express a preference for this or another solution." Evidently the final compiler or compilers of the dispatch are foreign to the formula itself.

The same may be said of the earlier formula "an agreement concerning Palestine which would satisfy Jewish aspirations." Of this the compiler or compilers observe, "if the above point of view is correct." He or they are transcribing.

In the memorandum too there are subterfuges which one would hardly wish to attribute to the Foreign Secretary. The words "a numerous and most influential section" of the Jews, which I judge to be Whitehall's own, disappear after utterance. In their place, at the close of the dispatch, is palmed the very different expression "the majority of Jews." It is very hard to make nationhood claims on behalf of a section of people, however numerous and influential they may be. But on behalf of the majority of Jews the claim (for what it is worth) can be made without offending mathematics. Hence in the course of the dispatch, the delicate replacement of the words "numerous and influential section" of the Jews by the words "majority of Jews" is allowed to occur.

Possibly the worst thing in the memorandum is the way in which it sets aside Mr. Lucien Wolf's ideals for Zionist colonization in Palestine in favour of the plans of the political Zionists. Mr. Lucien Wolf was an extremely well-known and very able publicist of the period, much versed in foreign affairs. He was the spokesman of some of the chief institutions in British Jewry such as the Anglo-Jewish Association and Board of Delegates of British Jews, whom indeed he was to represent four years later at the Peace Conference. Therefore the definition of Jewish aspirations in Palestine which he offered to the Foreign Office—at its request—was one which commended itself to the representative bodies of Jews in this country. It would I believe have commended itself to the Arabs of Palestine too, if they had known of it. There are no assumptions of ownership in it, no demands for unexampled privileges. Mr. Wolf and the other Jews for whom he spoke only asked that their colonists should have "equal political rights with other inhabitants," "religious and civil freedom," "reasonable facilities for colonization." In fine, the Jewish colonists would qualify for and would receive the normal rights of men.

We know, therefore, through this citation of Mr. Wolf's formula or plan, that in the spring of 1916 the British Government had its chance. A programme was set before it which had authoritative Jewish backing, which was the product of Jewish brains, which would have consorted with the obligations to the Arabs that it had just undertaken. Such were the merits of the programme that it could not be left unmentioned. But to mention it, to say indifferently that he "had no objection to it," and thenceforward to drop it for ever was all the Foreign Secretary did, or all the man or men did who were responsible for this memorandum sent in the Foreign Secretary's name.

The opportunity for following a policy which would have meant no "Palestine Question," no enmity with the Moslems, no jettisoning of the Christians, which would have meant an honourable programme for the Jews, was not merely missed but was consciously evaded. By now Whitehall was entangled with the arbitrary and ruinous schemes of the political Zionists. Some words of Mrs. Dugdale in this respect are worth quoting. "In the spring of the year 1916 the Zionists" (that is to say the political Zionists, Messrs. Weizmann and Sokolov) "began to make a little contact with the great Departments, whose goodwill would be at least as necessary as the sympathy of Ministers, when the moment really came for them to step into the arena of Allied politics. The spokesmen of certain bodies of non-Zionist Jews" (that is to say real "Zionists," who aimed at a spiritual Zion) "were beforehand with them at the Foreign Office, throwing all their weight into other plans for helping the Jews in the Russian Empire and elsewhere. They pressed upon the Foreign Office a formula for a Palestine policy acknowledging nothing more than 'the historic interest' taken in that country by their 'community.' The word 'race' was not used."

She continues: "The Zionists were in ignorance of the existence of this formula for some time after it had been submitted to the Foreign Office, and it is probable that the anti-Zionists were not fully aware of the interest in Zionism taken by some Ministers." This latter fact is very daintily phrased, but the reader will grasp what kind of a situation it was to which it refers.

What this "interest in Zionism" meant is made clear by the next succeeding sentences of the Petrograd memorandum. After declaring that the Foreign Secretary had no objection to Mr. Wolf's programme, the memorandum goes on to propound the very different programme to which, plainly, support was to be extended. Needless to say, this is not stated in so many words. Disclaimers accompany the paragraphs in which the Government's preference is made clear. The memorandum is as loud with disclaimers as the charge-room of a police-station. But the more the Government disclaims a preference for any particular solution, the more it indicates its preference for the special solution which will be "attractive for the majority of Jews."

It says, in what I may term the "betrayal-clause" of the memorandum, that a scheme in which the Zionist immigrants shall be enabled to grow sufficient in numbers to rival the Arabs and then shall be granted powers of government would indeed be "much more attractive for the majority of Jews." At the same time it says blandly that "the only object of His Majesty's Government is to devise some agreement which will be sufficiently attractive for the majority of Jews." If this does not point out, with just a touch of essential periphrastic humbug, that the Government desires the said scheme, then no words or phrases have any meaning at all.

Poor Mr. Wolf in his formula ingenuously had taken the inhabitants of Palestine into consideration. In the betrayal-clause of the Foreign Office memorandum the only reference to them lies in the arrangement for their supersession. They are not even to have the solace of an international protectorate because that would meet with opposition from "influential Jewish circles." These circles will have been the group of Messrs. Weizmann, Sokolov and their friends. Though the Sykes-Picot agreement was not to be signed for another six weeks or so, and was not known to this group, the international protectorate idea was in the air and clearly had been canvassed with them, as a separate proposition. They opposed it from the start, fearing that the influence of the Latin and Orthodox Churches, expressed through the representatives of the countries professing their beliefs, would doom the plans for Zionist hegemony.

A point to be mentioned is that the betrayal-clause varies in the two versions of the memorandum which have been published. As I have already said there are various differences between the version of Mr. Stein and the version of Mrs. Andrews. But there is nothing deserving of mention except in the text of this clause. Here, where Mr. Stein speaks of a scheme for "enabling the Jews, when their colonies in Palestine are sufficiently strong to be able to compete with the Arab population, to take in hand the administration of the internal affairs of this region," Mrs. Andrews's text is "a project which would grant the Jews, when the colonists in Palestine have attained a position which will enable them to rival the Arabs in strength, the administration of their own internal affairs in that country."

Mr. Stein's version assumes Jewish government of internal affairs; a

Zionist Minister of the Interior. Mrs. Andrews's version assumes Zionist self-government in Zionist areas. In order to resolve this discrepancy I applied to the Soviet authorities for a copy of the original text of the memorandum, inquiring at the same time was it indeed in English. They were very courteous, affirmed that the original was in English, and at first even said they would try and procure me a photostat facsimile. Both the Stein and Andrews versions were translations back into English from foreign texts.

There was a certain amount of delay, after which I received the text, not in English but in the official Russian version. A further appeal was met not by the English text but by a request that I should mention any particular passages of which I wished to know the original English. This was rather a disappointment, but I did as I was asked, since examination of the official Russian, itself a translation, was not satisfactory. In the reply which I received, the only quotation containing the original English of the passages I had mentioned which called for notice came at the end of the crucial clause. This was to the effect that Great Britain wished to find some arrangement to enable the Jews, when in sufficient strength to compete with the Arabs, "to take in hand the management of the internal affairs of that district."

Palestine therefore, in the memorandum communicated to M. Sazonoff by Sir George Buchanan for Sir Edward Grey, was described as a district and the Jews were to have the management of all its internal affairs (as in Mr. Stein's version) when their numbers were sufficiently large to compete with the Arabs. Palestine in fact, under this plan, was to be handed over to Zionist rule, without thought of its Arab people except of how soon they could be outnumbered, or could be reduced to parity. The Arabs' natural right to their country, and the bond into which we had just entered to give them their independence if they fought beside us, alike were disregarded.

That is enough concerning this deplorable document, the first of a series in which British policy and the aims of political Zionism were welded together. The alliance is reflected in the evidently composite text, passing as the voice of the Foreign Secretary alone.

There is but a single plea of any kind to be made on behalf of the memorandum. In one place it has a frankness of its own. At least the reasons for favouring political Zionism are stated without hypocrisy.

Of course, this message was not intended to reach the general public, and so hypocrisy could no doubt be left out. The Government refers in it to nothing but the main chance, and proposes acquiescence in the Zionist schemes as a halfpenny-for-you-penny-for-me politico-commercial transaction. Such bargains, it is true, are the common stuff of alliances. The alliance with the Arabs was a give-and-take affair also. But since nearly all those who have imposed the support of the arbitrary type of Zionism upon Great Britain have presented it regularly to the nation as radiant with a halo of selfless intentions, it is very satisfactory to have the reality disclosed in such business-like terms as "utilizing" the Zionist idea and "achieving important political results."

The way in which these results were to be realized is very interesting. Russia was an unfortunate ally at the time, in the sense that her maltreatment of her Jewish subjects had set the minds of Jews against her all over the world. Various violences done to them during the early War years, undisclosed in Great Britain, but published in the United States, had deepened the antagonism of the Jews in that country. This made them lukewarm to the cause of Russia's companions-in-arms. Indeed, as the Petrograd memorandum acknowledges, their attitude towards the cause of the Allies to a considerable extent was hostile. An espousal of political Zionism by the British Government might remedy this Jewish hostility. The Zionist leaders in England then, and later, guaranteed that it would. They gave a special guarantee for the United States.

They knew what they were about. About a fortnight after the Grey memorandum was presented to M. Sazonoff, a meeting of Jewish organizations from all over the country was held in Philadelphia. Mr. Justice Brandeis, of the Supreme Court, a close friend and counsellor of President Wilson, was one of those who addressed the gathering. It was resolved to take advantage of the conditions caused by the War to secure full rights for Jewish citizens everywhere. Any discriminatory laws or regulations under which they suffered were to be abrogated. This programme, excellent of course as it stood, "received the endorsement and approval of many officials of the Government, notably of the Secretary for War." (Kallen.)

It was a beginning. Before long the support of Zionist plans for a Jewish Palestine was to be grafted to the Philadelphia programme. Now, however, I shall leave the Zionists to these plans and return to the Arabs. The reader must not imagine that any chopping and changing in this narrative is done without a reason. Nothing is more essential than to underline the contrast between the way in which Zionism adopted and was adopted by our politicians, and the way in which the Arabs pursued their alliance on the field of battle and the scaffold.

Chapter 8

Preparation for the Arab Revolt. How the Arabs died in Syria. Feisal and Djemaal–The Revolt start.—The Sykes-Picot Treaty. The Zionist "October Programme." Political Zionism made "a complex problem. Political Zionism made "a small nation."

The Arabs did not break into revolt instantly upon conclusion of the alliance with Britain. There were good military reasons for this, especially the need of a larger stock of weapons and war material. Cairo itself counselled delay for a while. It may be said too that the Arabs had begun to fight for us long before one of them took rifle in hands. The Shereef, as we have seen, "had drawn the sting of the *jehad*" (Liddell Hart.) "He had already," says Temperley's standard *History of the Peace Conference*, referring to the period before the revolt began, "rendered service incalculably great to the Allies." This work does not use a term such as "incalculably great" unless it means incalculably great. Let us keep that estimation in mind.

When Hussein concluded the alliance the evacuation of Gallipoli had much improved the situation of the Turks. Freed of the Gallipoli menace, Djemaal Pasha, the commander of the Turkish forces in Syria, no longer needed to behave circumspectly towards the Arabs there. He was given presently too a further reason for the violent action he now began, through the incredible remissness—to say no more—of the staff of the French Consulate-General at Beyrout.

In the previous chapter it was said that M. Georges Picot, who had conducted an inquiry for the French Government in the Near East and then was given the task of negotiating the Anglo-French Arrangement with Sir Mark Sykes, was not a very happy choice for this work. He had been Consul-General at Beyrout till the War broke out, and as we have seen the French representatives in Syria had become heavily involved with the Arab preparations for a rising there against Turkey. The local negotiations had been very much concentrated in Beyrout. When Turkey joined the enemy, the Consul-General of course had to take his departure. In what followed he does not seem to have been personally to blame, but his general responsibility as chief of mission was engaged, and certainly it was tactless to choose him afterwards as an envoy in the Arab sphere. In the Consulate were many papers covering the transactions between the members of the Arab secret societies and the French or Allied authorities. A large number were destroyed by the staff of the Consulate before evacuation of the premises, but a considerable bundle which had been stored in an attic was forgotten.

The Consulate-General was placed under the care of the United States, but Djemaal, who cared nothing for the United States, had the seals on the doors broken, and a search made which revealed the forgotten papers. He already had got on to the track of the planned insurrection, in the July of 1915, and a number of leaders of the Reformist Society, the "Islahiyeh," had been arrested, in Baalbek, Damascus, Jaffa and other Syrian towns. Not long after, twenty-six arrests were made in the Acre and Tyre districts. A permanent court-martial was established at Aley, in the Lebanon, to try these and other Arabs arrested, for conspiracy with the enemy and for plotting insurrection. Five of the arrested, a former deputy and the Mufti of Sidon amongst them, were condemned to death.

But Djemaal's tribunal was still without absolute evidence against many Arabs who were deeply suspect to him. In the French Consulate he obtained the necessary evidence, in the spring of 1916, and after giving the Syrians involved some time to commit themselves further, he established upon this justification a reign of terror in Syria. Those whose names were found registered in the seized documents were brought to trial, as soon as captured, and were hanged in public. Nor were they the sole victims. Djemaal, whose nickname was "The Butcher," chose others as he pleased, or allowed his vindictive subordinates to choose them, on mere suspicion or upon general principles.

He began a policy, as near as he could, of destroying the whole population. Youths under age were rounded up and thrust into the army. Their fathers were sent into banishment, having first surrendered any little holdings of land which they held. These lands (or houses) were then sold over their heads by the military officials, who pocketed most of the proceeds. The evicted Arab householders or husbandmen were told they would receive compensatory allotments in Turkey in Asia. This was but a pretext for transporting them to Sivas or Angora or some worse spot still, where they were left to their fate. In some of the vilayets or provinces of Syria there were scarcely any Arab Christians left, for the Christians especially bore the brunt of Djemaal's fury.

The population shrank by something like a third. In Damascus and in Jerusalem there was terrible misery. Men fell down fainting with starvation in the streets of Beyrout.

The condition of Syria, even amidst the manifold horrors of the War, drew attention in all parts of the world. The neutral states tried to persuade the Turks to stop the general persecution of the population. They did not meet with much success at first, but Constantinople presently grew nervous of the universal feeling that was mounting up against its rule. So the Apostolic Delegate in the Turkish capital was permitted to organize the distribution of large sums which the Pope sent him on behalf of the sufferers. Other bodies followed suit. The world's almoners, the United States, dispatched three warships, the Tennessee, the Des Moines and the Chester, to the Egyptian ports, whence they crossed, to Jaffa mostly, and thence distributed relief.

The Jews in Palestine suffered along with the Arabs. A number of their colonies, especially those nearer the Egyptian border and the seat of war, were ravaged; the stock stolen, the trees cut down. Djemaal (later in the War) issued a proclamation against Zionism, for which there was no real cause since very few of the Jews then in Palestine professed political Zionism and most had come only there as to the sanctuary of their religious faith. He followed this up later by an order bidding them to quit the country "on military grounds." This was not enforced in Jerusalem, but altogether some 12,000 Jews were expelled in a penniless and miserable state. The United States warships transported them to Alexandria. I was in Egypt at the time and remember well the long lines of waggons filing through Alexandria, piled with refugees and their poor belongings, on their way to camps which had been established for them on the outskirts.

A very large number of the Jews in Palestine, being Russian subjects, became technical enemies of Turkey. Forty thousand or so acquired Turkish citizenship; some eight thousand who refused were imprisoned and expelled. Theirs was a preposterous situation: they had been driven from Russia by Russia's own ill-treatment of them. Now they suffered this fresh ill-treatment because they were Russians. As may be imagined, they had never taken the least interest in the Russian cause, and out of their tens of thousands only a handful had in any degree undermined Turkish rule. These latter suffered much as did the Arabs. There was the case of the Aaronson family, which had worked for Allied Intelligence. This was discovered, and a daughter of the house committed suicide to escape familiar forms of Turkish vengeance.

Several of the chief personages amidst the Jewish bodies then in Palestine were tried during 1915 and 1916 on trumped-up charges and after periods of detention were forced to leave the country. But the Jewish population had a certain safeguard in the presence of Zionist groups in

Berlin and Constantinople, and in New York and the chief neutral capitals. Through these the Jewish colonies could always mobilize influence to prevent the Turks from practising against them the extreme excesses they used against the Arabs. "In this way," the Zionist official Report on conditions in Palestine during the War states, "opportunity was given for help from abroad on every occasion of serious political or economic danger. Only through the protection thus afforded by the Zionist Organization can the fact be explained that the war period left the Yishub (the totality of Jewish colonies) in Palestine practically intact."

The German Consul-General in Jerusalem, Herr Brode, the head of the German military mission, General Kress von Kressenstein (the brains of the attack on the Suez Canal), and the Spanish and United States Consuls also, were other protective agencies. "The German officials in general received during the War instructions from the (Berlin) Foreign Office and from the Embassy and Military Mission in Constantinople to promote Zionist interests. These instructions on the whole were punctually obeyed by all officials, no matter whether as individuals they sympathized or not with Jewish aspirations." These were the conditions from 1914 to 1916, and into 1917 till the menace of the British approach brought a general kicking over the traces by Djemaal and others, and the expulsions en masse to Egypt began.

But the Arabs of course were differently placed. Their adhesion to the enemies of the Turks gave another character to their sufferings. The repression which they underwent was horrible in method, and upon a scale which even from a Turkish point of view was unwise. But in principle most of it was logical. They constituted, which the Jewish colonies did not, a present or potential peril to the Turks.

Conversely, what they suffered entitled them to the sympathy and the gratitude of the Allied Powers. If it was primarily for their own independence that they died on the scaffold or in exile, it was also in the cause of Britain and of France, who by every creed of honour were called upon to requite them in the hour of victory, let alone to keep the undertakings made to their race.

I have just said that their repression was horrible in method. Djemaal used to give execution-parties, inviting his friends to be present at the hanging of those found guilty of desertion, of connivance with the Allies, and of other such acts. A number of the victims came from Palestine. Twelve young men were hanged together one day in Jerusalem. The Mufti of Gaza, Ahmed Aref al Husseini, and his son were both hanged. They belonged to the same family as does Jemal Bey al Husseini, so often an Arab delegate to London, and now proscribed from Palestine amidst other leaders of the people. The Grand Mufti of Jerusalem, now in flight in French Syria, also belongs to it

A scion of the other great Arab family of Palestine, the Nashashibi, the Orsini to the Husseini Colonnas, also was hanged. So was Selim el Ahmed el Abdel Hadi, the uncle of Auni Bey Abdel Hadi, signatory of the Versailles Treaty and secretary of King Feisal, recently an internee of Surafend concentration-camp and since proscribed from re-entering Palestine. Before Selim Abdel Hadi was arrested by the Turks, warning had reached him, but he refused to fly, saying, "If I go, they will take revenge on my uncle Hafiz (Pasha), and I don't want him to be molested at his age. I shall stay here." He made a careful calculation of anything he owed, and signed a document for payments half an hour before he went to the scaffold, saying, "My hand does not tremble. Why should it? I die for my country."

Others condemned to death by the Turkish courts-martial at various periods were Abdul Hamid Zahrani (who escaped); Shefik Bey el Mouayid (M. Bompard's visitor; condemned for his relations with the Allies); Shukri Bey el Assali (for correspondence with M. Ottavi); Abdul Gani el Arisi; Seifuddin el Habib (for having signed a secret proclamation of Arab independence); Mahmoud el Makhmessani; Salih Bey Haidar; Refik Rizk Solloum; Abdul Wahib el Inglisi ("the Englishman"; a Crusader's descendant); Enmu Hamid; Arif el Shebab (for raising revolt amongst desert-tribes); Abdul Kerim el Habib; Sheikh Ahmed Tabbarak; Ali Effendi el Armenazi; Hafiz Bey el Said (of Jaffa); Mahmoud el Adjem; Nayf Effendi Tello; Mehmed Muslim ben Ahbedin; Said Effendi el Kermi; Selim Bey Djezairi (of the "Fatah"); Emin Lutfi Bey (for endeavouring to promote rebellion amongst his fellow-officers); Abdul Kader el Kharsa; Rushdy Shamaa; Mehmed el Shamli; George Haddad (of the Christian Lebanon Society); Said Akl; Petro Pauli. These were executed, and other names could be added to the list.

Hakki Bey el Assi, Sheikh Reshid Riza and Faris Nimr (Dr. Nimr, the owner of the *Mokattam* newspaper in Cairo, to which Great Britain owed much during many difficult years before and after the War) and fifty-one others were condemned to death in their absence, according to Turkish procedure. The judgment of the court-martial said of them:

> "These persons plotted to remove the Arab territories from Ottoman rule and to obtain their military occupation by England, which would create then an Arab Caliphate attached to Egypt. They also took an active part in all the transactions preparatory for rebellion. They prepared and took part in the organization of rebellion. All are at large."

Three hundred Palestine notables were exiled to Asia Minor and ultimate famine.

The Emir Feisal had arrived back in Damascus in the midst of this reign of terror. He had come ostensibly to resume his role as a Turkish officer, in reality to join relations with the secret societies and to coordinate action in Syria with the revolt now due in the Hedjaz. But he found all the Arab troops had been transferred and that the country was in Djemaal's grip. He sent messages home counselling delay till perhaps something could be arranged in the north to combine with his father's plans.

He was to have much to endure now, though. Djemaal made a special point of inviting him to be present at the executions. These were shockingly contrived. An eyetwiness said of the victims, "They are not exactly hanged, but suspended from a frame with their toes on a stool." In their spasms they would kick the stool from under them and slowly strangle. Feisal had to look on and to feign indifference. Djemaal would glance every now and then at him and make jocular remarks about the spectacle. He suspected, though he could not prove, that Feisal was involved with the societies to which the men belonged who were dying in his presence.

On one of these gruesome occasions, though I do not think Feisal was present at this, twelve victims suffered together. The most notable of them was a young lawyer—he had been called to the Bar in Paris— a kinsman of the Abdel Hadi family, named Mahmoud el Makhmessani. The scaffold had been raised in a square of Beyrout, which the Young Turk regime with ironic chance had renamed "Liberty Square." Outside a ring of soldiers a silent crowd stood watching. At the last moment the hangman turned to Mekhmessani and demanded whether he had any final wishes to express. He asked to be allowed to speak to the people, and cried out to them that he was guilty. "I am guilty," he said, "if there is any guilt in loving liberty and in wishing to set my country free. I have desired to free it, and far from repenting anything which I have done to win freedom, I am proud to be the first victim for its cause. It is intolerable for us Arabs, sprung of one of the most splendid civilizations which the world has known, to think of the humiliated condition to which we have been brought by the barbarous hordes of Anatolia. We have had enough of the base yoke of the Turk."

The hangman struck the young Arab in the mouth with such force that he bled, but he continued shouting, "We have done with your slavery. You assassinate us in vain. The cause we serve will outlive us, and deliverance is coming. Down with the Turks! Long live the Arabs! Long live France, the Arabs' friend!" He went on shouting and struggling till the executioner had overturned the stool and thrown himself with his full weight round his victim's neck. One by one, the remaining eleven met their fate, either calmly or crying out and invoking the independence of their race and the names of the Powers coming to its aid, as Mekhmessani had done.

What would these men have thought, immolating themselves for their country, and for the kindred cause of the Allies whom they saluted at the last, if they had known how in the end their allies were to treat them. It is not a topic upon which to dwell.

Amongst those who died in Feisal's presence there can scarcely have been one who did not know of his connection with the insurrectionary movement to which they belonged. But none of them ever betrayed him. At least a third of the Syrian population, it is computed, was affiliated to the secret societies, and yet there was not a man found amongst them to buy either his own life or liberty or the life or liberty of father, son or brother by a denunciation of the Emir. Not one man: though scores were hanged barbarously and many thousands died of famine and ill-treatment

Feisal's feelings as he watched these ghastly exhibitions can be imagined. Yet his demeanour was unshaken. Lawrence records that but once did he break down and "burst out that these executions would cost Djemaal all that he was trying to avoid. It took the intercession of his Constantinople friends, chief men in Turkey, to save him from the price of these rash words." Djemaal in high temper had threatened him with execution or banishment.

As far as the Turk commander was concerned Feisal from now on became a hostage. But Feisal must have played his game with extraordinary skill. He retained somehow these Constantinople friendships which saved him, and Djemaal himself was not quite sure of his real attitude. He cannot have had any illusions of Feisal's faithfulness to Turkey, but he thought that perhaps it suited Hedjaz policy for the moment to maintain the Turkish connection as a matter of expediency. And for the moment too, and for the same reasons, it suited Turkish policy to keep the Hedjaz connection. It was on this slender support that Feisal's safety rested.

But he never faltered through all that spring. He continued to keep contact with the remnant of the Arab underground organizations, though indeed by now the brain of the societies was rather in the Hedjaz than in Syria. Several leaders had escaped thither, and in Mecca or from Jeddah they conferred with the Shereef. Feisal also continued his treasonable correspondence with his father, through "old retainers of the family, men above suspicion, who went up and down the Hedjaz railway, carrying letters in sword hilts, sewn between the soles of sandals, or in invisible writing on harmless packages." (Lawrence)

Then in May Hussein boldly telegraphed to Djemaal, "You must drop the persecution of the Arabs. You must proclaim a general amnesty in Syria and in Mesopotamia." He dared telegraph in such terms because at the same time he had formed another military unit, a camel-corps, to support (supposedly) the Turkish army when Egypt was next to be invaded. His telegram had the air of being advice from a genuine ally. But the camel-corps got no further than Medina. It was intended by him really to be the nucleus of the force he would launch against the Turks. In any event, Hussein had always been contemptuous of the new rulers of Turkey. He had told Enver to his face that he was "an ignorant youth."

Feisal from Damascus counselled further patience, and from Egypt similar advice came. Arms and munitions were being sent to Hussein by Sir Reginald Wingate, the Governor of the Soudan, but it was a somewhat slow business, and "Sir Henry McMahon was urging the Shereef to delay his operations until it was possible to equip him more fully for his task." *(Official History.)*

Hussein's mind was made up, though. He summoned Feisal home under the pretext of completing the final arrangements for the dispatch of the camel-corps and of inspecting it before it took the field. Feisal asked leave of Djemaal for the purpose. But the "Butcher" was not quite duped or not quite satisfied. There must have been a leer on his broad face when he answered Feisal, "I shall accompany you myself, and the generalissimo Enver will be with us, and he will inspect your corps."

Whatever doubts Feisal may have had up till then, he knew now that the moment for the revolt had come. It was not that the opportunity was so favourable, but that after Enver and Djemaal had seen things with their own eyes in the Hedjaz it was certain that they would take such measures that no opportunity of any kind would ever occur there.

The two pashas and Feisal, then, went into the Hedjaz together, and the promised inspection took place. One of the most vivid passages in Lawrence's great *Seven Pillars of Wisdom* describes what ensued.

> "In the end matters passed off well, though the irony of the review was terrible." Enver, Djemaal and Feisal together watched "the troops wheeling and turning in the dusty plain outside the city gate, rushing up and down in mimic camel-battle, or spurring their horses in the javelin game in the immemorial Arab fashion. 'And are all these volunteers for the Holy War?' asked Enver at last, turning to Feisal. 'Yes,' said Feisal.
>
> 'Willing to fight to death against the enemies of the faithful?' 'Yes,' said Feisal again; and then the Arab chiefs came up to be presented, and Shereef Ali ibn Hussein, of Modhig, drew him aside, whispering, 'My lord, shall we kill them now?' and Feisal said, 'No. They are our guests.'"

Rarely has even the East seen such refinement of plot and of counter-plot as we read here. Every word on the lips of Enver or of Feisal had both its open and its secret meaning, and as they spoke each of the two played with the other's uncertainties of mind.

> "The Sheikhs protested further; for they believed that so they could finish off the war in two blows. They were determined to force Feisal's hand; and he had to go among them, just out of earshot but in full view, and plead for the lives of the Turkish dictators who had murdered his best friends on the scaffold. In the end he had to make excuses, take his party back quickly to Medina, picket the banqueting-hall with his own slaves, and escort Enver and Djemaal back to Damascus to save them from death on the way. He explained this laboured courtesy by the plea that it was the Arab manner to devote everything to guests; but Enver and Djemaal, being deeply suspicious of what they had seen, imposed a strict blockade of the Hedjaz and ordered large Turkish reinforcements thither."

The tenseness of this scene is so great you would think Feisal's spirit must have grown brittle and have broken. But all the way to Damascus he continued smiling and courteous to the friends he hated, to the enemies he cherished, gave all his mind to the protection of the rulers whose rule he gave all his mind to destroy, till the city at last came in sight. Now he in his turn seemed trapped. But his father played his part well. Hussein demanded Feisal's return. He must have him, he wrote, to control tribes which seemed not so certain in their allegiance, which were restless and were assembling in an ominous way.

Djemaal reluctantly let Feisal go. More plot and counter-plot: he counted on Feisal's restraining the tribes for prudence' sake, on his biding for a little longer a time which Djemaal for his part would take care should never arrive at all. Feisal set forth therefore homeward, but on a pretext all his suite were kept behind by Djemaal in Damascus. They were to be hostages.

Feisal reached Mecca on the 1st of June. "Four days later his suite took horse and rode out east from Damascus into the desert to a Bedouin chief." Theirs was a pre-arranged and timed flight. That 5th of June, Feisal displayed the Arab flag, and one more nation joined the Allies. "The German hope of the co-operation of Islam in the world-plans of the Kaiser passed into the realm of dreams," says Lawrence.

In Egypt those who were dealing with the Arabs were taken by surprise. Half because of the counsels of patience sent from there and half because of the delays which Feisal's strange situation entailed, such speedy action had not been foreseen. The Arab Bureau in Cairo was electrified by a sudden message from a sloop patrolling in the Red Sea. The warship passed on the message in the Shereef's own form that "his hour was at hand." He asked for some British representatives to be sent at once to meet his son the Emir Abdullah. The rendezvous he gave was "a desert shore south of Jeddah." It is a spot known as Sheikh Memijeh Bay. Commander Hogarth, who recounts this, was one of those who hastened thither in a cruiser. Instead of Abdullah they found his young brother Zeid, who told them that Abdullah could not be present because he had gone out already to raise the tribes, whom he had been preparing for months. He was responsible for the restlessness and for the "ominous gathering of the tribes," because of which Hussein had demanded the return of Feisal. The Shereef had imagined a fine piece of satire, and had played it with dry gusto upon Djemaal. Ali, the eldest of his sons, and Feisal himself already were converging on Medina. The rebellion had begun three days before. The Shereef came out on to the balcony of his residence with a rifle in his hand and fired the inaugural shot himself.

It began therefore haphazardly in some degree. But it was in the nick of time. Feisal, before leaving for home, had seen the preparations in Constantinople for the dispatch of the Turkish reinforcements. These were 3,500 strong, under Khairi Bey, and were stiffened by the presence of German troops and specialists of various kinds. After detraining at Medina, where the staff and headquarters organization of an army-corps awaited them, they were to march on Mecca and to suppress all Arab power. This Feisal learned through agents of the secret societies in the Turkish army.

Amongst the Germans there were political agents. The capture of the Hedjaz was but to be the preliminary for a great war-campaign of propaganda and bribery and of backdoors penetration of the British territories which gathered about the Persian Gulf and were the gate to India. The chief of the German politicals was a Major von Stotzingen, an able man who has gained an unkind niche in history because of a letter of introduction which he bore. This was from a member of an influential German family, Countess von Schlieffen, and the salient passage in it ran, "He does not obtrude his personality and has not those characteristics which often make Germans disliked in foreign parts."

As Captain Liddell Hart (on whose account of these events I draw gratefully) points out, if this Turco-German force had overrun the Hedjaz and penetrated south, the reinforcements it brought might have meant quite easily the fall of Aden, where the garrison was small. Our local forces there had been driven into Aden proper out of the hinterland and were besieged by a Turkish division. An Indian contingent raised the siege next month, but we remained on the defensive at Aden thenceforth. If the place had been taken before the Indians arrived we should have had an expedition for its reconquest to add another to all our anxieties of the time. Meanwhile from Arabia von Stotzingen's propaganda, moving like an army, would have outflanked us in Egypt. The interception of this danger, says Liddell Hart, "was not the least of the services to Britain achieved by the Arab revolt."

The 5th of June in 1916 is a date therefore to be remembered as one on which a great blow was struck for the cause of Great Britain and her allies. The Arabs, too, struck it themselves and began on that day to carry out their part of the engagements into which they and Britain had entered. They began in a generous, daring way; they began indeed rashly, if equipment for war alone were concerned. Feisal and his brothers had about 50,000 men at their disposition, but between every five warriors there was but one rifle and an old rifle at that. They had no artillery, no machine-guns.

The Turks had fewer men than the Arabs in the Hedjaz, 15,000, but they were disciplined and pretty well-found. They were supported by artillery, both field-guns and howitzers, and by a proportionate supply of machine-guns. Fortunately the Turks were divided into several garrisons, and the surprise attack of the Shereef's sons took them off their guard. They were driven from Mecca city within a week. Our warships and our naval airmen came swiftly to the help of the Arabs and by bombardment from the sea and bombing from the air took a large part in the fall of Jeddah on the 16th. The Turkish garrison of 1,400 men surrendered. Rabegh, and Yenbo, which is the port of Medina, were taken within the month. Sir Reginald Wingate shipped two mountain-batteries and half a dozen machine-guns at once to the Shereef's aid. Egyptian troops under Moslem officers manned these batteries, and they brought three thousand rifles of one kind or another and much ammunition with them.

In England, though the rising was acclaimed in the Press, no intimation was given that it was the result of an alliance. It was recorded that naval units had fired on the Turkish garrisons at Jeddah and other coastal places, but this much could be credited to normal hostilities with Turkey. The food-ship facilities we gave to the Holy Cities of Islam were noted as a token of friendship merely.

The Times published the news of the rising seventeen days after it began, and devoted its first leader to it. It recognized that now "the Arab national movement had come to a head," wrote appreciatively of the Grand Shereef and of his sons. After ten days or so, details grew sparse. At the time of course communications with the Hedjaz were difficult, and censorship was easy.

Even when the fame of Lawrence had grown and had spread the fame of the Arab revolt far and wide, officialdom kept its details strangely secret. The War was more than a year over before the dispatches concerning the Hedjaz operations were issued. Lawrence's personal exploits too were to give an atmosphere of derring-do to the Arab war, which has obscured what may be called the legal facts of it, especially the humdrum debit and credit between Britain and the Arabs.

That is why I have detailed at some length how the revolt began, and later shall detail how it ended. It must be emphasized that from 1916 to 1918 this revolt was not at all a piece of wild music, a sort of military Ride of the Valkyries, heard "off" the stage of the War. On the contrary, it was a definitely contracted part of the operations, developed in a clearcut way, and crowned with success in every fashion, except in proper full payment for it by those who had contracted for it. Where payment was evaded by the dominant partners was in Syria. In 1936, by the Franco-Syrian treaty of the 9th September, the French at last acknowledged their debt and when the treaty is ratified will have settled with their Arab creditors in their section of that country. We have settled too in Irak, but we continue to default in Palestine.

While Feisal was slipping from Damascus to dare all in the field, we had made, so to speak, first preparations for that default in England. The negotiations between Sir Mark Sykes and M. Picot had ended, and the arrangement which they drew up was ratified by their respective Governments, in May 1916. Having the value of an international agreement, it has generally been termed the "Sykes-Picot Treaty."

It was a neat plan with great stretches of Asia docketed with letters of the alphabet and tinted with several colours, and all the still unconquered Turkish territory parcelled off into five zones. France and Great Britain had each a zone of administration and also a zone of influence, and there was to be an international zone, corresponding roughly to Palestine. An independent Arab state in Syria was, whimsically, to be composed of the British zone of influence and the French zone of influence. That is to say, that over a triangular section of territory lying between the zones where Britain and France were to administer directly, there was to be established a native state under an Arab ruler with Damascus as its chief city. But the northern part of it was to be under French influence. Only the French were to supply advisers or foreign officials, and they were to have a priority right upon enterprises and loans. The south was to be under British influence and the character of influence was to be similar.

It is difficult to imagine anything more unworkable than this "Arab" State, of which the fantastic design might have come to its authors at the end of a dinner, from some dish of Neapolitan ice-cream, wherein vanilla and strawberry zones-of-influence were established over independent sweetmeat.

Quite in this order of ideas the fifth zone was coloured chocolate. This was the international zone of Palestine where "was to be established an international administration whose form shall be decided after consultation with Russia, and subsequently in accord with the other Allies and the representatives of the Shereef of Mecca." The two administrative zones gave Cilicia, much of central Anatolia and coastal north Syria to France, while Great Britain was dowered with Mesopotamia and the ports of Haifa and Acre in Syria.

This Sykes-Picot Treaty, later to be modified and remodified and to form the basis of the abortive Treaty of Sèvres, was of course altogether incompatible with our previous pledges to the Arabs.

The new treaty made a mockery of the Syrian Arab State, and Palestine was to be withdrawn from its territories. It took away from the Shereef what had been granted to him, and did so secretly, with no reference to him, at the very moment when his sons and his tribesmen were beginning battle to honour his word. On the face of it, therefore, the Sykes-Picot treaty is not a parchment with a place of pride amongst the national charters of England.

At the same time, if it was inequitable in general concept, it did possess some saving points and was not entirely disingenuous and false in the style of the subsequent Balfour Declaration. It won from the French acceptance of the principle of Arab independence. Hitherto France had jibbed at this, however qualified by French or British tutelage in its early stages. Now France gave her support to the principle, and after some half-hearted dealings, did contribute her part to the success of the Arab revolt, through the aid in particular of the gallant Captain Pisani and his guns. The terms of French support were contained in an instrument signed, also in May, by Sir Edward Grey and M. Cambon, the French Ambassador in London, by which it was declared that their respective Governments were *"disposed to recognize* and protect an independent State or a Confederation of Arab States under the suzerainty of an Arab chief." The italics are mine. Four months before we had already recognized Arab independence over the whole area of Arab habitation.

In the Sykes-Picot document itself this was ignored. That is to say, Article 2 of this Treaty alluded to negotiations with the Arabs as having to be continued, at a time when they were at an end. Whether this strange statement was considered as justified by the Shereef's proviso that he would leave the French claims over to be settled after the War does not appear. But as far as Britain was concerned the Arab negotiations were ended, and the recognition of "an independent State or a Confederation of Arab States" had been conceded definitely by her.

However, there was another saving point in the Sykes-Picot Treaty which seemed to show that despite the talk of continued negotiation, someone who had had a hand in the Treaty recognized the true situation between

Mecca and Great Britain. The point is one which has received no attention, but deserves a good deal. The treaty contained the provision for consulting the representatives of the Grand Shereef when the mode of erecting an international administration in Palestine should be determined finally.

It may be that this provision found its way into the treaty to satisfy the known good will of Sir Mark Sykes towards the Arabs. It was not his fault that the treaty curtailed their independence.

Such latitude as he had was in the direction of compromise with the French claims only, under which he agreed to include Mosul in one of their zones. This is a sure indication that, if he had full cognizance of the Hussein-McMahon Treaty, he had been instructed to overlook it, since in it the Mesopotamian area was reserved for British influence and it was not possible to replace this by French influence without obtaining—if Britain were to be faithful to her word—the consent of the Shereef, the other party to the transaction.

Whether he knew the terms of the Anglo-Arab Treaty or was ordered to overlook them, it was an unhappy role for poor Sykes. His only reward was to be abused later by Mr. Lloyd George, who, during the Peace Conference, ejaculated that "Mark Sykes was responsible for the agreement which is causing us all the trouble with the French. He negotiated it for us with Picot, the Frenchman, who got the better of him." (Riddell.) In fact Sykes had been instructed to go a long way to satisfy the French. As far as he was concerned his Treaty was not much more than a jig-saw he put together, of which the British pieces had been sent to him in the red-leather dispatch-boxes of Downing Street.

So while the clause for consulting the Shereef (or Sheikh, as the text had it) of Mecca may have been due to him, it is more likely that it was the work or drawn up under the orders of someone in Whitehall who had a conscience. Some person, perhaps more than one person, was disturbed by the violation of the covenant which guaranteed the Arabs, not an international, but a national regime in Palestine. To make up for such a violation, it was little enough that could be done. But it was something to obtain the inclusion of the Shereef's representatives amongst those who were to draw up the conditions of international rule. It was done in the hope, maybe, that when the time came for discussions the Arab representatives might be in a position to enter a caveat to the whole proceedings.

Apart from the prickings of conscience there was nothing to cause the inclusion of the Shereef's name in the document. Till the pact with McMahon had been made by him he had been but the guardian of the Moslem Holy Places in Arabia and the potentate of the Hedjaz. His situation as the spokesman of the Arab race, in Palestine or elsewhere, had only come to him through the negotiation of that pact. Whoever therefore, in what are called Government circles, extended to him this situation in the prospective negotiations upon Palestine under the Sykes-Picot Treaty was well acquainted with the Anglo-Arab Treaty, and understood the obligations to the Arabs which we had contracted in it.

There is no clue in this intricate and hidden situation to the identity of the man or men with a conscience who, even if the clause were Sykes's own, must have given that clause approval when the terms were submitted. To whom it was submitted must again be a mystery. Nominally it would have been submitted to the "Government," but which persons in which group of that strangely functioning body saw the Treaty through the Lord knows. The most likely honourably-minded individual in a position to insert the clause or to secure its retention was perhaps Sir Arthur Nicolson, the Under-Secretary at the Foreign Office, who previously had been the man to warn M. Picot of the existence of an Anglo-Arab pact. But that is surmise.

One thing which is evident is that the inclusion of Hussein's name in the Sykes-Picot Treaty puts the Petrograd memorandum of eight weeks before into an unenviable posture. In this memorandum the Arabs, so to speak, were only entered for purposes of erasure. The divergence between the two documents also serves only too well to show the incoherency of the policies of the period. Sir Mark Sykes actually was in Petrograd, by Sir Edward Grey's orders, to obtain Russian agreement to the internationalization of Palestine, upon the very same day, the 13th of March, upon which the Russians were handed the memorandum from Sir Edward Grey deprecating the internationalization of Palestine! What real part can Grey have had in these doings?

Whatever deserves to be said of them, we can observe to advantage the fashion in which the early foundations of Zionism were laid in 1916. Amidst all the incoherency and worse, one thing also can be isolated and be tacked down, the implicit acknowledgment in the Sykes-Picot terms of our existing obligations to the Arabs. Before many months passed a new Government reigned in London, and this lapse into integrity was corrected. But fortunately for the truth, it still stands to witness.

During the summer of 1916 there was a halt in the activities in Britain of the Zionist representatives. The start of the Arab revolt may have counteracted these activities for a space. But more likely they were banished from the field by great events: the battle of Jutland; the Somme attacks; the entry into the War of Roumania. Lamentable events banished them too: Kitchener was drowned off the Orkneys on the 5th of June. With him, alas! departed from ruling circles any realization of the Arabs as a human entity.

Mr. Lloyd George succeeded him as Secretary for War, and while the country and the campaign benefited by the new Secretary's zeal and his driving-power, yet to his unselective ear the whispers of Zionism presently came with the force of oracles.

After a gallant start, the Arab revolt suffered a first set-back. The impetuosity of the Arabs and the surprise of the first days were countered by the equipment which the Turks now brought into play. The Arabs had no artillery save the Egyptian guns, and these were ineffective because they were outranged by the Turkish pieces. Without better artillery support the Turks in Medina were too tough a problem to tackle. An attempt to rush the place had failed, though Feisal and Ali had ridden about amidst bursting shells to accustom their men to these (to them) terrible novelties. The Turks massacred the Arabs in the Awali suburb. "Hundreds of the inhabitants were raped and butchered, the houses fired, and living and dead alike thrown back into the flames." (Lawrence.)

We landed sailors at Rabegh, where Aziz el Masri set about training Syrian and Mesopotamian volunteers into regular troops. By the autumn he had two thousand in khaki, who were drafted to the force acting under the Emir Ali. Aeroplanes were sent to Rabegh, four good ones to balance "twenty-three guns, mostly obsolete, and of fourteen patterns." Lawrence, some time about the end of October, was detailed to the Arab Army. Feisal then was harrying Turkish communications. Abdullah "with three machine-guns" was "blockading" Medina.

After the news of the revolt reached Constantinople, the Turks had proclaimed the deposition of the Shereef Hussein, and had appointed one Ali Haidar in his place. Ali Haidar had been brought by them to Medina, where they were gathering an important force, which was to march on Mecca and to overthrow Hussein. As its probable route must lie through Rabegh, the Anglo-Arab parry to this move was to strengthen Rabegh, which was done with naval and air-force co-operation. But in Egypt, where military responsibilities and policies were bewilderingly divided, the Arab war had not too many friends. "Staff officers," says Lawrence, "prophesied its near failure and the stretching of Shereef Hussein's neck on a Turkish scaffold."

Meanwhile, far from desert warfare and from the perils of the scaffold, another cause was making its progress. *Bella gerant alii…* Zionism wedded itself civilly first to this country and then to that. In the United States it was organizing itself with marked success, which meant a great deal, since of all the Jews in the world at least three million were in the United States. These were concentrated too in the large cities where their influence had greatest play. On the 2nd of October most of the chief Jewish organizations issued a joint manifesto in which the Philadelphia resolutions had swelled to some purpose. This manifesto demanded for the Jews full rights wherever they lived in the world, as well of course as the abrogation of all extant laws or regulations prejudicial to them. "It being understood," explained the manifesto, "that the phrase 'full rights' is deemed to include

(1) Civil, religious and political rights;

(2) The securing and protection of Jewish rights to Palestine."

The second item needed all the 'deeming' and the 'understanding' which its authors could give to it, but they did not delay to argue their case. In or out of the United States they proclaimed it vociferously, and that on the whole was enough. But in England well co-ordinated action was taken by them.

Matters had reached such a stage [as an official Zionist Organization report was to explain later] that in October 1916 the Zionist Organization felt justified in putting forward a formal statement of its views as to the future government of Palestine in the event of its coming under the control of England and of France.

This was a big advance, co-related of course with the development in the United States. So far the Zionist Organizations views, even though incorporated in Foreign Office memoranda, had been laid unofficially before the British Government. Now these views were to be presented as a formal statement, officially, as though the Zionist Organization possessed an internationally established status which might be affected by the advance of England and of France into the Syrian territories. Whence this status was gained remains undiscoverable. But the document which presupposed it was adroitly presented by the Zionist leaders and was adroitly accepted by the British Government and thereby the said status, though it did not exist, was recognized. The document was rather a long one, divisible roughly under six heads.

One clause demanded that a Jewish Chartered Company should be established of which the purpose would be the resettlement of Palestine by Jewish settlers. This Chartered Company project was not a new one: the Sultan Abdul Hamid had been asked to consider something similar. It had British precedents of the most attractive character, and without doubt the Chartered Company was expected to dissolve in short course into a Government, more easily even than such Companies had dissolved into Governments in India and in South Africa.

Meanwhile, it was to have power "to exercise the right of pre-emption of Crown and other lands and to acquire for its own use all or any concessions which may at any time be granted by the suzerain Government or Governments."

Reading this, one is led to ask, "Why have a suzerain Government at all?" The Jewish Chartered Company of Palestine was to have at its disposal any land anywhere at any time in that country. Any concessions which anyone else might obtain or might have obtained were to be taken away from him and were to be bestowed on the Chartered Company. Nothing was left for the "suzerain" to do but the clerical work of surrendering everything and of expropriating everybody. (In fact, though it may not seem credible, the general scheme of this clause actually was enforced within about five years, in favour of the notorious Rutenberg concessions.)

Another clause ran: "Inasmuch as the Jewish population in Palestine forms a community with a distinct nationality and religion, it shall be officially recognized by the suzerain Government or Governments as a separate national unit or nationality."

Upon which clause it might well be observed that inasmuch as the Jewish population in Palestine then did not form a distinct nationality but was divided amongst all the nationalities of eastern Europe and some of western Europe and some of Asia; that inasmuch as at least three-quarters of that population had no sympathy with political Zionism and continued to repudiate it after it had come to Palestine; inasmuch as the identification of the Jews as a religious body or the adherents of a creed was then and still is rejected by the political Zionists; therefore there does not appear to be cause for official recognition here of anything but of three separate units of fallacy.

The most significant clause of all, though, was that in which the Arabs came in for mention. Astonishingly they did come in for mention in a Zionist document of that date. But in what manner?

> The present population, being too small, too poor, and too little trained to make rapid progress, requires the introduction of a new and progressive element in the population, desirous of devoting all its energies and capital to the work of colonization on modern lines.

The Arabs, the "present population" of the above paragraph, at the time numbered some 675,000, and Palestine is of merely county dimensions. These however were not facts to detain the Zionist Organization. It dismissed the Arabs without further consideration, after what seemed without doubt the conclusive remark that their population was "small and poor." To be small and poor is the supreme crime in a category of thought which, curiously, is itself small and poor.

Therefore these Arabs, exiguous in their hundreds of thousands, required "the introduction of a new and progressive element." Sentences of such surpassing effrontery as this one are rare, and it would be hard to find anything matching in insolence the whole clause. What right had the

Zionist Organization to talk of what the Arabs needed? None whatsoever.

Still, whether the clause or the whole programme of which it was a part were insolent or not, the programme of the Chartered Company was accepted as a foundation-stone by the British Government. "The Government," says the Zionist Report, "seems to have regarded the Zionist claims embodied in the programme as forming a basis for discussion." Negotiations thenceforth went on steadily.

Talks with individual statesmen "gave place to discussions of a more formal character. Zionism won recognition as one of the complex problems connected with the Middle East on the one hand and the question of small nationalities on the other." (Zionist Official Report.)

There it is. A better example could not be supplied of the sophistries by which the hapless Arabs were to be supplanted. Zionism, political Zionism, not alone was confirmed in the status it had acquired out of the skies, but now was advanced a stage beyond. Political Zionism became one of the "complex problems connected with the Middle East." All in a flash it was enrolled amidst the problems which by and by the Allies must face.

The role thus assumed by political Zionism was one unwarranted by any law, any deed, any political conditions which were then in existence, or previously had been for over a thousand years. Zionism as a political entity had owned no situation outside the brains of its own recent devisers. Political Zionism was not something engrained in the soil of the Near East, nor had it any place amidst the problems which the Ottoman Empire handed on so profusely to its successors.

The Ottoman Empire had been approached and had refused to introduce this amidst its many complicated factors. It would not have a Jewish enclave. No statesman in the world had toiled for years over Zionism, no statesman in the world had inherited dossiers in hundreds filled with the negotiations of his predecessors-in-office concerning it. It simply was not a problem at all. There was a Jewish problem in Eastern Europe; there was none in Palestine. It was intended now to introduce the problem where it had never existed, but that was to create a problem—something vastly different. In fact, to say that political Zionism was a complex problem connected with the Middle East was a thumping lie. Its true situation in the realm of politics was that of a theory just beginning to be exploited in London and Paris and New York.

The complexity attributed to it was wholly unreal. What was called complexity only meant the difficulty of finding a formula opaque enough to disguise the immediate or future annexation of Palestine.

But sophistry did not confine itself to slipping political Zionism in this way in among the problems of the Middle East. With the same stroke

Zionism also won "recognition as a problem connected with the question of small nationalities." Indeed it did. The operative word, as Mr. J. B. Morton says, is "connected." By more adroitness that which had been nothing, but had been transmogrified into a problem, was now again transmogrified from a problem into a small nation, by coupling it to various lesser lands.

The scheme for this can be visualized. In 1916 the small nations were already forming up to put their pleas to the (it was hoped) conquering Allies. Together they made a political caravan, a train if you like. When the moment came they would all set off together, the train would depart for the terminus where the victorious Peace was being prepared. The political Zionists were ready for this. Rapidly and unostentatiously a van labelled "Zionist Problem" would be connected to the last carriage. The train would puff away. Somewhere en route the label would disappear, and a van inscribed "Jewish National Home" would draw eventually alongside the arrival platform, behind Czechoslovakia, Lithuania, Latvia and all the others. The whole scheme is very simple. But the chance of watching the manoeuvre is not often given.

So much for this October programme. While the remaining two months of 1916 were consecrated in England to the "formal discussions" sprung of it, discussions of another kind were being held by Lawrence in the Hedjaz, with the Emir Feisal, with Mauled el Mukhlus, the first ex-Turkish regular of the Arabs to volunteer for the revolt, and with other leaders. They sat together at Hamra and talked of Djemaal's executions in Syria. Some of the young Mesopotamian "Fatah" stalwarts took Lawrence up sharply. Djemaal was within his rights, they argued, as the men he had hanged had been caught in correspondence with the Allies. These men had been ready to accept French or British suzerainty, too, and that was a crime against Arab nationality.

> "Feisal smiled, almost winked, at me. 'You see,' he explained, 'we are now of necessity tied to the British. We are delighted to be their friends, grateful for their help, expectant of our future profit. But we are not British subjects. We should be more at ease if they were not such disproportionate allies.'
>
> "Someone added of the sailors coming ashore each day from the warships at Rabegh, 'Soon they will stay nights, and then they will live here always, and take the country.' Feisal mused a little and said, 'I am not a Hedjazi by upbringing; and yet, by God, I am jealous for it. And though I know the British do not want it, yet what can I say, when they took the Soudan, also not wanting it? They hunger for desolate lands, to build them up; and so, perhaps, one day Arabia will seem to them precious.'" (Lawrence).

Can we blame Feisal now for these doubtful musings, even though we gave him Irak in the end? It was on the very first night Lawrence spent with the Arab Army that Feisal gave vent to them. Lawrence wandered about amongst the tribesmen "corrugated with bandoliers" next morning, and for some days more, then went back to Egypt, and reported against sending a British expedition to Rabegh. This pleased Military Headquarters and pleased the General Staff in London, which was averse to launching any sort of new expeditionary force, even if it only were composed of three or four brigades. By an odd stroke, this new military popularity of Lawrence's led the Staff in Egypt to be more lavish with stores and arms for his Arabs than normally he would ever have dared to expect. A few capable officers were dispatched too in order to stiffen the revolt. With their help the Arabs fought on. But in December they met with a reverse below Medina, which the enemy fortunately did not exploit.

There had been a reverse of another kind some six weeks or so previously. The Shereef had been proclaimed by the Mecca ulemas "King of the Arab Nation." This was injudicious ere he had come to a settlement with the Emir Ibn Saud, who even then was very powerful in his interior sector of Arabia, and with the minor chiefs who had niches of power here and there on the coasts. Hussein had promised also in the correspondence with the High Commissioner to respect existing British agreements with these chiefs.

But more than anything else the title was altogether too much of a disclosure of the concealed Anglo-Arab Treaty not to horrify London. So by a mixture of argumentation and of pressure Hussein was brought to acquiesce—till the situation was clearer, it was put to him—in the less clamant title of "King of the Hedjaz."

This was an ominous sign, possibly, had it been realized, for the future honouring of the Anglo-Arab Treaty. Other events, more than ominous, but hidden from the Arabs, occurred. Sir Mark Sykes, reappearing in Cairo and calling on the High Commissioner, "remarked to him in conversation, producing a map, 'What do you think of my treaty?'" (Liddell Hart.) It was the first word Sir Henry McMahon had ever heard of the conclusion of the Sykes-Picot Treaty! He did not remain in Egypt long after he had received this shock. "The workings against Sir Henry McMahon," says Lawrence, "came to a head, were successful, and ended in his recall to England."

In early December Mr. Lloyd George had replaced Mr. Asquith as Prime Minister. Sir Henry McMahon's successor took over office at the beginning of the ensuing January. 1917 had come, a year which was to witness a great victory for political Zionism, but a great defeat for political honesty.

Chapter 9

Political Zionism's first "official" steps in London. Brandeis and Balfour.—Lawrence and British pledges. Jewry versus Zionism.—First arrangements for the Mandate. Jewish opposition in the U.S. to Zionism.—France's recognition.

The Zionist Executive has recapitulated as follows the course of Zionism in Britain between 1914 and the critical year of 1917:

> "During the first months of the War the foundations were laid of a close understanding with the statesmen who guided the destinies of Great Britain. The time was not yet ripe for any formal assurance of support from the British Government. But an atmosphere was created in which, given favourable political conditions, it was possible to hope that such an assurance might be obtained. The friendly atmosphere was intensified during the following two years, and when Mr. Lloyd George became Prime Minister and Mr. Balfour Foreign Secretary, the seeds sown in 1914 were able to bear fruit."

This intensification of friendly atmosphere is a bland phrase for the collusive fog in which during 1916 members of the Government lost all track of each other's actions, and dim figures handed programmes out of the gloom to unseen recipients. However, the result of everything was that when the fog dissipated or was discontinued, the Zionist leaders were found standing on the steps of the Foreign Office. In February the first unobscured meeting between them and an appointed delegate of the Government took place. Sir Mark Sykes was the Government's representative.

During the six months or so of obscurity which had preceded this meeting, while the Zionist leaders had used it to the extreme advantage we have seen, they had also got a little lost in it between times. The fog had the defects of its qualities. Public events continued too upon a great and absorbing scale for the Government. The state of Russia, the preoccupations of France and of Britain with the Greek situation, the Cabinet troubles of Great Britain herself, had forced Zionist projects into the background. The Petrograd memorandum had been fairly well received in Russia, but then Russia herself had begun to break up.

Russia's defection had emphasized the need of acquiring the help of the United States for the Allied cause. In the United States the main obstacle to adoption of the Allied cause was thought to lie in the power of the German-Americans. But most of the German-Americans were Jewish. Therefore the lull of interest in Zionism ended as soon as it was put forward again, this time as presenting a means of winning round German-American sympathy.

Previous to that, though, and while the Foreign Office was passing from the hands of Sir Edward Grey into those of Lord Balfour, the Zionist leaders in England had been only intermittently in evidence. It is even possible that their October memorandum had shocked what may be called the "conscience-group" in the Foreign Office, which was in a position to keep them at a distance while their major protectors were engaged with first-class crises.

The fullest account of how relations with the new Government were now welded has been given by Mr. Samuel Landman, in some reminiscences contributed some three years ago, on the 22nd February and 1st March, to the review *World Jewry*. Mr. Landman, a leader of the Revisionists, the most advanced section of political Zionists, was M. Sokolov's secretary at the time, and afterwards was secretary of the World Zionist Organization. He was therefore in close touch with these affairs. There are some words of comment to be made upon his account, but a summary of the facts as he retails them may be given first.

He says, then, that Sir Mark Sykes, by the latter's own account, had been trying to get in touch with this Jewish German-American opinion without much success. Sir Mark Sykes, I may interpolate, was Assistant-Secretary to the War Office then, a position which however was not at all departmental. It was his official title, but in reality he acted as liaison officer between the War Office, the India Office, the Intelligence organizations, and other bodies of the highest importance. He used to visit all the seats of power daily, co-ordinating their information, besides interviewing generals back from the front on leave, ambassadors and ministers, people of every standing and of every position, provided they had something worth telling to tell him. He had the ear of the Cabinet of course, and was in sum a man of the greatest influence.

It is not difficult to perceive why he had not been so successful in his German-American endeavours. He, with the "conscience-group" at the Foreign Office very possibly, was trying to work through the leaders of British Jewry, through the moderate Lucien Wolf section, through various rabbis whose only aim was to establish a spiritual-cultural Jewish centre in Palestine.

I return to Mr. Landman. Sir Mark Sykes was regretting his insuccess one day in the presence of Mr. James Malcolm, "a prominent British-Armenian" as Mr. Wickham Steed designates him. Mr. Malcolm, a Balliol man, belonged to a family of Armenian origin but British for several generations. He was in contact with some ardent political Zionists, and he now told Sir Mark Sykes that it was to the political Zionists he should have turned. "You are going the wrong way about it," he said, "the well-to-do English Jews you meet and the Jewish clergy are not the real leaders of the Jewish people." Political Zionism or national Zionism, as Mr. Malcolm called it, was the key to influence over the Jewish body in the United States, and to more even than that. Mr. Malcolm said that there was a way to make American Jews thoroughly pro-Ally, and that he knew a man in America who was probably the most intimate friend of President Wilson. Through that man, if through anybody, the President's mind could be turned towards active participation in the War on the side of the Allies. (The man in question was Judge Louis Brandeis, of the United States Supreme Court.)

"You can win the sympathy of Jews everywhere," added Mr. Malcolm, "in one way only, and that way is by offering to try and secure Palestine for them." Sir Mark Sykes, with the chocolate internationalized Palestine of his own treaty before his eyes, said that this was impossible. Mr. Malcolm, who (in my opinion) knew more of the previous tractations of Lord Balfour and of Mr. Lloyd George than Sir Mark Sykes did, said that the latter ought to put the suggestion before the Cabinet at any rate. Sykes spoke to Lord Milner about it, and when he told Mr. Malcolm this, Malcolm spoke again of what might be accomplished through Judge Brandeis's influence. Mr. Malcolm's motives were disinterested; he believed in Zionism as a political force and thought it would be valuable to the Allied cause in America.

After more conversations it was agreed (the Cabinet, or such members of it as were approached, finding no obstacle apparently in contrary treaties) that negotiations should be undertaken, with the aim of obtaining Transatlantic support, on the basis of securing Palestine for the Jews. Mr. Malcolm had insisted that it was no good approaching Zionist leaders unless there was something in the way of a concrete offer to make to them.

Various persons now became involved, including Mr. Greenberg, the editor of the *Jewish Chronicle*. There were meetings at Dr. Weizmann's house in Addison Road, whither he had come from Manchester. Malcolm met Weizmann there, for the first time apparently, Mr. Greenberg having been, presumably, his point of contact with the movement. Then Sir Mark Sykes met M. Sokolov and Dr. Weizmann several times, with the knowledge and approval of Sir Maurice Hankey, the Secretary of the War Cabinet.

A passage *in extenso* may now be taken from Mr. Landman's article.

He writes:

> "After an understanding had been arrived at between Sir Mark Sykes and Weizmann and Sokolov, it was resolved to send a secret message to Justice Brandeis that the British Cabinet would help the Jews to gain Palestine in return for active Jewish sympathy and for support in the U.S.A. for the Allied cause, so as to bring about a radical pro-Ally tendency in the United States. This message was sent in cipher through the Foreign Office. One of the principal Under-Secretaries at the time was Sir Ronald Graham. He was in the confidence of Sir Mark Sykes and during the whole time he was at the Foreign Office he was of unfailing help to the Zionists. Secret messages were also sent to the Zionist leaders in Russia to hearten them and to obtain their support for the Allied cause, which was being affected by Russian ill-treatment of the Jews. Messages were also sent to Jewish leaders in neutral countries, and the result was to strengthen the pro-Ally sympathies of Jews everywhere.
>
> Through General Macdonogh, who was won over by Fitzmaurice [Mr. G. H. Fitzmaurice, Dragoman of the British Embassy in Constantinople for many years, a man of great influence], Dr. Weizmann was able, about this time, to secure from the Government the service of half a dozen younger Zionists for active work on behalf of Zionism. At that time conscription was in force, and only those who were engaged on work of national importance could be released from active service at the Front.
>
> I remember Dr. Weizmann writing a letter to General Macdonogh (Director of Military Operations) and invoking his assistance in obtaining the exemption from active service of Leon Simon, Harry Sacher, Simon Marks, Hyamson Tolkowsky and myself. At Dr. Weizmann's request I was transferred from the War Office (M.I.9), where I was then working, to the Ministry of Propaganda, which was under Lord Northcliffe, and later to the Zionist office, where I commenced work about December 1916. Simon Marks actually arrived at the Office in khaki, and immediately set about the task of organizing the office which, as will be easily understood, had to maintain constant communication with Zionists in most countries.
>
> From that time onwards for several years Zionism was considered an ally of the British Government, and every help and assistance was forthcoming from each government department. Passport or travel difficulties did not exist when a man was recommended by our office. For instance a certificate signed by me was accepted by the Home Office at that time as evidence that an Ottoman Jew was to be treated as a friendly alien and not as an enemy, which was the case with the Turkish subjects."

A most enlightening passage indeed. It is confirmed at one point by Mrs. Dugdale, who dates the period from which use of the official cipher began. Speaking of the submission of the October Programme she adds:

> "Something hardly less significant happened in the same month. Dr. Weizmann and M. Sokolov were allowed to communicate with each other, and with other Zionist leaders abroad, by sending telegrams through the Foreign Office, which transmitted them in code."

When Dr. Weizmann or M. Sokolov were on the Continent they had the same privilege through British Embassies or Legations.

With the quotation from Mr. Landman which has just been given, we reach in his account the "official" interview of February 1917, which followed on the transactions he describes. Concerning his account there is this to be mentioned. It subordinates the activity of Dr. Weizmann to that of Mr. Malcolm very considerably, at least in the earlier stage. No doubt the Zionist leader, and M. Sokolov too, were less in evidence in later 1916. But the Petrograd memorandum is definite proof that national or political Zionism and not internationalized Palestine was in the British Government's programme in the spring, and no one but Dr. Weizmann and his associates could have placed it there. Mark Sykes may have been ignorant of political Zionism. On Mr. Landman's showing he was; which implies that when he was negotiating with the Russian Government the Grey memorandum to that Government was not disclosed to him. This would correspond well with the sort of policy which was being carried out; pretty stuff indeed.

But the assumption that negotiations between the Government proper and Dr. Weizmann had come to a standstill, and that they were only rescued by the Malcolm intervention from breakdown and a consequent end of the Anglo-Zionist programme so far as it was composed then, seems overstrained. This can be said without belittling in any way the part played by Mr. Malcolm. The period of decline of one Government and of entry into power of another was bound to weaken relations with the Zionist leaders for a while, but with Balfour and Lloyd George in power it could only be a temporary delay. It must be remembered that the political Zionists have their own internal dissensions, which must colour their accounts of things. In the struggle for control which afterwards developed between the Weizmann group and the Brandeis group, the respective share of these leaders and of their sympathizers in maintaining the cause from the start bulks or shrinks according to the particular body to which the Zionist writer belongs, in whose text one reads of it.

It may also be suggested that Zionist exuberance sometimes makes convinced adherents of Zionist doctrine out of generals and under-secretaries who were merely following out instructions from their chiefs and eventually from the Cabinet. There is no clue to their motives, which may have been convinced, but may have been altogether utilitarian.

With these provisos, the tale of events may be resumed at the meeting of February 1917. This was held at the house of Dr. Moses Gaster, an able member of the increasing band of Zionist leaders, by whom Sir Mark Sykes had been much attracted.

By one of those fictions which give a cherished four-dimensional air to diplomacy, on that 7th of February, Sykes was not present at the meeting as Assistant-Secretary to the War Cabinet, but as himself, "in his private capacity." When drawing up his treaty with M. Picot, conversely, he had been present, not as himself, but as a Foreign Office Official.

At Dr. Gaster's he found, in addition to his host, Lord Rothschild, Sir Herbert Samuel, Messrs. James de Rothschild, Cowen, Bentwich, Harry Sacher, and of course Dr. Weizmann and M. Sokolov, all without doubt present in every conceivable personal and impersonal capacity.

It was indeed not a very specific gathering. The Rothschilds, who gave the dignity of their name to the assembly, were recent enough appearances at the prow of political Zionism, and were no more in the engine-room or at the helm of the movement than any other figureheads. Dr. Weizmann, Dr. Gaster, M. Sokolov and Mr. Cowen on the other hand directed its speed and course. Another exponent of the political movement was Mr. Bentwich, afterwards to be Attorney-General in the Palestine Administration. He had written, "State sovereignty is not essential to the Jewish national ideal." But he had predicated the concession to Zionist settlements and settlers in Palestine of "special rights" which were equivalent to sovereignty since they ousted the inhabitants of the country from control over either settlers or settlements.

He had also spoken of the territory stretching from the Mediterranean to the Euphrates as "Greater Palestine," had said that it was full of historical associations for the Jews, and that it cried for "a population to redeem it from the neglect and decay of centuries." He was of opinion that "Jewish colonization might extend" to this territory.

Sir Herbert Samuel represented the slowest form of evolutionary Zionism. He aimed at such form of Government in Palestine as would evolve in the long run into Jewish rule. Mr. Harry Sacher was a sort of proxy for Gentile interests and a direct representative of Manchester's guardian hand.

A composite group altogether. Everyone present was for a Zionist State, but some were "long-runners," like Sir Herbert Samuel, and some were "short-hoppers," along a scale in which long hops and short runs were not excluded. The gathering therefore put no positive proposals to Sir Mark Sykes. But in a negative way it spoke categorically. The Assistant-Secretary to the War Cabinet was told that there must be no internationalization of

Palestine, because Zionists desired a British Protectorate "with full rights to the Jews to develop as a nation." It was the first time the word "must" had been used to His Majesty's Government. In the Petrograd memorandum the quoted prohibition still had been veiled.

The meeting decided to narrow negotiations to fewer people (and incidentally perhaps to fewer policies) and M. Nahum Sokolov, who was the chief agent in Britain of the International Zionist Executive, was chosen to carry on conversations with Sir Mark Sykes. It was arranged that M. Picot should join them to represent the French Government. He conferred with Sykes next day. "Thus opened," says the Zionist report of the event, "the chapter of negotiations which ended nine months later with the Balfour Declaration."

The minutes of this meeting were communicated forthwith in cipher to the Zionist Organization of the United States. This cipher privilege certainly was a logical one. From now on the Political Zionist organization in the United States began to take a hand in the shaping of British policy and in the ordering of British affairs.

After this the meetings between Sir Mark Sykes and M. Picot with the Zionist leaders were continued and also there were some less formal meetings between Dr. Weizmann and various British statesmen and publicists. The month of February ended with little more to note—unless to cast a commiserating eye at the innocent Arabs, moving northwards now, against Wejh, on the limits of the Hedjaz territory, touching as they thought for the first time the borders of their new independence. Wejh was on the coast, more than two hundred miles north and west of Medina, and the occupation of it would mean that the railway which fed Medina with life was threatened on the flank, and Medina itself was in danger of isolation if that railway were cut.

Lawrence was with Feisal, and they marched or rode, five thousand men on camels, through the desert towards their half-real, half-figurative goal. The Arabs did the last fifty miles on water, with nothing to eat. But they made little of this because of the stimulus which now they felt. "The advance on Wejh," says Lawrence, "was their biggest effort: the first time in memory that the manhood of a tribe with transport, arms, and food for two hundred miles, had left its district and marched into another's territory without the hope of plunder or the stimulus of blood-feud." A young Bedouin chief pointed out to Lawrence, one night, the hollows of the sand-valleys "winking with the faint camp-fires of the scattered contingents. He called me to look, and swept his arm round, saying half sadly, 'We are no longer Arabs but a People.'"

Next night, so well every man knew the purport of their great adventure, a sheikh of another tribe repeated much the same thought to him, an old man this time, Auda ibn Zuweid. He corrected Lawrence, who had spoken of their army, and said gravely, "It is not an army, it is a world which is moving on Wejh."

A further Arab contingent, coming from another direction, outstripped them and took Wejh, the guns of a British warship cowing the garrison and sailors being landed in co-operation. The tribes now were pouring to the banners. "The roads to Wejh swarmed with envoys and volunteers and great sheikhs riding in to swear allegiance." Feisal made them take oath on the Koran "to wait while he waited, march when he marched, to yield obedience to no Turk, to deal kindly with all who spoke Arabic and to put independence above life, family and goods."

Words echoing in the sands! March saw more practical achievements in London. The Foreign Office sent a note to the War Cabinet endorsing the advantages of British support of Zionism. The Russian revolution had broken out on the 12th, and it was thought that as many Jewish personages were involved in the revolution they might be rendered more favourable to a continuance of alliance with the Western Powers if given this sop. The Zionist leaders took advantage of the position to come out boldly against the Sykes-Picot Treaty. They knew of the general British project for internationalizing Palestine, but they had not known that this was already the subject of an Anglo-French agreement. But now they got information of it, of the principal lines of it, from a French source.

Mrs. Dugdale supplies an account of what was the situation then. "Dr. Weizmann's first interview with Balfour at the Foreign Office"— the fresh gain in status will be observed—"in March 1917 was concerned with difficulties arising from French and Italian claims in Palestine. Balfour suggested that, failing agreement with France, it might be best to aim at a joint Anglo-American Protectorate. Dr. Weizmann felt doubtful of the prospects of working under two masters, whose general principles of administration might be far apart. But he and his friends were much more perturbed by rumours of a Franco-British division of Palestine, leaving Tiberias and part of Galilee in French hands. This was in fact the line of the Sykes-Picot agreement, news of which had leaked out."

That there were Arab claims to Palestine which nonsuited those of any European State and that the country was peopled by Arabs were facts of course sedulously ignored by Lord Balfour. He and Mark Sykes advised the Zionist leaders to go to Paris and to Rome to press their case. This they did. First they decided to try and see the authorities of the Quai d'Orsay. Mr. Landman may be quoted again:

> Malcolm again rendered immense service to the Zionist cause. As a member of the Armenian National Delegation he was personally

> acquainted with the leading French officials in charge of Near Eastern affairs—especially M. Gout, M. Picot and M. de Margerie. They were the three key-men for the Zionist purpose. Malcolm went first alone to M. Picot, and prepared the way for Sokolov. Sokolov had previously tried to invoke the assistance of French Jewry in getting an audience from the French Government. He had not been successful. The '*Alliance Israélite*' had used every effort to dissuade him from talking Zionism to the Ministers.
>
> Even Baron Edmond de Rothschild, the devoted friend of Palestine and of the Zionist leaders, could not very well ask the French Government to depart in favour of England from its traditional role of protector of Christians in the Near East. The position was such that Sokolov doubted very much whether he would be given an audience at the Quai d'Orsay. With the help of Malcolm however all the difficulties were overcome, and the leaders of French Jewry, to their intense amazement and annoyance, read in the *Temps* that M. Sokolov had been received by M. Pichon, the Foreign Minister. Not only that, but they found that M. Sokolov had actually been invited to stay to lunch. M. Jacques Bigart and M. Sylvain Levi, both of the '*Alliance Israelite*' telephoned to M. Sokolov's hotel to make sure they had heard aright, and finished up by inviting Sokolov themselves.

The backing of the British Foreign Secretary and of other personages of the Government is overlooked in this account. It was very helpful to M. Sokolov, who besides had met M. Picot in London, on the morrow of the February 7th meeting. Picot had not been encouraging then, but when M. Sokolov paid his Paris visit in March the French diplomatist knew how strong was the support gathering in England behind political Zionism.

What is most notable in Mr. Landman's account is his frankness about French Jewry. The situation in Paris was what it had been in London. The chief French Jews did not like this perversion of Zionism nor the proposals for the appropriation of Palestine. M. Sylvain Lévi, the most distinguished of French Jews, who belonged to the College de France, remained an ardent opponent of the political theories.

M. Sokolov and his companions stayed about a month in Paris, and in the end prevailed over the French Government's reluctances. "How they prevailed does not come into this story," says Mrs. Dugdale. Nor will come into any story probably, though the promise of altering the attitude of the United States no doubt played its part. "The upshot was cabled across the Atlantic by M. Sokolov from Paris to the American Zionists on April 24th. The French Foreign Office had agreed that an Allied victory in the Middle East would mean recognition of Zionism." (Dugdale.)

In Italy it is doubtful whether M. Sokolov had as definite an agreement to cable. But he seems to have been satisfied enough with his Roman visit, where Sykes had prepared his way for him amply at the Vatican, the Consulta, and the British Embassy. His conversations at the Vatican turned on the situation of the Holy Places of Christendom. From Rome "each achievement," relate Messrs.Wise and de Haas in their joint work, "was cabled to Zionist organizations over British-controlled cables." British messengers delivered them too.

It was proof of the growing power of the Zionist leaders, of which this telegraphic complaisance was an outward sign, that they should have tried to secure the annulling of the Sykes-Picot pact. What is more they succeeded in doing so, or in securing what was tantamount to the annulment of the portions which affected them. Not only did the French Government admit the recognition of Zionism, though it had no place in the Sykes-Picot provisions, but the international zone was deleted from the text. Nothing was stated or disclosed officially, but internationalization vanished, *spurlos versenkt*. When the revised Sykes-Picot documents became the basis of the abortive Treaty of Sèvres in 1920, the clause providing for internationalization was gone. With that clause disappeared too the conscientious stipulation that the prospective international ruling body of Palestine must consult Arab representatives before disposing of the future of that country and of its Arab populace.

To quote the Petrograd memorandum, "it had met with opposition on the part of the influential Jewish circles." Or as a pamphlet written by Mr. Sidebotham puts it, "in 1917 our views on the war-settlement began to take on a more idealistic tinge, which was confirmed by the entry of the United States into the War."

This entry of the United States into the War had important effects in several ways upon the fate of Palestine. A statement of war-aims in the Near East was issued under the auspices of the Government, which was directed in particular towards the Jews of the United States. It ran:

> It is proposed that the following be adopted as the heads of a scheme for a Jewish re-settlement of Palestine in accordance with Jewish National aspirations:
>
> *1. Basis of Settlement.*
> Recognition of Palestine as the Jewish National Home.
>
> *2. Status of Jewish Population in Palestine generally.*
> The Jewish population present and future throughout Palestine is to enjoy and possess full national, political and civic rights.

3. Immigration into Palestine.

The Suzerain Government shall grant full and free rights of immigration into Palestine to Jews of all countries.

4. The Establishment of a Chartered Company.

The Suzerain Government shall grant a Charter to a Jewish Company for the colonization and development of Palestine, the Company to have power to acquire and take over any concessions for works of a public character, which may have been or may hereafter be granted by the Suzerain Government and the rights of pre-emption of Crown lands or other lands not held in private or religious ownership, and such other powers and privileges as are usual in Charters or Statutes of similar colonizing bodies.

5. Communal Autonomy.

Full autonomy is to be enjoyed by Jewish communities throughout Palestine in all matters bearing upon their religious or communal welfare and their education.

What was this "British" statement of war-aims in the Near East? Again nothing other than a Zionist document taken over and re-edited. It is the programme of the previous October, complete with references to the "suzerain," and with several other of the original phrases reappearing.

When first issued, as the October Programme, it had been termed a "basis for discussion" between the Zionists and Whitehall. The basis had crept up by now and had become the main structure of the Government's statement of policy; a magic formation.

It is worthwhile indeed to stop a moment here to recapitulate the magic steps by which Zionism reached the astonishing position gained in this April statement. Consider its stages. First of all political Zionism floats in the minds of some adepts. A few books giving its theories, in the Russian or German tongues chiefly, come to England. A handful of the adepts also transport themselves to England, and translate, in both senses of that word, their doctrines to this country. In the mind of a Cabinet Minister of their race the culture finds an appropriate medium for growth, and expands, till he eases what has been thronging his brain into a memorandum on paper. This passes to his colleagues and working through them develops, with additions from the original adepts, into a further memorandum, the Petrograd document, which half inquires about this Zionism, half supputates the advantages of patronizing it, if a satisfactory form for it can be found.

In order to supply this form, the doctrine is tabulated thereon by its original propagators, in a manner which they dub official, but, since they have no status, is official for them alone. This is presented to British ministers, to the Ambassador in Paris. Shortly afterwards it is recognized, or rather is accepted as an official presentation by the Government. Upon which those who presented it by an inevitable process themselves turn into official persons.

The next step is for the now official Zionist leaders to submit a document, the latest embodiment of all that has gone before, the October Programme, and this the Government says it will take into consideration, thereby half sharing it. Soon, and finally, comes the Government's own announcement of war-aims, which proves to be, in all that matters, identical with this October document. So what began as a remote idea in the heads of a few strangers, in the far parts of Europe, has now become the mind and the policy of the British Empire. And though this development has been crammed into three years, the violence of the process has escaped observation, and has appeared to be in the order of nature.

In reality the growth of political Zionism had not been natural at all. It corresponded to nothing so much as the mango-tree trick, now in this political version of it practised upon the greatest scale and with the nimblest sleight-of-hand in the history of conjuring statesmanship.

The same month that the mango thus blossomed, another fruitful event occurred. Lord Balfour left England to visit the United States. The chief purport of his journey was to weld relations with that country, now that she had joined the Allies in the field. In this purpose he succeeded admirably. But the sub-motive of advancing the Anglo-Americano-Zionist project was also fixed in his mind. He encountered Mr. Brandeis, the Zionist leader and confidant of President Wilson, the trump-card of Zionism in the United States, very soon after landing, at a White House party. "You are one of the Americans I had wanted to meet," Balfour said, and "a day or two later they had the first of one or two talks.... It seems from such notes of these conversations as survive that Balfour pledged his own personal support to Zionism. He had done it before to Dr. Weizmann, but now he was British Foreign Secretary." (Dugdale.)

> "Mr. Justice Brandeis seems to have become increasingly emphatic during the course of the British Mission's visit, about the desire of the American Zionists to see a British Administration in Palestine. He gave no great encouragement to the idea of United States participation, observing that the bulk of American citizens were still opposed to the War, and would not wish to undertake responsibilities outside it. Dr. Weizmann's letters and telegrams were keeping him shrewdly informed of the British point of view. England, Dr. Weizmann said, was not yearning to annex Palestine, and would hardly care to oppose the internationalization which would be fatal to Zionist hopes, except for the attraction which the idea of large-scale Jewish settlement was beginning to have for her. Hence, Zionist policy must be to keep to that simple demand for a British

> Protectorate, rejecting all other schemes which would tend to raise fresh jealousies, and bring about some form of joint control. The American Zionists grasped the point."

Whereon Mrs. Dugdale, from whom I have taken this further citation, discovers triumphantly (though surely somewhat tardily) that "A Jewish national diplomacy was in being."

The "simple demand for a British Protectorate" containing some form of "joint control" had been defined already in Dr. Weizmann's memorandum of two years before. In this he had said: "I therefore thought that the middle course should be adopted: viz., the Jews take over the country: the whole burden of organization falls on them, but for the next ten or fifteen years they work under a British Protectorate." Very diplomatically worded, indeed. In consideration of what the taking-over of the country by the Jews meant for the Arab inhabitants, the description of that process as "the whole burden of organization" would not have displeased the author of *The Prince*.

However it was expressed, the Protectorate plan was that which Brandeis and the political Zionists of the United States adopted, which Mr. Brandeis instilled into President Wilson. "Mandates," of course, were not yet imagined. Balfour, before his visit ended, told the President of the Sykes-Picot arrangement (as of other embarrassing secret treaties), but Mr. Wilson does not seem to have paid much attention to them. Balfour made no mention, as far as can be gathered, of the Anglo-Arab Treaty, and this skeleton in the cupboard does not appear to have been communicated to Mr. Brandeis either.

While the Foreign Secretary was still in the United States, there had been an attempt to communicate the news of the Sykes-Picot Treaty in a very different quarter. Sir Mark Sykes and M. Picot went together to Jeddah to disclose it to King Hussein. This was done on Sykes's initiative, though the fact that the new Russian Government had denounced the secret treaties which divided the Near East, and was believed to be preparing the publication of their texts, supplied the Government with an additional motive for frankness. "To lessen the shock," says Captain Liddell Hart, "Sykes and Picot were sent to the Hedjaz early in May so that they might explain to Hussein and Feisal the broad provisions of the treaty and the intentions of the British Government." Before they reached the Hedjaz our first offensive in Palestine, launched by Sir Archibald Murray on the 26th March, with the object of capturing Gaza as a preliminary to an advance on Jerusalem, had failed in its objective. A second attempt was also unsuccessful, and the capture of Palestine clearly became unrealizable for some while.

This altered the two emissaries' plans. "By the time they arrived," continues Captain Liddell Hart, "the collapse of the British offensive against Gaza had made the vista of Syria remote, and hence the two commissioners deemed it best to leave their treaty in a gentle haze when interpreting it to Hussein. In this they were helped perhaps by the difficulties of translation into Arabic." They were indeed. On the day they met—it was the 19th of May—Sir Mark Sykes treated King Hussein to a long speech in parliamentary style which no one quite understood, and least of all the interpreter, who was a Greek. What the Greek passed on in a sort of Arabic was still less understandable to Hussein, who cried, "I don't understand," and slapped his thigh, where he kept his McMahon Treaty in a special pocket of his robe. He would never let it out of his possession. Sir Mark tried another speech. The interpreter floundered still more. King Hussein slapped his thigh again, cried, "This is good enough for me," and the proceedings terminated. The visitors insisted no more, as King Hussein had grown angry. The impression left upon him by what he could make of Anglo-Hellenic-Arabic was that the motive of their journey was to get him to renounce for good, there and then, the Arab rights to the coastal districts of north Syria, from which he had only consented to "avert his eyes" till the War was over.

The Emir Feisal accompanied his father on this occasion, which occurred in the environs of Jeddah, and so did several of the Syrian leaders who were in the Hedjaz now. They and he, though no more informed than Hussein, were disturbed, and Feisal asked Colonel Newcombe, Lawrence's companion-in-arms, who was there, what it all meant. Newcombe, trusting the promises he had heard, said simply to Feisal that "whatever he took was promised to him." Sykes and Picot departed the next day.

Rumours by then of the Sykes-Picot partition had reached the Arab camp in a ragged, roundabout way, through the Turkish lines. Lawrence recounts how he dealt with "old Nouri Shalaan" who apparently had been sent to question him. Nouri bore a set of documents and asked which of the British pledges therein was to be believed. Like Newcombe, with less trust indeed, but with the same unwillingness to destroy faith, Lawrence gave a reassuring answer. "In his mood, upon my answer, lay the success or failure of Feisal. My advice, uttered in some agony of mind, was to trust the latest-in-date of the contradictions." It is obvious that old Nouri Shalaan's stamp-collection of British pronouncements did not contain the really recent issues.

About the same time Lawrence was asked by other Arab leaders to endorse the British Government's promises of Arab independence. He had had "no previous or inner knowledge of the McMahon pledges and the Sykes-Picot Treaty," but his foresight told him that "if we won the War the promises to the Arabs were dead paper. Yet the Arab inspiration was our main tool in winning the Eastern war. So I assured them that England kept her word in letter and in spirit. In this comfort they performed their fine things; but, of course, instead of being proud of what we did together I was continually and bitterly ashamed."

As soon as he did gain accurate knowledge of the Sykes-Picot arrangement Lawrence took another line, and told Feisal openly of it. "Fortunately, I had early betrayed the treaty's existence to Feisal, and had convinced him that his escape was to help the British so much that after peace they would not be able, for shame, to shoot him down in its [that is, the Sykes-Picot Treaty's] fulfilment; while, if the Arabs did as I intended, there would be no one-sided talk of shooting. I begged him not to trust in our promises, like his father, but in his own strong performance."

But Lawrence and his Arabs once more must give way, as they did in life, to the progress of Zionism in two continents. In May something novel occurred to political Zionism: it suffered a reverse, something much more important than the mere passing decline of interest chronicled earlier in this chapter. The opposition amidst the Jews themselves to political Zionism, of which so little ever has been heard, came to a head. It spread even—but this was a little later—to the Government sphere. A door was dragged open; a breeze of the open air came to the heated ante-chambers, and under the jugglers' cloth the mango stopped in its growth.

The origin of this reverse lay in the increasing number of persons who had come to hear of the advancing situation gained by the political Zionist programme. It had gravely disturbed the principals of British Jewry and it occupied the Jewish Press. On the 20th of May Dr. Weizmann, presiding over a special conference of delegates from the Constituent Societies of the Jewish community in Great Britain, had expounded in a public declaration the policy of his party. (I shall quote presently what he had to say.) Moved by this, four days later Messrs. Alexander and Montefiore, Presidents respectively of the Board of Deputies of British Jews and of the Anglo-Jewish Association, in the name of the Conjoint Committee of these two bodies, dispatched to *The Times* a manifesto of protest.

They declared that, in view of the statements and the discussions lately published relative to a projected Jewish settlement in Palestine on a national basis, the Conjoint Foreign Committee of the above-mentioned bodies deemed it necessary to put on record the views which they held. They began by declaring their sympathy with Zionism, if it were carried out in a non-political manner. They declared their adherence to the formula of March 1916 (Mr. Lucien Wolf's, which the Petrograd memorandum had shelved). They went on to say that the "establishment of a Jewish nationality in Palestine, founded on the theory of Jewish homelessness, must have the effect throughout the world of stamping the Jews as strangers in their native lands and of undermining their hard-won positions as citizens and nationals of those lands."

They pointed out that the theories of political Zionism undermined the religious basis of Jewry. The only alternative to a religious basis would be:

> "a secular Jewish nationality, recruited on some loose and obscure principle of race and of ethnographic peculiarity. But this would not be Jewish in any spiritual sense, and its establishment in Palestine would be a denial of all the ideals and hopes by which the survival of Jewish life in that country commends itself to the Jewish conscience and to Jewish sympathy. On these grounds the Conjoint Committee of the Board of Deputies and the Anglo-Jewish Association deprecates most earnestly the national proposals of the [political] Zionists.
>
> The second part in the Zionist programme which has aroused the misgivings of the Conjoint Committee is the proposal to invest the Jewish settlers [in Palestine] with certain special rights in excess of those enjoyed by the rest of the population, these rights to be embodied in a Charter and to be administered by a Jewish Chartered Company. In all the countries in which Jews live the principle of equal rights for all religious denominations is vital to them. Were they to set an example in Palestine of disregarding this principle they would convict themselves of having appealed to it for purely selfish motives. In the countries in which they are still struggling for equal rights they would find themselves hopelessly compromised."

The letter of protest ended with these words:

> "The [political Zionist] proposal is the more inadmissible because the Jews are and probably long will remain a minority of the population of Palestine, and it might involve them in the bitterest feuds with their neighbours of other races and religions, which would severely retard their progress and find deplorable echoes throughout the Orient."

It is superfluous to point out how far-seeing and how justified is this document. What a different situation both Britain and the Jews would have had in the Near East today if these counsels had been heeded. But, to quote Mrs. Dugdale, "Dr. Weizmann and his group were now making superhuman efforts to mobilize the scattered nation (that is the Jews) in every Allied country for a united demand for a British Protectorate over a Commonwealth in Palestine." These efforts naturally reached their maximum on British soil, and valuable adherents had been included in the mobilization. So the then Chief Rabbi wrote to *The Times* to say that the Alexander-Montefiore letter had not been authorized by the Board of Deputies or by the Anglo-Jewish Association, and that these bodies at large had not had an opportunity of considering its contents.

Lord Rothschild wrote too, from Tring Park, that "we Zionists cannot see how the establishment of an autonomous Jewish State under the aegis and protection of one of the Allied Powers" can, or could be subversive of the loyalty of Jewish subjects to the countries of which they were members. "In the letter you have published the question is also raised of a Chartered Company. We Zionists have always felt that if Palestine is to be colonized by the Jews some machinery must be set up to receive the immigrants, settle them on the land and develop the land, and to be generally a directing agency. I can only again emphasize that *we Zionists have no wish for privileges at the expense of other nationalities,* but only desire to be allowed to work out our destinies side by side with other nationalities in an autonomous State under the suzerainty of one of the Allied Powers."

It is I who have italicized some of the words of the noble lord. The anonymity of the Allied Power which was to be suzerain is respected magnificently in his communication. But its chief interest lies in the appearance in it at this early stage of the pretension that the Zionists "only desire to work out their destinies side by side with other nationalities." As years have gone by this plausible "side by side" gambit has figured more and more in Zionist strategy for the winning of Palestine. But Lord Rothschild doubtless introduced it with perfect honesty. He had given no attention to the implications of the phrase "side by side." The expression suggests, and is used for propaganda because it suggests, the existence of two persons or bodies of equal power working heartily together at one task from which they draw equal benefit and obtain equal aggrandisement. But when in fact, as is the case in Palestine, one body is powerful and the other powerless, one body rich and the other poor, one body expert and the other simple; when also the two bodies seek contradictory destinies, then it is mendacious to use the expression "side by side" for the adjacent display of their activities.

More striking though than Lord Rothschild's letter at this juncture was the rejoinder of Dr. Weizmann himself, writing as President of the English Zionist Federation. He made two points. The first was that "it is strictly a question of fact that the Jews are a nationality. An overwhelming majority of them has always had the conviction that they were a nationality, which has been shared by non-Jews in all countries." Undoubtedly the thesis thus put forward by Dr. Weizmann is one which can be argued, nor is it likely that the division of opinion upon it would correspond to the line which divides people upon political Zionism. It is not with Dr. Weizmann's first, but with his second point that I am concerned:

> "The Zionists [resumed he] *are not demanding in Palestine monopolies or exclusive privileges, nor are they asking that any part of Palestine*

> *should be administered by a Chartered Company to the detriment of others.* It always was and remains a cardinal principle of Zionism as a democratic movement that all races and sects in Palestine should enjoy full justice and liberty, and Zionists are confident that the new suzerain whom they hope Palestine will acquire as a result of the War will, in its administration of the country, be guided by the same principle."

This was Dr. Weizmann addressing himself to the readers of *The Times*, that is to say to the members of the British public. There can be no better comment upon his pleading than to set down again the terms in which the Zionist Organization, of which he was the leader in Britain, had addressed itself to the members of the British Government in its "Formal Statement" of the previous October:

> 1. The Jewish Chartered Company is to have power to *exercise the right of pre-emption of Crown and other lands and to acquire for its own use all or any concessions which may at any time be granted by the suzerain government or governments.*
>
> 2. The present population, being too small, too poor and too little trained to make rapid progress, requires the introduction of a new and progressive element in the population.

It seems beyond belief that having made representations of this sort to the Government in the autumn the Zionist leader should venture to declare to the public in the spring that Zionists demanded no privileges nor monopolies for themselves, and predicated for all races in Palestine full justice and liberty. But let us follow Dr. Weizmann further. The situation, to use the phrase of his own organization, requires the introduction of a portion of that speech of his of the 20th of May which in the first instance had induced Messrs. Alexander's and Montefiore's protest.

This was no chance utterance. The conference at which he delivered it was specially convened and was attended by a particular audience. It was held in order that "a communication on the political situation, as it affected the Jewish National movement, might be made to the Jewish societies through their delegates." Before speaking the orator consulted those members of the Government with whom he had had dealings, and his discourse was in agreed terms. The italics in the citation which I give are my own. Dr. Weizmann said:

> "I shall try to outline, as much as is possible to do so, what are our plans and how we think we shall be able to carry them out. And before I do so let me do away with one or two which perhaps I may call misunderstandings or what may be called wrong phrases. One reads constantly in

> the Press and one hears from one's friends, both Jewish and non-Jewish, that it is the endeavour of the Zionist movement immediately to create a Jewish State in Palestine. Our American friends went further than that, and they have even determined the form of that State by advocating a Jewish republic. While heartily welcoming all these demonstrations as a genuine manifestation of the Jewish national will, we cannot consider them as safe statesmanship. Strong as the Zionist movement may be, full of enthusiasm as the Zionists may be at the present time, it must be obvious to everybody who stands in the midst of the work of the Zionist Organization, and it must be admitted honestly and truly, that the conditions *are not yet ripe* for the setting up of a State ad hoc. States must be built up slowly, gradually, systematically and patiently.
>
> We therefore say that *while a creation of a Jewish Commonwealth in Palestine is our final ideal—an ideal for which the whole of the Zionist Organization is working—the way to achieve it lies through a series of intermediate stages. And one of these intermediary stages which I hope is going to come about as a result of the war is that the fair country of Palestine will be protected by such a mighty and a just Power as Great Britain. Under the wing of this Power Jews will be able to develop and to set up the administrative machinery which, while not interfering with the legitimate interests of the non-Jewish population, would enable us to carry out the Zionist scheme. I am entitled to say that His Majesty's Government is ready to support our plans."*

The first thing to be said about this speech is not pertinent to the immediate issue, the internal Jewish differences and the character of the proposed Chartered Company. But it is so pertinent to the supreme issues of the whole Palestine question that immediate reference to the point in question is necessary. The speech was made in May of 1917, two and a half years before the League of Nations came into being, and nearly three years before the Palestine Mandate was "conferred" on Great Britain. So that all the "Mandate" chicanery is excellently exposed by it. All the prating about "Britain's obligations" is exposed for the humbug it is. In the middle of 1917 the business had been privately arranged already. The "fair country of Palestine" was to go to Great Britain, and under her wing the Zionist scheme was to be carried out. The plan had been nurtured between the two parties, and Dr. Weizmann (unguardedly) had been allowed to affirm the British agreement to support the Zionist scheme. Good: there is no getting away from that.

Reverting to the immediate issue, four days after delivering his speech Dr. Weizmann wrote to *The Times* that Zionists were not demanding privileges or monopolies in Palestine. Yet what was his speech but a declaration that the whole Zionist Organization was working for that supreme monopoly, a Jewish Commonwealth, as he called it. Zionists, as he explained, under British rule would be able to set up the administrative machinery which would enable them to carry out this scheme in Palestine, through a series of intermediate stages. Gradually the country of the Arabs was to be turned into a Jewish one, and His Majesty's Government was ready to support this plan.

Plan is a polite name for the scheme. The reader may be left to judge it, and to judge especially the Government which supported it, in the terms which will spring most suitably to his mind.

Shortly after the publication of Dr. Weizmann's letter, a further manifesto was sent, on the 1st of June, again to *The Times*, by eighteen prominent Jews of British birth, who declared their solidarity with the protest of Messrs. Alexander and Montefiore. Amongst these were Lord Swaythling, Sir Matthew Nathan, Messrs. Isidore Spielmann, Ernest Franklin, Laurie Magnus and Israel Gollancz. Though the Weizmann influence was growing powerful the signatories received plenty of support from their fellow-Jews, and during the months which followed they continued their opposition to political Zionism. "Just as the leading French Jews tried hard," acknowledges Mr. Landman, "to keep Zionism away from their Government, so did the leading Anglo-Jews do their utmost to keep Zionism away from the British Government."

Mr. Landman details what happened next:

> "Sir Mark Sykes informed us that something must be done to impress the Cabinet, and the Zionist leaders were compelled to take up the challenge. It was absolutely essential to convince the Cabinet that Anglo-Jewry was Zionist in sympathy and outlook, in view of the constant denial of this which they heard from the leading Jews.
>
> A rapid campaign amongst the members of the Jewish Board of Deputies was organized, and when it was seen that a majority was obtainable, a pro-Zionist resolution was introduced and carried by a majority against the wishes and the speeches of the President, David Alexander, K.C., and other honorary officers. The President and Mr. Henriques resigned, thus leaving the field clear for the Zionists."

The only error in this is the presumption that all the Cabinet required convincing. Some members of it did not care to take action in the face of Anglo-Jewish recorded opposition. But Mr. Lloyd George and Lord Balfour were quite indifferent to the wishes of Anglo-Jewry. They were determined upon the political Zionist plan, and only desired that the Zionists should find them some means of evading, with greater or less reasonableness, the Jewish obstacle of which they took no heed in itself.

The whole matter, it should be added, despite the references of both Dr. Weizmann and of his adversaries to "constant discussions in the Press" passed unnoticed by the bulk of the British people. The Jewish Press, in which indeed it had held a large place, does not circulate outside the Jewish community. The daily papers read by the overwhelming majority of the public dealt cursorily with the passing Zionist crisis, if they dealt with it at all. The letters and the speech which I have cited were minor news during the space of a week, and though the letters did appear in the premier newspaper of the kingdom, it is not a journal read by millions. *The Times* itself consecrated a single leader to the subject, one which leaned to the Weizmann thesis, yet in *The Times's* best Tower-of-Pisa manner, impressively but without leaning too far.

With that the controversy dropped out of print, till on the 17th June came the meeting of the Conjoint Committee, of which Mr. Landman speaks. There was a hot debate, and the resolution disapproving the Alexander-Montefiore protest was passed by a majority of five votes, fifty-six to fifty-one. While Mr. Alexander resigned his Presidency of the Board of Deputies, on the other hand (which Mr. Landman does not record) the Anglo-Jewish Association stood by Mr. Montefiore. A singular pronouncement was made on this occasion by Lord Rothschild, who denied "most strenuously," but surely much more astoundingly, that "any Zionist plan had yet been submitted to the Government, or that any was contemplated which would not preserve the fullest possible rights to all inhabitants of Palestine irrespective of race or creed."

After this the battle of opinions was lost to public sight, but raged on upon its own field of action, and was transported too outside Great Britain. Feeling against the new doctrines of political Zionism rose in the United States. A number of protests were made there by leading Jews, chiefly upon the ground that political Zionism destroyed the Jewish religion as the core and the rallying-point of all Jewry. To the great credit of some who protested, they added that political Zionism meant unjust treatment and dispossession of the Arab population of Palestine.

The first point Mr. Jacob Schiff declared, "I believe that I am not far wrong if I say that from fifty to seventy percent of the so-called Jewish Nationalists are either atheists or agnostics and that the great majority of the Jewish Nationalist leaders have absolutely no interest in the Jewish religion."

At Buffalo, in June, the President of the Annual Convention of the Central Conference of American Rabbis thus addressed his audience:

> "I am not here to quarrel with Zionism. Mine is only the intention to declare that we as rabbis, who are consecrated to the service of the Lord, whose lips are to guard knowledge and from whose mouth the people are to seek the Law because we are the messengers of the Lord of Hosts, have no place in a movement in which Jews band together on racial or national

> grounds, and for a political State or even for a legally-assured Home. Upon us rests the obligation to take up and to sound unremittingly the keynote to which the Jew has ever given expression. The religious Israel, having the sanctions of history, must not be sacrificed to the purely racial Israel of modern planning. If it is sacrificed, the religious demand of the Jews of our age, apart from other considerations, cannot be satisfied."

In this address one of the root-fallacies of political Zionism was well exposed: Its invocation of "historic rights" on behalf of a mere piece of the most modern "town-planning."

On the second point Mr. Mayer Sulzbacher, who had been President of the Court of Common Pleas in Pennsylvania, spoke out well. His legal accuracy of mind stood him in good stead. "Democracy," he stated, "means that those who live in a country shall select their rulers and shall preserve their powers. Given these principles a Convention of Zionists" (such as the Political group was then holding) "looking to the government of people who are in Palestine would be in contravention of the plainest principle of democracy. It can have no practical meaning unless its intent is to overslaugh the people who are in Palestine and to deprive them of the right of self-government by substituting the will of persons outside, who may or may not ever see Palestine."

"Overslaugh" is a rare juridical word, of Dutch origin, meaning to pass over illegitimately the legal claims or rights of an individual in favour of any other unqualified person or persons. The judge used an exact description of the improper act which was preparing against the rights of the Arabs.

Opinion contrary to the proposals of the political Zionists manifested itself upon the Continent of Europe too. In Italy Signor Luzzatti, a former Prime Minister and himself a Jew, demanded that Jews should seek to live in Palestine as free citizens and not as sovereigns. In France M. Reinach announced himself to be a resolute adversary of Zionism. "Jerusalem belongs to all the religions," said this noted Jew. "We know its history for three thousand years. The Jewish kingdom endured scarcely five centuries." It was a pity he did not take up the point of its dimensions during those centuries.

But the issues raised by these pronouncements, both in America and in Europe, were met by their being ignored. In England, Mr. Lloyd George, Lord Balfour, Lord Milner and presently General Smuts, imbued with an indescribable mixture of false idealism, of ingenuity and ingenuousness, of biblical dilettantism and Hebrew pedantry, of expediency and of gratefulness and of bargaining statesmanship, were bent upon the political Zionist plan. Lord Cecil also (Lord Robert Cecil he was then), who had been in charge of the Foreign Office while Balfour was in the United States, was "already almost as convinced a Zionist as Balfour" (Dugdale). Dr. Weizmann expounded to him in the Foreign Office the "objections to an Anglo-French division of Palestine, which he called a Solomon's judgment of the worst kind" (Dugdale). No doubt they discussed this with entire seriousness, letting no thought intrude into their minds of what sort of a Solomon's judgment was the greater division of the whole of Syria.

Towards the end of April, according to Mrs. Dugdale, "the Foreign Office recognized *with some dismay*" (my italics) "that the British Government was virtually committed." But it is difficult to see how "the Foreign Office" can possibly have been dismayed by what the Foreign Minister found supremely encouraging. He returned home in June, delighted with the spread of the Zionist entanglement. In Washington he had proclaimed "I am a Zionist," and had come back to England "assured by his conversations with Brandeis, and by what he had learned from him of the President's attitude, that there would be active sympathy there" (Dugdale).

So it seems reasonable to assume that the dismay which Mrs. Dugdale attributes to the whole Foreign Office was confined to one or two of its members. Here at least is a further suggestion that in the said Office some men may have remembered the Arabs and our commitments to them. On the other hand the "conscience-group" may have been dissolved or dissipated by now and the dismay may have sprung only from fear that Lloyd George and Balfour were forcing the pace.

Meanwhile, in Paris the counterpart of the Foreign Office, the Ministry of Foreign Affairs, also had espoused the Zionist cause. M. Cambon produced on behalf of his Government a note which spoke of the Allied Powers, "as a deed of justice and of reparation," assisting by their protection "in the renaissance of the Jewish nationality in that land from which the people of Israel were exiled so many centuries ago."

This French recognition of Jewish nationalism in Palestine was cabled with exultation, need it be said, over the telegraph systems of the world. It was an obvious preliminary to a public pronouncement by the British Government, and the first formal step towards this was taken shortly after. Lord Rothschild and Dr. Weizmann called together on Lord Balfour at the Foreign Office and "put it to him that the time for a definite declaration of support and encouragement had come." (Dugdale).

Chapter 10

How the "Balfour Declaration" was written—Its real authors. Tactics of Judge Brandeis.—The "Brandeis regime". Jewish opposition in England.—Publication of the Declaration.

The arrival of the two Zionist delegates at the Foreign Office with their plea for a declaration of British support was no surprise of course to the Secretary of State. All the negotiations since February had tended to the sole end that Britain should adopt the Zionist cause publicly, and various formulas, such as that of the previous October, had been elaborated with this in view. The delegates' visit to Lord Balfour and their request for a pronouncement therefore were so much stage-play. It was not that the time had come for him to issue a declaration, but that the time had come for him, in the Army phrase, to be issued with a declaration. Balfour knew his role in a performance so much after his own mind: he took his cue, and asked the visitors for "a draft that he would put before the War-Cabinet for sanction."

His Majesty's Government, be it noted, was to define its policy in the forthcoming document. The Foreign Secretary's way of setting about this was to ask Dr. Weizmann, and his honorary companion, to furnish him with a draft of this policy of His Majesty's Government. As soon as he got it, Lord Balfour would put Dr. Weizmann's policy of His Majesty's Government before His Majesty's Government for approval. The walls of the Foreign Office without doubt have enclosed many a singular scene, but they might well have inclined together to hide from view the spectacle of a Secretary of State asking a visitor from Russia to give him a draft of his own Cabinet's measures. The situation was what is called Gilbertian, or would have been so but for the great issues of national honesty involved.

The Zionists at once set about preparing their draft out of their store of material. This was entrusted in August to a "Political Committee," composed of members of the Zionist Organization. Some of them were residents in this country; others were from various Continental countries, but from time to time, as they visited England, they were gathered in to serve. On the Committee were Messrs. Achad Ha-Am, Cowen, Ettinger, Hyamson, Marks, Sieff, Léon Simon, Tolkowski, Jabotinski, Harry Sacher; and Mr. Landman was secretary.

The names of these gentlemen are of great interest, since it was they, along with the noted leaders, who now (as far as Europe was concerned) set to work on framing what was to be known as the "Balfour Declaration." We owe our acquaintance with their share in the work in the first instance to the Zionist Organization, which in a mood of vainglory disclosed transactions in its reports which Whitehall would have kept secret.

Besides the above-mentioned collaborators, there were others who worked at the "Balfour Declaration," in the United States. Reference has been made already to the importance of Zionism in the United States as a factor in this affair. But not half, not a quarter enough is known of the immixture of American Zionists in the conduct of policy by their Administration, as by the British Administration. In writing this book, my outstanding regret is that I have not been in a position to cross the Atlantic to inquire into what happened in the political ante-rooms of the United States before the proclamation of the Balfour Declaration, and in particular into the circumstances under which President Wilson came to espouse the Zionist thesis. I do not mean by this that there is any reason for attack on the President's good faith. Not at all. He erred, it is fairly clear, through ignorance of the far-off country whose fate he attempted to settle. There was an excusable side to his ignorance; it was not the wanton ignorance of Mr. Lloyd George nor the determined ignorance of Lord Balfour. When rumours of the real conditions in Syria came to him, the President was responsible for one act at least which goes far to absolve his memory. None the less, without a full understanding of what occurred in what may be called the Court circles of the White House, any account of the story of modern Palestine must remain incomplete.

Some addition can be made, however, to what is known generally in this country concerning events in America, and it welds naturally into the tale of the few months which preceded the Declaration. It will be necessary with this aim to make a brief digression into past history before linking up again the American and European action in the summer of 1917.

A good deal in the United States sphere turns on the action of Mr. Louis Brandeis, who at the time had become without doubt the most influential Zionist in the country. He was a lawyer of proved ability, whom President Wilson had wished to make Attorney-General in the year before the War; but this fell through. In 1916, though, he was appointed to the Bench of the United States Supreme Court. The President himself affirmed the closeness of his relations with Brandeis. "I have tested him by seeking his advice," declared Woodrow Wilson, "upon some of the most difficult and perplexing public questions about which it was necessary for me to form a judgment." (de Haas.)

Brandeis indeed came next to Colonel House upon the double scale of friendship and of influence with the Chief of State. He had not been a Zionist from youth. His biographer, Mr. Jacob de Haas, had introduced Zionist doctrines to him in Boston, when he was already a prominent man. Brandeis made his first speech on behalf of the creed in 1913. "Early in the fall of 1914," adds Mr. de Haas, "Brandeis perceived the identity of purpose in American idealism and Zionist aims. Hence he did not hesitate to approach President Wilson, who sympathized fully with Brandeis's Zionist views, and then proceeded to discuss the future of Palestine with the British and the French Ambassadors in Washington."

It may be said therefore that Zionism began as a world-force in the United States. It was elevated there to the rank of a national consideration considerably before this occurred in England. This is an instructive and little-known point. Mr. de Haas goes on to give a curious piece of information. He says that Sir Cecil Spring-Rice, then our Ambassador in the United States, was already at that date in accord with the Zionist Palestinian policy. "He reported the British Government as favouring a programme for Jewish settlement in Palestine that was far more concrete than was later stipulated in the famous Balfour Declaration."

This talk of a "concrete programme" does not tally in the least with the attitude of Mr. Asquith, Prime Minister in the autumn of 1914. He had got no further along the Zionist road than to raise his eyebrows as he read Sir Herbert Samuel's initial memorandum concerning it. Nor did he ever get any further. What then is the explanation? Either Mr. de Haas is quite wrong in his facts, or some plan for "Jewish settlement" was elaborated and sponsored by other members of our then Cabinet without the knowledge of the Prime Minister. This seems altogether outrageous, despite the chaotic conditions in Whitehall during those early months of the War, which have been described in Chapter 7. A possible explanation may be that in the course of Sir Edward Grey's misty philanderings with the Zionist cause, some document from his chief reached the British Ambassador in Washington, and that by the time news of it had got through to the Zionist watchmen round the State Department and the White House, Grey's feelers had been exaggerated into a "concrete programme."

Another, and perhaps likelier, explanation would be that the document in question had its origin not in London but in Washington. One of the Zionist programmes in circulation was sent to England, to the Foreign Office. Any expression of benignity towards it, reported back to Washington, and retailed from person to person, easily might be turned into a proposal to adopt it.

What seems clear in any case is that a contact with political Zionism had been established by the British Embassy at Washington at the very beginning of the War. Nothing much appears to have come of it during 1915, but in the spring of 1916 the connection was resumed. The courting of the Zionists by our politicians was growing more definite: it was the moment of Grey's extraordinary dispatch to Russia. Diplomatic discussions, according to Mr. de Haas, were resumed with President Wilson and with the British Ambassador. He details the conditions of the time which led to this resumption, but does not indicate who carried on the discussions upon the Zionist side. But the assurances received, "reduced to a six-line memorandum with the initials 'W.W.' were wholly satisfactory," he concludes. More knowledge of the six-line Presidential memorandum would be worth having, but we shall not be far from the truth in assuming that it was a pledge of support for the claims of Zion in Palestine, if and when the chance came to push them.

Next year, with the entry of the United States into the War, the opportunity had come. President Wilson's situation was predominant in Allied counsels. In May, even before the Balfour Mission came to America, he "took occasion to afford ample opportunity for the discussion of Zionist Palestinian projects, and the occasion was not neglected." Again Mr. de Haas, from whom I continue to quote, might have been more explicit. (I think that I should explain that Mr. de Haas is one of the foremost Zionists of the United States. I do not agree with him, but I recognize in him a man anxious to expose the truth as he sees it, and to give facts. He takes his readers to the right door always, even if, as just above, he has a trick of only half opening the door for them. He played a principal part in the Anglo-Americano-Zionist pourparlers and is in a position therefore to give an authoritative account of what occurred.)

The situation in the early spring, before Balfour arrived, was rather curious. I summarize Mr. de Haas's account of it. The State Department, the United States Ministry of Foreign Affairs that is, was averse to a Declaration in favour of Zionist aims by Great Britain till both France and Italy should have chimed in. The President also, while determined to aid the Zionist cause, was opposed to a project of Balfour's, which was high in the air at the time, that the United States should take over or should share with Great Britain the prospective suzerainty of Palestine.

"Suzerain" was the word of the moment, figuring, as we have seen, in the various Zionist and other documents dealing with the future of Palestine. "Mandates" were not yet invented. What made the situation curious was that the United States were not at war with Turkey. "There was therefore some confusion for a time in the British Palestinian project [that is, confusion was produced by the project] which appeared to recognize the Suzerain Government. The belief that Turkey was to remain the Suzerain created considerable excitement, but after an exchange of heated and perplexing cables it was made manifest that the British by 'Suzerain' meant the United States, though they left a door open for themselves." Thus Mr. de Haas. As far as the question of suzerainty went, Lord Balfour's play with the idea of an Anglo-American condominium, or even an American stewardship, had been a diversion only. Neither of these ideas ever approached the sphere of practical politics.

The much more important point springing from the confusion of mind in the United States about the identity of the forthcoming Suzerain is that it shows the alienation of all those concerned from the realities of Palestine. They knew nothing about it. Foremost in ignorance was Mr. Brandeis himself, who in a speech had declared that "Zionism was not a movement to wrest from the Turk the sovereignty of Palestine." Since Brandeis, however he erred about Palestine, was in principle elsewhere a genuine democrat, it only shows how little he knew of Palestine, when he protested that he was not engaged in a movement to oust the Turks. He thought them to be the native occupants and inhabitants of the country, with natural rights to sovereignty, and evidently was as unaware of the Arabs as President Wilson was. Both the President and Brandeis were to learn of the Arabs later on, and to profit by what they learned in their different fashions.

The next step in Zionist progress in the United States came with the arrival of Lord Balfour, who brought a considerable Mission with him. Some of the details of his stay there have already been given, but there are others to add. He and the members of his Mission found the whole Administration, except in some degree the more wary and knowledgeable State Department, thoroughly fecundated with the Zionist thesis. This was the work in the main of Mr. Brandeis. He was a great organizer, very much what is called the practical man. His doctrine was that Zionists should not merely hold meetings and write literature to spread their views. Zionists might do these things, but what was essential was that Zionists should make themselves useful in all the emergencies and in the novel situations which a state of war upon American territory created. They had the advantage of relations through kinsfolk all about the globe. This doctrine was not entirely propaganda, of course; there was a spirit of true philanthropy in Brandeis. But at the same time it was propaganda; superb propaganda. If a United States senator, or civil servant, or soldier, or consul, or simple citizen found that he could generally be helped in his difficulties by some active, intelligent man, and learned, sooner or later, that he was a Zionist, the senator or civil servant or whatever he was quite naturally concluded that this Zionist idea must be a good one.

Mr. de Haas describes the Brandeis plan very clearly. To the defensive policy (of keeping the Zionist Organization clear of German influence, which was not so easy), "there was added," says Mr. de Haas, "a constructive and novel aggressive policy. By freely rendering service to American officials the American Zionist Organization won the friendship and the goodwill of those who could not be influenced permanently by importunate effort. The objective was not merely to maintain the esteem and the willing co-operation of President Wilson himself, but to permeate every avenue of his Administration, *and the whole British service in this country*" (my italics) "with a sympathetic understanding of Zionism."

Mr. de Haas had his own share in this campaign of useful usefulness. It was he who suggested to Brandeis the "Transfer Department," for example. The "Transfer Department" took over the transport of funds from persons in the United States to their relatives in the European and extra-European war-zones. Here is its author's description of it:

> "The Transfer Department served Jew and non-Jew alike, without cost to sender or recipient, and its ramifications extended through all the war-zones occupied by the Allies, and throughout Turkey, Syria, Palestine, to Trans-Jordan and Baghdad. It became a department that sought and found people worlds asunder. It safely delivered money under romantic circumstances and often at considerable risk to the messenger. Practically not a cent of the millions handled was lost. Starting by using the good offices of the U.S. Department of State (Foreign Office) as a means of communication and deposit, it became so successful and so reliable that it was employed by the Treasury of the United States to deliver moneys and messages which the Government could not handle successfully.
>
> An Arab in Boston desired to send a few dollars to a friend in Petra. A Greek in Terre Haute, Indiana, wanted to befriend someone in Anatolia. The Greek Church in the U.S.A. wanted to reach the Metropolitan in Constantinople. Jews wanted to help their families in Poland. Chadissim forced out of Jerusalem were located in the refugee-camps in Alexandria. Money collected in America found its way into the prison at Damascus, into the detention-camp at Aleppo, and even reached the prisoners at Broussa.
>
> For a time the green receipt of the Z.P.E.C. (Zionist Provisional Executive Committee, of which Mr. Brandeis was Chairman) Transfer Department was "current money with the merchants" throughout Palestine, and thus set at naught the Turkish decision to close the Zionist banks.
>
> ... Perhaps the senders appreciated what was done for them at no cost, perhaps afterwards some of them learned how gold was carried through the Taurus passes. This Transfer Department in its non-sectarian

> service was unique in Jewish history. The rank and file of Zionists probably never gave it a thought, but governments knew. They appreciated the endless improvisations in transmission which the changing war-front demanded, to the point that Embassies in European capitals advanced cash on the requisition of the Executive Secretary in New York."

These details given by Mr. de Haas speak for themselves. The "Transfer Department" was part of a general scheme which in itself was admirable. No one would wish to deny it the praise it deserves for its serviceableness to great and to small, for the humanity of its concept, and for the ability of its execution. But—as Mr. de Haas himself is at pains to show—it brought in its own rewards to the organization which created it. It put the United States Governmental machine, and in part the governmental machine of Allied countries, in a situation of moral debt to Zionism. It created an enormous predisposition in favour of the Zionist cause among a great many people, and particularly among those whose sympathy was likely to be valuable.

> Zionism [says Mr. de Haas] numbered its adherents in every American city. This vast army of humans was gradually inventoried, and as the need arose employed to render those services which in war time aroused the goodwill and the respect of those men whose signatures counted in great affairs. The cost of all such services, an infinitesimal amount, was paid by the Zionist organization. The returns were in a form of reliance on the capacity for performance which created wide confidence in the movement.

That is to say, to recast the somewhat involved final sentence, "men whose signatures counted" saw what Zionists could do, and gave their trust to a movement created by such capable men. Mr. de Haas cites, as an example of eventual guerdon, the privileges extended to the American Zionist Medical Unit, when it sailed for Palestine, which put it on a par with the American Red Cross organization. The passports of this Unit were stamped officially with the "Shield of David." Thus a national-international status was conferred on the Zionist symbol. How was this achieved? Not alone through friendship in the highest circles, be it noted.

> The open sesame which made such a combined act possible could not come from above. To the contrary, the task was accomplished from the ground up, and was only possible because under the Brandeis method of arousing individual interest in the cause, an appreciation of Zionism penetrated every Government department, and wherever needed *there was an understanding Zionist ready to smooth and cement the necessary contacts.* (My italics.)

As the Departments involved included the War Department, the Treasury, the Passport Division, the Navy and the Army, it will be seen how far Zionism held the passes in the United States. What chance had the Arabs in such a situation? How little they knew by the far Red Sea of the influences assembling to deny them their patrimony and to conceal their very existence.

I return to the active preparations for the "declaration of support and encouragement." In Washington, in that spring of 1917, Lord Balfour and his Mission fitted well into the Zionized Administration. Balfour "while in Washington summarized his own attitude in a single sentence, 'I am a Zionist.'" (He and Mr. Brandeis conferred, as we have seen.) "But while Balfour and Brandeis met as often as circumstances demanded, other Zionists met and discussed the Palestine problem with all those members of the British Mission whose understanding it was thought desirable to cultivate." (de Haas.)

Balfour returned home with a thoroughly cultivated Mission, gave his formal interview to Dr. Weizmann and Lord Rothschild, and the drafting of the Declaration began on both sides of the Atlantic. In England "many different versions of the suggested formula were drafted by various members of the (Zionist) Political Committee." (Zionist Official Report.) Drafts went back and forth to the Foreign Office.

They also went back and forth over the ocean. "A considerable number of drafts were made in London and transmitted to the United States, through War Office channels, for the use of the American Zionist Political Committee." (de Haas.) President Wilson himself lent a hand to the drafting, or at least bent a supervising eye upon the text of the suggestions from England. "The field of international discussion was accordingly widened, and all the drafts of the proposed Declaration were submitted for approval to the White House." (Wise & de Hass.)

Most of these earlier drafts were on the lines of the proposed Charter of the Jewish Company; of the War-Aims statement, Zionist in origin of course, issued in the previous April; of the October programme, and so forth. Generally they were elaborations, and the Government found them too long. "Some of the Zionist drafts were detailed and elaborate," says the Report of that Organization, "but the Government did not want to commit itself to more than a general statement of principle." Still apparently quite unable to produce such a statement itself, the Government set its Zionist prompters to work on a shorter formula.

The new general statement of principle was tabulated quickly. On July 18th, after it had been approved by President Wilson, Lord Rothschild forwarded the Balfour Declaration to Lord Balfour, and all seemed finished.

These were its terms:

> His Majesty's Government, after considering the aims of the Zionist Organization, accepts the principle of recognizing Palestine as the National Home of the Jewish people and the right of the Jewish people to build up its National life in Palestine under a protection to be established at the conclusion of Peace, following upon the successful issue of the War.
>
> His Majesty's Government regards as essential for the realization of this principle the grant of internal autonomy to the Jewish nationality in Palestine, freedom of immigration for Jews, and the establishment of a Jewish National Colonizing Corporation for the resettlement and economic development of the country.
>
> The conditions and forms of the internal autonomy and a charter for the Jewish National Colonizing Corporation should, in the view of His Majesty's Government, be elaborated in detail and determined with the representatives of the Zionist Organization.

This was the Declaration which Mr. Lloyd George and Lord Balfour would have issued, be it observed, but for something which now happened. It was the intention of the Government to recognize all Palestine as the National Home, and to give "internal autonomy" to the Jewish nationality from the start. Zionist immigrants were to land as rulers. Immigration was to be free, without obstacle, and the Chartered Company or Chartered Corporation, as it had become, was to "resettle" the country, as though it were empty.

But all was not finished. The above draft had been shown round a good deal by then, so that it had come to the knowledge of the chief personages of English Jewry.

Men like Lucien Wolf or Claude Montefiore or Sir Matthew Nathan had not been asked of course to take part in writing it themselves. They knew, though, that it was being prepared, and after they had procured its text they repeated their struggle of the spring. They sent to the Cabinet "representations antagonistic to Zionism." That is how the Zionists describe the signatories' protest against the proposed Declaration.

The result was that the Cabinet had the Declaration redrafted. The Chartered Company disappeared, though a reason for this may have been that its promoters found difficulty in raising adequate funds to launch it.

The new formula was:

> 1) His Majesty's Government accepts the principle that Palestine should be reconstituted as the national home of the Jewish people.
>
> 2) His Majesty's Government will use its best endeavours to secure the achievement of this object and will discuss the necessary methods and means with the Zionist Organization.

This was ready on September 18th, after two months of negotiations and exchanges of views with various parties. It was approved by President Wilson. But the British Jews who had opposed its predecessor fought as resolutely as ever against the new version. This still handed over all Palestine for "reconstitution" to the Zionist Organization, and under the second clause autonomy and free immigration and the other provisions of the July text could be introduced at once.

Edwin Montagu, Sir Philip Magnus and their associates in British Jewry by the stand they made enjoy the everlasting credit of having prevented either of these Balfour Declarations, of July or September, from being issued. It is a rider of importance upon the character of political Zionism that it was Jews who prevented it from carrying out the arbitrary seizure of Palestine which it intended. The Arabs therefore owe a great debt to these upright Jews.

What stands out most, though, is that but for their action the British Government too would have handed over Palestine to the Zionist Organization. In both formulas the Government passed the Arabs by completely, as though they did not exist. Here therefore is an absolute answer to the countless subsequent protestations during twenty years that the British Government never, never intended to put Palestine into Zionist hands. These protestations are falsehoods. Mr. Lloyd George, Lord Balfour and their confederates in the matter did so intend. Here is the documentary proof of it.

But now, faced once more with the difficulty of issuing on behalf of Jews a document against which Jews fought might and main, the Prime Minister and the Foreign Secretary were driven to have the Declaration remodelled again. A new draft was prepared. It was sent to Dr. Weizmann, M. Sokolov, Sir Philip Magnus, Mr. Montefiore, Sir Stuart Samuel, Mr. Leonard Cohen and to the Chief Rabbi (Dr. Hertz), with a request for their opinions upon it in writing. Mr. Landman speaks of this as a move upon which a great deal hung, but it is hard to believe this. The Government knew that a majority of those consulted would be in favour of the new draft, which, if not all that previous drafts had been, yet remained satisfactory to the political Zionists, who, as will be seen, had their usual part in its compilation.

In the new draft Palestine was no longer mentioned as the National Home of the Jewish people: instead the Government signified its desire to establish "a National Home for the Jewish people" in Palestine. A vast deal of printers' ink and a vast deal of speakers' breath has been wasted upon the exact significance of this change of formula. All that it signified in fact was a lack of courage on the part of the Governmental persons involved.

Confronted with Jewish opposition, they took fright at announcing that they would patronize the turning of Palestine en bloc and at once into a Jewish National Home.

They decided to announce their patronage only of a first instalment of this process. They suffered no change of heart: they did not reconsider their position in the light of the McMahon-Hussein Treaty: they made no effort to consult any Arab representatives or to preconize as essential and to promise such a consultation as soon as it should be possible. They went on with their illegitimate deal, but they phrased it differently and began to develop it more warily.

The men who had forced them to this more cautious action were not deceived. Mr. Leonard Cohen, the Chairman of the Jewish Board of Guardians, Mr. Montefiore and Sir Philip Magnus, who was Member of Parliament for London University, continued to protest on behalf of British Jewry. One of their chief objections was to the maintenance in the text of the word "National." They were quite right in this, of course, for the retention of the "National" qualification was of paramount importance. "National" was a key-word.

For Jews to have not a social or religious home, but a "National Home," meant that the germ of the future Jewish State in Palestine was implanted in the formula. Also the attribution of a national quality to the so-called "Home" extricated the Jews who formed it from allegiance to any State founded upon the popular suffrage of all denizens of Syria or of any section of Syria.

Zionist apologists of all shades do not pay much attention to this point. They prefer to sheer away from the clear implications of the maintenance of "National" in the new draft, and to lose themselves in empty dialectic upon the different effect of a definite or an indefinite article in front of that word, upon the rival meanings of "a National home" and "the National home." But there is no reason at all for the reader who wishes to get to the bottom of the business to waste his time upon Lord Balfour's little Janus-faced parts of speech.

Despite the efforts of Sir Philip Magnus and his friends, this key-word "National" was kept in succeeding drafts by the Government. The political Zionists insisted upon it and so, for the matter of that, did their supporters in the Cabinet. But the opposition did not give up battle. A staunch advocate and leader was found in Mr. Edwin Montagu, who, as Secretary for India, could put the case to the Cabinet itself. Faced with Balfour's just quoted July draft, or rather the Zionist draft Balfour patronized, he had "opened his offensive in late August with a memorandum of passionate protest." (Dugdale.) What is more, he carried the day. For a brief period the Government of Great Britain was about to drop its pro-Zionist policy.

We have the testimony of Mrs. Dugdale for this. "The Cabinet," she says, "was more than shaken, for on September 24th, Balfour replied to a grumble" (against the delay) "made by one of his own F.O. people, 'Yes. But as the question was (in my absence) decided by the Cabinet against the Zionists I cannot do anything till the decision is reversed.'"

As his niece points out, Balfour was in no doubt about being able to have the decision reversed. The conditions under which the Cabinet met then will have helped him, quite apart from his own power. The meetings of the War-Cabinet were very variably attended. Balfour himself was not a member, but had been invited by Mr. Lloyd George to come as often as he liked. He attended by deputy sometimes: he or his deputy were present at four-fifths of the meetings. General Smuts also had a free invitation to be present that summer. Regular members were the Prime Minister, Lords Curzon and Milner, Messrs. Bonar Law and Henderson, Sir Edward Carson. Sittings were very numerous; every morning, and on occasion even two or three times a day. A lot of other people often were present, since members of the War-Cabinet could bring in departmental officials and experts to give testimony or advice. Sometimes the business before the Cabinet was decided there and then by all its members, but the business might equally well be left for individual members to submit a decisive report upon it, or might be left for settlement to a committee. Everyone was at the highest tension and very overworked.

Montagu had prevailed at some gathering of this loose assemblage. It was not difficult for Balfour to turn the tables when Montagu was out of the way. Montagu, unfortunately for Palestine, had to depart on the 14th of October on a pre-arranged voyage to India in connection with the reforms which bear his name. Of the other members, besides Balfour, Smuts, Milner and Henderson (and Barnes who succeeded Henderson) were all pro-Zionist. "Lloyd George, the Premier, bluntly stated that he could not understand the anti-Zionist Jews. Mr. Balfour, General Smuts, Lord Milner and Mr. Barnes, the representative of Labour, were all frankly in favour of a declaration, and naturally they too were perplexed by the attitude of the Jewish opposition." (de Haas.) No doubt Mr. Lloyd George was blunt, but I doubt whether he failed to understand the anti-Zionist Jews' arguments. What he will not have understood was their allowing their feelings to interfere with the grasping of a ripe opportunity, full of political dividends. It is characteristic enough of this extraordinary politician, who always has been saving his country on Monday and ruining her on Tuesday, that he could entrust to Mr. Montagu's ability the most far-reaching changes of policy in our Eastern Empire, while he could refuse to listen to his advice upon a subject to which Montagu brought this same ability and in addition every endowment of blood and of experience.

In 1923, at his house in London, Edwin Montagu spoke to me himself at some length upon the way in which the pro-Zionist declaration was pushed through by the Prime Minister and Lord Balfour. It was a personal conversation, much on the lines of that which I had with Asquith, but longer and fuller, and it was Montagu himself who asked me to visit him. He said that not the slightest consideration was given to our previous pledges to the Arabs. The whole question was treated as a close preserve between Great Britain and the Zionists.

Nothing was thrashed out properly. As the autumn came on, members of the Cabinet were overwhelmed with their several duties and with the general crisis of the time, when the Allies' fortunes were at a very low ebb indeed. There was a marked disposition for each Minister to stick to his particular province and to accept the word of the others upon theirs. The Premier and Balfour tried to push the Zionist project briskly through, both of them possessed with an *idée fixe*. Up to the time of his departure for India, said Mr. Montagu, the terms of the Declaration and its consequences had never been properly analysed by all members of the Cabinet, and certainly had not been grasped by the non-partisan members after a fashion which would enable them to hold out against their pro-Zionist colleagues.

Even so, some resistance or some doubt did survive in the Cabinet, chiefly through Lord Curzon, and this was reinforced by the continued Anglo-Jewish opposition outside. Curzon was unconvinced by political Zionism. Towards the end of October he penned a memorandum on Palestine in which he detailed a policy there such as Lucien Wolf had set forth, by which all creeds would be secured in peaceable possession of their Holy Places, all individuals secured in equal rights, and "some scheme for land-purchase and for the settlement of returning Jews might be undertaken."

"If this be Zionism," wrote Lord Curzon, "there is no reason why we should not all be Zionists, and I should gladly give my adhesion to such a policy. But in my judgment it is a policy very widely removed from the romantic and idealistic aspirations of many of the Zionist leaders whose literature I have studied, and whatever it does, it will not in my judgment provide either a national nor material nor even a spiritual home for any more than a small section of the Jewish people."

This shows that Lord Curzon's attitude was somewhat entangled. He thought that the demerit of the policy of which he approved was that it did not embrace many Jews. He did not approve, though, of "romantic" political Zionism, which did embrace many. His position is complex. His opposition to the Declaration evidently was not on the strongest grounds, and he gave way at last.

He may have been forced to give way. In the end, as the pronouncement went on hanging fire, the Zionists lost patience or grew disturbed and brought pressure to bear through the United States. "The leverage for forcing action was in the United States," says Mr. de Haas, and again, "Dr. Weizmann looked for American support to counteract the opposition in London, where the political situation was somewhat disconcerting." Hints were given to the British Government (not for the first time) that Zionism might be driven into the arms of the enemy. A final memorandum asking for the Declaration was handed to Lord Balfour by Lord Rothschild and Dr. Weizmann. This suggested that

> "the problem be considered in the light of imperial interests and of the principles for which the Entente stands.... We therefore now humbly pray that this declaration may be granted to us, and this would enable us to further consolidate Jewish public opinion in the Entente countries *to counteract all the demoralizing influence which the enemy Press is endeavouring to exercise by holding out vague promises to the Jews.*" (de Haas and Wise)"

The italics are mine. Other pro-Zionist testimony (given to me myself in 1923) is more explicit still. It was considered that in an article of mine I was not doing justice to Dr. Weizmann's services to the Allies (which indeed I do not think of questioning), and I was informed that at the juncture under consideration he "by his personal intervention turned the Zionist scale to the side of the Allies and defeated a standing German offer which at the time was being considered seriously by the non-Allied branches of the Zionist Organization."

It was after the above warnings and the Rothschild-Weizmann ultimo-memorandum, so to speak, that the American influence was brought to bear decisively. Writers to the Zionist signet deal with this last stage in different ways. Mr. Leonard Stein confines himself to saying that "there was some delay before a public statement was formally approved by the Cabinet," though of an earlier phase he mentions that "when the hour of decision was reached in the middle of 1917 the President supported the Zionists with the full weight of his influence."

Mr. Philip Graves puts it that, "Finally the negotiations came to a successful issue, owing in part to the intervention of President Wilson, who had been approached by Mr. Justice Brandeis, one of the best-known American Zionists." The official Zionist Report, compiled in Europe in an atmosphere jealous of the increasing American control, says that the

President sent "a personal message to the British Government, intimating his agreement with the idea of a pro-Zionist announcement."

We must turn to Messrs. Wise and de Haas for genuine knowledge of what occurred. Mr. de Haas's individual version is: "The American ascendancy in the war-councils led the British to ask for President Wilson's consent and approval of the terminology of the declaration before its issuance. *The draft cabled from Government to Government was handed to the Brandeis regime for its approval.*" (My italics.)

No bettering is possible of the phrase found by the author to describe at once those who then managed the President and the character (as regards Palestine) of the Administration—"the Brandeis regime." The text sent by the British Cabinet for approval in these quarters was thus worded:

> "The Cabinet after preliminary discussion suggest the following amended formula—His Majesty's Government view with favour the establishment in Palestine of a National Home for the Jewish race and will use its best endeavours to facilitate the achievement of this object, it being clearly understood that nothing shall be done which may prejudice the civil and religious rights of existing non-Jewish communities in Palestine or the rights and the political status enjoyed in any other country by such Jews who [sic] are fully contented with their existing nationality and citizenship."

This was passed to the Brandeis regime, which was not satisfied with the finish of the British version—in the small degree that this multigenerate mixture was British. Mr. Wise and Mr. de Haas subjected it, in their own words, "to the most necessary revision." In the view of the members of the regime it placed Zionism "on a principle of discontent, which is most undesirable." "They therefore proposed to Colonel House on October 15th to limit the final clause to read 'or the rights and political status enjoyed by Jews in any other country.'" "The final draft," they explain in their joint work, *The Great Betrayal*, "was amended by the authors of this book. After consultation with Justice Brandeis it was submitted to Colonel House, who transmitted this version to President Wilson, upon whose agreement and express authority the final text was issued by the British War Cabinet."

It was on the 17th of October that Wilson cabled his approval of this text as amended by Messrs. Wise and de Haas. By now, the character of the declaration should be clear enough for anybody. The Declaration was not only in England based upon Zionist drafts, but the American share in it, what is called the "American share" under the assumption that it was the work of the President or of his Ministers, was also Zionist work. Mr. Wilson and Colonel House were but automata signing or transmitting ex-parte texts, which were given all the prestige which should have been attached only to the independent pronouncements of the President and Administration of the United States.

With this edifying state of things the story of the immediate origins of the Declaration and of the circumstances of its issue comes to an end. In London the word "race" was changed to "people": the de Haas-Wise alterations were accepted. There was a fortnight's delay before the pronouncement appeared on the Cabinet's agenda. On the 2nd of November the final scene of all was played.

Some of the Zionist leaders must have been waiting in an adjoining chamber on that day, for the event, as Mr. Landman records, was announced by Sir Mark Sykes (who later was to regret his part in all this). He came excitedly out of the Cabinet Room, and ejaculated very appropriately to the group of assembled fathers, "It's a boy."

Officially, the product of polyandry was dispatched in the form of a letter from the Foreign Secretary to Lord Rothschild, as follows:

> Foreign Office,
>
> November 2nd, 1917.
>
> "Dear Lord Rothschild,
>
> I have much pleasure in conveying to you on behalf of His Majesty's Government the following declaration of sympathy with Jewish Zionist aspirations, which has been submitted to and approved by the Cabinet.
>
> His Majesty's Government view with favour the establishment in Palestine of a national home for the Jewish people, and will use their best endeavours to facilitate the achievement of this object, it being clearly understood that nothing shall be done which may prejudice the civil and religious rights of existing non-Jewish communities in Palestine or the rights and political status enjoyed by Jews in any other country.
>
> I should be grateful if you would bring this Declaration to the knowledge of the Zionist Federation."
>
> Yours sincerely,
> Arthur James Balfour.

Nothing more cynically humorous than the final couple of lines of this letter has ever been penned.

Chapter 11

Analysis of the Balfour Declaration. Its sham character and deceptive phraseology.

There is a great deal which has to be said now concerning the Declaration which, like water seeking its source, came to the Zionist leaders on that 2nd of November in 1917. But the first thing of all to be said of the Balfour Declaration is that it was a pronouncement which was weighed to the last pennyweight before it was issued. There are but sixty-seven words in it, and each of these, save perhaps the Government's title and a few innocent conjunctions, was considered at length before it was passed into the text.

This too memorable document is not so much a sentence of English as a verbal mosaic. Drafts for it travelled back and forth, within England or over the Ocean, to be scrutinized by some two score draftsmen half co-operating, half competing with one another, who erased this phrase or adopted that after much thought. At long last, out of the store of their rejections and of their acceptances the final miscellany was chosen, ratified and fixed. There never has been a proclamation longer prepared, more carefully produced, more consciously worded.

Commentators of all views agree upon this. In his *Zionism* Mr. Leonard Stein says, "The Balfour Declaration was by no means a casual gesture. It was issued after prolonged deliberations as a considered statement of policy." In Temperley's *History of the Peace Conference of Paris,* it is stated that "before the British Government gave the Declaration to the world, it had been closely examined in all its bearings and implications, and subjected to repeated change and amendment." M. Nahum Sokolov, in his *History of Zionism*, another fundamental work, writes that "every idea born in London was tested by the Zionist Organization in America, and every suggestion in America received the most careful attention in London." "The Balfour Declaration was in process of making for nearly two years," writes Mr. Wise, who indeed was in a position to know. "Its authorship was not solitary but collective." Mr. Lloyd George himself, speaking in Wales in 1930, assured his hearers, in curious terms, that the Declaration "was prepared after much consideration, not merely of its policy but of its actual wording."

So there is one point upon which there is no doubt. Whatever is to be found in the Balfour Declaration was put into it deliberately. There are no accidents in that text. If there is any vagueness in it this is an intentional vagueness. If it is vague, the admiral is vague who orders his destroyers to emit a smoke-screen.

It is most important to have this established before more is said, for the reason that for some time past the controversy concerning Palestine, in so far as the Declaration is concerned, has been given a false turn. A secondary apologia has been evolved, which bypasses the bona fides of Lord Balfour's pronouncement to concentrate upon its terminology. It is described as "uncertainly phrased," or as "containing implications not foreseen when it was written," or as "not so definite as was thought"; or contrariwise it is said that "too much has been read into it."

Behind this apologia often enough there may have lain a good intention. The Balfour Declaration, alas! has been made by a series of our Governments the pedestal of British policy in Palestine. Because of this a number of persons have reasoned that the Declaration must be accepted as it stands, "with all its imperfections." Scrutiny of it might reveal that it was written in bad faith. But to expose bad faith in the Declaration would be the same as exposing it in the conduct of the country itself, since one Government of Great Britain published it and subsequent Governments have confirmed it. The people who have shrunk from scrutinizing it may not have put their thoughts to themselves as starkly as that, but it was thus they did think in their hearts' recesses. Therefore, as they conceived, the only course which lay open to them, if the country's honour was to be saved, was to assume that the Declaration had been loosely composed, and to lead the controversy on to that ground. They made great show of riddling out what it meant, with a little deprecatory criticism thrown in.

In this way they could escape perhaps having to acknowledge that this nationally issued and nationally endorsed document was nothing but a calmly planned piece of deception. That is why for years past we have heard statesmen, publicists and politicians, and members of the public too, assert that the authors of the Declaration either did not mean what they appear to say in it, or did not succeed in saying in it what they meant. Other apologists have given their own interested versions of its meaning. In this order were the explanations of Mr. Winston Churchill, as intricate and as lasting as worm-casts in the sand.

Behind excuses and shifts of the kind there may lie, in this way, something of good intention. But it is an intention deplorably translated into practice, and I am not going to follow the example thus set. Since the Balfour Declaration was without excuse, I see no reason to excuse it.

There is no pleasure in taking such a course (as I have said before now): there is no relish in exposing one's country or in exposing at least the men who spoke in her name. But the world of 1939 has no room for displays of patriotic cowardice. Nor is there any sort of advantage in them. We want an England which can confess her sins, and thereafter take her place at the head of the nations in the strength of her cleared conscience.

With this borne in mind, let us return to the Declaration. It reached the general public on the 9th of November, when Lord Balfour's letter was reproduced in the newspapers. It was given forth, of course, under the guise of an entirely British communication embodying an entirely British conception. Everyone concerned was made the victim of this false pretence. The British people were given to believe that it was an unadulterated product of their own Government. To the mass of Jews it was presented as a guarantee sprung of nothing but the conscience of the Cabinet—and thereby it served to allure them towards political Zionism. As for the Arabs, when it was proclaimed eventually upon their soil (which was not till much later), to them too a text in which Zionists of all nationalities had collaborated was announced as the voice of Britain. They were told that it was a pledge made to the Zionists: they were not told that the Zionists had written most of it. They were asked to respect it on the ground that it was given to the world by the British Government out of its native magnanimity, after the said Government had extended its profound, solitary and single-minded consideration to the "problem of Palestine."

Let me be quite clear about this. The onus of deception does not lie upon the Government of 1917 because before issuing its Declaration it consulted the Zionists. As far as the mere form of the proposed pronouncement went (leaving aside other considerations), the Zionists could have been asked quite reasonably to submit their ideas upon the species of "support and encouragement" for which they hoped. The Government could have examined whatever the Zionists submitted, and have consulted further with them, till both had agreed upon a final text. Had this text been published for what it was, an agreement between the two parties which the British Government was willing to sponsor, then the form of the Declaration would have been blameless. The form would have been honest, even if the policy was indefensible.

When however the bipartite Declaration—and to call it bipartite even is to swell the Governmental share in its drafting—was given out as the composition of His Majesty's Government alone, a plain deception was committed. In subsequent years too these synthetic *ipsissima verba* have been paraded with unyielding obstinacy to the Arabs as a sacred obligation of Great Britain to the Jews, even after it had been disclosed that all the time various Zionists had themselves framed the obligation to themselves. This makes later Governments partakers in the deception of the 1917 Cabinet, a deception only mitigated by culpable ignorance in the case

The Zionists themselves are in a better position in the matter than their British collaborators are. To do them justice, it was they who made known the real conditions under which the Declaration was composed. They did so after an interval which I cannot give exactly, since I have not read all Zionist publications and writings that ever were. But the Zionist Organization certainly had divulged its share in the Declaration within four years of its publication, and for all I know this may have been divulged earlier. I shall not say that the motives of the Zionist Organization were of the first rank. Everything seemed to be going swimmingly for their cause then and some members or other of the Organization staff could not resist gathering kudos in the eyes of the mass of Zionist supporters by disclosing the important part which their body behind the scenes had taken in the Declaration. Still, their statement was a frank one.

And now to analyse the text of the Declaration. "*His Majesty's Government view with favour the establishment in Palestine of a national home for the Jewish people....*" This first clause is often printed with the words "national home" with capital initials. But in the original copy, as reproduced in *The Times*, Lord Balfour used the discreeter apparel of what printers call "lower-case" letters for his protégé. Neither he nor his colleagues can claim the invention of this title, which has been imagined by Leon Pinsker in Odessa thirty-five years before. Pinsker himself did not intend it to apply to Palestine. He said, "We must not attach ourselves to the place where our political life was once violently interrupted" (Stein), though he did his best to establish colonies there as elsewhere. But Balfour and his colleagues adopted the title from the Zionist programmes and drafts, and made use of its ambiguity. For most people in 1917 "National Home," with or without capitals, was a new phrase. Naturally no one could give it a meaning, for it had no established meaning, and was put into practice in Palestine without one.

But in a formal document announcing the support of the British Government for this institution, it was indicated by all rules of statesmanship that ere committing itself to such support, the Government should define for the nation what exactly it was supporting. Not to do so was to pledge (without touching on the right to give a pledge) the aid of Great Britain for no one could say what. The same culpable lack of definition was to be found in the preamble, wherein the Declaration was described as "a declaration of sympathy with Jewish Zionist aspirations," but no clue was supplied to these desires. What were Jewish Zionist aspirations? They were not identified. How could a British Government guarantee its sympathy to an enigma?

The truth of course is that these unfathomable phrases were employed just because they were unfathomable and could be interpreted to pleasure. They had the air of promising Government support of what the Zionists wanted in Palestine, a Jewish State, to be reached through a fictitious condominium of Jew and Arab. This was the meaning which the Zionists who helped to draw up the Declaration accepted in the end, and this was the meaning which Zionists and Jews in general were given to understand the Declaration would hold.

They were disappointed no doubt that they did not receive full ruling rights immediately. But they were confident that they could engender conditions in Palestine involving a more rapid finish for the transition period than might be expected. The Government on its part did mean to give as much of the Zionists' sense to the Declaration as was safe, from the very start. As the margin of safety grew, as its own hold on the land became stronger, as a menial prosperity enticed the mass of Arabs, and the opposition of the remainder had been measured and met, then the Government would increase its support of the Zionist establishment in widening degrees, till the Jewish State at last arose.

On the other hand, the Government kept a way of retreat open in case some formidable opposition, in Britain or outside, might make headway against official alliance with political Zionism. In that event, the Declaration was phrased so that it could be explained away as nothing but an expression of unengaged, friendly interest in the Zionist movement. If it came to that, what *did* "view with favour" amount to as a gage of support? Pretty little. It could be taken to signify no more than that the Government would cast a benign eye upon the "national home," pleased if the Zionist plans worked out, regretful but quite unimplicated if they failed.

To sum up: the paths of the Government and of Zionism had crossed: the Government had liked the wanderer's look: the pair had dallied, and then they had agreed to walk on together. So far so good. But if trouble arose on the way before home was reached, well, the path which the Government had crossed the Government, in a manner of speaking, could cross again.

The final drafting of the Declaration was a great play of wits, in fact. The opposition to the previous drafts had brought it home to the Government that it must be more careful. So in the final draft, while still conceding everything to the Zionists in its own intent, the Government achieved a wording which would allow it an exit, if needs were, from any definite obligation of any kind. In this the Governmental drafters outwitted the Zionist drafters, who thought that they had the Government securely tied up. The Government was anxious for these ties, which it had invited, but it preferred now to draft so that even they could be slipped in the last resort. All first-class chicanery, but how far fitting in a Declaration by Great Britain is another matter.

In the succeeding clause the same dubious skillfulness prevails as in the first. The Government *"will use their best endeavours to facilitate the achievement of this object."* What is to be understood of this facilitation? To "facilitate" may signify to lend a hand, actively, but also it may just as well signify to put no hand in the way, passively. The sentence in fact is composed upon the same lines as its predecessor, that is, it covers the private intention of giving active help, provides a public screen of passive interest, and in the last resort contains a way out. As in the preceding sentence the situation of the Zionist drafters was that they considered that the nucleus of their special intentions was contained in the words used.

However, it is not till we reach the third and final clause of the Balfour Declaration that its character is quite revealed:"... *it being clearly understood that nothing shall be done which may prejudice the civil and religious rights of existing non-Jewish communities in Palestine or the rights and political status enjoyed by Jews in any other country."*

The first part of this clause is the supposed "safeguard" of the Arabs of Palestine, which protects them from Zionist encroachment. As far as protection goes, I am reminded of the experience of a relative. When about to land from a ship in a lonely corner of some docks in a distant country, he was warned to take very little money with him and, above all, "to beware of the police." A similar warning applies to this "protective" clause.

At first sight it does not seem so craftily phrased as the earlier clauses. The will-to-deceive in it is so patent; the description of the Arabs as the "non-Jewish communities in Palestine" is so obviously slippery. At the time the Declaration was issued the population of Palestine was in the neighbourhood of 670,000. Of these the Jews numbered some 60,000. These are broad figures, but reasonable: there is no accurate census to quote: in an interim report to the League of Nations drawn up by the military administration the Jewish total was put at 55,000; in a note of the 1920 Government it was put at 65,000.

Deductions can be made from the pre-War Jewish population. Estimates of this vary from the caution of the official Shaw Report, which says it must have been at least 60,000, to the futuristic 100,000 of Mr. Bentwich. Mr. Stein says well over 80,000, and quotes Ruppin's 1916 estimate of nearly 85,000. Accepting this last estimate, and allowing for a fall of 25,000 during the War, which tallies with the figures of those lost by death or exile (Arab wartime losses being infinitely greater actually and proportionately), a 60,000 total for 1918-19 is a fair assumption.

Therefore we have Palestine with 91 percent of its people Arab and 9 percent Jew at the time of the Declaration. It was an Arab population with a dash of Jew. Half of the Jews were recent arrivals.

Before this unpalatable reality, what did the framers of the Balfour Declaration do? By an altogether abject subterfuge, under colour of protecting Arab interests, they set out to conceal the fact that the Arabs to all intents constituted the population of the country. It called them the "non-Jewish communities in Palestine"! It called the multitude the nonfew; it called the 670,000 the non-60,000; out of a hundred it called the 91 the non-9. You might just as well call the British people "the non-Continental communities in Great Britain." It would be as suitable to define the mass of working men as "the non-idling communities in the world," or the healthy as the "non-bedridden elements amongst sleepers," or the sane as "the non-lunatic section of thinkers"—or the grass of the countryside as "the non-dandelion portion of the pastures."

But of course there is more than mere preposterous nomenclature in the use of the phrase "non-Jewish communities in Palestine" to describe the Arabs. It is fraudulent. It was done in order to conceal the true ratio between Arabs and Jews, and thereby to make easier the supersession of the former. It was as though in some declaration Highlanders and Lowlanders had been defined as "the existing non-Irish communities in Scotland" in order that the Irish colonies might be deemed the essential elements of the population north of the Tweed. The Scots themselves thus would appear to be nothing but sporadic groups dotted about the Caledonian soil. Upon which, dispossessive action against the Scots could be attempted more easily. It was a pity indeed that Lord Balfour was not forced to try in Scotland what he and his Zionist friends carried through in Palestine: one airily disingenuous statesman the less would have been left in power.

Just now it was stated that at first sight this phrase seemed not so crafty, because it was too manifestly deceitful. But on second examination it is perceived to be adroit in its mean way. It plays upon general ignorance. What in 1917 did the war-worn British public, what did the deluded Jews of Russia, what did any general body of people outside the Near East know about the composition of the population of Palestine? Nothing.

It was upon this, then, that the drafters of the Declaration played. They concealed the Arabs' very name and called them "existing communities in Palestine," as though they were packets of monks who had strayed into the country and here and there had got a foothold in it. The qualification "existing" provides the finishing touch. The impression given is that these Arabs have just managed to survive, that an explorer has returned and reported to Lord Balfour that he has discovered non-Jews existing in the hills.

Consequently the average citizen, when he read the Declaration, concluded, if he gave the matter any further thought at all, that proper steps would be taken under its terms to safeguard the occasional remnants of other races than the Jews who might be found in the Holy Land. This was what it was intended he should conclude. As for any odd individuals who in the thick of war might have sufficient interest to question the phraseology employed, for them what may have been thought a neat reply had been prepared. "Community is the correct word to use since the population of Palestine is divided into the Moslem, Christian and Jewish communities." The Druses and Samaritans might have been added for effect: otherwise there is no more to say about this equivocation. It is enough to write it down to expose it. Words are wasted on it.

But the Declaration was not issued merely to falsify the status of the Arabs. It was also to offer them a spurious guarantee, in the phrase, *being clearly understood that nothing shall be done which shall prejudice the civil and religious rights*" of the aforesaid so-called "communities." That their religious rights should not be prejudiced, indeed, was satisfactory, though there was not very much in that. Happily, it could be taken for granted. Wherever Britain rules religious rights are preserved.

The crux arrives with "civil rights." What are "civil rights"? All turns on this point. If civil rights remain undefined it is only a mockery to guarantee them. To guarantee anything, and at the same time not to let anyone know what it is, that is Alice in Wonderland legislation. "I guarantee your civil rights," said the White Queen to Alice in Palestineland. "Oh, thank you!" said Alice, "what are they, please?" "I'm sure I can't tell you, my dear," said the White Queen, "but I'll guarantee very hard."

If only the Declaration had been as innocent as the text of *Alice in Wonderland.* Its nonsense is deceptive nonsense, written with vicious intention. The Arabs were guaranteed civil rights, again because to the unalert ear it sounded as though they were being assured a man's normal rights, the freedom to choose the government of his country which every decent man should enjoy, the common political rights of a democratic regime.

But in fact the Arabs were not assured these at all. The effect, and the aim, of the clause actually was to withdraw from the Arabs (fighting or suffering for us at the time under promise of independence) those very rights of independence for which they had contracted; to say nothing of their natural title to them. By sleight of tongue civil rights were substituted for political rights. If civil rights meant anything, which was uncertain and would take long legal proof (which was never offered) they meant most likely civic or borough rights, or such rights as a foreign householder can exercise in a country of which he is not a citizen. But this was untested theory. As practice went, "civil rights" was an expression which was left without any interpretation, and so had no existence as a surety or guarantee at all.

When in Jerusalem, once I asked a High Commissioner himself what were civil rights, and the answer of the High Commissioner was that "Well, they would be very difficult to define." Which is precisely why they were guaranteed to the Arabs. It was a triumph of draftsmanship, of course, to take everything away from them in terms which appeared to safeguard them. A skilful ruse of the drafters, if a knavish one.

There can be no doubt that the authors of this particular "guarantee" were the Zionists themselves, and that the phrase was introduced from America. The clause "it being clearly understood" and what follows has enough of a turn of its own to arouse attention. It is not automatic phraseology: it is no oft-employed cliché. If it were to be found in some previous document relating to the question, then obviously it was transferred from there into the Balfour Declaration.

It is so to be found, and it was transferred. When the September version of the Declaration was dropped because of the Magnus-Montagu opposition, the Cabinet or the Zionist camarilla in it gave its own attention to finding a substitute. But this attention, as before, consisted largely in picking and choosing amidst the Zionists' suggestions.

Baulked of the open mastership of Palestine which the September version would have given them, and driven to pay lip-homage to the Arabs, the Zionists, on one side of the Atlantic or the other, evidently offered a suitable formula drawn from the manifesto of the Jewish organizations of the United States, of the 2nd of October, 1916, a year or so before (quoted in Chapter 8).

In this manifesto the said organizations, *inter alia*, had demanded full rights for the Jews wherever they lived. The manifesto went on to define these, and the definition was thus worded: "it being understood that the phrase 'full rights' is deemed to include civil, religious and political rights."

There most certainly is the source, the rough copy of the celebrated Balfour guarantee. The identity of words is not to be dismissed as a mere coincidence. The juxtaposition of "it being understood that" and of the table of rights which follows points unmistakably to reproduction.

Observe, though, what a difference occurred in the new use of the formula. In the United States the Zionist drafters had employed the formula to define their own rights. In the Balfour Declaration they had to employ it to define, for safeguarding purposes, their own rights, but also, so to speak, to undefine the Arabs' rights. They conceded therefore to the Arabs the notorious "civil rights": for themselves they dropped this word "civil" altogether. They had seen from the beginning that it had no value, since in the manifesto they had taken care to demand religious and political rights in addition to civil rights. In the Balfour Declaration they took the same care.

But they improved the phraseology in the "Balfour Declaration." Not only was "civil" jettisoned, but with great agility the cardinal word "political" was shuffled from "rights" on to "status." To have granted in the same clause only civil rights to the Arabs but to the Jews political rights would have been too glaring a contrast. It might have drawn attention even from the indifferent eyes of 1917. Therefore, for the Jews their "rights" were left apparently unclarified but really expanded in principle through the removal of the constricting adjective, while "political status" was brought in as something of another order peculiar to the Jews, and to do the work of a definite guarantee.

Let me halt for a space to explain why it was essential to have such a guarantee. Without it when Palestine became a Jewish State all Jews might be conceived as belonging to it. This might occur even during the preliminary stage, during the illusory period when Jew and Arab running in harness were building up a new Palestine together (or whatever mixed metaphor best describes this atrocious mixed metaphor of policy). Antisemitism spreads easily, and an agitation might arise in any country to dispatch Jewish citizens to Palestine, or if not to expel them, to catalogue them as aliens, citizens of Palestine, and to deprive them of the vote.

The insertion of the guarantee is further proof, besides, of the character of the regime intended under the Declaration in the Holy Land. If the "National Home" was to be something innocuous, a mere "national home from home" with a modicum of establishment receiving a stream of visitors, an institution without any political status, then there was no need to guarantee hosts or guests against losing their overseas or overland political status in their place of origin. If "National Home" meant a State or quasi-State, there was every need for the guarantee.

The "guarantee" clause of the Declaration, then, with its deceptive text by which the Arabs were to be deprived of their citizenship, sprang undoubtedly from Zionist brains, though it was adopted of course by Balfour and the others and issued by him as though the British Cabinet had thought it out. Considering the joint authorship of the Declaration, this perhaps might have been expected. Its British drafters were mostly guided by expediency: the Zionist drafters were doctrinaires. The British thought it necessary to shut their eyes to Arab rights; the Zionists were convinced or convinced themselves that the Arabs had no rights as men, save those the Turks might have conceded them.

Mr. de Haas, the American drafter, proclaims their attitude very clearly. "We draw a distinction," says he, "between Jewish rights and Arab claims. Whether the Palestinian population in 1914 possessed any tangible political rights is for those versed in Turkish law to say. In practice we know that such rights did not exist, even though the young Turks had created a paper Parliament. Djemaal Pasha ruled in Palestine with an iron hand, as every Turk had done before him, though he too may have indulged [sic] the people in paper rights. The term '*Political rights*' [Mr. de Haas's own capital and italics] does not appear in the Balfour Declaration. The phrase used is civil rights, and as we have made abundantly clear every word of that document was weighed by more than a score of authorities."

From one of the principal drafters of the Declaration, who scissored its terms, this statement clinches the matter. Under the Declaration the Arabs were to get no political rights, whether they had them in principle or not. According to the Zionists' thesis, of which Mr. de Haas is such a notable exponent, they did not hold any in practice and it was very unlikely that they held any in theory.

A couple of pages later in his work, Mr. de Haas has the air of recoiling momentarily from this thesis, or else of having forgotten in the heat of writing that he had just developed it. He says, in passing, of the Arab case, "The Arab case, apart from the rights which inhere from living in a country…" But having mentioned this natural dower thus fugitively he does not allude to it again.

Mr. de Haas is not alone in this attitude, nor is it the attitude alone of the Zionists of the United States. The same point of view prevails amidst British Zionists: it must so prevail, since to recognize that the Arabs have political rights is to recognize that the "National Home" cannot be imposed upon them. As an example of British Zionist opinion I may quote from Mr. Herbert Sidebotham, amongst Gentiles the most assiduous apologist of the cause. His role in Manchester has been mentioned already. He is an absolute apostle of Zionism, and I think he might be described not too maliciously as the inside-out Paul of the movement.

It is very significant to see the effect which his gospel has upon him. Here is a man, very properly admired by his colleagues in journalism, and to be read with respect when he comments on other topics. But when he turns to the defence of Zionism and starts to justify its behaviour, he propounds the most extravagant theories as though they were founded in reason and matured in experience. This is no unusual phenomenon.

A blind spot of madness seems to form in the outlook of everyone who succumbs to the Zionist germ.

Mr. Sidebotham differs from Mr. de Haas in that he concentrates on the status of Palestine rather than on the status of its inhabitants. But he reaches a similar result. He deprives the Arabs of any birthright. I quote from a memorandum of his, somewhat hurriedly entitled *British Policy and the Palestine Mandate: Our Proud Privilege*. This begins "We are in Palestine by a conjunction, made by the accidents of war and not designed, between the oldest national idea in the world's history and *certain political and moral interests peculiar to Great Britain*." (I cannot refrain from italicizing the final phrase. Could anyone?)

At the close of his first chapter Mr. Sidebotham writes: "Palestine, in fact, had no separate national or geographic existence apart from that which the classic history of the Jews had given it, and this disappeared with Jewish independence. In assigning Palestine therefore as a national home, Mr. Balfour was not giving away anything that belonged to someone else. It was a ghost of the past which two thousand years had not succeeded in laying and which could assume an actual physical existence only through the Jews. To the Christian Palestine was the Holy Land… To others Palestine might indifferently be regarded as an appendage of Egypt or a part of Syria or Arabia. Only to Jews could Palestine be a country by itself…" Or again, "Palestine as a country did not exist before the Balfour promise. To the Turk it was a part of the vilayet of Beirut, to the Arab it was the southern part of Syria."

I fancy that it is a just description of the line of argument in the above quotation to say that it is pleasantly extravagant. It has a side to it which is so fantastic that it is almost entertaining. Palestine, declares Mr. Sidebotham, is not a country unless the Jews occupy it. Only their presence can make it one.

There is no reason on earth why Palestine should be a country. It is too small, its boundaries are artificial in the main, there is nothing to distinguish it from the territory just to the north, its sacred character has not the slightest national quality. The little province is in fact nothing but a section of Syria. Its existence for centuries has been provincial. Mr. Sidebotham recognizes this. In the eyes of the Arabs it is, he says, no more than "a part of Arabia," or is "only the southern part of Syria."

It is now that he becomes odd. Because Palestine is only a part of Arab territory he would take it from the Arabs' ownership. No doubt he allows that the Arabs have a right to a country somewhere, but to the parts of this country their right vanishes. If the Jews come along and propose to turn part of an Arab country into a whole Jewish country, then the Arabs lose that part automatically. As an entity the part is untenable. But by argument on these lines we might get so far as to find our claim to the whole of England unsound, if we lay claim to it as part of the inheritance of the British race, as part of the British Commonwealth. For that is the way in which the Arabs lay claim to Palestine, on the ground that it is part of the inheritance of the Arab race, part of the Arab commonwealth or nexus of lands in Arab occupation.

To return to the general issue, the situation laid down for the Arabs of Palestine by typical Zionist writers is that these Arabs are political slaves, persons not having the right of ownership of their place of birth, a place indeed which in their hands politically would not exist.

Let us go back to the Declaration. After it had been published an event occurred which is closely attached to this particular question of national prerogatives, and may serve to close the discussion of it. The Zionist leaders approached the chief Allied Governments with a request for pronouncements of encouragement and support similar to that which Great Britain had given them.

A deception awaited them. From the French, on the 9th of February, 1918, they received a note which was no more than adequate. Mr. Sacher, or any other of the Political Committee, would have turned out something much more attractive. It ran:

> *M. Sokolov représentant des organisations sionistes, a été reçu ce matin au Ministère des Affaires Etrangères par M. Stephen Pichon, qui a été heureux de lui confirmer que l'entente est complète entre les Gouvernements français et britannique en ce qui concerne la question d'un établissement juif en Palestine.*

Not really a satisfactory statement, it will be seen. The French evaded giving the Zionists any direct guarantee. They confined themselves to saying that they were in agreement with the British Government's policy. This left the onus of the policy upon the British, and the Quai d'Orsay spokesmen gave no pledge at all that they would continue in agreement with it as it developed. Moreover, the French note was sent with a covering letter in which M. Sokolov was complimented upon the *"dévouement avec lequel vous poursuivez la réalisation des voeux de vos co-réligionnaires."* A very back-handed compliment. It discounted the whole nationalist and not religious platform which the devoted M. Sokolov was straining to construct.

But it was when Italy was approached that this best-laid scheme really went agley. Here is the Italian pronouncement, given in London on the 9th of May, 1918, to M. Sokolov by the Marchese Imperiali, the Italian Ambassador, "by order of Baron Sonnino":

> *In relazione alle domande che gli sono state rivolte il Governo di Sua Maestà é lieto di confermare le precendenti dichiarazioni già fatte a mezzo dei suoi rappresentanti a Washington, l'Aja e Salonicco, di essere cioé disposto ad adoperarsi con piacere per facilitare lo stabilirsi in Palestina di un centro nazionale ebraico, nel'intesa pero' che non ne venga nessun pregiudizio alio stato giuridico e politico delle già esistenti comunità religiose ed ai diritti civili e politici che gli israeliti già godono in ogni altro paese.*
>
> [In connection with the requests which have been made to it His Majesty's Government is happy to confirm the previous statements made through its representatives in Washington, The Hague and Salonica, that is to say that it is prepared to take steps with pleasure in order to facilitate the foundation in Palestine of a Jewish national centre, on the understanding however that no prejudice shall arise through it to the legal and political status of existing religious communities and to the civil and political rights already enjoyed by Israelites in any other country.]

The Italian Government in its pronouncement put in the missing words which made all the difference. Since the petitioners who had asked for a declaration had caused the Palestine population to be divided into "communities," the Consulta took care to signify that this division was a religious one. It spiked the guns of Lord Balfour and Dr. Weizmann who had used the religious idea to make the division into communities, but thereon had treated the communities as national divisions.

More important and more meaning still was the insertion of the words "legal and political status." The Italian Government guaranteed that the National Home should not prejudice those very fundamental rights of the Arabs which the Balfour Declaration deliberately had excised. With entire politeness it indicated that it was not deceived by the terms of the Balfour document, and that it would not be party to the suppression of native rights.

It is impossible not to admire the neatness of the rebuke; the hoisting of the political Zionists with their own petard by rejecting their claims under guise of confirming them—just as they had drafted for the Arabs; the elegant assumption that Lord Balfour had intended a genuine guarantee and that Italy would make it more to his mind by making it watertight.

This Italian guarantee was given, need it be said, long before the days of Fascism, by the old Italian Kingdom, democratic and liberal, so that it cannot be ascribed to rivalry or spite or other such motive. If it puts Italy in a strong position at present, it is simply an example of how honesty can indeed be the best policy. Not surprisingly, it has been kept rather quiet. The version of it with which Mrs. Andrews credits M. Sokolov in her *The Holy Land Under Mandate* is not exact. Mrs. Andrews quotes Italy as safeguarding only the "civil and religious rights of existing non-Jewish communities or the legal or political status enjoyed by Jews in any other country." The Italian Declaration is turned thus into another Balfour Declaration. The true version, given by M. Sokolov, in the original Italian just cited, is very different, and stands to this day, with formidable implications attached to it upon which it is unnecessary to dilate.

Chapter 12

Illegitimacy of issuing the Declaration.
The motives for issuing the Declaration.
The Declaration as payment for services rendered.

So much for the Declaration as a declaration. There are a trio of other points of view from which it yet has to be considered. The first is: Apart from the abuses in its deceptive terms, was the mere publication of the Balfour Declaration legitimate in itself?

The point is a recapitulatory one, which the general burden of this book has answered. It requires to be repeated now, though, for the order of the argument, and can be dealt with quickly. The Government had no business to issue a declaration enacting, let alone crystallizing the situation of the Zionists in Palestine. The preceding Cabinet had covenanted to recognize the independence of this Arab land "in every sense of the word independence." This agreement was still standing: the Arabs were carrying out their side of it by waging war upon the Turks. Therefore the Government had no right to father and to patronize officially the special action in Palestine of a third party, which did not intend to ask any permission for this special action from the Arabs, and so contravened their independence. That is the position in short. The Balfour Declaration, barred by the treaty with King Hussein, and issued without any previous consultation or consent of the Arabs, was illicit.

The excuse has been made that under the circumstances of the time, with most of Palestine still in enemy hands, it was not possible to have consulted the Arabs. In which case obviously the only legitimate course was to wait till Palestine was out of enemy hands, and then to consult them. Two other courses also were open.

(1) To have held preliminary negotiations with King Hussein, in which that monarch could have probed the meaning of "National Home" and the meaning of the British promise of patronage. He would have been able to demand a definite statement from the Zionists whether or not they were willing to develop their activities under the licence and within the frame of the forthcoming Arab State.

(2) It would have been possible (if not so sound) to have issued a contingent declaration, subject to Arab agreement before it came into force.

Neither of these evident and easy courses of action was adopted, nor any of the kindred courses which suggest themselves without difficulty. So the weak excuse that it was not possible to consult the Arabs expires at once.

Another sort of excuse is so common that it must be mentioned also. As an excuse it is worth just as much as the gold in a farthing. Nothing ought to be more astonishing than the facility with which such a silly thing is repeated. But it has gained currency because it suits so well the too common laziness of mind which does not wish to make the least effort of inquiry into the rights or the wrongs of any question. The exercise of the brain is escaped by saying of any such question that it is all wrongs, that the situation of everyone concerned in it is deplorable, and that it is a waste of time to search for shades of culpability amidst them. "Drop grudges and start afresh" or "keep out of it," says the excuse-broker, and gets off to his golf.

In the case of Palestine, the excuse is that we have made promises all round, to Arabs and to Jews, in public and in private. The only common-sense, straightforward course therefore is to cancel "the lot of them" and to make a new beginning. So runs a plea which is as ignoble in attitude as it is indefensible in argument. If there were any basis to it, what a prospect it would open.

Anyone who had repented of a contract which he had made could slip out of it always, by making another and later contract or contracts which were incompatible with the previous one. If the person to whom he was contracted ventured to hold him to their bargain he could go to court, display his documents, and plead "All these engagements of mine are in contradiction one with another." The judge, finding that they were, would announce, "So they are. The court annuls them all therefore." What morality and what nonsense!

No, when an individual invokes a plurality of contracts, or a nation protests a superfluity of treaties or of official declarations, there is but one means of deciding which of them holds good. Which was the first of them? If that was duly transacted, it is by that the citizen or the cabinet must adhere.

The Balfour Declaration was issued over two years after the pact with King Hussein had been made. It is incompatible with this previous pledge and therefore it is null and void. It has no more status than have the vows made to a woman before the altar by a man who has a discarded wife still living. The best description in fact of the Balfour Declaration is that it is a bigamous declaration.

The worst of bigamy is the suffering it inflicts upon two persons, the true wife and the false "wife." In the present example of this crime, many thousands of Jews—I do not say their leaders—have been decoyed to Palestine by the junior marriage-lines to which Balfour set his name. Between these immigrants and their leaders the responsibility is their own affair. As far as we are concerned, who have inherited the responsibilities conferred on Britain by the 1917 Cabinet, we owe to these poor people a considerable reparation, which we shall have some difficulty in paying. But we do not owe it to them to install them in the situation of the lawful spouse, or side by side with her in her home.

The second point to be considered comes now. It also is in some degree recapitulatory. It deals with the causes of the Declaration, and it has been seen already that the publication of this was part of a bargain. It was the reward given to the Zionists for tipping the balance in the United States on to the side of participation in the War. That at least has been the main reason alleged for the deed of the 2nd of November. But other reasons or causes are alleged too, and some curious witness has been borne concerning them, which calls for examination.

In addition there is the question of how far the bargain made was a useful one. There is a historical interest in seeing what actually was carried out, and what was gained or was lost at so great a price.

On the Zionist side there is no inquiry to be made. The cause of their entry into the Declaration bargain was the desire for their version of Zion.

Of the British side, however, there is more to be said. The outstanding point is that the celebrated "historic rights," by which the Zionists claimed entry, counted for little or nothing, despite all the orating about them, in the concession of the National Home. The Government did not issue the Declaration because the whole Cabinet was penetrated with a romantic determination that the Jewish race should enjoy its own again. Jacob has had its Jacobites, but there were not many of them then in high places. Of those in the Cabinet, there was probably but the protagonist, Lord Balfour, who did not act with the Zionists on the *do ut des* principle. Balfour, if he can be acquitted of nothing else, can be acquitted of the bargaining which was the predominant Governmental motive.

He had a theory to demonstrate, which was that the world had not paid the Jews sufficiently for their contributions to civilization. The world was backward in its payments, and it was a piece of intellectual bookkeeping for Balfour to balance the payments. This supplied him with a sort of *do quia dedisti* motive; a reasonable gratitude. But his strongest impulse was the putting into practice of his own theory. It was such a moral theory to him that he did not care how immorally it was put into practice.

So it was that Balfour, despite everything that happened following upon his Declaration, after all the outcries and the riots, after all the protests and the testimony of misdoing showered forth by the Arabs, still went on professing in his chair of Zionism with the placidity of unconcern. His theory satisfied himself: interruptions were tiresome, but could be lived down.

Mark Sykes, on the other hand, who had done most for Zionism next to Balfour in the official world, and had been more physically active on its behalf than even Balfour, began to doubt about it before he died, too soon, in 1919. "From being the evangelist of Zionism during the War he had returned to Paris with feelings shocked by the intense bitterness which had been provoked in the Holy Land," writes his biographer Shane Leslie. "Matters had reached a stage beyond his conception of what Zionism would be. His last journey to Palestine raised many doubts."

Balfour's own first and last journey to Syria, when he nearly fell, in the northern zone, into the power of an infuriated Arab mob, raised no doubts in him. Ere then, in the southern zone, like another Catherine surrounded by bevies of Potemkins, he had been led, with his armed escorts hidden from view, through the permanent set of the Zionist colonies, and had been heralded by the cheers of their permanent chorus. The set delighted him: it was the Palestine he wanted to see, something remote from the realities of the situation.

This attitude of his has induced some to call him a dilettante in politics. He was and he was not. He pursued politics with iron determination, and yet it was out of politics, despite his tennis and his golf, that he won his supreme entertainment. In all his statesmanship there was a strain of recreation and he would not be baulked of it. He was like a man who will have his exercise, and goes trudging over other people's gardens and wheatfields in the honest cause of health. The Arab acres of Palestine lay on the route of Balfour's mental exercise, and he led his Zionist companions into them, exclaiming on the emptiness of the site and its suitability for occupation as he trampled the corn and strode past the vociferating owners

To accomplish and to vindicate his theories, then, Lord Balfour signed the Declaration. He was not ignorant of course of the material advantages which might come of it, but these hardly provided him with a motive. There is a piece of advice which says not to marry for money but to go where there is money. It was on these lines, as far as the nuptial settlement went, that Balfour married Britain to Zionism, very much *en secondes noces*. He would very probably have been even more satisfied if his rarefied idea of getting the United States to take over the lady had been accomplished. The United States as an Oriental ruler under an untried scheme was so irresistibly unlikely and therefore so fascinating.

Beside Balfour, however, there is that other dominating figure, the Prime Minister, Mr. Lloyd George, to be considered. What were his motives? He did not say much about them at the time of the Declaration, but he has explained them on various occasions since. Three years ago, in the House of Commons, he gave his view of "Jewish historic rights" in Palestine. A general debate on Palestine was going on, and it was in the course of an indication of the special points to which he would speak that he threw out a reference to the "historic rights." It was just in his style to pass casually, as he did, over what was a primary question, but the little he said upon it was categoric enough.

"I am not now putting the case," he said, "that the Arabs are only a modern introduction into Palestine and that the ancient inhabitants were the Jews. There is nothing in that case, because, after all, the Jews turned out the Hittites and the Ammonites." This was only a quarter of the truth, which left out the factors of the brief duration and of the minor extent of Jewish occupancy, and left out the Arab inheritance from the "Ammonites and Hittites." But even so it is quite enough.The Zionists claimed the right of establishment in Palestine on the grounds of historic right, on the grounds that they were the ancient inhabitants. "There is nothing in that case," said the ex-Prime Minister, yet it was on that very case, which was the only ostensible case, that he encouraged and supported their entry in 1917. What is to be said of such action? Really there is no canon, no axiom of justice, no propriety which has not been violated in the endeavour to install the Jewish National Home in Palestine.

However, if this one was not, what was Mr. Lloyd George's real motive, as head of the Government, in issuing the Declaration and in supporting the case in which he saw nothing. He himself has named for us two motives which do not agree altogether, but have something in common. The one is personal: he supported Zionism as a reward for Dr. Weizmann's help in manufacturing chemicals during the War. The other is impersonal: he wanted to win over the Jews in general to the Allied cause. In his speech of June, 1937, in the Commons he made an explanation which merged the two, so it may be quoted.

> "It was [said he] one of the darkest periods of the War when Mr. Balfour prepared his Declaration. Let me recall the circumstances to the House. At the time the French Army had mutinied, the Italian Army was on the eve of collapse and America had hardly started preparing in earnest. There was nothing left but Britain confronting the most powerful military combination the world has ever seen. It was important for us to seek every legitimate help we could get. We came to the conclusion, from information we received from every part of the world, that it was vital we should have the sympathies of the Jewish community. I can assure the Committee that we did not come to that conclusion from any predilections or prejudices. Certainly we had no prejudices against the

> Arabs because at that moment we had hundreds and thousands of troops fighting for Arab emancipation from the Turk.
>
> In these circumstances and on the advice which we received we decided that it was desirable to secure the sympathy and co-operation of that most remarkable community, the Jews throughout the world. They were helpful in America, and in Russia which at that moment was just walking out and leaving us alone. In these conditions we proposed this to our Allies. France accepted it, Italy accepted it, and the United States accepted it. And the Jews I am here to bear testimony to the fact—responded nobly to the appeal which was made. I do not know whether the House knows what we owe to Dr. Weizmann, with his marvellous scientific brain. He absolutely saved the British Army at a critical moment when a particular ingredient which it was essential we should have for our great guns was completely exhausted. His great chemical genius enabled us to solve that problem. But he is only one out of many who rendered great service to the Allies. It is an obligation of honour which we took, to which the Jews responded. We cannot get out of it without dishonour."

There is much omitted in this account of the circumstances of the Declaration. There is, amongst omissions, no word to recall that the Arabs were fighting for us, that Hussein and his sons were risking their position and their lives. There is no mention of our obligations to the Arabs. As for Allied acceptances of the Declaration, the reader has seen already how France accepted and how Italy accepted: he has seen something of the way in which "acceptance" took place in the United States. In the matter of the obligation of honour to the Jews, he has also seen that there remains to many innocent parties amongst them an obligation, but an obligation of a kind. To speak of an "obligation of honour" in respect of an engagement which in itself was dishonourable, since it violated human rights and a previous pledge, is arrant nonsense, and something more.

But the question of Dr. Weizmann's invention remains and must be pursued further. There is no occasion, happily, to dispute its usefulness. Dr. Weizmann is a great chemist who worked with infinite zeal and rendered admirable service. The question is whether in describing the extent of this service Mr. Lloyd George's imaginative mind has not been at play.

He went into further details in a speech he made where the atmosphere was more conducive to detail perhaps than round the Treasury Bench. This was in May of 1925 after the lecture given by Mr. Philip Guedalla before the Jewish Historical Society in London, to which I referred in an early chapter. After thanking the lecturer, who had spoken of an appeal which Napoleon I made to the Jews, Mr. Lloyd George said, "We also made an appeal to your great people. Unlike Napoleon—let us be quite frank—our motives were mixed." The speaker then explained the motives which sprang in his own breast from natural sympathy with a people with whose history and biblical literature he had been imbued since his childhood.

He went on:

> "There we were, confronted with your people in every country of the world, very powerful. You may say you have been oppressed and persecuted—that has been your power. You have been hammered into very fine steel and that is why you can never be broken. Hammered for centuries into the finest steel of any race in the world! And therefore we wanted your help. We thought it would be very useful. I am putting the other side quite frankly. We had had already very great help. I personally owe a deep debt of gratitude to Dr. Weizmann, and I am his proselyte. In the Ministry of Munitions I was confronted with one of the most serious crises with which I was ever beset. It was one of those unexpected things that come upon you like a cavalry charge coming up against a chasm. And I found such a chasm. As I marched from gun to gun, from shell to shell, I suddenly found that we had not got one of the great motive powers to make cordite—wood-alcohol. I turned to Dr. Weizmann.
>
> Alcohol had to be made out of wood, and he trained little animals—I don't know through how many generations—to eat sugar, and the alcohol was made out of maize, and then there was plenty of 'corn in Egypt' and we were saved. I felt a deep debt of gratitude, and so did all the Allies, to the brilliant scientific genius of Dr. Weizmann. When we talked to him and asked him, 'What can we do for you in the way of any honour?' he replied, 'All I care for is an opportunity to do something for my people.'
>
> It was worth anything to us in honour, or in coin of the realm, but all he asked for was to be allowed to present his case for the restoration of his people to the old country which they had made famous throughout the world. Acetone converted me to Zionism.
>
> So the case was put before us, and when the War Cabinet began to consider the case for the Declaration, it was quite unanimously in favour. I think we secured the co-operation of the French at that time, and the famous Balfour Declaration was made."

In his great work of war reminiscences Mr. Lloyd George repeats this account in closer scientific terms when describing Dr. Weizmann's device. He remembers how it was C. P. Scott of the *Manchester Guardian*, who brought Weizmann to his notice as a likely chemist to solve the acetone problem. When there arose some difficulty in obtaining maize, owing to the submarine blockade, horse-chestnuts were introduced instead. This was in the autumn of 1917. A national collection of horse-chestnuts was organized. The factory at King's Lynn which had carried out the maize process, altered to the chestnuts, "and though at first the poor quality of the material hampered output these difficulties were overcome, and the Weizmann process was turning out acetone from horse-chestnuts by the time the factory was closed in 1918."

> When our difficulties were solved through Dr. Weizmann's genius [continues Mr. Lloyd George] I said to him, "You have rendered great service to the State, and I should like to ask the Prime Minister to recommend you to His Majesty for some honour." He said, "There is nothing I want for myself." "But is there nothing we can do as a recognition of your valuable assistance to the country?" I asked. He replied, "Yes. I should like you to do something for my people." He then explained his aspirations as to the repatriation of the Jews to the sacred land they had made famous. That was the fount and origin of the famous declaration about the National Home for Jews in Palestine.
>
> As soon as I became Prime Minister I talked the whole matter over with Mr. Balfour, who was then Foreign Secretary. As a scientist he was immensely interested when I told him of Dr. Weizmann's achievement. We were anxious at that time to enlist Jewish support in neutral countries, notably in America. Dr. Weizmann was brought into direct contact with the Foreign Secretary. This was the beginning of an association the outcome of which, after long examination, was the famous Balfour Declaration which became the charter of the Zionist movement. So that Dr. Weizmann with his discovery not only helped us to win the War, but made a permanent mark upon the map of the world.

These quotations are conclusive evidence, I think, of the motives which inspired Mr. Lloyd George. He gives them to us in the proverbial nutshell; at least, in two nutshells. "Acetone converted me to Zionism" and "The co-operation of Jews, notably in America, converted me to Zionism." The second nutshell is a combination of my own, it is true, but it is composed out of his own words and in faithfulness to the sense of his three discourses. But, whether it was the physical acetone of Dr. Weizmann in England, or the moral acetone of Jewish aid in the whole world, which converted him to Zionism, one thing is manifest: there was no question of Zionism converting Mr. Lloyd George to Zionism. In his own words, "There is nothing in that case." The Balfour Declaration, as far as it concerned the Prime Minister, was a salary he paid the Zionists for their services, no more, and if the metaphor be taken to the end, I fear it must be said that it was paid out of Arab trust-funds. It is evident he should have inquired into the character of the territorial cash at which, in his impulsive manner, he grabbed.

His account of what happened, besides the omissions mentioned, contains minor inaccuracies, and one not at all so small. He says that when the War Cabinet began to consider the case for the Declaration it was quite unanimously in favour. This appears a mere playing with facts, for if it can be said that at some early sessions the members of the War Cabinet present fell in with the scheme, a situation soon developed in which there was Cabinet dissension about it. As we have seen, the scheme once was actually voted down: "I cannot do anything till the decision is reversed," said Balfour. Of this Mr. Lloyd George gives no hint, nor does he give a word to Edwin Montagu's considerable and persistent opposition. So that the picture given is anything but correct, and only achieved by allowing hearers or readers to believe that the attitude of some Ministers at a given moment remained the attitude of all continuously, which it did not.

Since he was inaccurate about his own Cabinet, it seemed as well to learn something of the acetone story from other sources besides Mr. Lloyd George. This, in short, is what happened. In 1912 Dr. Weizmann was associated with a firm named Strange and Graham, which was engaged in analytical research and in production in the field of chemical supply. In the month of March of that year a Mr. Kane, one of Strange and Graham's chemists, made a discovery of some importance, which was that among the products of the fermentation of starch, a process he was studying, there was acetone to be found. Acetone was at the time a necessary ingredient for the manufacture of certain high explosives. This discovery was made known to Dr. Weizmann, in a current way, as part of the work of the firm.

There the matter remained. Then Dr. Weizmann left the employ of Messrs. Strange and Graham. But Kane's discovery had interested him. He did not think that it had been sufficiently followed up. Acting now entirely upon principles of his own, he attacked the question of extracting acetone from starch as found in various substances, and developed a new process.

When the War broke out, the production of acetone became important. Dr. Weizmann gave fresh attention to his process. His old firm, using the original Kane system, was manufacturing acetone. The explosives experts of the Government, inquiring into production, heard of Dr. Weizmann's process. Sir Frederick Nathan, who at the time was adviser to the Admiralty on cordite supplies, was struck by the report he received on the Weizmann process from a Mr. Rintoul, who was at the head of the Research Department of the Nobel Explosives Company. Sir Frederick Nathan got into touch with Dr. Weizmann and advised him to patent his process. This he did in October 1915, and it was adopted by the Government and was substituted for the Kane process or for whatever version of the Kane process was in use.

There was, as it happens, a technical dispute after the War upon the patent rights, and a case was brought in 1926 before one of the judges of the High Court, in which Dr. Weizmann was the plaintiff. Evidence showed that the new process, though of course it started from the initial discovery of Kane, owed nothing at all to his subsequent methods or those of his firm in developing it, since Dr. Weizmann had hit upon an essentially different form of extraction. Judgment therefore was conclusively given in Dr. Weizmann's favour.

Work on the Weizmann process began in June 1916 (as stated by Mr. Lloyd George), on the 19th, the raw material used being maize. From that date to the last day of the year the average weekly production of acetone under the process was 4 tons 8 cwt. 68 lbs. During 1917 the average was raised to 5 tons 3 cwt. 14 lbs. It then declined with a declining demand for acetone and during 1918 the factory at King's Lynn, where the process was concentrated, worked intermittently and finally ceased. It had also been employed in other factories, but not for so long. The process was also used more extensively in Canada during 1917.

A summing-up of the matter which I have had from authoritative quarters is that the acetone process was theoretically right, and was used to some extent by the army, but not a great deal. The bacteria—the "trained little animals" of Mr. Lloyd George's speech—fermented starch from maize, and afterwards from horse-chestnuts, and wood-acetone and an alcohol were produced. These were separated and the acetone was suitable for making cordite. But because acetone, from all sources was scarce—according to Mr. Lloyd George himself a single British factory was producing it—the army adopted a propellant which did not require acetone. Its requirements of course entirely swamped other demands for propellant.

If there had been plenty of acetone, the army would have gone on using it, no doubt. But there was not plenty. The army supplies were made independent of it therefore; alternative solvents were used to make another form of propellant known as R.D.B.

It is the fault of the ex-Premier that I have to make this rectification, which seems ungenerous towards Dr. Weizmann perhaps. But if Mr. Lloyd George had not magnified what Weizmann did in the interests of justifying the price which he paid him, there would have been no occasion to write these paragraphs upon the degree of accomplishment of a man who served the country valuably and steadily throughout the War.

As it is, the price paid is preposterous beyond belief. Reading Mr. Lloyd George's text you would imagine that there had been some scaling-down of payment, but what happened was just the contrary. Mr. Lloyd George with some artfulness screens with Dr. Weizmann's refusal of any honours for himself (to which I render entire homage) his suggestion of colossal honours, if they can be called honours, for a body to which he was attached. Far from scaling down the price paid for the acetone, the Prime Minister by accepting this suggestion consented to give for it a reward beyond all price. A Grand Cross of the Bath or an Order of Merit given to Dr. Weizmann, however valuable to the recipient, would have cost the State nothing. But, even supposing that Dr. Weizmann had "absolutely saved the British Army," to confer upon him and upon his in return proprietary rights in a country which was in possession of another race and was secured by treaty to that race, was this the reward applicable to the occasion? If land was the only possible recompense, there were the Isle of Wight and the Isle of Man, and other British places in Britain's free gift, ready to be handed over.

No British commander obtained more than an earldom from the Great War. No commander of any of the belligerent Powers on land or on sea, from Foch and Jellicoe downwards, some of whom at least must have saved armies or navies sometime, by the very order of things, no commander of them all received more than title, or decorations, or grant of money. Yet for Dr. Weizmann history is turned inside out, geography is suppressed, a people is disfranchised and an empire is forsworn. All in return for a formula for making propellant-paste, which was valuable for a while and after a while was superseded.

The thing is outrageous. The whole sum of war-profiteering is a mite in comparison with this. Even if the Palestine prize were not given for acetone, but for the enlistment of Jewish support in the United States and other countries (Mr. Lloyd George's alternative essential motive) what then? It would still be outrageous, it would still be the most gigantic and most intolerable "deal" of the War.

But possibly the truest comment on the reward paid to the Zionists is to examine what in sober reality was gained for the Allies by the "National Home" transaction. So much is assumed upon this point, and so little is established.

Certainly one of the anticipated recompenses never came to hand. "The Foreign Office," writes Lord Balfour's biographer when dealing with the October-November period, "was now in fact anxious to reap all the immediate advantages there might be in the Declaration." She goes on, "It was expected apparently to have some direct results on the Russian revolution, then passing out of its Menshevik phase. Lenin and Trotsky took power in the same week of November 1917 that Jewish nationality won its recognition." There is much unrealized satire in this last sentence. However, the direct results which were expected will have been that Russia would go on fighting. This Russia did—at Archangel.

But it would be unfair to suppose that Zionism was to make its real return for the Balfour Declaration in Russia. This was only dangled as an attractive possibility. The real return was to be in the United States, where

Zionist adherents and the Zionist machine were (as we have seen more than once) to tip the trembling scale and bring the great Federation into the War.

It is sustained that they did so, but I have never read any satisfactory proof of it. I agree that it would be a difficult thing to prove, for there was no day or short critical period when you could say at the end of it that the United States changed over from opposing participation to favouring participation. If there had been such a critical instant, there would have been some chance of showing who or what supplied the decisive twist. But there was no such occasion, though certain events provided factors to participation. Therefore there is this difficulty of proof.

At the same time, it is clear that the obstacles in the way of proving the case do not permit it to be assumed. If the Zionists cannot easily show how they brought America in, they are equally unentitled to say without producing evidence that they did bring America in, and to profit by this unverified assertion.

Such evidence as there is on the whole tells altogether against their being the deciding factor. No doubt they were one factor amongst a quantity. They won a number of their own people over from indifference or semi-support of the other side, but they have made claims as though they were the factor which brought in the United States. It is an interesting point that in the volume of Mr. Lloyd George's memoirs which treats of the American entry into the War he makes no mention of Zionism as a contributory cause. We have the sinking of the *Lusitania* and of various United States merchant-vessels, the Zimmerman dispatch to Mexico, and other such events. We have an exposé of President Wilson's developing opinions, and so on. But of Zionist help, nothing. It seems to me that if it had been so valuable as all that, had been as valuable as Mr. Lloyd George is by way of sustaining in other passages of his memoirs (such as have been just quoted), then it should not have slipped his memory completely at the moment of cardinal computation.

The run of the evidence in fact does not square with Zionist help having been the determining factor. The leaders such as Brandeis and de Haas had enough to do, it is quite evident, in gathering supporters for the Zionist cause itself and in trying to counteract the anti-Allied sentiment amidst these supporters, particularly amidst all the seniors who had been in Russia or remembered Russia. This was excellent subsidiary work for the Allies, which deserves every recognition, but it was negative and preparatory, not positive and final. You may not be able to make a road till you have removed the rocks and undergrowth on the site, but you cannot exact payment for the completed road while you are still digging at the bushes and your tractors are dragging the surface rocks away.

"From the fall of 1914 to the summer of 1915 the Zionists had no real Press of their own," avows Mr. de Haas, "no stirring publicity department, and had only intermittent support from the Yiddish Press, which was still in doubt as to the correct war-policy, and therefore hesitated to support ad hoc the Brandeis pro-Ally programme." From 1915 to 1917 the activity of Brandeis and his associates increased the number of Zionist adherents enormously, but the Zionist body was still eminently Zionist and had not been made pro-Ally.

The organization had to contend with the obvious difficulty that many Jews could not swallow the avowed support of the Allied cause [Mr. de Haas explains, when detailing its upward struggle]. Brandeis [says he in a general exposé] unhesitatingly banked on Allied victory when he took office as Zionist leader, but the Zionists in Europe were naturally divided according to each local allegiance. Russian Jews were however not in sympathy with the Russian cause, and thousands of Jews everywhere rightly felt that every Russian victory in Eastern Europe was a gain for the forces of oppression. *It was not until the fall of Tsardom* [six weeks before the Balfour Declaration was issued] *that a simple pro-Allied attitude became possible in this country* [U.S.] *and elsewhere.* Moreover there were Zionists who were pacifists and conscientious objectors to war in every form.

This mixed situation created an excellent opportunity for German propaganda both in America and Poland. Therefore until America came into the War the American Zionist organization had to be handled with considerable skill in order to maintain its pro-Ally alignment.

[German blunders helped.] The Brandeisian policy throughout this situation was to keep all Germans and all German propaganda at arm's length. This decision required tact, determination and a mass of information. The Zionist Organization had no secrets to hide, *but to keep it clear of German influence,* disguised in the most benevolent and insidious forms of intrigue, *was no light task.* It was however accomplished. [Italics in this passage are all mine.]

The gist of this is that the definite tipping of the scale in the United States towards participation in the War cannot be claimed by the Zionist leaders, who had all they could do to maintain any sort of pro-Allied attitude even within their own body. Once more the enormity, in every sense, of the grant to them of the Balfour Declaration with its lien upon Palestine stands out.

It might perhaps be asserted that the Balfour concession, as it were, was given in exchange for Zionist influence amidst just a few men in the United States, the great Jewish bankers and financiers and other magnates.

But that assertion cannot be borne out either. Mrs. Dugdale herself records that Balfour when in the United States found "the Jewish magnates hostile to the national [that is, Zionist] movement." Two months after the Declaration was issued our Ambassador at Washington "reported on Brandeis's authority that the Zionists were violently opposed by the great Capitalists." More evidence could be cited, but this is evidence enough. Any great Jewish financial interests in the United States which came to our support did not do so because of the pleadings of any Zionist.

Yet generalizations upon what the movement accomplished in America have been and continue to be fluid and free. A typical and recent example is provided by Mr. Landman, enunciating in a pamphlet that in the Balfour Declaration contract the main consideration "given by the Jewish people—represented at the time by the leaders of the Zionist Organization—was their help in bringing President Wilson to the aid of the Allies."

Accurate specification of this aid, and of exactly how it was all-important, is never provided. No doubt Judge Brandeis helped and encouraged the President in his plans. But that is all that can even be surmised. No one, amongst the Zionists themselves, has dared to sustain that the President and his circle of advisers would have reached contrary conclusions and have remained neutral but for Mr. Brandeis.

Once the United States had entered the War, the United States Zionists undoubtedly were very helpful. Brandeis was able to point out to the President that the Jews in general (by no means all of them Zionists) had contributed far more enlistments to the armed forces of the Republic than their ratio to the total population warranted.

But whatever the Zionists did, after war was declared, was upon another plane. It was done in allegiance to the Stars and Stripes. No doubt they had their personal motives in addition to their motives as citizens, but necessarily it was as citizens that they acted thenceforth, in common with their fellow-citizens of every extraction. The existing non-Zionist communities in the United States upon their own initiative had resolved on war, and this resolution whelmed the minor actions of all pro-war bodies in the greater action of President and people. The official Zionist policy was no longer an individual course up the stream, but in the general turnover from neutrality merged and ran headlong with the flood of the nation. The Zionists of the Union can hardly demand Palestine for doing their American duty.

The third and final point comes up for consideration now. It is the question of responsibilities. The largest share of them must be borne by the 1917 Government. The Zionists have a big burden to carry, but their action would have come to nothing without first the acquiescence, and later the collusion, the backing and finally the incitement of Whitehall.

They were inspired too by an ideal, even though it was ill-interpreted and should have been carried out in a purer way. Unfortunately their leaders rejected the pilgrimage to Zion in favour of the appropriation of Palestine. But the presence of an ideal, however subverted, does attenuate in a minor degree their fault, and there is not much counterpart to be found for it in the bargaining motives of our own Government.

No doubt the Government was in some straits because of the perils of the war at the time. In the then Prime Minister's own words, "It was important for us to seek every legitimate help we could get." The help though had to be legitimate. It could not be that form of help which is helping oneself to another's property. The Government was, indeed, fighting to save England, and that would seem to supply it with a motive equal, or superior to the Zionists'. But it was precisely to save England that the members of the Government were waging the war. It was to preserve the England which had come down to them, not to substitute for it an England of easier conscience and then to claim this as a survival.

There was the question too of position and of setting an example. It was for the British realm to set the example, not to conform to the standards of the Zionists. Methods understandable from a self-appointed fresh-made caucus such as the Zionist Organization were beyond belief when proposed by the heirs of a hundred Parliaments.

The responsibility for not taking this view must lie therefore upon the Cabinet of 1917, and principally upon Lord Balfour, who insisted on working out, in a sphere which the War placed at his mercy, an academic thesis of his own, in a particular way. When that way was barred to him by facts, he scorned them and scorned that elementary justice which was altogether too much in the foreground for his style of seeing things. He persisted wilfully in his course, and as we have seen, it was he who broke every opposition.

"From the first," his biographer assures us, "he threw his whole weight on the side of the Zionists, and without it they might not have prevailed." "The Balfour Declaration," say the officials of the Zionist Organization in their report upon it, "is justly so-called, not only because it fell to Sir Arthur Balfour as Foreign Secretary to write the historic letter, but also because he, more than any other single statesman, is responsible for the policy embodied in the Declaration."

As happens now and then in the course of public events, words which were written to be a eulogy have stayed to be an impeachment.

With this the immediate examination of the Balfour Declaration may end. These were its principal characteristics:

1. Its publication broke our pledged word to the Arab race.

2. Its object was to establish the Jews in a privileged position in Palestine without the assent of the population, as a prelude to the absorption of the latter, under plea of their co-operation, in a future Jewish State.
3. It was written in great part by those who were supposed only to have received it, and was deliberately worded so that the truth might be hidden by it, its guarantees to the Arabs be useless and its promises intangible.
4. It was ostensibly a recognition of Zionist aspirations to return to Palestine under the sanction of historic rights, but in reality it was the published clause of a private bargain by which war-spoils were to be given in payment for war-help.

There is relief in quitting this subject. The Balfour Declaration will recur in the remaining chapters, but at least in combination with other proclamations or papers or speeches and in conjunction with other events. So it will be less prominent.

But it is a pity that it cannot be lost from sight, and a greater pity that it has not yet been removed from our public records. Unlawful in issue, arbitrary in purpose, and deceitful in wording the Balfour Declaration is the most discreditable document to which a British Government has set its hand within memory.

Chapter 13

First consequences of the Balfour Declaration.
Mr. Ormsby-Gore appears on the scene.—Allenby's campaign.
The Arabs' exact part in it.
Allenby leaves the Balfour Declaration unpublished in Palestine.
The reasons for this.

In their report upon it, the Zionist Organization officials declared that the publication of the Balfour Declaration was "the signal for an unprecedented outburst of joy and enthusiasm throughout the length and breadth of Jewry." A commentary upon this is provided in a letter written on the 11th of November from India by Mr. Edwin Montagu. "I see," he wrote, "that Balfour has made the Zionist declaration against which I fought so hard. The Government has dealt an irreparable blow at Jewish Britons and has endeavoured to set up a people which does not exist." The then highest-placed Jew in the country showed therefore neither joy nor enthusiasm, and there were plenty of Jews who thought like him.

But a great deal of enthusiasm undoubtedly did follow in other quarters. "The text was cabled through the War Office and the Foreign Office to Jews in the remotest corners of the earth. Sheaves of cables were taken by us to the War Office," writes Mr. Landman, "for this purpose." The response was on a similar scale. Russian Zionists sent an address to the British Government to give thanks for the "inspiring declaration." Similar messages came from most European countries and of course in great numbers from the United States. The most interesting result however occurred in Germany. The German Zionist Association passed a resolution greeting with satisfaction the act of the British Government in "recognizing the right of the Jewish people to a national existence in Palestine."

This, Mr. Horace Kallen points out, was "tantamount to defiance of their rulers." So it was, but the rulers were hardly aware of the defiance, they themselves were so annoyed to think that they had not got in first with this bid for universal Jewish support. Everybody at the time seems to have taken for granted that universal Jewish support was going to turn the tide of the War. Never was there better evidence of how general the belief is in that power of international Jewry, and in the existence of international machinery for using it, which most Jews themselves so consistently deny. On this strange occasion though, the Jews not merely did not deny it, but appear to have encouraged the story of their international power, and to have done their best to spread popular credence in it. A little more and they would have rescued the "Protocols of Zion" and other such rubbish from the waste-paper baskets of the world and have gone about brandishing them, and crying to the belligerents, "See what we can do when we league together."

Ludendorff himself, if he did not send a telegram of congratulation to Lord Balfour, declared that his Declaration was the cleverest bit of propaganda the Allies had accomplished. The statement is attributed to him, at least, and seems likely, for under German General Staff orders an undignified scramble began at Constantinople, where the German and Austrian ambassadors sought somehow to extract imitation Balfour Declarations from the Turks. They had no success worth mentioning.

Not very consistently, the Germans spread the text of it by wireless through the regions under the control of the Central Powers, on the chance of gaining something by exposing it wherever they did not or could not imitate it. It came to Palestine first in this manner. But the military position was too acute for much effect to spring from this. Allenby's winter offensive began only some three weeks after the Declaration was published, and he entered Jerusalem on the 9th of December. The one act of any possible usefulness to the enemy cause which was achieved was that the Balfour text, through the Turks, was passed to the Emir Feisal, in the hope of shaking his adherence to Britain. But of what followed upon that we shall see later.

At the moment the point to be made is that those Jews who scout the stories of consciously exerted world-wide Jewish influence might well turn for their proofs to the period of which I am writing. What was the result of all the wild bidding for the Zionist international help? What did we in particular gain by our apparently winning nod? Nothing tangible. Resolutions in Zionist coteries in Berlin and in Petrograd did not go far to give us a victory.

As in the case of the United States, all the talk of the rally of world-Jewry to the Allies in Europe never seems to get beyond the statement that there was such a rally and that extraordinary results flowed from it. But what were these results? What did world-Jewry accomplish? No doubt world-Jewry did something. But what did it do on a great scale, what did it do that can be traced and expounded?

In Russia there is not even a suggestion of accomplishment. Indeed Russia went the other way, and we were fighting her before long. In Germany none of the great Jewish supporters of the imperial regime ceased their part in the struggle for German success. And when the imperial regime collapsed, the scissions in the will-to-win of the German people did not come from Zionist streams percolating through the national system. It was not by Zionist aid that the Allies conquered Germany, but by their arms.

However, in the fictitious atmosphere of the time promises showed full of promise and the Heavens were alight with congratulations. A later epitome of the situation condenses them. "For once," says Mr. Kallen, without a smile, "for once justice, internationalism and imperialistic interests were in harmony." To celebrate this meeting of strong waters in the newly issued Declaration a great assembly under Zionist auspices was held in London at Covent Garden in early December. All manner of people discoursed in many tongues.

Some of the speeches have gained importance with time, as they are records of sentiments and of intentions which their authors now probably would like suppressed. Some, on the contrary, stand to the credit of those who delivered them. The Chief Rabbi spoke to his auditory of the rights of the people of Palestine, and did not qualify these rights in any way. Sir Mark Sykes pronounced a discourse which his hearers cheered, without taking the broad hint which it contained. "You will always," said he, "look back with joy to the fact that when the promise was held out to you of reparation you thought of your fellows in adversity, the Armenians and the Arabs." As regards the Armenians it was a deserved commendation: as regards the Arabs Sykes was to be disillusioned.

Lord Cecil declared, without any sign of examination into what he was saying, that "Our wish" (he represented the Government at the meeting) "is that Arabian countries shall be for the Arabs, Armenia for the Armenians and Judaea for the Jews." He went on to give a perfect example of that strange directional idealism of his, which focuses on some chosen result which appeals to him and leaves surroundings, circumstances, origins, and everything else in darkness he makes no effort to dispel. "I say," continued he, "that one of the great causes for which we are in this war is to secure to all peoples the right to govern themselves and to work out their own destiny, irrespective of the threats and the menaces of their greater neighbours."

Yet, when he made this speech, the great cause for which he was there was to abstract from the people of Palestine the right to govern themselves. The inner object of the gathering he addressed was that the people of Palestine should not work out their own destiny, but instead have it worked out for them in the way which the majority of those whom he was addressing desired. The very event which he rose to celebrate was the drafting of the terms under which the will of a "great neighbour" was to be forced upon a small people.

What is the lesson of such an extraordinary display? A very useful one. It is that in this affair of Palestine no one need be moved or influenced by the great names or the altruistic reputations of those who have espoused or patronized the Zionist cause. That men such as Lord Cecil or General Smuts should be on the Zionist side is no guarantee at all that the Zionist side is the right one. It only means that men such as Lord Cecil or General Smuts are human, and can be and have been as foolish, and as perverse too, as any minor persons. Their names only guarantee them as men of good intentions generally. They do not guarantee the ration of good intentions which they apportion to any given situation, nor even their knowledge of it.

When and how was General Smuts, for example, to learn, during his African campaign, of the composition of the population of Palestine, of the character, extent and length of the Arab occupation of that land? I am ready to run all risks of lèse-majesté in South Africa by saying that in every probability at that time he was ignorant of these essential points. Afterwards, unfortunately, he became contumaciously ignorant of them, in the Balfour manner.

In those early, all-important days no Arab got through to tell the truth to high-placed personages. The Arabs indeed were not considered to be men worthy of consultation or with a right to it. In any event, they were out of reach, in part far away fighting, in part inhabiting the scene of war, dissipated here and there, and themselves unaware as yet of the trick which was being played upon them. Official Britain, official Dominion statesmen and others in similar positions who were to "confirm" the Balfour Declaration, accepted in good faith the version of Palestine's conditions which was prepared for them by the Zionists and handed out by those in Governmental and Civil Service posts who were in liaison with the Zionists.

Nobody realized the perfidy of the Balfour Declaration. Men such as Lord Sydenham, later to be one of the greatest Arab champions, sent messages of congratulation upon its issue.

There were speeches at the Covent Garden meeting, however, which should have served as warnings to friends of the Arabs of the situation intended for the latter, wherever their presence impeded the realization of Zionist aims. Dr. Gaster made a very important speech. He was one of the directing group, a Declaration-draftsman, and the owner of the house where the first official Anglo-Zionist conference had met in February. He spoke therefore with much authority. "What Zionism stands for," said he, "must be clearly apprehended, and also what the declaration of the British Government is expected to embody.... What we wish to obtain in Palestine is not merely a right to establish colonies or educational or cultural or industrial institutions. We want to establish in Palestine an autonomous Jewish Commonwealth in the fullest sense of the word. We want Palestine to be Palestine of the Jews and not merely a Palestine for Jews. We want the land to be a land of Israel. The ground must be ours."

As there is so often occasion to remark, nothing could be clearer. Did any of Zionism's Gentile supporters, present in force, disclaim Dr. Gaster's proposals? Did Lord Cecil offer a twitter of demur to them on behalf of the Government? Did another primary supporter of the cause disclaim them, one whose name now enters upon the scene, the recent Colonial Secretary, Mr. William Ormsby-Gore?

They uttered no dissentient word. On the contrary, when it came to Mr. Ormsby-Gore's turn to speak, this is the essence of what he had to say: "The Jewish claim to Palestine is to my mind overwhelming.... From the moment I met their Zionist leaders, whether in Egypt or in this country, I felt that there was in them something so sincere, so British, so straightforward, that at once my heart went out to them.... I have done what little I can to help forward the movement, and in the future, if you are looking out for a friend, count me as one of them."

There is not much of a disclaimer about this pronouncement. From the start Mr. Ormsby-Gore helped to set the tone of the pro-Zionist policy which year by year has been destroying further and further our ancient good name and high status in the Middle East. We shall see him at work.

A few days after this meeting Sir Mark Sykes made another speech; in Manchester. There was more than a hint that the Arabs should be remembered in this speech; he warned the Jews to "look through Arab glasses."

The warning was of no avail. A trifle of lip-homage was paid to the Arabs for a week or so, and then they were put out of sight. In the last week of the year a meeting was convened of the Jewish National Fund Commission for England, to consider the financial needs of the Zionist project. M. Sokolov himself was present. Mr. Ettinger, another of the Declaration-drafters, outlined a scheme for the colonization of Palestine. "All that the present generation can do," he said, "is to lay the foundations of the community. But the Commission has in mind the settlement of two million Jews, with eight hundred or a thousand cities, garden-cities and towns."

This statement of Mr. Ettinger's, so rich in prospect for the Arabs, may be said to have marked the close of a period, the period of theory. Till now, all that had been arranged for Palestine had been arranged theoretically, upon paper, at a distance from its soil. The Arab armed forces from the Hedjaz, it is true, in the course of their action against the Turks, certainly were approaching that soil. In their simple pedestrian way they were advancing under Lawrence upon Akaba. But the Zionist advance had been carried out by proxy, in London and New York.

This situation was drawing to an end. The physical occupation of Palestine by Britain was about to begin, and thereby of course to introduce quite a new turn of events.

If British occupation of Palestine had not begun earlier, it had not been for want of desire. As soon as he became Prime Minister in 1915 Mr. Lloyd George had pressed for an advance from Egypt into the Holy Land. He saw the great prestige to be won from a capture of Jerusalem, if no more than that could be accomplished.

Sir Archibald Murray then commanded the forces charged with the defence of Egypt. Technical difficulties prevented him from turning his defensive role into anything of an offensive nature in the direction of Palestine till January of 1917. Early in that month the first British soldiers—New Zealanders from Auckland—crossed the frontier. But Murray was short of men and could not obtain reinforcements. In January some 40,000 Turks faced him. He had four divisions. Fortunately the Arab revolt had kept 12,000 more Turks in the Hedjaz and upon the lines of communication leading to there.

Operations against Palestine were postponed eventually till the autumn and a division was withdrawn from Murray for service on the Western Front. None the less in the spring he undertook the so-called "offensive-defensive" against Gaza. Assaults were delivered in March and in April, but both failed. Our losses were considerable, and whether the second assault should have been delivered at all is very doubtful. The responsibility for it rests in the main with the General Staff, though Murray's dispatches after the first attack were over-optimistic and created in London a wrong impression of the position. "The second attack on Gaza," writes Lawrence, "which London forced on one too weak or too politic to resist.... I heard how we went into it, everybody, generals and staff-officers, even soldiers, convinced that we should lose." In June Sir Archibald Murray, "like the commanders of many other British 'advanced guards' sent to open a campaign with insufficient forces" *(Official History of the War)* was superseded. General Allenby was sent out to take his place.

Allenby landed in Egypt on the very day, the 6th of July, that the Arabs under Lawrence captured Akaba by skilful manoeuvre. They had taken two months to reach their objective. The six-hundred-mile route "was so long and difficult that we could take neither guns nor machine-guns, nor stores nor regular soldiers." They started out from Wejh, a mere reconnaissance-group on camels, and raised their force by degrees from the Arab tribes through or near whose districts they passed. Two Syrian officers formed Lawrence's "staff," ready for the entry into their native territory. They picked their way over lava and through desert scrub, in solar heat and often enveloped by sandstorms. "Some even of the rough tribesmen broke down under the cruelty of the sun, and crawled or had to be thrown under rocks to recover in their shade." But they ran about and showed themselves at all points to give an impression that they were more numerous than their real numbers.

"The hill-sides were steep and exhausted our breath, and the grasses twined like little hands round our ankles as we ran, and plucked us back. The limestone tore our feet, and long before evening the more energetic men were leaving a rusty print upon the ground with every stride. Our rifles grew so hot with sun and shooting that they seared our hands. The rocks on which we flung ourselves for aim were burning, so that they scorched our breasts and arms, from which later the skin drew off in ragged sheets. The smart made us thirst, but even water was rare with us."

The Turks fired vainly on them with mountain-guns. The Arabs on their camels charged Turkish infantry formations and broke them. They captured one strong outpost of Akaba by favour of an eclipse of the moon. By their methods of fighting the Arabs shattered the Turks' morale, and they had already deceived them upon their objective, so that when they came down finally upon their goal the garrison, and the men of the outposts driven in to it, hesitated, parleyed and surrendered. The five hundred Arabs took prisoner seven hundred Turkish men and forty-two officers.

"Strategically," says Liddell Hart, "the capture of Akaba removed all danger of a Turkish raid through Sinai against the Suez Canal or the communications of the British Army in Palestine … it ensured the Arab ulcer continuing to spread in the Turkish flanks, draining their strength and playing upon their nerves."

From Akaba Lawrence rode the hundred and fifty miles to Suez, and thence went to Cairo. Allenby soon sent for him, and they had an interview at which the role of the Arabs in his coming campaign was settled. With the taking of Akaba, the liberation of the Hedjaz, and of well beyond it, was completed. There was still a Turkish garrison in Medina, but it was locked up there in a safe of its own making, reinforced by Arab strategy. The Arabs now could turn to the further and greater part of their task, to joining the British Army in setting free their Mediterranean patrimony.

Feisal and Lawrence had settled this between them long before. Lawrence went back to Arabia, saw King Hussein at Jeddah, and told him of the arrangement made with Allenby by which the Arabs, under Feisal, should form the flying right wing of the British forces. Hussein accepted at once the transfer of his son and his men to Allenby and, says Lawrence, "took the opportunity to stress his complete loyalty to our alliance."

Equipment, munitions and funds presently were furnished in generous quantities to develop the new fighting-force. Its military role was to protect Allenby's right, as he advanced, from any Turkish attempt at envelopment from the east. In this direction, the Turks possessed an important centre at Maan, on the Hedjaz railway, about half-way between Akaba and the Dead Sea. Von Falkenhayn himself had gone to Maan to superintend its reconstruction as an entrenched camp, where some eight thousand men and proportionate artillery and aircraft were stationed. It might have been made a troublesome offensive centre.

But the result of the Arab action, with which our Air Force combined, through the summer and autumn was that Maan was turned into a second Medina, into which the Turks recoiled to shelter from eternal forays and railway destruction. They locked themselves up there. The continuous loss of their railway-engines also "was sore upon the Turks. Since the rolling-stock was pooled for Palestine and Hedjaz, our destructions... began to pinch the army about Jerusalem, just as the British threat grew formidable."

At the end of October Allenby struck, taking Beersheba on the last day of the month, Jaffa on the 16th of November and Jerusalem on the 9th of December. By the end of January, 1918, all southern Palestine west of the Dead Sea came under British control.

In this first stage of the conquest the Arabs had played their part well, and had played exactly the part which had been assigned to them. This was true both of the forces under Feisal and Lawrence and of the Arabs behind the enemy lines in Palestine and the other portions of Syria. It is necessary to emphasize this, for in the interests of Zionism every Arab role has been minimized or left unmentioned, or even discredited. Zionist commentators have a way of contracting all the Arab forces in the field to the single figures of Lawrence and of Feisal, and of belittling even these two. "The Anglo-Asian adventurer and mystery-monger Colonel T. E. Lawrence," is Mr. de Haas's description of Lawrence.

However, the motives of Zionists in this are so evident that it does not matter so much what they say or what they leave out. When however their British backers adopt the same tactics of depreciation, the matter becomes more serious. As a conspicuous example of these tactics may be chosen the words spoken in the House of Commons, during the Palestine debate of June, 1937, by Mr. Herbert Morrison, the Chairman of the London County Council. "The Arabs of Palestine," said he, "happened to remain passive throughout General Allenby's campaign. I am not complaining that someone remained passive in those exciting days, but it upsets the doctrine, so far as Palestine is concerned, that there were particular obligations in regard to that territory."

In the first place, even if the Arabs of Palestine had remained passive in the sense that Mr. Morrison implied, that would have made no difference to the obligations of this country towards the Arabs in general. We contracted with all the Arabs as a unit, and it was officially recognized by our civil and military authorities (as will appear) that the Arabs had carried out their share of the contract. That is all that matters legally and in equity. To seek to evade our obligations, as Mr. Morrison does, on the supposed grounds that some Arabs were remiss, though the Arabs as a whole satisfactorily finished what they promised to do, is paltry. Would the London County Council evade paying a builder who had erected a block of flats perfectly to time and to specification, on the plea that one batch of his workmen was reported to have been idle? I should like to see the London County Council try to escape payment. There is nothing like a homely parallel such as this to show the sophistry of the argument used for the larger issue.

But what makes Mr. Morrison's shift to avoid honouring our engagements a really mean shift is the fact that the Arabs of Palestine did not remain passive, in any honest understanding of the word. The Arabs of Palestine (to say nothing of those who had perished on the scaffold already) now did what Lord Allenby required them to do. They were not asked to rise, which Mr. Morrison, for all his disclaimer, suggests as the necessary basis of the contract between Britain and them.

Allenby, for several reasons, did not desire the presence of an Arab irregular force operating on his own front. For one reason he did not wish his manoeuvres complicated by groups of ill-armed peasants not cognizant of his intentions and escaping from his orders. And a "rising" would only have been an affair of a few poor groups. Palestine had been denuded of its able-bodied young men, who had been conscripted into the Turkish Army, and sent to distant fronts. As for their elders, Djemaal Pasha had seen to them. The first British official report on conditions in Palestine describes how far the country was in a condition to provide an insurrection. "When Allenby's army swept over Palestine," says the relevant passage, "it occupied a country exhausted by war. The population had been depleted: the people of the towns were in severe distress: much cultivated land was left untilled: the stocks of cattle and horses had fallen to a low ebb: the woodlands, always scanty, had almost disappeared: orange-groves had been ruined by lack of irrigation: commerce had long been at a standstill."

In fine, the farms and the fields were going to ruin because there were no men left to till them. Yet Mr. Morrison demands of the missing thousands that they should have risen. He argues that people who had been decimated and exiled for the cause of the Allies defaulted because they were not there when the Allies arrived.

However—to complete the real picture—apart from the impossibility of a rising, the Arab role was fixed in the conferences between the British commander and Lawrence. At this first stage of the campaign, it was a triple role. Arab soldiers left in the Turkish Army were to be invited to desert and to join Feisal's forces in the east. The local peasantry was to give any little help it could with food-supplies, which of course was very little. The principal occupation enjoined for the peasantry was to act as guides to the British troops and to serve as spies and intelligence agents, at a capital risk of course.

These plans were exactly carried out. A proclamation signed by King Hussein was dropped in large quantities by our aeroplanes over the Turkish lines, calling on any Arab soldiers to "come and join us who are labouring for the sake of religion and the freedom of the Arabs so that, if God wills, the Arab kingdom may again become what it was during the time of your fathers." (Additional proof that the promise of Arab independence in Palestine was acknowledged formally and spread by the British military authorities.)

The Arabs, as has been seen, were no longer numerous on this front. When they had been in greater numbers, in 1916, they had deserted freely. The German general Kress von Kressenstein, who had led the attack on the Suez Canal and afterwards had commanded in Sinai, complained of his heavy losses from Arab desertion. His Arabs left him and disappeared into the countryside. Afterwards when the Arab forces were centred at Akaba for the forward move into Palestine many of them joined Feisal. Those of them who were natives of Palestine and had been living concealed in their villages were employed now as guides and agents on the British front.

Lawrence's words concerning the role of these men, and of the population in general, are instructive. "We on the Arab front," he wrote, "were very intimate with the enemy. Our Arab officers had been Turkish officers and knew every leader on the other side personally. They had suffered the same training, thought the same, took the same point of view. By practising modes of approach upon the Arabs we could explore the Turks, understand, almost get inside their minds. Relations between them and us was almost universal, for the civil population of the army area was almost wholly ours without pay or persuasion. In consequence our intelligence service was the widest, fullest, and most certain imaginable." Earlier in his book, contrasting the mishandled situation in Mesopotamia with that in Palestine, he had written of the "freedom of movement and the elasticity of Allenby in Syria, who entered the country as a friend, with the local people actively on his side."

Under these conditions, then, after the battle of Beersheba, in which Allenby and his soldiers showed themselves worthy of one another, the British Army took Jerusalem. The news of the victory stirred the whole world. Two days later, on the 11th of December, Allenby entered the Holy City by the Jaffa gate, on foot.

This reverent, edifying act was barely accomplished there before political ambition restored a secular atmosphere in which it was more at home. Allenby had brought with him the Sykes-Picot Treaty, almost it might be said in the flesh, for both Sir Mark Sykes and M. Picot accompanied him. The parts played by the two men however were divergent. It had been Sykes who had suggested that the conqueror should enter the city of the Sacred Passion on foot. Picot's very different suggestion is best described in the words of Lawrence, who had been summoned to be present.

After the formal entry lunch was served to the principal personages. "The aides pushed about and from great baskets drew a lunch, varied, elaborate and succulent. On us fell a short spell of quiet, to be shattered by Monsieur Picot… who said in his fluting voice, 'And to-morrow, my dear general, I will take the necessary steps to set up civil government in this town.' … A silence followed, as when they opened the seventh seal in Heaven…. We turned to Allenby and gaped. Even he seemed for the moment at a loss. We began to fear that the idol might betray a frailty. But his face grew red: he swallowed, his chin coming forward, whilst he said, grimly, 'In the military zone the only authority is that of the commander-in-chief—myself.' 'But Sir Grey, Sir Edward Grey …' stammered Monsieur Picot. He was cut short. 'Sir Edward Grey referred to the civil government which will be established when I judge that the military situation permits.'"

The French Government, whose impulsive mouthpiece had thus been checked, still hankered after internationalization of Palestine, or the establishment therein of a ruling commission of some kind, of which the members would be nominated by Great Britain, France and Italy in the first instance, neutral Powers coming in later perhaps, as it were after allotment.

The British Government had not said no to this plan. It was involved in it under the Sykes-Picot pact, but it was equally involved in opposition to it under the Zionist bargain. That M. Picot should have stammered out to Allenby "Sir Grey's" name as a warranty for an international regime was topsy-turvy enough, since, as we have seen, Sir Edward Grey had started discounting such a regime in his memorandum to Russia of a year and nine months before.

But being involved on behalf of and against a plan at the same time necessarily produced a certain indefiniteness of attitude in the British Government. It remained silent when the French Foreign Minister declared in the Chamber of Deputies, a fortnight after the capture of Jerusalem, that neither France nor Britain would govern in Palestine, but that there would be set up there an international regime, one, he added reassuringly, *"fait de justice et de liberté."* And Mr. Stein, who mentions this, also chronicles a statement of Mr. Page, then United States Ambassador to Great Britain, that as far as he could ascertain the British Government did wish Palestine to be internationalized.

This internationalization implied that Palestine was to have control of its own local affairs, as Page understood, but that "some Great Power or number of Powers should see to it that none of the races that live there should be allowed to impose upon the other races." The terminology makes it evident that the Ambassador had been talking to Lord Balfour, and innocently had absorbed the latter's agile method of evicting the Arabs from the occupation of their native land. Balfour's pet project, which he pursued with some persistence because of its unrealizable charm, also was repeated to Page, that is, to install the United States in Palestine to take the position of what came to be known later as a Mandatory. Not that he ever expected this to occur. There would not have been much object in issuing his Declaration unless it was Great Britain who was to be suzerain in Palestine. But Balfour liked to play with the idea of an American, or a joint Anglo-American suzerainty.

All his Palestine schemes came under this intellectually recreative heading. He drew an interest from them akin to the study he gave to a Royal Society experiment, some altogether fascinating experiment with untried components and an impudent formula. He believed perhaps that his heart had gone out to the cause of the Jews. But a closer analysis would have shown that his interest in Zionists resembled a chemist's interest in chlorides or what not. He watched them lovingly in the Palestine retort, hoping to extract from them all sorts of dazzling precipitates which chlorides had never yielded before.

The peril of the man was that no one knew when he was entertaining himself with politics and when he was putting up with politics, which latter was the period in which he accomplished his true political work. Also when he was on the track of an experiment he was ruthless with unwanted factors. The Arabs were so much dirt in his dish, and he cleaned it free of them before he put in his first Zionist dilutes.

In this strain of mind no doubt he talked engagingly to Mr. Page about American or Anglo-American "internationalization" of the territory which was coming under British control. But he knew at heart that there would be no internationalization.

Allenby's bluff impromptu to Picot probably saved the Government a good deal of trouble. After all a military administration was the only one possible or permissible for the moment, and this could be prolonged on one plea or on another till the French had been persuaded out of their present intentions.

The military occupation of the country, despite its being as yet incomplete, brought things to a new stage. Two problems were presented immediately: the reaction of the Arabs and the reaction of the Zionists to the opening-up of Palestine. London would have overlooked the Arabs, but for the first time, it may be said, the Arabs were beginning to show symptoms of doubt, or were making inquiries which verged on doubt. Lawrence had encountered the absolute beginnings of doubt in the Hedjaz the previous year, as has been described. But that was a private issue, which he settled there and then. Now there were signs of the matter being brought to public view. The Arabs manifested some inclination not to be overlooked.

As soon as the text of the Balfour Declaration reached Egypt a committee of the leaders of the Syrian or Arab community in Cairo, a very important and representative body, sent a deputation to protest against its terms.

It was not surprising that they protested as soon as they read the Balfour document. They saw the implications in it before anyone else did, but this was not merely a feat of insight, because they had a very different document to compare with it. This was a pledge given them, a confirmation to them of the Arab independence already promised to King Hussein, which they had received on the 11th of the previous June (1918) from the British Government through the High Commissioner. This assured them that pre-War Arab states and Arab areas freed by military action of their inhabitants should remain entirely independent, "subject to the interests of France."

Lawrence writes of it "at this juncture the British Cabinet, in joyous style, gave with the left hand also. They promised to the Arabs, or rather to an unauthorized committee of seven Gothamites" (Lawrence never cared for urban Arabs) "in Cairo, that the Arabs should keep for their own the territory they conquered from Turkey in the War. The glad news circulated over Syria."

Allenby, as we know, arranged that the Arab forces should be placed on his right wing as a definite part of his army, and as a part of that army they conquered Palestine. It is well to interpolate this in case Mr. Morrison might argue that because they were not in the centre or on the left wing therefore they did not free the territory conquered in centre or left by Allenby's army.

As a matter of fact, these seven Arabs were not all civilian Gothamite wiseacres. Several of them were Arab officers who had deserted from the Turks and were interned in Egypt till the opportunity of creating a regular

Arab force arrived. They were members of the Ahad Society. One such was an officer named Aziz Ali. Among the civilian members of the committee were, I believe, MM. Iskandar Amoon, Rashid Rida, Rafeek al Athem and Kamel Kassab.

In January the Balfour Declaration was communicated to King Hussein, that is to say a copy was taken to Jeddah and was shown to him. This act, by the way, contains its own significance. If Palestine had lain outside the area in which he had contracted for Arab independence, why show him this effusion? Details concerning the really excluded areas (that is those in the French sphere) were not communicated to him, so there can be no excuse put forward that he was shown all documents dealing with areas where any Arabs lived, as a mark of courtesy or good will. The communications he received dealt with matters which rose between the British Government and himself in the areas covered by his pact with Sir Henry McMahon. So the very fact that the Balfour Declaration was shown to him at all is a subsidiary proof that Palestine, to which it related, was one of these areas, and therefore was one of the areas promised independence.

King Hussein was not so quick as the Cairo Committee to perceive the implications of the Balfour document. The fact was that he paid no real attention to it, trusting, poor man, to his treaty with us. Hogarth says that "he took it philosophically, contenting himself with an expression of good-will towards a kindred Semitic race, which he understood (as his phrase made clear) was to lodge in a house occupied by the Arabs."

He imagined that the Jews who came to Palestine would be citizens of the Arab State, and, as upon a previous occasion, those who visited him did not dare nor care to undeceive him. It is to be remembered that the Declaration, too, will have been translated into Arabic for him, and in the translation the fraudulence of its text may have been hidden.

But the real trouble was to come upon the Arab front. The revolutionary Government of Russia had found the Sykes-Picot Treaty in the national archives and had published it. Through the Germans this had reached the Turks quickly. The division of Syria according to the desires of the Powers, without reference to the Arabs, was a terrible revelation of bad faith, whatever extenuating circumstances may have accompanied it. Djemaal Pasha "read the most spiteful paragraphs at a banquet at Beyrout" (Lawrence), and conveyed the whole text to Feisal through the Turkish lines.

But Lawrence, as we have seen, had by now told Feisal of the Sykes-Picot Treaty, and Feisal was inwardly armed against it. The Turkish disclosures, though, and perhaps the Balfour Declaration, clearer to others than to Hussein, on top of it, spread the knowledge of what had occurred beyond Feisal and his immediate circle. In later days he himself told Mrs. Steuart

Erskine of what was the result. The Arab forces were now all concentrated at Akaba when the Turks sent the news through. "Feisal, who" (says Mrs. Steuart Erskine) "spoke to me at some length about this crisis, said that a wave of indignation swept over the army which had already accomplished so much in the cause of the Allies, and that it nearly ended in an insurrection. As a result of the high tension he telegraphed to his father, saying that he could not continue the war in these circumstances."

King Hussein, through the British representative at Jeddah, Colonel Basset, sent at once a demand to London to know whether it was true that the British Government proposed to partition Syria in contradiction to the terms of the treaty he had signed, and whether or not the British Government would abide by that treaty. On the 8th of February, 1918, Colonel Basset sent from Jeddah the reply of the Government. It had been dispatched by Lord Balfour as Foreign Secretary. It is another of the notable documents of the Palestine question. Here is a translation of the text, sent of course to King Hussein in Arabic, into which it had been turned in Cairo. It is not presented as a letter-for-letter version of the English text, which has not been made public; but is taken from a literal version in English of the Arabic text Hussein received.

> I have been ordered by the Viceroy [that is, the High Commissioner] of His Britannic Majesty to communicate to Your Majesty the cable which has been received by His Excellency from the Foreign Office in London. The British Government has addressed the cable directly to Your Majesty. Its text is as follows:
>
> The goodwill and perfect frankness which Your Majesty had displayed in forwarding to the Viceroy the correspondence sent by the Turkish commander in Syria to His Highness the Emir Feisal and to Jafaar Pasha has made an excellent impression upon the Government of His Britannic Majesty. The action which Your Majesty has taken in this matter is but another proof of the friendship and the frankness of intercourse to which the close relations between the Hedjaz Government and His Britannic Majesty's Government have always testified. It is scarcely necessary to point out that the aim of Turkish policy is to create doubt and dissension between the Allies and the Arabs, who are assembled under the wise leadership and good guardianship of Your Majesty to exert their energy to regain their ancient freedom. Turkish policy continues to sow this dissension by false and evil insinuations to the Arabs, such as that the Allies intend to occupy Arab territories, in the hope that the Arabs thereby will be influenced to alter their plans of action and to abandon the goal which they have set themselves. But the intrigues of provocative persons should not be allowed to rouse discord between those who are joined in a single hope and a single purpose.

> The Government of His Britannic Majesty and its Allies remain steadfast to the policy of helping any movement which aims at setting free those nations which are oppressed. It adheres to its decision to stand by the side of the Arab nations in their struggle to create an Arab world in which law and the Shar' shall replace Ottoman oppression, and to defy the industrial competition which the official Turkish institutions have engendered. *The Government of His Britannic Majesty repeats its previous promise in respect of the freedom and the emancipation of the Arab peoples.* The Government of His Britannic Majesty has always adopted and pursued a policy of emancipation, and intends by a straightforward and determined maintenance of this policy to preserve those Arabs who have not yet been set free from the disaster of falling back into their former condition, as well as to aid those Arabs who are still under the yoke of the oppressor to win their freedom.

I do not know how far the reader will find the preamble of the Government message sincere. However, the important point in the reply is that in the passage which I have italicized, reproduced exactly from the original, the Government guaranteed again the fulfilment of the pact with Hussein. The Government of His Britannic Majesty repeats its previous promise—nothing could be more explicit. The previous promise was "to recognize and support the independence of the Arabs within the territories included in the limits and boundaries proposed by the Shereef of Mecca." So beside the solemn promise of 1915-16 there is the official confirmation by the Foreign Secretary of 1918.

It makes no difference that the guarantee was given by Lord Balfour within three months of the issue of his Declaration which set out to prevent that guarantee's fulfilment. Whether he and his companions in the Cabinet meant to fulfil it or not, they gave this confirmation to the Arabs, in order to retain them as allies, and thereby they engaged their country's faithfulness, if they had none of their own. From that day the scandal of the treatment of the Arabs grew worse.

King Hussein was so satisfied with Lord Balfour's assurances, as well he might have been on the face of them, that he sent a sharp message to Feisal. "He said that the realization of the Arabs' aspirations was guaranteed by his honour and by the honour of his family, ending his message with these words, 'If you do not continue the war I shall consider you a traitor.'" (Steuart Erskine.)

Feisal may have telegraphed to his father in a moment of discouragement that he could not continue the war, but it is more likely that he did so to stir Hussein and to obtain through him such a renewal of the British pledge as the King received. This would be more in keeping with Lawrence's account of Feisal's mind and policy at the time. One way or another, the

British response having been received, the Arab army continued its share in the campaign.

A plan had been drawn up between Allenby and Lawrence, who had already discussed it with Feisal, by which the Arabs were to advance from Akaba when railway communications had advanced enough to ensure supplies and if possible to arrive at the Jordan before the end of March. In a raid they burned the lighters and launches of the Turks and stopped water-traffic on the Dead Sea before January was over.

Jafaar Pasha trained a nucleus of an Arab regular army: there were some four battalions of them in February. On the 28th of this month further and more elaborate plans for the Arabs were concerted. But as the spring advanced the possibility of carrying out the advance into northern Palestine and to Damascus faded away. Troops were taken from Allenby, as from Murray, for the Western Front, then endangered by a German offensive. On 5th of May Allenby told Lawrence the Arabs would just have to hold on for the present.

He softened this blow by allotting to them two thousand riding camels which the dissolution of a Sinai force had put at his disposal. This was the chief of a number of allocations of personnel, material and stores to his Arab right, to which he now gave considerable trust. To the Arab political cause Allenby made a species of gift too, a negative one perhaps but having its value. He would not have the Balfour Declaration published in Palestine.

Arabs in official positions, those who read British newspapers, and others such got to know of it, of course, and as far as they could, began at once to attack it. But from the mass of the people it was kept hid, though there was Zionist complaint of this. "No official instruction seems to have been given by Whitehall in London to General Headquarters in Cairo as to bringing their action into accord with the new idealist character which the Palestine offensive, in view of the Balfour Declaration, had acquired." *(Zionist Official Report.)* The new idealist character! A pleasant concept, this, of Allenby and his mundane army being regenerated by the Balfour Declaration.

Mr. Graves suggests that the Declaration was not published (it was only proclaimed in Palestine after two years had passed) because "when the result of the War was in grave doubt it was not a fitting moment to make any official proclamation of our intentions as regards hostile territory."

What of the Balfour Declaration then? For whom too was a proclamation not fitting? For the enemy? The enemy had spread it about the world as widely as the enemy's wireless-service permitted. For the nations of Europe? For India? For the American continent? They all knew it from universal publication in the Press.

The only people who could be, and were ignorant of the Declaration were the inhabitants of Palestine and the adjacent war-zones, who probably had not ten wireless-sets between them nor any access to newspapers. So that Mr. Graves unintentionally leads us to the chief reason why the Declaration was not published, which, as it happens, the Zionists themselves have confessed. As they put it, "There can be no doubt but that General Allenby knew by the time that such a Declaration had been issued. But the military authorities obviously thought that any official mention of that fact in the newly conquered territory might mar the jubilation of certain sections of the population. Naturally anxious to avoid any friction which might hinder the freedom of further military operations, they preferred to abstain from any mention of the fact that the British Government had promised to support Zionist aspirations." *(Zionist Official Report.)*

There is one part of the truth expressed with some marvellous phraseology. In plain English, the Government had issued a Declaration so high-handed, so improper that it would have been a danger to the progress of the army. It had to be suppressed.

The general evidence points to Allenby having suppressed it himself. There is reason to believe too that while he felt that publication of it would have injured his campaign, there was a stronger reason still for his action. He did not think it was legitimate for him to publish it, because it contravened the Hague Convention to which Great Britain had subscribed. Under the Hague Convention an occupying army must not introduce a new political regime. (This question will be treated fully in a later chapter.)

However that be, the non-publication of the Declaration introduces an unescapable dilemma. If Allenby suppressed it himself, the Government had to be censored by its own forces in the field. If it was suppressed by order or agreement of the Government then the Government knew the Declaration was a betrayal of the Arabs, and preferred to conceal it from them till their country was in the Government's control.

Chapter 14

The Zionist Commission in Palestine.—Close of the War.
The Arabs' military achievement.
The Joint Anglo-French Proclamation promising Independence to the Arab populations.

The second problem before the Government when Allenby occupied southern Palestine was how to content the Zionists, who expected immediate results from the Balfour Declaration, and results in Palestine. But the occupied portion of that country was little more than a military camp, and the Declaration itself was an obstacle to victory, and could not be proclaimed there. So it was not too easy to find a means of beginning the installation of the National Home.

However, a plan was evolved between the Zionists and the Foreign Secretary or was drawn from pigeon-holes where it had been waiting. This was to send into the occupied territory a delegation of the Zionist bodies in Great Britain and the Allied countries. This delegation could be given a free hand in Palestine, if it took upon itself the organization of succour for the Jewish colonies, which had suffered so severely during the War, and of other kindred benevolent activities.

This does not mean that the programme was all a piece of window-dressing. The little Jewish community did need relief very badly, and their fellow-Jews of course were genuinely anxious to purvey it to them. This part of the programme was entirely sincere. But the advantage of it was that if the delegates' terms-of-reference were made loose enough, then they could extend their situation by and by, could involve themselves in the administrative system, and in sum could form the nucleus of a future Jewish establishment with governmental attributes.

The delegation was to be known as the Zionist Commission. When Lord Balfour made the first announcement of its functions in the House of Lords, he declared that these would be "to investigate the present condition of the Jewish colonies in Palestine, to organize relief-work and to supervise reparation of damage done to Zionist colonies during the War, in so far as circumstances will permit."

But before the Commission left England in March, the necessary change was made to enable it to slip from benevolence into political activity. This was most ingeniously done, by granting to the Commission supplementary terms-of-reference masked as a "definition of status." In order supposedly that both the Army authorities and the Delegation itself should know where the latter stood, it was announced from the Foreign Office that the Zionist Commission was "to represent the Zionist Organization in Palestine and act as an advisory body to the British authorities there in all matters relating to Jews or which may effect the establishment of a national home for the Jewish people in accordance with the Declaration of His Majesty's Government."

These second and effective terms-of-reference were everything that the Zionists could have dreamt, if they ever dreamt instead of making specific arrangements. In the first instance the new Commission was placed in quasi-authority over all Jews in Palestine, since it was made the intermediary between them and the British administrators. Advantage was taken of the war-conditions to give the members of the Commission an illegal status. The Jews in Palestine were of various nationalities, about half being Turkish subjects by now perhaps. As Turkish subjects these Jews should have shared the lot of the other ex-enemy subjects, the Arabs, pending the formation of a new regime on the conclusion of peace.

If the Jews were of other nationalities, then their recourse in communications with the temporary British Army authority lay through their consuls, in accordance too with the Capitulations, if they were nationals of a Capitulatory Power.

Instead of this a Commission of Zionists was appointed, themselves of a variety of nationalities. Dr. Weizmann was Chairman. The other British members were Messrs. Joseph Cowen, Eder and Leon Simon. Professor Sylvain Lévi came from France. Two Italians, Commendatore Bianchini and Signor Artom, joined later. (The United States Zionists did not appoint members because the United States was not at war with Turkey. Mr. Walter Meyer acted unofficially as an American "observer," in the Geneva manner.) Their sphere of action was so vaguely and widely indicated—"in all matters relating to Jews or which may affect the establishment of a national home for the Jewish people"—that the Commission could claim upon pretty well any issue in which a Jew was or would be concerned that they were the persons indicated by the Government to handle it.

The Jews of Palestine were extra-territorialized in this way: they got back that "internal autonomy" which had been removed from the too frank earlier drafts of the Balfour Declaration. They were taken from the ranks of the Syrian population at large and were put into the care of the

Commission. They could always say in any juncture that the Commission had been appointed to "advise" the Administration on their behalf, without any intervention of native authorities, if the latter by any chance were established. In all "matters relating to the national home" any authority but British or Zionist was eradicated. Thus, by the proverbial pen-stroke, though their name was not mentioned even, the unfortunate Arabs again were deprived, carefully and in advance, of that independent control of their soil which was their natural inheritance and had been secured to them by formal and repeated engagements.

Zionists everywhere, regaled with rights which had been taken from the Arabs, did all they could for their Commission's success. Behind the scenes, Judge Brandeis had thrown himself "with great vim into the task of helping the Commission to proceed to Palestine." (de Haas.) "He regarded this move as a recognition in substance." The United States Zionist Organization, explains Mr. de Haas, "freely supplied Dr. Weizmann with money, just as it had liberally financed the political tasks of the English organization the previous year."

"Equally unostentatiously Brandeis began the draft of a charter for the future Jewish homeland." This covered the general objectives of the Commission. Land, water-rights, all other natural resources and all concessions, he wrote, "must be secured for the whole Jewish people." There was to be no exploitation by individuals: the Commission was to guard against this.

With these recommendations, or instructions, in its dispatch-boxes, the Commission arrived in Palestine early in April. By now the trend of events was growing evident to the Arabs of Palestine, and as the aims of the Commission became still clearer, through its members' own speeches and actions after landing, the Arabs began to protest. It is well to record this, because it is sometimes alleged that the Arabs were contented to accept Zionism at the beginning, and only took up a hostile attitude under various influences later on. That was not so. The Arabs protested as much as they could from the start, but they were cut off in their corner of the world. The War was being waged there; censorship controlled the cables. Such news as came from there was only military news sent by a couple of correspondents attached to the forces.

What made more galling the inability of the Arabs to present their position to world-opinion was that the Zionist Commission, by Government arrangement, was granted the freedom of the military cables and telegraphs and telephones. The Arabs were gagged, through lack of machinery to publish their case: all the machinery which existed was put at the Zionists' disposition for their communications in Palestine and from Palestine throughout the world. It is only too characteristic of the Arabs' lot that their enforced silence should have been used as proof of their indifference, or even welcome, to Zionism.

But the Arabs did react as best they could, though their complaints remained unknown outside the country. Dr. Canaan records that a formal protest was laid before the High Commissioner in Egypt immediately after the publication of the Balfour Declaration.

The relations of the Commission with British G.H.Q. had been cordial at the beginning, but soon enough they disimproved. Representation had to be made to its members asking them to curtail their political activities and to have less to say upon the preponderant situation which the Government had accorded to the Zionist body in Palestine.

The response was remarkable. "The Commission fully aware of the exigencies of the military situation, agreed that friction in the country might handicap operations, and that a full display of the Government's pro-Zionist attitude had better be postponed till after the victory." (Z.O.R.) Here is the truth nakedly exposed.

So the activities of the Commission had to be limited on the surface to relief-work (this work was excellently carried out), and to Jewish organization, which was not quite so innocent, since it involved preparations for creating a "Jewish Constituent Assembly." Another act was the laying of the foundation-stone of the Hebrew University on Mount Scopus by Dr. Weizmann.

Under the auspices of the Commission the "Jews of Jaffa and Jerusalem" held a conference at the former town in June to make arrangements for the summoning of the "Constituent Assembly." Amongst those present was then Major Ormsby-Gore. His invitation to the Zionists made at Covent Garden in December ("in the future, if you are looking out for a friend, count me as one of them") had been answered promptly. When the Commission left London he was attached to it as "Political Officer" and accompanied it all over Palestine. The Commission had power to go where it pleased through the occupied area in a semiofficial manner.

The Commission could even obtain travelling (and commercial) facilities for persons not belonging to it. More than three years later this fact was cited in the official Haycraft Report as one of the early causes of Arab discontent. Those whom the Commission recommended, who naturally were Zionist Jews, "enjoyed greater facilities than Arabs in the matter of obtaining permits to travel on military railways and to import merchandise by them, owing to the fact that the Zionist Commission was accepted by the Administration as sponsor for the Jews."

To return to the Jaffa Conference, Mr. Ormsby-Gore's presence there was taken as giving an official British patronage to the meeting. That to give this patronage was his intention was evident when he rose to make a speech, in which he referred to the information he would lay before the Government when he returned to England:

> What do we understand by the Jewish National Home? We mean that those Jews who voluntarily come to live in Palestine should live in Palestine as *Jewish nationalists* [my italics] That is, that they should be regarded as Jews and nothing else, and that they should be absolutely free to develop Hebrew education, to develop the country, and live their own life in their own way in Palestine freely, but only submitting equally with all others to the law of the land.
>
> ... I can say (to the British Government) when I go back, that whether you come from Russia, from Salonica, from Bokhara, from Poland, from America, from England, or from the Yemen, you are bound together in Palestine by the ideal of building up a Jewish nation in all its various aspects in Palestine, a national centre for Jewry all over the world to look to. This is the ideal of the future, an ideal which I am convinced will be realized without doing any injustice or injury to any of your neighbours here.

The final paragraph of this oration shows that Mr. Ormsby-Gore was in no ignorance of the complaints of the Arabs. He followed the Balfour method of falsifying the situation by speaking as though the Jews had a number of environing races around them—"any of your neighbours here"—so that the real issue between the solitary components, the one great Arab majority and the one tiny Jewish minority, might, as so often, be sloughed over. That he could be convinced that the Zionists were not doing an injustice to the Arabs when manifestly they were ousting them from the control of the country only serves to show the character of his convictions. But the main interest of his words lies in his acknowledgment, one of a kind which cannot be too often tracked down, that the idea of all present was the building-up of "a Jewish nation in all its aspects," and that Jews in Palestine were to be Jews and nothing else.

He continued by asking his hearers to "be patient with the British Government," which by international law was obliged to carry on the Turkish system of rule, so long as the administration remained military. His peroration began with an announcement which deserves to make the name of Ormsby-Gore famous for ever: "The Zionist movement is not merely a political move, but a spiritual force."

There was an allusion in his speech to the Jewish recruits who now were being enrolled, drawn from the youth of the Jewish colonies. So it is a convenient moment to speak of the Jewish military effort, by which I do not mean the service of those Jews who fought side by side with Gentiles in the ordinary forces of the Allies, but the special units which were raised as a sequel to the Zionist policy of the British Government and especially in reward for the Balfour Declaration. Earlier in the War a mule transport-corps, about 500 strong, had been recruited amidst the Jewish refugees from Palestine in Egypt, and had done fine work at Gallipoli. Mr. Vladimir Jabotinsky and Mr. Pinhas Rutenberg, both of whom for different reasons were to win much later notoriety, had agitated at the time for a Jewish legion. Mr. Jabotinsky wrote to *The Times* to advocate it. But they did not get support, and the mule-corps was the sole result.

Mr. Jabotinsky, a man of determination, stuck to his idea however and after the issue of the Balfour Declaration he now gained the backing of the Zionist Organization and finally of the War Office. It was intended at first to create a "Jewish Regiment." "Jabotinsky and the Zionists were agog with delight," says Mr Horace Samuel [in *Unholy Memoirs of the Holy Land*], who served as an officer in the unit when it was formed, and provides a detached account of its activities. They saw in the Jewish Regiment the nucleus of a Jewish army, which, having won Palestine, would then garrison it so as to keep the Arabs permanently in order." Just so.

But strong Jewish influence in London, the same influence which had fought in vain for the reasonable Wolf programme in Palestine, the Montagus, Montefiores, Magnuses and other leaders whose names have been cited, struggled, this time with greater success, against the formation of a "Jewish Regiment." They knew the intentions which lay behind it and they resented the segregation of Jewish soldiers from other soldiers of the Empire. So instead a Jewish battalion of the Royal Fusiliers was created, the 38th, under the command of a Gentile, Lieutenant-Colonel Patterson, who had commanded the Gallipoli mule-corps. It contained a mixture of Jewish and of Gentile officers. "A few Jewish officers were Zionist, a few were definitely anti-Zionist." (Horace Samuel.)

After an imposing send-off from the City of London, the battalion, which contained American Zionist volunteers, crossed Europe and shipped from Taranto to Alexandria. "On the 1st of March the regiment made through the streets of that city one of those self-advertising marches which were always one of its chief characteristics," says Mr. Samuel. "For so far as the Jewish regiment was concerned, not merely fighting, but propaganda, was the thing. As Jabotinsky himself once remarked: 'We are not merely a regiment—we are a political performing company.'"

The battalion went into training in Alexandria and later on was joined by another battalion, the 39th. There were some difficulties with Russian-born privates who when Russia abandoned the war thought they might follow suit, but "the officers and N.C.O.s managed to preserve the morale of the regiment," and in June it was moved into the line on the Nablus road, about twenty miles from Jerusalem. "It held with adequate efficiency for a few weeks the villages of Abwein and Jiljilia."

To follow Mr. Samuel's account, he was drafted back at the expiry of this period to Cairo to take command of a company of the Palestinian recruits, mentioned in his speech by Mr. Ormsby-Gore, who declared frankly of them that they would go "as missionaries of Jewish nationalism in Palestine." "They were very different stuff," says Mr. Samuel, "from their brethren who had been conscripted in London. They were out for fighting. They were anxious to drive out the Turk, and then constitute a permanent Jewish garrison amid a hostile Arab majority. More evidence commended to the reader.

The further history of the recruits may be found by the curious in Mr. Horace Samuel's pages. I may say that he, who served as a judicial officer for two years in Palestine after the War ended, is not a foe of Zionism, whom it has served my purpose to quote. I believe he is a Zionist, but, as I have said, somewhat detached. He is no particular friend of the Arabs, holding for example the opinion that if the Army had faced up to the Arabs from the beginning and really "impressed on all and sundry that the policy of the Balfour Declaration was the unalterable policy of the British Government," then "there would have been an end of the whole matter."

"So far as the Palestinians were concerned," says he, "it was certainly unfortunate that the War came to an end so soon, and that they were never given an opportunity of active service. I think it fair to assume that that very superfluity of patriotism which made them so undisciplined in camp would have made them correspondingly heroic in the actual field." With which most will be disposed to agree.

The Fusilier battalions took a creditable share in the final offensive in Palestine, not a prominent one perhaps, but as soldiers they had to act under orders in the positions allotted to them and they did as well as their opportunities permitted. Sir Ronald Storrs records the extraordinary gallantry of one of their scouts. The 38th and 39th battalions lost an officer and thirty-seven men. There would be no reason to mention the matter of the whole Zionist (not Jewish) military effort at all, save that one might be accused of leaving it out in order to exalt the Arab accomplishment. And it does provide evidence of those early Zionist aims of armed occupation of Palestine which it is so necessary to establish.

By the summer the Commission was working amidst an Arab population now quite antagonistic to it. "The Arabs of Palestine, backed by the sympathy of Arabs everywhere, assumed an attitude of sullen opposition." "The Zionist Commission, which had been in Palestine since March" (this should be April) "had, through its vigorous activity, aroused the anger of all the local population. Indeed the repulsion against the immigrant foe was goaded on by Arabs far beyond the boundaries of Palestine—those who had followed the tragic efforts for independence." (Andrews.)

The adjective "tragic" in this American estimate is no misnomer. It is a curious commentary upon it that while the Zionist Commission, mindful no doubt of Judge Brandeis's behests, was thus pursuing its course, Judge Brandeis's friend the President had issued his "Fourteen Points" address to Congress, of which the twelfth point directly affected Palestine. These celebrated points were to be the piles on which the platform of peace was to be constructed, according to the idea of Mr. Wilson. The twelfth point ran: "The Turkish portions of the present Ottoman Empire should be assured a secure sovereignty, but the other nationalities which are now under Turkish rule should be assured an undoubted security of life and an *absolutely unmolested opportunity of autonomous development.*" [My italics.]

This declaration, made in January, reached the occupied part of Palestine through foreign and Egyptian newspapers and so became known to the Arabs. Versions of it, altered and magnified no doubt by passing from mouth to mouth, were circulating generally when the Zionist Commission arrived. The contradiction between President Wilson's promise of self-government and the peripatetic sample of Zionist government which they beheld increased the rising dissatisfaction of the Arabs. In July Mr Wilson endorsed his previous statement in a speech containing the following words:

> "The settlement of every question, whether of territory, of sovereignty, of economic arrangement, or of political relationship (should be) upon the basis of the free acceptance of that settlement by the people immediately concerned, and not upon the basis of the material interest or advantage of any other nation or people which may desire a different settlement for the sake of its own exterior influence or mastery."

This sentence might have been composed specially to rebuke our Government and the Zionists, whose aims for Palestine were in such contradiction to the principles therein laid down. I cannot find whether this Presidential announcement became known in the occupied territory before Allenby began his great final offensive in September. The chances are that it did not become known, but I place it here where it belongs chronologically and where it helps to illustrate how blandly the noblest sentiments can be ignored, even by those who have uttered them. For, fresh from his Twelfth Point and from this declaration President Wilson within two months wrote a letter to Rabbi Stephen Wise, President of the

American Zionist Federation, in which he spoke of "the satisfaction I have felt in the progress made by the Zionist movement in the United States and in the Allied countries since the declaration by Mr. Balfour on behalf of the British Government." It is true, of course, that the President as yet had only the haziest ideas of conditions in Palestine.

He drew his information from his pro-Zionist intimates, who saw no connection between the Fourteen Points and Palestine. Judge Brandeis, beside supporting the dispatch of the Zionist Commission, had been busy developing a whole programme of action—and other things.

> No publicity was given to the organization (by Brandeis) at the beginning of 1918 of a group devoted to a careful study of the resources of Palestine, and a survey from historic sources of the boundaries of Palestine together with an estimate of the boundaries that in view of economic conditions would best serve the purpose of a large Jewish settlement.
>
> Illustrative of the view of the British and the American Governments' interest in the Jewish Homeland is the fact that the boundaries projected in New York in 1918 included the El Arish section of the Sinai Peninsula, extending eastward to the line of the Hedjaz railroad, and north from Tyre to a line skirting the Hermon, thus including the whole of the Jordan watershed.

Presumably what Mr. de Haas understands by "illustrative of the British and the American Governments' interest in the Jewish Homeland" is that the said Governments would be satisfied to let their Zionist friends in New York design the boundaries of Palestine as imaginatively as they pleased. The actual map-maker was a Mr. Moisseiff, who must rank amongst thwarted inventors.

From this unpublicized activity Mr. Brandeis went on to the preparation of the programme of the Zionist Convention held that summer in Pittsburgh. "It was the apogee of American Zionism." (de Haas.) The first of the five clauses of this programme may be quoted now: "We declare for political and civil equality irrespective of race, sex, or faith, of all the inhabitants of the land (Palestine)." Whatever happened to the other clauses, this primary one was struck rapidly as a match, lit nothing, and was thrown away.

The Pittsburgh Convention and the Jaffa Conference preceded a military council held by Allenby, at which he determined that he would make a general offensive upon the Turkish Army in Palestine in late September. He was receiving reinforcements from Mesopotamia and India now, and felt that a general attack might be ventured.

But like most great military strokes, it was a venture. Some of the conditions enforced upon Allenby made his plans hazardous. He was obliged to launch his main attack upon his left, in the coastlands, because only there did the railway enable the necessary supplies to be gathered. "This seemed so obvious that he could not dream of the Turks staying blind, though momentarily their dispositions ignored it." (Lawrence.) The Turks were indeed very weak towards the coast: they were of opinion apparently that the attack would come from the British right, extended by the Arab forces. Success, as Lawrence says, hung on maintaining them in this fatal misappreciation, for which end the Arab units were of paramount importance, since it would be the business of the Arabs to press the enemy as though the attack was to come from their direction. But Lawrence was warned that the Arabs must not be engaged in a position from which they could not escape, since if the Turks got wind of what was afoot and withdrew a few miles on the coast the British forces would be left with all its "railways, heavy artillery, dumps, stores, camps misplaced, and without orange-groves in which to mask its concentration next time."

Feisal and Lawrence therefore had no easy situation to handle with their Arabs. In Lawrence's case things were complicated at this critical juncture by the conviction, which daunted his energies every other while, that the Arabs might be betrayed of the independence for which they were fighting. "And for honour, had I not lost that a year ago when I assured the Arabs that England kept her plighted word." In August Feisal received from Allenby through General Dawnay a further "warning message" not to do anything rash, "as the British push was a chance, and if it failed the Arabs" (because of their situation under the offensive-plan) "would be on the wrong side of Jordan to be given help. Particularly Allenby begged Feisal not to rush upon Damascus…Feisal smiled wisely at Dawnay's homily, and replied that he would try this autumn for Damascus though the Heavens fell, and, if the British were not able to carry their share of the attack, he would save his own people by making separate peace with Turkey."

Djemaal Pasha had followed up his information of the Sykes-Picot Treaty by sending letters to Feisal begging him to come to a composition with Turkey. Djemaal was alarmed for the safety of the Moslem world, which he saw collapsing, and there was some genuineness in his letters, though how far he personally could be trusted, if success came the Turkish way, Feisal knew well. He judged it useful to go on with the correspondence, which provided a valuable sidelight on Turkish conditions.

Lawrence, who was cognizant of everything, encouraged continuing it in part for this reason, and in part because as the correspondence grew and involved secretly more and more important personages in Turkey (including its future ruler, Mustapha Kemal-Ataturk) it weakened the enemy's unity. Feisal even made a fictitious offer of quitting the field if the Turks would evacuate the Transjordan province of Amman.

He forwarded all the relevant correspondence to his father in Mecca, but old King Hussein was aghast at what he read, and "sent a vehement telegram of protest, to the effect that he would never countenance such a pact and that the Turks should be told, "Only the sword lies between us.""(Liddell Hart.) In all the convolutions of this story no one stands so straight as King Hussein.

Lawrence's and Feisal's motives in continuing the correspondence were not however sprung entirely from its value as a source of military intelligence. Lawrence particularly felt that it was not fair for all contact with the Turks to be lost by the Arabs. "We could not close all avenues of accommodation with Turkey. If the European War failed, it was the Arabs' only way out: and I had always the lurking fear that Great Britain might forestall Feisal and conclude its own separate peace, not with the Nationalist, but with the Conservative Turks. The British Government had gone very far in this direction, without informing her smallest ally. Our information of the precise steps, and of the proposals (which would have been fatal to so many of the Arabs in arms on our side) came, not officially to me, but privately."

Lawrence's information was accurate, of course. A year before this discussions had begun in Switzerland between Turks and British agents. The Englishmen were not formal envoys. They were in a betwixt and between situation. They did not engage the Government, but on the other hand the Government had engaged them. They were asked to go and to report on what the Turks had to say. They knew Turkey well and had old friends amidst the Turks generally. The Turks were men of some status and belonged to a group, gradually forming then, of politicians and soldiers who thoroughly disliked the German connection, which they thought would involve Turkey in ruin. The Turkish Minister in Switzerland and indeed all the Turkish Legation were secretly on their side; the diplomatic bag being employed for correspondence with Talaat Pasha, with whom negotiations were engaged. They were not entirely Conservatives: there was one member of the Committee of Union and Progress amongst those in Switzerland. As Lawrence explains, Mustapha Kemal himself was prepared to act against Enver, from Arab territory, if Feisal came to an agreement with him. Whether Mustapha Kemal was in touch with the Swiss negotiations is not clear. There was a main group negotiating, but there were individual threads too, not always linked, and not necessarily friendly to each other.

The main group was Anglophile above all, and preferred to carry on conversations with Great Britain rather than with any other of the Allies.

It produced a detailed scheme, which was dispatched to London, of which the preamble began:

> "A new party shall be formed to work for conciliation and for the safeguarding of the common interests of England and of Turkey. The promoters of this scheme believe that its accomplishment will only be possible through the withdrawal of Turkey from the German grip. In order to prepare Turkish public opinion both for this change of policy and for the introduction of a sober and healthy system of government, it will be indispensable to hasten the collapse (in any case inevitable) of the Committee of Union and Progress. Today the omnipotence of this band of vultures depends solely upon the existence of certain leaders of high station who are at the head of the chief departments of State and of the Central Committee. Once the terror inspired by these active personalities will have dissipated by their elimination, their Government would cease to exist for ever."

There was more upon these lines, which deserves citing to show how definite were the negotiating group's plans for a rising or for whatever the suspicious word "elimination" stood for. But the proposals were double-barrelled, for they also envisaged the New Party's inability to oust the Germans as long as the War lasted. In this event the party had ready a contingent programme, under which consideration had been given to the condition of the non-Turkish sections of the Turkish Empire. The programme ran:

1. As regards the government of the provinces administrative autonomy shall be accorded to the various ethnic elements of the Empire. Only the Valis (governors), the commanders of the military forces and the heads of the religious communities shall be named by the Sultan.
2. The remaining administrative personnel in each vilayet shall be appointed and be chosen by the local native authorities.
3. A certain number of foreign specialists—preferably British—shall be attached to the administrative authorities of the vilayets.
4. Each vilayet shall pay a due contribution to the general expenses of the Empire.
5. In case the "Union and Progress" Government should be overturned while the War is still in progress, in conformity with British interests, through the action of the New Party, then Great Britain shall guarantee the reimbursement of the Ottoman Public Debt. At the same

time, Great Britain shall engage herself as from now to provide Turkey with the financial assistance needful to ensure the smooth running of a satisfactory government for that country, even in the case of the signature of a treaty disadvantageous to the Porte.

6. In case the "Union and Progress" Government should be overturned while the War is still in progress Great Britain will recognize as an obligation to bring about the cessation of all hostilities by her Allies against the Ottoman Empire.
7. Great Britain will use her influence with the Great Powers to obtain the retrocession of Lemnos and Mitylene to Turkey.

There were several Turkish negotiators, and various schemes and programmes not differing very much from the above were in existence. They were considered by Mr. Lloyd George, and no doubt by Lord Balfour and other members of the Cabinet.

Besides these proposals, the Turkish Government itself had been dallying with peace proposals as far back as the spring of 1917 and had received through a British intermediary in Switzerland a "personal opinion" that if the Turkish Government made an official announcement to the Allies that it was willing to treat for peace, then the offer would be considered. The Turkish Government, or Talaat Pasha at least, had decided to make some such announcement, and Talaat had prepared his terms.

Under these terms, in matters touching the Arabs, Mesopotamia would become autonomous, sending delegates to a federal parliament at Constantinople. Syria "might be granted" the same autonomy. Arabia proper would be given a form of autonomy, but not under a King of the Hedjaz.

These semi-governmental proposals came to naught because the collapse of Russia, the possibility of a British defeat in Mesopotamia, and other factors intervened to make the Turks believe that they might win through after all and share in the Central Powers' victory.

It was when these latter hopes fell away that Talaat turned to the more individual conversations by which the security of the Committee of Union and Progress were menaced. It must have been a great shock to him when Allenby gained his victory at Gaza, for he had believed that British forces would never be able to capture Palestine, and that an arrangement on his own lines would have to be made with him.

I have given an account of the Turkish proposals at a little length to show what a serious menace the consideration of them by Great Britain was to the independence guaranteed to the Arabs. In 1918 they were mingled with the offers to Feisal, to which he and Lawrence responded in the way we have seen.

Whatever safeguard of correspondence he maintained for his people's sake and whatever went on behind his back, Feisal threw his heart now into the preparations for the offensive. An unexpected difficulty was provided by King Hussein, who was piqued at the importance, in fact the predominance in the Arab forces now being gained by Jafaar Pasha, and other Mesopotamian or Syrian officers. He was annoyed at Jafaar's having received a general's rank (there were some ten thousand Arabs fighting by this time in all sectors) without the matter having been referred to him. But by a ruse Lawrence patched things up between the King and his son and his son's officers. "Now, sirs," said Feisal on this occasion, to his staff, facing the last stage of their campaign, "praise God and work."

The prospective Arab work was of two kinds, each as vital to Allenby as the other. There was a third intention too, not so regularly covenanted for by the army commander. The first (touched upon a few pages ago) was to make the Germans and Turks believe that the offensive, which the enemy expected, was coming from their sector. This already had been suggested to the enemy in many ways by Allenby's staff. There had been the celebrated ruse for example of the lost dispatches, which had been written specially to be lost and were altogether misleading to the enemy, a ruse imagined and carried out by Colonel Meinertzhagen.

But the Arabs had a primary means of action upon the enemy's dispositions which surpassed any secondary ruse. A number of Ahad members, instead of deserting, had stayed in the Turkish ranks, kept in regular contact with their brethren in Feisal's army, and—this was more valuable service than any—made their plans to disorganize the forces they commanded. Very subtly, for complete safety's sake, these officers were left to imagine, by their correspondents in Feisal's force, that the blow would fall on the Turkish left, instead of the right. They were only asked to confuse their sectors tactically, which of course at the supreme moment would prevent troops being moved from wing to wing of the Turk army, in so far as any such movement would be practicable. "They were conjured," says Lawrence, "so to dispose their troops as to be ineffective both ways."

Another trick accomplished by the Arabs was to buy secretly from a chattering tribe well behind the Turkish left all its barley-crop "futures." This, the tribesmen were told, was to provide against scarcity of fodder for the animals of the British and Arab forces when "they had broken through," but they were enjoined on no account to mention this. But, as was expected, the news got out and reached the Germano-Turk command, confirming the Staff in the belief that it was their left that Allenby meant to attack.

The second main task of the Arabs was to envelop Deraa, the chief junction of the enemy railways, and to cut the lines at important points, so as to wreck the enemy's communications.

The third task, or rather the Arabs' third and more or less private intention was at last to raise in insurrection those tribes in whose territory the Turkish left wing would have to manoeuvre. It was only in this quarter, away from cities, where Djemaal's terror had not penetrated, that intact and useful potential forces for the Arabs lay. These tribesmen had long desired to revolt. At the time when Mr. Morrison (with not a few others) speaks of the Syrian Arabs as inert, Lawrence tells how he received continuous demands from the tribes round Deraa to be allowed to revolt. But Lawrence had forbidden this. He was not satisfied (and events proved him right) that Allenby then would be able to reach the level of Deraa in his coast-sector. So the Arab rising would be isolated and lost. "Deraa's sudden capture (which the Arab chief of the district had promised), followed by a retreat, would have involved the massacre or the ruin of all the splendid peasantry of the district. They could only rise once, and their effort on that occasion must be decisive."

These considerations, in the autumn of 1917, had made Lawrence order a postponement of the rising. Now, in the autumn of 1918, the hour for the rising had come.

The Arabs had the honour of beginning the great offensive. Allenby had demanded that three days before he moved the Turkish forces in Deraa should be enveloped and the railway cut. "Deraa was a vital point, for there centred the rail communications of all three Turkish armies and the line of retreat of the fourth. Only the Arabs could reach it. Upon them much depended if the Turkish dispositions were to be paralysed before Allenby's stroke descended."(Liddell Hart.)

By nine in the morning of the seventeenth "the southern ten miles of the Damascus line was freely ours," recorded Lawrence of that first day of battle. "It was the only railway to Palestine and Hedjaz, and I could hardly realize our fortune, hardly believe that our word to Allenby was fulfilled so simply and so soon." "Lawrence's preparatory task on behalf of Allenby was complete," says Liddell Hart in his study of the campaign. "By his three-sided cut at the focal point of the enemy's communications he had gone far to hamstring the Turkish armies just as Allenby was to jump on them. The stroke had the physical effect of shutting off the flow of their supplies temporarily—and temporarily was all that mattered here. It had the mental effect of making Liman von Sanders send part of his scanty reserves towards Deraa. More significantly still, he sent German troops, the precious cement that held together his jerry-built armies."

On the 17th an Indian deserter had warned the German staff that the main British attack was to be delivered in the coastal area. This was two days before Allenby was ready to move. But the Arab attack at Deraa made the Germans believe that the deserter was sent to fool them.

On the 19th Allenby gave the signal for advance. He crashed through to his great victory. There is no space to go into all the details of how the Arabs conquered too. They took Deraa on the 28th. And on the 30th September Damascus was captured and the Arabs' flag hoisted on their ancient capital. "Ali Riza Pasha himself, who had so long combined the dual function of Turkish commander and head of the Arab Committee, was not present to inaugurate the change. He had just previously been dispatched to take charge of the Turks' last line of defence, a duty that he had accepted as a conveniently early chance to join the British. .He so much enjoyed telling how he had selected heavy artillery positions that could not be occupied for want of water that in his merriment he upset the table on which breakfast had been laid."

Between that 5th of June in 1916, when the Arabs with such wild daring had begun their haphazard revolt, to this 30th September in 1918 the Arabs' action had steadily increased in importance and in value to the Allied cause. The greatness of its final accomplishment is summed up best by Captain Liddell Hart, the recognized chief military commentator of our day. He writes:

> In the crucial weeks while Allenby's stroke was being prepared and during its delivery nearly half of the Turkish forces south of Damascus were distracted by the Arab forces; pinned east of the Jordan by the subtle feints and the nerve-paralysing needle-jabs that Lawrence conceived and directed. Those forces comprised the 2nd and 8th Army Corps as well as the garrisons along the Hedjaz railway between Maan and Amman. Together these totalled some 2,000 sabres and 12,000 rifles. The ration strength appears to have been about three times as large, i.e., about 40,000 to 45,000 out of a total ration-strength of 100,000 south of Damascus.
>
> As a consequence Allenby was able to concentrate three Army Corps totalling 12,000 sabres and 57,000 rifles against the other half approximately of the Turkish forces. In the sector chosen for the decisive stroke he obtained odds of 5 to 1—44,000 to 8,000.... it created a whirlpool which sucked down almost half the Turkish Army, indeed more than half of it, if, as is just, we count the 12,000 Turks cut off in the Hedjaz. And even this reckoning leaves out the Turkish forces in Southern Arabia.
>
> What the absence of these forces meant to the success of Allenby's stroke it is easy to see. Nor did the Arab operation end when it had opened

> the way. For in the issue it was the Arabs almost entirely who wiped out the Fourth Army, the still intact force that might have barred the way to final victory. (They had taken 8,000 prisoners and killed a number that was estimated at nearly 5,000, besides capturing 150 machine-guns and thirty cannon.)
>
> This was the arithmetical factor. But there was also the biological. The wear and tear, the bodily and mental strain on men and material was applied by the Arabs, under the guidance of Lawrence's mind, who prepared the mind of Liman von Sanders so that he arranged his forces in the way that produced their defeat.

In another passage Liddell Hart says:

> Why had the enemy stayed to be pulverized instead of making a timely recoil? We know now that Liman had been anticipating a big attack, and that at the beginning of September he had thought of frustrating it by a withdrawal to a rear line near the Sea of Galilee. But "I gave up the idea," says he in his memoirs, "because we should have had to relinquish the Hedjaz railway, and because we could no longer have stopped the progress of the Arab insurrection in rear of our army."

Thus ended the war in Palestine and the Arabs' splendid part in the liberation of their territory. They had fulfilled their obligations, setting indeed no term to them and all through the campaign taking on obligation upon obligation as each emprise they were called upon to accomplish came to its end. As Lawrence, identifying himself with them, declared, "Our bond had been most heavily honoured." It was now the turn of Great Britain to reward them in conformity with the promises she had made to them. It was not such an extraordinary reward, after all, since it was but to recognize them as masters of the soil which they had occupied for so many centuries. The enemy himself had offered them not so much less, if they had been willing to abandon the Allied cause.

The local armistice was signed by Turkey on the 31st of October, soon to be followed by the great armistice in the West. The military authorities in Palestine now had to give themselves entirely to the problems of administration. The whole of Syria soon was in the Allies' control. It was the control of the Allies, not of Great Britain alone. Small French and Italian detachments had accompanied Allenby's army to maintain formally the inter-allied quality of his force, and the Union Jack was not hoisted when Jerusalem was captured. Allenby entered Jerusalem with a French and an Italian officer on either side.

With all Syria occupied it became necessary to adjust its government to the concept of general Allied control. The arrangements for this had to be carried through at once, and were treated as temporary till the heralded

Peace Conference should draw up the terms of peace for Syria, as for other parts of the world of which the future depended upon the result of the War. It was decided between Great Britain and France, not too easily, that the principle of the Sykes-Picot Treaty should be followed, and so Syria was divided into four sections known as O.E.T.A. (Occupied Enemy Territory Administration) North, South, East and West respectively. O.E.T.A. North and West were to be governed by French forces dispatched to Syria for the purpose, O.E.T.A. South by the British, and O.E.T.A. East by the Arabs.

Roughly put, the French held the coastal parts of Syria north of Palestine and the British the southern or Palestine parts. The Arab holding, with Damascus as capital, was an enclave into the other two, with Aleppo and Amman as chief places over against the French and British sectors respectively. Lord Allenby in July of 1919 was put in general control over all the O.E.T.A.s, though in practice he did not act outside the British area except in consultation.

It was after consultation between the French and the British Governments that on the 9th November a proclamation was issued by him, addressed to the inhabitants of Mesopotamia and of Syria, which might be described perhaps as the most striking document of all that were to appear in relation to the affairs of Palestine. It is true that it is not a fundamental item in the way that the Hussein-McMahon engagements were. It was only corroborative of these.

But it is so categorical, so plain in what it asseverates, and so unescapable in the evidence it provides of our faithlessness, that it stands out amidst all others. There is reason to suppose that Sir Mark Sykes, already on the road to repentance, had a share in the drafting of it, though it was first completed in the French language. Allenby's share in it was that he demanded it. The Arabs had kept their word to him, and he now, as their governor, insisted that it was necessary we should give in earnest of our intention to keep our word to them.

But it is a Governmental document. The responsibility for it lay upon the Governments of France and of Great Britain. It was studied and passed by the two Governments. M. Picot and Lord (Robert) Cecil went over it together. Finally it was submitted to Mr. Lloyd George and to M. Clemenceau, who ratified it and ordered its publication. The statesmen's motives were not quite those of Allenby, the soldier. They wanted to appease local trouble: he to carry out a bond. Already in the Near East there was wide irritation and unrest which had to be placated. This was because of the small evidence of the promised control over the irredeemed territories being conceded to the Arabs. In Mesopotamia fighting had broken out because of Arab dissatisfaction.

Feisal had been not so much given, as allowed to remain in, the Damascus area which (following Lawrence's advice) he had wisely conquered with Arab arms. But his tenure was uncertain. The French had rushed troops to North Syria and had the air of installing themselves for good in the portions of the country of which the allocation had been left for consideration at the close of the War. We were digging in with as permanent airs in Palestine and in Mesopotamia.

It was quite true that a mass of practical obstacles obstructed the immediate delivery of large territories to a race which had no administrative machine in being, and had had no great experience of self-government on any scale, though in the Turkish civil system and in the Turkish Army it had had more experience of this administrative work than was generally credited to it. Still, these obstacles had been recognized by Hussein himself on behalf of his fellow-Arabs, and a transition period in allowance for them had been foreseen in his treaty determining the future of the Arab lands. So it was not so much the physical solidity of the regimes being established by British and French in these redeemed territories as the lack of any definition of their character which disturbed the Arabs. It led to talk such as Lawrence had listened to in Hamra from Mesopotamian officers and from Feisal himself in the far-back first days of the revolt (cf. Chapter 8). If the French and British would declare that their installations in Syria and in Mesopotamia were only stop-gap (however permanent of appearance owing to national habits) the Arabs would be placated.

Therefore it was to assure the Arabs of the transient nature of the British and French administrations in their lands that the Allied statesmen had the proclamation issued on the 9th November which is known as the Joint Anglo-French Proclamation. It was posted and circulated all through Palestine: there was not a village where the news and the text of it did not circulate.

It will be best to give its text first in the original French:

> *Le gouvernement français, d'accord avec le gouvernement britannique, a décidé de faire la déclaration conjointe ci-dessous pour donner aux populations non-turques des régions entre le Taurus et le golfe Persique, l'assurance que les deux pays, chacun en ce qui le concerne, entendent leur assurer la plus grande autonomie afin de garantir leur affranchissement et le développement de leur civilisation:*
>
> *"Le but qu'envisagent la France et la Grande Bretagne en poursuivant en Orient la guerre déchainée par l'ambition allemande, c'est l'affranchissement complet et définitif des peuples si longtemps opprimés par les Turcs et l'établissement de gouvernements et administrations nationaux puisant leur autorité dans l'initiative et le libre choix des populations indigènes.*

> *Pour donner suite à ces intentions, la France et la Grande Bretagne sont d'accord pour encourager et aider l'établissement de gouvernements et d'administrations indigènes en Syrie et en Mésopotamie actuellement libérées par les Alliés ou dans les territoires dont ils poursuivent la libération, et pour reconnaitre ceux-ci aussitôt qu'ils seront effectivement établis.*
>
> *"Loin de vouloir imposer aux populations de ces régions telles ou telles institutions, elles n'ont d'autre souci que d'assurer par leur appui et par une assistance efficace la fonction normale des gouvernements et administrations qu'elles se seront librement donnés. Assurer une justice impartiale et égale pour tous, facilite le développement économique du pays en suscitant et en encourageant les initiatives locales, favoriser la diffusion de l'instruction, mettre fin aux divisions trop longtemps exploitées par la politique turque, tel est le rôle que les deux gouvernements alliés revendiquent dans les territoires libérés."*

That is:

> The French Government, in agreement with the British Government, has decided to issue the following joint declaration in order to give to the non-Turkish populations between the Taurus and the Persian Gulf the assurance that the two countries, each in its own sphere, intend to secure for them the amplest autonomy, with the aim of guaranteeing their liberation and the development of their civilization:
>
> "The end that France and Britain have in pursuing in the East the war unloosed by German ambition is the complete and definite freeing of the peoples so long oppressed by the Turks, and the establishment of National Governments and Administrations deriving their authority from the initiative and the free choice of the native populations.
>
> "In order to give effect to these intentions, France and Great Britain have agreed to encourage and to assist the establishment of native Governments and Administrations in Syria and in Mesopotamia, now liberated by the Allies, and in the territories whose liberation they seek, and to recognize them as soon as they are effectively established.
>
> "Far from wishing to impose any particular institutions on the populations of these regions, their only care is to assure by their support and efficacious assistance the normal workings of the Governments which these populations freely shall have given themselves. To ensure impartial and equal justice to all, to facilitate the economic development of the country by promoting and encouraging local initiative, to foster the spread of education, to put an end to the divisions too long exploited by Turkish policy—such is the role which the two Allied Governments claim in the liberated territories."

There could not possibly be a clearer or more definite promise to establish Arab—because native—rule in Palestine and the other Arab lands. So definite is this proclamation, so binding are its exemplary terms that one cannot but believe that, whatever their motives, the British and the French statesmen who issued it had some temporary intention of carrying it out. To believe anything else would be to think too ill of human nature; no man carrying the heritage of Adam could use such phrases to deceive his fellowmen. Indeed during a debate in the French Chamber in the last week of December Monsieur Pichon spoke of a firm intent to honour it. Referring to the coming Peace Conference, and to the agreements between France and Britain specified in the second paragraph of the Proclamation, he declared, "Of course we admit the complete freedom of the Conference, and its right to give these agreements their proper conclusions, but these agreements are binding both upon England and upon us."

So far so good. But unfortunately more remains to be said. The text as I have given it in French, the original text drawn up between Britain and France, was duly published in France, and may be found in several of the Paris papers. It appeared, for instance, in the *Journal* and *Petit Journal* of the 9th of November. This was on the very verge of the great Armistice of the 11th of November, and the Near Eastern proclamation of course was obscured in the vast excitement of the close of war upon the Western Front.

The Proclamation was published in England too, but was obscured in the same way there, occupying in *The Times* a position at the end of a column on a minor page. Its position, though, was the least of things. What is of first importance is that in the British version, given to the Press by the Government through the usual official information services, the preamble had disappeared. It has never been published in this country: its existence is unknown in this country. The preamble was worded so that the two governments might introduce it in the same terms, changing the words "French" and "British" about, i.e., the British version would run, "The British Government (or His Majesty's Government), in agreement with the French Government, has decided, etc., etc."

Why did it disappear? We may well wonder. It is to be observed that in the preamble it is carefully stated that the Proclamation applies to all non-Turkish populations between the Taurus Mountains (which are the northern boundary of Syria and Turkey) and the Persian Gulf, so that no one, not even Dr. Weizmann nor Mr. Ormsby-Gore, could say that it did not apply to Palestine.

The preamble was officially written by the French Government in agreement (as it states) with the British Government, and we know that the Proclamation was submitted to and ratified by the leading British statesmen, by the testimony of the official History of the War. Why then was the preamble expunged or dropped in Great Britain?

Expunged or not, it is there in the French version to bear witness to the completeness of the pledge to the native race in Palestine (as in the other Arab lands), that the Allies would make it their mission to see that the Arabs only had such governments as they would have freely given themselves, and that the Allies would support and assist these Governments— in due pursuance naturally of the McMahon-Hussein Treaty. Even without the preamble the terms of the Proclamation itself obviously refer to Palestine, as part of Syria and as being "liberated by the Allies" at the time. Allenby published it in Palestine as in a country for which it was intended.

Chapter 15

Proposals for making Palestine "a Jewish country" approved by Balfour.
Zionist preparation for the Peace Conference.
The siege and investment of Feisal.—The "Treaty of Friendship."
The "Frankfurter letter."

Since the fate of Syria apparently was to be settled at the coming Peace Conference in Paris, the chief persons who were concerned, or wished to be concerned, in its fate now made their way to Europe. Dr. Weizmann himself had quitted Palestine for London as far back as September. He had established good personal relations with the Army authorities during his stay in Palestine, and was the one member of the Zionist Commission who had done so.

During the previous May, when the Zionist Commission had reached Akaba during its tour, he had had a conference with the Emir Feisal. It was their first meeting. Various British persons were present too, and the chief merit of this meeting in Zionist eyes will have been that the Zionist chief appeared to the Arab prince under the aegis of Major Ormsby-Gore and in an aura of British officialdom.

Nothing precise sprang of this meeting. Zionist aims were something new to Feisal, and attracted him after a fashion at that early stage, when they were presented to him crowned with a vague but bright nimbus of benevolence and clad in the "art-silk" robes of Semitic fraternity. Feisal always was to hear more of common aims and of mutual upbuilding of Palestine than of the details of the National Home project. But even at this first meeting at Akaba he made clear that Palestine, despite the universality which attached to it as the world's greatest sanctuary (which he recognized), yet was an Arab country, and he specified that any Jewish settlement in it must be in an Arab domain and under Arab suzerainty. He was not told that this conflicted with the Zionist plans.

There can be little doubt that then, on the eve of the Peace Conference, the Zionists as they reckoned up the factors of the situation saw that Feisal represented their only hope of any sort of "understanding" with the Arabs.

The polite prince, transported from contact with the native soil and with the native public, going round and round, as they half foresaw, in the circling vortex of the self-centred Conference, under the continuous social pressure of their own British friends, presented the only conceivable means of deflecting an Arab to their intentions.

Nothing was to be hoped from the mass of the Arabs. The experiences of the Zionist Commission had shown this, and the agitation too which had resulted in the Anglo-French Proclamation.

But in any survey, of the situation, after all, Feisal only represented a secondary factor for the Zionists. He would have to fall in probably with what was arranged for him and his by the treaty-makers of the Allied and Associated Powers. These treaty-makers were the prime factors and the persons to be secured. In London, in December, Dr. Weizmann had an interview on the subject. As might have been expected, it was with Lord Balfour. Balfour told him that the Zionists "probably would be heard at the Peace Conference when the national problem with which they were concerned came up," and that "Great Britain was pledged to the policy of a National Home and would support it at the Conference." This showed that the formula devised for the Conference, when Palestine came up, would be that of the very, very difficult national problem in that country which had to be faced with full consideration of its long-tangled items. An elaborate falsehood of course, for the Conference in reality would not be facing but creating a problem, through the introduction into Palestine of entangling items of its now fresh manufacture where there had been none.

Besides the European Zionists, extremely important Jewish delegations from the United States came to Paris via London. Chief of these was the American Zionist Delegation, the representatives of the Brandeis dominant group, composed of Dr. Stephen Wise, Mrs. Fels (wife of the millionaire soap-boiler), Messrs. Bernard Flexner and Louis Robison, who were joined later on by Messrs. de Haas, Frankfurter and Gans. The American Jewish Congress, held in Philadelphia on the 16th December, sent a large body, the members of which brought with them a resolution passed at the Congress. By this "the representatives of three million Jews demanded such political, administrative and economic conditions [in Palestine] as will assure under the trusteeship of Great Britain, acting on behalf of such League of Nations as may be formed, the development of Palestine into a Jewish Commonwealth."

The presence in the United States delegations of Messrs. de Haas and Wise is to be noted, since it is they, particularly Mr. de Haas, the Zionist historian in the United States, who provide valuable information of what now occurred. Mr. de Haas in his *History of Palestine* says that before leaving for Europe the members of Dr. Wise's delegation received instructions, or "advice," as he puts it, upon their attitude. He does not say who gave it. The person in a position to give advice to a delegation of the American Zionist Organization was its Chairman, Mr. Brandeis. In the interim he had been publicly appointed by President Wilson to a position of immense importance for the Zionist cause. He was "to collate the material upon which the eventual peace should be published." This appointment dated as far back as October 1917.

But Mr. Brandeis's views do not seem altogether consonant with these instructions to his delegates. He had given his favour to the plan of a "British Palestine," while this advice which the delegates had received was to aim at a Jewish rather than a British Palestine. "The neutral Jewish status of Palestine," they were told, "means freedom of action in the direction of settlement and emigration. We can tell the Jews to go to their Homeland. We will give no political offence [sic] in doing this, but it will be difficult to preach 'Go to British Palestine.' Ormsby-Gore evidently sees this when he suggests a Jewish passport."

With Major Ormsby-Gore suggesting (by what authority?) Jewish passports and therefore the recognition of a Jewish nationality based on Palestine, with one Zionist body bearing are solution for a Jewish Commonwealth, with another having an official compiler of plans for the treaty as its Chairman, the outlook just before the Peace Conference already was ominous for the Arabs. The official United States delegates, too, before leaving for Europe had been prepared for their task. "All the important members of the Wilson Mission who were likely to be consulted on Palestine or on the Jewish phase of any European problem, were deliberated with prior to their leaving New York. Strong in the possession of the President's personal interest—Mr. Wilson having said that the Jewish Homeland was one of the two permanent new achievements that would come out of the War—the members of the Brandeis Zionist administration proceeded to London and Paris." (de Haas.)

What a picture! One is reminded of those court proceedings of the olden days in which the verdict was prepared before the trial began. Certainly it might be said that the Palestine verdict journeyed back and forth from New York and London to Paris ere it was delivered. For all that, the Zionists gathering in London were not satisfied. They wanted more than the surest of mere prospects. So a proposal was laid before Lord Balfour early in December for a method of putting his Declaration into practice which would ensure:

> "An unfettered development of the Jewish National Home in Palestine —not mere facilities for colonization, but opportunities for carrying out

> colonizing activity, public works, etc., on a large scale, so that we should be able to settle in Palestine four to five million Jews within a generation, and so make Palestine a Jewish country. (de Haas)"

Lord Balfour "approved this," Mr. de Haas informs us. Yet only a month had passed since the Anglo-French Proclamation had been promulgated throughout Palestine by the Government of which Balfour was a member. Nor did Balfour and his group confine themselves to theoretic approval. They helped where they could. "The interpretation of Jewish National Home into Jewish Commonwealth was cabled to his associates in New York by Dr. Wise at the suggestion of British officials." (Wise and de Haas.)

There was but one cloud darkening the Zionist outlook in these halcyon days. It was of the Zionists' own making. They did not agree altogether amidst themselves; there was dissension between the Americans and the Europeans. Dr. Weizmann and the Europeans saw the Americans, secure in their wealth and in their close connection with President Wilson, more and more disposed to seize control of the movement. Brandeis made plans for Palestine like an emperor. He intended particularly that if a British Mandate were created, then Britain should sign a formal contract with the Zionist Organization, which was to act on behalf of the "Jewish people." "His Majesty's Government of the one part and the Zionist Organization, acting on behalf of the Jewish people, of the other, mutually agree and bind themselves . . that was the sort of document he wished to see, with the "Jewish people" thereby accepted as a negotiating Power.

The Weizmann European group on the other hand, in closer contact with the British Government, and attached to the *do ut des* policy, had formulated another plan. The American delegates complained that they were presently confronted with it. It proposed:

> "a liberal land reform policy, visualized Palestine as a type of British Crown Colony with a Jewish Governor, the recognition of the Jewish flag and Jewish festivals and Sabbaths. Hebrew as one of the official tongues, and political conditions *that would give the Jewish minority majority-rights in Palestine* [my italics]. The proposed settlement was about five thousand Jews a year. The plan moreover contained a clause for the creation of a Jewish council with its seat in Jerusalem. (de Haas)."

In fact the plan was very much the same as the Mandatory regime which was set up later, which in fact was based on an emendation of these proposals. The main difference was that under the Mandate the Jewish minority was not given majority-rights, which would have been too venturesome for a start. They were given something to which they had as little claim though, that is they, the minority, were given equality-rights with the Arab majority, the Arab majority conversely being reduced to a level with a group numbering only one-tenth of their own numbers.

At the time the bluntness of the minority-into-majority proposals flustered some officials, if not Balfour, in the Foreign Office. "British officialdom which at that juncture believed there were only twenty thousand Jews in Palestine, was fearful of the Arabs, urged prudence, and the formulation of as little as possible." (de Haas.) Someone, Lord Cecil I fancy, wrote a minute insisting on the desirability of this unformulating prudence until the Zionist settlers should have established "by precept and example a life and civilization worthy of the highest and noblest ideal of Deuteronomy and Isaiah."

Minutes of this type appealed to the American Zionist group, and with this one sounding as psalters in their ears the Americans withdrew to evolve "a new set of proposals based on the Pittsburg programme which they believed would prove as acceptable to English idealism as it would conform to the aspirations of the Zionists." (de Haas.) The first clause of the Pittsburg programme, which was disregarded instantaneously by its very devisers, has been quoted already. The other clauses predicated in the National Home the national ownership of the soil though it might be sub-leased; public control of all natural resources and of general utilities, with due regard to existing rights; free schooling; the organization of most undertakings upon the co-operative principle.

Whatever the American group produced out of the four-fifths of the programme which its members retained, the result was not found in conformity with "English idealism and the aspirations of other Zionists." Differences were patched up, however, between the Europeans and the Americans and both bodies collaborated in the memorandum which ultimately the Zionist Organization presented to the Peace Conference. This did not occur though till the end of February, and in the meantime the Zionists began what may be called the investment of the Emir Feisal. Their aim, and the aim of the Government, was now explicit—to extract from this passably cozened prince some document compromising the Arab claims before these could be put forward by the Arabs as a body.

It was certain that the mass of Arab nationalists would try as speedily as they could to establish some kind of council or assembly. Already the members of the "National Committee," which had been formed at Damascus in 1914 and had instructed Hussein when he opened negotiations with Great Britain, were trying to get into touch again with each other and to find a place and means of assembly in public. Once an organization on any kind of representative basis could be created, it would be sure either to speak out directly on behalf of the Arab race, or to instruct Feisal as his father had been instructed. The kind of instructions which he would receive, the Zionists knew well by now, meant their own doom, or meant at least the doom of any pretence that the Arabs at large would fall in with the Zionist programme.

But while Arab representation was still loose, and undefinedly in Feisal's hands, there was an opportunity of securing from him an agreement favouring their projects. The Government, which shared these hopes and was equally alive to the opportunity, was on its part particularly anxious to obtain from Feisal an acceptance of the Balfour Declaration.

Is there any need to point out how unreal and how unfair was the situation which enabled the Conference to begin under these conditions, with Feisal exposed to every pressure, the Zionists represented by well-found delegations, and the Arabs, whose lives and territories were to provide the theme of discussion, with no delegations at all? It was not the fault of the Arabs, since before a representative Arab delegation could appear, how much would not have to be accomplished?

Two problems faced the Arabs as preliminaries. They had to find means of assembling, and they had to determine upon those who were to assemble. Wherever they chose to meet, the process of meeting would take time. Transit in their countries, of its nature slow, had been disorganized further by the War and by the restrictions on free movement which had succeeded it. But if it was hard for the Arabs to assemble save after much delay, it was still harder for them to decide who amongst them were to do so.

They were scattered over a great area in the ruins of a collapsed empire, which had never had a wide, organized democratic elective system suited for producing delegates on the scale now required. They were faced with the great difficulties of regionalism and federalism. Were they to have one federal assembly, or something like the Austro-Hungarian Imperial Delegation, or something like our own loose but effective Empire connections?

All these were enormous problems with which the Arabs were confronted at the very outset of their existence as a nation or group of nations. They should have been matters for the most serious consideration of the Peace Conference. It is true that the members of the Conference might have declared, with some reason, at the start of its labours, that it was not possible for such elaborate processes to accomplish themselves ere making peace with Turkey. (In the sequel four years actually were to pass before peace with Turkey was signed at Lausanne, but this was not to be foreseen at the start.)

If, however, the Allied chiefs thought, as 1918 passed into 1919, that they could not wait, they at least could have arranged some temporary kind of representation for the Arab nations as a whole. They might have summoned to Paris the 1914 Damascus Committee, deputations of the "Fatah" and of the "Ahad" and so forth. Such an arrangement would have been makeshift and transitory, it is true, but it would have answered its purpose. Feisal, by his connections with these bodies, would have been designated as the obvious head of their delegacy, but he would have had something of a constitutional situation.

It would not, however, have been possible so to sustain the figment that the affairs of all the Arabs could be treated as a personal affair between the Allies and Feisal: which was no doubt the reason that nothing of this sort was done by the Conference.

But as the sittings of the Conference progressed, and it became evident that there would be more time to spare than had been first imagined, the onus which lay upon the Conference of considering Syrian opinion became heavier.

In Mesopotamia within two years the whole kingdom of Irak with all its appurtenances was launched by Great Britain. The preparations for this began at once in 1919, when the army of occupation, under orders from home, canvassed the population for its views upon the character of the country's future institutions. This inquiry in practice proved difficult, the Mesopotamians for one thing being less advanced than the Syrians. Still, difficulty was to be anticipated, and the great thing was that then a beginning was made, that the principle of Arab independence was recognized at the first possible moment, and that the measures taken fructified in a couple of years.

There was no reason why the same procedure should not have been followed in Syria. There would have been difficulties in Syria too, such as that presented by the little Christian Lebanon, to which the Turks had been forced by the Concert of Europe to grant autonomy. The Lebanon was anxious to conserve its privileged status. Whatever real or imaginary difficulties there were, however, they could have been met, and the very fact that we had grappled with the difficulties in Mesopotamia made it necessary to grapple with them in Syria.

We could not be treaty-keepers in Mesopotamia and treaty-breakers in Syria, honest in Baghdad and dishonest in Jerusalem, straightforward on the banks of the Euphrates and shifty and elusive on the banks of the Jordan. Yet that was what we became, and our very virtue on one side of the new frontiers became suspect and lost its pristine value because of our conduct upon the other side. How could generous intentions be credited to us in Irak under the circumstances? Men recognized that what we did there was well done, but they now looked for the policy, for the reason of state which lay behind this generosity and this faithfulness to our word. Was our undoubted amity oleaginous? Did the line of conduct follow the course allotted to a coming pipe-line?

Thus by our action in Palestine did we tarnish the good we did in the sister-country. Our rulers did not care. They were bickering with the French in private over the division of the Syrian mandates and they were as determined as Tartar conquerors to impose upon Palestine the rule which pleased them.

So there was no summoning of Arab delegates from Syria to Paris to proclaim unwanted truths before the Conference, and in Syria there was no sequel given by British or French to their Anglo-French proclamation. It was a terrible thing thus to address in noble words a confiding race, and immediately thereafter to act as though those words never had been spoken. In Syria we were like hosts who ran welcoming the Arabs, grasped their hands, patted them on the shoulder, led them to our doors, and then shut the doors with a bang in their faces.

As a result in Paris, while the Zionists were (as a loose phrase well puts it) more than fully represented, the Arabs as Arabs were not properly represented at all. Feisal, as his father's representative, did what he could within his limits. Two colleagues joined him presently, the Mesopotamian Rustum Bey Haidar and the Syrian Auni Bey Abdel-Hadi who had taken a prominent part in the Arab Congress of Paris before the War and had lost a kinsman on the Turkish scaffold. They acted as Secretaries of the Delegation.

Meanwhile, in November, Feisal accompanied by Lawrence had reached London. From the moment of his arrival he was much lionized. He was too distinguished of temperament to care for lionizing for its own sake, but he was gratified by the warmth of his reception, which had its genuine side of course, and was a recognition by the public of all that the Arabs had accomplished. But soon the manoeuvring began, very adroitly. A kind of political massage, persistent, dulling, soothing and smoothing, was applied to Feisal, till his whole being seemed whelmed in its movements. Everyday at receptions and at meetings, more and more into the Allied victory. It merged gloriously indeed: Feisal now found himself cast as one of the leaders of the great world-triumph.

But it merged, and in the process of merging the very definite contracts which the Arabs had carried out, in the Hedjaz and in Syria, were lost to sight. As a helper and minor creditor of the great Allies Feisal would have had a political bill to present to them for settlement, a plain business. As one of the board of Allies he began to perceive himself involved in culling the rewards of supremacy in an undefined way with nothing fixed or guaranteed but largeness of prospects. And he was invited to take into account all sorts of considerations which could not have been imposed upon him as an Arab, but were part of his new outlook as an Allied statesman.

Foremost of these was an "understanding" with the Zionists. He had been subjected already at Amman, as we have seen, to the lure of Zionists coming to settle in Palestine, to use his father's words, as "lodgers in the Arab house." Such Jews as he knew had indeed lived there as lodgers of the Ottoman Sultan. Now a development of this state of things was proposed to him, a scheme for Jewish colonies leading an autonomous life, upon terms afterwards to be worked out. Feisal had no clear idea then that such autonomy was intended to initiate Zionist co-partnership in Palestine, and from co-partnership was to evolve into ownership of the country. Nothing was very clear to him at the time, for new projects which he did not understand (as he was to tell me later on himself) continually were being mooted to him. The League of Nations was shaping, and the word "Mandate" was just creeping into use.

The question of language too was a perpetual difficulty for Feisal. He had only a few words of English, depended a great deal on Lawrence to expound texts, and Lawrence's Arabic, for all its fluency, was not that suited to texts. "At the beginning my Arabic," as Lawrence testifies himself, "had been a halting command of the tribal dialects of the Middle Euphrates (a not impure form), but now it became a fluent mingling of Hedjaz slang and north-tribal poetry with household words and phrases from the limpid Nejdi, and book forms from Syria. The fluency had a lack of grammar, which made my talk a perpetual adventure for my hearers. Newcomers imagined I must be the native of some unknown illiterate district; a shot-rubbish ground of disjected Arabic parts of speech."

Continually pressed to make engagements he never quite understood, which were translated to him as part of an adventure, with a generous but dangerous freedom, Feisal had days of revulsion. He complained then that the Arabs were being deprived of their access to the Mediterranean, were being driven into the desert, and he demanded flatly the fulfilment of the pledges made to his father. But governmental hands grasped his in iron friendship and led him to Dr. Weizmann, and the much-desired document was extracted from him on the 3rd of January.

It was not published till three years ago, 1936. Dr. Weizmann himself then made it known, in an article he contributed to *The Times*. That he should have waited through seventeen years, during which Palestine suffered unrest and bloodshed deepening into insurrection, before he did publish his *bordereau* is indication enough that it was valueless. If the Emir

Feisal had written a valid acceptance of the National Home and of the Balfour Declaration, it would have been rushed to the Press before Feisal's signature was dry upon it.

But it deserves reproduction for two reasons. It is one of the "Feisal documents" which are all that the Zionists have ever possessed with which they can make the least show of having gained Arab acquiescence in their plans. Secondly, when it was produced in 1936 some Zionists and pro-Zionists—Dr. Weizmann himself was more careful—based upon it resounding and absurd claims, such as that it superseded the Hussein-McMahon Treaty. Till then these gentlemen mostly had ignored the Hussein-McMahon Treaty, or had refused to consider it a treaty at all, but they did not mind now acknowledging its existence in order to supersede it.

Dr. Weizmann, on the 10th June, 1936, then wrote:

> The present disturbances in Palestine have given renewed currency to the story that the promise to set up a National Home for the Jewish people in Palestine was inconsistent with promises made to the Arabs during the War. I desire here to refer to one aspect only of this matter namely the attitude adopted at the Peace Conference by the Arab Delegation itself towards the establishment of the National Home in Palestine.
>
> When Feisal came to Europe in 1919 we submitted to him our plans. Both Feisal and Lawrence approved of them, and early in 1919 these conversations culminated in the Treaty of Friendship, a copy of which is appended. The text of that treaty was approved by Lawrence, who discussed it with Feisal.
>
> The agreement, the original of which is in my possession, opens as follows:
>
>> His Royal Highness the Emir Feisal, representing and acting on behalf of the Arab Kingdom of Hedjaz, and Dr. Chaim Weizmann, representing and acting on behalf of the Zionist Organization, mindful of the racial kinship and ancient bonds existing between the Arabs and the Jewish people, and realizing that the surest means of working out the consummation of their national aspirations is through the closest possible collaboration in the development of the Arab State and Palestine, and being desirous further of confirming the good understanding which exists between them, have agreed upon the following articles:
>
> The articles (some of which have been summarized) were:
>
> - Article I. The Arab State and Palestine in all their relations and undertakings shall be controlled by the most cordial goodwill and understanding, and to this end Arab and Jewish duly accredited agents shall be established and maintained in the respective territories.

- Article II. provided for the determination of the boundaries between the Arab State and Palestine.
- Article III. In the establishment of the Constitution and Administration of Palestine all such measures shall be adopted as. will afford the fullest guarantees for carrying into effect the British Government's Declaration of November 2nd, 1917.
- Article IV. All necessary measures shall be taken to encourage and stimulate immigration of Jews on a large scale, and as quickly as possible to settle Jewish immigrants on the land through closer settlement and intensive cultivation of the soil. In taking such measures the Arab peasant and tenant farmers shall be protected in their rights, and shall be assisted in forwarding their economic development.
- Article V. provided for full religious freedom.
- Article VI. The Mohammedan Holy Places shall be under Mohammedan control.
- In Article VII. The Zionist Organization undertook to assist the Arab State with the advice of its economic experts.
- In Article VIII. they agreed to act in accord on the matters embraced in the pact before the Peace Congress.
- In Article IX. they agreed to submit any dispute to the British Government's arbitration.

> Feisal signed the pact [continued Dr. Weizmann] in London on January 3rd, 1919, with a reservation in Arabic—a translation of which was attached in Lawrence's own handwriting and is given below in facsimile—making his obligations under the pact dependent on the fulfilment by the British Government of the demands put forward in the Arab Memorandum of June 4th, 1919.

Dr. Weizmann closed his letter with references to Feisal's appearance before the Supreme Council and other matters which may be left to await their turn. But before dealing further with this document of his, I should explain that an unfortunate misprint is to be found in the printed version of the original article, as it appeared in *The Times*. The very last words, "Arab Memorandum of June 4, 1919" should read, "Arab Memorandum of January 4, 1919." In the appended facsimile [Author's note: from *The Times*, from which his text is quoted] in Lawrence's own handwriting he wrote "Jan. 4," in short, and *The Times* printers by mistake transcribed this as "June 4." It is an evident misprint, since Feisal could not speak in January of demands already put forward, if in fact these were not made till four months later.

The reservation or codicil in facsimile, as reproduced in *The Times*, with the date corrected, ran as follows:

> "If the Arabs are established as I have asked in my manifesto of Jan. 4 addressed to the British Secretary of State for Foreign Affairs, I will carry

> out what is written in this agreement. If changes are made, I cannot be answerable for failing to carry out this agreement."
>
> Feisal ibn Hussein.

[The signature was in Lawrence's handwriting too.]

Such is the "Treaty of Friendship." To anyone who reads in the wide spaces between the lines of Dr. Weizmann's letter, the "treaty" is revealed as a mere proposal between him and Feisal which never advanced any further. It never reached treaty stage. Dr. Weizmann does not say so, for his letter is void of all precisions. He does not explain which was the manifesto of January 4th, though the whole agreement depends upon it. He does not indicate what happened to this manifesto. He does not even give an inkling of its contents.

Obviously the one point of interest is whether the demands of Feisal's manifesto were or were not carried out. It is all very well to talk of Feisal (or of the Arab delegation) as having a certain attitude, but if this attitude only existed in case of the occurrence of specified events, then it is absurd to make capital of the attitude without ever disclosing whether the events occurred.

It is still more absurd to act in this fashion when the events did not occur. Yet this is what Dr. Weizmann did in his letter. He tried to make capital for the existing situation out of Feisal's attitude towards a situation which never existed.

It never did exist, though, as I say, Dr. Weizmann leaves us in the dark about it. I felt that the dark ought to be pierced, as after much search I could identify no document of January 4th. In the end I applied and learned from official sources, for which information I beg to express my sincere gratitude, that "regarding a memorandum or manifesto mentioned in the reservation attached to the Treaty of Friendship signed between Dr. Ch. Weizmann and Feisal ibn Hussein on the 3rd of January 1919… the manifesto was in fact the Emir Feisal's statement of claims addressed to the Peace Conference and not directly to His Majesty's Government. The document has not been published by His Majesty's Government."

This cleared the situation. There is no contradiction between the explanation and Feisal's codicil. His manifesto went no doubt to the Foreign Secretary, but it did not go "directly" to him, that is for his guidance the Foreign Secretary received a copy of the document to be presented to the Peace Conference, but it was not addressed to him. In his own codicil Feisal does not observe this diplomatic distinction, which, however, has its own importance. But what matters chiefly is—what was in the document, and did the Conference or the Government accede to its demands?

Feisal's statement of claims before the Conference may be summarized here. We shall return to it. He demanded that the independence for which his father had covenanted should now be granted to all Arab territories in Asia which hitherto had formed part of the Turkish dominions. This independence (in accord with the McMahon terms) was, he said, "in no wise to be limited by the Allies, except in so far as the Arabs themselves might ask assistance." With regard to Palestine he specified that "on account of its universal character I shall leave Palestine on one side for the mutual consideration of all parties concerned."

He adjourned the Palestine settlement in consequence of all the pressure which had been brought to bear upon him. Notably he had been told in London that if he were amenable about Palestine it would be much easier to support his rights in northern Syria. It is to be borne in mind that at the time the immediate peril to the Arab state in Syria lay in the presence of French troops in Beyrout and in the northern coastal regions. The attitude of the French was already hostile in principle and in manner to the Arab O.E.T.A. government at Damascus, the nucleus of Arab rule which the victorious Arab troops had so hurriedly installed. At the time the Zionist menace in Palestine seemed less no doubt to the troubled Feisal. He wished at all costs to keep control of the ancient Arab capital, Damascus, and the price of British help was this amenability to ask no immediate decision in Palestine.

But the issue concerning us now is not his postponement of any Palestine issue, but whether his demands in general for the Arabs were accepted. They were not accepted, since the French were given the districts which he claimed for the Arabs and, more than this, his own little kingdom round Damascus presently was invaded by them and its territory taken and administered under French Mandate, without opposition from the British Government. In no spot of Syria was an Arab independent State established.

Therefore, the safeguard in his codicil applied, since the Arabs did not obtain the situation he had demanded. So this "treaty", which depended for its existence upon his general demands being accepted, never came into being, and was improperly invoked by Dr. Weizmann.

That is not all. Feisal's misgivings about these documents which he was induced to sign and these statements he was led to make were deeper than appears from Dr. Weizmann's text. The reservation or codicil, complete with Lawrence's holograph translation, displayed with such airs of authenticity in *The Times* article, is only half authentic. I do not mean by this that it is not a genuine document or that Dr. Weizmann intentionally is using a piece of evidence which is not accurate. But it just happens that the codicil he gives is not the codicil as Feisal composed it and understood it, and that there is marked difference between the two versions.

Dr. Weizmann's codicil is Lawrence's unsatisfactory English translation. Feisal's own codicil, that attached to his own copy of the "Treaty," is very different. It is in Arabic, his native tongue, and not in the English which he did not comprehend. I have been able to obtain a guaranteed translation from Feisal's codicil, which is in his archives, made by a scholar with entire mastery of both the English and the Arabic tongues, and this is its text:

> "If the Arabs obtain their independence as demanded in my memorandum of the 4th January 1919 to the Foreign Office of the Government of Great Britain, I shall agree to the contents of the above clauses. But if the slightest change or modification is made I shall not then be tied or bound by any of its provisions, and the agreement will then be null and void, not binding and of no account, and I shall not be liable in any manner whatsoever."

To this are appended the signatures both of the Emir Feisal and of Dr. Weizmann.

In Dr. Weizmann's codicil "Arab independence" disappears, and the forceful disclaimer made by Feisal becomes a pallid "I shall not be answerable." One thing is abundantly evident from Feisal's own text, that he was at heart scared by the engagement he had been induced to take. Here then is Feisal faced by an English text which was not what he thought it to be, and Dr. Weizmann by an Arabic text of the accurate terms of which he alike was ignorant. Obviously he was, or he would not have given his English copy as the sole official rendering. The value of the whole document is shown clearly for the nothing it was, an ornamented zero.

Dr. Weizmann never could have gained anything for his cause by it. What was Feisal's situation at the Peace Conference? He represented his father. King Hussein, and his father's royal status only proceeded from the fulfilment of the obligations into which Hussein had entered with Sir Henry McMahon on behalf of all the Arabs. A kingdom, it is true, was not specified to him as a reward for Arab participation in the War, but his kingdom sprang from nothing but that participation. It has been said, in fact it is too generally said, that Hussein assumed his title of King. What happened was that the Ulema of Mecca, the clerico-legal Moslem hierarchy, met in assembly there and recognized him as King of the Arab Nation. He was installed by them on the 6th of November in 1916. As has been seen, Great Britain shrank from recognizing this title and reduced it to King of the Hedjaz. But the lesser title had its origin in the greater and came to him as a result of the situation won by the revolt of the Arabs.

Hussein himself in the text of the pact which contracted for that revolt clearly and regularly defined his status as signatory to be that of the spokesman, not of Mecca or of the Hedjaz, but of the Arab peoples. It was with him in this character that Great Britain negotiated, and consequently it was in this character that he was recognized and accepted as a sovereign by Great Britain and, in his son's person, given a seat at Paris.

"Everything," Hussein had stipulated in a passage of these negotiations, speaking of himself and of the Arab peoples, "everything was the result of the conditions and the desires of our peoples. We are but transmitters and executants of such decisions and desires in the position they have pressed upon us."

But Feisal, as his father's representative, could have no other powers, no further powers than those which his father possessed. He had to act within identical limits. On his own authority he could take no decisions for the Arabs. He could but make proposals and transmit them to his father for his father's acceptance. In his turn Hussein's role, as he clearly defined it, was but to transmit the decisions and the desires of the Arab peoples to the British Government.

In default of a National Assembly to instruct him, Feisal's sole directive lay in the Hussein-McMahon Pact. Outside this he had no power to negotiate. Obviously he had no power to modify or renounce the pact. In an affair which involved the honour of Britain as a partner in this treaty with all the Arabs, Feisal should never have been decoyed—as efforts were made to decoy him—off the grounds of his legitimate activities.

Had the tricks to this end succeeded, it would have been only a short and false paper success. Nothing is more certain than that if any endeavour had been made by him to put arrangements with any Zionists into force by his sole authority, then Feisal would have been disowned by his father, rejected by his fellow-Arabs, and never would have mounted the throne of Irak.

The entry of the French into the Arab zone, combined with the workings of his untrammelled self in that salving codicil of his, set him free of this peril. But intrigue encompassed him during those early days of the Peace Conference, and he never indeed was set free from its toils. Before long he was again in the jaws of a trap of a kind. This was in March, a couple of months later. Some events occurred in the interval, such as the presentation of the Zionist case to the Peace Conference, to which allusion has not yet been made. But it is best to have done with the documents of the early cabal about Feisal, and to mention at once this other, the second of the pair.

In March it was not a "treaty" which Feisal was brought to sign, but a letter he was brought to send. He had had an interview in Paris with some of the Brandeis group of Zionists from the United States. The outcome was this letter, addressed to Mr. Frankfurter, a member of that particular delegation, who, as Mr. de Haas says, had been specially summoned to London to "aid in advancing the American idea of mass-action speedily accomplished."

The latent rivalry between the United States and the European Zionists, even when, as at the time, they were working better together, and paying compliments to each other, was always cropping up in some fashion. In what is known as the "Frankfurter letter" the Americans may have secured or thought they secured an offset to the "Treaty of Friendship."

This is the text of the letter:

> Délégation Hedjazienne,
> Paris,
> March 3rd, 1919.
>
> "Dear Mr. Frankfurter,
>
> I want to take this opportunity of my first contact with American Zionists to tell you what I have often been able to say to Dr. Weizmann in Arabia and Europe. We feel that the Arabs and Jews are cousins in race, having suffered similar oppressions at the hands of powers stronger than themselves, and by a happy coincidence have been able to take the first step towards the attainment of their national ideals together. We Arabs, especially the educated among us, look with the deepest sympathy on the Zionist movement. Our deputation here in Paris is fully acquainted with the proposals submitted yesterday by the Zionist Organization to the Peace Conference and we regard them as moderate and proper. We will do our best, in so far as we are concerned, to help them through. We will wish the Jews a most hearty welcome home.
>
> With the chiefs of your movement, especially with Dr. Weizmann, we have had and continue to have the closest relations. He has been a great helper of our cause, and I hope the Arabs may soon be in a position to make the Jews some return for their kindness. We are working together for a reformed and revived Near East, and our two movements complete one another. The Jewish movement is national and not imperialist: our movement is national and not imperialist, and there is room in Syria for us both. Indeed, I think that neither can be a real success without the other.
>
> People less informed and less responsible than our leaders and yours, ignoring the need for co-operation of the Arabs and Zionists, have been trying to exploit the local difficulties that must necessarily arise in Palestine in the early stages of our movement. Some of them have, I am afraid, misrepresented your aims to the Arab peasantry and our aims to the Jewish peasantry with the result that interested parties have been able to make capital out of what they call our differences.
>
> I wish to give you my firm conviction that these differences are not on questions of principle but on matters of detail, such as must inevitably

occur in every contact of neighbouring peoples and as are easily adjusted by mutual goodwill. Indeed nearly all of them will disappear with fuller knowledge.

I look forward, and my people with me look forward, to a future in which we will help you and you will help us, so that the countries in which we are mutually interested may once again take their places in the community of civilized people of the world."

Believe me,
Yours sincerely,
(Signed) Feisal.

This mawkish effusion in some respects leaves the "Treaty of Friendship" far in the rear. It is hard to conceive what the Arabic version of it can have been like, if there ever was an Arabic version. Nothing of the sort in Arabic seems to have survived amidst Feisal's papers. But since he spoke French, a French translation may have been made for him out of the American-English of the text, to match the heading of his note-paper.

What bosh this letter is, with its "we Arabs, especially the educated amongst us" and "we are working for a reformed and revived Near East" and its other phrases straight from self-help conventions in Illinois or Connecticut.

Enough of the Frankfurter letter. Like its congener, the "Treaty of Friendship," it was the fruit of a stratagem to obtain an Arab document of acquiescence in Zionist designs which no Arab body would ever have imagined, much less granted. However, the Frankfurter letter is more stupid than malign. The views put forth in it as those of "us Arabs" are so grotesquely unreal, that it was raw and childish to get Feisal to put his name to them.

He was being pestered to death at the time to sign this and that. In Paris he complained bitterly to his secretaries about it, and said he did not know what it all meant. Of Dr. Weizmann's approaches he said, "What does this man want? I would do anything to get rid of him. He tires me out by his long speeches."

A decade later he summed up very neatly his own opinion of his letter to Mr. Frankfurter. The chance of doing so came to him in this fashion. When the Commission of Inquiry into the recent disturbances was sitting in Jerusalem in 1929, some misguided Zionists introduced into evidence copies of the letter. Auni Bey Abdel-Hadi, acting then as chief Arab counsel, at once cabled to Baghdad as follows:

To His Majesty the King of Irak, Baghdad.
"It has been said before the Inquiry Commission that in your letter

> to Mr. Frankfurter you consented to the Zionist policy. Please cable me to correct this report."

The reply came from Rustum Bey Haidar, King Feisal's Private Secretary at the time. Since Auni Bey Abdel-Hadi and Rustum Bey Haidar had been the other members of the Delegation which, according to the letter, was alleged to have regarded the Zionist proposals as "moderate and proper," their attitude towards it in 1929 was an answer in itself. But this was the reply sent from Baghdad by the royal secretary:

> His Majesty does not remember having written anything of the kind with his knowledge.

Delightfully phrased. An answer which disposes of everything, except perhaps of the question of who drafted Feisal's letter.

Chapter 16

The Peace Conference.—The Zionist role there.—Feisal's vain speech. Weizmann enounces Zionist demands. "Palestine to be as Jewish as England is English." The private meeting of the "Big Four" at Mr. Lloyd George's flat. Mr. Lloyd George and the Hussein-McMahon treaty. President Wilson insists on sending a Commission to find the desire of the Syrians.

The first plenary session of the Peace Conference was held on the 18th of January. The chief representatives were MM. Clemenceau and Pichon for France, Mr. Lloyd George and Lord Balfour for Great Britain, Sigg. Orlando and Sonnino for Italy, and for the United States, President Wilson and Mr. Lansing. Thirty-two States, which had fought the Central Powers, or had broken off diplomatic relations with them, took part in the proceedings.

There were more than enough participant countries, therefore, for the peace-gathering to have been called a Congress, as there had been Congresses at Berlin and Vienna. Whatever it was that caused the adoption of the other title of Conference, the change was justified. Never was there an assembly to compare with this one for pure conferential power. It was an incessant series of small meetings where a few persons of mark confabulated and two or three men drew up together constitutions for the world. The plenary sessions were the least significant: they were formal occasions, when President Wilson read his encyclicals and chief personages orated. Or else lesser peoples held the field in an atmosphere like that of a medieval tourney.

The champions of small countries and of minor causes, housed in the most astounding quarterings, rode in amongst buzzes of excitement, waved their lances and proclaimed the superior virtues of their ladies. On the dais the French spectators were bored; the Italians basked in the sunshine; President Wilson watched and had all the points of the performance hurriedly and wrongly explained to him; Mr. Lloyd George, lavish with smiles and glances, was the fickle Queen of Beauty.

Afterwards he would resume his normal political sex, and over cigars next day "get down to it" with the rest of the Big Four in a deadly quiet talk at his flat.

At this extremely personal, almost private Peace Conference, the great thing was to be admitted to the privacy of the principals. The Zionists had all the necessary admissions, as inner Peace Conference history attests. In another world from the public conferrings, far from tournaments, in movements easeful and triumphant as high summer's, like bees visiting and fecundating flowers, Messrs. Weizmann and Sokolov and Wise flew from the President to House and from House to Balfour and Balfour to Lansing and from Lansing to Tardieu, and from Tardieu to Lloyd George through long honey-making days. M. Tardieu was the one really receptive Frenchman, or thought he was.

Yet the Zionist group was the sole group in Paris which almost could have dispensed with these intimate visits. In one sense the Zionists scarcely needed to have anyone working for them in Paris at all, since it was superfluous to court principals, half of whom (and the dominant half of whom) were themselves vowed already to the Zionist dogma. Of the various Zionist delegations in Paris the chief was the official delegation of the British Government. Lloyd George and Balfour! Acetone and accessory! The next in importance was the official delegation of the United States of America. When Feisal presented the Arab case to the Council of Six he did so before men who had helped to create the Zionist case.

A summary has been given earlier of Feisal's speech on this occasion. He spoke in the first week of February, before the Zionists did. It was an unsatisfactory affair, for no one has ever known exactly what he said. His speech was unfinished at the close of the hearing and does not appear ever to have been completed.

On the morrow of it the Council of Six was transformed into the smaller Supreme Inter-allied Council, the "Big Four," and the rest of Feisal's speech was put off to an unfixed ulterior date at the convenience of the new body. But no date ever was found for it.

Feisal spoke in Arabic, from manuscript notes. There was no official interpreter. Lawrence translated at intervals, and questions were put to Feisal. But Lawrence, as we know, was not at all a sworn interpreter. Neither the Emir nor his secretaries (at the time) understood what Lawrence said in English, and of course none of the Europeans there but Lawrence had any Arabic. Whether Lawrence compiled an official version of the speech in English at the time is not clear. It seems more likely that he did not, for *The Times* had not even a résumé to publish next day, such as it published of the speeches of all other chief personages then. The *Temps* had a condensed few lines about the Emir's "*vaste programme du rêve panarabe.*" The official document of Arab demands seems to have been composed and deposited with the officials of the Conference before then. It is this which ranks as the manifesto to the Peace Conference by Feisal, cited in the previous chapter.

The gist of Feisal's speech, the important point in it, was that the Allies were asked to recognize that the Arabs generally formed a unit in blood, in history, in faith and in speech. There was no question of trying to place them all under a single Arab Government, but they would form a natural confederacy, of which each section, the Hedjaz, Nejd, Syria, Irak and so forth would govern itself according to its own traditions and desires. But the whole should be placed under the supervision of a single Mandatory European Power which would superintend the construction of roads, telegraphs and such matters. Feisal laid some stress on the construction of a transarabic railway by one branch of which Jerusalem and Mecca should be linked, and by the other Aleppo be joined to Baghdad and the Persian Gulf. The two lines would meet at Aleppo.

As we have seen, he also asked for the postponement of any decision on Palestine. No doubt he thought that this was the best he could do for Palestine to prevent the immediate development of the non-Arab projects, and—as we have seen—to get British help in saving Damascus. But his endeavours in this direction, and anything that he said indeed, were destined to be fruitless, for the Zionists already had arranged with the Conference leaders for their form of Mandate in Palestine, and by the 30th of January the division of Syria between Britain and France tacitly was agreed upon.

When in due course the Conference proceeded to the creation of the League of Nations and the insertion of the Mandatory system into its constitution, once more the key-men were the Zionists' men. Most of the original plan for these institutions, as will be seen, was drafted by General Smuts, and in lesser degree by Lord Cecil. After Balfour there were no more ardent and no blinder propagandists of Zionism than these two. Colonel House, another participant in League making, was yet another friend of Zionism.

Yet Mr. de Haas can state that "the Jews had no official status at the Peace Conference" and can go on to declare that because of this Mr. Lansing devoted himself to the details of the Zionist hearing, of the hearing, that is, given by the Council of Ten to the Zionist leaders. In this statement of Mr. de Haas's—it must be interpolated—the use of the word "Jews" as though it were synonymous with Zionists will not do at all. There were in Paris other Jews attending the Conference, who went there to oppose

Zionism, or having gone to Paris to further the interests of their people in quite different matters, encountered Zionism and opposed it. Lucien Wolf was there, for example, to present a memorial on behalf of the Board of Delegates of British Jews.

When the Zionists were given their hearing, it was not possible to avoid also hearing these Jews who protested against Zionist policy. Their spokesman was Professor Sylvain Lévi, who held a chair in the celebrated College de France and had opposed M. Sokolov's first manoeuvres in France. He had not long returned from Palestine where he had gone to represent French Jewry upon the Zionist Commission. He had joined the Commission in the belief that it was a relief organization only, to succour the Jews in the Holy Land. Here, therefore, was a man who had been undeceived, a man of talent, with unmatched experience and with the ability to explain what he had seen and heard. But what was his lot? Mr. de Haas informs us, "At the formal hearing given the Zionist leaders the members of the Supreme Council not only listened approvingly to the Zionist claims, but they showed marked displeasure at the arguments advanced by a French-Jewish anti-Zionist."

Contact with realities in Palestine had made an anti-Zionist of Professor Lévi, a condition of mind bound to arouse displeasure amidst the statesmen whose programme envisaged no reality. Their attitude was that of the French minister to whom an eye-witness reported upon certain riots or troubles which had occurred in one of the nearer French colonies. This first-hand account of causes and results did not at all chime in with the account which the Minister intended to deliver in the Chamber. Rapidly turning over the unwelcome pages of the report, he shook his head and said to his subordinate, "*Ne craignez-vous pas d'avoir été un peu influencé par ce que vous avez vu?* [Don't you fear that you have been a little affected by what you have seen?] "

This reproach could not have been addressed to M. Sokolov and Dr. Weizmann when they presented the Zionist case at this hearing upon the 27th of February. It was the old, arbitrary case we have seen persisting through a number of guises in a number of documents. But before it was ready, there was to be a good deal of making-over of still more documents and texts. The proposals which had been produced in London in December served as a beginning. Mr. Charles Thompson in his *The Peace Conference Day by Day* relates the next development, due to the mellifluous activities of Rabbi Stephen Wise amidst the chiefs of the Conference.

> Following his talk with Balfour and Colonel House and later with Tardieu, Dr. Wise wrote out a statement which disclosed that a very definite plan was under way. This statement included three propositions:

(1) that a Mandate be given to Great Britain as the trustee over Palestine;
(2) that a Mandate be given to France as the trustee over Syria;
(3) that a Mandate be given to the United States as the trustee over Armenia.

The text of Dr. Wise's plan deserves quoting a little. He wrote:

> "Great Britain should be given, and I believe will be given, the Mandatory of Trusteeship over Palestine, which trusteeship, I have reason for saying, Great Britain will not accept save by the common consent of such disinterested peoples as our own. Great Britain's trusteeship over a Jewish Palestine will be because of the summons or mandate of the League of Nations, and for the sake of the Jewish people and the Jewish Commonwealth which they are in time to realize."

What is noteworthy about these unconsciously satirical words about disinterested peoples and the rest is that they were composed early in January. Mr. Thompson mentions them in his notes of the 5th. Now at this time the Mandate scheme had not yet come into existence. It was only after a week's discussion by the Council of Ten, which at times was stormy, that on the 30th of January a communique was issued announcing that "a provisional agreement had been reached upon the German colonies and the occupied territory of Turkey-in-Asia." "The provisional agreement referred to in the communique," Mr. Thompson recorded on the 30th, "is the Smuts-House plan approved by the President and the British Imperial Cabinet. The reference to Turkey-in-Asia discloses for the first time that Mesopotamia, Palestine, Armenia and Syria come within the scope of this new colonial policy, so that if England and France divide up Turkey when the break comes, they must do it under 'mandatories.'"

Dr. Wise, therefore, more than three weeks before Mandates were born, was writing with aplomb about the British Mandate in Palestine being exercised for the sake of the Jewish Commonwealth. He knew that the Mandate would be given to Britain and he knew the terms of her "acceptance," to use that word for the firm determination of our Government to appropriate the Mandate.

In its antepenultimate stage the Zionist case, as prepared for the ultimate presentation on 27th of February, was a compound of the ideas of all the Zionist delegates. At first the American ideas bulked more in it. Before the final text was chosen these were largely to disappear, chiefly, as it seems to me, because they were too frank. The process of assimilation by which the Zionist constrictor was to absorb the Arab rabbit was too clearly stated in the American draft. First there was to be an "initial transition period during which the Mandatory would exercise control and establish government and carry out land-reform. In the second period when the Palestinian Commonwealth should come into existence, the mandatory as trustee would have its functions limited to protecting the interests of the League of Nations [whatever those were] and direct the foreign policy of Palestine." (de Haas.)

Then there was to be local autonomy of a "progressive" character. This meant that as the Zionists extended their holdings each was to obtain self-government, till by and by the whole of Zionist Palestine would be "locally autonomous."

There was to be a Jewish Council with its seat in Jerusalem, to be elected by a world congress, which also was to define the Council's functions. This of course would bring into being a fluid Jewish or Zionist nation of double nationality. Its citizens, or whatever they were to be called, could be, for example, United States' subjects and yet govern in Palestine through the aforesaid Council, which was to have considerable power. It was even, according to Mr. de Haas, to have the right to "issue obligations." The Zionists, he adds, undertook to establish an interim Council before 1920. (Of this plan a version was to be reintroduced in six years' time.)

Colonel House, who rose from a sick bed to aid the American Zionist delegates, "met these plans with hearty approval." He "enlisted the support of the American technical advisers" for the already-mentioned scheme for stretching the boundaries of a Zionist Palestine thirty miles or so beyond the existing frontier, into Sinai. "The demand for a larger area impressed him and President Wilson with the idea that the Zionists meant to create a real settlement in Palestine," blandly says Mr. de Haas.

All the provisions for such a "settlement" certainly were ready; everything was organized beforehand down to the limit of the preliminary stage under British Mandate. "Informally it was understood that the transition period, from administered area to self-governing commonwealth, would last about ten years." These cut-and-dried arrangements made a great impression, it seems, upon "all the American peace-experts." They "warmly seconded this draft which particularly appealed to them because it was the first attempt to present a concrete picture of a 'Mandate' in action." Heaven help them, the "American peace-experts" declared this seriously.

None the less, the concrete picture did not survive. But it is well that its terms should be known, for they demonstrate what went on behind the scenes of the Conference what were the inner intentions of the Zionists, and how far ranking delegates of the United States were secretly involved in the Zionist machine. They were quite ready to legislate for Palestine without a thought of its inhabitants or a care for those individual rights-of-man so dear to them on their own soil, or on any other soil but Palestine's soil.

I do not pretend, naturally, that our British delegates were unaware of what was being planned. If the American-Zionist draft was withdrawn through British influence, that influence was only exerted from "safety-first" reasons, was only prompted by the feeling that everything should not be let out of the Palestine bag, or that the bag should not be overfilled at the start.

Messrs. Wise and de Haas, themselves principal agents in the drafting, declare that the American draft was on the point of being adopted. "The substance of the American proposals was accepted as the text to be presented to the Peace Conference as the 'Zionist proposals.' To the final form the signatures of a group of Europeans and Americans were joyfully attached. French and Hebrew translations were prepared and the new phraseology, 'transition period,' 'trustee' and 'Commonwealth' presented intense but thrilling problems for the Hebraists, Yiddishists, and other clerical assistants."

Mr. de Haas has a way of leaving out names, just when they most should appear. One would like to know who were the signatories on the European side who provided these intense but thrilling problems for the clerical staff. Nor does he exactly apportion the responsibility for the subsequent over-riding of the American proposals. But it is clear that Dr. Weizmann had a large share in this. He had disagreed (by cable) with Mr. Brandeis over the question of the Jewish Council. It had been proposed that the "World Zionist Congress" which was to elect or establish the Council should meet in New York. When it was seen that this would mean the attendance of seven hundred and fifty American Zionist representatives, and that the European Zionist representatives would be very much in a minority, Dr. Weizmann would not accept this part of the scheme.

Another important cause of disagreement was, according to Mr. de Haas, that he himself wished to use the expression "Palestinian Commonwealth" while Dr. Weizmann "demanded references to Jewish Palestine and Jewish Commonwealth in the proposed mandate." It is rather odd that the Americans, on other points so frank, should have wished to be discreet about this.

For these internal reasons, then, the American draft did not win unanimous approval. Besides the internal reasons too, there were external influences which told against the American programme. The flustered group in the Foreign Office continued to be nervous of any manifest disclosures of the intended policy. The adjective it found to qualify Dr.

Weizmann's phrase "Jewish Palestine" and even the homely formula "Jewish Commonwealth" was "premature." Mr. de Haas, again failing to provide a name, quotes from a communication received from someone he describes as "a leading British official," who certainly incarnated official doubtfulness and caution.

> To this phraseology ["Jewish Palestine," etc.] a leading British official took exception. He regarded this terminology as "political Zionism" which "can but embarrass the British Government," a condition he wished to avoid becoming public at the Zionist Conference which was about to be held in London. He was uneasy over the proposed functions of the Jewish Council for Palestine. "I don't like," he wrote, "political or extra-Palestinian control of such a body. I want to see it perform effectually the gigantic task of agricultural and industrial development, of organizing immigration as a great non-profit-making public-utility society without the addition of political functions."

The American Zionists may not have realized it, but the "leading British official" was giving them a lesson. He was teaching them how to mask designs and was introducing them to that intricate form of self-deception under which you do not deceive yourself but put up a pretence by which you might be deceived, and act as though you were. In this instance he stacked up lofty phrases such as "gigantic task," "agricultural and industrial development," "non-profit-making," "public-utility society," into a species of hoarding, which hid what would happen behind them in Palestine, and round which he took good care not to peer. He knew as well as anyone, of course, that all the activities in which he encouraged the Zionists to engage "instead of politics" would be in fact fraught with great political consequences. He knew that agricultural and industrial development on the scale the Zionists intended would place them in a position of dominance in Palestine. He knew that colonization and immigration would destroy the natural ratio of power in Palestine. He knew as well as anyone that the gigantic task to which he gave a non-political character was in fact the gigantic task of supersession of the Arabs. He knew it all, but he showed the raw American Zionists how to place one's knowledge so that one does not see it. It is possible that the reader, comparing the two methods, may prefer Mr. de Haas's.

As it happened, despite all the endeavours to make the Zionists cautious, and despite the relative caution of the text which Dr. Weizmann and M. Sokolov presented to the Conference on the 27th of February, the unexpected happened and the truth was blurted out. Their text itself was long, developed the "Historic Title of the Jews to Palestine," indicated boundaries which would be found satisfactory, enumerated proposals for the Mandate, for the establishment of a Land Commission, for the creation of a Jewish Council in Palestine to represent the resident Jews, for the recognition of Hebrew as an official language, for a naturalization system, for everything, in fine, that appertains to the life and government of a country.

Further, it proposed that the sovereign possession of Palestine was to be vested in the League of Nations and that Great Britain was to be made the mandatory Power. But the Mandate was to be subject to the following proviso:

> "Palestine shall be placed under such political, administrative and economic conditions as will secure the establishment there of the Jewish National Home and ultimately render possible the creation of an autonomous Commonwealth, it being clearly understood" [and so on, introducing the last paragraph of the Balfour Declaration].

The text adopted contained, as is apparent, watered versions of some of the American Zionists' proposals, and the indiscreet "Jewish Commonwealth" was included in an anonymous form. But all the care and the circumspection thus spent upon it were wasted and the gammon of it was made manifest because Mr. Lansing, the United States Foreign Secretary, took it into his head to ask a question.

When the sitting began there had been no prospect of anything untoward occurring. It is true there had been a little introductory incident. The Zionist report of the event says, "The Conference began at three-thirty. Monsieur Clemenceau left in a few minutes." That unambiguous man!

But afterwards everything continued in the expected order till suddenly Mr. Lansing interjected his question. He asked Dr. Weizmann what in fact was meant by the "National Home." The President of the United States had already welcomed and sponsored this institution without asking what it meant. Enough if Mr. Brandeis recommended it cordially. The chief of the State Department felt it due, one supposes, to the mere technique of his office to inquire for more explanation. Or his inquiry may have been a hint to Dr. Weizmann. Whatever Lansing's motives, Dr. Weizmann at once provided him with the fullest explanation. It is likely that he had been chafing at the bonds in which the flustered department of the Foreign Office had bound him.

Now the opportunity of freeing himself had been given to him. He threw the protocol to the winds and answered that the "National Home" meant that there should be established such conditions ultimately in Palestine that "Palestine shall be just as Jewish as America is American and England is English." The precautions of the "leading British official" and of others of his kidney had been in vain. The cat had bounded out of the bag, had torn its way out of it, rending the material with its claws and miaowing on its highest note.

This celebrated avowal of Dr. Weizmann's has never been forgotten by the Arabs, and the reader should remember it with the same fidelity. Many an endeavour has been made in the intervening years to lose it from sight, to pass swiftly over it, to obscure it with argumentative detail, but to no purpose. There it stands like a peak rising out of a flat place, visible from far and tangible from near, and never to be explained away as a cloud or as an illusion formed of some passing dust. Palestine to be as Jewish as England is English. The Arabs in consequence to "get out or to get under."

If confirmation had been needed that Dr. Weizmann had disclosed the aims of his movement, he supplied it himself on the morrow. In an interview printed in *The Times* of the 1st of March he set out the Zionist programme with great clarity. He began with the customary disclaimer, but presently passed to facts.

> "We do not [he said] aspire to found a Zionist State. What we want is a country in which all nations and all creeds shall have equal rights and equal tolerance. [That is the 60,000 Jews, plus future immigrants who were foreign subjects, were to have the same voting and executive power as the 670,000 native Arabs.]
>
> We cannot hope to rule in a country in which only one-seventh [in fact, it was not even one-tenth] of the population at present are Jews. We understand that the Peace Conference has practically decided to place Palestine under the League of Nations. This is entirely in accordance with our wishes, but we go further. We indicate the power which we wish to be the Mandatory of the League. That Power is Great Britain. The British Imperial System, which has provided for almost every description of State, can take into itself without friction a Jewish Palestine held in trust for the League of Nations.
>
> The British system educates the dependencies so as to fit them ultimately for self-government, and when they are ripe for self-government freely and gladly confers on them that boon.
>
> By the establishment of a Jewish National Home we mean the creation of such conditions in Palestine today as will enable us to move large numbers of Jews into the land, to settle them there, to render them self-supporting, and last but not least to establish schools, universities and other Jewish institutions so that the country may become as quickly as possible as Jewish as England is English. We hope that an administration will be created that will enable us efficiently to carry out this programme.
>
> I see no reason for differences between ourselves and the Arab non-Jewish population. There is plenty of room for us both in Palestine. It will hold five or six millions if properly developed, whereas the present

> population is less than 700,000. It is not likely that there will ever be an "Arab question" in Palestine: non-Jews need not fear that they will suffer at our hands. For two thousand years we have known what it means to be strangers. We Jews know the heart of the stranger: are we likely to deal out oppression?
>
> Moreover we have never proposed that a Jewish minority should rule over the rest. Palestine will only become a Jewish self-governing commonwealth when the majority of its inhabitants are Jewish."

Shortly after making this statement to *The Times*, Dr. Weizmann repeated much of his explanation in a report to the Zionist Conference then being held in London. On the 5th of March he told the Conference that the "Zionist Organization has every reason to be satisfied with the reception that has been accorded to their delegates. I consider that our historic claim to a Jewish National Home in Palestine has been conceded by the Powers." By a Jewish National Home he added that he meant the establishment of such political, administrative and economic conditions as would enable them to settle, say, 50,000 Jews a year in the country, to foster their own language and schools, to develop an administration suitable for these purposes, and ultimately to make Palestine as Jewish as England was English.

The Peace Conference was captivated by Dr. Weizmann's epigrammatic précis of his programme to Mr. Lansing. Lord Balfour—who must have been a trial to some of his Foreign Office staff—was delighted by the Zionist leader's comprehensiveness. M. Tardieu was even over-responsive. In the Whitehall phrase, he now showed himself "premature." He sailed with French contempt for hypocrisy through face-saving formalities and declared bluntly that there would be no objection by France to the formation of a new Zionist State in Palestine in (sic) the League of Nations, under a mandate granted to Great Britain.

Only in Palestine did the news that the country was to be made as Jewish as England was English meet with a hostile reception. The people, already incensed by the ways of the Zionist Commission, broke into protest. Cables were sent to the Peace Conference delegates and to the British Press. A representative protest was that from the Moslem and Christian Committee of Jaffa, which put the cardinal point at issue clearly when it said, "We are the born sons of the Holy Land." No formal attention was paid to these protests, but they were to have a temporary effect.

President Wilson had gone back on a month's visit to the United States and was absent when Messrs. Weizmann and Sokolov spoke to the Council of Ten. But the Zionists did not lose sight of him. A memorial on the "Jewish Title to Palestine" was handed to him on the 1st of March at the White

House. This was on the customary lines, for the most part. A new justificatory phrase was found for Jewish immigration: "the land needs rehabilitation." Great Britain was again designated as the suitable Mandatory. Any constitution given to Palestine was to embody the Zionist statement before the Peace Conference, and was to contain the Balfour Declaration. Local autonomy was to be established, and granted or enlarged in proportion to the abilities of localities to maintain proper standards of administration. (A proviso not unrelated to the supposed backwardness of the Arabs and the undoubted forwardness of the Zionists.) The established rights of the present population were to be equitably safeguarded; the point being that the population was thought to have no *established* rights. (Cf. de Haas *supra*, Chapter 11)

It was the familiar programme, peptonized with fair words for the President's better digestion, and he replied in amiable innocence.

> "As for your representations touching Palestine, I have before this expressed my personal approval of the Declaration of the British Government regarding the aspirations and the historic claims of the Jewish people in regard to Palestine. I am, moreover, persuaded that the Allied nations, with the fullest concurrence of our own Government and people, are agreed that in Palestine shall be laid the foundations of a Jewish Commonwealth."

The President, therefore, was slightly at cross-purposes with his co-workers, who were indeed lacking in uniformity, judging by some of their statements. Dr. Weizmann "did not aspire to found a Jewish State"; the President concurred in its foundation; Lord Balfour was delighted by it; the Foreign Office thought it premature; M. Tardieu said there was no objection to it; the American Zionist plans for a Jewish Palestine were replaced by Dr. Weizmann's plans for a Jewish Palestine", and Mr. Lloyd George was in agreement with everybody for the time being.

Then the President returned to Paris, and within a week of his arrival an important event for the story of modern Palestine occurred. This was the private meeting at 23 Rue Nitot, where Mr. Lloyd George was living, of the chief Conference delegates, to consider the situation in Syria. It was a meeting not at all in the course of recent proceedings; it had no connection with the presentation of the Zionist case, and was the means indeed of preventing any immediate or quick sequel to that event. It was not therefore a meeting which most of those who took part in it desired: it was driven upon them.

It came with something of the force of gravity exerting itself finally after long strain against an entangled system of props upholding some top-heavy superstructure. All the inconsistencies of the war policy in the Near

East, the covert bargains, the treaties which negatived their predecessors, the pledges suppressed, the secrecy of ally to ally, had collapsed together under the natural pressure of events in Syria. The Arabs, expecting the McMahon-Hussein agreement to be honoured, found that the French would not yield to them the occupation of three of the four principal Arab towns of north Syria therein mentioned, Homs, Hama and Aleppo. There were French detachments in these places and they would not depart.

The French on their side demanded that the Sykes-Picot Treaty should be put into force and that the seaboard—widely understood—of Syria from Tyre to the Taurus should be granted to them, under the alias of a Mandate later if the British and others insisted upon it.

These counter-demands were not merely upon paper; Arab and French soldiers made them face to face on Syrian soil, and the position there grew steadily more tense and brittle. It was a position which could no longer be left to itself and the British Prime Minister came to the decision that a consultation should take place upon it. He summoned this secret session of the Peace Conference chiefs and brought Lord Allenby to Paris from Syria to attend it. Lord Balfour was there too, and Sir Maurice Hankey made one of his earlier appearances as the perpetual squire of the Cabinet. Lord Allenby's Chief-of-Staff, Sir Louis Bols, came with him. France was represented by MM. Clemenceau, Pichon and Berthelot, Italy by Sigg. Orlando and Sonnino. M. Mantoux was interpreter. No account of what occurred in the Rue Nitoton that 20th of March reached the British public, and even now it is from the private papers of President Wilson that our knowledge of it remains drawn, and it is to the revelative zeal of Mr. Ray Stannard Baker, the American historian of the President's share in the peace-making, that we owe it.

As soon as the meeting began, it was seen that Mr. Lloyd George meant to call the French severely to order. He adopted an attitude which kindled understandable fury in their breasts. Fresh from his own plannings with Mr. Wise and the other Zionists to dispossess the Arabs in Palestine despite of the Hussein-McMahon Treaty, he took in hand the very document he had just discarded and flourished it at the French delegates to prevent their dispossessing the Arabs in North Syria. "The League of Nations," he declared to M. Pichon, "cannot be used for putting aside our bargain with King Hussein. It has the status of a treaty."

True as this was, and notable as was the Premier's acknowledgement of the status of the agreement with King Hussein, yet there was something stupendous in the way that Mr. Lloyd George could admonish the French for using the League of Nations to put aside the bargain with King Hussein in North Syria, while he and Lord Balfour were making ready to use the

League of Nations to put aside the bargain with King Hussein in South Syria.

Beside this, he ventured to confront M. Pichon with the date of the Hussein Treaty, six months earlier than the Sykes-Picot Treaty and therefore the valid treaty of the pair. This fact again was true and it was highly proper that it should be made clear. But Mr. Lloyd George's airy disregard of the morality of his own Government in concluding the Sykes-Picot Treaty under the circumstances, and his endeavour to confound the French with our double dealing as though it were a phenomenon beyond our control—these were attitudes to rouse the rage of any hearers. The most colossal presumption of all, though, was to impugn the Sykes-Picot Treaty and to say nothing of the Balfour Declaration, issued in cold blood nearly two years after the Hussein Treaty which it so scandalously and flagrantly set at naught. But Mr. Lloyd George, untroubled by all this, suspended the moral constitution and took stand by some rule-of-thumb to which he and Balfour had the clue.

With the French though, who had no traditional privilege of escaping from issues of right or wrong by acting practically, Mr. Lloyd George was extremely stern for seeking to set aside the British agreement with King Hussein. Monsieur Pichon retorted—I should imagine with some Gallic feeling—that France was accused of setting aside a bargain which she had never made. France, he said, had no agreement with King Hussein: it was a British agreement.

Mr. Lloyd George, at the height of his form, replied that the whole of this pact of 1916, the Sykes-Picot Treaty, was based on a letter from Sir Henry McMahon to King Hussein. He took the McMahon treaty in hand and read out the passage by which the four towns of Damascus, Horns, Hama and Aleppo fell within the boundaries wherein Great Britain had stated she was prepared to recognize and support the independence of the Arabs.

M. Pichon: "This engagement was made by Great Britain alone. We never saw it till a few weeks ago, when Sir Maurice Hankey handed me a copy of the text."

Mr. Lloyd George: "The agreement may have been made by England alone, but it was England who organized the whole of the Syrian campaign. There would have been no question of Syria but for England. Great Britain has put from 900,000 to 1,000,000 men into the fight against Turkey, but Arab help has been essential to us. That is a point upon which Lord Allenby can speak."

Lord Allenby then testified that the Arab help "had been invaluable." He went on to say of the present position that when he had, in accord with the Sykes-Picot Treaty, put French administrators into the 'blue' area of

Syria, the Emir Feisal had then told him that he could not maintain the command of the Arab army if the French were allowed to occupy the ports. Such a French occupation would mean that the "Arabs were to live in a house without a door." On this, Lord Allenby had pointed out to the Emir that he was in charge of the Administration as Commander-in-Chief and that the French officers whom he had appointed must be looked upon, not as French officers but as Allied officers whom he had appointed in his capacity as Commander-in-Chief. The Emir Feisal had answered him that he would admit this for the present, but he had asked, "Would it last for ever?" General Allenby had reassured him on this point, saying that the League of Nations intended to give the lesser nations the right of self-determination.

After this acknowledgement of his reconfirmation of the Allied pledges by Lord Allenby, Mr. Lloyd George returned to his argument where he had left it. "It was on the basis of the letter I have quoted [from the McMahon-Hussein documents]" he said, "that King Hussein put all his resources into the field, and this helped us most materially to win the victory. In signing the 1916 agreement France for practical purposes accepted our undertaking to King Hussein." He pointed out that it was not M. Pichon, but his predecessors who had accepted. (For what occurred at the time the reader may refer back to Chapter 8.)

M. Picot had been shown the McMahon-Hussein Treaty in the Foreign Office on the 23rd of November, 1915. He had also been told of a special message from Hussein, transmitted through Cairo, that the Arabs would oppose French occupation of the four cities by force of arms. On the 21st of December M. Picot told Sir Arthur Nicolson that the French Government agreed that the Arabs should administer the four towns. But all this information seems to have been secreted in the Quai d'Orsay and never communicated to M. Pichon when he took office.)

"I am bound to say," concluded Mr. Lloyd George, "that if the British Government now agreed that Damascus, Homs, Hama and Aleppo should be included in the sphere of direct French influence we should be breaking faith with the Arabs, and we could not face this." "We could not face this except in Palestine," he should have said, to be accurate.

The President of the United States now took up the burden of discourse, and introduced another note. It was the first he had ever heard of the Hussein-McMahon Treaty, he said. He was interested to know of it but it was not permissible for him to express an opinion upon it. He continued,

> "The point of view of the United States is however indifferent to the claims both of France and of Great Britain over peoples, unless these peoples want them. One of the fundamental principles to which the United States adheres is the consent of the governed. From the point of

> view of the United States of America the only idea is whether France will be agreeable to the Syrians. The same applies to Great Britain, whether she will be agreeable to the inhabitants of Mesopotamia. The only way to deal with the question is to discover the desires of the populations of these regions."

The President might have envisaged things more clearly. He did not seem to know that Great Britain in Mesopotamia actually was trying to discover the desires of the inhabitants. He did not seem to grasp that the McMahon-Hussein Treaty, whatever its imperfections, was based on the Arabs' own claim to independence: it was an Arab claim to which Great Britain gave her assent. The President perhaps argued that British assent was not needed, that the disposal of Arab lands was the Arabs' affair. It is evident then that he might have examined his own conscience in regard to Palestine, where the principle of the consent of the governed had not been mentioned by him, as it is improbable that when he spoke of the Syrians he included the inhabitants of Palestine.

But for all this, he did formally enunciate that freedom to decide their own lot was the right of the peoples which had been under the Turks, and thus willy-nilly he included the people of Palestine. More important still, he laid down that the only way to find out these peoples' wishes was to find out from the peoples themselves.

Nor did the President confine himself to the pious expression of his sentiments. He clenched the argument there and then, in Mr. Lloyd George's rooms, by declaring that an International Commission of Inquiry into the desires of their populations should be dispatched to the ex-Turkish countries. This was something for which the Emir Feisal had asked several times in private. He had also spoken of it in his speech before the Council of Six. Professor Temperley says that he is "reported" to have done so, showing thereby how little is known accurately of the speech. Auni Bey Abdel-Hadi tells me, however, that Feisal did mention it, and, as I say, had broached it before then when he had met the Allied chiefs.

The proposal was one which was much less pleasing to them than it was to the President. As though aware of this and foreseeing that his hearers would fail him, Mr. Wilson ended determinedly with a declaration that, "I shall send it, with carte blanche to tell the facts as they find them."

Whatever their inner feelings, the others did not demur at the time, except Balfour. The Anglo-French Proclamation of the previous 9th of November had been quoted at the meeting, and it would have been difficult to demur in face of it. At this stage the Anglo-French Proclamation had not been hustled out of sight. Mr. Lloyd George announced that he had no objection to an International Commission. The French delegates said they would take the President's plan into consideration. The Italians implied that they would be guided by the trend of common action.

So matters hung for a fortnight. Relations between the French and the Arabs went on disimproving. The Paris Press treated the Emir Feisal as an adventurer. These attacks, and the news which came to Feisal from Damascus, nearly led to his packing-up and withdrawing from the Conference. But British influence, exerted through Mr. Wickham Steed, the editor of *The Times*, kept him at his post. Mr. Steed even managed with great tact to bring him and Lawrence into conference with some of the chief Foreign Office officials of the French Government.

President Wilson meanwhile had been confirmed in his intention to dispatch the Commission because of various conversations he had with Americans who had enjoyed long and special experience of the Near East. It is indeed probable that the idea of a Commission had been implanted originally in his mind before he had left for the United States. In the second week of February he had received Mr. Howard Bliss, the President of the American College at Beyrout. Mr. Bliss had with him M. Chekri Ganem, who had been President of the Syrian National Committee, and the two, though nothing was reported of it, testified before some of the chief delegates. M. Ganem had claimed that the population should be consulted in Syria, both as a matter of natural right and because of the promise of the Anglo-French Proclamation.

These depositions and conversations had stuck in Mr. Wilson's memory, and after his return other Americans visited him and impressed him further. Some of them brought singular propositions to the President, such as the transfer of rule in the Near East to a board of "social workers," but all were disinterested enough to press him, whatever he did, at least to consult the Near East peoples upon the type of government the latter would wish to have, or if they were to be given mandatory governments, upon whom they would wish to have as Mandatory.

Moved by these various considerations, increasingly doubtful whether the facts hitherto presented to him were genuine, he determined at all costs to dispatch the Commission to Syria as soon as possible. It was an act which had great consequences, and one which should always be remembered to the man who made it. Afterwards he fell away from the standard which now he set and allowed his associates at the Conference to have their own way with the distribution of Mandates. But when this happened his health was failing; he had become overwhelmed; he was talked out of his thoughts by a multitude of voices and was jostled out of his plans by a multitude of affairs.

As American members of the "Interallied Commission on Mandates in Turkey" (the title which was adopted for it) the President nominated

Mr. Henry King and Mr. Charles Crane. They were assisted by Professor Albert Lybyer, Mr. G. R. Montgomery and Captain William Yale (a descendant of the founder of the University). Another Army officer, Captain D. M. Brodie, acted as secretary. Dr. Haddad, instructor in the School of Medicine at Beyrout College, acted as chief interpreter, and there was a competent clerical staff. Mr. King was a prominent scholar and author, who had directed the religious work of the Y.M.C.A. during the war in France, and had since been appointed to the staff of the United States Peace Conference delegation. Mr. Crane, a Chicago manufacturer for twenty-five years, had gained diplomatic experience in 1917 when he had been appointed to the U.S.A. mission to Russia. He also was a member of the Conference delegation, and was to become United States Ambassador to China. All the assistant members of the Commission had already made some study of the questions of the Near East.

But April dragged through without the departure of the Commission seeming to grow any nearer. M. Clemenceau said that he "wanted the Syrian business put on a satisfactory basis before any International Committee of Inquiry should start." In other terms, France must be installed in Syria as she desired, and after she had been settled the Commission could go out and inquire how anything left over from her occupation was to be settled. This showed what M. Clemenceau at least thought of the Commission and how much attention he was likely to pay to any report the Commission produced. Professor Lybyer was told by the M. Gofit of the Ministry of Foreign Affairs, who had been approached two years before by Mr. Malcolm on behalf of Zionism, that the French Government "refused to make final appointments (they had mentioned names of possible Commissioners) unless the English would first agree upon the most important matters that were undecided, and especially that they—the French—should be placed in charge, in a way, of O.E.T.A. East, and that it should not be the British function, but theirs, to pay the subsidy to the Emir Feisal." (Andrews.)

The French, in fact, wanted Feisal to be taken out of our pocket and put into their pocket. M. Clemenceau was in a very annoyed mood about it all and growled about the impossibility of knowing where you were with the British. Mr. Lloyd George "had expressed himself to me," as he complained, "entirely in favour of a French Mandate for Syria." (Steed.) And now Lloyd George had tacked and was opposing this Mandate. A little later he complained again, "Lloyd George has told me that he intends to demand a mandate for Great Britain in Mesopotamia and Palestine. I can't see why he should allow his people to contest our mandate in Syria." Yet a motive was plausible; to try and cover an anti-Arab policy for Palestine by a strong pro-Arab policy in the rest of Syria.

It is never quite easy, however, to follow the workings of Mr. Lloyd George's mind, because he has always leapt from good to bad and back, and supported himself on contradictions. He may have acted now merely on the principle of accepting anything for a start. But it looks as though he thought well of the Commission a while, for British delegates were provisionally appointed, and instructions were framed. The chosen delegates were Sir Henry McMahon and Commander Hogarth, Lawrence's old Oxford mentor, who had helped so much at the start of the Arab revolt. The distinguished Mr. Arnold Toynbee was to be secretary. The three came to Paris early in May, and conferred with Messrs. Crane and King.

Paris was as far as the British representatives ever went. Mr. Lloyd George's interest in the Commission or his determination that Britain should take part in it came to an end. Nothing clear was said or done, but if he had any sincere sentiments on the point they loosened, grew dishevelled and frayed away. It may be that he had become aware that the Commission would not skate over Palestine and confine itself to the French area.

This was in later April. On the 7th of May, falling in with the French desires, the British delegates agreed in principle to the partition of Syria by Britain and France as Mandatories. The *chose jugée* was established.

President Wilson, however, would not recognize this or would not be deterred in his own intentions. He insisted that the Commission should leave. Neither the French nor the Italians ever had appointed delegates. The question was whether Mr. Lloyd George would send his Englishmen out with the Americans, who were to go whether anyone else went or not. He withdrew them. Their appointments were cancelled on "practical" grounds, understood to be lack of Anglo-French agreement in time concerning the Commission. So the Americans went off alone on the 29th of May. Feisal preceded them to Syria that same month, the situation there clearly calling for his presence.

The Conference had not of course been occupied at this period entirely with the question of the Commission. Amongst its thousand occupations one which had relation to Near Eastern business was the question of "national minorities." All the Jewish delegates in Paris, not alone those who were Zionists, worked hard to obtain in the forthcoming Peace Treaty two things. The first of these was that an end should be made of political discrimination against Jews both by the established nations involved in the Treaty, and by those nations who were coming into existence through it. The Jewish delegates at the Conference were determined that Jews in all countries new or old should enjoy those full citizenship rights, which in some instances had been denied to them by previous regimes.

The second aim of the Jewish delegates was to obtain proper protection for Jewish schools and proper recognition of the Jewish religion. Both these aims, needless to say, were admirable and there was nothing better in the Treaty than the clauses which eventually secured them.

But the political Zionists used the opportunities which this "minority campaign" gave them. There were other minorities engaged in it besides those that were Jewish, and the Zionists took up their causes.

> "All the lesser nationalities of Eastern Europe emerged from the darkness of history to put forth their claims for self-determination. And each turned to the American Zionist Organization for aid in the presentation of its case. It was perhaps the only time that Jewish international-mindedness was acknowledged useful by Moldavians, Transylvanians, Finns, Georgians, Ukrainians, Ruthenians, Lithuanians, Latvians and Croatians. Each was accorded a hearing and each given that quiet aid which history and circumstances warranted" (de Haas).

There was no wrong in so doing, of course, but each of these frustrate or accepted nationalities might be trusted in return to give to the Zionist cause the same quiet aid—which history and circumstances did not warrant. It is easy to see the working out of the process by which so many small countries, young or old, when it came to ratifying the Balfour Declaration put their pens so readily and so blindly to the dotted line.

This, however, was not the only business at the time of the political Zionists. They tried also quite a different plan, which is well described in the *History of the Peace Conference,* edited by Professor Temperley.

> "As is well known [runs the account] there were considerable differences among the representatives of the Jews as to the objects which they desired to secure. On the whole it may be said that the English Jews tended to confine their efforts to securing for their co-religionists the widest personal liberty and full opportunities for the use of their own religion and the maintenance of their own customs. There was, however, a party which went further than this and aimed at getting official recognition of what they called Jewish nationality. They seem to have hoped that the Conference would give official recognition to the Jews in Poland and in other States as an organized corporation, with definite political rights, and there are indications that if this had been secured they might then have pressed for representation of this Jewish nationality on the League of Nations. It need not be said that any suggestion of this kind was ruled out from the beginning. M. Clemenceau's letter specially points out that the clauses of the Treaty "do not constitute any recognition of the Jews as a separate political community within the Polish State."
>
> The recognition of "national rights" of the Jews in Poland would have been completely inconsistent with the territorial sovereignty of the

> State, which is the basis of our whole modern political system. It is in accordance with this that, for instance, the educational control of the schools assigned to the Jews is given, not to one general committee supervising the Jewish education for the whole of Poland, but to "committees" which are clearly intended to be mere local bodies.
>
> *The view taken by the British Delegation throughout and supported by the Plenipotentiaries, was that if there was to be a Jewish nationality, it could only be by giving the Jews a local habitation and enabling them to found in Palestine a Jewish State.* [My italics.] Any Jew, however, who was a national of a Jewish State would naturally cease *ipso facto* to be a Polish citizen."

The "party which aimed at getting official recognition of what they called Jewish nationality" was, of course, formed of political Zionists. Their manoeuvre is worth recounting as it shows how the plan of slipping into the Conference amidst all the "small nationalities" and of getting thoroughly mixed up with them and so adopting their situation (cf. Chapter 8) was put into practice. The historian's comment upon the scheme too, is valuable. He gives independent testimony to the real intentions which the British delegates nourished for Palestine, if any more such testimony be needed.

I can add a rider of some interest myself. I was in Poland in December of 1918, when the country was rising to life again. A species of rough census was made about then, and the Poles found that very many of their Jews wrote themselves down as "Jewish" or "Zionist" citizens. The Poles said that the Jewish action had been instigated by the Zionist organizations, and were exceedingly wrath about it. It developed still further during the next month or two, during the early days of the Peace Conference, and the connection between this claim of Jews in Poland to be Jewish nationals and the Zionist manoeuvres in Paris is evident enough. In Lvov, as I remember, there was hardly a Jew but wrote himself down as a subject of the Jewish State.

This did not mean that the Jews of Lvov wished to emigrate en masse to Palestine. Some wished to go, but most informed the exasperated Poles that they intended to stay where they were born, but in an extra-territorial situation, as foreigners in Poland, which they preferred to any national rights. That was a reason why the Poles, when it came later to conceding these national rights, were less willing and prompt about it than might have been expected.

In May the Council of Four appointed a special Committee to deal with the minorities question, and in the end guarantees to protect the Jewish minorities figured in the treaties signed by Austria, Bulgaria, Hungary and Turkey. Poland, Czecho-Slovakia, Greece and Roumania consented to special protocols of the same import. There was no one apparently in Paris to rise and demand that the rights of the Arab majority in Palestine should be guaranteed by Great Britain. This suppression of a majority, unexampled in political practice, is the most extraordinary as well as the most baneful legacy of the Treaty of Peace.

The Crane-King Commission, in the interim, had reached Syria. It was originally intended, I think, that it should go to Mesopotamia also, but perhaps because the British authorities there were conducting their own inquiry, it did not make this journey. Reference to the conditions of Mesopotamia, however, formed part of the Commission's report.

Before coming, however, to the account of the Commissioners' work, something should be said of the situation in Palestine the Commissioners found at the time of their arrival. Palestine was under the Army Administration set up in accordance with the laws of war in captured territory, under supreme command of Lord Allenby, and established under the circumstances already narrated.

Eight months of occupation, of the entire territory, had developed great antagonism between the Army and the Zionists. From the start military support of Zionism may be said to have been confined to the Jewish battalions and to Major Ormsby-Gore. The Jewish battalions themselves were not so thoroughly Zionist as the major, and he did not belong to the forces of permanent occupation. As time passed the rest of the army grew increasingly resentful of the attitude and the acts of the Zionist Commission. As soon as Dr. Weizmann returned to England the relations between the Army and the Commission disimproved rapidly. Of the numerous members of the Commission who came and went thereafter, for its personnel often was changed, there were some, such as Dr. van Friesland, whose personality and methods were appreciated, but they were not many.

Within a mere couple of months of the Turkish defeat, "the attitude of practically the entire military administration was considered by every Jew and every Arab in the country as strikingly opposed to both the spirit and the letter of the Balfour Declaration," a Zionist Organization Report itself testifies.

How this attitude developed, and the result of this development, will appear later on, but here it is necessary to record the fact of its existence at the time the members of the Crane-King Commission landed in Palestine. The army had the historic habit of British soldiers, which is to make friends with the inhabitants of a country which they occupy or garrison, and the army sympathized with the Arabs in general when it perceived the Zionist intrigues to supplant them.

British soldiers are the least politically minded beings on earth, only concerned with their regimental duties and with sport, but they are alive to injustices and have their own way of venting their opinion of them. Mrs. Stuart Erskine supplies a vivid little picture of a batch of them, returning through Jerusalem to their barracks, and intoning as they went a current chorus:

> "And they sold the Holy City
> To the Zionist Committee."

A rude approximation, but the voice of the Army, and a sound military précis of the Balfour Declaration.

Another notable factor of the Palestine situation as the American Commission found it, was that the junior private of that army was as well placed to learn the details of the sale of Palestine as were the senior and the most important of its Arab inhabitants. The army received newspapers from home and read Reuter bulletins on mess notice-boards: it could follow something of the doings of the Peace Conference. On the other hand the main characteristic of the condition of the Syrian public at the time of the arrival of the American Commission was its enforced ignorance of the details of what was happening in Paris.

The few Syrian publications were local pamphlets. The main source of news in the vernacular lay in the Egyptian papers, arriving irregularly in Palestine or the other parts of Syria long after the events which they chronicled. These papers themselves, ably as some of them were conducted, were not wealthy enough then (though they have expanded since) to maintain their own world services of continuous cables and telegraphs. Their special news sent to them by compatriots in London or Paris was nearly all by letter, arriving with a lengthy time-lag. For cabled and telegraphed news two of them had understandings with daily papers in London, by which their representative in London, or an Englishman so acting, every evening might see the proofs of next day's paper and select from it matter to send. This formed the backbone of the Arabic newspapers' Conference news, but this backbone was made of news sent to London on subjects likely to interest the British public by British correspondents. British correspondents did not send to Fleet Street matter which might be of prime importance in Jerusalem or Damascus but in the United Kingdom would appear esoteric.

The Arabs, therefore, dependent in the main upon such copies of the Arabic papers of Cairo and of the European papers as reached their shores irregularly and long after events, were at the most extraordinary disadvantage. How could they fight their cause in Paris? How could they mobilize national opinion at proper moments and make Paris aware at once, in any important juncture, that they were the most vitally affected body of all, and that account must be taken in full of what they thought and desired and were determined upon. They could not do this: they had no chance. They were placed or fell into the role of a far-off, unconcerned, uninterested body. It was a miracle when their occasional protests arrived within hailing distance of the happenings which had aroused them. How could they manifest with effectual speed against what was being done to them, when they did not even know what was being done to them, and the Conference, with Zionists fleeting through its corridors, took no measures to have them informed.

Chapter 17

The first Arab parliament.—Feisal summons the Syrian Congress. The Damascus Programme.—The Crane-King Commission's Report.

Once he was back in Syria, Feisal, however, had something of his old independence of mind restored to him, and presently took an important step in which his Conference mentors certainly had no part. He called into being a national assembly. This was not quite an individual move, it is true. If he had not convoked the assembly, it was on the way to convoke itself. The principal Arabs in Syria had been working towards it, and many of them had gathered in Damascus. But he co-ordinated and rounded off the popular movement and gave it the benefit of his prestige in the West by summoning this "Syrian Congress," as it was called.

It is probable too that one of his reasons for calling the Congress was to re-establish his own position amidst his countrymen, which must have been impaired by his inability to obtain from the Conference in Paris the fulfilment of the war-time promises made to them.

There were in fact a number of reasons for summoning the Congress, which was an inevitable gathering. Its convocation was a set-back to the Zionists. The hope which they had nourished of wheedling some form of acquiescence in the "National Home" from Feisal, in order to give a specious validity to their pretensions before the Arabs could organize, had faded. They had got the "Treaty of Friendship" and the Frankfurter letter, but the one, quite apart from its ultimate validity, was void on its own showing, and the other had never had any value of any kind, and was grotesque.

So their fishing season, so to speak, was over, and Feisal had not been netted. They had to reckon with an Arab Congress now, and however much they and their friends might try to ignore it (as they did), the Congress was there, and it altered Feisal's situation.

The brunt of the organization of the Syrian Congress fell on the members of the 1914 Damascus Committee and their friends, the men who had helped to prepare the Arab revolt with King Hussein, and had armed his hand in the negotiations of the time with Great Britain. The Congress therefore was in lineal sequence from the early gatherings of Arab exiles in foreign countries and the meetings of the secret national societies under the Turks. Through the warfare of the last three years these had now developed from the first open convocation of Arab deputies upon Arab soil to the nucleus of an Arab parliament.

The Congress was limited to Syria. In the future a federal Congress for all the Arab lands might come. The great difficulty which confronted it, as we have seen, was the election of its members. The British and the French authorities refused to allow elections of any kind in their respective spheres. Whether this refusal was justified or not is a difficult point. The only available roster was the Turkish one, so that any elections which might take place would have been according to the extant Turkish law and therefore in consonance with The Hague regulations for occupied territory. But the occupying forces were not entitled to hold elections, and Arab authority in the British and French areas did not exist. On the other hand in their own area where they were the recognized authority of the O.E.T.A. and they were employing the Turkish system, the Arabs seem to have been quite in order.

It was six of one and half a dozen of the other. The Congress too, whatever the rights and wrongs on this intricate point, was representative. The secondary electors for the Turkish Parliament of 1908, according to the Turkish system, named the members or deputies of the Congress. The American Commissioners themselves agreed that it represented the will of the population, a conclusion they reached after widespread inquiry amidst the Arabs and through their own intercourse with disinterested informants not of Arab race.

The American Commission did not reach Damascus till the 26th of June, sixteen days after its disembarkation at Jaffa, but the preparations for it began to assail its members immediately. In their report, speaking of their earliest inquiries, they say, "For the most part the question of a Mandate was referred, either in writing, or more often in response to questions, to the approaching Syrian Congress at Damascus, at which they [the first Moslem delegations heard] would have representation." Also the popular demand for independence, expressed to the Commissioners in general terms at the very beginning, very soon began to take more shape, as the deputies in Damascus started consultation upon it. This was even before they met officially. When they did meet, they gave it definite, tabulated form in what was called "The Damascus Programme."

So it will make for simplification if the "Damascus Programme" is given here at once, preceded by that twenty-second Article of the Covenant of the League of Nations to which it refers. So far I have not quoted at any length from the Covenant or dealt with it more than was incidentally needful. The Covenant and the Mandate for Palestine will be examined together, when the time comes to consider the Mandate, since their texts are entwined.

But as the "Damascus Programme" turns so much on the twenty-second Article, the relevant clauses of the Article had best be cited textually, as the Commissioners gave them to the Arab public in Damascus. The first four clauses are all that need now be quoted. The remaining five refer to Africa, to the Pacific and to the inner relations of Mandatories with the Council of the League of Nations. The four clauses call for a deal of criticism, but for the moment any other criticism than that expressed by the Syrian Congress must wait.

Article 22 of the Covenant of the League of Nations

1. To those colonies and territories which as a consequence of the late war have ceased to be under the sovereignty of the States which formerly governed them and which are inhabited by peoples not yet able to stand by themselves under the strenuous conditions of the modern world, there should be applied the principle that the well-being and development of such peoples form a sacred trust of civilization and that securities for the performance of this trust should be embodied in this Covenant.
2. The best method of giving practical effect to this principle is that the tutelage of such peoples should be entrusted to advanced nations which, by reason of their resources, their experience or their geographical position, can best undertake this responsibility, and which are willing to accept it, and that this tutelage should be exercised by them as Mandatories on behalf of the League.
3. The character of the Mandate must differ according to the stage of the development of the people, the geographical situation of the territory, its economic conditions and other similar circumstances.
4. Certain communities formerly belonging to the Turkish Empire have reached a stage of development where their existence as independent nations can be provisionally recognized subject to the rendering of administrative advice and assistance by a Mandatory until such time as they are able to stand alone. The wishes of these communities must be a principal consideration in the selection of the Mandatory.

The fourth clause created what are known as the A Mandates, to which the Palestine Mandate belongs. The B and C Mandates were in Africa and Oceania.

The answer of the Arab Congress to this Article, for their "Programme" amounted to a rejoinder, was as follows. I quote from the Report of the Commissioners, to whom the first copy of the Programme was tendered. They state of it that "Much evidence goes to show that the programme prepared represents well the wishes of the people of Syria."

The Damascus Programme of the General Syrian Congress.

We, the undersigned, members of the General Syrian Congress, meeting in Damascus on Wednesday, July 2nd, 1919, made up of representatives from the three Zones, viz., the Southern, Eastern and Western, provided with credits and authorizations by the inhabitants of our various districts, Moslems, Christians and Jews, have agreed upon the following statement of the desires of the people of the country who have elected us to present them to the American Section of the International Commission. The fifth article was passed by a very large majority. All the other articles were accepted unanimously.

1. We ask absolutely complete political independence for Syria within these boundaries. On the North the Taurus system. On the South Rafeh and a line running from Al-Juf to the south of the Syrian and the Mejazian line from Akaba. On the East the Euphrates and Khabur rivers and a line extending east of Abu Kamal to the east of Al-Juf; and the Mediterranean on the west.
2. We ask that the Government of this Syrian country should be a democratic civil constitutional monarchy on broad decentralization principles, safeguarding the rights of minorities, and that the King be the Emir Feisal, who carried on a glorious struggle in the cause of our liberation and merited our full confidence and entire reliance.
3. Considering the fact that the Arabs inhabiting the Syrian area are not naturally less gifted than other more advanced races and that they are by no means less developed than the Bulgarians, Serbians, Greeks and Roumanians at the beginning of their independence, we protest against Article 22 of the Covenant of the League of Nations, placing us among the nations in their middle stage of development which stand in need of a Mandatory Power.
4. In the event of the rejection by the Peace Conference of this protest for certain considerations that we may not understand, we, relying on the declarations of President Wilson that his object in waging war was to put an end to the ambition of conquest and colonization, can only regard the Mandate mentioned in the Covenant of the League of Nations as equivalent to the rendering of economic and technical assistance that does not prejudice our complete independence. And desiring that

our country should not fall a prey to colonization and believing that the American Nation is farthest from any thought of colonization and has no political ambition in our country, we will seek the technical and economic assistance from the United States of America, provided that such assistance, does not exceed twenty years.

5. In the event of America not finding herself in a position to accept our desire for assistance, we will seek this assistance from Great Britain, also provided that such assistance does not infringe the complete independence and unity of our country, and that the duration of such assistance does not exceed that mentioned in the previous article.
6. We do not recognize any right claimed by the French Government in any part whatever of our Syrian country and refuse that she should assist us or have a hand in our country under any circumstances and in any place.
7. We oppose the pretensions of the Zionists to create a Jewish Commonwealth in the southern part of Syria, known as Palestine, and oppose Zionist migration to any part of our country, for we do not acknowledge their title, but consider them a grave peril to our people from the national, economical, and political points of view. Our Jewish compatriots shall enjoy our common rights and assume the common responsibilities.
8. We ask that there should be no separation of the southern part of Syria, known as Palestine, nor of the littoral western zone, which includes Lebanon, from the Syrian country. We desire that the unity of the country should be guaranteed against partition under whatever circumstances.
9. We ask complete independence for emancipated Mesopotamia and that there should be no economical barriers between the two countries.
10. The fundamental principles laid down by President Wilson in condemnation of secret treaties impel us to protest most emphatically against any treaty that stipulates the partition of our Syrian country and against any private engagement aiming at the establishment of Zionism in the southern part of Syria: therefore we ask the complete annulment of these conventions and agreements.

The noble principles enunciated by President Wilson strengthen our confidence that our desires emanating from the depths of our hearts shall be the decisive factor in determining our future, and that President Wilson and the free American people will be supporters for [sic] the realization of our hopes, thereby proving their sincerity and noble sympathy with the aspiration of the weaker nations in general and our Arab people in particular.

> We also have the fullest confidence that the Peace Conference will realize that we would not have risen against the Turks, with whom we had participated in all civil, political, and representative privileges, but for their violation of our national rights, and so will grant us our desires in full in order that our political rights may not be less after the war than they were before, since we have shed so much blood in the cause of our liberty and independence.
>
> We request to be allowed to send a delegation to represent us at the Peace Conference to defend our rights and to secure the realization of our aspirations.

In publishing the above communication the American Commissioners added a paragraph of comment, as follows:

> The Programme mostly speaks sufficiently for itself. Various points in it are commented upon elsewhere in this Report. It is the most substantial document presented to the Commission and deserves to be treated with great respect. The result of an extensive and arduous political process, it affords a basis on which the Syrians can get together and as firm a foundation for a Syrian national organization as can be obtained. The Mandatory Power will possess in this Programme a commitment to liberal government which will be found to be very valuable in starting the new State in the right direction.

In another part of their report they stated that "there can be no doubt that the main elements of this programme represent the popular will as nearly as that can be expressed in any country." They were in good position to say what did represent the popular will, for they had taken the utmost pains to discover what it was.

Between their arrival at Jaffa on the 10th of June and their departure from Adana on the 21st of July they received and studied 1,863 petitions, visited 36 of the more important towns, and heard delegations from other important centres. In addition they received delegations from, as they say, "hosts of villages," according to their records from 1,520 villages. It may be said of them that they passed a microscope over Syria, and were made aware of every grain of opinion in the land. In Palestine they heard major delegations in Acre, Beersheba, Gaza, Bethlehem, Haifa, Hebron, Jaffa, Ludd, Jenin, Ramleh, Jerusalem, Nablus, Nazareth, Safed, Tiberias, Ramallah, Richon-le-Sion and Tel-Aviv; they listened to or read the opinions of mayors and municipal councils, administrative councils, councils of village-chiefs, sheikhs, Arab societies, Moslem-Christian committees, 5 economic or trade groups, 53 Christian groups, 18 Moslem groups, 14 Jewish groups, and a group each of Druses, Samaritans and Persians.

An analysis of the petitions which they received shows clearly how well the Damascus Programme represented the feelings of the population. Fifteen hundred of the petitions demanded a United Syria. This, the Commissioners explain in a footnote, "means a Syria without Palestine treated as a separate country. In effect it is intended as a declaration against Zionism." Only eleven petitions were received definitely in favour of a Jewish State in Palestine and of extensive Jewish immigration. These petitions were all from Jewish delegations. Eight petitions approved the Zionist colonies, without entering further into the Zionist programme, four of them being statements by Arab peasants that "they were on good terms with the Jewish colonies." The fifteen hundred petitions thus aimed against Zionism were the largest percentage for any one request presented to the Commission (80.4 percent).

The second largest percentage, 1,370 petitions (73.5 percent) was for "Absolute Independence." Of this the Commissioners state:

> It is certain from the oral statements that accompanied the petitions that the term "Absolute Independence" was seldom used in the sense of an entire freedom from any foreign guidance, such as that of a Mandatory under the League of Nations, inasmuch as the request was frequently combined with a choice of Mandate or a request for foreign "assistance." While a few of the young Arab clubs certainly desired freedom from all foreign control, the great majority asked for independence and defined a Mandate to mean only economical and technical assistance, because of a widespread fear that the mandatory arrangement would be used to cloak colonial annexation.

Eleven hundred and two petitions asked for the type of kingdom specialized in the Damascus Programme with the Emir Feisal as king.

Ten hundred and sixty-four requests were made for American "assistance," failing which there were 1,073 for British assistance. Petitioners sheered off from asking for any given Mandatory, because of the suspicions concerning the character of a Mandate. For an American Mandate there were 57, for a British 66.

Nine hundred and eighty-eight protests were made against secret treaties, especially treaties dividing Syria, and against private agreements. The Commissioners stated of these that "the Sykes-Picot agreement and the Balfour Declaration are not mentioned, but it is usually understood that they are referred to."

Against the twenty-second Article of the League Covenant there were 1,033 specific protests. In 1,350 petitions a specific protest against the Zionist programme, mentioned by name, was registered. "The anti-Zionist note was especially strong in Palestine, where 222 of the 260 petitions declared against the Zionist programme."

The Commissioners schedule 1,129 "general anti-French statements." Of anti-Arab of the same general type there were 35, and it is pleasant to learn that of anti-British there were but three.

This analysis, and the other quotations so far made, are taken from the complete Report of the Commission. It is a long document of some 50,000 words. It is not possible therefore to reproduce it in full and indeed much of it is not germane to the Palestine issue. I shall confine myself therefore to citations or summaries from the following portions of the Report: (1) Report of the Commissioners upon their experiences in "the Area under British Occupation," O.E.T.A. South or Palestine; (2) a section under the heading of "General Considerations"; (3) extracts from other sections which are pertinent; (4) the final Recommendations of the Commission; (5) some points from the Confidential Appendix."

1. The Area Under British Occupation

I summarize this with an occasional quotation. The inquiry was carried out mainly without British help. In all sectors the Commissioners endeavoured to remain independent of the aid of the administration. But they record that the British officials from Major-General Sir Arthur Money, in command of O.E.T.A. South, down to the youngest officer, were courteous, obliging and helpful. As a body they give an impression of ability, efficiency, and a serious effort to administer the country for the good of the people.

Lord Allenby detailed Lieutenant-Colonel J. K. Watson to accompany the Commission, of whom the Commissioners speak in the warmest terms.

Moslems were practically unanimous for the independence of Syria, in the form which the Congress should desire it. Christians were mostly in favour of a mandatory power, exercising real control. The Commissioners visited two Jewish schools, and lunched at Richon-le-Sion colony where they met prominent members of several other Jewish colonies as well as the members of the Zionist Commission.

The Moslem and Christian population was practically unanimous against Zionism, usually expressing themselves with great emphasis. The Jews of Palestine declared themselves unanimously in favour of the Zionistic scheme in general, though they showed difference of opinion in regard to the details and the process of its realization. The elements of agreement may be stated as follows:

(a) Palestine, with a fairly large area, to be set aside at once as a "national home" for the Jews.

(b) Sooner or later the political rule of the land will become organized as a "Jewish Commonwealth."

(c) At the start authorization will be given for the free

immigration of Jews from any part of the world, for the unrestricted purchase of land by the Jews, and for the recognition of Hebrew as an official language.

(d) Great Britain will be the Mandatory Power over Palestine, protecting the Jews and furthering the realization of the scheme.

(e) The Great Powers of the world have declared in favour of the scheme which merely awaits execution.

Differences exist especially along two lines:

(a) Whether the Jewish Commonwealth should be set up soon or after a considerable lapse of time.

(b) Whether the chief emphasis should be upon a restoration of the ancient mode of life, ritual, exclusiveness and particularism of the Jews, or upon economic development in a thoroughly modem fashion, with afforestation, electrification of water-power, and general full utilization of resources.

The Commission suggested that a Commission for the Holy Places should be set up containing representatives of all creeds.

2. *"General Considerations"*

Under this heading the Commission spoke of the importance of the Anglo-French Proclamation.

Our survey made it clear that this Anglo-French Declaration and similar utterances of the Peace Conference, and President Wilson's Fourteen Points, had made a deep impression upon the Syrian people and lay in the background of all their demands. The promises involved not only cannot justly be ignored by the Peace Conference, but should be faithfully fulfilled. This is particularly true of the British-French Declaration, for it is completely in accord with the repeated statements of the aims of the Allies, and was expressly directed to the Arabic-speaking portions of the Turkish Empire, especially Syria and Mesopotamia.

The sincerity of the professed aims of the Allies in the War, therefore, is peculiarly to be tested in the application of these aims in the treatment of the Arabic-speaking portions of the former Turkish Empire. For the promises here made were specific and unmistakable.

The War and the subsequent breaking-up of the Turkish Empire, moreover, give a great opportunity—not likely to return—to build now in Syria a Near East State on the modern basis of full religious liberty, deliberately including various religious faiths, and especially guarding rights of minorities. It is a matter of justice to the Arabs, in the recognition of the Arab people and their desire for national expression, and of deep and lasting concern to the world, that an Arab State along modern political lines should be formed. While the elements are very various and the interests often divisive and much of the population not yet fitted for self-government, the conditions nevertheless are as favourable as could be reasonably expected under the circumstances to make the trial now. The mixed and varied populations have lived together with a fair degree of unity under Turkish domination, and in spite of the divisive Turkish policy. They ought to do far better under a State on modern lines and with an enlightened Mandatory.

The trial at least could safely be made under a sympathetic Mandatory Power, and made with good promise of success. If the experiment finally failed, division of territory could still follow. But to begin with division of territory along religious lines is to invite increasing exclusiveness, misunderstanding and friction. As Dr. W. M. Ramsay has said concerning certain other portions of the Turkish Empire, "The attempt to sort out religions and settle them in different localities is wrong and will prove fatal. The progress of history depends upon diversity of population in each district." And there is real danger in breaking-up Syria into meaningless fragments.

Any policy adopted, therefore, for Syria, should look to the establishment of a national government and administration deriving their authority from the initiative and the free choice of the native population, and should treat it as far as possible in harmony with its natural geographic and economic unity. This is the natural course to be taken, if at all feasible. It is directly in line with the expressed purpose of the Peace Conference. And it is the plain object of the desires and ambitions of a large majority of the population concerned.

3. *Extracts from other Sections*

Here and there in the Report there are statements which must be recorded. At the beginning the Commissioners, speaking of their encounters with the public, said:

> We were not blind to the fact that there was considerable propaganda, that often much pressure was put upon individuals and groups, that sometimes delegations were prevented from reaching the Commission, and that the representative authority of many petitions was questionable. But the Commission believes that these anomalous elements in the petitions tend to cancel one another when the whole country is taken into

> account, and that, as in a composite photograph, certain great common emphases are unmistakable.

They recurred to the question of irregularities later, saying that a number of the petitions showed signs of organized propaganda. They had resemblances and identities of phrasing. Printed forms were used sometimes.

The same Arab agent was observed in four cities of Palestine assisting in the preparation of petitions. Similar activities on behalf of French sympathizers were observed in Beyrout. In addition to this general propaganda, which was entirely legitimate as well as natural and inevitable, it is certain that a small number of petitions were fraudulently secured. [The Commissioners gave evidence of five cases.]

Facts of this kind, and others, diminishing in any degree the value of the petitions as a true estimate of public opinion in Syria, were carefully collected by the Commissioners under five headings. But they concluded:

> Yet despite these five qualifications, it is believed that the petitions as summarized present a fairly accurate analysis of present political opinion in Syria. The great majority of irregularities offset one another. The preponderance of Christian petitions in Palestine is balanced by the flood of Moslem appeals at Aleppo. The petitions are certainly representative. It was generally known throughout Syria that the American Commission would receive in confidence any documents that any individual or group should care to present… In the few cities in which the military authorities sought to exert control, directly or indirectly, over the delegations, without exception the opposition parties found opportunities to present their ideas to the Commission, if not always orally, at least in writing.

The Commissioners defined their own terms of reference and the origin of their powers with care. "The action creating the Commission, of which the Commissioners now reporting make the American section, was taken by the Council of Four." They quoted their instructions, drawn up by this body before the split upon the question of the Commission. These indicated that the Commissioners were to make inquiries in the portions of the Turkish Empire which were to be separated from that Empire and to be placed under Mandatories, in accordance with the terms of the resolution of the 30th of January, 1919, passed at the Peace Conference, and incarnating the twenty-second Article of the Covenant. The instructions continued—and this part of them is to be noted very particularly:

> And it is agreed that the administration of these Mandates shall be in the spirit of the following document, which was formally presented to the President of the United States on behalf of the Governments of Great Britain and France.

Upon which the Anglo-French Proclamation was quoted. We shall return to these important instructions.

I pass now to 4.

4. The Recommendations of the Commission

The findings of the Commission were given at considerable length, and for the most part I summarize them, with, I trust, absolute faithfulness.

The Commissioners recommended to the Conference that

(1) The Mandate should be for a limited term, the period to be fixed by the League of Nations when experience has been gathered through annual reports to it and in other ways.

(2) The term of the Mandate should however be long enough for the Mandatory to carry through the undertakings necessary for the foundation of the new State which will follow.

(3) The Mandatory should devote himself especially to educating the people and cultivating their national spirit.

(4) From the start the Mandatory should train the people in independent self-government, which should be established as rapidly as possible. The institutions of a democratic State should be set up.

(5) The Mandatory should expedite self-government on the principle that government should aim not at the accomplishment of "certain things" but at the development of citizens.

(6) Complete religious liberty must be ensured, and "a jealous care be exercised for the rights of all minorities."

(7) The Mandatory should be careful not to involve the new State in any considerable indebtedness nor should its finances be entangled with those of the Mandatory Power. The established privileges of foreign subjects, schools, commercial concessions and the like should be respected, but be subject to review and modification by the League in the interests of Syria. "The Mandatory Power should not take advantage of its position to force a monopolistic control at any point to the detriment either of Syria or of other nations, but should seek as rapidly as possible to bring the new State to economic as well as to political independence."

These seven clauses were tabled by the Commissioners as their primary recommendations, to which the Peace Conference should give effect if it wished to be true to the principles of the Covenant. By so doing the Conference would protect the essential interests of Syria, however the machinery of administration might be organized.

The report then continued:

> We recommend in the second place that the unity of Syria be preserved, in accordance with the earnest petition of the great majority of the people of Syria. The territory concerned is too limited, the population too small, and the economic, geographic, racial and language unity too manifest to make the setting up of independent States within its boundaries desirable, if such division can possibly be avoided. The country is very largely Arab in language, culture, traditions and customs.

The precise boundaries of the country should be fixed by a special commission, after the territory in general had been allotted. The Commissioners did not think the claim of the Damascus Congress to include Cilicia in Syria proved in any way. They urged that the Lebanon should constitute part of the Syrian State with a large measure of its traditional autonomy.

In the third place, the Commission recommended that Syria should be placed under a single Mandatory Power.

> No doubt the quick mechanical solution of the problem of difficult relations is to split the people up into little independent fragments. But, in general, to attempt complete separation only accentuates differences and increases antagonism. Granting reasonable local autonomy to reduce friction among groups, a single Mandatory ought to form a constant and increasingly effective help to unity of feeling throughout the State, and ought to improve steadily group relations.

In the fourth place, the Commission recommended that the Emir Feisal should be made head of the new Syrian State. "There seems to be no reason to doubt that the great majority of the population of Syria sincerely desire to have Emir Feisal as ruler."

The Commission then came to the question of Zionism. Because of its great importance I give the text of this part of the Report in full, as follows:

> We recommend, in the fifth place, serious modification of the extreme Zionist programme for Palestine of unlimited immigration of Jews, looking finally to making Palestine distinctly a Jewish State.
>
> (1)The Commissioners began their study of Zionism with minds predisposed in its favour, but the actual facts in Palestine, coupled with the force of the general principles proclaimed

by the Allies and accepted by the Syrians, have driven them to the recommendation here made.

(2) The Commission was abundantly supplied with literature on the Zionist programme by the Zionist Commission to Palestine, heard in conferences much concerning the Zionist colonies and their claims, and personally saw something of what had been accomplished. They found much to approve in the aspirations and plans of the Zionists, and had warm appreciation for the devotion of many of the colonists and for their success, by modern methods, in overcoming great natural obstacles.

(3) The Commission recognized also that definite encouragement had been given to the Zionists by the Allies in Mr. Balfour's oft-quoted statement [the Balfour Declaration], and in its approval by other representatives of the Allies. If, however, the strict terms of the Balfour Statement [sic] are adhered to—favouring the "establishment in Palestine of a national home for the Jewish people," "it being clearly understood that nothing shall be done which may prejudice the civil and religious rights existing in non-Jewish communities in Palestine"—it can hardly be doubted that the extreme Zionist programme must be greatly modified.

For a "national home" for the Jewish people is not equivalent to making Palestine into a Jewish State, nor can the erection of such a Jewish State be accomplished without the gravest trespass upon the "civil and religious rights of existing non-Jewish communities in Palestine." The fact came out repeatedly in the Commission's conference with Jewish representatives that the Zionists looked forward to a practically complete dispossession of the present non-Jewish inhabitants of Palestine, by various forms of purchase.

In his address of July 4th, 1918, President Wilson laid down the following principle as one of the four great "ends for which the associated people of the world were fighting"—"The settlement of every question, whether of territory, of sovereignty, of economic arrangement, or of political relationship upon the basis of the free acceptance of that settlement by the people immediately concerned, and not upon the basis of the material interest or advantage of any other nation or people which may desire a different settlement for the sake of its own exterior influence or mastery."

If that principle is to rule, and so the wishes of Palestine's population are to be decisive as to what is to be done with Palestine, then it is to be remembered that the non-Jewish population of Palestine—nearly nine-tenths of the whole—are emphatically against the entire Zionist programme. The tables [drawn up by the Commission] show that there was no one thing upon which the population of Palestine was more agreed than upon this. To subject a people so-minded to unlimited

Jewish immigration and to steady financial and social pressure to surrender the land would be a gross violation of the principle just quoted, and of the people's rights, though it kept within the forms of law.

It is to be noted also that the feeling against the Zionist programme is not confined to Palestine, but shared very generally by the people throughout Syria, as our conferences clearly showed. More than 72 percent—1,350 in all—of all the petitions in the whole of Syria were directed against the Zionist programme. Only two requests—those for a united Syria and for independence—had a larger support. This general feeling was only [i.e., but] voiced by the "General Syrian Congress" in the seventh, eighth, and tenth resolutions of the statement already quoted in the Report [the Damascus Programme].

The Peace Conference should not shut its eyes to the fact that the anti-Zionist feeling in Palestine and Syria is intense and not lightly to be flouted. No British officer consulted by the Commissioners believed that the Zionist programme could be carried out except by force of arms. The officers generally thought that a force of not less than 50,000 soldiers would be required even to initiate the programme. That of itself is evidence of a strong sense of the injustice of the Zionist programme on the part of the non-Jewish populations of Palestine and Syria. Decisions requiring armies to carry out are sometimes necessary, but they are surely not gratuitously to be taken in the interests of a serious injustice. For the initial claim, often submitted by Zionist representatives, that they have a "right" to Palestine, can hardly be seriously considered.

There is a further consideration that cannot justly be ignored, if the world is to look forward to Palestine becoming a definitely Jewish State, however gradually that may take place. That consideration grows out of the fact that Palestine is the "Holy Land" for Jews, Christians and Moslems alike. Millions of Christians and Moslems all over the world are quite as much concerned as the Jews with conditions in Palestine, especially with those conditions which touch upon religious feeling and rights. The relations in these matters in Palestine are most delicate and difficult. With the best possible intentions, it may be doubted whether the Jews could possibly seem to either Christians or Moslems proper guardians of the Holy Places or custodians of the Holy Land as a whole.

The reason is this. The places which are most sacred to Christians—those having to do with Jesus—and which are also sacred to Moslems, are not only not sacred to Jews, but abhorrent to them. It is simply impossible under these circumstances, for Moslems and Christians to feel satisfied to have these places in Jewish hands or under the custody of Jews. There are still other places, about which the Moslems must have the same feeling. In fact, from this point of view the Moslems, just because the sacred places of all three religions are sacred to them, have made very naturally much more satisfactory custodians of the Holy Places than the Jews could be. It must be believed that the precise meaning, in

> this respect, of the complete Jewish occupation of Palestine has not been fully sensed by those who urge the extreme Zionist programme. For it would intensify, with a certainty like fate, the anti-Jewish feeling both in Palestine and in all other portions of the world which look to Palestine as the Holy Land.
>
> In view of all these considerations, and with a deep sense of sympathy for the Jewish cause, the Commissioners feel bound to recommend that only a greatly reduced Zionist programme be attempted by the Peace Conference, and even that be only very gradually initiated. This would have to mean that Jewish immigration should be definitely limited, and that the project for making Palestine distinctly a Jewish Commonwealth should be given up.
>
> There would then be no reason why Palestine should not be included in a united Syrian State just as other portions of the country, the Holy Places being cared for by an International and Interreligious Commission, somewhat as at present, under the oversight and the approval of the Mandatory and of the League of Nations. The Jews of course would have representation upon this Commission.

These were the recommendations of the Commission concerning Zionism, and with them extracts from the Report proper may end. But there was drawn up at the time—5 in my list—a "Confidential Appendix" to the Report, from which I take a few quotations. It was intended that this appendix should be for the use of Americans only, because, as its preamble stated:

> There was material involving criticism of our Allies that ought not to come into a report to be put into their hands, and yet that the American Delegation to the Peace Conference and our own State Department ought to have, as involved in a complete statement of the case.

The criticism of Great Britain in this appendix is not notable. "Two or three military governors seemed to have taken some action to procure votes for Britain. Orders had been issued at Jaffa against declaring for complete independence." But on the other hand it is recognized that "much enterprise on the part of members of the Arab Government at Damascus," the distribution by agents of printed forms and of instructions, and other such activities, were not hindered by British authorities. Complaint and tribute fairly cancel each other out.

But an important note follows.

> Some British officers showed signs of disappointment at the declaration in favour of the Americans as first choice. One of them in consequence recommended to His Government to decline a Mandate over Syria, and the Commission was informed that Mr. Balfour sent

a message to this effect, which General Allenby conveyed to the Emir Feisal.

This can have been no great surprise to Feisal, who knew of the Sykes-Picot Treaty. Feisal, the Commissioners learnt, before their arrival in Damascus, had tried but failed to get certain councils to request a British Mandate. The Commissioners recognized that Feisal preferred the prospect of a British Mandate to an American one, though he said to them that America or Britain would be equally satisfactory to him.

> It may be that because of the benefits he has received and continues to receive from England, and because of the better prospect of a speedy larger Arab union if Syria and Mesopotamia and other areas are under the same supervision, he prefers in his inmost heart the Mandate of Britain. Lord Allenby "and many British officials" on the other hand, thought that an American Mandate over all Syria might be the best solution of the difficulties between Britain and France. If Britain withdrew then France could more easily withdraw her pretensions too.

In the appendix the absolute situation as regards "Complete Independence" was made very clear, as was the attitude of the Commission to it.

> The nations in forming the League have pronounced in the Covenant that Syria should be under Mandatory control. The Commission did not find reason to recommend modification of this decision, but abundant cause for holding it to be just. The 4th Article of the "Damascus Programme" provides for the possibility of a Mandate, defining it as "equivalent to the rendering of economic and technical assistance that does not prejudice our complete independence." Here also the restriction may be too great. The Mandatory Power should have a real control over the administration, so as to eliminate as far as possible corruption, waste, inertia, serious errors of judgment, etc.
>
> In spite of all that was said in favour of complete independence, it is altogether probable that either America or Britain would be allowed without resistance as much control as the council of the League of Nations judges to be wise. In fact, assurance was given on very high authority that the demand for complete independence is to an extent artificial, being in part motivated by the fear of a French Mandate, and in part by apprehension of the conversion of mandatory control into permanent possession. If adequate assurances be had against both these possibilities, the objectors to a Mandate, limited so as to secure its exercise in the interests of Syria, will be reduced to a small and impotent group. In time, when all things are ready, a true and lasting "complete independence" can be awarded by the League of Nations.

Chapter 18

Importance of the Damascus Programme and Crane-King Report. The Crane-King Report suppressed. Syria divided between France and Britain.— Another letter of Feisal's. The Zionist Commission takes governmental attributes to itself. Resentment and vain appeals to London of the Army Administration.

The preceding chapter was made up chiefly of the texts or parts of the texts of the twenty-second Article of the Covenant of the League of Nations, of the Damascus Programme, of the Syrian National Congress, and of the Report to the Peace Congress of the United States Commission of Inquiry into Turkish Mandates. It is significant and ominous in the history of modern Palestine that of these three documents which concern it so deeply, the extract from the Covenant alone is a familiar one. For all that most people know of the other two, they might just as well never have been written.

While reproducing them, so far I have added little comment. As the United States Commissioners said indeed of the Damascus Programme, they speak for themselves, and it was preferable to let them speak uninterruptedly. But if what they have to say is very clear, it is not quite all that needs to be said, and I turn to them now.

First the Damascus Programme. When one reads it, and when one compares it with the programmes and the resolutions evolved by the Paris peacemakers, it is the words of the men "not able to stand by themselves" which shame the words of the men who so dubbed them. The feeling arises that these Arabs of Syria, in their pitiful disregarded charter, showed themselves more worthy of respect than the heads of great States advertising so widely, and so much in the way of business, the absolute purity of their principles.

The Damascus Congressmen showed no satisfactory title to Cilicia, indeed. But in all their programme there is nothing else at which to cavil, and whatever they proposed they proposed knowing that they must execute it, should it be accepted. Not for them the stillborn clauses of Article 22. A tutelage of some kind would be imposed upon them, as they were well aware, and they knew that their tutor or Mandatory, or whatever the supervising State was to be called, would see that they were true to the promises which they made.

They showed wisdom; they asked for a State of a loose, decentralized character suited to the varying units of their race. They made due arrangements for safeguarding the rights of minorities. At a time when to their knowledge the Zionists were planning to supersede them in their native land they restrained themselves to a dignified protest against this, and thereafter guaranteed to their "Jewish compatriots" the enjoyment of common rights and the sharing of common responsibilities. What a contrast to the rapine of political Zion and to the cabals of Whitehall.

Their claim to be no less well developed than were the Bulgarians, the Greeks, the Serbians and the Roumanians at the moment when these peoples were freed from Turkish rule was so apposite, such an exemplary parallel, that in itself it was proof of the political capacity which the Covenant-makers denied to them. There was, at the least, a certain incongruity in treating people as politically deficient when their immediate reply to that imputation was charged with very perceptive political knowledge.

When they came to the question of the Mandate, they did not really demur to it. They demurred only to the depreciatory way in which it was imposed upon them, and their real fear was in fact that they would *not* be placed under a Mandate. They feared that the protectorate decreed by Paris would turn out to be anything but a Mandate, in any genuine sense of that word, that it would be instead a cloak for indefinite occupation of their territory and for legislation against their will. Heaven knows, in these fears they gave absolute and conclusive proof of how politically competent they were.

Their final request is very notable. They asked for the Emir Feisal as their ruler, declared that he had merited their "full confidence and entire reliance." When they said this they looked back upon the manner in which he had led them in the War, and the manner in which he might lead them in peace, if he were but left to himself and could act untrammelled by the coils which always were twisted around him in the West.

But they did not ask for him to be their representative in Paris, or at least to be their sole representative. To the Peace Conference they asked to be allowed to send their own delegation. Nor did Feisal disapprove of this decision, which tallied with his own motives in summoning the Congress. The Congress by now knew what had been happening to Feisal in Paris and in London, and saw the difficulties which beset him. How could he face gracious but alert Britain over the Zionist question? How could he evade the match-making schemes of the most veteran chaperone in the world, bent upon throwing him and all the *ingénues* of Zionism continually together?

He had been brought to Europe in British warships; all the expenses of his Hedjaz delegation in Paris were paid by Britain. He received from her a subsidy of £150,000 a month for the sake of carrying on his government, and so far she had defended Arab rights everywhere outside Palestine. Feisal could not forgo the funds upon which his administration depended, he could not endanger the only help he had against the immediate peril of French appropriation of North Syria. On the other hand, thus beholden to Great Britain, he could not escape from her insistent suggestioning that in return for what had been done for him he should give some proof of friendliness to her plans in Palestine.

But if instead of Feisal, or more likely, if in addition to Feisal, a delegation of Congress members were sent to Paris, or to wherever the negotiations for the Turkish treaty would continue, then responsibilities would be spread amidst the Syrian Arabs as a whole instead of resting on the solitary Emir. Furthermore these envoys of Congress would have to report to Congress, and could not be asked to sign Treaties of Friendship and other such inveigling papers on a supposed individual authority. They would not be princes saddled, caparisoned and bitted with personal obligations to the British Government and with personal connections in London, and for them it would be easier to offer a courteous but sturdy resistance to all the proposals for entanglement in the Zionist scheme.

Besides these motives was the plain fact too that in asking to be allowed to send a delegation to the Peace Conference they were but asking for their bounden right. Theirs was a request which should have been made months ago by the Supreme Council to the Arabs instead of being made now by the Arabs to the Council, just as the Conference was coming to an end. The way in which the Arabs made this request, however, was notable enough. Politely, they asked to be "allowed" to represent themselves. The Zionists in Paris had neither made nor needed to make any such polite appeal. They had taken their tickets to Paris without a by-your-leave, and had put them into pockets heavy with Conference letters-of-introduction and bulging with Conference latch-keys.

Finally, it is to be observed that, apart from the demand for the Cilician districts, the Arab Congressmen only asked for what had been promised to their race by Great Britain, subject to arrangement with France in the northern coastal area. Yet all this display of reasonableness, all this manifest readiness for accommodation has not prevented the Arabs from being entitled intractable, obdurate, entirely unreasonable, and I know not how much more.

I turn now to the Report of the Crane-King Commission. It is a full document and a frank one, amply argued. Its recommendations are well presented and were perfectly feasible. More than anything else, though, its main accomplishment was to expose unhesitatingly the aims of Zionism in Palestine—"practically complete dispossession of the non-Jewish inhabitants."

To have this established at the outset by men of the independence and the ability of Messrs. Crane and King—before he appointed them President Wilson had said, "I want to put the two ablest Americans now in Europe on that Commission"—was damning for the Zionist projects then. It is more damning if possible now for Mr. Lloyd George and the other Conference chiefs and cabinet ministers who were responsible for imposing these projects upon Palestine. The Americans informed them flatly that "nine-tenths of the population were most emphatically against the entire Zionist programme."

If after reading the Report these statesmen entered upon a pro-Zionist policy in Palestine, they did so in full knowledge that they would be imposing it by force upon an unwilling and helpless people. If on the other hand they did not read the Report, because they did not want to have it in their hands, then their ignorance was culpable and their policy was no whit less guilty.

But at this point the question surely will come, how was it possible for them to disregard the Report at all, since thus to act counter to its findings must have been to arouse some degree of international feeling against themselves. The answer is a simple one, and possibly may not prove so surprising in the light of the previous doings, herein detailed, of men of mark. No public feeling was evoked by the Report: no member of the general public read a line of it: there was not a paragraph concerning it in the Press—for the sufficient reason that it never appeared. The Crane-King Report was suppressed.

Exactly how it was suppressed is still much of a mystery. How could President Wilson stifle or allow to be stifled this testimony, which he had thought essential in the interests of justice, and needful for the proper fulfilment of the Covenant? He himself had fought in the teeth of every opposition to secure the Report. How under these circumstances could he permit himself to be overruled by others who did not wish the Report to be made public?

Something may be attributed, in explanation, to the tardiness of the document. This was not the fault of the Commissioners, but was due to the way in which the negotiations upon the Commission between the President and Messrs. Lloyd George and Clemenceau, not by accident, had dragged on and on. When at last Wilson cut the cables of discussion and dispatched his American envoys alone to Syria, their departure was long overdue. The

Peace Conference was ending: the Treaty of Versailles was signed indeed while they were in Damascus. By the time their Report was ready the Versailles Treaty was three months old. This will have militated against its publication, though in truth it was still eminently timely, as no treaty with Turkey had been concluded or was within sight of being concluded.

On another count the frankness of the Report, if it had become public, might have affected American relations with France, for it was as explicit about French aims and methods in North Syria as it was about Zionist aims and methods in the south. The British Government, too, would have been excessively annoyed by the undesired disclosure of the attitude of the Palestine population to Zionism. Thus the general unity of the Allied and Associated Powers, obtained not too easily at Versailles, might have been impaired. A particular result of any estrangement between them would have been, or might have appeared to be, a setback to the progress of the League of Nations. The President at the time was obliged to entrust his infant League to the ministrations of the European Powers, since his own America had refused to nurse it. A nettled France might have been sparing of these ministrations. Her rulers at the best took a lukewarm interest in the child.

One would have expected, however, that such considerations would not have weighed with President Wilson on the morrow of the Syrian Commission's report. The very aim of his gospel in those hours was to make an end of national acts dictated by expediency.

The most likely answer to the general quandary is to be sought therefore in something else, in the breakdown of the President's health. The relevant dates seem to confirm it. The Report just failed to appear beneath his great rainbow span, during that period of his power when his imagination was bright and his intentions circled the earth. From the day he fell grievously ill, he could no longer sustain the struggle for a justice such as the Crane-King findings propounded, and his illness coincided only too well with the completion of the Commission's work.

He had received, it is true, a summary of the Report on the 10th of July. It was however a brief cabled precis, which could but have had the effect of making him anxious to see the full document. This was not ready till two months later. The Commissioners reached the United States again in mid-September. It was on the 27th of that month that they were able to dispatch a copy of the entire report to the White House for the President. But only the day before Mr. Wilson had collapsed during the speaking-tour which had taken him away from the Capital.

His recovery, such as it was, was protracted, and in the meantime the Report was lost to sight. Mr. Ray Stannard Baker, the President's biographer and intimate, assures me that "there is no record of his having seen it at the time, nor of his having taken any action in regard to it." When, in preparation for his celebrated works upon the Peace Conference, Mr. Baker went through the papers in Mr. Wilson's strongbox, he expected to find amongst them this special "President's copy" of the Crane-King report. But it was missing. It had disappeared from the White House, and what became of it is not known, though it is surmised that it may have been transferred to the State Department during the President's illness.

The State Department—the United States Foreign Office—never published it, though it was through the State Department that copies reached the British and French Embassies and became at the confidential disposition of the French and British Cabinets. There is evidence that the French Government, unpleasantly stirred by what it saw in the Report (as has just been suggested), brought very strong diplomatic pressure to bear to prevent its publication. In the biography of Mr. Henry White, who was a member of the American Commission to Negotiate Peace, by Mr. Allan Nevins, there is a note of his protests at its suffocation "under pressure from France—the Report having stated that a French Mandate would be wholly unacceptable to the (Syrian) people." What the British Cabinet said or did concerning it is not known, but clearly it was enough for the Cabinet's purposes to have the Report quashed through French intervention. The result was the same, indeed the result was superior, for Whitehall could obtain precisely what it wanted and yet seem unimplicated.

The ownership of the Report too never appears to have been settled. The Commissioners themselves did not feel they were empowered to issue it privately. After Mr. Wilson went into retirement he seems to have regarded it as his personal property.

When at last he did give Mr. Stannard Baker permission to print extracts from it, this did not occur till just after the two Houses of Congress had voted a joint resolution confirming the Balfour Declaration, and the League of Nations Council had approved the Mandate for Palestine as proposed. The Congress resolutions were passed in May and June and the Mandate was approved on the 24th of July, 1922. The first revelations of the Commission's Report, long extracts from it, appeared in Mr. Baker's syndicated articles in the *New York Times* in August, too late for the Congress meetings, where they would have exerted a powerful influence against the confirmatory resolution. In December Mr. Wilson allowed the publication of the entire Report in a technical journal of New York, the *Editor and Publisher,* which deserves the gratitude of us all for its determination that the Report should be known. I owe my extracts to it.

Under whatever circumstances this happened, then, at the close of 1919 the American Report was withheld, and once more the prestige of the West, this time of the great nation of the far West thought so superior to European manoeuvres, suffered in the Near East a shocking decline. The Commission had come to Syria acting with authority and vested in credentials. Everywhere the people had thronged to lay their case before the long-anticipated tribunal, and everywhere the Commissioners had made most meticulous inquiry. Honest dealing, the Arabs thought, was to be their portion now. They were being treated as intelligent persons, as men competent to discuss their own future, and no longer as dead stones, which were to be built into the constructions the Allies meant to raise upon their soil.

The Commission departed and the Arabs waited, at first with confident impatience, and then with increasing disquiet. They waited and waited, but nothing was said, nothing done. By degrees the old silence and boycott closed round them again, worse this time because of their spent hopes. The sullen feeling of being tricked possessed them more heavily than ever, and of resentment against the parties responsible.

The immediate and tangible effect of non-publication of course was that the labours of the Syrian Congress came to naught, though the members continued restively in session till the 1st of December. Feisal, tired and very worried, returned to Europe to try and discover what was to be the fate of his countrymen under a Convention which had been signed between Great Britain and France on the 15th of September, after a couple of months' negotiation.

Negotiations upon various points had been going on in lesser or greater quiet during the months just before and just after the signing of the Versailles Treaty. Sometimes the quiet ended in a little hubbub, as in May, when "it suddenly emerged that British and French commercial interests were negotiating for the laying of a pipe-line from the Mesopotamian oil-fields to the port of Tripoli." The emergence unfortunately was into the midst of American treaty-making circles, and protests rained on Mr. Lloyd George. He said he knew nothing of the business, and had written to M. Clemenceau to cancel the whole of the negotiations. However, the question of oil was not to disappear. But later conversations took a more official turn, and gushes of oil-news were kept under restraint.

Zionist negotiations, which did not come to the surface, also went on with both French and British Governments. Dr. Weizmann and M. Sokolov, who generally conducted them, were by now so sure of the eventual identity of the National Home with all Palestine that they concerned themselves seriously with the future boundaries to be assigned to the country. "Every effort was made to urge upon the British and the French Governments the justice and the necessity of the Zionist proposals in regard to the boundaries. Mr. Balfour was particularly impressed in conversation with

Dr. Weizmann and Mr. Brandeis in August with the economic arguments in regard to the northern boundary." Next month, in Paris, MM. Pichon and de Caix "formally promised Dr. Weizmann that Zionist representatives would be heard when the question of the Syria-Palestine frontier was discussed between England and France." (Z.O.R.)

I have found no record of whether the Zionist leaders were in Paris when the Anglo-French Convention of the 15th of September was signed. If they were not there physically, they were there in spirit, because the Convention, though not a final one, marked the beginning of the division of Syria into two, according to Zionist desires and to those of the British Government. On the surface it dealt with the northern areas to be evacuated by British and to be occupied by French troops, but in practice Britain then created Palestine as a unit, which thenceforward she intended to occupy. France did the same by North Syria, though there difficulties arose through the presence of the Arab administration, and the dispersion of Arab troops.

A provisional Franco-British frontier was arranged across the middle of Syria, by which military occupation was demarcated on Sykes-Picot lines. Mr. Lloyd George quoted the biblical limits "from Dan to Beersheba" as the boundary he would desire. He used the phrase with inner realization, without doubt, of its comprehensive vagueness. M. Clemenceau, who was carrying on the negotiations with him, listened and endured. The Convention was signed "without prejudice" to any future alterations which might ensue when the Turkish Peace Conference should determine what Clemenceau unbiblically described as "the political organization of the Levant."

A compromise was reached concerning the four cities of the Sykes-Picot: "A" zone; Damascus, Homs, Hama and Aleppo. The British troops were to quit them, but the French were not to enter them. It was to the French, however, that in this area the Arabs were to appeal for "help and advice." From now on the Arabs' eyes in this matter of help and advice were to be fixed in a perpetual squint, their right eye to the French, their left to the British. One of the most genial arrangements of the post-war period.

All this prenatal determination of Mandatory areas happened a full half-year before Great Britain and France were formally "chosen," by each other and friends, as Mandatories for their respective halves of Syria.

A French semi-official statement covering the Convention evidenced too the gentle seep of the oil of Irak back into consideration. It ran, "It does not appear that the district of Mosul is included in the regions wherein Great Britain feels that she can cease to be responsible for the maintenance of order."

When Feisal arrived in London to inquire into the lot of the Arabs under the Convention he had several interviews with Mr. Lloyd George and with Lord Curzon, who in January had succeeded Balfour as Foreign Secretary. As early as October 1918 Curzon had taken over the London direction of the Foreign Office while Balfour was kept in Paris. Three months later he took over the official position of Foreign Secretary itself. Balfour, however, stayed in the Cabinet with a sinecure office, exercising his influence in Paris upon the conduct of the Peace Conference.

The intention of Curzon's appointment without doubt was to have a Foreign Secretary who could attend to current affairs in the Foreign Office in the midst of the appropriate staff, instead of one who was abroad, dissociated from his own headquarters, and only able to give attention to the rest of his work in the time he could spare from one special section of it, the Peace Treaty.

But things did not turn out as had been hoped. Balfour in his seemingly careless way stuck to most of the attributes of the position which he had resigned, and the practical sequel of the change was that Great Britain now had two Foreign Secretaries, one at home, and one abroad. Curzon himself has described the resultant situation, seven months after he had taken office, in August. There had been confused and lengthy Cabinet meetings about Turkish affairs. Two of these lasted for five hours. But no headway was made. In Lord Curzon's words, "A.J.B. is in Paris pursuing one policy. I am here pursuing another. No one knows what ought to be done, and we go on getting deeper and deeper into the mire." (Ronaldshay.)

Therefore from the point of view of the Arabs the arrival of Curzon at the Foreign Office, as long as Balfour stayed in power in Paris, did not make much difference. It remains hard to disentangle Lord Curzon's own attitude towards them and their country. He seems to have given most of his intention to the purely Turkish part of the Turkish Treaty. Perhaps the most notable indication of his attitude is to be found in the very slight reference to the affairs of Palestine in Lord Ronaldshay's biography of the Marquess.

Curzon and Lloyd George together received Feisal on a couple of occasions, and assured him that the promises made to the Arabs would be kept. Mr. Lloyd George declared that "the engagements taken by Sir Henry McMahon were as valid and important as the [Sykes-Picot] 1916 agreement between Britain and France." Excellently proper as this acknowledgement was, it was in style equivalent to saying that a first-born was as much the eldest son as a cadet.

In a noble mood at a Downing Street meeting the Prime Minister declared that "The Arab forces have redeemed the pledges given to Great

Britain, and we shall redeem our pledges." But afterwards he explained to Feisal that in Syria this British redemption would take place only at the expense of French demands. He and Curzon informed Feisal that they considered the "main point" of British pledges to the Arabs to be the inclusion in the Arab area of the four towns of the desert-fringe, Damascus, Homs, Hama, and Aleppo.

Feisal was given no choice, and had to take what was offered to him. He accepted the French "help" of the September Convention. With superb irony, which escaped all comment, arrangements were made for a neutral zone to be delimited in order to keep Feisal's area safely separate from the area of those to whom he was to turn for advice and assistance. When he went to Paris, too, to discuss details, he learned from M. Clemenceau that "the undertaking of the French not to occupy the four towns was conditional on the ability of the Damascus Government to keep order and to suppress anti-French propaganda." All this recalled the Austrian demands upon Serbia in July of 1914. The *vieux routier,* Clemenceau, was taking in fine the old road to intervention.

By now Feisal had gained much experience of Allied leaders. Someone was misguided or mischievous enough to ask him one day his opinion in general of these statesmen. The Emir, who had been visiting art exhibitions, answered, "They are like impressionist pictures. The effect is excellent from a distance." Of Mr. Lloyd George in particular he said, "I ask him for independence and he gives me memorandums." One of these memorandums Feisal, after hearing its contents, would not even take into his hands out of Mr. Lloyd George's. He "refused it with the greatest energy," very likely with as much energy as it had been proffered to him.

Between times, in London that autumn, in October, Feisal gave an interview of some importance to a member of the staff of the *Jewish Chronicle,* an influential, active and well-written organ of English Jewry. This interview is useful for its bearing on his real attitude towards Zionism. He told his interviewer that "Palestine is and must remain part and parcel of Syria." Arab Palestine, he went on, was not a country but a province. There was no natural boundary between the two "countries" (the future French "Syria" and Palestine). He added that he raised no objection to Dr. Weizmann's proposals. But it seems evident that he still had no clear idea what these proposals meant, or that they had never been told him fully, for his interviewer had to explain plainly to him that the whole of Jewry, relying on the Balfour Declaration, looked to setting up in Palestine a "National Home" which would be ultimately a Jewish State.

Feisal answered that "such aspirations clashed with Arab ideas." He appealed for the co-operation of the Jews in the formation of an Arab kingdom, when a concentration of Jews into it might make of Palestine "a sub-section of the Arab kingdom."

Mr. Kallen throws some further light upon Feisal's idea then of an arrangement with the Zionists, saying "Feisal was to give a sort of Mandate for Palestine, and was to guarantee Jewish rights there by means of a minority-treaty such as the Jews had promulgated for themselves in Central Europe." With regard to this, it must be remembered that this or any other treaty or arrangement must have been submitted by Feisal to his father, who at the time could not have disposed of it himself, with the Syrian Congress in being. King Hussein, incidentally, had refused to ratify the Versailles Treaty though Feisal had signed it, because of the failure of the Allies to concede in it, or to give surety of conceding in any subsequent treaty, the Arab independence which Great Britain had guaranteed. We had promised not to conclude a treaty with the enemy without enshrining this independence amidst the conditions. Though the Versailles Treaty was with the German enemy only, Hussein was afraid that if he let the matter pass, he might be considered to have abdicated the principle of the inclusion of Arab independence in any subsequent treaty.

Feisal's interview in the *Jewish Chronicle* was productive of some Zionist reaction. As Sir Herbert Samuel was the party concerned it will be best to give his own account of it, which occurs in a lecture upon "Great Britain and Palestine" he gave before the Jewish Historical Society of England, at University College in Gower Street, on November 25th, 1935. It was the second "Lucien Wolf Memorial Lecture," though trust it will not be taken amiss if I say that the one thing which the learned society and the distinguished orator did on this occasion was to forget Lucien Wolf.

"Later in that year (1919)" [said Sir Herbert Samuel] "some misunderstanding arose owing to the terms of an interview with Feisal which had appeared in the *Jewish Chronicle* of London, and I had taken steps to remove it. Among my papers relating to that time is a letter signed by Feisal, of which the following is a translation from the French:

Peace Conference,
Secretariat of the Hedjaz Delegation,
Paris,

December 10th, 1919.
Dear Mr. Samuel,

I have been very glad to learn that you had taken the opportunity of the second anniversary in commemoration of the Balfour Declaration to dissipate the misunderstanding created by the publication of the

> interview with me in the newspaper, the *Jewish Chronicle*, last month. I am firmly convinced that the mutual confidence established between us, and the perfect accord in our point of view, which has permitted a perfect understanding between Dr. Weizmann and myself, will prevent similar misunderstandings in future, and will maintain that harmony between us which is so necessary for the success of our common cause.
>
> Accept, dear Sir, the assurance of my highest consideration.
> Feisal.

"It is impossible" [commented Sir Herbert Samuel] "that a letter should have been written in such terms by the authorized representative of the Arab Movement if there had been at that time any real sense of grievance against the policy which was being pursued, or any feeling that the Balfour Declaration was itself a violation of pledges that had previously been given to the leaders of the movement."

In this comment Sir Herbert Samuel strayed somewhat from those good standards of his own which it has been so satisfactory to acknowledge. It was not just and it was utterly incorrect to suggest, as the terms used by him did suggest, that in writing this letter—as indeed in writing or in signing the Frankfurter letter and the "Treaty of Friendship"— Feisal acted on behalf or by the desire of the "Arab Movement," or of its leaders. There was not a leader or a sub-leader, there was not one simple adherent of Arab nationalism who had authorized these documents. They began with Feisal and ended with Feisal, and as Feisal's own production, unsubmitted to his father or to the other "leaders of the movement," they have not the slightest value as final expressions of Arab policy.

The very reverse of Sir Herbert Samuel's argument is true. It was perfectly possible that a letter should have been written in such terms while there was a real sense of grievance against the policy which was being pursued. Such a letter could be written by an isolated and badgered man in Paris, committing himself to nothing, and it was so written. The vagueness of it will be noted. What was the misunderstanding? Upon what was there perfect accord? Was Feisal in complete accord that the Arabs should lose supremacy in Palestine? It is not to be believed. If he had nourished any such designs, he would have been sent packing by those he represented, like any other negotiator who had overstepped his role and exceeded his instructions.

The unfortunate prince, after this third tooth, as it were, had been extracted from him under the gas of cordiality, remained in Europe for another couple of months, to no particular advantage. There was a lull in Near Eastern affairs, though the Zionists continued their lobbying. Curzon and Milner were induced by M. Sokolov to agree to give their support to the frontier-line which he and Dr. Weizmann proposed. Dr. Weizmann, who had gone to Palestine, "won Lord Allenby's support from the military standpoint." (Z.O.R.)

Lord Balfour, back in London, enjoyed himself in Parliament. He announced in shocked tones that it had been "openly stated" that Great Britain meant to remain the dominant Power in Syria. "There is not now," said he, "and never has been any shadow of truth in that statement. It is an utter and total perversion of the truth." Loud and prolonged cheers greeted this exhibition of probity.

1920 arrived, a year of great moment. It saw the suffocation of what little Arab rule had been left in Syria and the end of military government in Palestine. It saw also the arrival of the first High Commissioner to establish there mandatory administration, under a Mandate, however, which was not yet in existence.

The reasons for this latter sufficiently astonishing move will be discussed in due course. But it may be said now that it sprang principally from the desires of the Zionist leaders that there should be a change in the character of government. The rift between their followers in Palestine and the Army Administration, especially between the Army Administration and the Zionist Commission, was widening to a chasm. Conflicts of authority had occurred on a certain scale, and the chief of them will be recorded. Much of what happened was stifled. The British people, that is to say, never heard of it. But Palestine itself was alive to the incessant disputes between the Zionist Commission and most of the British officers in charge of the territory. By this time the Zionist Commission was fulfilling altogether the inner intentions of those who had dispatched it to the Holy Land. It had extended its size gradually, till in the spring of 1920 it consisted of a full hundred members, eked out by camp-followers of every degree of administrative sutlership. It had arrogated to itself the privileges of a ruling hierarchy, and was endeavouring to act as a Government within the actual Government, and outside of it also, through its intimate relations with statesmen in England.

The members of the military Government were driven into continual protests against it, protests which, alas, were disregarded studiously in London. "A complete administrative machine is operating, in fact its departments correspond in numbers exactly to my own. This Administration within an Administration renders good government impossible, and the Jews look to their administration and not to mine, while the Moslems and Christians can only see that privileges and liberties are allowed to Jews which are denied to them."

Whose words are these? Those of the Chief Administrator of Palestine himself, written in the month of April.

The Zionist Commission was modelled upon a Cabinet. Its ministers kept changing, but the following list represents it at a given period of that spring of 1920, and the Cabinet-character of the body is evident.

Zionist Commission.	
Chairman	Chaim Weizmann
Vice-President	Mr. M. Ussishkin
Members	Messrs. Ruppin, Yafee and Eder
Treasurer	Dr. Van Vriesland
Controller	Mr. R. D. Kessel
Secretary	Mr. Max Nurock
Chief Accountant	Mr. J. Braude
Departments.	
Political	Dr. Eder.
Relief	Dr. de Sola Pool
Agriculture and Colonization	Dr. J. Ettinger
Technical Affairs	Messrs. Wilbushewitz, Hecker and Rutenberg
Legal Affairs	Dr. J. Thon.
Statistics	Mr. I. Wilkanski
Publicity	Messrs. Agronski and Almalich
Trade and Industry	Mr. I. Epstein
Immigration	Mr. Shenkin
Education	Dr. Lurie
Finance	Dr. van Vriesland
Loans	Mr. M. Cohen
Labour	Mr. J. Papper
District-Commissioners.	
Jaffa	Mr. E. Y. Levin-Epstein
Haifa	Mr. A. Abrahams
Galilee	Dr. M. Glicken
Safed	Mr. I. Hibbashan
Tiberias	Mr. I. Yankowski.
Cairo	Mr. A. Alexander
Alexandria	Mr. I. Idelowitz
Port Said	Mr. M. Mirovitch

A list comprehensive enough for Whitehall, and even extended by a species of bijou consular service in Egypt.

The ways in which this body interfered with the Administration's prerogatives and countered the Administration's actions were only too diverse. The Zionist Commission held elections for a "Constituent Assembly" without reference to the Chief Administrator, the aim of these elections being to consolidate in this Assembly, under the control of the Commission, all the Jews of Palestine. This was done despite the protests of the Orthodox Jews, who then were at the very least a quarter of the Jewish community. Their leaders, Chief Rabbi Zonnenfeld and Rabbi Diskin, protested to the Government against these elections. They were, said they, nothing but an endeavour to drown the voices and to dominate the lives of those Jews who looked on Palestine as the shrine of their religious faith, and not as a mere hub of Jewish racialism.

The Commission established permanent courts for the trial of ordinary civil cases. A formal complaint against these courts was made by the Administration, but in the absence of any instruction or any sort of support from London it could do nothing but complain.

The American Zionist Medical Unit (that which had obtained special Zionist passports for the journey), good as its work was in itself, would not hear of acting under the control of the Public Health Department. It toured the country without authorization, and was involved in quarrels with Arab municipalities because it carried out inspections of Moslem houses through its own uniformed inspectors, who entered them without the consent of the inhabitants and as though enjoying the very Governmental authority which its members had refused to accept for themselves.

The Commission made open protests against Government measures which were not to its taste. One notorious example was when the Administration instituted a fund to help native agriculturists with loans at 6½ percent. Under the Turkish regime there had been an Agricultural Bank making such loans, but its funds had been carried off by the retiring Turks. The Administration now determined to replace this and made an arrangement for the purpose with the Anglo-Egyptian Bank. Proper care was taken that any loans already made by Jewish banks or by similar bodies should be safeguarded. A Jewish bank, the Anglo-Palestine, was issuing loans to agriculturists at the time, but its charges were twice those of the official fund. Obviously, therefore, the official fund, as far as loans to Arabs at least were concerned, would be preferred by everyone to the Jewish Bank. Because of this the Zionist Commission protested against the creation of the fund, and the protest was made not merely in Palestine but also in Whitehall. From London orders actually were sent to suspend the fund. This despite the representations of the Chief Administrator, who had pointed out that "the Zionists cannot fairly ask that the Fellaheen should be left helpless and a prey to usurers, who would be their only resource had not the Administration come very rightly to their aid." Words of significance, when it is recalled how often Zionist writers have tried to make capital out of Arab usurers.

When Dr. Weizmann went back to Palestine he perceived the unreasonableness, to say no more, of the Commission's demand, and through his influence resumption of the Administration's loans was allowed in the end. The whole affair was debated in the House of Lords eventually, when Lord Sydenham, that great champion of justice for the Arabs, received a remarkable reply from Lord Crawford on behalf of the Government. It ran, "This question is the key to the future and especially to the Zionist future of the country, and the Zionist Organization maintains that it should not have been settled without previous consultation with them." That is to say, the Government tacitly accepted that the Palestine Government (as Lord Sydenham said) "had no right to act without consulting a self-constituted body, largely composed of aliens," and the Cabinet spokesman pleaded the dictum of the Zionist Organization as though it came from a body entitled to lay down procedure for the British Army. As far as practical usage was concerned, Lord Crawford was not so far from the truth after all.

Another source of friction in Palestine was the insistence of the Commission upon the installation of Hebrew as an official language, to a level with which Arabic, the common tongue of the country, was to be reduced. Most of the Jews then in the country spoke Yiddish, and objected to the vulgarization of Hebrew. The revival of Hebrew was quite artificial. Furthermore, its adoption as an official language by the military Government of Occupied Enemy Territory was illegal under the Hague Convention, by Article 45 of which the occupying army was not permitted to make changes in the existing forms of administration. (The whole question of this disregard of the Hague Convention will be fully treated in a later chapter.)

The unlawful use of Hebrew as an official language, which no action of the superior military authorities nor of the British Government itself could rectify, was frequently resisted by individual officers. But whenever they tried to confine official forms to the Arabic and English tongues—the two permissible—the Zionist Commission intervened and succeeded in having Hebrew reimposed.

The Jaffa Municipality had passed a by-law making Arabic compulsory upon all signboards. In an Arabic-speaking country it was a necessary regulation, and the British Military Governor of Jaffa counter signed it. But one of the earliest actions of the Zionist Commission was to obtain the cancellation of this by-law. "The Zionist Commission intervened and the by-law was quashed." (Z.O.R.) I ask the reader to transpose this act to England, as may so often be done to advantage, and to imagine a by-law of a corporation or urban district council ordering the use of English upon signposts being quashed by the intervention of a committee of strangers who had never been in England till a year or two before.

On a later occasion the then Chief Administrator himself, Major-General Money, was subjected to Zionist complaint because he had ordered that tax-forms and receipts were to be printed in English and in Arabic, despite these being the languages which he was bound to employ.

Yet another source of discord for long was the payments which the Zionist Commission made to Zionist clerks and others who entered Government service. Government salaries, calculated on the scale obtaining in the country,' were not sufficient for Europeanized Jews. But by paying subsidies to those of them who were willing to serve, a certain number were maintained in the Administration, and into the bargain were a perpetual source of leakage of official information. The abuse of this was so great that in the end the subsidies were stopped, but too late to arrest the evil of leakage.

All these things increased tension between the Commission and the Palestine authorities. But what caused more than tension, what brought Army and Commission into open hostility was the manner in which Zionist influence in the high places of England was brought to bear against officers who offended the Commission or the political Zionist caucus in Palestine. When this occurred the average soldier doing his best by the standards of the Service stood no chance against his accusers in London. He had to recant or to resign.

> In London [runs the official Zionist account of these very dissensions] the political atmosphere was very different [from that in Palestine]. The position of Zionism in all influential circles and *the personal authority of Zionist leaders* [my italics] was very strong. It seemed psychologically impossible to reconcile the melancholy reports from Palestine with the cloudless benevolence pervading every Government office in London.

Cloudless benevolence!—the words are amply descriptive. In London mere Zionist appeals had ceased. The leaders walked in upon Cabinet Ministers and stated their needs, which thereon were fulfilled.

There is no least exaggeration in this statement. The occurrences which followed the visit of Mr. Brandeis to Palestine may be given in evidence. In the summer of 1919 Mr. Brandeis sailed for Europe, his main object being to proceed to Palestine. He was accompanied by Mr. de Haas, whose account therefore of ensuing events is first-hand. It is to be found in three of his books but more fully in his autobiography of Brandeis. In London they met Dr. Weizmann, and from there went on to Paris which they reached on the 28th of June, the day that the Versailles Treaty was signed.

Mr. Brandeis and his companion "ignored the hilarity in the streets" and spent a couple of crowded days calling on President Wilson, on Colonel House, on the Italian Ambassador, on Lord Balfour, on Baron Edmond de Rothschild and, it seems, upon the entire French Cabinet. Balfour, of course, "gave the Justice every assurance of his seeing eye to eye with the Zionists."

Every prospect pleased indeed till, a few days later, the travellers reached Egypt, when the horizon assumed the traditional Egyptian darkness.

> The visitors found General Allenby indifferent to Foreign Office policies, whether they concerned Arab interests or promises to the Jews. The repercussions of the Crane-King Commission were met in Palestine. The population was naturally restive and all sorts of interpretations were evolved from the American investigation. Jewish complaints of British hostility were almost overwhelming.
>
> Brandeis had set out to make a leisured inspection of Palestine, but his brief conferences in Paris led him to decide that it was advisable to change his Palestinian tour into a political visit. The ascendancy of the military party in British Near Eastern policies was a fact, and one that needed to be handled firmly, and it was in that spirit that Brandeis left Egypt and crossed the Sinai peninsula.
>
> The British Commander-in-Chief and his military and civil aides regarded the Balfour Declaration as a forgotten episode of the War. The civilian aides [Mr. de Haas means by this the staff-officers engaged in civil administration] took advantage of every economic opportunity to strengthen the British foothold, ignoring all Jewish considerations, and treating the Arabs as "natives" in the approved colonial manner. The Jews, ignorant of this divided policy [the divergence between the aversion of the British Army and the cloudless benevolence of the British Government] brought eloquent testimony that Palestine was already slipping away from the vision of a Jewish homeland they had conjured out of the text of the Balfour Declaration.

As soon as Mr. Brandeis had grasped this situation, he started to handle the British Army as firmly as could have been wished by Mr. de Haas or by anyone. He went straight to Headquarters on the Mount of Olives, and, according to his chronicler, "expressed some definite opinions on the matter to General Money." Mr. de Haas does not tell the events of the visit, but what happened was that Mr. Brandeis told the Chief Administrator that, "ordinances of the military authorities should be submitted first to the Zionist Commission." General Money was taken aback, naturally, at such a mode of address: his A.D.C., who was present, said with some warmth to the visitor, "For a Government to do that would be to derogate its position." "As a lawyer you realize this," he added.

Brandeis was not abashed at all, and continued, "It *must* be understood that the British Government is committed to the support of the Zionist cause." "Unless this is accepted as a guiding principle, *I shall have to report it to the Foreign Office"* he concluded, in words deserving of the italics I have given them. Dining later on with one of the principal officers of the Administration, this singular Justice repeated much the same admonitions, but towards the close of the dinner turned to cajolery. He pointed out the opportunities awaiting a man of ability and of ambition in Palestine who appreciated the merits of the National Home. "If you'll give us a word of adherence," he declared, raising his glass, "I drink to the future Governor of Palestine. What I say to Wilson goes."

An offer, without doubt, not couched in the language of the Bench and not intended for publication, but eminently deserving of it. By and large, indeed, the recent history of Palestine resolves itself into the publication of deeds and of sayings which their authors never meant to make known. Mr. Brandeis's offers and his threats in this case were treated with equal coldness and contempt by his soldier hosts. So he carried out the threats and as soon as possible "reported to the Foreign Office." "He unbosomed himself," explains Mr. de Haas. Knowing where to obtain instant compliance with his desires, Mr. Brandeis did not delay to reach London for the unbosoming. "It was to Mr. Balfour that he spoke," in Paris.

The talk was instantly fruitful.

> A few hours later the British Foreign Office through the British War Office was reminding the military authorities in Egypt and Palestine not only of the verbal contents of the Balfour Declaration, but also that it was *chose jugée.* A number of Palestinian officials immediately sought desirable exchanges, and Colonel Meinertzhagen, a pronounced pro-Zionist, was dispatched to Palestine. [There is no suggestion that Colonel Meinertzhagen, who had taken a distinguished part in Allenby's campaign, had any knowledge of Mr. Brandeis's intrigues. He proceeded on orders to Lord Allenby's headquarters and was attached to his staff.] There had been no stirring of the troubled waters, no protest-meetings. The Brandeisian direct-action diplomacy had achieved results. The result was so clear to Palestinians that the silent but efficient Brandeis is still a golden memory. [de Haas.]

The date upon which this insolent intruder visited his convenient Balfour seems to have been the 4th of August. On that day, at least Balfour sent "detailed instruction for the Palestinian authorities." Its main points were: that the American and French Governments were equally pledged to support the establishment in Palestine of the Jewish National Home; that this should be emphasized to the Arab leaders at every opportunity; that the matter was a *chose jugée*, and that continued agitation would be useless and detrimental. It would be unfair," continues the Zionist Organization statement from which I quote this corroboration,

> "to say that this Instruction *[the capital letter is used]* bore no fruit at all. Certain changes in the Administration's attitude became at once notable, partly due to Mr. Balfour's Instruction, partly perhaps, to Major-General Money's departure. During the short period of Major-General Watson's Administration some improvements were introduced. We have already mentioned that concessions were made as regards the use of the Hebrew language in official documents and publications. The number of Jewish clerks and policemen was also increased. Unfortunately, no change could be detected in the essential attitude of the British personnel, although Major-General Watson himself seemed to be quite unprejudiced."

The Zionist Report here quoted tries to steal from Mr. Brandeis a little of the kudos for the "Balfour Instruction" and for its sequels, and it attributes Balfour's action to "the energetic representations made by the Zionist Office in London to the British Government." On another page it declares that

> Mr. Louis Brandeis's visit to Palestine in July 1919 was of great assistance. Short though his stay was, it enabled him to get an unbiased view of the situation and to report on it after his return to England. Soon afterwards Major-General Money was replaced, as Chief Administrator, by Major-General Watson, and some of the crudest infringements of the principle of equality—especially with regard to the position of the Hebrew language—were removed.

But Mr. de Haas, accompanying Brandeis, was better placed than anyone to know exactly what happened. The sequence of events evidently was that after Balfour had complied promptly with Brandeis's requirements, the latter went on to London and there in conjunction with the Zionist office continued his short but effective cutting-out campaign. In fact Mr. de Haas partly confirms this, saying of his chief that he "proceeded to London, elated that his visit to Palestine had produced such excellent results."

One way and another, between the pressure brought by the Organization chiefs in London and by Brandeis of the golden memory, British officers who did not, like Balfour, see eye-to-eye with the Zionists, began to lose their posts. They were either forced into resignation or removed. "One of the chief saboteurs of the Balfour Declaration was removed through his (Mr. Brandeis's) influence," writes Mr. Kallen, a cautious commentator. Our faithful Zionist Organization Report, too, has something to say of the last days of Major-General Money's rule. He had made a speech condemning the policy of creating "separate institutions for different communities," whether charitable or educational.

> Shortly afterwards a circular letter was sent from Headquarters to all Military Governors asking their opinion as to the advisability of creating mixed Government schools, for Arabs and Jews alike. The Zionist Commission, it goes without saying, energetically resisted all these attempts, and it is possible that its endeavours, as well as representations made by the London Office to the Home Government had something to do with Major-General Money's recall from the post of Chief Administrator.

As it happens, General Money already, and for the second time, had tendered privately to Lord Allenby his resignation from his thankless post. But if he had not decided to retire it is evident enough that he would have had to retire. He is not to be confounded with the "chief saboteur of the Balfour Declaration" just mentioned. This was Colonel Vivian Gabriel (now Sir Vivian Gabriel). Colonel Gabriel was Assistant Administrator of O.E.T.A. South. Before the War he had held several highly responsible positions in the Indian Civil Service. In 1914 he had been attached to the Headquarters Staff in Egypt. He then became a member of the British Military Mission to the Headquarters Staff of the Italian Army. At the time he was Financial Adviser to the Palestine Administration. He does not appear to have pleased the Zionists for a number of reasons. Among them, "he busied himself in promoting British commercial interests. His circulars betrayed in culpable language the belief that Palestine was part of the British Empire." (Wise-de Haas.)

Lord Sydenham, when the opportunity occurred, some months later during a Lords debate, directly accused the Government of taking action against British officials, under Zionist influence. "The military Administrator at the time," said he, "found that his position had become impossible, and then a most capable Indian Civil Servant, appointed by the War Office as Financial Adviser, and specially commended for good work, was suddenly dismissed. He was condemned unheard, because it was stated that he had adopted "an attitude inconsistent with the Zionist policy of the Government." Lord Curzon, who closed the Debate for the Government, had not a word to say in reply.

Chapter 19

The Emir Feisal proclaimed King of Syria.
He asks for recognition of Syrian independence by the Allies and cites the McMahon-Hussein pact.
Fall of the Kingdom of Syria.—Arabs and Jews clash in Palestine.
The Chief Administrator of Palestine tells Mr. Lloyd George some truths about the country.

The year 1920 opened politically with the return of Feisal to Syria. He reached Beyrout from France on the 15th of January, bringing with him nothing but the memory of indecisive interviews in England and of disquieting admonitions in France. Nearly seven months had passed since the treaty-signatures had been written in Versailles, and yet not an inch of tangible progress seemed to have been made towards the start of the other peace, that with Turkey, upon which the whole status of Syria must depend.

Protracted secret negotiations with the Zionists concerning the form of the Palestine Mandate were one of the causes of this great delay. A principal cause was naturally the change of regime in Turkey itself and the stiffening of attitude when Mustapha Kemal and his companions came to the front and took charge. Far from ending in the East, the War had broken out again between the French and Kurdish-Turkish bands, mixed regulars and irregulars. When the British troops were withdrawn in the north, in accordance with the Lloyd George-Clemenceau Convention, there were insufficient French troops available to take their place. The Turks seized the opportunity to cross the line drawn at the Armistice and to recapture as much as they could of their old territory. To oppose them at the beginning the French had little else but a corps of Armenian volunteers.

Little French garrisons were besieged here and there by overwhelming forces. In one such affray a general and two reduced battalions were thus isolated for a fortnight. An outnumbered French force was obliged to evacuate Antioch, and sporadic warfare between small French units and enemies, of all degrees of discipline, including Arab irregulars, went on from Cilicia to the borders of Palestine.

Brigandage was general throughout the distracted country. Feisal's government in Damascus could not cope with the situation. Its indefinite status, its inability to extract any declaration firmly establishing it from the Powers, its terrible lack of money, Feisal's own long and profitless absences—all this bereft his government of power and of the means to exert it. In addition there was the quarrel with the French, whose own situation was complicated by their fighting the Turks as well as sparring with the Arabs

Various nomadic tribesmen, over whom Feisal at the head of a putative State could exert no real control, engaged freely in looting and forays against outlying posts. The Arab Government had perhaps eight thousand regulars in and around Damascus, a nucleus which it was most undesirable to disperse. As it was, those Arab detachments which had established themselves in some coastal centres had been ordered to evacuate these by Lord Allenby, who had no choice in the matter, as he was given orders to execute the Lloyd George-Clemenceau Convention, which excluded Arab regulars from the nominal French zone. In this way Antioch was emptied of Arab troops, who only departed, as from Beyrout also, after the Commander-in-Chief had given peremptory commands and threatened to use force if they did not obey.

That the few French who replaced the Arab troops had to retire presently and that large numbers of the Arab population of Antioch were driven to flight before the advancing Kurds shows something of the anarchy which the political situation induced in Syria during the late winter and spring of 1919-20. To these conditions Feisal returned in January, to find himself out of touch with the crisis and with the feelings it had engendered in the country. His task, to try and bring about some order, was all the more difficult because he had become an object of considerable suspicion. He was paying now for the Frankfurter letter and his conversations with Dr. Weizmann. There was deep distrust of the webs which had been spun round him in London and Paris. His role as the spiders' protégé was not one which his fellow-Arabs found very convincing, despite Feisal's endeavours to persuade them that some day, in some way, the promises made to them would be carried out and that their natural rights would be respected.

Deputations came continually to him, tribal leaders, sheikhs from country districts with their villagers behind them, and adjured him in fervent tones not to forget his country's cause. He was urged to take a strong line with the Allies, on the ground that this was all the Allies understood. Turkish agents caballed against him with some of the young hotheads who were tired of delays, and a *coup d'état* actually was planned against his rule. But the Arab prince to whom Feisal's place was offered very patriotically and honourably refused to have any part in the business and the plot came to nothing.

Feisal himself made one more endeavour to obtain from the chiefs of the adjourned Peace Conference a message with which to placate his people. The result was a cabled intimation that the Allies "had not forgotten Syria," and of all things, yet another demand that he should quit the country and come to London to plead his cause all over again. (On the 2nd of February the first meeting of the Supreme Allied Council had been held in London.) He might as well have resigned his position as leave Syria then.

On the top of this invitation to London came a minatory communication from his father. King Hussein telegraphed, "I repudiate any action compromising the independence of Syria which you may take." The members of the Syrian Congress now pressed for a definite declaration of this independence, and though Feisal would have preferred to have negotiated a little longer, and though he tried to obtain his father's consent to at least a postponement while he informed the Allies that he must make such a declaration, he did not shake Hussein nor alter the opinions of the Congress members.

Accordingly, he agreed to the proclamation. Perhaps, after all, he thought, it might be best to place the Allies before an accomplished fact. Statesmen often conformed to conditions which they had refused to install. He summoned the prorogued Congress for the 6th of March, and the Congress decided on the proclamation of independence for the 8th. The proclamation duly took place, and on the following day the new State of Syria was declared to be a kingdom. Feisal accepted the throne and was proclaimed King of Syria, Palestine and the Lebanon. The independence of Mesopotamia, or Irak, had also been announced and its throne had been offered to Feisal's brother, the Emir Abdullah.

Feisal's proclamation as king was ceremonious. It took place in the town hall of Damascus, to which the Emir rode in the midst of a great escort of cavalry through the thronged and cheering streets. His throne was an ornamental chair inlaid with mother-of-pearl.

The erection of the Kingdom of Syria and the proclamation of Arab independence was notified to all the Allied and to the other principal countries. Notifications were sent also to Lord Allenby and to General Gouraud. What Allenby's answer was is not known, but Gouraud dispatched a very courteous telegram in which, while emphasizing that as High Commissioner of the French Republic he could not in any way recognize the action which had occurred, he tendered to the new king his personal congratulations.

In his notifications to the French and British Governments Feisal had demanded formally the withdrawal of all British and French troops from

Arab soil, that is to say, the evacuation of northern Syria by the French and of Palestine and of Mesopotamia by the British. In addition to these announcements and demands, he also sent a letter to President Wilson recalling the visit of the Crane-King Commission, and appealing for his help in attaining the unity and independence of Syria, instead of its being parcelled into zones under control of the Allied Powers. Personal letters were sent by him in addition to the Allied Premiers, explaining the reasons which had led him to the step he had taken, and how far certain points of the proclamation might be regarded as formal.

With this state of things I was to come into close contact. I had been in Egypt following the proceedings of the Milner Commission, which was to report on Anglo-Egyptian relations. Early in March the gravity of the state of Syria and the fear that the fighting in the north might spread to Palestine, brought me to leave Egypt and to land at Haifa. Scarcely had I arrived when it appeared as though the extension of disorder into Palestine was at hand. Bedouin raiders came pouring out of the gorges of the Yarmook valley, crossed the Jordan and attacked the post of Semakh, on the lip of the Sea of Galilee. It was the frontier-post of the British zone, occupied by Indian cavalry. The Bedouin were driven off with losses, but continued to make raids afterwards. These raids were on a lesser scale, but much damage was done in remoter villages and to a couple of Jewish farms, while cattle were stolen in some numbers. The Bedouin also attacked the Damascus-Haifa train, of which the route ran down this same Yarmook valley. Steaming at full speed the train regained Deraa, and communications with Damascus, poor and intermittent at the best, were broken.

Feisal's Government, however, sent a few hundred troops to the district and when the next Arab train mounted the valley I took the opportunity and boarded it at Semakh. I remember well that day, the portal of experiences which have influenced me ever since; how between the gorges of the Yarmook the low, black tents of the Bedouin showed at intervals, lying close as strawberry nets to the mountain slopes; how we came out on the great tableland of the Hauran, and skirted the Lejja, a gloomy fastness which looked the seat of all outlawry. It closed the plain like a wall, an ashen wilderness of lava, broken only at one point by a pair of domes and what seemed a couple of ruined leaning towers, but all forbidding and pitchy, like a small Italian town dead and gone black.

But no outlaws or raiders attacked us, and in the valley the Bedouin only congregated excitedly and made much delay at stopping-points.

At the end of the day the unlit train crept into Damascus. The city itself was dark under the stars, and seemed impenetrable. The ensuing week opened it to me. Political life there had resemblances to political life in

Poland or in Greece: minor political clubs and party-cenacles abounded, prone to acute differences upon unessentials. But upon essentials, upon the main point of Syrian independence all were agreed. One party-centre transcended every other one in importance, the "Arab Club," which was inconspicuously housed near the railway station. The Arab Club was the focus and the spring of opinion, by which the Congress was animated and, through the Congress, the Cabinet of the new Government and Feisal himself. The Cabinet had been carefully chosen amidst men with experience of affairs. Of the eight ministers half were Moslem, half Christian.

The more I met Congressmen and Arab Club members the more evident it was that they had not altered their general attitude and their real hopes since Messrs. Crane and King had interviewed them nine months before. Their tempers had been tried by the Allies' delays and they felt very insecure of the Allies' plans, but they knew at heart that Syria needed our help. Its very conditions at the moment made this plain to them. But they asked that our help to them should be reasonably disinterested, that their country should not be dismembered, and that their fundamental proprietorship of it should be respected.

This was very much what Feisal himself said to me, when I saw him a few days after my arrival. He was living then outside the city, in a simple grey-painted house on the hillside, above the famed almond-orchards. It was the first opportunity he had had as King to speak to the British and European public, and my interview was endowed with some formality.

"Our action was quite justified," he said to me. "Long ago the Allies promised us an independent Arab State where we have proclaimed it. But what immediately forced Congress to take the step of proclamation was the never-ending delay of the Peace Conference in coming to a decision concerning us. The Arab people have waited a very long time, and during this delay all kinds of contradictory reports have been spread about the fate which will be doled out to them. Men have lost their confidence: they are convinced that the Allies mean to leave Syria divided into three parts as it is now, and that the promised union of the Arab people in an Arab kingdom or confederation is a myth. The result is that the most dangerous public opinion has been formed in the country and will not hear of further postponements."

"Couldn't you have been patient just a little longer," I said to him, "the conclusion of the Turkish Treaty cannot be so very far off, and the status of Syria must be defined in it. Couldn't you have waited that short while?

"*I* could have waited," said Feisal, "I *would* have waited myself, for I am sure of the Allies' good intentions, but the public opinion of this country cannot be reined in any longer for a period of unfixed length.

Violent propaganda has been at work here against the Allies. Its source is in Anatolia, and the story has been spread abroad that the treaty negotiations are being delayed deliberately by your statesmen, and that we shall have to wait as we are another couple of years for a decision. I could not dare ask the people to go on waiting any longer, with feeling as high as it is."

"The British and the other Allied governments were warned from here, warned repeatedly, that the growth of popular feeling was reaching an irresistible stage. I have been given kindly assurances in return, but I don't think that the gravity of my position has been realized. No doubt," and he shook his head, "no doubt they have great preoccupations, but they don't realize anything."

"Weren't you asked," I said, "to appear in London and to lay your people's demands before the Allied meeting there?"

"Yes," he said, "and in principle I shall be glad to go to London or elsewhere, as soon as I *can* go. But as to the Arab demand, that demand is for one thing, which is the recognition of the independence of an integral Syria, instead of its division into three zones. Those who demand it most are the classes whom I have trained, as far as I have had the opportunity, to lead the country, to command the army, to engage in public administration, to one form or another of superior service. I have no clue to the decisions the Conference which is to make the peace with Turkey will take regarding my country. If I were to return from a Conference to tell these men, these leaders of the people, that the principle of an undivided Syria had not been granted but that today's zones of influence were to continue, I tell you I cannot foresee the condition into which the country might not fall nor foresee what would be the position of my own person."

He paused, and spoke with slow phrases, as though the words weighed on him, "I have made them—many promises—on behalf—of the Allies." Then, recovering himself, and smiling at the prospect, "If only the Allies would recognize the fundamental independence of Syria and of Mesopotamia, then I should be delighted" (*ravi* was his word; we talked in French) "to go to England and to discuss the practical side of it. When we get into negotiations I have every intention of safeguarding British interests here and in Mesopotamia. Our desires and the interests of Great Britain could be secured without hurting the principle of independence." "But your proclamation demanded the withdrawal of our troops," I objected. "Do you expect that to be carried out?"

"We could not accept continual occupation," he answered, "but there will be plenty of time to see the date at which your troops might have to retire. It is difficult to put these matters into a few words, but believe me I don't think that we and you are so far from agreement or can fail to find agreement, because we remember what England did for us during the War, and surely England will remember what we did for her. Did not Sir Henry McMahon, too, in his pact with my father the King of the Hedjaz promise us what we now ask, an Arab state within the boundaries we claim? The reservations made for Basra and Baghdad we shall observe."

I asked him for some information upon the McMahon pact and then inquired what would be his attitude towards a Mandate.

Feisal smiled and spread his hands, as much as to indicate that a Mandate was a wide term. He said, "I've not yet arrived at a clear understanding of what a Mandate means. It may mean nothing but friendly support and relations: it may mean colonization. It is too elastic a phrase. Everything depends upon how the 'Mandate' would be exercised."

I spoke of the difficulty of treating the Syrian question as a whole at present owing to the divided occupation of the country between British and French. "I think I might come to an agreement with the French too," said Feisal. "When I was in Paris M. Clemenceau told me French troops did not intend to stay in Syria, when I put the question to him. Unfortunately we reached no official conclusion, though a basis of agreement had been laid. Once our independence were acknowledged some arrangement for the installation of French counsellors holding their authority from the Arab Government might be reached more easily."

"What of the pro-Turkish movement here?"I asked.

"There is no love of the Turks in Syria," he answered. "But if Turkish rule over us was bad, the Arabs at least were a united element under the Ottoman regime. That in the main is what people are saying today. If, however, they are being pushed into the hands of the Turks you must find it excusable. There is a proverb of ours which says that when a man is drowning he will cling to a serpent to save himself. But don't let us talk of the Turks. The British and the Arabs have been allies from the beginning of the war here, and Britain is our chief ally since she laid the basis of our State. Even if she had no interests in Syria I should be happy to call on her to restore our material prosperity and to act as our friend and guide and adviser."

Then I turned to the Lebanon. What was his government's attitude towards this special enclave of Syria? He thought that provided the Lebanon did not place itself under foreign occupation it might have entire independence within the Syrian orbit.

I came to the Zionist question last. He said, "I arrived at an understanding satisfactory to us both with Dr. Weizmann, and *I* am ready to carry it out," with emphasis on the *I*. He referred to the "Treaty of Friendship," which had been drawn up a year before (discussed in Chapter 14).

That is the general burden of my interview with Feisal, of which I have kept my notes and draft. I regret sorely now, of course, that I did not pursue the Zionist business further with him, but I had come newly to it, and at the time in Damascus it was overshadowed altogether by the perils of Franco-Arab conflict, which indeed was but a few months distant. With the rest of the country in chaos the conditions of the relatively quiet British zone were not clamant for attention.

As it happened too, just when Feisal had spoken to me of his agreement with Dr. Weizmann, his swarthy young half-brother the Emir Zeid, had broken into the room, listened a moment, and then, after presentations, had plunged into rapid conversation with the King. The subject was a Druse foray, requiring their full attention, and this had brought the interview to an end.

But if I had known then all that I know now, I should have arranged for another meeting with Feisal, with Zionism and the National Home as its subject. None the less, what Feisal said to me in that March of 1920 is of as much consequence now as when he spoke, more than anything else because he recognized, in what he said, the strict limitations of his own authority. It clarifies too his personal attitude, though that is of lesser importance. It disposes absolutely of any idea that he accepted the permanent division of Syria into zones, or that he stood for anything less than the independence of the whole area of Syrian soil.

It confirms that King Hussein did intend to include Palestine in the territory for which he stipulated Arab independence. That is, of course, manifest in itself in the text of the pact made to that end. But if confirmation were needed Feisal gave it. He knew his father's mind when he spoke to me in Damascus, and he quoted his father's pact as a surety for his own kingdom, and for his own title. That title specified that he was "King of Palestine," lest there should be any doubt concerning this point through the misuse by the Western Powers of the word "Syria" for the northern part of the country only. Hussein, too, had just threatened to repudiate him if he did not proclaim Syrian independence exactly in the terms which in fact were employed at the proclamation.

A point of great additional interest is that—as far as I have been able to discover—when Feisal cited the McMahon-Hussein pact to me, this was the first time the Arab claims under it had been put forward in the Press. In his address to the Peace Conference a year before I do not think that Feisal mentioned the pact by name. All Feisal did at the Conference was to make a general claim without introducing the geographical guarantees of the pact. In any event this Peace Conference speech of his was, as we have seen, scarcely quoted. It might almost as well have been delivered *in camera*.

The reason Feisal had in bringing the pact by name now into the open in our interview was easily discerned. He was getting doubtful about our memory and our faithfulness. Whatever he said to me of his confidence in Britain's memory, he felt that it was time that there should be a public record of what had occurred. He was beginning to doubt whether the pact would be remembered in London, if it remained for the British public an unidentified and unannounced document.

Unfortunately, his purpose in speaking to me of it was in great degree frustrated by myself. I did not emphasize the point at all, or explain how we were committed under the pact, simply because at the time I had never heard of it, and believed that it was a current document which had been duly published in the previous year. During the Versailles peace-making I had been in distant countries and indeed had been cut off for long from all knowledge of what was passing in the West. I had been in Egypt in the early part of 1915, but had left there before the negotiations with King Hussein had begun.

When King Feisal told me of the pact, I confessed my ignorance of it to him, and asked him for some account of it *"pour ma gouverne,"* a phrase always used in interviews of this type when the interviewer himself needs something explained to him, not that he may reproduce it but that he may be able to conduct his interview. This he gave me, but never explained that the pact was unpublished. I was content to make mere reference to it, therefore, assuming that when my cable reached London the subeditors would insert the details of its text. The correspondent of a newspaper does not waste money upon telegraphing texts of documents which are available in his home-office, as I wrongly imagined this to be available.

When I returned to England other matters intruded: Feisal's kingdom had been swept away. The interview went quite out of my mind, and it was not till I started going through old papers methodically for the purposes of the present book that I realized the interest of Feisal's revelation of the McMahon pact to me in March of 1920. It might, if I had but realized the situation, have been made known in its essential details during the period of the Turkish Treaty negotiations at Sèvres and San Remo and have been brought to the notice of the League of Nations in good time. My short reference to it had failed to awake attention in our London office, in the throes of nearer and resounding crises upon the Continent, though it was noted in Parliament.

A further corollary from Feisal's declarations to me deserves mention. From them it is shown again that his understanding with Dr. Weizmann (dependent as it was upon conditions which Dr. Weizmann himself was working to prevent) was nothing but a subsidiary arrangement for establishing a Jewish settlement owing allegiance to the Arab Government. There could be no Jewish rule in a country of which Feisal had been proclaimed the monarch, from which he had demanded the evacuation of the occupying British troops, albeit he was ready to give them "plenty of time in which to retire."

When, therefore, to cite a major example of misrepresentation, it is stated in the Peel Report (on page 27) that "if King Hussein and the Emir Feisal secured their big Arab State, they would concede little Palestine to the Jews," the implication that either father or son was willing for Palestine to become a Jew-ruled country is unwarrantable. The version of Feisal's situation, as given in the Report, also requires to be emended.

In the paragraph from which the above quotation is taken the Report goes on to state that the Emir Feisal, in concluding his agreement with Dr. Weizmann, "was not, it is true, directly representing the Arabs of Palestine: but the Arabs regarded Syria as one country, and in Syria the Emir's leadership had been accepted." The argument is that, therefore, the Arabs of Palestine were co-responsible for their leader's acts, and that so they too, tacitly or automatically, "conceded little Palestine to the Jews."

Whereas the situation was nothing like this. The Emir's undefined leadership was given as soon as possible a concrete form, concerted between him, his father and his fellow-countrymen. He became a constitutional sovereign, accepting his throne from the people, as represented in Congress, which drew up an Act of Succession. As his words and his deeds in Damascus testified, he recognized himself as only the agent of the Arab people in Syria, and as one who, when presenting projects to Congress, might or might not find those projects endorsed. This was his second phase. During his first phase he had been his father's representative, and even then his father emphasized that he himself only acted as a spokesman of the Arabs. In his own Hedjaz Hussein still ruled personally; beyond it he also was a mere representative. Feisal at no time was ever anything but a middleman in matter of authority. While he was "leader" he had represented and had been answerable to his father: when he became king by his oath he was made answerable to the National Assembly.

As he avowed to me, the touchstone of the whole future set of decisions of the Allies for Syria was not the reception which he might give to these decisions, but the reception they would get from Congress when, as a returning envoy, he laid them before that body. What was true for the Allies' decisions was true in the lesser field of negotiation with Dr. Weizmann. If Feisal's position as "leader in Syria" had endured, and if the conditions had entered into being under which the "Treaty of Friendship" became feasible, it never would have been anything more than feasible merely. It would not have become, as the Peel Report seems to imagine, immediately operative. It would have had to take its chance before Congress with other proposals awaiting ratification. Far from being the source of a more "peaceful development of the situation in Palestine" than has ensued, its chances of survival would have been nil, if its indefinite phrases had been focused into any escape of the Jewish citizens of Palestine from national suzerainty.

Feisal himself was well aware of the fact by now: his statement to me was that *he* was ready to carry out the Weizmann agreement. He was always courteous in public, and since he had negotiated with the Zionist leader to satisfy the British Government, he did not decry his own negotiations. That was all.

Poor Feisal! In this affair the political Zionists and their British friends have made him the fastest galloper and the greatest ground-coverer of all stalking-horses, and of all men of straw his effigy has been carried further by them and has been placed in more poses. He resented deeply the part assigned to him and chafed at the public silence which, as King of Irak, he had to observe concerning Palestine and the rest of Syria. But we have seen his response to the Frankfurter letter. On the occasion of his final visit to Jerusalem he said to some of the Arab leaders, "What can I do for you? My heart bleeds for you." The kingdom over which he had reigned so briefly was indeed always close to his heart, and he gave it almost his last thoughts. He had been in London, and travelling south had stopped in Berne to rest. He did not rest much there, though, for he wrote a long memorandum in his own hand upon the situation throughout Syria. Next day Rustum Haidar Pasha and Nouri Said Pasha, who were with him, perceived how ill he seemed, and begged him not to worry about any political affairs for the present. But he paid no attention and would not be satisfied till they had promised him that they would return in his name to Paris and London to take up again the questions of Palestine and the Franco-Syrian area. To soothe him they pretended that they would leave next day. By then he was dead.

That troubled sojourn of his in Damascus, which must have recurred so forcibly to him in those final hours at Berne, was brief enough. His kingdom of Syria lasted only four months. In May his Government rejected the Mandate over north Syria which France had assumed in April, declaring that it was unacceptable to the mass of the Syrian population. Thenceforward relations with France worsened rapidly. A mixture of fighting and of tangled negotiations ended in mid-July with an ultimatum from General Gouraud, by which the Syrian Government was to accept the Mandate within four days, though Gouraud guaranteed that the Mandate would not take the form of annexation or of direct administration. Feisal tried to be conciliatory, and actually did accept the ultimatum. But his acceptance reached Gouraud too late. The French advanced. Final parleys were swept away by a tide of tribesmen and regulars who rushed out to give battle to the French. They were crushed, and on the 25th of July Damascus fell.

Feisal took refuge in Palestine, and after a period in Europe, about a year later he was installed as King of Irak, under a promise from Great Britain of temporary mandatory aid, of accruing national responsibility and presently, of independence. All of which has been carried out, so that in Irak at least our engagements have been honoured and the proprietary rights of the Arabs respected.

The kingdom of Syria, on the other hand, never had much of a chance. It could not attain recognition of its independence from the Allies till it accepted the Mandates, and it could not accept the Mandates without abandoning the independence of two-thirds of its citizens. It could not suppress disorder till it was given help, and it was refused help till it had suppressed disorder. Inside that revolving vicious circle it turned and turned and was abraded away.

I went back to Palestine after a month in Damascus and in other parts of the country. I found it, to say the least, in a more disturbed state than in March. The clash between Arabs and Jews had occurred in the interval. "*The* clash," not "a clash;" for there was no trace of accident about the affair. The policy of the Home Government had ensured it. When it took place there was naturally an uproar amidst Zionists throughout the world, and in the House of Commons a number of questions were asked. The Zionists said, and some members of Parliament too, that the authorities in Palestine were responsible for the rioting and bloodshed because they had not taken proper police or military precautions either before or during the crisis.

This was not the true case. The authorities in Palestine could not prevent an explosion which the Government in London had foreordained from the time of the Balfour Declaration. The Arabs would not have been mortals if they had remained quiescent with the signs of Zionist power increasing daily and the whole future, as they saw now, dedicated to its development. The authorities might have delayed the rioting by displays of force here and there for a while, but they could not have displayed force always and everywhere. The national feeling which manifested itself in the riots was universal, and would have found another vent if the Jerusalem outbreak of early April had been stifled.

This outbreak began during the Nebi Moussa festival at Eastertide, and lasted sporadically from the 4th to the 8th. There was both fighting and looting. By the time the troops had established order five Jews had been killed and over two hundred of them wounded. Four Arabs were killed and twenty-one of them wounded. In comparison with what was happening in northern Syria and in Cilicia this was an inconsiderable business, but as it had occurred in Jerusalem, where strife is so repugnant, it made more noise. As the casualties show, the Jews suffered much more than the Arabs, but it was no one-sided massacre, and both parties were armed. As for its immediate origin, the Arabs were mainly, but not everywhere, the aggressors. The initial act sprang from or was accomplished against a Moslem procession, which was cheering for independence and for "Feisal our King."

The Arabs at the time repudiated the charge that they were on any occasion the aggressors, and it is probable that they would still repudiate it. But they might well have conceded the point. They would have acted to more advantage if they had not spent themselves upon the detail of happenings, but had declared that, while they were guilty of assaults upon the lives and the property of individuals, yet such things must occur when the life of their country itself was being continuously and covertly assaulted. For this was what was happening. Bi-nationalism, a status under which the Zionists were deemed as much the owners of an Arab land as the Arabs were, was being fed to them now in preliminary small doses. It would be fed to them like a deleterious drug weekly, monthly, yearly, in extending doses, till feebleness, then dependence on the drug, and finally assimilation with the will of the drug-givers ensued.

A judicial Commission of Inquiry into the causes of the riots was hastily formed, with orders to report to the Foreign Office. This was called the Palin Commission, from the name of the general who presided over it.

Besides the Palin Commission, the ordinary military justice set up courts to try various persons, Jews and Arabs, for offences leading to the riots. One trial made a great deal of stir, that of Mr. Vladimir Jabotinsky, who as Lieutenant Jabotinsky had shown such zeal in the creation of the Zionist Mule Corps for Gallipoli and the Jewish battalions of the Royal Fusiliers (cf. Chapter 14). His own record as a soldier included a mention in dispatches for gallantry at the capture of a ford of the Jordan under enemy fire.

He had organized in relative secrecy a "Self-Defence Corps" amidst the younger Jews, and he and others had procured arms for them, which had been used for the purpose the name of the corps indicated but had not, it was alleged, only been so used. In any event the existence of the Haganah, as it was named in Hebrew, was an aggravation to the Arabs, a contribution to unrest, and a defiance of the law of the land, so Mr. Jabotinsky was condemned by the court to fifteen years' penal servitude; a "savage sentence," says Mr. Horace Samuel.

But there was no great reality about this sentence. The trial was not so much a trial by law as a trial of strength between the forces represented by their champion, Jabotinsky, and the Army of Occupation. He flouted his judges by telling them to their faces in court that whatever sentence was given him would be quashed. To which they retaliated with the fifteen years. He also produced in evidence deciphered official documents which had been drafted in a code of sufficient importance for the Chief of Staff to wear suspended to his neck the key of the safe where the coding-memoranda were kept. (Some words of the Peel Report, dealing with this period, may be interpolated here. "It was obvious that the Jews had created a very efficient intelligence department, from which *(as is indeed the case today)* the Administration could keep little secret." The frank admission about today is worth underlining.)

Mr. Jabotinsky was quite correct. His imprisonment was changed quickly to detention in the second division for a political offence, which meant transference to the sea-coast at Acre, where he bathed and played tennis. I do not know that anyone would grudge these privileges to Mr. Jabotinsky, a straightforward man, free of the cant Zionist pretence of nourishing the Arabs by digesting them.

Later he was sent to Egypt, and after six months was released, his sentence duly being quashed as he had said it would be.

All these happenings had left the population of Palestine in a ferment. Its dissatisfaction had begun ripening to dangerous anger about two months before, when the Zionist Commission had tried to counter the Arabs' first measures for political organization. An "Islamo-Christian Association" had been established to consolidate Arab action and as a counterpoise to the Zionist Commission itself. This of course was not at all to the taste of the Commission, which had grown increasingly arrogant under the direction (after the departure for home of Dr. Weizmann) of M. Ussischkin. M. Ussischkin came from Russia and had a Muscovite manner, was "by nature instinctively opposed to all things British" (de Haas). Under his aegis the Commission now demanded that the Chief Administrator should refuse the Islamo-Christian Association or other Arab gatherings the right of free speech.

The new Association was proposing then to hold various meetings and had asked permission for this from the Chief Administrator, in accordance with regulations. The request was reasonable in itself, and was justified further by the quantity of meetings and of assemblies of all kinds which the Zionists had held up and down the land, from that earliest and memorable Jaffa meeting when Mr. Ormsby-Gore had preconized the "building-up of a Jewish nation in all its aspects in Palestine." But the Commission none the less "strongly protested" against the Arabs being allowed equal right of public meeting.

There was another Chief Administrator by now, Sir Louis Bols, who had been Allenby's Chief of Staff in France. "A little, brave, quick, pleasant man," Lawrence had called him, and might have added that he was extremely conscientious. He disregarded the Commission's interfering protest, and the Arabs held their manifestations which, as might have been expected, "had a frankly anti-Jewish character" (Z.O.R.), heightened, of course, by the Zionist Commission's endeavour to silence them.

It is probable that the Arab manifestations would have had a still more frankly Jewish character and the riots might have been precipitated rather earlier if they had known all that was happening in England. Dr. Weizmann had presented a memorandum to Lord Curzon in which he proposed that some 200,000 Jewish immigrants should be granted entrance to Palestine and that in particular Transjordania, as the country east of the Jordan was named then, should be peopled by 60,000 to 70,000 Jews from beyond the Caucasus range, meaningly described by him as "good fighters and colonists." The proposal to introduce the warrior-husbandmen had not even the excuse that there already were Jewish holdings in Transjordan, which needed development and/or defence. In 1920 it is believed that one Jew lived in Transjordan. By 1923 the Jewish population had precisely doubled itself.

After the Jerusalem disorders, Zionist proposals in London grew even more martial. Mr. Joseph Cowen, Chairman of the Zionist Federation and one of the drafting-overseers of the Balfour Declaration, at a London meeting declared that "the Jews would be glad to undertake the garrisoning of Palestine. Let the British people put us back there and they will find that the more Jewish they make Palestine the more British it will be." This was a view which will have commended itself to Downing Street more than to Government House in Jerusalem. There had been serious complaints of the local Zionist recruits who did happen to be "garrisoning Palestine," as part of the occupying force. They had been withdrawn from Haifa as a result of an affray with the Egyptian Labour Corps.

> Many of the men recruited in Palestine [ran the official account of the affair] regarded themselves as a Palestinian militia, and when ordered to Cyprus a large number went on a strike organized by a battalion soviet. This very unmilitary way of expressing their feelings does not appear to show that they considered themselves as British subjects. The authorities may find a way of satisfying the local patriotism of the Jewish volunteers

> without exciting the hostility of the Arab population, by establishing a depot and training centre away from any large town, but it should be clearly indicated that soldiers are servants of the State and not their own masters.

It is not probable that any notice was taken of these recommendations. When I passed through Palestine (having been recalled home so that I might be sent to Ireland), all the officers of the Administration whom I met complained of their impossible situation. The Home Government never listened to any request or recommendation sent to it. General belief was that London wished to force Sir Louis Bols to resign. He could not even wring from Whitehall any inkling of the policy which he was to pursue. The Home Government probably did not care to put its policy on paper.

The Chief Administrator had an invidious lot, and the dignity of his post was destroyed, as the information not vouchsafed to him came regularly to the Zionist Commission. Sir Louis Bols made another protest to the Home Government that information was being supplied to the Commission which was withheld from the responsible ruling body in the Occupied Territory. This leakage of information, of course, may have been due less to Cabinet indiscretions than to the knowledge the Zionist Organization in London naturally held of a policy which it was helping to make. It passed along to the Commission the news of its own work. Sir Louis Bols may not have realized this when, sadly rather than impatiently, he asked that "at least equal reticence or equal confidence should have been shown to both the Administration and the Zionist Commission."

He had come into office anxious to govern with the utmost fairness, and the Zionists themselves agree that there were "indications that when assuming the duties of Chief Administrator his intentions were rather friendly, and he seemed quite prepared to support the Jewish element with perhaps the only exception of the Jewish battalions." (Z.O.R.) But when he perceived that he was expected to run his Administration in harness with the coursers of the National Home, and when first he received hints, then was informed of requirements, and finally was presented with plain orders (as he was) from the Zionist Commission, his attitude necessarily changed.

It is probable that he doomed himself and his Administration in mid-March, when he wrote home his comments upon a speech which had been made by Dr. Weizmann in London the month before at a meeting held in the Cannon Street Hotel. He felt it to be his duty to controvert several of Dr. Weizmann's assertions concerning Palestine, and to warn the future Mandatory Powers of the danger of accepting them as a true picture of the state of the country.

"It must be understood," he wrote, "that approximately 90 percent of the population of Palestine is deeply anti-Zionist. This opposition comprises all Moslems and Christians and a not inconsiderable proportion of Jews."

He went on to explain that the cause of their opposition was in part religious and in part the fear that the "ancient dwellers of the land would eventually have to give place to Zionists who were backed by big financial concerns." The Chief Administrator had tried to calm these fears by assuring the people that no forced land-sales would be permitted and that a guarantee would be demanded from the new owners, when land was voluntarily sold to them, that tenants and the peasantry employed thereon would not be disturbed and would continue in their employment.

Sir Louis Bols in making these announcements had shown more acquaintance with equity than with the intentions of the Government, but this was hardly his fault. He continued now, in his communication for the benefit of the Mandatory Powers, by saying that if the policy outlined by Dr. Weizmann in Cannon Street were followed rather than the course he had just indicated, that is, if exclusively Jewish labour were employed and Government lands were handed over to the Zionist Organization, then the situation would become untenable. In words which deserve to be recorded because of their foresight he declared, "I wish to state clearly that if such a policy is proposed it is certain that a revolution would ensue which would result in the Jews being driven out of the land unless they are covered by powerful military forces of the Mandatory Power."

Great works such as the electrification of the country, the making of railroads and ports should be carried out, he added, by the Government of the country and not by one small section of the community, however rich it might be. If this course was not followed antagonism would be aroused beyond allay and the Zionist cause would suffer consequently.

> The policy of working hand in hand with the Arabs seems to be reversed by Dr. Weizmann's speech, and a desire is indicated to fight for the country economically [proceeded Sir Louis Bols]. I desire to impress my view that such an aim is not possible of achievement. The inhabitants of Palestine are not savages but comprise industrious labourers and well educated and exceedingly clever landowners and professional classes. These are men whose families have been in Palestine for centuries, who look to Great Britain, as she is the likely Mandatory Power, for fair treatment in every respect. In the conclusion of his speech Dr. Weizmann says that there is "a certain amount of Arab hostility to Zionism in Palestine." I wish to emphasize the statement I have made that 90 percent of the population of Palestine is deeply anti-Zionist.

So the reader perceives that the Government was informed exactly of the situation in Palestine as it was. What the Crane-King Commission had reported, Sir Louis Bols affirmed in his turn.

Here, then, is additional specific proof, to be set beside the Crane-King Report and other testimony, that for what Mr. Lloyd George and Lord Balfour and other ministers did in Palestine no excuse of ignorance of local conditions can be invoked. Excuses of this sort have appeared recently, an adroit form of apologia, which is masked as half-apologia. In the Peel Report there are touches of it. The statesmen are exculpated by being not quite exculpated. Their deeds are not concealed beneath suspiciously staring whitewash, but are dimmed with a greyish distemper which has the appearance of having been there always. The special touch of the half-apologists is to name no names, but to give to the acts of individuals an impersonal value, saying that "the position in Palestine was not appreciated at the time the National Home was launched," that "it was not realized then that Palestine was almost wholly Arab," and so forth, nobody being specified as not appreciating or not realizing.

No doubt in 1920 the British public was as ignorant of the balance of population in Palestine and of the sentiments of its inhabitants as it was of either of these matters in Azerbaijan or in Herzegovina. But the Prime Minister and his colleagues were by no means in the same boat as the general public. The only kind of ignorance they could have was that for which Balfour indeed was already notorious, studied and accomplished ignorance. Full information had been supplied to them of the exact constituents of the Holy Land's population and of the rejection of the Zionist enterprise by 90 percent of its people. The essential facts had been sent to them or made available for them by the head of their own government in Palestine and by an official Commission of the United States of America. They had been informed early, while the Mandate was unassumed, while the Turkish Treaty was unmade, while they themselves were uncommitted: and they had been informed later, with all the strength of a last hour warning, when they were on the verge of commitment.

But to all this information, which they had no desire to receive, they kept themselves blind, and contumaciously they proceeded with their plans.

Chapter 20

The San Remo Conference.
The covert assumption of the Mandate for Palestine by the Prime Minister.
Mandatory Government illicit as no Mandate yet possible.
Governmental secrecy, and its reasons. Dr. Weizmann blurts out the aims of the Premature Mandate.

The San Remo Conference, where these plans fructified, held that April, has proved a very perishable conference, perhaps the most withered of all the post-War conferences which have shrunk so considerably in men's memories.

While it was sitting, however, the San Remo Conference occupied everyone's attention, though not for the causes which best merited this. What drew attention was the family quarrel between Allies. England and France seemed totally at variance upon the policy to be pursued across the Rhine. They were divided upon the culpability of German behaviour in the Ruhr, upon the degree of disarmament to be imposed upon Germany, and upon various kindred questions which make strange reading nowadays. For a while Europe shook with the peacemaking. Then the disagreement was remedied, mainly by the skill of Mr. Lloyd George, and a joint manifesto brought the Conference to a resonant close.

What now has to be observed of San Remo is that this forgotten great Anglo-French hubbub prevented much regard being paid to anything else which occurred there. So much so that there is a temptation to suggest that it was used as a screen, behind which the other concerns of the Conference, especially the vital questions of the Turkish succession, were whisked to hidden completion. It would be extravagant to assert that things were exactly so, but it is fair, I think, to say that some persons must have been satisfied enough when the Anglo-French divergencies did happen to throw the Turkish deliberations into the shadow. In that shadow the plenipotentiaries were able to carry through matters of singular importance and—if anyone had examined them—matters of very singular aspect, without any sign of notice from the public and even, by a species of covert understanding, without any sign of notice from themselves. These matters were the (so-called) award made at the Conference of the Mandates for Palestine and Mesopotamia to Great Britain, and of the Mandate for "Syria" to France. The smooth suddenness, the sleight of hand and of mind, the privacy with which this embarrassing act was accomplished are scarcely to be believed. Let anyone examine the files of the Press of 1920 if he doubts it, particularly the files of the official-toned organs.

This, though, is looking forward a trifle. The immediate preliminaries of the Conference most certainly call for mention first. The sessions at San Remo were really but the prolongation of parleys which had begun in London, as a sequel to the Peace Conference, with the meeting of the Supreme Allied Council on the 12th of February. This was the meeting to which Feisal had been invited. The London Conference ended as such on the 3rd of March, but its work was continued by a sub-Conference of the Allied Foreign Ministers under Lord Curzon's chairmanship, which in some fifty sittings drafted a treaty for presentation to Turkey.

Therefore Feisal's final appeals, before the proclamation of Syrian independence was made, reached England while the Supreme Council was sitting. At first thought it might be imagined that they must have come, to the exclusion of other business, before the assembled Premiers, and must have remained before them till they had enjoyed thorough consideration. But a little recollection of the circumstances of the time makes one realize that nothing could stay prominently before the Premiers, unless it were set aside as part of the programme of a special gathering. Unscheduled sensations arriving without an appointment could not expect more than a transient glance. Or, to put it in another way, there were too many questions projecting for any of them to stand out. It was only when Allied leaders were run through by something painfully acute that they could or did give real heed to it and extracted it, somewhat pettishly, from their invulnerable frames.

So when Feisal had said to me in Damascus that he knew the Allied leaders had great preoccupations, he showed a thoughtful understanding of their lot. During March and April of 1920 Mr. Lloyd George had to take into consideration and had to propound decisions upon the control of the Dardanelles and the Bosphorus; upon whether the Sultan and the Turkish Government were or were not to stay in Constantinople; upon the fate of Smyrna; upon the future of Fiume and of Zara and upon the whole Adriatic question, which involved him incidentally in a lengthy and sub-acid correspondence with President Wilson; upon the enormous dilemma of relations with Russia; upon the massacres of Armenians now bloodily renewed by Turks and Kurds; upon the dispute with Germany over the trial of war-criminals; upon the surrender of the Kaiser, which was the subject of a curious correspondence with the Dutch Government; upon the terms of peace with Hungary; upon the high post-War prices which were taking the decencies of life out of reach of the European multitudes; upon the rehabilitation of currencies and of international exchanges; upon the settlement of the complicated but pressing Egyptian situation; upon the terrible Irish disorder just arriving at the stage of insurrection.

It is but fair to the then Prime Minister to give at this juncture this list, doubtless incomplete, of his anxieties. Presumably he shared some of them with Lord Curzon and Lord Balfour and in a lesser way with other Cabinet Ministers. But even so, for him to have given full consideration to all these questions, most of them major crises, at one and the same time, was beyond human capacity. This is to be remembered when his actions in Syria—one more crisis to ponder—come under review. If there was evidence that in this matter he only erred and stumbled, because of the weight of his burden and of the continual call for speed in decision, then one would forgive him a great deal. The trouble is that his stumbling, if there was stumbling, seemed to be in the right direction. After which, only too swiftly, he recovered, pulled himself together and went wrong.

Throughout March there was scarcely any mention of the happenings in Damascus: certainly no inkling of their importance was given. Three days after the proclamation of Feisal *The Times* had a single line announcing it, and four days later a couple of paragraphs recounting how he had been offered the crown of Syria by the National Assembly and how it had been accepted and conferred. No indication was given of the extent of the proclaimed kingdom nor any of the inclusion of Palestine in the royal title and domains.

In the House of Commons, on the 18th, Mr. Lloyd George, however, answered a question by Mr. Ormsby-Gore. "It appears," he said, "that the Emir Feisal was proclaimed King of Syria, including apparently Palestine and Syria, by a Congress at Damascus on March 8th, but of whom this Congress was composed or what authority it possessed is not yet known. As it is obvious that the future of the territories which have been conquered from the former Ottoman Empire can only properly be determined by the Allied Powers assembled in conference for the purpose, the Emir Feisal has been informed by the British and French Governments, acting in concert, that they cannot recognize the validity of the proceedings, and the Emir has been invited to come to Europe to state his case." "Is that the case only with regard to Palestine?" asked the vigilant Ormsby-Gore. "He is invited to come to Europe," answered the Premier, "to state his case in regard to the whole of that territory."

Again, on the 22nd, and again in reply to Mr. Ormsby-Gore, Mr. Lloyd George spoke. He said, "The question of Syria will shortly be examined with a view to arriving at a settlement in accordance with the declarations that have been exchanged between the British, the French and the Arab Governments." His questioner had put a leading question: was the Emir, he had asked, going to be "reassured" that the Allies would adhere to their pledges to King Hussein and to the Anglo-French Proclamation of November 1918.

No doubt some of Mr. Ormsby-Gore's friends were worried by the form of Mr. Lloyd George's replies. If Feisal was to be "reassured" on the basis of Britain's legitimate pledges to the Arabs (to which public reference now had been made), then the Balfour bargain was left out of consideration. If Feisal was to state his case for the whole of the territory whose independence had been proclaimed, what had happened to the exclusion of Palestine from Syria, which had been arranged in Zionist interests?

Here I enter the realm of supposition, but I do not imagine that these worries lasted very long in London. Explanations descended to the Zionist leaders from Downing Street and consentments mounted back to there, or else in that street the forces both of gravity and of capillary attraction had ceased to ply. But in more distant places, where no such explanations were available, the Commons statements must have appeared disquieting. It is a possibility that my own interview with Feisal, in which he made the identical claim based on the pledges to his father, will have deepened this disquiet. It was published in the *Daily Mail* on the 30th, in the nick of time. It must have been noted, brief as it was, and retelegraphed outside and about Europe because of the penury of news in other journals, and have suggested to suspicious minds collusion between Lloyd George and Feisal.

Just previously, on the 28th, the former had made a full-dress speech in the House of Commons which will have provided further grounds for this impression. It was a general statement upon Governmental policy. When the Premier came to discussion of the Near East, he said nothing at all of Palestine or of any part of Syria—conceivably a hint of Governmental disassociation—while of the parallel province of Mesopotamia he spoke in perturbing terms. "The Government of Mesopotamia," he proclaimed, "must be Arab. We shall respect the solemn undertaking we entered into in November 1918 upon that subject." Since this solemn undertaking also had been promulgated in Palestine it looked as though the next step must be a guarantee that the undertaking would be respected in Palestine also, and the Zionists, or certain Zionists, now took fright.

Probably this fright was unjustified. It is of course impossible to gauge what was in Mr. Lloyd George's mind when he made his various pronouncements. But he had no understanding with Feisal such as the Zionists feared: to have been in Damascus, where the one thing Feisal prayed for was some, was any kind of understanding, however informal, was to know this. Why, then, did Mr. Lloyd George speak in the way he did? Was it that for a brief space, with so many preoccupations assailing him, he did actually forget all the coil of plans for the National Home which he himself had helped to twine? Was there some interval indeed within which the Zionists and all their friends were cut off from access to him and could not remind him of these bonds? Had he some flash of thoughtless plain-dealing, some vision of settling with the Syrians the affairs of Syria? Did that once fluent sympathy for a coerced people, which years ago had carried the young Welshman to unreckoned power, now rise upon the ebb and flood some private, unprofitable vein of the reckoning statesman? Or was everything that he had said but a marking-of-time with a little loose-gaited phraseology?

The last supposition, unfortunately, is the more probable. If there were any satisfactory reassurances they went to the Zionists and not to Feisal. Feisal was still waiting then for a reply to another appeal he had made, in which he had adjourned the question of the recognition of his kingdom, and had asked that an "assent to independence" in general terms should be conveyed to him privately. If he received this, he would leave at once for England.

But the Zionists who had taken fright did not know this. They were in the United States and took the pronouncements of the Premier at what seemed their value. There was a coolness between them and their colleagues in London at the time, and they either had received no explanation from the latter or had distrusted any they had received. So a sharp recall to order was sent to the British Government. It was indirect, but the more telling perhaps for this reason.

Out of the blue then, a week before the San Remo Conference was to open, came a cable from *The Times* correspondent in Washington, and was printed to advantage upon the principal page of that paper. *The Times* correspondent all of a sudden had grown worried about the future of Palestine.

> The Balfour Declaration [he cabled] was made the basis by the Peace Conference for an arrangement whereby the Zionists should get Palestine under something tantamount to a British protectorate. It is now stated that we have recently been trying to break the agreement and to substitute for a British protectorate an arrangement giving the Emir Feisal a mandate for Palestine under which the Jewish minority-rights would be guaranteed...There may be good reason for the new proposal, but from the point of view of Anglo-American relations it is distinctly

> explosive. The Jews are very powerful here. To turn Palestine over to the Arabs would disgust our friends and encourage our enemies.

A peremptory communication, but also one of a rare frankness. The correct description of the approaching Mandate as "an arrangement whereby the Zionists should get Palestine under something tantamount to a British Protectorate" was enough to cause Mandate-drafters, busy in the basements of Downing Street illuminating in white and silver the initial "M" of the patent, to drop colours and brushes to the ground. Texts, blessed by Lord Cecil, about Jews and Arabs working out together the future of their common fatherland, fluttered down beside them, as the dexterous fingers which had been limning them in pure gold lost their grip and opened in dismay. In their place stretched the gross layers of newsprint, stamped mechanically in their midst with those rough, down right, almost vulgar words, "an arrangement by which the Zionists should get Palestine."

Those rough words bespoke their origin, whoever had transmitted them from Washington. The "Brandeis regime" had got to work. Its members had been gathered round President Wilson's sick bed in February, and now that he was convalescent they were recovering along with him. Through spokesmen of the White House or (improbably, for the style discounted it) through the President, or (most probably) from the lips of the regime itself the intimation to Great Britain had come straight, or quickly had filtered, to the correspondent who had dispatched it. The genuine "Brandeis direct-action diplomacy," so remote from diplomacy, so indifferent to European face-saving, had manifested itself again, with its wonted force.

No doubt the cable from Washington was superfluous, and most annoying to Mr. Lloyd George, but, besides being an imperishable record of facts, it was a proper dispatch for the Conference and shows the conditions under which this began. It began on the 19th, housed in the palatial "Villa Devachan," and was attended by Messrs. Millerand and Lloyd George, Signor Nitti, Lord Curzon, Marshal Foch, General Badoglio, Sir Henry Wilson, Sir Maurice Hankey, Mr. Philip Kerr and a number of others. The soldiers were present to arrange and to advise upon the military clauses of the Turkish Treaty and questions relating to the German Army. There were also various unofficial delegations, representing bodies which had or thought they should have an interest in the Turkish Treaty. There was even an "Arab delegation" in San Remo, led by one of the wealthy Loutfallah family, but it was not dispatched by the Congress nor by King Hussein nor by King Feisal, and was no more than a group of spectators with a watching-from-afar brief.

Of course there was a Zionist delegation there too, on a very different rung of the ladder. "Perhaps," quaintly ventured a report of *The Times* mentioning the variety of delegations, "perhaps the Zionists are most active," and went on to announce that before the first sitting of the Conference Mr. Lloyd George's secretaries had been almost submerged by telegrams and cables from Zionist associations in the United States and in the British Isles, urging that Great Britain should obtain the Mandate for Palestine.

The Premier also received early on the following resolution:

> At meetings held in London this week the Parliamentary Labour Party, the Executive Committee of the Labour Party and the Parliamentary Committee of the Trades Union Congress have adopted resolutions to remind the British Government of the Declaration made on November 2nd, 1917, that the Government would endeavour to facilitate the establishment of a Jewish National Home in Palestine, a declaration that was in harmony with the declared War Aims of the British Labour Movement, and which was cordially welcomed by all sections of the British people and was reaffirmed by Lord Curzon on November 2nd, 1919. The National Labour Organizations indicated now urge upon His Majesty's Government the necessity of redeeming this pledge by the acceptance of a Mandate under the League of Nations for the administration of Palestine with a view to *its being reconstituted the National Home of the Jewish people.* The National Committee desire to associate themselves with the many similar representations being made to the Government urging the settlement of this question with the utmost dispatch both in the interests of Palestine itself as well as in the interest of the Jewish People.
>
> *(Signed)* J. R. Clynes; H. S. Lindsay; W. H. Hutchinson; J. H. Thomas; C. W. Bowerman (as Chairmen or Secretaries of the organizations named).

I draw attention by italics to the phrase in this resolution which shows that the Labour Party, or its leaders, also intended that the Zionists in 1920 were "to get Palestine," though their language was more circumspect than that from Washington. Their petition asked that entire Palestine, no mere portion of it, should be reconstituted as the Jewish National Home. This is not the moment to compute the guilt, or the innocence in every sense of that word, of the Labour movement in this affair. Enough to disclose that it took its part in the disfranchisement of the Arab people and that it entreated the Prime Minister to accept (sweet word!) the Mandate.

The Times had also seized the opportunity of urging him, in a leader upon its Washington dispatch, to be true to the Balfour Declaration. "The Government have made a solemn promise which they cannot break without doing untold harm. They might indeed do worse than register it, once and for all, in the treaty of peace with Turkey," said a leader. Now to register it after this fashion was exactly what the Prime Minister and his associates had in mind. Through its wide connections *The Times* will have been aware of this. So the stroke of suggesting registration was very neat, and doubtless was found insufferable by Mr. Lloyd George, who at the time was on the worst of terms with Printing House Square. He now saw himself placed in the position of following its obnoxious advice.

So in these several, not altogether pleasant fashions, by Labour and by Conservatism and from either side of the Atlantic, Mr. Lloyd George was now thoroughly reminded of his indentures. It is not to be imagined though that these doings bulked as largely on the general scene as they must, perforce, in this account. *The Times* matter was published on a single day; the Labour, the Zionist and other such cables, letters and resolutions passed from post-offices to pigeon-holes. The House of Commons replies were not promoted to reproduction in the news-columns of the Press with appropriate comment, but were read by the few who read through the columns of Parliamentary debates in the fewer newspapers which provide them. There was no public perception of the matter at all.

Indeed, though it was spring, the silence of a summer noon might be said to have brooded over the soft and breathless passage of the Palestine Mandate into the arms of Great Britain. At San Remo there was but one short bout of purposeful bustle. Dr. Weizmann arrived punctually there on the 19th. On the morrow Lord Balfour, perversely in Cannes, was summoned by telegram. The communique of the first day's session said simply that "the Turkish Treaty was discussed." The Turkish delegates, it was arranged, should be called to Paris upon the 10th of May to receive the treaty.

On the 20th, the second day of session, it was learned that "financial questions had been discussed, largely in connection with the Turkish Treaty." This may have had relation to the Anglo-French agreement for the distribution of the Mosul oil-fields output, which agreement was to be completed in San Remo itself, in sequel to the conversations of the previous year, by Sir John Cadman and M. Berthelot. During the 21st, according to the still pigmy communique, the "consideration of the Turkish Treaty was practically completed." Lord Balfour had a long conversation with Mr. Lloyd George. It came out afterwards that one more invitation was sent to Feisal to appear before the Conference and "state his case." That was Wednesday, Feisal was in Damascus under the conditions we know, and in San Remo it was generally anticipated that the Conference would end on the ensuing Monday, the 26th. The invitation, of course, may have been dispatched before Wednesday, on the 19th or the 20th. Even so, it was the sort of invitation that it was.

In the House of Commons a member or two, dissatisfied with the meagre news which the country was receiving, put questions to discover what was happening. They were curtly informed that the affairs of Palestine "were under consideration by the Conference." That was enough about Palestine. The Anglo-French disagreement over Germany now occupied most minds and nearly all the considerable space which the Press gave to the Conference. The Turkish Treaty was relegated to minor paragraphs in the messages from the Press, and took on the air of a gleam in a low corner of the otherwise darkened sky, brought in to finish correspondents' telegrams on a consolatory note. Or at the most there might be a laconic special reference. One, dispatched early the previous day, appeared on the 24th, which said, "It is expected that the Palestine question will come up today, and before the Conference this morning Sir Herbert Samuel and the Zionist delegates had a conference with Mr. Lloyd George and Lord Curzon." Any comment on this conference before the Conference is scarcely necessary: it should have been printed as the Conference before the conference.

But it may be explained that Sir Herbert had just returned from a prolonged tour of Palestine, bearing a report upon conditions there. Subsequently Lord Curzon made unnecessary mystery about this report, in a speech in the Lords. He disclaimed that it was an official report, said that Sir Herbert Samuel had really gone out to Palestine in a private capacity, at the suggestion of Lord Allenby. Thereon he had toured the country and had drawn up this report "which he afterwards allowed me to see."

Lord Curzon did not know that Lord Allenby's suggestion for the visit sprang from a super-suggestion of Dr. Weizmann. I do not remember whether the Arabs shared Lord Curzon's ignorance, but they had been greatly disturbed by Sir Herbert's presence in Palestine. They had no personal feeling against a man whose pleasant demeanour and genuine desire to placate them were in such happy contrast with the ways and intentions of the Zionist Commission. But they feared his literary pursuits.

When Sir Herbert Samuel came to San Remo, Mr. Lloyd George, like Lord Curzon, was allowed to see the Report. It was never made public, however, though, as Lord Curzon testified, "there was nothing in it in the least unsuitable for publication."

Presumably, therefore, after he had read through Sir Herbert Samuel's report, and certainly after he had conferred with him and with Dr. Weizmann, the Palestine question "came up" before Mr. Lloyd George and his fellow-delegates on the 23rd. It reappeared before them on the 24th, the official communique dispatched that same evening saying, after mention of those present, "The Council continued its discussion of the territorial clauses of the Peace Treaty with Turkey affecting Armenia. It later examined the question of the Mandate for Palestine and the establishment there of a national home for the Jews, as well as questions affecting the religious communities there."

The next day, the 25th, was a Sunday. Two communiqués were issued that same evening, and appeared in some of the papers on Monday. The first said: "The Supreme Council met at 11 a.m. today at the Villa Devachan. There were present Signori Nitti and Scialoja, MM. Millerand and Berthelot, Mr. Lloyd George, Lord Curzon, M. Matsui and Mr. Underwood Johnson. [Mr. Johnson was the United States "observer." He did not take an active part in, nor have any responsibility for, the proceedings.] The question of the Mandate for Palestine, Syria and Mesopotamia was discussed, and the question of the new Armenian State was settled. The Council finally discussed the resumption of commercial relations with Russia with special reference to the negotiations now proceeding with the Russian Commercial Mission at Copenhagen."

The second communiqué, issued later, dealt with the afternoon session, and held no reference to the Near Eastern countries, as the Adriatic question and Germany's attitude to the Treaty of Versailles were the subjects of debate.

So that the sole official information given to the world upon what had happened at the morning session of the 25th, as far as the Near Eastern countries were concerned, was that "the question of the Mandates for Palestine, Syria and Mesopotamia was discussed." Discussed, indeed! During that session, which lasted for three hours, the "examination of the Palestine question" which had begun upon the Saturday had been concluded, and Britain had been granted, or awarded, or indemnified with the nomination as Mandatory. And at this session, or between this session and the previous day's session, the Balfour Declaration had been inserted into the draft-Mandate which was being prepared as part of the coming Treaty.

In fine, Sunday the 25th was the fateful day, the day of days, and that particular session was of pre-eminent interest, was a moment when the destinies of the most sacred land on earth were determined for, at the very least, a long period. A type of government, too, never before essayed in human society was inaugurated, or was introduced after some fashion, and the countries which were to govern thus unprecedentedly were named.

Yet no faintest suggestion of what had been done was vouchsafed by the Conference chiefs in their official report of their transactions. They said that the question of the Mandate for Palestine (and for the other Arab lands) had been discussed, as though there had been some talk about it, and then they had gone on to other matters. More than this they never disclosed. The nearest they reached to any sort of explanation of their business was the last sentence of the previous day's communique, stiff with constraint and wariness.

It is true that official communiqués are noted for their reticence. It is also true that international Conferences are fatiguing affairs, and that at the end of a long day tired men may cut their labour by giving the shortest possible account of what has happened. But reticence, not saying much about the event of the day, is one thing, and concealing it altogether when it is a final decision is another. The crucial meeting in this case was held in the morning, and there was ample time to announce what had taken place during it. The news could have been given in less than twenty words, in as many words as were employed to obscure it.

That 25th of April something of great moment had been accomplished, though the absolute character of the act remained undefined. It was, therefore, the duty of the Allied plenipotentiaries to make clear in an official statement what (in the current phrase) "they thought they were doing." That they made no such explanation shows how ill at ease they were about the character of the day's work.

Babies born that April morning have become young men and women, and yet we are about as ignorant as they were in their mothers' arms of what occurred at the Villa Devachan. This only we know, that the Balfour Declaration was slipped into the Mandate, and that it was Signori Nitti and Scialoja, M. Matsui, Lord Curzon, Messrs. Berthelot, Millerand and Lloyd George between them who somehow nominated as Mandatories the countries represented by MM. Berthelot and Millerand and by Lord Curzon and Mr. Lloyd George. It was a very intimate occasion, so intimate that four of those present suffered from ingrowing functions, nominating and being nominated at one and the same time. The sole clue to what a spectator might have witnessed of their proceedings from start to finish is to be found in the statement of a correspondent that "One cheerful feature about the Conference so far is the progress made in settling the Turkish Treaty. Discussions have run on the most cordial lines." Indeed they had done so.

This is the most living account of what happened which we possess. The League of Nations' own account of the birth of Mandates is highly significant because, in an Irish way, there is no account. "There is no record of the conversations by which Great Britain was selected as Mandatory for Palestine," confesses the League's official handbook.

Under such circumstances, it is impossible to prevent imagination from playing with the scene at the Villa Devachan. One pictures the bustling but superfluous helpfulness of the other delegates as Mr. Lloyd George efficiently levered the Balfour Declaration into the draft-Mandate. But the assumption of the draft-Mandate itself is not so easy to picture.

Did Signori Nitti, Scialoja, Millerand and Berthelot segregate themselves and then propose Great Britain as Mandatory for Palestine? Did

Mr. Lloyd George simper and blush acceptance, or look sternly before him and say duty was duty? Did the French delegates then go to the chairs at the foot of the table? Did the British delegates take the vacated seats at its head, along with the Italians and the Japanese, meditate their choice with them for a pensive second, and then in chorus with them offer "Syria" to France? Whereon did the French delegates, with national immunity from humbug, nod and thank the British for carrying out the arrangement of the previous September?

Maybe it happened after this fashion: more probably it did not. Procedure demanded that all the Principal Allied Powers should nominate the Mandatory, so Mr. Lloyd George and poor Lord Curzon, completely out of his element, one imagines, will, in some way that we cannot guess and upon which unhappily silence has been maintained, have taken part in nominating themselves.

The official silence concerning the details of this odd performance has not prevented a hundred writers and orators in the service of the Zionist thesis from projecting ever since, through the best part of two decades, moving pictures of the moral glory which descended on the Villa Devachan that day. Mr. Lloyd George has been presented, as upon the screen, in the role of the world's knight, bending a knee to receive Britain's obligations in Palestine. Like an accolade they were laid upon his shoulders by the incarnate kingly conscience of mankind. Whatever happened then, this did not. At San Remo the nomination of Mandatories, after the manner of the dubbing of knights, was not practicable, or rather was not picturable. Britain and France had long fixed their respective Mandatory spheres between them, and the story of their being "chosen" now for these positions is only elaborate and disingenuous pretence. Mr. Lansing, the American Secretary of State till that February, who knew all that was afoot, passed on these League and Mandate manoeuvres a judgment so apt that it must be quoted here. "If the advocates of the system," said he, "intended to avoid through its operation the appearance of taking enemy territory as the spoils of war, it was a subterfuge which deceived no one. It seemed obvious from the very first that the Powers, which under the old practice would have obtained sovereignty over certain conquered territories, would not be denied mandates over these territories."

Pure clap-trap also is the story of the resigned acceptance by the Mandatories of their nominations, which in fact they "accepted" with the resignation of stockbrokers accepting profits. Mr. Lloyd George, as Lord Lugard and others regretfully chronicle, already had blurted out in one of his unguarded moments that "France would be compensated for the oil-wells of Irak by the Mandate for Syria." As for what are called "obligations," it would have been a rash statesman who would have dared to refuse a full load of them to Mr. Lloyd George himself. That was the real situation. The chivalrous parties concerned were each responsible for his own knighthood, and even such a political gymnast as the same Lloyd George could hardly have laid his obligations upon his own shoulder and have bade himself to rise without throwing his frame and his features into contortions too unmannerly ever to be displayed to the public. Why, the secret of the scene could not even be risked by one word about it in a turgid little communique!

The correspondents in San Remo, however, did not keep utter silence upon the momentous session. But their information from official sources was meagre. It was clear that, with one exception, they had encountered from delegates and from official spokesmen marked reserve. Reuter, the general handler of public pronouncements, had a short note:

> This morning's session of the Conference lasted three hours. The question of the Mandates from Mesopotamia, Syria and Palestine was settled, the Mandates from Mesopotamia and Palestine being entrusted to Great Britain and that from Syria to France.

The odd use of the word "from" suggests how little was made clear to the writer, whose message was given as Reuter's own, not as an official message.

It was *The Times* which held the exceptional information, and *The Times,* despite its being at odds then with the Prime Minister, was the evident vehicle for disseminating it at home and abroad. *The Times* had a quality no other newspaper had, was like a long matured cask which gave a value to the wine which came from it. News drawn from it had the true character of *"officieux"* news, that is, news recognizable as official in origin yet having an independent stamp. The French, who had invented the word, had never got the right blend in their own *officieux* information, for which they used the *Temps.* Their news never seemed to have sojourned in the *Temps* cask, but to have been poured in and drawn off within an hour.

Whereas *The Times,* by a miracle of its own, could reproduce with fidelity the views of a Prime Minister and yet by reproducing them give them a certain cachet. Information passed through it rather as bills passed through the Houses of Parliament, and everything which it reported had an indefinable yet unmistakable air of having received the Editor's consent. It was indeed the only paper in the world which could be official and independent at once. *The Times* was the perfect vehicle for the sort of announcement which was to be made now.

But again it must be observed that the news about Palestine, though in such a great organ, did not bulk largely. It was appended, a final paragraph, at the tail of a lengthy telegram upon the Anglo-French tension, and ran as follows:

> It is agreed that Britain be given Mandates for Mesopotamia and Palestine. The Holy Land will be looked upon, in the terms of Mr. Balfour's Declaration, as the home of the Jews, but Jews settling in Palestine will not lose their original nationality save by the ordinary processes of law. Steps will be taken to respect the rights of the Arabs. The Syrian Mandate will be given to France, but it is well to state that these decisions have been taken more as a matter of political expediency at the present moment than as forecasting the moment of assumption of Mandates. The whole series of questions relating to the frontiers of these new Mandatory regions has indeed yet to be settled, as well as all points still open with the Emir Feisal, who has been asked to come to Europe to discuss them. The decision however will enable civil administration very largely to replace the military occupation in these areas.

The above obviously inspired message skated over what had happened within the council-chamber of the Villa Devachan. To cover official silence, something clearly had to be said somewhere about the proceedings, and in this message the announcement was made, guardedly. But even so, the phraseology of the message showed how difficult it was, for the best of reasons, to frame in words the business which had been transacted at the Villa, and showed too why there had been no official definition of the transactions. If there had been one, it would have been necessary (confining the outlook to Palestine) to have announced that either (1) Great Britain had been nominated as prospective Mandatory for Palestine—which would have been true but would not have suited the Premier's plan, or (2) that the Mandate for Palestine had been entrusted to Great Britain—which would have suited the plans but would have been false. Reuter had committed himself to formula No. 2, but obviously enough in unwitting error.

For Great Britain was not awarded the Mandate for Palestine on the 25th of April, 1920. She could not be awarded what then was not in existence. The Mandates were sequels of the Peace Treaty, and the Peace Treaty with Turkey was not yet concluded. The flower could not appear in the air before its stem had risen from the soil. There were no Mandates in being as yet, and none could be created till the Peace Treaty had been concluded and ratified.

It was not therefore Mandates which were awarded to the two Powers at San Remo. It was nominations as prospective Mandatories which they received, a very different thing. The former would give them rights, the latter gave them no rights at all.

But the Allied leaders were not anxious for the world to realize that their countries were only prospective Mandatories. They wanted to start straight off as (supposedly) invested Mandatories, having the full privileges of that status. They had their reasons for this desire, Mr. Lloyd George's being that he was anxious to bring the military administration of Palestine to an end, so as to set up a civil Government.

None the less the Allied leaders, while they meant to act as though they possessed Mandates, shrank from putting evidence of their intentions upon paper. They were not quite so sure as they gave out that the Treaty with Turkey was going to be concluded at once. There was the possible prospect before them of a sort of no-man's-time, between nomination to the Mandate and the Mandate's entry into being. This period might be short. On the other hand, in the Irish phrase, it mightn't yet. If it were short, how they described themselves during it would not matter much. But it would matter a good deal if it were not short, since in that event to write themselves down as Mandatories in an official announcement would be to leave written proof that they had presented themselves with Mandates in advance of their existence.

Therefore they preferred, as long as they could at least, to make no written claim. The respite of hazy definition indeed might not be long, but every week gained was something. They would be returning home soon, and if they had to make definitions when they got home, these would be by word of mouth, and the whole atmosphere of their parliaments and peoples would have been felt and tested by them. Nobody at home might prove to be very much alive to what was or was not possible under Mandates, or to where these new political contraptions began or ended. Meanwhile, in respect of Britain, the announcement in *The Times* would do to go on with.

So it did, unfortunately. It was not analysed, though well it might have been. What did "forecasting the moment of assumption of mandates" mean? In itself it was an obscure phrase, and the obscurity was increased by its being presented in the announcement not as an absolute alternative to "political expediency," but as rather an alternative or partly an alternative. The Mandate and the alternative to the Mandate were to be used together, though how this was to be done passes comprehension.

Mandates did not come piecemeal: you had a Mandate in full or you had no Mandate at all: you could not forecast one. If you did establish your Government there on a basis of forecast mingled with expediency, then gibberish was your title-deed to Palestine.

As for the phrase itself, "forecasting the moment of assumption of the Mandate," if it meant anything, deserved to be interpreted in the sense of forecasting the moment of cashing a cheque without the formality of having an account at the bank. But it was obscure enough to conceal what it meant, and no one bothered to pierce through its mists or to ask how the San Remo decisions could erect a Mandatory Administration where there was no Mandate. Till the Peace Treaty was ratified there *could* be no Mandate.

This was the inescapable fact which at San Remo Mr. Lloyd George was endeavouring to escape. He had his Mandatory Government for Palestine, and by now his Mandatory High Commissioner, Sir Herbert Samuel, up his sleeve. But he was determined to withdraw them both from this overcrowded receptacle, and to establish them in power without delay, despite the legal obstacles which absolutely hindered this. For, just as a Mandatory Administration could not exist till the completed Treaty with Turkey installed it, so the military Administration could not cease to exist till the completed Treaty with Turkey abolished it.

One thing does mitigate the Prime Minister's proposal, the chance at the time that the Turkish Treaty would be signed the following month, or soon afterwards. Probably he thought that, even though the Treaty looked like being delayed, still by the time the first practical steps were taken to expel the old and to install the new Administration in Palestine, he would indeed possess the Mandate. He considered that what he was about to do was a minor irregularity which would right itself, since the no-man's-time, if it did lengthen out a bit, would not go on and on for months and months.

But if there is any mitigation here, there is precious little of it. If the signature and then the ratification of the Turkish Treaty were reasonably close, that was all the more reason that he should have waited for them. If they were not reasonably close, it was unpardonable to forestall them. A proper explanation of the position too, of the dependence of the Mandate on the completion of the Treaty, should have been given by him at once. To let it be implied, as he was letting it be implied, that the Conference decisions enabled civil Administration to be set up in Palestine there and then, was false.

These considerations, however, did not come to Mr. Lloyd George, or were set aside by him. He was in too great a hurry to get rid of the Army Administration which in Palestine was standing in the way of the desired development of the National Home. The riots in Jerusalem had brought matters to a head. "It was felt on both sides," said the Executive of the Zionist Organization in its next year's report, "that the last stage of the conflict had been reached, and that the question at issue was now reduced to its crudest and simplest form: either the Jews or the military Administration would have to go."

That was the situation put in accurate words. Mr. Lloyd George's decision, to which possibly his colleagues in the Cabinet had rallied or had been rallied, was that of the two it was the Army which was to go, and go without any more delay. "What you want in Palestine," he had said at San Remo to Dr. Weizmann, "what you want in Palestine, Weizmann, is men who really care for the National Home policy."

Undoubtedly this was what Dr. Weizmann did want in Palestine. At San Remo Dr. Weizmann must have felt that the earth was his and all who trod thereon. He gave evidence of such feelings in an interview which he now conceded to Reuter's correspondent. This was something very different from Reuter's diminutive note of information, though note and interview were the product of the same day. Dr. Weizmann unbosomed himself exultantly, prematurely and recklessly to his interviewer. What he told him threw official silence into the sharpest relief (if the metaphor will pass for a silence which had been manufactured to shape). In principle Dr. Weizmann's talkativeness should have undone all the effects of the uninformative communiqués. He made public what they kept in their narrow breasts.

But for the third time, and not too often, it must be explained that this interview, like all the events here described, was muted by the din of Anglo-French fraternization, and in *The Times* (where it was at its best) was diverted to a quiet column and clad in unassuming letterpress. There is no evidence that it caused any stir. So much was going on in the world: readers, in their sphere, resembled the Prime Ministers who were trying to cope with too many things. They read distractedly and did not weigh the news. To follow the Peace-play they watched those cards which the larger headlines dealt into their sight. This was not so, of course, in Zionist circles or even in Jewry as a whole. San Remo's news gained the fullest publicity in the Jewish Press, and in the United States all fears were dissipated, and Zionists hurried from their houses and stood at street-corners, laughing and greeting each other and shaking hands.

The Arabs, too, were widely informed of what had happened, though more slowly because of their poorer means of inter-communication. But what Arabs knew, or thought, or said, or did, was so unimportant that in this account it must not further delay Dr. Weizmann's elated interview.

Speaking of the morning's session of the Conference, he said:

> Two decisions have been reached which are of the utmost importance. The first is the embodiment of the Balfour Declaration in the Treaty, thus giving it international sanction. We have always considered Mr. Balfour's Declaration as the charter of our liberties, and international sanction is the turning-point in Jewish history. The second decision is that the British Government, which is the Mandatory Power in Palestine, [Note "is." Not "*is to be*"] has agreed that a civil administration shall be set up

> immediately in Palestine to carry the Balfour Declaration into effect, always having regard for the *legitimate* [my italics: Dr. Weizmann's distinction] interests of the non-Jewish communities. The Zionists are satisfied that the intentions of the Government will be carried out without delay. We are most anxious to begin reconstruction, for the last two years in Palestine have brought about general demoralization. The painful period is over, and the beginning of the reconstruction work will be hailed both by the Jews and the Arabs as delivery from a nightmare.

I am afraid that for some of the things said by Dr. Weizmann in this statement, such as the final guarantee that the Arabs would hail Zionist reconstruction of their country as a delivery from nightmare, the only suitable qualification is the candid North-Country one of "brass." It was molten metal of the purest ore, worthy in its way of an eminent chemist. Next day the Arab "delegation" dealt with the matter, protesting vehemently against the splitting into two of Syria and against the Mandate contrary to the "desires of their people who had accepted solemn and repeated promises of independence."

But the most important remarks of Dr. Weizmann came at the start of his interview. He revealed that *The Times's* recent advice had been very timely indeed. The Balfour Declaration had been embodied in some way (we shall see the method later) in the text of the draft-Treaty to be presented to Turkey. Officialdom had breathed no word of this in the "*officieux*" message of *The Times.* He also revealed, though not so clearly, the reasons for it. The Balfour Declaration, so inserted, as an article of the Treaty would become binding upon Great Britain and upon her co-signatories of the Treaty, as an obligation both between the victors on the one part, and on the other part as an obligation of the victors to Turkey. This was the international sanction of which Dr. Weizmann spoke. But how typical of the unreality of the affair was this plan, one escaped from a musical comedy, by which Great Britain bound herself to Turkey to execute a policy which Turkey always had refused to execute.

Dr. Weizmann also revealed that the true object of setting up a civil Administration in Palestine simply was to carry out the National Home project. Zionist representations had achieved this and also had secured the agreement that "reconstruction" would start without any wait for the materialization of the Mandate. "The Zionists," as he put it, "are satisfied that the intentions of the Government will be carried out without delay." The Zionists will have shared the Prime Minister's hope that the Treaty with Turkey would be signed in a month or so, and they shared or, more probably, were at the back of his unwillingness to wait even that short while.

Chapter 21

Mr. Lloyd George violates the Covenant of the League of Nations. The Chief Administrator of Palestine recommends the suppression of the Zionist Commission. Intervention of the United States against monopolies in Palestine. Parliament uninformed and unconsulted upon the Mandate. End of the Military Administration in Palestine. The Army judges political Zionism.

Dr. Weizmann had explained the importance of two decisions taken by the San Remo Conference, at the instance, he might have added, of the British delegates. From a more objective point of view, the main achievements of Mr. Lloyd George and his colleagues at San Remo had not been two, but three. First of all, unwatched and with great celerity they had got what passed as the full-fledged Mandate for Palestine into their possession. Secondly, under their auspices a settlement had been reached with France for the distribution of the oil from the Mosul wells. There had been no secrecy or covertness about this latter transaction: its terms were published as a White Paper. As has been stated, France received a quarter of the output.

But of the third achievement, not a word was spoken or printed in any sort of communication, official or other. Yet it was a considerable and noteworthy act to break the solemn Covenant of the League of Nations within twelve months of having composed it and signed it. The twenty-second Article of this Covenant, that under which Mandates were established, has been mentioned already. Its text was recorded, in Chapter 17, wherein was underlined the contradiction between the immaturity which it ascribed to the peoples with which it dealt and the maturity and competence of the formal resolutions with which one of these peoples, the Arabs of Syria, had replied to it. This was the article which, even such as it was, now in one important respect was overtly broken at San Remo. In a sense it was more than broken. Some of it was not even taken into consideration: an essential part of a clause was expunged. The maltreated clause was the fourth: I repeat its terms.

> Certain communities formerly belonging to the Turkish Empire have reached a stage of development where their existence as independent nations can be provisionally recognized subject to the rendering of administrative advice and assistance by a Mandatory until such time as they are able to stand alone. The wishes of these communities must be a principal consideration in the selection of the Mandatory.

Whether the first part of this clause had been honoured at San Remo could not yet be said, since only the text of the Mandate when published would show whether the above-mentioned recognition of the right to independence was enshrined in it or was not. What certainly had been disregarded was the second part. During the mysterious ceremony at which the Mandatories had been selected, the selectors had evaded that principal consideration of the wishes of the aforesaid communities, to which they were sworn under the Covenant. Of these wishes the selectors, as we have recently seen, all were well aware except, barely possibly, M. Matsui of Japan. If by accident he was ignorant of the Arabs' wishes, the other delegates now had their chance to enlighten him.

But at San Remo the other delegates kept the twenty-second Article sedulously from sight, just as before San Remo they had sedulously eschewed any move to consult the population in Palestine or in "Syria." Instead, Mr. Lloyd George had consulted Dr. Weizmann at length (to mention but him among Zionists), who was not a native of Palestine. If he had been one he could only have spoken for the Zionist-minded Palestine-born Jews, a very small proportion of the Jews in the country and a decimal speck of its total of inhabitants.

So here was a flagrant breach of the Covenant, a shocking act, because it showed such cynical appraisement of the new tables-of-the-law, which those who now broke them were even then proffering to the peoples of the world, to lead them out of the bondage of secret understandings and of false international promises. Theirs was a treble betrayal.

By their act they betrayed the young League of Nations whose Covenant was to be inviolable. They betrayed the small peoples to whom they preached commandments which they themselves did not keep. They betrayed those of their own kin, the throng of men and women in the greater countries who were seeking to make of the Covenant the Constitution of a new and juster international polity.

Could any excuse be found for them, even by themselves? They might say that the wishes of the population involved, of the so-called communities, were known to them and had been taken prominently into their minds, in accordance with Article 22. Article 22 only laid down that the said wishes must be "considered." It did not say that the wishes must be hearkened to. So that if they took the wishes of the communities into their minds, but presently, after a short but intense spasm of consideration, regretfully decided to eject these same wishes from their minds, then they would have kept faith with Article 22.

I do not know whether such an excuse may have seemed sufficient to them, but to other minds it will appear wretched hypocrisy. However, a perusal of the Covenant shows that the envoys of the principal Allied Powers can scarcely have paid that document even this tribute of sham nominal attention. The French text of the Covenant, of equal value with the English, and the text in the hands of many delegates, went further than the English and said that the wishes of the Communities were not merely to be a principal consideration, but were to be considered first, before any other considerations entered at all. "*Les vœux de ces communautés doivent être pris d'abord en considération pour le choix du Mandataire.*"

If any attention had been paid to the clause, the marked difference between the English and the French texts must have been a matter for question and arrangement, and even the unpublished whispers of what passed at San Remo hold no echo of either.

The excuse too might have been made that in effect the people of Palestine were willing to have Great Britain as Mandatory, that this was known, and that in demanding the nomination for themselves the British delegates conformed with the wishes of that people. This excuse again would be an unworthy subterfuge. What was known was that the people of all Syria, Palestine included, were well disposed towards a British Mandate, provided that it acknowledged their independence and that it did not comprise the establishment of the "National Home." These desires of theirs had just been reasserted: the kingdom which was the image of them had been proclaimed at Damascus.

So that excuse was no excuse. There was indeed no excuse at all, and with a wilful breach of the Covenant of the League of Nations the Mandatory era under the supervision of the League of Nations symptomatically began.

Two months passed before its formal opening, however, and were rich in events. The last few days of April were marked by a touch of unrest in the House of Commons. The speed and the silence with which the Mandates affair had been carried through, the extraordinary absence of any official news from San Remo, led to some disturbed questioning of the Under-Secretary for Foreign Affairs. Members wanted to know what was the truth in the fragments of information which they read in the Press. "Was it true," asked one of them, "that Palestine had been given back to the Jews?" The Under-Secretary knew nothing. Even the Ministries in London had been included in the zone of silence radiating from the Italian littoral. To be obliging, he said now that certainly he would telegraph to Italy to find out from the delegates whether Press statements were true.

But then the delegates returned to England. On the 29th of April Mr. Lloyd George at last indicated to the House that "the Mandate for Palestine has been given to Great Britain with a full recognition of the famous Balfour Declaration in respect of the Jews." The ticklish moment passed without a supplementary question. The speaker of course did not explain *how* the Mandate had been given, and when pressed for details of its terms would not supply them, declaring that "he did not think this desirable till they were submitted to the Turks."

Lord Cecil followed, saying how satisfied he was that "it was now finally and definitely settled that the Palestine Mandate was going to this country. The Mandatory," he warned members, "will have exceedingly complex racial questions to solve." This phrase of Lord Cecil's deserves the same consideration as that given to its predecessors: innocent in appearance, it was extremely misleading. If another man had used it, he could be accused of deliberate begging of the question. But Lord Cecil, of course, would not be culpable of anything more than *petitio principii.* In this elegant and classic pursuit he was now engaged, giving to his hearers the impression that as Mandatory Great Britain was about to take over a duty more tangled than she guessed, that Palestine was a land fraught with innate, intricate national problems. Whereas Palestine had been a country free of any such problems till men of Lord Cecil's way of thinking decided to introduce them. In a country where 91 percent of the population was of one race, complexity of racial problems was a contradiction in terms.

Meanwhile, in Palestine itself, Sir Louis Bols on the 1st of May read to a gathering at Nablus the terms of the Balfour Declaration. It was the first time that the words of Balfour and Milner and Wise and Sokolov and de Haas and uncle Tolkowsky and all had been communicated officially to the Arabs, two and a half years after its publication in London. After the news from San Remo and the House of Commons statement, the Chief Administrator judged that it might as well be published. A gentlemanly version of what it might mean, put forth in Palestine by Sir Herbert Samuel, had led the General to believe that it would be interpreted in some fairly tolerable fashion. His scruples were rather more at rest about it, and the die was cast in any event, so he thought that the Arabs had better hear what was before them.

Sir Louis Bols, however, was as near the end of his patience as he was of his office. He could no longer stand the behaviour of the Zionist Commission. This junta knew now that the Military Administration was on its last legs, or was to be bundled out whether its legs were sound or shaky, and in consequence treated the Administration with ever-increasing contempt. The Commission sent absolute orders to the Governorate.

> Our attention [ran one such] has been drawn to the fact that of late several Jewish candidates for the gendarmerie have been accepted without recommendation from or reference to this Commission. We take the liberty to point out that it is the wish of the Zionist Commission that all candidates should pass through their hands. Their credentials should be scrutinized by us so that we may be certain that only the right men are finally presented to you for acceptance. Only by this method can the Zionist Commission be able to exercise an indirect [sic] control and be in any way responsible for the efficiency of the Jewish gendarmes. We feel certain that you will appreciate the validity of this argument and express your agreement with the desirability of the principle we submit—namely, that no Jewish candidate be accepted who does not bear a recommendation from this Commission.

This missive was signed by Mr. Max Nurock, then Secretary of the Zionist Commission, and presently to be awarded with a post as Assistant Secretary in Government House, under the civil regime. What is more, Sir Louis Bols found that he was unable to escape these orders sent by Mr. Nurock. He had to comply, though, as he said, " Many excellent Jewish recruits, Palestinians of the best type, object to the authority of the Zionist Commission in this matter, and have thereby been lost to the force."

He had also to cope with insubordination from secret agents of the Criminal Investigation Department which had been set up by the Zionist Commission, with violent attacks, in the Commission-controlled Hebrew newspapers, upon schools where English was the language of instruction, and with a number of similar abuses. Complaints against his Administration, laid or backed by the Commission, were without end. His summing-up of these complaints was pithy.

> The complaints against the present Administration [said Sir Louis Bols] fall under two heads:
>
> 1. Unfair discrimination against the Jews.
> 2. Failure to give preference to the Jews.

During the riots in Jerusalem, the climax was reached in a letter sent to the General by M. Ussischkin and M. Yellin, who represented Jerusalem Jews. This was an absolute ultimatum, asserting that Sir Louis Bols's promises of protection for the community were not being kept, and declaring that if within two hours their safety were not completely assured and their protection fully guaranteed, the Jewish population would "find themselves forced to realize that they cannot leave their fate in the hands of others, and will as one man rise to defend themselves and their brothers who are being maltreated and murdered before their eyes."

Sir Louis Bols's comment upon this was,

> "I cannot allocate the blame [for the riots] to any section of the community or to individuals while their case is still *sub judice*, but I can definitely state that when the strain came the Zionist Commission did not loyally accept the orders of the Administration, but from the commencement adopted a hostile, critical and abusive attitude. It is a regrettable fact that with one or two exceptions it appears impossible to convince a Zionist of British good faith and ordinary honesty. They seek, not justice from the military occupant, but that in every question in which a Jew is interested discrimination shall be shown in his favour. They are exceedingly difficult to deal with. In Jerusalem, being in the majority, they are not satisfied with military protection, but demand to take the law in their own hands. In other places where they are in a minority they clamour for military protection."

Just after the Conference had opened at San Remo the Chief Administrator sent home a considered statement of the whole case, of which the conclusions are memorable. After detailing various of the acts of the Commission which have been quoted, he went on:

> "It will be recognized from the foregoing that my own authority and that of every department of my Administration is claimed or impinged upon by the Zionist Commission, and I am definitely of opinion that this state of affairs cannot continue without grave danger to the public peace and to the prejudice of my Administration.
>
> It is no use saying to the Moslem and Christian elements of the population that our declaration as to the maintenance of the status quo on our entry into Jerusalem has been observed. Facts witness otherwise: the introduction of the Hebrew tongue as an official language; the setting-up of a Jewish judicature; the whole fabric of Government of the Zionist Commission, of which they are well aware; the special travelling privileges to members of the Zionist Commission; these have firmly and absolutely convinced the non-Jewish elements of our partiality. On the other hand the Zionist Commission accuses me and my officers of anti-Zionism. The situation is intolerable, and in justice to my officers and myself must be fairly faced.
>
> This Administration has loyally carried out the wishes of His Majesty's Government, and has succeeded in so doing by strict adherence to the laws governing the conduct of the Military Occupant of Enemy Territory, but this has not satisfied the Zionists, who appear bent on committing the temporary Military Administration to a partialist policy before the issue of the Mandate. It is manifestly impossible to please partisans who officially claim nothing more than a "National Home," but in reality will

be satisfied with nothing less than a Jewish State and all that it politically implies.

I recommend therefore, in the interests of peace, of development, of the Zionists themselves, that the Zionist Commission in Palestine be abolished."

Sir Louis Bols was a brave man to write in these frank terms and to dare to make such a recommendation. His words remain to establish the obduracy of the Home Government, its trick of what may be called lying-with-the-eyes, by refusing to contemplate the truth, and its determination upon the very course of which the injustice was exposed by the Chief Administrator in his memorandum. "The Zionists, he had said, "appear bent on committing the temporary Military Administration to a partialist policy before the issue of the Mandate." On what else was the Cabinet now bent than on committing a temporary Administration to a partialist policy before the issue of the Mandate? The proof of its guilt is absolute.

In the light of his experience, Sir Louis Bols, though, hardly can have expected any attention to be paid to his supreme recommendation. Yet he had studied the point and had drawn up a scheme for the creation of an advisory Jewish Council, attached to his Administration and under his orders, which would have replaced the Zionist Commission. So that his proposal was no mere vent to his own feelings. He wrote it, one fancies, as his political testament, to stay on record for those who came after. That is how it stands today, and, not for the first time in our history, makes the reputation of a British soldier where statesmen have lost theirs.

There is no record, to my knowledge, of any reply to Bols's memorandum. Whether it went to San Remo or not is also unrecorded, though I am inclined to believe that it did go there, and that it contributed to Mr. Lloyd George's decision to get rid of the Military Administration as quickly as possible. It would be no surprise to learn indeed that General Bols's words were what prompted him to remark to Dr. Weizmann that what was wanted in Palestine were men who really cared for the "National Home."

That remark spoke of the native assurance of its utterer, beneath all the caution and doubts which restrained his official speech. And when the embarrassments attending the assumption of the Mandate had thus far gone unnoted, when the House of Commons duly had applauded his brisk little statement announcing it, Mr. Lloyd George presently must have been pretty contented. Perhaps he was a little too contented. In any event the shock which Providence so often reserves for complacent content was at hand.

It seems unbelievable that there should be occasion to relate a check now to the all but unobstructed advance of the Ziono-Governmental plans. One does not expect a reversal of current in full stream. During some five years those plans had suffered but one setback, due to the enlightened Jews who in 1915 had tried to stem political Zionism. They had restrained it from immediately arbitrary acts, but that was all they could achieve. Their warmest words had been left to get hotter with disconsideration and to boil themselves away.

True, there had been also an adverse Cabinet decision, but Balfour himself had treated this affair as little more than an accident. He would see that the Cabinet's decision was reversed speedily. So it was, too. Balfour spoke to the culprits, and that was that, with complete identity of demonstratives.

Thenceforward, as readers will have seen, the whole plot went forward steadily to its accomplishment. Hindrances of any kind, reports, memoranda, Arab outcries, were circumvented or treated as non-existent. They all came from persons or from bodies that could be ignored with safety. No one had moved amidst the few, individuals or States, powerful enough to stand in the way of the plotters. All who had power were deceived or were indifferent to what passed in Palestine, or were engrossed elsewhere.

But now, all at once, a powerful marplot did stand forth, the most powerful of all, the United States. The United States unhappily were not interested in the Arabs' rights, now that the interlude of the Crane-King Commission was over. Not Messrs. Crane and King, but the Brandeis regime reigned securely in Washington. The United States, though, were deeply interested in their own rights in the Near East, or were deeply interested in the scheme of universal rights created by the Covenant, in which they felt that they owned perhaps a founder's share.

The American Republic was touched, in a way which no one at San Remo had envisaged, by an item of the proceedings there. The trouble arose out of the second of the achievements of our own delegation, mentioned at the start of this chapter, the oil-arrangement concluded with France, by which the Mosul output was to be divided *pro rata* between Great Britain and France. This, together with the news of the "assignment" of the Mandates, had been notified to the United States as to other countries, and the affair had seemed finished.

But on the 12th of May the United States Ambassador, Mr. John W. Davis, presented a note to the Foreign Office. After acknowledging receipt of the San Remo notifications, he went on to observe that the Government of the United States consistently took up the position that the future peace of the world required that as a general principle any alien territory which should be acquired pursuant to the Treaties of Peace with the Central Powers must be held and governed in such a way as to assure equal treatment in law and in fact to the commerce of all countries.

The representatives of the Principal Allied Powers [Mr. Davis pointed out] in the discussion of the Mandate principles, expressed in no indefinite manner their recognition of the justice and far-sightedness of such a principle, and agreed to its application to the Mandates over Turkish territory.

In crude oil terms, the United States objected to the Anglo-French monopoly which had been established at San Remo. Later on, in the course of the Ambassador's longish note, he indulged in some light sarcasm about authoritative reports of work going on in Mesopotamia preliminary to oil-production and about the permitted researches of certain individuals whose activities, though stated to be wholly on behalf of the civil administration, were attended by circumstances which created the impression that some benefit at least would accrue to British oil-interests.

Coming to business, the note demanded that:

> "... no exclusive economic concessions, covering the whole of any mandated region or sufficiently large to be virtually exclusive, shall be granted. It is believed that the establishment of monopolies by or on behalf of the Mandatory Government would not be consistent with the principles of trusteeship inherent in the Mandatory idea."

The note ended with a request for an early expression of the views of His Majesty's Government.

This United States note was double edged. It could mean interference with the plans for "reconstruction" of Palestine which were in the front drawers of the Zionist Organization's desk. The reader will remember the monopolies which had been a feature of Zionist memoranda, from that of October 1916 onward. Their schemes still embraced such monopolies.

But it was not this edge which made the United States note immediately wounding. Nor was the interference with the oil arrangements themselves so very distressful. Over both questions the Foreign Office could be trusted to argue with its wonted ability. The real cause of immediate anxiety was the fact that there would have to be argument at all, since arguments meant the taking of time, and delay perhaps to the Mandate. So far the attitude of the United States towards the Turkish Treaty had been that of an interested spectator. The note handed in by Mr. Davis held suggestions of a change from outside interest to interference in the proceedings.

Quite suddenly therefore the Prime Minister and his Cabinet were faced by the sight of something in the distance which looked like a traffic control tower, in the midst of the road along which they had meant to speed. The prospect was unnerving, and all the more so since the surface of the road itself on which they were travelling was growing increasingly uneven. The differences between Mustapha Kemal in Anatolia and the

Turkish Government in Constantinople were widening. Kemal's grip on the Anatolian provinces, the body of Turkey, was growing very firm, and the power of the Ottoman Administration to act for Turkey grew weaker and weaker. The prospects of a May treaty, for this and for other reasons, already had vanished.

This was the start of an unhappy period in the home-life of Whitehall. On the brink of success, when the long-meditated scheme for installing Zionism in Palestine was about to come into action, things suddenly went askew. It was a surprise, though it should not have been one, considering the scheme's moral flimsiness. But undoubtedly the Mandate business was turning into a first-class dilemma. Mr. Lloyd George was bound to his Zionist friends to establish civil Administration immediately, while the right to establish it kept flitting further and further from his grip.

He was trying to act in one way towards the Arabs of Mesopotamia and in another way towards the Arabs of Palestine, in spite of the identical pledge which covered his conduct in both lands. He was brandishing the 1918 proclamation in Mesopotamia and tearing it to pieces in Syria, though it covered and had been proclaimed for all Arab territory from the Taurus to the Persian Gulf. When to these troubles were added those others which sprang from the growing ascendancy of Mustapha Kemal in Turkey and from the prospect of American interference with all his Near Eastern hopes, it was not surprising that the situation got rather beyond his management.

Statements and replies to questions in the House of Commons became less uniform. Volubility crept in: there are times when two words are voluble. Other Cabinet Ministers and Undersecretaries made announcements, not always using the Premier's wave length. He himself veered about: in one part of a speech he spoke as though the Government had been invested with the Mandate, and later on in the same discourse as though the Mandate was yet to come.

Possibly this looseness of vocabulary was accelerated by the apparent inability of the country to grasp what the Government was doing. It did not seem to matter much what you said. When the real facts were given, the impossibilities and the contradictions of the policy thus revealed seemed to go unnoticed. There did not appear to be much object therefore in shrouding these facts, or in beating about the bush. Mr. Bonar Law, Privy Seal and Leader of the House, who gave several important replies, rejected bush-beating from the start.

So the next few months saw some statements made about the Turkish Treaty and the Mandate which should have been collected together and placarded on walls and doors throughout the British Isles.

Mr. Bonar Law led off with the most startling statement of all. Asked in the House of Commons whether no definite acceptance of the Mandate would be undertaken without the assent of Parliament, he answered quite calmly, "The assent of Parliament is not required for the acceptance of a Mandate."

Astounding as this declaration was, the more astounding thing is that the House seems to have put up with it. The Lord Privy Seal after making it threw a sop to Members by adding that "doubtless an opportunity will occur for discussing the situation in Palestine in connection with the Turkish Treaty, out of which the proposal arises." To which Commander Kenworthy replied by pointing out that the expenses for the Mandate must surely come before the House. Then, appealingly, "does not that in fact give us the right to decide?"

"Very likely," said the Privy Seal with a fine indifference, "but there were no expenses in connection with the matter," and yawning (I suppose) resumed his seat. The Commons of England said no more. No one asked by whose authority Parliament was deprived of its prerogative of assent. No one asked—since *someone* must have assented to the Mandate for it to have been accepted—who had assented instead of Parliament. No one asked who was in a position to act for Great Britain, for the whole British Empire, without parliamentary control being applied to his acts.

The position leaves one at a loss for adequate comment. If Mr. Bonar Law had said that the assent of Parliament was not required just yet, that would have been bad enough. But what was this compared with his comprehensive declaration, made so off-handedly, that Britain could be saddled with the government of a foreign land without the consent of the Legislature. Parliament never would have a chance of voting for or against upon the sole issue. "Doubtless," as Mr. Bonar Law had said, in some indirect fashion, when opportunity occurred for discussion, "in connection with the Turkish Treaty," as he vaguely had phrased it—doubtless then if they were willing to reject an entire Peace Treaty, the Commons could assert themselves and reject the Mandate along with the Treaty.

But that did not remove the interference with Parliamentary supremacy. An act of enormous political importance could be begun, and could continue for an unspecified time, accumulating crises, involving the forces of the Crown, effacing the rights of a people, without Parliament being able to prevent it. Without Parliament being able to prevent it even when, as in the present instance of Palestine, the act meant at once the setting-up of a so-called civil Government which had no legal warrant behind it and for three years was to involve King, Lords and Commons in unauthorized legislation.

Early in June Mr. Lloyd George began to sink deep into contradictions. On the 7th he declared that there would be no decision upon the future Administration of Mesopotamia till the Peace Treaty with Turkey had been signed and "the Mandates settled." A proper legal view. But that very same day he announced the appointment of Sir Herbert Samuel as the first High Commissioner of Palestine, at the head of the Civil Government to be established there forthwith. So in Palestine the Administration was not to wait till the Peace Treaty in Turkey had been signed and "the Mandates settled." He made the appointment knowing well now that the Peace Treaty was not in measurable sight, confessing to the House of Commons in answer to a question, "I am not sure when the Peace Treaty will be signed."

A fortnight went by. Sir Herbert Samuel was on his way to Jerusalem. At long last a Member of Parliament put a pertinent query. It was Mr. Wedgwood Benn, whose solitary intervention entitles him today to much respect. "Are we to understand that the Mandate has already been settled in Palestine?" he demanded. "No," answered Mr. Bonar Law, in the simplest Doric style, though not a month before Mr. Lloyd George, standing by the same dispatch-box, had announced, "The Mandate for Palestine has been given to Great Britain."

"Then how can you appoint a Governor?" cried Mr. Wedgwood Benn, with irresistible reason. Mr. Bonar Law became aggrieved. "You must take," he said, "preliminary steps to set up a Civil Administration. I should have thought that that was desirable from every point of view." Alas, Mr. Benn failed now. He might have scored a triumphant hat-trick by one more question. Perhaps it was not his fault, perhaps the rules of the House prevent three probing questions in a row to a Minister.

However that be, he let the opportunity pass. He might have indicated that the very cause of his anxiety was that the preliminary steps of which Mr. Bonar Law spoke were coming to an end. How was it legal, he should have asked, for the Government to bring preliminaries to an end, and to embark on the Administration itself? To this question there would have been no answer, whatever were uttered in lieu of one. Assuredly the confession would not have been made that the civil Administration was being set up, legally or illegally, in accordance with a miserable compact, in order to oust the Army and to introduce the "National Home" into the Holy Land.

Two days later, though, Mr. Lloyd George was in a sense to rub this in upon his own conscience, which however withstood the friction. During a full-dress debate on Mesopotamia he described Great Britain correctly as "designate Mandatory of the Powers," and explained that the legal document under which the Mandate came to her was, or would be, the Turkish Treaty. "As far as the legal document is concerned, the legal document will be the Turkish Treaty. Under the Turkish Treaty we shall be receiving the Mandate from the Allied and Associated Powers. We shall have both a moral and a legal right to this position." He used the future tense. In the present tense he was without legal or moral right to the position.

Meanwhile in the House of Lords Earl Curzon too struggled with the subject of the Mandates. On the 25th he spoke of Mesopotamia, but in places his words applied to Palestine. The Government, he said, had declared that "there would be no annexation of any of these territories by Great Britain. It is the object of His Majesty's Government to set up an Arab Government or Governments of the liberated areas and not to impose on the populations any Government which is not acceptable to them."

He said, too, with a simple honesty, "We, as the party principally concerned, have been engaged in drawing it (the Mandate) up ourselves." He described procedure for laying the resulting document before the League of Nations, and continued,

> Under this draft-Mandate Article 1 provides for the framing of an Organic Law. An Organic Law is really a synonym for the future Constitution of the country, and the phrase employed is as follows:
>
> "This Organic Law shall be framed in consultation with the native authorities, and shall take account of the rights, interests and wishes of all populations inhabiting a Mandated area."

Admirable, and the reader perhaps may look for this Organic Law in the Palestine Mandate. He will have long to look before he finds it. Other people were drawing up draft Mandates besides Lord Curzon, if indeed Lord Curzon himself was allowed to draw anything up at all, and their influence was far greater than his. Article 1 of the Mandate now reads: "The Mandatory shall have full powers of legislation and of administration, save as they may be limited by the terms of this Mandate." Nor will the reader find any mention of consultation with native authorities in any part of the Palestine Mandate. Organic Laws indeed!

Afterwards Lord Curzon spoke directly of Palestine. He said that we had gone into Palestine first for military reasons, to protect the flank of Egypt. "My Lords, our interest in Palestine never has been, and I venture to say, never ought to be measured in terms of £. s. d. It certainly has not been the view from which Englishmen have ever looked at Palestine, from Cœur de Lion to the present day." This was said of course long before any of our Insurance Companies began to take a benevolent interest in the development of Zionist industry in the land of the Crusades.

Lord Curzon went on to consider the military value of that land. Lord Lamington, who had spoken earlier, had questioned this, and Curzon now suggested that if Lamington were to ask the authorities at the War Office what they thought about it, he would not find that they agreed with him.

> If he went to the War Office and put the proposition in this form: "Would you, the authorities at the War Office, be willing to see another Power, and possibly a hostile Power, in the future in possession of Palestine? Would you consider your position safe in Egypt in these circumstances?", I doubt if he would get an affirmative reply.
>
> However that may be [Lord Curzon continued], we were drawn into Palestine for military reasons, and conquered Turkey, and there then remained the question—what was to be done? Broadly speaking, the question which we had to put to ourselves was, "Should we go?" I do not know whether it is a tribute to our sincerity or to our powers, but nobody wanted us to go. Everybody insisted on our remaining.... It was as the result of the practically unanimous request of all parties that we, by no means eagerly or joyously but very reluctantly, accepted a Mandate for Palestine which we could not refuse.

The attitude which Lord Curzon describes in that last sentence of his may be credited to him, read it as we may with the wryest of smiles. He was about the only man in Governmental circles who could have taken over the Mandate with such motives, and it is to be supposed that he believed that these motives prevailed amidst his colleagues. He was singularly out of touch with the Prime Minister.

In a later part of his speech he broached the Arab-Zionist question, and here he too propounded the customary fallacies about the wealth, the enterprise, the resources and the fervent spirit of the Zionists being necessary for the "development" of Palestine.

But I have no quarrel with Lord Curzon, a lonely figure handling phrases and projects not of his world with courteous lack of inquiry into their credentials. It did not occur to him to doubt them: presently he was assuring his hearers that "indiscriminate mass-immigration, whether of Jews or of non-Jews from Russia or from other parts of the world, will most certainly not be permitted."

It was on the 29th of June that he made his speech. The following day was the last day of the Army Administration of Palestine. I am not sure whether Sir Louis Bols, and his Chief of Staff, Colonel Waters-Taylor (a great bugbear to the Zionist Commission), remained to the end to hand over the government formally, but I fancy they did not. Mr. Horace Samuel says that shortly after the Mandate was conferred at San Remo "the heads of the Chief Administrator and his Chief of Staff were duly served up on chargers for the edification of the French and the Zionists." I have heard too, from an officer then serving at Headquarters, that by one of those accidents with which Fate relieves the monotony of its duties the first intimation the Chief Administrator received that his reign was closed was not the official announcement from the Home Government, which tarried. His first tidings were a personal cable from Sir Herbert Samuel, running "Anxious retain services your cook," or words to that effect.

Whether Sir Louis Bols outlasted his cook or not, his Administration was terminated. Mr. Horace Samuel, a writer always anxious to put his case fairly, as befits one who was a judge in the military courts, makes some general comment upon Sir Louis Bols and his Chief-of-Staff at the moment of this *(de facto)* termination which merits to be quoted. It enshrines, in the few sentences I take from it, the criticisms most frequently made against the Military Administration.

The two officers, says Mr. Samuel, were not unreasonably blamed by the Zionists for the riots of the preceding Passover. Not that these officers, he is careful to observe, "in any way exhorted the Arabs to start attacking the Jews. What, however, they did do, and what was certainly open to challenge, was to make every Arab realize that it was absolutely an open question whether a Zionist or an Arab policy was to be eventually adopted; to allow the impression to be spread broadcast that the actual Administration favoured an Arab policy, and that the policy of Great Britain could be deflected by the requisite amount of vim and determination."

This charge, or half-charge, does nothing to injure the name of those against whom it is brought. On the contrary, it enhances their reputation. The writer who brings it leaves out of consideration the legitimacy of the policy which he would have had them adopt with decision. Yet this is a factor which cannot be ignored. The Administration in Palestine was faced with the soldier's duty of observing the laws of war and of military occupation. It could not adopt a course which meant abrogating or altering these regulations because these did not fit in with the policy of Mr. Lloyd George and of Lord Balfour. This policy, as a matter of fact, had not been properly disclosed to members of the Administration. But had it been disclosed to them, they still would not have been able to carry it into effect and would have been obliged to point out to the Home Government that it contravened the laws under which their Administration must act.

The Government thereon, it is possible to conceive, would have had the resource of application to The Hague for absolution from observance of the established military code in Palestine. It is doubtful, though, whether a tribunal, of which the duty is only to interpret laws, could have so absolved the Government, which would have been under the necessity therefore of reassembling an International Congress to re-enact regulations for military occupation of enemy territory. So there was little chance of legalization of Government policy.

Thus, as things were, the soldiers had no choice—if they had had any other desire—but to be fair to the Arabs, not to prejudge the future by predicating the adoption of any given line of action, and above all not to present the policy of the Home Government as one which could not be altered, when well-founded protestations were made against it with "vim and determination."

As for "allowing the impression to be spread broadcast that the actual Administration favoured an Arab policy," Mr. Samuel need not have spoken of a mere impression. The Administration *did* favour an Arab policy, in the sense that it was fighting all the time to maintain the rights of the Arabs against the improper Zionist pretensions. Upon this point there is an important rider which may well be introduced here before the subject of the conduct of the Army in Palestine is left.

Various Zionist controversialists, with their usual skill, when dealing with this matter, do not so much blame or attack the Army as write regretfully of its ignorance and its lack of comprehension. They say that the Army never really grasped the merits of Zionism, or "only half understood the Balfour Declaration " (Leonard Stein) or did not appreciate the policy of the "National Home." The suggestion is that if only the Army had not been quite so dull, it would have perceived the value of all these things, and then would have thrown all its weight upon the Zionist side or at the very least have shown itself entirely sympathetic to Zionist claims.

Now the truth is that far from not grasping or only half-understanding or not appreciating Zionist policy, the British Army in Palestine grasped and appreciated it and understood it all too well. That is the absolute clue to the Army's attitude.

Nor was the Army a dull body, drilling unappreciatively through life. It had eyes and ears and used these organs. It was composed of a sound average body of British citizens. Sir Ronald Storrs records that "apart from a few professional soldiers our administrative and technical staff included a cashier of a Rangoon bank, an actor-manager, two of Messrs. Cook's assistants, a picture-dealer, an Army-coach, a clown, a land-valuer, a boat-swain, a distiller, an organist, a cotton-broker, various architects, British civil-servants, a taxi-driver, two schoolmasters and a missionary." This was the staff of his Governate, inherited from the Army, a sample of the diversity of the whole military body.

The Army, therefore—and this is what is so important—was the sole large category of average British citizens which had direct access to the facts of the so-called "Palestine problem," the sole such category which had encountered Zionism in Palestine and had experienced what it meant. It was the sole such category which was aware of the Arabs' true situation, which knew that they were not the fantastically dubbed "non-Jewish community" which the home politicians called them, but the people of the land of Palestine, whose native rights had been guaranteed and now were about to be betrayed. The humblest of private soldiers possessed a first-hand acquaintance with the realities of the subject which was denied to the united faculties of all the learned societies of the British Isles. Those privates' commanders, the authorities of the military administration, had a knowledge of the subject which the Prime Minister and other Cabinet Ministers of Great Britain had not acquired, and indeed had steadfastly refused to obtain.

So the undoubted fact that the Army in all its ranks was, with the fewest exceptions, anti-Zionist, that hostile catchwords borrowed from the Arabs, such as "*Yehoudi Mushquais!*" ("Jews no good!") were on the lips of the soldiers, that, as the Zionist Executive complained, "jeers and gibes at the Zionists, at the Jewish colonies, at the Commission, were heard in every officers' mess from Dan to Beersheba," is but the most convincing proof that officers and men were alert to what was going on around them. They reacted, more earnestly than politely, against the great wrong planned in the interests of the "National Home" against the population amidst which they lived. Their estimation of the wrong may be traced in their behaviour. It takes something phenomenal to cause the easy-going British soldier, who never even hates his foes, to turn to gibes and to jeers.

One of the least politically minded units amid all our institutions, our Army when it gives attention to politics must have a very powerful reason to impel it. In Palestine it had one, and the lesson of its espousal of the Arabs' cause is instructive beyond anything. There never will be a better proof of the justice of that cause than this favour shown to it by the one mass of ordinary Britons who came into contact with it and knew more than any other persons about it. As the Army at that time was constituted, its soldiers sprang from every class and were of every type of the British people, and the whole evidence was before them. In a way, they were empanelled by their presence upon the scene, and it was in a great trial by jury that they returned their verdict of "Guilty" upon Zionism as practised in Palestine.

Chapter 22

The first High Commission of Palestine.—Sir Herbert Samuel. The Prime Minister's equivocation.—The Treaty of Sèvres. The Covenant again violated.—The farcical frontier of Palestine. President Wilson's "bomb-shell" letter.

The Civil Administration of Palestine began on the 1st of July. Need it be said, the appointment of Sir Herbert Samuel as High Commissioner was a blow to the Arabs. That a man of Jewish blood should be placed at the head of the Government surpassed their fears.

The leading Zionists, too, made small secret of their predominant part in securing the nomination of the first High Commissioner. As time went on, they made no secret at all. In a discourse in the United States the following year Dr. Weizmann declared, "I was mainly responsible for the appointment of Sir Herbert Samuel to Palestine. Sir Herbert Samuel is our friend. At our request he accepted that difficult position. We put him in that position. He is our Samuel."

Dr. Weizmann spoke then, in an exuberant mood to an exultant gathering. Towards the close of Sir Herbert Samuel's term of office, a different kind of announcement is attributed to Dr. Weizmann. It may have been fathered upon him; it may really have been one of the American Zionists who said it. Whoever said it, it was uttered in a less satisfied mood, and declared that Sir Herbert Samuel was 110 percent British.

This showed that Sir Herbert had not altogether satisfied the Zionist Warwicks who had brought him to the High Commissioner's dais, and the occasion of the remark will have been some refusal of his to be 110 percent Zionist. There is no doubt that the best item in the new Administration that July was its chief. He brought to his duties a conscientiousness which impressed all those who came into contact with him.

During his term of office, though it served to introduce the forcible imposition of Jews from Eastern Europe upon the soil of Palestine, he remained a curb upon extreme action by local Zionists, threw his influence against dumping of great numbers of immigrants at once, and did what he could to make the Arabs regard him as a close friend. Considering his public task, this last endeavour was an impossibility. But he did, I think, win a large meed of respect from the Arabs, and continues to hold it.

As High Commissioner of Palestine and protector of the "National Home" his presence could only be unrelished by them. But as Herbert Samuel they found him a good-hearted man, a zealous administrator, and that marked rarity, a Zionist with scruples. His mission was bound to fail, for he was sent out as the Head of a permanently premature Government, and his own role, whether he realized it or not, was that of a large juicy apple on top of a basket of rotten policy. But even Sir Herbert Samuel could not conceal the rest of the fruit from its unwilling purchasers.

All who have concerned themselves with the affairs of Palestine will pay their tribute to his merits. One thing particularly distinguished him during his term of office: he was willing to learn. He has not ceased to learn. The modification of his views, as years have passed, is best demonstrated by his speech in the House of Lords in the June of 1937, condemning the Government's proposals for Partition. It is true that he envisaged a wealthy, industrial Palestine, produced with the full co-operation of the Zionist movement as it is. Whereas the real role of Palestine, or of an Arab Confederation containing Palestine, will be to abjure wealth and much industry and most of what is called "modern progress." But for all that, his speech showed how he had thought and how he had profited by experience.

Almost at once Sir Herbert Samuel in July of 1920 was to give proof of his scrupulous conscience. His new Administration had to be staffed for the most part by officers hitherto belonging to the military Government. Demobilized, they re-entered service in Palestine as civilians under the Colonial Office. Clearly, till new cadres could be trained and ordinary Civil Service entries drafted to Palestine, there had to be this arrangement. On the whole these ex-officers brought to the new regime the attitude of the old, which conflicted with official policy, so that a number of them were weeded out in the course of the next few years. They had seized the chance of continuing work which they liked, and they had not given much thought to the change, or had not realized the difficult situations in which they would be placed.

But there was one at least who had meditated upon the altered conditions, and before re-engaging in the Palestine service he asked to be received by Sir Herbert Samuel. He was a senior officer, whose rank entitled him to this consideration, Colonel E. L. Popham. He had been one of three Assistant Administrators at Military Headquarters, and was acting as Governor of Jerusalem and of the surrounding district at the time of the change-over, while Sir Ronald Storrs was in temporary general charge. He now said to the Chief Administrator that as the new Government had been announced as adopting the establishment and advancement of the

"National Home" under the Balfour Declaration as a basis of its future policy, he felt that before taking service under it he should know to what he was bound. Would Sir Herbert be able to start his Administration with an intimation to the people that the "National Home" excluded any idea of Jewish governmental control at any time over Palestine?

Sir Herbert Samuel replied very straightforwardly at once. "I regret," he said, "that I cannot reassure you about this. The policy of His Majesty's Government, which I have come out to execute, is to encourage the immigration of Jews until a point shall be reached—it may be fifty or even a hundred years hence—at which their interests shall be sufficiently predominant to warrant the establishment of Jewish government in Palestine."

Sir Herbert had offered, very understandingly, a way out of his dilemma to the soldier whose faithfulness to principle he will have appreciated. He suggested that since the Jewish State might only be formed in the distant future, the chances therefore of the Governor having anything to do with its actual instalment were very remote.

But this way of looking at the situation did not dissipate the scruples of his hearer, who had his own reasons also for believing that the creation of the Jewish State might not be so very distant. He had had a conversation some while before with Dr. Weizmann, during which the latter had tried to win him over to the Zionist side. To this end Dr. Weizmann had insisted particularly on the military safeguard to the Suez Canal which would be constituted by a Jewish State, an argument which would have had no meaning if the said State or Commonwealth were not to be founded till forty or fifty or a hundred years on. The argument evidently presumed the installation of the State with the least possible delay.

So Colonel Popham thanked Sir Herbert Samuel, but resigned his position as Governor there and then, and went straight from the room where the interview had occurred to his own office, to put his resignation formally upon paper. Before he did so, however, he first wrote down at once the declaration of policy which had just been made to him by the High Commissioner, so that there might be no doubt about it. Colonel Popham now lives in South Africa, but I have been in correspondence with him, and it is from his own account of what happened that I quote.

It is of the highest interest to note the difference between Sir Herbert Samuel's frank avowal of governmental policy and Mr. Lloyd George's later endeavour to conceal it and, in so doing, to deny his own child.

Sir Herbert Samuel honestly acknowledged that the aim of the Government was to introduce Jews into Palestine till in the end there were enough of them to set up a Jewish State. As for what Mr. Lloyd George said, here is his evidence upon the point, given to the Peel Commission, and recorded, on page 24 of its Report. The passage deserves to be cited in text-books as a perfect example of equivocation.

> The idea was, and this was the interpretation put upon it at the time, that a Jewish State was not to be set up immediately by the Peace Treaty without reference to the wishes of the majority of the inhabitants. On the other hand, it was contemplated that when the time arrived for according representative institutions to Palestine, if the Jews had meanwhile responded to the opportunity afforded them by the idea of a national home and had become a definite majority of the inhabitants, then Palestine would thus become a Jewish commonwealth.

The right analyst for this statement would be a moral theologian, or perhaps Sir Bernard Spilsbury, but in their absence let us do our best. In general, what did it mean? It meant that while a Jewish majority of inhabitants in due time was to make of Palestine a Jewish State, yet an Arab majority of inhabitants must not at any time make of it an Arab State. The way in which this was concealed and a false air was conveyed of entire impartiality between Jews and Arabs is really very dexterous. The impression is given that first of all British policy was governed by the wishes of the Arabs, in deference to which no Jewish State was created. Reasonably therefore, after some time, the Jews would have their turn, and British policy would be governed by their wishes, which would be for the establishment of a Jewish State.

This study in practical deceit was the treatment which a Prime Minister of Great Britain contemplated for the Arab people in Palestine. Yet in his statement how thoroughly he conceals his part. To read it who would think that he and certain colleagues were entirely responsible for the entry of the Jews into Palestine? Who would think that he meant to deny their natural rights to the Arabs? Who would believe he had any responsibility for the calculated outnumbering of the Arabs by the Jews? He speaks, of events which he himself arranged, with complete detachment, as though he had nothing to do with them, as though the Jews fell into Palestine like the rain, by force of gravity, and he was a mere civil engineer observing and fitting his plans in with the climatic conditions imposed on him by Providence.

It is a pity that he is not the only detached observer of this type. But the Peel Report cites other prominent personages in the same class. "Lord (Robert) Cecil in 1917 and Mr. Winston Churchill in 1920," says the Report, "spoke or wrote in terms which could only mean that they contemplated the eventual establishment of a Jewish State." General Smuts was no better. His "contemplation" took the form of spurious prophecy. Speaking in Johannesburg in 1919, he "foretold an increasing stream of

Jewish immigration into Palestine and in generations to come a great Jewish State rising there once more." How false is this "foretelling." General Smuts, a prime agent in the introduction of the Zionist flood into Palestine, stood there like a lock-keeper with his hand on the lever of the sluice-gates, and foretold an increasing stream of Jewish immigration.

Nothing for many decades has been so wounding to a sense of national probity as the behaviour in relation to Palestine of these men, who were the first men of our day. By this behaviour they abstract their own figures from the small heaven of honest gods whom we have tried to revere. In whom are we to believe at all if they, who in other matters have earned our regard, yet in this matter so debase themselves by their hocus-pocus explanations and their prophecies of events which they themselves have ensured. At a time when the world is in such a parlous condition, when there is such a penury of strong minds and faithful hearts, none of us would wish to lose our faith in a Churchill or a Smuts, or in a Lloyd George in some of his aspects. Yet how can it be maintained in the face of the quibbles and the prevarications which I have just set down? What is to be said of Mr. Winston Churchill, with full knowledge that the policy of the Government—and his own policy—was the eventual production of a Jewish State, addressing the Arabs as he did? "When it is asked," said he in a too notorious official statement during his term as Colonial Secretary, "when it is asked what is meant by the development of the Jewish National Home in Palestine, it may be answered that it is not the imposition of a Jewish nationality upon the inhabitants of Palestine as a whole."

Whether Mr. Churchill wrote this explanation or not, he published it as his own, and he is responsible for it. What answer, what excuse has he to make for it? Did he satisfy his conscience by saying to himself when he spoke that Jews and Arabs were to form an amalgam in Palestine, that they were all to be "Palestinians" together, and that so they would not have to adopt Jewish nationality, though on his own showing they would cease to have Arab nationality. No other excuse than this is apparent, and it is a sorry one. Has Mr. Churchill any other? If he has any true excuse, he owes it to his otherwise great reputation to produce it now. If he has none, he must be left to bask amidst those terminological inexactitudes which Sir Herbert Samuel would not adopt on the threshold of his term of office.

As that term of office progressed, the situation in or out of Palestine did not improve. The Mandatory Government was physically established, but the terms of the Mandate, under which presumably it was to rule, remained undisclosed. Shortly after the inaugural ceremony in Jerusalem, Sir Philip Magnus, who had fought so hard against political Judaism, demanded in the House of Commons to know when would its terms be laid before the

House. He begged the Prime Minister not to let the Mandate be confirmed by the League of Nations before its terms had been so published.

Mr. Bonar Law, replying, could name no date for publication of the terms. This, he said, depended on the date of the Turkish Treaty. As for Sir Philip Magnus's plea that the Houses of Parliament should be made aware of the text of the Mandate before this was confirmed by the League, he answered coldly, "I do not see any advantage in adopting the course suggested." Once more Parliament was put in its place, and Parliament sat down in its place.

Soon afterwards Lord Balfour made a speech in the House of Lords which was to be much quoted. It was altogether in his best ingenuous manner. He said that he was not sure that he did not rate highest amidst the difficulties before Zionism "the inevitable difficulty of dealing with the Arab question as it presents itself within the limits of Palestine." (As one might say that the British question as it presented itself within the limits of England was an inevitable difficulty before immigration from abroad could swamp our island.)

Lord Balfour, continuing, trusted that the Arabs would remember that most especially it was Great Britain who had freed them from their brutal conqueror who had kept them under his heel for centuries, Great Britain who had established the sovereignty of the Hedjaz, Great Britain who was preparing the way in Mesopotamia for a self-governing Arab State. "And I hope that, remembering all this, they will not grudge that small notch—for it is no more geographically, whatever it may be historically—in what are now Arab territories being given to the people who for all these hundreds of years have been separated from it."

The small notch was the gate of the Mediterranean and the way out of the desert. A perfect example of Lord Balfour's distraction from facts of which he did not desire to remind himself.

In August Feisal, a king without a kingdom, came to Europe in response to the San Remo invitations. But the main event of that month was the abortive Peace Conference with Turkey, which was attended by the Ottoman delegates. A treaty actually was signed, but never was ratified, the so-called "Treaty of Sèvres." The text of the treaty had been sent to the Constantinople Government not long after the close of the San Remo Conference. It was a fit product of that Conference, the Sultan's delegates in San Remo not being allowed to query any of its clauses. "The Ottoman delegation," explained the *Temps* to its readers in late April, "only has the mission of receiving the Treaty and going back with it to Constantinople to submit it to discussion by the Council of the Empire." The Council itself was free to discuss it, but not to alter it.

Sir Harry Luke in his notable *Making of Modern Turkey* describes the character of the treaty and its effect upon the Turkish people:

> "The effect of the Treaty of Sèvres [he writes] to which the Sultan's Government had perforce given its signature, would have been to have handed Thrace to the Greeks, Eastern Anatolia to the Armenians, Adalia to the Italians and Cilicia to the French, with Constantinople as an international centre, while Turkey would have been deprived of her armed forces and would have ceased to be, save in name, an independent State."

On another page Sir Harry Luke writes of the peace terms, that the Government of Constantinople was:

> not allowed, however, to discuss them. Helpless, they [the Ottoman delegates] had no option but to sign, on the 10th August, the Treaty of Sèvres, whose only practical result, seeing that it implemented in part the secret inter-Allied arrangements giving Italy and France spheres of influence in certain regions of Asia Minor remaining in Turkish hands, was to drive those Turks who were still wavering between the Sultan and Mustapha Kemal into the arms of the latter. Beyond rousing Turkish patriotism still farther, the Treaty of Sèvres remained a dead letter, for by now the whole of Turkey not in Allied occupation was in Nationalist hands.

Mustapha Kemal in fact had already set up a formal new Government at Angora while the plenipotentiaries at San Remo were conning the hollow provisions upon which all of them, but none more than Mr. Lloyd George, hoped to build so high. There never was any hope of the treaty being ratified, as the Sultan's Parliament had been dissolved by him in April. His own authority hardly extended beyond Saint Sophia. Under these circumstances, even our own Government made no move to ratify the Treaty.

There would seem therefore to be no reason to concern ourselves here with the Treaty of Sèvres at all. Nor do I propose indeed to delay upon it. But I ask the reader to follow me for a page or two in an examination of the most important aspect of it. The particular clauses to be examined were stillborn like the rest of the treaty, but the intentions enshrined in them were maintained in the Mandate when it came, and they serve also to expose thoroughly the at once absurd and crooked doings at San Remo. What was done at San Remo found form in the Sèvres Treaty; what was written down and signed at Sèvres had been prepared and arranged in San Remo. The Sèvres Treaty too was meant by its makers to become law: it was their intention to govern Palestine and the rest of the Turkish Near East under its provisions. Therefore it is essential to disclose at the least the main character of these provisions, so that the conduct of the responsible parties may be exposed, much as in a court of law the preparations of an accused man for a deed, which some accident has prevented, are possibly a primary part of the evidence.

In the Treaty of Sèvres the fate of the Arab countries was detailed in a couple of clauses, 94 and 95. By clause 94 Mesopotamia and "Syria" were to be recognized, in accordance with the already famous Article *22* of the Covenant, as prospectively independent States, "subject to the rendering of administrative advice and assistance by a Mandatory till such time as they are able to stand alone."

This formula came, as we know, from the fourth clause or paragraph of Article 22, and was itself a shorter repetition of the gaudy phrases of paragraph 1 about the well-being of these as yet unstable States or peoples being a sacred trust of civilization, and so forth. The third paragraph said that "the character of the Mandate must differ according to the stage of development of the people, the geographical situation of the territory, its economic conditions and other similar circumstances."

The important thing about the fourth paragraph was that it specified the communities or peoples recently subject to Turkey as those which were ripe for provisional recognition of independence. The next two paragraphs, 5 and 6, classified the other Mandated peoples, in Africa and in the Pacific, as not ripe for this prospective independence. Those in paragraph 5 were to have the territories in which they lived administered by the Mandatory for them "under conditions which will guarantee freedom of religion and of conscience" and would prevent such abuses as the slave trade, the arms and the liquor traffic. The Negro peoples of Central Africa were especially envisaged by this paragraph. As for the sixth paragraph it concerned small, remote, sparsely populated places such as South-West Africa and some of the Isles of the Pacific. These, for various reasons, were to be administered as integral parts of the Mandatory's territory, with due safeguards for the interests of the native population.

These three paragraphs, 4, 5 and 6, developed paragraph 3.

Paragraph 3 said there would be Mandates of differing character according to the circumstances of the various cases.

Paragraphs 4, 5 and 6 explained that the need for differing Mandates would be met by having three classes of them, and specified which peoples were to belong to which classes.

This division into classes was made still clearer by the official application by the League of Nations of the first three letters of the alphabet to distinguish the three types of Mandate. This device was employed when Mandates first began to be drafted in 1919 and was adopted by the League. The ex-Turkish peoples were said to have A Mandates, the African and Pacific peoples B and C Mandates.

I trust this is quite clear. Because of their development and various attendant circumstances the peoples of Mesopotamia, "Syria" and Palestine received the A Mandates, given to the group of peoples who, in the words of Article 22 of the Covenant, had:

> "... reached a stage of development where their existence as independent nations can be provisionally recognized."

Under the circumstances, it would have been expected that the Treaty of Sèvres, which only dealt with this group, would have included the arrangements for all their political futures in one and the same clause. But no. Clause 94 only dealt with Mesopotamia and "Syria." Palestine was separated from its sisters and put into a separate clause by itself, clause 95. Mesopotamia and "Syria" in clause 94 had the requisite provisional independence duly allotted to them. Palestine, the remaining class A Mandated territory, did not receive it.

In clause 95, no mention of provisional independence was to be found. There was no word about Palestine being placed under the Mandatory's advisory tutelage pending the moment when she could stand alone. The Covenant was mentioned, but there was no single word in accordance with the Covenant in this clause, though it was in accordance with the Covenant that the Allies were sworn to make the Peace Treaty. Not one line, not one phrase was there from the Covenant. In place of it was an announcement concerning the Jewish National Home as follows:

> "The High Contracting Parties agree to entrust, by application of the provisions of the Covenant of the League of Nations, the administration of Palestine, within such boundaries as may be determined by the principal Allied Powers, to a Mandatory to be selected by the said Powers. The Mandatory will be responsible for putting into effect the declaration originally made on November the 2nd, 1917, by the British Government and adopted by the other Allied Powers, in favour of the establishment of a national Jewish Home, it being clearly understood that nothing shall be done... " [Then came the rest of the Balfour Declaration text.]

The above few lines with the Balfour Declaration text made up clause 95. An astounding piece of work, this clause 95. It spoke of applying the pro visions of Article 22 of the Covenant. But to say that it applied these provisions was a piece of colossal effrontery. Article 22 proposed provisional independence for the ex-Turkish peoples and said their wishes must be consulted in the choice of Mandatory, and said absolutely nothing else. Clause 95 arranged the establishment of the Jewish National Home, and arranged absolutely nothing else.

So that not merely did clause 95 *not* apply the provisions of Article 22, but it contravened them. Not merely did it fail to apply the terms of the Covenant, but it suppressed the Covenant for Palestine. It erased the words of Article 22 and put in their place the bastard Balfour Declaration, with its twenty fathers, a thing which had no place or status or part whatsoever in the Covenant, which had no connection in the world with the Covenant. And having carried out this substitution, the drafters of clause 95 ventured to say that they were applying the very provisions which they were removing. They tore Palestine from the protection of the Covenant which predicated its independence, thrust it under the Balfour Declaration which precluded its independence, and then dared to maintain that they were following the code which they had violated. Never has hypocrisy been so luscious: never has perjury worn a bolder face.

The reader sees that it has been only too worthwhile to examine into the intricacies of the Treaty of Sèvres. It is not surprising to learn that the Hedjaz delegate refused in the name of King Hussein to sign this dishonourable paper.

Besides being such a grave infraction of honour and of justice, the Treaty was grotesquely farcical in its treatment of Syria. Since clause 95 denied to South Syria the independence which clause 94 conceded to North Syria, under the rules of the game, as they were enounced officially, this could only be because North Syria was "able to stand by itself under the strenuous conditions of the modern world," but South Syria, Palestine, was not. This absurdity appears the more frolicsome when it is remembered that at the time there was no true frontier between North and South Syria. In fact the rest of 1920 was to be spent by the Zionist chiefs in trying to secure for the section of the country which was to become their National Home a frontier which would include the whole of the Yarmook valley, the headwaters of the Jordan, and generally in trying to get the upper boundary of Palestine put as near to the North Pole as possible.

The present 1938 frontier had to be artificially delimited by a Commission. In 1920 what was being used and proposed as a frontier was the line drawn on a map, in London or Paris, by Sir Mark Sykes and M. Picot four years before. These two gifted artist-geographers themselves would have been stunned to think that their humble and transitory pen mark was to prove an absolute demarcating line between the Syrians who were intelligent enough to rule themselves by and by, and the Syrians too feeble of mind for this privilege. The more so since those to the south of it, the Sykists, were brothers and cousins and kinsfolk of the Picotians to the north. Nor does absurdity even end there.

As the definite boundary was still unknown at the time of the Treaty, and indeed was being hotly debated with the French, a large class of hapless Syrians in the centre of the country, who might be apportioned to "Syria" in the north or just as well to Palestine in the south, were in a state of suspended capacity. If they were put in the north they came under clause 94 and would be worthy of self-government, if in the south they came under clause 95 and would not. Their personal development therefore, their degree of culture, their mental powers, all hung in the balance. They were to prove progressive or retrograde, ancient or modern, wild-eyed Asiatics or sagacious sons of the Mediterranean, according as Dr. Weizmann's demand for rivers and plains prospered with the experts of the French Government.

To the east of the Sea of Galilee and round Banyas and Metullah and such places the nervous tension of the inhabitants, if they came to know what was afoot, must have been extreme. The men of Tyre, fit for independence if the frontier was fixed below Tyre, unfit for independence if the frontier was drawn above, wakened every morning unaware whether, when night fell, they would be reflective citizens or dull innocents. Eventually, when the frontier was fixed and the great division was made, the Tyrians were recognized as persons able to stand alone prospectively, and so were the people of Banyas, though these latter only won the verdict of ability by, so to speak, the shortest of foreheads. On the other hand the inhabitants of Metullah, some twelve miles to the north-west of Banyas, proved to be incapable of self-government, being caught at the very tip of a wedge of sequestered incompetence which projected into North Syria.

That will do for the Treaty of Sévres. The particular scandalous manoeuvre of the plenipotentiaries at San Remo by which they withdrew Palestine from the operations of the Covenant failed through the demise of the treaty. They of course were not to be baulked by this, and shaped their plans in another way. But the failure of the treaty none the less placed the Prime Minister and his Government in the most awkward situation which yet had confronted them. This failure was evident by the time that September was half way through, and there were they with no Mandate for Palestine, with no prospect of obtaining one within sight, and yet with a "Mandatory" Government set up and perforce soon obliged to begin legislation.

What made everything worse was that the American menace had developed. Mr. Davis's ominous note of the 12th of May concerning economic monopolies and concessions in the prospective Mandatory areas had been left unanswered. I do not know whether private appeals had been made to the United States' Ambassador in the interval to settle the matter out of court, or whether mere pious hopes had been entertained that the

State Department would forget all about it. Appeals or hopes, they came to naught, for Mr. Davis returned to the charge with another note at the end of July, a sharp one, requesting an early expression of the views of His Majesty's Government upon its economic policy in the Mandate regions. The request was made despite the fact that, as the Ambassador sardonically put it, "the Government of the United States appreciates that, with respect to the inauguration of the administration of the Mandate territories, His Majesty's Government will consider it necessary to proceed with due deliberation." The last quality which marked the action of His Majesty's Government then was due deliberation, and both parties to the correspondence knew it.

The dispatch went on to say that the United States Government had noted the publication of the San Remo oil agreement between Britain and France, and did not see how this corresponded with the principle of equality of treatment for all nations in Mandated areas, a principle understood and accepted during the Peace negotiations in Paris. It seemed to the United States Government that the conclusion of this agreement "resulted in a grave infringement of the Mandate principle." At the close of the dispatch a further request was made that "in an early reply to the note of the 12th of May His Majesty's Government will find it possible to elucidate fully its policy regarding the Mandated territory of the Near East and other regions.

Lord Curzon replied in August, taking the war right into the enemy's camp, pointing out that the delicacy of the United States about oil privileges consented for each other by Britain and France in Mesopotamia was rather offset by the fact that 80 percent of the petroleum production of the world was under American control and that "United States predominance in regard to oil-production was assured for many years to come." He quoted instances of distinctly unaltruistic American action towards non-American oil-concessions in Haiti and in Costa Rica, and generally showed the wide knowledge and the lively powers of self-defence possessed by our Foreign Office.

On the general question, which is that which interests us here, because it involved the danger of delay to the already overdue Mandates, the Foreign Secretary was as categoric as he dared to be. He said that the Draft Mandates for Palestine and Mesopotamia which were being prepared would, after approval by the Allied Powers interested, be communicated to the Council of the League. While he "fully appreciated the suggestion for discussing with the United States Government the various propositions mentioned," none the less he thought the "terms of the Mandates can only properly be discussed at the Council of the League of Nations, by the signatories of the Covenant."

This was a diplomatic way of asking the Americans to be so good as to mind their own business and to leave the whole Mandate affair in the hands of the British and French personages who had given themselves the Mandates (and in this matter manipulated the Council and all the other embodiments of the League of Nations as they pleased).

The Americans, however, had every intention of continuing to mind what they considered to be their business. They intimated that they did not think the matter closed by Lord Curzon's note and that a reply and a resumption of their demands were to be expected in due course. This reply was not sent for some months, and in the meantime the field was held by the long-drawn-out parleys upon the frontier. From the time of the Peace Conference the Zionists, as I have just mentioned, had been jockeying and lobbying to obtain a location of the northern frontier in their favour. The Sykes-Picot frontier gave to the prospective French Mandated area the waters of the Litany river, and of the Upper Jordan, as well as the Yarmook valley leading to the plains of the Hauran. The Zionists desired these waters and areas to be included in "their Palestine," for they already had in mind, and by 1920 to some extent had on paper, the celebrated Rutenberg scheme for harnessing all the water-power they could for the benefit of their projected industrial and commercial enterprises. The French however clung to the Sykes-Picot frontier.

The negotiations which this Zionist demand for a more northern boundary brought about were tedious and there is no need to follow them in geographical detail. But from another point of view they are very noteworthy, because in the course of them the ramifications of Zionist influence were displayed to perfection, and another great example was given of how on major occasions the leading Zionists themselves wrote the documents which afterwards were made to pass before the world as the genuine self-sprung utterances of Governments and of chiefs of Governments.

> During 1919 and 1920 every effort was made by the Zionist leaders to urge upon the British and the French Governments the justice and the necessity of the Zionist proposals in regard to the boundaries. Mr. Balfour was particularly impressed in conversation with Dr. Weizmann and Mr. Brandeis in August 1919 with the economic arguments in regard to the northern boundary. In France M. Pichon and M. Robert de Caix formally promised Dr. Weizmann in September 1919 that Zionist representatives would be heard when the question of the Syria-Palestine frontier was discussed between England and France. Sir [then Mr.] Herbert Samuel was in close touch with the Zionist leaders, and used his influence to keep the question of the Zionist boundaries constantly before the British Government.

> In November 1919 M. Sokolov had interviews with Lord Milner and Lord Curzon, both of whom agreed to support the Zionist frontier-line. Further Dr. Weizmann, then in Palestine, won Lord Allenby's support from the military standpoint. In the early part of 1920 M. Sokolov had long interviews with President Deschanel, M. Millerand and M. Leon Bourgeois in Paris, and endeavoured to weaken the French attitude of unwavering insistence on the Sykes-Picot line.
>
> In February 1920 renewed efforts were made to mobilize American Jewish and non-Jewish opinion in our favour. The American Press was emphatic in its protest against the mutilation of Palestine and in insisting on the vital need of the Litany for its development. The American Ambassador was instructed to make representations.

So far the 1921 Report of the Zionist Executive, which after detailing these activities and achievements, adds with almost naive regretfulness, "More than this at the time it was impossible to expect." Indeed, one would have thought so, and yet more was not merely expected, but was effected. For their own reasons, or from lack of information surprising in such an official document, the members of the Zionist Executive in their 1921 Report do not mention what next occurred. What did occur was that the Zionist leaders in the United States sent a letter to President Wilson, then on his sick-bed. This letter ran as follows:

> "Negotiations in Paris on the Turkish settlement have reached so critical a stage in their effects upon the realization of the Balfour Declaration in Palestine as to compel me to appeal to you.
>
> My associates of the Zionist Organization wire me from Paris that in the conferences on the Turkish Treaty France now insists on the terms of the Sykes-Picot agreement—one of the secret treaties made in 1916 before our entrance into the War. If the French contention should prevail it would be disastrous to the realization of the establishment of the Jewish Homeland in Palestine, inasmuch as the Sykes-Picot agreement divides the country in complete disregard of historical boundaries and natural necessities. The Zionist cause depends upon rational northern and eastern boundaries for a self-sustaining, economic development of the country. This means on the north Palestine must include the Litany river and the watersheds of the Hermon, and on the east it must include the plains of the Jaulon and the Haulon. Narrower than this is a mutilation.
>
> If the Balfour Declaration subscribed to by France as well as the other Allied and Associated Powers is to have more than paper value there can be no compromise as to the guarantees by which the Balfour Declaration is to be secured.
>
> I need not remind you that neither in this country nor in Paris has there been any opposition to the Zionist program, and to its realization the boundaries I have named are indispensable. The Balfour Declaration,

which we know you made possible, was a public promise. I venture to suggest that it may be given to you at this time to move the statesmen of Christian nations to keep this solemn promise to the hope of Israel. It is your word at this hour to Millerand and to Lloyd George which may be decisive."

Mr. de Haas, to whom we owe the publication of this text, does not say who signed it, as one man must have done since it is couched in the first person singular. But we are not likely to be wrong if we assume that it was Mr. Brandeis of the golden memory. I reproduce it just as it is printed, the command that Palestine "must include the Jaulon and the Haulon" corresponding so well to the American Zionists' grasping ambitions in a land of which clearly they knew but little. The plains in question are the Jaulan and the Hauran. In an affair where there is such small comfort of any sort to be found, this much satisfaction at least has been vouchsafed to us that the Brandeisian order was disobeyed by the French, and Palestine was not dilated by either the Jaulon or the Haulon.

But the suggestion at the end of the letter that "it might be given" to the President to move the European statesmen, coming from the quarter from which it did, had the effect intended. I quote Mr. de Haas:

"One April morning the British Cabinet received from the stricken American President a cabled letter so tensely worded as to the honour of Christendom being involved in providing the Jewish Homeland with adequate boundaries, that Premier Lloyd George described the message as "a bomb-shell". The coastline of Palestine was moved north to the ladder of Tyre and inland to Merom."

This information is to be found in Mr. de Haas's life of Mr. Brandeis. But in his *Great Betrayal,* written in collaboration with the Rev. Stephen Wise, the fuller truth is told. The tensely worded letter which moved Mr. Lloyd George, to say nothing of the frontier, was none other than the letter written by the Zionist leaders. The letter, Mr. de Haas explains, "was addressed to President Wilson, *who immediately ordered it to be sent to the British Cabinet as his personal opinion.*"

The text of the document appears to have undergone some alterations first, for Mr. de Haas reproduces a holograph of its typewritten text with handwritten corrections, in rather illegible writing. These do not amount to very much, but perhaps it will be more in order if I reproduce this version, which presumably was that which was alchemized into President Wilson's personal opinion:

Negotiations in Paris on the Turkish settlement have reached so critical a stage in their effects upon the realization of the Balfour

> Declaration of a Jewish Homeland in Palestine as to compel me to appeal to you.
>
> My associates of the Zionist Organization cable me from Paris that in the conference on the Turkish Treaty France now insists upon the terms of the Sykes-Picot agreement—one of the secret treaties made before our entrance into the War. If this contention of the French should prevail it would defeat full realization of the promise of the Jewish Homeland; for the Sykes-Picot agreement divides the country in complete disregard of historic boundaries and of actual necessities. Rational northern and eastern boundaries are indispensable to a [here is an indecipherable word] and the economic development of the country.
>
> On the north Palestine must include the Litany river and the watersheds of the Hermon. On the east it must include the plains of the Jaulon and the Hauron [nomenclature is improving]. Less than this would produce mutilation of the Jewish Homeland.
>
> If the Balfour Declaration subscribed to by France as well as the other Allied and Associated Powers is to be made effective, these boundaries must be conceded to Palestine.
>
> Neither in this country nor in Paris has there been any opposition to the Zionist programme. The Balfour Declaration, which you made possible, was a public promise. I venture to suggest that it may be given to you at this time to move the statesmen of Christian nations to keep this solemn promise to Israel. Your word at this hour may be decisive to Millerand and Lloyd George."

It can but be assumed that when this letter was cabled to London as the President's *cri de cœur* the last five words were left out. Shorn of these, it certainly would have the air of a special appeal, or rather of a special injunction, to the Prime Minister. Mr. de Haas, otherwise a valuable recorder, is very remiss about giving dates, but apparently the April morning upon which this bomb-shell struck Mr. Lloyd George was just before he went to San Remo, and it was at San Remo that, with its splinters goading him, he did succeed in getting the French to listen to the biblical dimensions of Dan to Beersheba as those for Zionist Palestine.

In the end, though, all the trouble taken by the Brandeis regime over President Wilson was wasted, for the French Cabinet, afraid of the Foreign Affairs Commission of the Chamber, retreated considerably from its concession. The negotiations were taken up all over again.

> The Zionist leaders utilized the frequent postponements to bring pressure to bear on both parties, though, as far as the British Government was concerned, there was no need to do anything but strengthen the hands of the Government, which was as anxious as were the Zionists to secure the desired boundaries. (Z.O.R.)

The Zionist Report continues by giving details of how remarkably (though it does not say so) the Zionists could assemble forces all over the world on their behalf.

> In October and November 1920 influence from every possible quarter was mobilized in view of the meeting of the Supreme Council then about to be held. Sir Herbert Samuel, as High Commissioner in Jerusalem, urged the British Government not to accept the Sykes-Picot line. The Advisory Council of Palestine, in the name of all the inhabitants of the country, also passed a resolution in the same sense. The American Zionists, of course, threw their powerful weight into the scale. In addition, the Canadian and South African and Australian Zionists were successful in inducing their respective Prime Ministers to cable to the British Government in support of the Zionist boundary, particularly in regard to the need of not taking away from Palestine the sources of the Jordan, the headwaters and tributaries of the Yarmook, and access to the Litany waters. In London, the Parliamentary Committee for Palestine Affairs, established in the early part of the year, was kept fully informed through Lord Robert Cecil and the Hon. W. Ormsby-Gore of the progress of the negotiations. The Committee conveyed to the Prime Minister on November 9th a resolution supporting the Jewish standpoint both in regard to the Mandate and the frontiers. *The Times* and the *Manchester Guardian* supported the same view in leading articles.

One is reminded, on reading this, of the companies which are formed in the realms of finance, all to the same end and all by one group of associates, but under varying names. The high-sounding Parliamentary Committee for Palestine Affairs, what was it but a holding-company for the Zionist programme, with Lord Cecil and Mr. Ormsby-Gore as directors? What did the Dominion Prime Ministers know of the river Litany?

On top of this cumulative propaganda the views of various eminent engineers were obtained upon the feasibility of a hydro-electric scheme for Palestine and upon the necessity of an adequate water-supply for running it. These documents, favourable on purely technical grounds, were sent to the Government in support of the Zionist desires, and to Mr. Lloyd George and Lord Curzon Dr. Weizmann emphasized both Palestine's physical need for water-power and that in "the view of experts the territory in dispute was of little or no value to the country on the north." The Zionists said that they were willing to accept the decision of an impartial arbitrator if the matter were brought to arbitration.

Lord Curzon showed his personal interest in various ways and "it is beyond doubt that the Foreign Office used every effort to induce the French Government to accept the boundary set out in the Zionist proposals." But the French stayed unmoved.

> Just before Christmas, Great Britain and France made an agreement readjusting the boundaries of the Mandated areas of Palestine, Mesopotamia and Syria, so as to allow Great Britain to construct a railway and a pipe-line entirely in her Mandated area connecting the Hedjaz Railway with the Mosul oil-region, and to permit France also to tap this oil within her Mandated territory. (Wright.)

The Palestino-Syrian roundabout had to endure those losses which were made up by the Mesopotamian swing, and the northern frontier was adjusted very much on the lines of the Sykes-Picot Treaty, starting at Ras en Nakoura on the sea-coast midway between Acre and Tyre and going pretty straight inland till at the end it rose in a rough parallelogram to include Lake Huleh and make, as we have seen, the people of Metullah unfit to rule themselves. Accurate delimitation was entrusted to a Boundary Commission later to be formed, and another Commission, to which Zionist engineers were to be appointed, was to examine into the use by Palestine of the waters of the north Jordan and Yarmook districts.

These were consolations for the Zionists' failure to get the boundaries made to their order. However, if they had not obtained the boundaries as they desired them, they had the Administration which they desired. To the subject of that Administration we may return now.

Chapter 23

The "Civil Government" of Palestine set up in 1920 an unlawful government. Violation by the Lloyd George Cabinet of Great Britain's pledges at the Hague. Proofs of the illegitimacy of the Palestine Government.

At the period which we have reached the Prime Minister and his friends started to act in Palestine as though under the impression that if they flouted all law there consistently enough, then they would establish a new order of conduct. From now on they pursued a regular course of illegality, through the deputy action of the Government which they had established in Palestine and, fundamentally, through the very establishment of this Government. For it is impossible to find that the supposititious Mandatory Administration for the three years between August 1920 and September 1923 had any Mandatory status or any legal status whatsoever. It was called a Government, but it had none of the title-deeds or rights of a Government. It was not a Government.

Its deeds were all null and void, and presumably remain so to this day, in the absence of any remedial act. Among these was the quite arbitrary series of enactments by which Zionist immigration into Palestine was set on foot, as well as the enactment of the Constitution under which the country continues to be ruled. So the matter is of the first importance and it involves some very serious considerations.

It being granted that the Mandate eventually came into force, in September of 1923, how can this legalize what was done by the Palestine Civil Administration before that date? The statutes passed then were invalid, and leave at least some doubt as to what can be the value of more recent legislation which sprang out of that which was enforced during those three years.

This question of the illegality of the 1920 Administration has been introduced already, of course. The reader has seen how this Government was hastened into being so that Zionism might be established and the Balfour Declaration be operated in the territory which had been administered as O.E.T.A. South. He also has seen how the Military Administration, though obliged by pressure from the Home Government to infringe in lesser degree the laws which limited its action, yet would not compound with the entire disregard of those laws which full acceptance of the Home Government's policy entailed.

But the far-reaching result of Mr. Lloyd George's haste has not been advanced yet, and now that it is advanced, the whole question naturally demands closer inspection, particularly in the light of the documents and pronouncements which support what I assert. These have been kept obstinately out of the writings and speeches which, in the Palestine question, have been the all but universal fare of the general public.

The character of the Civil Administration during the three years in question was announced clearly enough when the Administration was installed. It was proclaimed as a civil government supplanting the military government. It governed under the Mandate, since it passed laws and erected a Constitution which were not possible under military government. "Sir Herbert Samuel has been appointed High Commissioner in Palestine," Mr. Bonar Law had told the House of Commons, "for the purpose of instituting a civil administration to replace the existing military administration." So civil was the administration that officers who took service in it had to be demobilized first, and were only allowed to wear their uniforms till they could obtain plain clothes.

Accordingly, if the Administration over Palestine ceased to be a Military Government it ceased to hold a Military Government's rights and powers. It could not supersede a Government and suppress its powers and yet keep the powers which it had suppressed, nor could it remain the Government which it had extinguished.

On the other hand, as a civil government, it had to possess a title. M. Hymans, the Belgian statesman, doing his best for legality in the difficult circumstances of the League Council at San Sebastian, when the Mandatory question first came up, pointed out, "It is not enough, however, that the Mandated Powers should be appointed. It is important that they should also possess a legal title. A mere matter of form perhaps but one that should be settled."

What was to be the legal title of the new Civil Government? Mr. Lloyd George himself was so good as to explain this to the House of Commons on the 23rd of June, just before he installed it. A Member had questioned the moral and legal right of the country to the Mandates in ex-Turkish territories. The Prime Minister replied (to repeat words of his already cited), "As far as the legal document is concerned, the legal document will be the Turkish Treaty. Under the Turkish Treaty we shall be receiving the Mandate from the Allied and Associated Powers."

But the Turkish Treaty was not signed till August in 1923. From 1920 to 1923 there was no Treaty and consequently the only legal title or foundation for a Mandatory Government was missing.

What then was the status of the Government of Palestine under the High Commissioner? It had lost all military powers. It had not gamed any civil powers. A cursory observer might say that it had fallen between two stools, but its situation was worse than that, since it could not pick itself up and choose one of the stools. The first stool, or, in the occasion, the governmental throne, the military one, had been removed from the presence-chamber in Jerusalem under the expectation that the civil throne would be ready. But the construction of the civil throne could not even be begun without a Peace treaty, and so there was nothing, throne or stool or anything, to bring into the room. Thus the Palestine Government was obliged to sit flat on the floor, upon its own frame, and from that imaginary and base elevation it attempted to draw administrative powers. In plain fact, the Government had no legal backing, no document, no warrant, no title, no powers whatsoever. There are various formal texts available to demonstrate this. Let us examine them.

The Peel Commissioners in their Report (on page 153), make two quotations from the Manual of Military Law, a codex of the laws which govern the actions of all civilized nations in a state of war. It is the standard official publication issued by the War Office and distributed for the instruction of officers and soldiers of the British Army. The first of these quotations deals with the technical fashion in which taxes and other financial dues must be collected by an army occupying enemy territory. The second deserves full reproduction. It is taken from paragraph 354 in Chapter 14 of the Military Manual, and declares that "It is no longer considered permissible for him [i.e., the occupant of conquered enemy territory] to work his will unhindered, altering the existing form of Government, upsetting the Constitution and domestic laws, and ignoring the rights of the inhabitants." A most salutary quotation, the printing of which does the Royal Commissioners credit as far as it goes. But unfortunately they seem to have shrunk from using it except with reference to the period of O.E.T.A., and, more notably still, they have refrained from quoting other paragraphs of the same manual, even though they lay beside paragraph 354.

The Manual, it should be said, enshrines the conclusions of the Hague Convention of 1899, of which the text was amended and accepted by the signatory nations, including of course Great Britain, in 1907. In this Manual, then, under paragraph 3 of Chapter 14 comes the primary statement that

The laws of war are legally binding. Usages are not.

The distinction between laws of war and usages is evident. Usages are arrangements commonly made by or between combatants. The laws of war are the rules laid upon combatants by international enactment, and proclaimed in the Hague document. In paragraph 266 of the same chapter follows a definition of importance in the present issue:

> An armistice is not a temporary peace. It merely supersedes hostilities without putting an end to the war.

Palestine was governed under such an armistice, concluded with Turkey on the 30th October, 1918. It lasted till the Treaty was signed in August 1923. Therefore, when the "Mandatory Government" of July 1920 was set up by Mr. Lloyd George and his Cabinet, Palestine was in a state of war under which the laws of war were legally binding upon whatever government represented Britain in Palestine. Apart from the moral obligations of civilization making it incumbent on a British Government to obey these laws, His Majesty's Government had adhered to them under the Hague codification.

So we were thoroughly bound. To what were we bound, though? Let me cite first two essential paragraphs, 353 and 355, the two precisely which lay on either side of paragraph 354, but failed to catch the eye of any of the Peel Commissioners.

Paragraph 353:

> "The occupation of enemy territory during war creates a condition entirely different from subjugation through annexation of the territory. During the occupation by the enemy the sovereignty of the legitimate owner of the territory is only temporarily latent, but it still exists and in no way passes to the occupants. The latter's rights are merely transitory, and he should only exercise such powers as is necessary for the purposes of the war, the maintenance of order and of safety and the proper administration of the country."

That a Government should be set up in Palestine, legislating not as the military occupant, but by virtue of untraceable external authority, that it, for example, should order the immigration of alien subjects to begin as by right and should replace the existing Constitution by a new one— these were as open violations of this law of war as could be conceived.

Paragraph 355 provides further evidence of the violation of law by the 1920-3 Government:

> "The occupant therefore must not treat the country as part of his own territory or consider the inhabitants as his lawful subjects. He may,

> however, demand and enforce such measure of obedience as is necessary for the security of his forces, the maintenance of order, and the proper administration of the country."

The 1920-3 Government did treat Palestine as part of its own territory and did consider the inhabitants as its lawful subjects. It actually imposed upon them legislation under Orders in Council. The High Commissioner promulgated compulsory Ordinances. Zionist immigration was begun under an Ordinance promulgated the month after he assumed office.

The next paragraph to be cited, paragraph 361, has the most damaging effect of all. It lays down that:

> "It is of little importance whether the government imposed by the invader is called military or civil government, for in either case it is a government imposed by the necessity of war, and so far as it concerns the inhabitants and the rest of the world, *the laws of war alone determine the legality of its acts.* [My italics.]"

Here is the truth stated with absolute plainness. The acts of the 1920-3 Government were illegal if they were not in accordance with the laws of war. But the Government of 1920—3 consisted of a High Commissioner, assisted by an Executive Council, whose very presence "altered the existing form of government; " who issued edicts on the authority of an external State and thus "upset the Constitution;" who introduced Zionists into the country without the assent of the inhabitants and thereby most obviously "ignored their rights." By the laws of war, none of these things were any longer considered permissible (under paragraph 354), and they of course infringed the laws cited in paragraphs 353 and 355. The circle of illegality is complete and offers no escape from it.

Still, can anything be ventured in the "Civil Government's" defence? Can, or at the time, could any provision of the Hague code be cited on its behalf? There was paragraph 362 which said:

> "Political laws and constitutional privileges are as a matter of fact suspended during occupation. For instance, the laws affecting recruitment and those concerning suffrage, the right of assembly, the right of bearing arms and the freedom of the Press."

Paragraph 366 said:

> "It is within the power of the occupant, if demanded by the exigencies of war, to suspend any existing laws or to promulgate new ones."

After full search, this couple of paragraphs is all that can be found which might in any degree be adaptable for the purposes of an advocate seeking to defend the 1920 Government. I give them in order to avoid any imputation of Royal Commissional short-sight for these pages, but there is nothing in them to controvert the proof just given of that Government's illegality. The suspension of political laws and constitutional privileges, as the examples attached to paragraph 362 testify, means simply that those processes of enemy rule cannot be allowed to continue upon occupied soil which would be equivalent to a continuance of war there against the occupant. Recruiting for the Turkish Army, election of deputies to the Turkish Chamber, assembling of adherents of the Turkish system, carriage of arms which might be used against the occupying troops, freedom to attack the latter or to defend the Turks in newspapers and in other writings—that is all which is suspended by paragraph 362, and it is but common sense that such things should be suspended. The existing form of government was not suspended, though, and the introduction of an altogether different form of government was not permitted.

By paragraph 366 the occupant can promulgate new laws, but only, as previous paragraphs show, within the frame of the existing constitution and still more within the frame of the laws of war themselves, both of them flouted by the Orders in Council and the edicts of the 1920-3 Government. The new laws allowed under this paragraph can be little but by-laws. The occupant is forbidden even to introduce legislation for new taxes. When the Germans occupied Belgium, they could and did introduce military by-laws, some of them abusive, to say no more, but they did not and could not introduce German Imperial legislation to replace Belgian Royal legislation.

When our own army more leniently occupied Cologne it did not attempt to establish British civil law in place of German civil law. Nor for the matter of that did our army in Palestine. But the forged Mandatory Government of 1920—what else was it but a forged Government?—after ousting the army, introduced Orders in Council and organic legislation by self-authorized decrees, all to the end that a small people might be robbed of its future.

The proceedings of Parliament itself give further proof of how improper was that Government and its action. In July of that year, 1920, the Under-Secretary for Foreign Affairs, in answer to a written question, declared that "the international status of inhabitants of Palestine who were Ottoman subjects by birth will not be changed so long as the treaty of Peace with Turkey has not come into force. When it does come into force such persons will become citizens of Palestine."

Here, therefore, is a formal recognition on the part of the Government that the inhabitants of Palestine who were Ottoman subjects by birth remained so till the Treaty was signed. This was the position of all the

Arabs of Palestine. Therefore, till the state of war ended, to impose any other government upon them save that conducted under the military code which employed the Ottoman code was manifestly illegal, and the acts of such a government broke international law.

The accusation that the Government was breaking the law was brought against it actually in the Lords during the session of the 29th of June, 1920. Lord Lamington quoted Article 354 and emphasized that, under it, it was not permissible to alter the existing form of administration, to upset the constitutional and domestic laws or to ignore the rights of the inhabitants. "That," said he, "is what we are doing now. Therefore we have violated the very principle with which we entered the war."

To this charge Lord Curzon, who spoke for the Government, could make no answer. He passed on without offering a defence.

Therefore there is no getting away from the real character of the action of the 1920-3 Government. It broke international law repeatedly, broke it as a matter of habit, and broke it in affairs of the utmost gravity. The greater shame of this is that international law is law of a superior temper. The French call it the *"droit des gens"*—the rights and the code of the people and of the peoples in one—and it corresponds between nations to the laws of honour between men. It is something naturally incumbent upon all nations. To break it is like breaking one's word, or not paying a debt of honour, or betraying a trust, things which are more binding on men of conscience than the formulated precepts of jurists. Therefore, for the Home Government, through its alias in Palestine, to break during three years not merely laws, but the laws of honour, was the nadir of its descent.

There comes the query now: Admitted that the acts of the 1920-3 Government were illegal, was the Government necessarily illegal itself? It is difficult to see that it could be anything else. It functioned as a civil Government, itself governing under civil, external laws, when the only legitimate form of Government in Palestine that could be was a military Government, governing under military, native laws. The Government proper to the situation was one exercised by persons subject to a military commander-in-chief, as the vehicle of power in the occupied territory, designated in paragraph 367 of the code in the Military Manual, thus:

> "The Commander of an occupying army is expressly prohibited from declaring, either in his own name or in that of his Government, extinguished, suspended or unenforceable in a court-of-law the rights and actions of enemy subjects."

Sir Herbert Samuel was not the commander of an occupying army, and all his subordinates who had belonged to the army were, as we have seen, carefully demobilized before they transferred from O.E.T.A. to the "Civil Administration." The whole reason of existence of himself and of his Administration was to excise military rule. It can hardly be claimed that the members of the Civil Government were soldiers in spite of themselves. In any event it was not the quality of bearing arms that would have given validity to a genuine Government. It was the quality of being amenable to the laws of war, which on the face of it was utterly absent from Sir Herbert Samuel's Administration from the day it began till September three years later.

One single official attempt was made to establish a claim to legitimacy for the 1920 Administration, but it recoils disastrously upon those who made it. This attempt did not occur till early in 1923. However extraordinary it may seem, up to that date the Home Government had succeeded marvellously in hushing up the status of its unconventional infant, the Palestine Government. Then, as now, there were so many other things going on which distracted attention from the Holy Land. Readers must have perceived, at the moment of writing, how difficult it is for the informative world to manage several crises at once. Spain, China and Czecho-Slovakia are alternated in the news: now one comes to the fore, now another, and there is no guarantee about regular turns. In the early twenties Palestine did not stand the ghost of a chance beside the Ruhr. The Palestine Government came into being, and in expectation of the Turkish Treaty no notice of its character was taken. Europe drifted into acceptance of its existence and forgot about it as time passed.

As it happened, in the autumn of 1922 I returned to Palestine, stayed there through the winter, and on my return wrote a long series of articles for the *Daily Mail* in the new year. The most important thing I perceived on my arrival there was that the Mandate was not in force. This was not realized at all then, except by official persons who were careful to keep their realizations to themselves. There has never been a subject of such immense concern concerning which there has been such general ignorance as that of Palestine, nor has there been a subject concerning which more information has been withheld. At the time there was indeed a good deal of fuss about the money which was being spent over Mandates, but that in Palestine the money was being spent upon a Mandate which did not exist—a matter infinitely more important—not one man in ten thousand, in fifty thousand, was aware.

I remember well that I felt it necessary, in order to support my statement that there was no Mandate, to quote an official declaration of the Spanish Government, which I had asked the Spanish Consul in Jerusalem, with whom I had become friendly, to procure for me from Madrid.

When the real situation was thus brought prominently to public notice a certain amount of perturbation was caused. The obvious corollary that if the Mandate was not in force, then the Mandatory Administration of Palestine itself was not in force, entered the minds of a good many people. There had been, it may be repeated, some desultory inquiry upon the point in Parliament three years before. Beside the query put to Mr. Bonar Law (already quoted) the chief intervention had been that of Mr. Asquith who had said:

> "We are told that arrangements have been made for the future administration of Palestine upon the footing that Great Britain is the Mandatory ...I do not know anything except hearsay about the particular terms of that Mandate, but has it been submitted to the League of Nations? Is Sir Herbert Samuel going to Palestine as Mandatory of the League, or is he going there as an officer of the British Government selected by His Majesty's Ministry to perform a duty, not to the League of Nations, but to those who dispatched him from these shores? That is a very simple question and surely demands a very simple answer."

Balfour, who replied for the Government, significantly ignored the demand, though of an ex-Prime Minister, for an explanation of Sir Herbert Samuel's status, confining himself to an explanation of the character of Mandates in general. The matter was not pursued and in Parliament as elsewhere gradually dropped from sight during the next three years.

But in 1923 what I had written reopened it—I had seen Lords Islington and Sydenham and various members of Parliament about it—and questions were put in the House upon the status of the Palestine Administration, notably one demanding what right that body possessed to order, as it had just done, the holding of elections. The answer was supplied by Mr. Ormsby-Gore who in the interval had sidled on to the benches of a new Government. He was Under-Secretary for the Colonies, and when the Mandatory Government was set up at Jerusalem, the affairs of Palestine had been transferred from the Foreign to the Colonial Office.

The chief of minor pro-Zionists now was installed as the mouthpiece of the Government. Mr. Winston Churchill, who had become Colonial Secretary, did not answer Palestine queries so much. So Mr. Ormsby-Gore on this crucial question got up and tried to explain things away:

> "The position is [he said] that the Mandate for Palestine was conferred upon His Britannic Majesty by the Principal Allied Powers in April 1920. On the 3rd of October 1921 the President of the Council of the League of Nations communicated to the then Prime Minister a request that His Majesty's Government should continue to *carry on the administration of Palestine in the spirit of the draft-Mandate* [my italics] which had previously been submitted to the Council, until such time as

> the position had been definitely regularized. On the 24th July 1922 the Council of the League approved the terms of the Mandates for Palestine and Syria, and passed a resolution that they would enter into force automatically and at the same time, as soon as the Governments of France and Italy had notified the Council of the League that they had reached an agreement on certain particular points in regard to the Syrian Mandate. It is true that agreement has not been reached, but this in no way affects the Administration of Palestine.
>
> On the 10th of August 1922 a Palestine Order in Council, of which the draft had been officially communicated to the Council of the League on the 1st of July 1922, and which provided for the holding of the elections referred to by the Honourable Member, was passed by the King in Council. This order took effect on the 11th of September 1922, when it was published and proclaimed in Palestine."

This, to my knowledge, is the sole defence ever offered of the legitimacy of the 1920-3 Government. It would have been better surely if such a defence had never been made. To begin with, Mr. Ormsby-Gore maladroitly based his case in the end, as far as he based his case anywhere, upon the very acts which were most fatal to it, the Orders in Council. He cited one of these as authority for holding the elections. By the elections—as the project for them proposed—a "Legislative Council" was to be established under the presidency of Sir Herbert Samuel. Administrative officials were to have a controlling number of votes upon it: Jews were to have seats upon it as Jews: the Arabs were to be divided and have seats as Moslems and as Christians.

The whole project was a blazing infraction of the law which the Administration should have observed, as the Council violated the Ottoman Constitution in force. It was only made worse by "authorizing" it under Orders in Council which, as we have seen, themselves flagrantly contravened the permissible activities of the occupant of Palestine by assuming a sovereignty which had "in no way passed to the occupant." (Paragraph 353.) As an advocate, the Under-Secretary had chosen very unfortunate arguments to support his plea.

But while basing his case on the very acts which destroyed it, Mr. Ormsby-Gore rested it on his way upon the request of the President of the Council of the League of Nations that His Majesty's Government should "carry on the administration in Palestine in the spirit of the draft-Mandate." Yet what was the legal value of the request to "carry on" from the League of Nations (which really sprang from a sub-committee of the League)? None at all. It has as much effective (or legal) value as the "Carry on, London!" which an announcer of the B.B.C. gives during a weekly item, amidst murmurs and hummings, marching and the music of bands. Inside the B.B.C. studio one would see probably the lonely announcer give leave to London by putting a record on the turn-table of a gramophone.

So it was with the League, putting on its turn-table a disc of shellac or whatnot, and producing sounds of authority. "Carry on, Draft Mandate!" A request from the League to "carry on" had no conceivable legal value. To make use of such a request as the credentials of authority was absurd. What is more, the President of the Council of the League himself would have acted very improperly if he had suggested that his request was to be interpreted as conferring credentials.

It is not possible to know quite what passed in the bosom of the League, between the President of its Council and the sub-committee which was the source of the statement or request made to the British Government. What is certain is that Mr. Ormsby-Gore's version of the League's request gave it a tone which its authors never gave it. The Recommendation of tine sub-committee was:

> "With regard to A Mandates, the sub-committee *would only express the hope* [my italics] that so long as the transitory conditions continue the Administration of the territories in question will still be carried out in the spirit of Article XXII of the Covenant."

From this to communicating a "request that His Majesty's Government should continue to carry on the Administration of Palestine in the spirit of the draft-Mandate" a considerable change in wording occurred. Whether the change in wording occurred when the Council interpreted and developed the sub-committee's Report or whether the development occurred in Mr. Ormsby-Gore's speech cannot be said. The sub-Committee's recommendation, as the italicized portion shows, certainly did not extend beyond a pious and empty hope that the Palestine Government would stick to the morality of the Covenant. It did not attempt to confer any title on H.M.'s Government, whereas in Mr. Ormsby-Gore's version it was phrased to give that effect.

The League, in any event, had not the slightest power or status itself in Palestine or over the affairs of Palestine, and could not confer a jot of status or power upon any would-be Government in that country. Till the Treaty with Turkey should be concluded the League not alone had no commands or authorizations to give on Turkish soil, whether occupied or not, but it had no connection of any kind with Turkey. Till the signing of that document brought forth the League as an entity in the Treaty, the League of Nations did not even exist for Turkey. Prior to the Treaty Turkey remained in the political world which was in being when the War started, in which there was no League. The League, on its part, born of the Treaty, could have no cognizance of anything save through the Treaty.

Therefore no injunction—if there ever had been an injunction—from the League bidding the British Government to carry on in the spirit of the draft-Mandate was worth a brass farthing. The President of the League Council, anxious to be helpful in some way, might just as well have requested the Government to carry on in Palestine in the spirit of a draught Guinness. Enough of this or of any other of the national beverages soon would have convinced the Colonial Office of its possession of all earthly powers, and the prescription would have been far more comfortable and homely, and infinitely closer to the Covenant than was the draft-Mandate which at the time a collection of statesmen and experts and a posse of Zionists were blending and adulterating between them.

Mr. Ormsby-Gore's poor apologia, it is worth observing, has been dismissed too by the open or covert acknowledgements of most of the commentators who have dared to pay any attention to this matter. Mr. J. de V. Loder (now Lord Wakehurst and Governor of New South Wales) has some relevant words upon it in his *The Truth about Mesopotamia, Palestine and Syria.* This excellent work, however, just does not attain, as regards Palestine, the first-class value which it might have had, if only its author had been more candid. Trying to make things easy, to gloss over things just a little, in the interests of the Government, he finds for example the phrase "anticipatory rights" to denote the rights which the Government assumed from the Mandates before it possessed them. Lord Wakehurst, it may be, used this phrase sardonically: from the context it is not easy to judge. If he did, I withdraw the interpretation I have given to his words, and pay my respectful tribute to a thrust so well delivered.

Later, though, he says, speaking of the Mandatory territories, that:

> "No legal basis for a change of status exists until a peace-treaty with Turkey is ratified, and the League of Nations has strictly speaking no competence as yet to deal with the regions under discussion."

This was written some months before the Lausanne Treaty was signed, and it confirms amply all I have maintained. What impairs it as a picture of the situation is that, in order to hide realities (here there is no doubt about this), the words "strictly speaking" and "as yet" are inserted. They have no business where they are. If Lord Wakehurst's second sentence had run "and the League of Nations has no competence to deal with the regions under discussion" it would have been an exact statement of the situation at the time he was writing. Instead of this he brought in the future in order to hide the starkness of the present, and mitigated the League's incompetence with "strictly speaking." But there are no two ways about it. Either the League was competent or was not competent.

This small bowdlerization of Lord Wakehurst's is not a matter of such moment that I should draw attention to it, if it were not for this—it shows how a blunt representation of facts in the Palestine Question has always been wanting. None the less, in his person a distinguished writer did acknowledge the illegalities of the Government and the irregularities of the League, and spoke as much of the truth as he dared.

Besides Lord Wakehurst's there are other statements which might be quoted, but it will be enough to give one, which could not be bettered, since it is the common work, in a sense, of the Foreign Office and of the United States Department of State. On the 29th of December, 1921, Sir Eyre Crowe, the Permanent Under-Secretary, writing for his chief, the Marquess Curzon, sent to the State Department a dispatch in which the following passage occurs in relation to the territories under Mandate in the Near and Middle East:

> "The position with regard to these territories has not materially changed. A state of peace with Turkey does not yet exist, and the Council of the League has not yet formally approved the provisions of the draft-Mandates. The consequent delay and uncertainty causes His Majesty's Government considerable anxiety in Palestine. In these circumstances the peculiar religious and racial problems in that country and the particular conditions which attach to His Majesty's Government's acceptance of the Mandate as set out in the draft provisions are daily rendering more onerous the task which His Majesty's Government have assumed. For these reasons His Majesty's Government intend to invite the Council of the League of Nations, at the forthcoming session on January the 10th, formally to express their approval of the terms of the Mandate for Palestine as drafted in spite of *the dependence of the final legalization of the status of the Mandatory upon the entry into force of a treaty of peace with Turkey.*"

This dispatch contains the usual periphrastic description of the endeavour to impose the "National Home" through the Balfour Declaration as "the peculiar religious and racial problems in that country" and the usual euphemism by which the appropriation of the Mandate is called its "acceptance." But the words I have italicized are not so usual. They are a confession both that the status of Mandatory had been assumed in Palestine, and that this status was not legally assumed, and was known not to be legal by those who were responsible for creating it and for maintaining it.

The watering of the unpleasant word "legalization" by the adjective "final" was but another and, coming from the great Department of State from which it did, and from the pen of one of its chief servants, an almost pathetic little bowdlerization. As has just been observed of the question of League competence, there are no two ways about it. The status of the Mandatory was legal, or it was not legal. When it became legal, it would become so all at once and entirely. Previously it remained at all points and at all times illegal. Legalization did not creep slowly like a blush across the ivorine cheek of the Mandatory Government, nor flow like rainwater through its executive channels, so that June 1922 was rosier and more legitimate than June 1921, or February 1923 more liquidly lawful than the February of 1922. No, all was illegal and pallid and dry till, on the 29th of September, 1923, in one swift movement the water was turned on, or, as you like, the permanent rouge was dabbed upon the Governmental cheeks.

An American reply to this Foreign Office note was addressed to Lord Curzon by the United States' Ambassador in London, Mr. George Harvey, on the following 5th of April, 1922. The relevant passage runs:

> "In the communication of December 29th, 1921, Your Lordship drew particular attention to the situation in Palestine. A state of peace between the Allied Powers and Turkey does not yet exist. Nevertheless the United States appreciates the desire of His Majesty's Government to remove the existing uncertainties regarding the terms of the mandate for Palestine in order that *a legalized civil administration may be established as early as possible.* [My italics.]"

There is the truth, with no veil upon it save the very gossamer "legalized" in the place of "legal." What Sir Eyre Crowe had nine-tenths admitted the United States' Ambassador on his Government's behalf specified. It was a legalized or legal civil administration which Great Britain desired to have in Palestine, in the place of her present administration which was not legal. No other interpretation is possible.

Finally, to make assurance doubly sure, may be quoted the words of the Permanent Court of International Justice of The Hague, which in a judgment which will be the subject of a later chapter, declared on the 26th of March, 1925: "The document termed "Mandate for Palestine" was not yet in force in 1921." In which case, the Mandatory Government was in the same position evidently as the Mandate.

Here the main study of this affair may end. Whatever the "Civil Administration" purported to be was something which had no right to exist and for the matter of that was unable to exist. A military Administration governing under a Mandate not in force or a Mandatory Administration governing by military law were alike impossibilities. Therefore from July 1920 to September 1923, the so-called Civil Administration of Palestine under Mandate was an illegal, unsanctioned entity, usurping powers which it did not possess; breaking the laws which any Administration in that country was obliged, by bond and by honour, to obey; without authority, and enforcing its will upon people not subject to it by a series of spurious acts and decrees. This was done by the command of the Government of Mr. Lloyd George, the Palestine Administration itself being but a reflection of the will of himself and his partners, of whom Lord Balfour was both the most prominent and the most guilty.

The essential burden of responsibility for incurring an accusation against Britain of a type which has not lain upon her for centuries, if it has ever lain upon her at all, must rest in the first instance upon the shoulders of these two men, whose blameless private life was not matched in all their political actions. It is true that Mr. Lloyd George's Cabinet resigned in October 1922, and that the succeeding Cabinet, under Mr. Bonar Law, supported the illegal Government for about eleven months, till the conclusion of the Treaty of Lausanne legalized it. Mr. Bonar Law, though, was then a failing man, and it would be hardly fair to visit any more responsibility upon him than such as had come to him previously as a subordinate member of the Lloyd George Cabinet.

No doubt also a number of Ministers in both Cabinets had no real notion of what was being accomplished in the Holy Land in their name. Mr. Edwin Montagu, as I mentioned in an earlier chapter, told me that his colleagues of the 1917 Government mostly knew absolutely nothing about the Palestine Question as it presented itself then, and there is no reason to suppose, in their utter lack of access to unbiased information, that the bulk of Ministers of the later Governments knew anything more. Nor have Ministers of the various Cabinets between 1923 and this day, outside the responsible Ministry, the Colonial Office, and in a minor degree the Foreign Office, possessed any fuller knowledge or lesser ignorance than their predecessors. As time has passed, obviously they have grown to know less and less, indeed.

It is but fair to emphasize this point, because public opinion never seems to allow for want of knowledge amidst statesmen and politicians in general. They are always thought to be so fully informed upon any given matter that, according as their actions disclose themselves later on, they are judged to have acted in respect of it either with entire honesty or entire dishonesty. This is far from being true: one of the first things a journalist learns from contact with major politics is that highly placed persons can be quite ignorant and can act in ignorance. It is fortunate in the present instance that this should be so. If it were not so we should have had a strange selection of rulers governing this country for the last fourteen or fifteen years.

The Palestine Question has reached by now a stage in which those who have to take the greatest decisions concerning it may have the least information upon it. Ministers of today can only draw their information from the papers supplied to them by too interested Departments. Can anyone imagine that our present Prime Minister, Mr. Neville Chamberlain, has descended into the recesses of the matter? Or that he has ever had an opportunity of descending? Not for an instant is it to be believed that he has had such an opportunity. Till a short while ago, he has had to depend, for his information, upon a Colonial Office at the head of which was Mr. Ormsby-Gore. What did Mr. Baldwin know of the realities of Palestine? I have not the least hesitation in asserting that he knew nothing at all.

From these moderately comforting considerations concerning later Governments we may return to the unhappy acts of their chief predecessors of 1920-3. Two points now arise. It is all the more essential to consider them, since they provide, or if they could be proved would provide some degree of excuse for the incriminated Ministers in question.

The first point may be put as a question. Granted that the Palestine Administration of 1920-3 was illegal, is it not begging reality to harp upon this? Palestine had been conquered by the British Army, the blood of British and Australian soldiers had been shed profusely to win it, it would not have been torn from Turkish rule without these many lives so bravely sacrificed. Is it not begging reality to accuse a British Government of being illegitimate where the return of peace, the prospect of plenty and the whole existence of civilized government had depended upon British arms?

This argument has been put forward by some who have not thought much before they spoke, and by others who have masked a good deal of subtlety with a covering of bluff patriotism. The underlying assumption of it is that the soldiers who fell in Palestine fell fighting to provide there that form of government which Mr. Lloyd George installed. The 5th Norfolks, the 8th Hampshires bled so that the Sèvres Treaty might not die: the men of the 53rd Division left six hundred casualties on the Samson Ridge so that the nine subterfuges of the Balfour Declaration might pass unchallenged: the Australian Light Horse charged crying, "Advance the National Home!"

Was anything ever further from the truth? We know why our soldiers died—in loyalty to their country. Some of them too will have reflected as they marched to battle that they were going to redeem the land of their Saviour: all of them will have had some consciousness of this side of their emprise. If there was anything for which they did not die, it was that a British Government should use their bones as the foundation of a quibbling State unable to disclose its beginnings or avow its ends. It was for no such State in Palestine, nor for any political nostrum or thesis that they fought, and least of all in order that through their faithfulness their rulers should have ample opportunities for infidelity.

They expected of course to inaugurate some kind of British rule, in their soldiers' way, as part of the campaign; but they looked no further. If they thought of the matter at all, they thought of a coming military Government by their chiefs. This was what they died to establish, if you will: and who disestablished it? Is it maintained that the fallen men of the British Army in Palestine cried out from their graves that the survivors of the British Army must cease in 1920 to govern the land in which they lay, or else their own sacrifice was in vain?

If there is one plea in the world that will not do, it is this one that because of the Army's victory and for the sake of the dead lying on the battlefields, the tricks and the perfidies of statesmen must be condoned. More than in any other place it is intolerable in Palestine, where the Administration formed by the leaders and the comrades of the dead was ejected by these very statesmen. In 1920 there was no necessity for O.E.T.A. to come to an end. It was the legitimate vehicle of rule under the conditions of armistice. All that could be said against it was that it was lasting a long while and that it cost money. But both of these things were disadvantages such as might be expected to spring from a great war: neither had the faintest pretension to rank as a lawful reason for ending the regime. Whatever the expense, too, of continuing O.E.T.A., a genuine effort could have reduced this, and indeed an administration on a restricted scale, physically and morally, would have been more apt for the country. Nothing, in fine, permitted the termination of the Military Government in order that the pseudo-Mandatory Administration might replace it.

Moreover, the Chief Administrator at the time had made every provision for the continuance of the Military Government. In an earlier chapter I spoke of Sir Louis Bols's scheme for reshaping and re-organizing the Military Administration in prospect of the lengthening period of Armistice. I called it his "political testament": it made provision for Jewish needs in a legitimate way. Since writing this I have read in Sir Ronald Storrs's *Orientations* reference to it, thus: "There seemed to be no suspicion that our (O.E.T.A.) regime was not to continue indefinitely, for quite late in May 1920 I was shown at Headquarters the elaborate scheme of an apparently permanent Military Administration, elegantly engrossed, providing for a Chief-of-Staff, assisted by a galaxy of Colonels and Majors in charge of the familiar A, Q and M departments."

The Army therefore, was ready and willing to continue the task which it alone had the right to undertake, and any plea of justification for ousting it founded upon its own valour, is patently absurd, to say no more.

There is a variant of this plea, however—the second of the two points I have mentioned—which is more acceptable at first sight. It may appear a separate argument. It is said that we conquered Palestine, and that so we annexed it. Any and all forms of government we introduced there, Mandatory or non-Mandatory, were accordingly installed by right of conquest, at our proper pleasure, and any one of them was as legal as another, and all were legal.

Lord Balfour himself chose this line of resistance, when he found it necessary to defend Governmental policy in Palestine before the Council of the League of Nations. That lends it some interest, if no value, for when Balfour took this line he contradicted an earlier statement of his own before the Peace Conference. It was in May of 1922 that he informed the League Council that "a Mandate is a self-imposed limitation by the conquerors on the sovereignty which they exercise over conquered territory."

His feline agility of mind was displayed here in the seemingly accidental use of the plural, which he followed by a development of his dictum as though he had used the singular. Conceding any basis to his interpretation, it was *all the conquerors together* who imposed this limitation upon their *joint sovereignty.* No individual conqueror acting apart from the others could lay any claim to sovereignty, and none of them therefore had any sovereignty which he himself could limit.

But in any event the idea of annexation, and of the sovereignty which accompanies it, had been abandoned by the Allies, each for all and all for each, in the most unmistakable terms in respect of the ex-Turkish dominions, not to mention the other regions conquered by their arms. There were good intentions behind this abandonment, but not good intentions alone, since very notable advantages came to the Allies from such a policy. The relinquishment of annexation bound the United States fast to us, and gave us their Gordian sword to sever the knotted West Front. It also gave us a position of moral superiority towards the hostile Central Powers which was one of the main causes of the latter's defeat, and was exploited by us to the full.

The Mandatory system, which replaced annexation, however misused in practice, was in principle founded on a proper estimate of the rights of peoples. It was not a limitation by the conquerors of their own sovereignty. It was a postponement, arranged by them, of the exercise of sovereignty by the mandated races, whose sovereignty was itself predicated thereby. If the Covenant had been followed the Mandated peoples would all have had first voice in choosing the Mandatory, and so would have given their consent to this mandatory tutorship and to the postponement of their inherent rights. Everything thus would have conformed comfortably to equity. As it turned out, this stipulation was disregarded in the case of Palestine. But the disregard did not alter the truth that the people of that country, along with the other peoples of the A mandates, though provided like youths not of age with mandatory trustees, were yet always the owners of the property which the trustees administered on their behalf.

There was therefore never any British sovereignty in Palestine, and never any automatic legalization of governments there proceeding from annexation. A few testimonies may be cited to confirm this. President Wilson made a clear statement in January 1919 before the Council of Ten (of which Lord Balfour was a member), while the Mandatory system was in the making, that "the basis of this idea—trusteeship by the League of Nations through the appointment of Mandatories—was the feeling which had sprung up all over the world against further annexation..."

Lord Balfour, having heard the character of a Mandatory charge thus explicitly defined, next day "intervened in the discussion" with the observation that "the British delegation did not reject the idea of a Mandatory Power. I myself am strongly in favour of the principle. The [British] objection applies not to the areas conquered by British arms and managed from London, but to areas conquered by self-governing Dominions" i.e., (such as those captured during Botha's campaign in South Africa or as the Pacific isles captured by the Australians).

An unmistakable declaration. The British Government in the areas conquered by British arms and managed from London, of which Palestine was one, excluded the theory of annexing territory, and so of sovereignty over it. This was within a few months of the victory.

Earlier still, before victory had come, on the 5th of January, 1918, Mr. Lloyd George himself had asseverated that there was to be no annexation should it smile on our arms. "Armenia, Mesopotamia, Syria and Palestine," he announced in a speech, "have the right to see their separate national existences recognized."

Balfour, when later, in 1922, he spoke to the Council of the League and put forward his new doctrine of "self-imposed limitation over sovereignty exercised," either had forgotten or did not care what he had said in 1919. This was very like him. Once during that same 1919, in Paris, after an important meeting of the Council of Ten, next morning he was shown by a secretary (my informant) the minutes of the previous day's meeting. He perused them distantly like a bill of fare, and then inquired, "Does this purport to be what I said yesterday?" "Yes, sir," said the secretary, "it is an exact draft, taken down as you spoke." "Well," said Balfour upon some further inspection of the document, "I wish it to be understood clearly that these words I appear to have used do not represent the opinion of His Majesty's Government." Then, after a pause, as he dropped the minutes indifferently beside him, he added, "Nor, indeed, do they represent my own."

It was about this time too that Mr. Lloyd George, asked how "A.J.B." was getting on at the Peace Conference, replied "Oh, quite well. But he is settling nothing." (Riddell.) However, when Balfour disowned conquest before President Wilson he did help to settle something, whether he felt like remembering this afterwards or not.

A testimony to put beside President Wilson's is that of M. Poincaré who in February 1921 treating of the situation in the French area of Syria, epitomized it thus: "*il fera comprendre à tous que nous n'avons pas à établir en Syrie ni notre protectorat, ni à plus forte raison notre souveraineté.*" ("He [General Gouraud, the French High Commissioner] will make it plain to all that we are not to establish a protectorate in Syria and all the more are not to establish our sovereignty.") The situation of the French in North Syria and of the British in South Syria was identical. What was true of their regime was true of ours.

Then, in the July of 1920, Mr. Ormsby-Gore contributed his opinion, in an article published in *The Covenant*, a review issued by the League of Nations Union. "During the progress of the War," said he, "the leading statesmen of the A and A.P. were continually repeating that their war aims in regard to the ex-German Colonies and to the emancipated races of the Ottoman Empire did not and would not involve any policy of 'annexation.'"

In another passage he emphasized that, "The Mandatory Power has not complete sovereignty in respect of the territory in which it is to exercise tutelage, as its sovereignty is limited and circumscribed by the terms of the Mandate which it holds from the League." That is to say the Mandatory power has no sovereignty at all, for sovereignty here means unlimited power, and to talk of "limited sovereignty" is merely loose English.

As Secretary of State for the Colonies Mr. Ormsby-Gore confirmed, or reiterated, officially his 1920 statement. This was during the lengthy debate in the House of Commons upon the Government's policy for Palestine, upon the 21st of July of last year. "We are only temporary trustees in Palestine," said he, "trustees on behalf of the League. It is not our territory."

The Council of the League of Nations itself, on the 6th of September, 1929, declared that it adhered to a declaration upon the matter made by it in 1927. The Council enunciated, "There is no reason to modify in any way this opinion, which states implicitly that sovereignty in the traditional sense of the word does not reside in the mandatory Power." The British member of the Council which gave this decision was Mr. Arthur Henderson.

Finally, a practical and concrete proof has been afforded by the Belgian

Government, which in 1932 desired to effect a change in the frontier of its Mandated area of Ruata-Urundi, in Africa. Before doing so it sought the consent, not only of the League of Nations, but also of the United States. The consent of Italy and of Japan, it would appear, should have been sought too, but Belgium at least recognized that she possessed no sovereignty in this territory, even though she, as an African Mandatory, had ampler powers there than were possessed by A class Mandatories in the Near East. Native ownership of the soil was not definitely predicated in (B and C) African Mandates. Still less therefore was or is Great Britain sovereign in Palestine, where this ownership was predicated.

That, I think, deals abundantly with the two points which may be raised to claim legitimacy for the 1920-3 Government in Palestine or for its acts. There was no annexation of that country either before or after the Mandate came into force, nor did a situation ever exist in which moral or legal authority, such as that Government assumed and exerted, came to it before September 1923.

There is one subsidiary and final point, however, upon which a few paragraphs may be spent before the question is left. Purveyors of red herrings as standard diet may plead that, despite all this illegality, the 1920-3 Government was one which benefited Palestine, restored the country, improved the lot of the people, and in general was extremely praiseworthy.

This plea, of course, has nothing to do with the point at issue, which is not whether Sir Herbert Samuel's Government had any good aspects during those three years, but whether it *was* a Government. Some of its acts were good, some were indifferent, and some were as bad as possible. If because of its moiety of good acts, a government can waive the need of any title-deeds, things are being made easy for despotism and for lawless occupation. In Palestine the Civil Government walked into the house, using the key of the proper O.E.T.A. housekeeper, whom it had sent packing. No amount of tidying-up or of repair or of installation of new furniture justified it in making free with what was not its own, and nothing nullified its trespass.

The Government of 1920-3 had an admirable side to its activities, its municipal or county-council side, which dealt with personal welfare, with road-making, crop-improvement, repair of the damages of war, education and many other things. Even this municipal side, though, held a latent peril in it for the Arabs, if the State machine were over-developed for the size of the country. In any event, too, these merits were accompanied by another set of its activities, in the political order, which imposed the Zionists, produced projects for unrepresentative Legislative

Councils, substituted private agreements for tenders in public works, and issued deceptive statements of its own aims.

The one side was composed by the labours of an Administration tackling local needs in the spirit and according to the traditions of British rule, the other side was made of the schemes of distant statesmen who disregarded this spirit and broke these traditions. Nothing the officials did can cancel what the statesmen did. British officials worked for the Arabs' present while British statesmen worked against the Arabs' future. The officials tended them as men while the statesmen maltreated them as Arabs. The officials promoted their individual survival: the statesmen prepared their national sterilization.

Chapter 24

Ersatz Israel.

Appropriately, it was during the three years of arbitrary rule that the situation of Palestine, as we see it today, took its form. By the end of 1923, when the Mandate finally did arrive, the long-planned Zionizing regime was firmly in command, and the course of the country had been fixed. A Constitution had been adopted; "authorized" immigration had been begun; the Rutenberg development schemes were wedged into place; the Zionist Commission had been made a constituent item in the national policy; the United States had withdrawn the opposition which was interfering with Lord Balfour's designs.

A second outbreak of rioting, with much more bloodshed, had been followed by a second Commission of investigation, thus establishing the series of outbreaks attended by Commissions which was to become a recognized feature of Palestine's life under British control. Chief of all, the Arabs had laid their case formally before the Home Government in London, by the mouth of chosen representatives who journeyed thither.

They received their answer from the Colonial Secretary, then Mr. Winston Churchill, who in this way was obliged to frame the Government case in response. It included a denial of any obligations under the McMahon Pact, as well as a statement of the Government's understanding of what was meant by the "National Home." So that during this period the primary issues in Palestine were brought forward and, if the Government was to be believed, the rights and the wrongs of them were settled for good and aye.

Whether this, however, was the truth now remains to be examined. The reader will see for himself what bearing the various events just mentioned, of which I shall now treat in turn, have upon the general story, and will see, when we come to it, what there was in the full-scale Governmental case thus presented to the world, and so often repeated since.

Immigration had best be taken first, because after all it is enforced immigration which is at the root of the whole Palestine Question. At this point what requires to be specified is not alone the numbers of the Zionist immigrants during these three years, and the circumstances under which they entered. It is even more necessary to identify the character of the immigration, which in 1920 was a change of style from pre-War Jewish colonization. What was there in the new immigration—quite apart from the peril of its increasing volume—which rendered it obnoxious to Palestine? What exactly did the new immigration represent? Did it even represent the rebirth of a Jewish nation, as it purported to do?

These matters of principle are more vital than any mere account of happenings, and whatever did happen can only be properly understood if they are understood first.

During the period under review Zionist immigration, as far as numbers went, did not injure the Arab status. The registration of immigrants had begun, with some difficulty, under O.E.T.A. in 1919, and in that year 2,000 were admitted, most of whom were cases of repatriation. The rate quickened with the coming of the Civil Administration, and in 1921 there were 9,000 entries. In 1922 and 1923 it slackened to between 7,000 and 8,000. In all, between February 1919 and the close of 1923, in round figures 31,000 recorded Jewish immigrants entered Palestine. This was a net total, for there were other figures to subtract before it was reached. During 1922 and 1923 no less than 10,000 Jews *emigrated from Palestine.* Of this phenomenon little has been heard, of course, since it tallies so badly with Zionist assumptions.

No doubt the majority of these Jews departed because of the difficulty of earning a livelihood under the very hard conditions of the time, but there were plenty among them, as I was to learn from their own lips, who went off because they found the country antipathetic and wished in the ordinary way to "better themselves." Generally these men had been transported to the National Home at the expense of the Zionist bodies. Now they all had to pay out of their own pockets to quit it, and quitted it, not as exiles leaving their country, but as emigrants disappointed with one foreign land and anxious to try their luck in another one. When every allowance has been made for the compulsion of poverty and misfortune, this is a light upon the National Home which is sufficiently revelative.

The 31,000 immigrants of 1919-23, despite the loss of the 10,000 emigrants, restored the Jewish population to about its pre-War level. Therefore, as has been said, there was nothing so much in their numbers to alter the status of the Arabs. It was their new footing which altered that. It was this arrival of the Jewish immigrants "by right and not by sufferance," as Mr. Churchill was to define it, which destroyed the status of the Arabs, who found themselves changed in a flick from being the owners of their home to being one of a pair of lodgers in it. That was hardly what King Hussein had foreseen when he had spoken of lodgers.

Hitherto the Turks had been their landlords indeed, but the key of the house had been the Arabs' and the Arabs' only. Now the Arabs were presented with latchkeys to their own hearths, Zionist strangers were given identical latchkeys, and in a day or two were pointing out the rooms in which they had been born.

There was this too. The immigrants of the early twenties brought with them ideas and schemes of life which were incompatible with their own pretensions. Later on, as their numbers grew, these ideas and schemes, developed and propagated, were to threaten the extinction of Arabism. For the moment what they signified was, of all things, the extinction of any Jewish national sense there might have been in Palestine, and of any basis of unity there might have been there between Jews and Arabs.

The political Zionists often enough advise attention to the good terms on which the pre-War Zionists of Palestine had lived with the Arabs. They add that if it were not for the intrigues of various interested parties these good relations would have continued with themselves. The Arabs draw a different moral from the same fact. They point out that the pre-War Jews were on pretty good terms with the surrounding population primarily because they made no attack on the position of that population, and secondly because their ways and customs fitted in reasonably well with the ways and the customs of the land itself.

What follows from this deserves every consideration. The ways and customs of the pre-War Jews, which thus fitted into the Arab scheme of things, were essentially Jewish. Therefore when Jews were real Jews and real Zionists, Zionists by devotion and not by "right," they were acceptable enough to the Arabs (the question of peril through mass-immigration not having arisen). When Jews, however, clamoured to enter the Holy Land as though it was theirs by title, yet the moment they were inside behaved as non-Jews and erased or hid the Scrolls of the Law beneath voters' lists, by-laws of the G.F.J.L. (General Federation of Jewish Labour), agenda for Rutenberg company meetings and other such Occidental common places—then the Arabs would have nothing to do with them. They could accept into their midst Jews who had some national character. They would not accept the new Zionist immigrants who had no national character at all, yet were full of bold and outrageous claims based upon something which they did not possess, and presented Trades-Union certificates and Directors' reports as the insignia of Moses.

The pre-War Jews had held traces of cousinship with the Arabs, but they had never tried to make capital out of this fact, nor indeed had mentioned it at all. But cousinship had been pressed incongruously upon the suffering Feisal by Jews of the new type, such as Dr. Weizmann and Professor Frankfurter and various gentlemen from New York and Boston, who had no trace of it. The Weizmanns and the Frankfurters were men of ability, but when they proffered themselves as "cousins of the Arabs" they were ludicrous.

The immigrants of the new "mandatory" disposition, certainly all those younger ones who set the note for the attitude of the Zionist mass were of this Frankfurter type, though they did not come from the United States. Mostly those young people came from Eastern Europe, but were hardly at all Eastern. They were European in a generalized way, without territorial connections but breathing the ideas in the European air. There had been indeed not so much physical side to their lives. Theirs was a disembodied existence, with no real home save in what was thought or spoken. They had grown up in books, and they lived in speeches.

Jewish Palestine, as they found it, did not please them in the least. They thought the old P.I.C.A. or Rothschild colonies, founded by Baron Edmond de Rothschild, parasitic. They found even such self-supporting farm-settlements as Zichron Jakob or Petach Tikvah not at all to their taste: I was to hear the latter called an "agricultural ghetto." As for the Jews of traditional type, the Jews of the "Wailing Wall" and of the pockets of survival round Safad, they thoroughly despised them.

The Jews of the "Wailing Wall" were found good enough by them, it is true, as a means to an end, as living evidence for their claim of historic succession. But that was for the benefit of the outer world. Amongst themselves the newcomers hardly regarded their predecessors as alive. They looked on them as faded parchments employed either as proof of pedigree, or as fossilized strata on which they had to gain a foothold ere rearing on the site their own brand-new, blue-print, political, *lucus a non lucendo* Zion.

Some of the apologists of this Zionism, aware of the deadly self-contradiction in its spurning of traditionalism, tried to mask this as a breaking-away from the subservience and the squalor of the ghetto. That excuse will not do. If the newcomers had but set their faces against dirt and overcrowding, there would have been no criticism to make of them, of course. But what they set their faces against was the distinctively Jewish life which lay beneath any superficial dirt and overcrowding.

It was in squalid passages and peopled tenements and small dark synagogues that the Jewish ideal had persisted at its purest and most individual. This was the experience, not of the Jews only, but of all subjected clans or nations or races. Their national life continued in the houses of the poor and the conservative. The men afterwards called national liberators or revivers came respectfully and lovingly to the homes of the traditionalists, caught from them the vital breath, drew deep of it and exhaled it in power.

It was not so in Palestine. The political youth who now began swaggering in by right wanted no feeble breaths from the chinks of the past mingling with their modern air-conditioning. *They* were Zion, or rather Zion was and would have to be what they were. It was take-it-or-leave-it for the spirit and the sanctuary. Once the ancestral deposit in Jerusalem had served its documentary purpose, they had no use any more for the bearded and ringleted Orthodox, who found themselves discarded and driven for self-preservation into violent dissensions with their very determined supplanters.

So while the new Zionists, in the early 'twenties, outside of Palestine were making all possible capital out of Jewish tradition, inside Palestine, on the other hand, they were doing their utmost to relegate to limbo the pre-War Jews, the only Jews who represented tradition. These latter were appealing continually for redress against the politicians' endeavours to reduce their status, to contaminate their customs, to force them into politically-framed representative bodies. Petitions from them flowed to the Administration, to the Home Government, to the League of Nations, to private visitors of mark even, in a continuous stream.

Their supersession betrayed the falsity of the whole political Zionist movement. If there was such a thing as the Jewish nation it was the traditional Jews who represented it. The other kind of Jews had, it is true, a vast deal of achievement to their credit. The history of Western civilization was alight with their names. As poets, musicians, thinkers and—in the material order—as men-of-business, they had been amidst the principal makers of that civilization. There was no branch of it to which they had not contributed. But they paid the penalty of being whelmed by what they created. The Disraelis, Heines, Rubinsteins and Einsteins vanished as Jews in the Western world which they helped to construct.

But the religious observances, the ways of life, the writings of the traditional Jews—that was something other men had not got, something the West had not absorbed, a separate culture. To have forced this on the Arabs would have been wrong, but at least it would have been something individual to force.

Whereas the new immigrants and their leaders, Dr. Weizmann and Mr. Brandeis and all the rest, had nothing of their own, even to force. The leaders talked so much of the Jewish nation and of Jewish culture that it was not seen that they had neither of these things in their baggage. They brought culture with them, but it was not Jewish: they brought Jews with them who proceeded to regenerate Palestine in a way any Occidental might have employed.

They made great play of their introduction of Hebrew, which they caused to be made into an official language. On the very postage-stamps of Palestine they had the words *"Eretz Israel"* ("the land of Israel") placed. But it would have been nearer to truth if the inscription had been *"Ersatz Israel."*

They might talk Hebrew, but there was not a Hebrew deed done by them; they had, in a sense, to translate all their acts into it.

The Hebrew with which they covered the surface of the National Home was like one of those figures in eighteenth-century farthingales which some people use to cover their telephone. That appliance, in fact, might well serve as an illustration of what, under their veil of Hebrew letters, the political Zionists represented. They were as utilitarian, progressive and scientific as telephones, and not a whit more national. In those early 'twenties the immigrants no more brought to Palestine the first fruits of a distinctive culture and civilization than these would have been brought there by the importation of 31,000 telephone instruments.

Nor, during the years which have passed since then, have their successors contributed the overdue crop. Just the reverse. As their numbers and their power in the country have increased, all they have done has been to suck more and more national life out of it. Their institutions have grown more and more extraneous, to culminate in their monstrous Tel-Aviv, a great false hump strapped on to the shrinking back of Palestine.

There are over 100,000 Jews in Tel-Aviv and none but Jews in it, yet it is as much a Jewish city as is London by Aldgate, or any other "Jewish Quarter" in any other Western metropolis. In these "Jewish Quarters" who but the Jews have been assimilated? The Kosher notices, the shop signs in strange characters, all the emblems of the sort meeting the eye, are nothing to set against the anglicization of Aldgate's denizens. Jewish life in the "Jewish Quarter" has no doubt its faithful core, but for ever-increasing thousands it becomes a matter of a few labels, a few dishes of food, a round of Saturday Sabbaths approximating more and more each year to the dechristianized Sunday Sabbaths of the enveloping multitudes.

Tel-Aviv is the embodiment of these conditions. It is nothing but the largest of all "Jewish Quarters," and, since its inhabitants come from so many sources, possibly the least individual, least nationalist, most heteroclite of any.

This is a staggering thought, when it is remembered that by their own title, falsified though it be, the political Zionists were imposed upon Palestine in order to install there a thoroughly Jewish national civilization. Despite all their ability they have been unable to produce anything of this save here and there some of its unwarranted outer symbols. The truth is that their ability has no Jewish character, and only aims at producing the common occidental type of public works and places of instruction and of entertainment. The university, the technical schools, the laboratories, the experimental farms, the friendly societies, the discussion-groups, the symphony orchestras—they have them all, and a host of like institutions.

The National Home has even blossomed into "lidos" in the Hyde Park manner, imitations of imitations. As an ingenuous British Jew said to an acquaintance of mine, to whom he was discoursing enrapturedly of developments on the Zionist rivieras, "It's wonderful what they've done in a few years. It'll soon be like Ramsgate." Precisely.

Nothing but Ramsgate indeed in its least Kentish aspect or some Central European spa was ever to be expected. In trivial and minor things the National Home population always has had the mentality and the practices which have corresponded to those of its leaders in weighty and major things. The Zionist leader summoning Mr. Ormsby-Gore to heel, the Zionist scientist spending long vigils at his experimental bench, the Zionist schoolmasters in their classrooms, the Zionist industrialist popularizing some product, the Zionist shopkeeper arranging some spring or autumn sale, the Zionist builder, lawyer, or commercial agent—all are part of the familiar socio-political circle in which our Western world gyrates, and gyrates till its dingier rims appear. Thereabouts, in Palestine, overfleshed women, dowdily nude, sunning themselves in shorts, form a section of circumference accustomedly vulgar to ourselves, but impious and ever rankling to the Christians and Moslems of that land.

In major matters or minor, in meritorious or meritless or indifferent things, these people, these political Zionists, have shown themselves in fine capable of establishing in Palestine an up-to-date community, but from the start incapable of establishing one that was Jewish.

Like so many other things, this deficiency of theirs has remained hidden, or unmentioned. It may be that to mention it now will only provoke the retort that to condemn the political Zionists because they are not national is unfair. The one thing which they are trying to achieve, it will be said, is this very nationalism, and if they have not achieved it immediately that is because of the enormous handicap upon them. Dispersed about the world, they have not been in a position to acquire any form of culture except the non-Jewish culture of the particular place in which one group or another of them has lived. For whatever task they may undertake their equipment is un-Jewish, and it is unreasonable therefore to expect them to transform their holdings in Palestine into a centre in all respects Jewish at once.

The plea is plausible, but is no answer to the charge. Evidently enough the political Zionists could only bring with them to Palestine an un-Jewish equipment (considering this now, for argument's sake, as an involuntary act of theirs). But what they could have brought with them, what it was necessary they should have brought with them for any sort of self-justification, was the Jewish spirit. If they were what they said they were, Jews and nothing else, they were bound to possess this; it must be automatically in their keeping. With the Jewish spirit directing them, their practical handicap of un-Jewish education would not have mattered, for the spirit would have shone through in their own new, untrammelled surroundings. From those first days of 1920 it would have manifested itself as an instinct to do everything in as Jewish a manner as they could. Most important of all, it would have manifested itself in open compunction if this or that handicap forced them into developing their unique National Home in any commonplace international way. However fine the work they might accomplish in the international style, they would have been dissatisfied with working thus. They would have been trying continually to alter their manner of work. They would have given voice to their discontent too, for their natural feelings must have welled up in them altogether beyond containing.

That was an acid test of their genuineness: would they show compunction? It was a test in which, then and since, they have failed. Not compunction but contentment has marked their attitude from the beginning. They have been self-satisfied to think that their National Home reproduced so exactly the chief institutions of the countries in which they were born or in which they made their way. They have been proud of their carbon copies of all the latest gospels, and have said so. They have vaunted the perfect parallelism of their lectureships and of their statistical bureaus and of their board-rooms with those most recently established in the West.

Besides, their attitude to the surviving Jewish culture was proof in itself of their lack of the Jewish spirit. They were determined to compel those rabbis and layfolk who clung to this culture to subject it now to the political Zionist doctrine. "We are being compelled to make common cause with these false Zionists," Chief Rabbi Zonnenfeld protested to me when I came to Jerusalem and met him. "The Government aids and abets them by declaring that there must be a single Jewish Community in Palestine representing all Jews, and that one under the control of the so-called Zionist Organization. We are to sit with people who desecrate the Sabbath, we, who are the true moral foundation of Zionism. In Palestine alone we number four thousand fathers of families, the delegates of at least a million Orthodox of the Ashkenazi in the world."

This was the major compulsion, this driving of the Orthodox into the service of a profane ideal. In much the same way, the Hebrew tongue was driven into the service of political propaganda. The politicians scored a point by using Hebrew as the common tongue. Gentiles thought it a proof of their innate Judaism. But for the Orthodox, for the true Zionists, Hebrew was a tongue sacred to prayer, too sacred to be debased to ordinary uses. For common intercourse they mostly used Yiddish or such

Western tongues as they knew. But now the immigrants were compelling the use of Hebrew for everything. They were like innovators devalorizing poetry by driving everyone to shop and to gossip in pseudo-Shelley or practical-Keats.

But it was not the restored Hebrew of the immigrants which contained the Jewish spirit, it was the Hebrew of the altar and the Yiddish of the Orthodox. Their Yiddish had become the vehicle of Hebrew thought, which was the soul of Jewry. The Hebrew of the immigrants, the Hebrew of the politicians, the Hebrew of the Zionist Organization, was on the other hand full of Yiddish thought. That is to say that at its best it was used by them for the grafted ideas, the part-Germanic, part-British, part-American, part-Danubian theories which they professed. Their Hebrew was the dialect of professors and of publicists in all tongues, unnational.

Thus, then, in outlook and in act, the new immigrants, the political Zionists, showed themselves not the heirs but the changelings of Israel. Far from bringing anything national to Palestine, they did not even know their own true nationalism when they encountered it there amidst their pre-War population. To them it seemed nothing but an archaic religiosity.

This must be said for them, however, that the young immigrants possessed the virtues of their defects. If they had not the Jewish spirit they had the most selfless devotion to undefined Progress. Their character was best typified in the "*chalutzim*" or "pioneers" who formed their vanguard. These were students and intellectuals, worthy of high respect for their courage. They came to Palestine to act as manual workers, to labour on the land. They wished both to remove the reproach which lay upon the Jewish race of having no contact with the soil, and to build up their new settlement. They were ready to endure every hardship, and to encounter death itself, as large numbers of them did in the reclaiming of malarial swamps. Others led hard comfortless lives road-making, navvying, bricklaying.

The *chalutzim,* and the new immigrants generally, were accused of being all Bolsheviks or Communists of the most blood-red type. This was not true. They were brought into Palestine under the auspices of the Zionist Organization, which worked through local committees in the towns of Galicia, Roumania and such places. There was therefore some degree of safeguard over the prospective immigrants, though the lists made by the local committees were prone to include an agitator or two, included to avoid enmities or because of personal friendship. As a second safeguard, accordingly, the British Consul of the district had to visa the lists and could refuse any particular names upon them.

Consequently the majority of the recorded immigrants to the National Home had been passed through some sort of sieve and were not hotheads of revolution, by Western standards. What they were by Arab standards is a totally different matter.

The same could not be said of the "unrecorded" or clandestine, smuggled immigrants. There were a great many of these, as there have always been, and at the start as in recent years the proportion of them to registered entries was very high. The Peel Report estimates that 22,400 "unauthorized settlers" (how characteristic of the Report's special pink-wash is the use of "settler" to hide the starkness of "unauthorized") came into Palestine during the two years 1932 and 1933. In the early 'twenties figures were not far below this. During a given nine months of 1921 a thousand Jews a month entered by clandestine methods, generally by night journeys across the northern frontier and from vessels which hove to at lonely places on the coast.

This smuggling of immigrants became an organized business, of which Galatz was a notable centre in Europe. There was also a forged-passport bureau in Berlin. In Beyrout a Jewish hotel-porter received a regular salary of £400 a year as a principal agent in the traffic.

The Palestine police and immigration officials could do little to stop it. Their numbers were absurdly few for such a task: at Semakh, for example, where the railway from the Hauran and Damascus entered Palestine, the immigration staff consisted in those days of "one competent Soudanese." The police proper not only were very few, but too often found that the measures they took were countered elsewhere. The railway police had rendered good service by discovering and by arresting clandestine immigrants, but presently these policemen were removed by higher orders. The police authorities then detailed their own C.I.D. detectives to the task, only to see their work negatived by the disclosure of information through Zionist clerks in the Intelligence Department. It was impossible to keep any plans secret.

The headquarters of the Zionist Organization may be acquitted of any share in the smuggling of immigrants. But the same cannot be said of the Zionist Commission in Palestine. It connived at the secret immigration. If it did not arrange it it was thoroughly aware of it, and felt no call to bring it to an end or to give to the police or the immigration authorities any information of value concerning it. (Cf. the Peel Report upon present-day illegal immigration. "Jewish public opinion has declined to assist public authority in the detection of illegal Jewish immigrants.") The books of its Immigration section when examined were found to contain gross discrepancies between the recorded numbers of arrivals into the country and those notified as settled to the Immigration Department.

It was amidst the clandestine immigrants, as might have been expected, that some active Communists made their way into Palestine. They actually organized themselves into a formal group (*"Mitlagat Poalim Sozialistim"*), generally called the M.P.S. or Mopsi, of which the leaders were men named Chaldi, Lomosoneff and Myerson. All the Mopsi were not necessarily clandestine immigrants, but most were. Once they were in the country they were adepts at securing papers and in other ways at obscuring their origin. Within a month of Sir Herbert Samuel's arrival, Myerson went off to Moscow as a delegate to a Jewish Congress held there, at which no less a personage than Trotsky was chief spokesman and a committee for "Propaganda and Agitation" in Palestine was appointed. M. Trotsky recommended that "other objects be used as a cloak."

In November of 1920 a demonstration was held in Jaffa; in December a secret meeting in Jerusalem, when it was decided to "organize the railways." By February of 1921 there were known to be a full two hundred members of this group in Palestine, and in March they issued a handbill-proclamation calling on all workers, Jew or Arab, to join their ranks as members of the Red Army of workers. Arms had been smuggled in as a precaution against the hostility of the Arabs.

The hostility of the Arabs had increased considerably, as may be imagined. They knew about the arms and the clandestine immigration, and they saw their country becoming a mere depot for alien and incomprehensible bodies, which made the Holy Land the theatre of squalid disputes. The Mopsi were on the worst terms with the moderate group called "*Achduth Avodah*" ("Unity of Work"), which was affiliated to the 1st and 2nd Internationals, whereas the Mopsi were attached to the 3rd.

One of these internal Zionist quarrels precipitated the riots of May 1921. It was the 1st of the month, and the Achduth Avodah had been holding a large, official and duly licensed demonstration-procession in honour of Labour Day. To the Arabs the Labour side of the demonstration was all gibberish: what they very naturally saw in it was a triumphal gathering and march of the flock of strangers who were settling like starlings upon their country.

The Mopsi held a counter-procession, which had a collision, noisy but more verbal than physical, with the Achduth Avodah, and cannoned off their ranks to a tract near the seashore, on the fringe of the Arab town. The Mopsi procession was thoroughly unofficial and unlicensed and indeed before this brush had been vociferously decrying British Imperialism. The meeting between the two processions had raised the general temperature, and when the Mopsi came down to the seashore to demonstrate, Arabs gathered in the lee of their houses, and blows soon followed and then firing. The Arabs seem to have struck the first blows, but really the affair was like the coming together of two chemicals which if heated to a certain point burst into flame upon contact.

The outbreak was not so much a riot as a miniature rising against the presence of the Zionists. If military forces had not been there to quell it and the Zionists had had no arms there would have been some sort of Sicilian Vespers. As happens so often on such occasions, the majority of the victims were not active participants in the demonstrations, but a group of luckless older immigrants of the quieter sort who were awaiting transfer in the Immigrant Hostel maintained by the Zionist Commission. The Arab mob had reached that state of frenzy which seizes Orientals, and only saw in the Immigrant Hostel the centre and the symbol of their supersession. Thirteen of the inmates, including a woman, were murdered.

From Jaffa the outbreak spread into the countryside and several Jewish colonies were attacked, notably Petach-Tikvah, which had a narrow escape from being sacked. Since Petach-Tikvah was a pre-War, non political colony, wherein (unlike the political colonies) Arabs were given work, the berserk state of mind of the populace was patent. Martial law was proclaimed on the 2nd, but it was a week before any semblance of order returned, and the country stayed excited and agitated for weeks. Close on 200 Jews were killed or wounded in the disturbances and some 120 Arabs. The majority of the Arabs were killed or wounded by the troops, but after the first surprise the younger Jews had drawn on their private arms supply and had defended themselves, here and there passing to the offensive. Some of the Arab police were convicted of taking part in the attack on the Immigrant Hostel.

Most likely what contributed most to the restoration of peace was that Sir Herbert Samuel took the decision to suspend Zionist immigration, which he had introduced in the previous August by an "Immigration Ordinance," enacted by himself as High Commissioner. It was a courageous decision to take, since of course the cry rang out in the Zionist ranks that he was yielding to mob-law. "The High Commissioner certainly lost the confidence of the Zionists for the time being. The idea was even canvassed of making representations to the Colonial Office to get him recalled there and then." (Horace Samuel.)

But on the 7th the appointment of a Commission of Inquiry was announced by the Palestine Government and this served to divert attention. The members of the Zionist Commission, who were the persons most discontented with Sir Herbert Samuel, turned to prepare their case. The Commissioners named were Sir Thomas Haycraft, the Chief Justice of Palestine, Mr. Harry Luke, Deputy-Governor of Jerusalem (now Sir Harry Luke and Governor of Fiji), and Mr. J. N. Stubbs of the Legal Department, with Jewish and Arab assessors to aid them. The terms of reference of the Commission were "to inquire into the recent disturbances in the town and neighbourhood of Jaffa and to report thereon."

The Haycraft Commission thus had general latitude in respect of its report, though the inquiry was focused on Jaffa. It was the second of the series of Palestine Commissions, which, as I have said, were to be appointed almost as a matter of course on the morrow of any bloodshed and disorder in Palestine. So much in fact did the appointment of these bodies come to be expected, that in 1929 when an experienced British official heard through his window the first shots of the outbreak of that year, his immediate reaction was to exclaim, "Good Lord! Another Commission!"

The first Commission of Inquiry, which had followed the outbreak of 1920, the already-mentioned Palin Commission, had reported about the time that Sir Herbert Samuel assumed office. On his advice its Report was not published: he thought that, just as he was trying to make a start at pacification, it would only revive discords to no purpose. No doubt Sir Herbert was right, in so far as the general end of avoiding particular incitements to breaches of the peace was served. But the very policy which the High Commissioner had been sent to Palestine to establish was the source of the "discords," and produced a regular supply of new ones as the days passed. To suppress the Palin Report, yet to continue with the policy which was responsible for the subject-matter of the Report, was not a piece of remarkably clear thinking, though in this the High Commissioner is not to be regarded as primarily responsible. The Home Government was responsible, and it had not the faintest intention of thinking clearly, or of thinking at all.

Despite the restrictions laid upon its members by the limited scope of their inquiry, the Haycraft Commissioners managed to include in their report some very notable judgments. These had all the more weight since the Commissioners were conversant with the country and understood the mentality of its population.

Very significant was the refusal of the Commission to allow the mere details of the Jaffa affray to be given over-prominence. At the time Zionist writers and Zionist witnesses before the Commission naturally endeavoured to make the most of these details, which were in their favour. Next to them they were anxious to give prominence to the real or alleged defects of the British officials of the Administration in not taking due precautions for public order before the May Day demonstrations began, or in not taking swift enough and unsparing enough action after the start of the outbreak.

If the inquiry had been kept upon these points, the real underlying causes of the outbreak, the Government's insistence upon the National Home and the growing peril to the Arabs in Zionist immigration, would have been kept out of sight. The country would not have been shown to be riven right through at the good pleasure of Whitehall: the outbreak would have seemed a simple question of police and military carelessness in allowing too much latitude to the inconsequential roughs of Jaffa and the countryside. But what was the verdict of the Commissioners upon the question?

> "The immediate cause of the Jaffa riots on the 1st of May was an unauthorized demonstration of Bolshevik Jews, followed by its clash with an authorized demonstration of the Jewish Labour Party. The racial strife was begun by Arabs and rapidly developed into a conflict of great violence between Arabs and Jews, in which the Arab majority, who generally were the aggressors, inflicted most of the casualties."

In another passage they declared:

> "When we come to consider the causes of the disturbances we find an immediate cause which of itself would not have been sufficient to give rise to more than a street-riot of the ordinary kind … the M.P.S. demonstration and its clash with the procession of the Jewish Labour Party."

So, while the culpability of the Arabs for making the attack is duly stressed, it is made clear that its immediate cause was of no importance, and that something graver lay behind it. In itself the clash between the two parties of Jews was nothing, but their very presence and the offence of their demonstrations produced "racial strife." There was no responsible personage in London who could read this Report and not perceive the implication that a condition had been created in Palestine where real racial strife might spring from any minor occurrence.

The Commissioners could not speak about the responsibility of the Government, but they could speak of the responsibility of the Government's avowed partners:

> "We feel bound to express the opinion arrived at in the course of this inquiry that the Zionist Commission, which is the representative of the Zionist Organization in Palestine, has failed to carry conviction to the Arabs on the point of the National Home benefiting Arabs as much as Jews. As far as we can judge, the only sentiment it has inspired in them is one of profound mistrust… The distrust inspired in the Arabs by the Zionist Commission has been in our opinion an appreciable factor in creating the feeling, but for which probably the Jaffa riots would not have taken place… The Commission has desired to ignore the Arabs as a factor to be taken into serious consideration, or else has combated their interests to the advantage of the Jews…. Furthermore, the influence exercised, or believed to be exercised, by the Commission over the framing of legislation and in the selection of Government officials has

> done nothing to lessen the distrust with which it is regarded by the Arabs, who have no similar body to exercise corresponding influence on their behalf.
>
> It is not for us to say that the activities, real or alleged, of the Zionist Commission were or are illegitimate: we can, however, say that in our opinion the Commission's conception of its duties and functions has exercised an exacerbating rather than a conciliatory influence on the Arab population of Palestine, and has thus been a contributory cause of the disturbances which are the subject of our inquiry."

Nothing more damaging to the National Home and to the Zionist leaders has appeared in this book itself than these official words. The Commissioners, too, hinted openly at the restrictions encompassing them and preventing them from eliciting the whole truth. "It is not for us to say that the activities of the Zionist Commission were or are illegitimate." Nor did they content themselves with generalities. They questioned most closely the chief Zionist witnesses, and closest of all Dr. Eder, the head of the "Political Department" of Dr. Weizmann's shadow-Administration in the spring of 1920, and at the time of the outbreak Acting Chairman of the Zionist Commission.

Until the Commission came to examine Dr. Eder, Acting Chairman of the Zionist Commission, we were unaware to what extent such expressions of opinion [amidst Zionists] as those we have quoted were authorized by responsible Zionists. Dr. Eder was a frank witness in expressing his views of the Zionist ideal. He gave no quarter to the view of the National Home as put forward by the Secretary of State and the High Commissioner [to be mentioned presently]. In his opinion there can be only one National Home in Palestine, and that a Jewish one, and there can be no equality in the partnership between Jews and Arabs, but a Jewish predominance as soon as the numbers of that race are sufficiently increased. He declined to admit the word "dominion," but chose "predominance." As Acting Chairman of the Zionist Commission Dr. Eder personally exposed in all points the Zionist creed, if such there be, and his statements are therefore most important.

There is no sophistry about Dr. Eder. He was quite clear that the Jews should, and the Arabs should not, have the right to bear arms, and he stated his belief that this discrimination would tend to improve Arab–Jewish relations.

He considered that with regard to the High Commissioner for Palestine the Zionist Organization should be allowed either to formulate objections to the selection of the British Government, or to submit a list of its own nominees for consideration.

Dr. Eder, besides contributing his wonderful dictum upon Arab disarmament to the anthology of the Palestine Question, was certainly plain-spoken. He made quite clear what the Arabs had to expect under the National Home. The Commissioners observe that there was no sophistry about him, as though, on the political horizon, they knew of others who were sophists. We cannot assume that Cabinet Ministers were in their minds, but Dr. Eder's plain-speaking was vastly preferable to the utterances of statesmen who never let one lobe of their brains know what the other was thinking. These statesmen most certainly looked forward, along with Dr. Eder, to the predominance of the Jews over the Arabs, but the term they used for it was the "union of Jews and Arabs," or they said they looked forward to the "adherence of Jews and Arabs to the service of their common fatherland," or employed some such phrase smooth with the unmelted butter in their mouths.

There is another passage of the Haycraft Report which is as valuable today as when it was written, because it deals with a contention which has been put forward, over and over again, year after year, by the Zionists and the spokesmen of successive Home Governments. The Haycraft Report really disposed of it, but the Governmental mouthpieces and the Zionists go on reiterating none the less. Nine years afterwards, as we shall see, the Shaw Report was forced to dispose of it all over again. Yet the utterers of this calumny continued, after this second exposure, as they continue now, to repeat it as though it had never been exposed. It is too easy for them to do so. Who reads official Reports in elderly and inaccessible Blue Books?

This contention or allegation is that amidst the bulk of the Arab population there never has been any deep-seated or fundamental objection to the National Home and all it betokens, that most of the Arabs have been nothing but the tools of the leaders, of the Mufti of Jerusalem, of the Arab Higher Committee, of the sheikhs, of the whole crew of land lords, lawyers, usurers and such, who batten on the impoverished multitude. Under the Turks these sirrahs exploited the multitude to the top of their bent, and if they had a government of their own they would continue to do so. But the National Home bars the way to this government. Hence their campaign against the Home.

The Gentile protagonists of the Zionist cause are especially given to this argument, and seem to think that they have worded it to perfection when they say that the Arab agitation only aims at maintaining the subjection of the *fellaheen* to the *effendis*. There is a magic for them in the word effendi. They use it in a half-revolted, half-convinced manner, as though on the one hand they had but to mention it to win their case, and on the other hand as though it were a sort of verbal poison dangerous to retain upon the tongue. It figures and has figured in countless articles and speeches, in the sense of "capitalist" or "exploiter."

In fact effendi is a singularly modest agnomen, about equivalent in English to "educated esquire." In our own country a man who makes a little money, and thereby rises if only ever so little in the world, wins automatically the title of "esquire." In Arabic lands the man who acquires a little knowledge is raised about as much over his fellows by being dubbed "effendi." (The difference in the source of the improved status will be noticed.) It is therefore as much nonsense to talk of effendis as though they were slave-driving capitalists as it would be to say that the poor are trodden down by esquires in England. Effendis are not a class at all, but comprise people of all views and all pecuniary conditions. A group of effendis in Britain would include, say, Maxton Effendi and Wedgwood Effendi, to say nothing of Sidebotham Effendi and Sacher Effendi, and most definitely would have included Snell Effendi ere he was advanced to the equivalent of Snell Pasha.

This necessary correction having been made, let me quote now what the Haycraft Commission had to say upon the supposed diversion of the Arabs into hatred of the National Home by effendis or by Arab leaders with self-seeking motives:

> "It has been argued before us that the present state of popular feeling is due to an artificial agitation promoted by men who suffer by the change of Government [i.e., from the Turkish Government] who, having lost the advantages they enjoyed under the corrupt regime, are anxious to embarrass the British Administration by any means and to bring about a change of Government, and that they have chosen the obvious method of attacking the Jewish policy. They say also that the sheikhs and money lenders fear to lose their influence over the people if the Jews become a power in agricultural affairs. There may be some truth in these arguments, and it is not improbable that there are persons of the above categories who do what they can to promote discontent. But that is not enough to explain the present state of things. The educated people are sons of the soil, and they talk politics. They are too numerous to have as a body any substantial interest in a reversion to Ottoman Government."

And again:

> "A good deal has been alleged by Jewish witnesses about the instigation of the Arab mob to violence by their leaders. If this means no more than that while educated people talk and write the mob acts, then there is truth in the allegation. But if it means that had it not been for incitement by the notables, effendis and sheikhs there would have been no riots, the allegation cannot be substantiated. To some extent the

motives that influenced different sections of the Arab population were not the same; but the general belief that the aims of the Zionists and Jewish immigration are a danger to the national and material interests of the Arabs in Palestine is well-nigh universal among the Arabs, and it is not confined to any particular class. All that can truly be said in favour of the Jewish view is that the leaders of Arab opinion not only make no secret of what they think, but carry on a political campaign. In this campaign, however, the people participate with the leaders, because they feel that their political and their material interests are identical."

This is pretty decisively put, and it is as appropriate a reply to the loose charges of today as to those of eighteen years ago. In 1921 the bogey was that the Arabs wished to change back to Turkish government; in our days the bogey is that they wish to change over to Italian government or to coalesce in some way with Italy. But there has never been any mass-sympathy for any other European Power in Palestine, except in so far as we have made another Power appear more friendly by our own less friendliness. I take a final quotation from the Haycraft Report:

"We consider that any anti-British feeling on the part of the Arabs that may have arisen in the country originates in the association of the Government with the furtherance of the policy of Zionism."

Equally true of 1938. No doubt anti-British feeling has developed in the interval, but so has the association of the Government with Zionism developed. If the situation is worse than it was, that is our fault and ours alone.

Mr. Churchill, when the Report was published, murmured in his official capacity that it was "ably compiled, lucid and well-reasoned," and that was about all that happened. No notice worth mention was taken of its lucidity or of its reasoning. The Colonial Office had for some while been busy with more congenial prospects, those of the "development" of Palestine.

The first public notice of these had come from the mouth of Mr. L. C. Amery who, speaking for the Government, had stated in the House of Commons on the 4th of April, a month before the Jaffa riots, that:

"... the Secretary of State for the Colonies is considering the adoption of a policy whereby permission to entertain applications for concessions for constructional developments and for schemes providing for the employment of labour might be granted to the Palestine Administration provided that (1) the terms of the draft Mandate for Palestine are strictly observed, and (2) the concessions are not in conflict with any existing concessions with which it may be necessary to deal under Article 311 of the Treaty of Sèvres. No modification of the decision not to

> grant concessions for working or prospecting for minerals and oils pending the entry into force of the Treaty of Sèvres is, however, at present contemplated."

The first and principal comment to be made on this is that the Secretary of State was proposing to adopt a policy which he had no earthly right to adopt. Neither he, nor Sir Herbert Samuel as his proxy, had any power to grant concessions in Palestine. So long as there was no legal Mandatory rule there not all the king's horses nor all the king's men could grant them. What is more, the Colonial Office knew this well. There had even been formal recognition by the Government of its inability to allow concessions.

At the close of the War a British engineer had put forward a scheme for the very type of constructional developments of which Mr. Amery had spoken. His plans included electrical development and, *qua* project, were well founded enough to secure the support of the Department of Overseas Trade. But when this engineer, whose name was Bicknall— he had served in Palestine during the War—informed the Foreign Office of his application, he was told that the Government was powerless to grant any concession.

Just before the Armistice this was confirmed to him by letter, sent on behalf of the Foreign Secretary himself, as follows:

> "Mr. Balfour understands that the position in regard to the matter has been explained to you verbally and that you are now aware of the fact that the Government has no power, under present circumstances, to grant commercial concessions in Palestine."

The circumstances under which the Government had no power to grant concessions continued unabatedly from 1918 through 1919 and 1920. In the April of 1920 Mr. Bicknall, however, believing that the Turkish Treaty was about to be concluded and that therefore the new Administration under the Mandate now would be able to grant concessions, sent in another application. But the Foreign Office again replied to him, and informed him as categorically as possible that "pending a settlement of the future status of that country [Palestine] at the conclusion of a Treaty of Peace with Turkey no concessions can be made."

This letter was dispatched to Mr. Bicknall rather over three weeks before Sir Herbert Samuel was installed in Jerusalem, and during the rest of 1920 and all through 1921 the Treaty with Turkey remained un-concluded and, in the words of the Foreign Office, "no concessions could be made." Yet Mr. Churchill, with the approval and instigation of the Prime Minister, had the daring to set about granting them to Zionists in that April of 1921. Agreements granting them in principle were signed in the autumn, the agreements for the too-celebrated Rutenberg concessions. The first of these, for harnessing the waters of the Auja Basin to obtain electric power, was signed on the 12th of September. The agreement for large-scale concession for the utilization of the waters of the Jordan and the Yarmook to the same end was signed by the Crown Agents for the Colonies and delivered to Mr. Rutenberg on the 21st.

The case against the Colonial Secretary and the Government admits of no defence. By ensuring the Rutenberg concessions under conditions which according to its own acknowledgment forbade the granting of any such concessions the Lloyd George Government of 1921 committed one of the most flagrant and contumacious acts of illegality on record.

The provisos inserted in Mr. Amery's preliminary statement only serve to show that the Government was perfectly conscious of what it was doing. It was aware that there was no authorization, no warrant for what it intended to accomplish in the interests of Zionism, so by its spokesman the Government endeavoured to surround its arbitrariness with the appearances of lawful legislation. The concessions, said Mr. Amery, must conform strictly with the terms of the draft Mandate.

It is a source of wonder that reassurances so patently preposterous as these could be uttered by anybody. It was moonshine to talk of subjecting concessions strictly to the terms of a draft document, which, being a draft, therefore had no fixed terms at all. It is only when a document has ceased to be a draft that it can be observed. At the time Mr. Amery spoke the text of the Mandate was completely in flux. Later on even, during the August preceding the September signature of the Rutenberg Concessions, the current draft of the Mandate was itself dubbed slightingly by the American State Department "a so-called final draft." Upon this particular draft the United States and Great Britain debated before reaching the real final text of July 1922.

In this real final draft the two Articles of the Mandate governing such matters as concessions did indeed survive with little change from the texts of two years before. One of them, Article 11, was not changed at all. But this does not alter the falsity of the Government's supposed safeguard. These articles might have been altered at any minute. When Mr. Amery said that the concessions would only be granted providing the terms of the draft were strictly observed, there was every probability indeed that these particular articles would have to be altered out of recognition. Up to April 1922—a year after he spoke and five months after the Rutenberg Concessions were staked through the agreements—the insertion of a provision in the Mandate which would have forbidden any monopolistic concessions in Palestine, and so have blown Articles 18 and 11 and the

Rutenberg Concessions with them sky high, was being insisted upon by the United States. If it had not been for a desperate and heretofore secret appeal of Balfour's (of which presently) the Mandate as constituted would have fallen in pieces. Of all this the Government was quite cognizant when it proposed to anchor concessions to the draft Mandate, for the United States' objections to the concession Articles had been begun (as we have seen) in formal diplomatic notes a year before Mr. Amery spoke.

In any event, had the terms of the draft Mandate been settled and been engraved in gold letters on tablets of marble in May of 1921, the legality of the Rutenberg Concessions would not have been an atom advanced by the observation of these terms. The draft Mandate, it must be repeated at the risk of growing tedious, had no legal value or situation whatsoever, and it was no more possible to base concessions upon any of its transient and unratified provisions than it was to base them on the aforementioned draught Guinness, or on a draught of air.

Chapter 25

The granting of the Rutenberg Concessions. Suffocation of other applicants by the Government. The real aim of Zionist Concessions. The Arabs given no say in the matter.

A very considerable treatise might be written upon the Rutenberg Concessions alone. Nothing on such a scale can be attempted here, but some account of the chief features of this affair certainly must be given. It was a good deal discussed in its time, but these discussions are lost today in back numbers of the newspapers and of Hansard, while one feature of the Concessions was never properly discussed at all. Yet it introduces one of the primary considerations of the Palestine Question.

Most of the other aspects of the Rutenberg affair were covered in a Commons' debate upon the 4th of July of 1922, when the late Lord Brentford (then Sir William Joynson-Hicks) thoroughly disclosed the character of the contract and of the transactions which had ended in it. In his speech he gave the details of the Bicknall letters which I have just quoted. He said on this occasion, "I have had some experience of contracts in the City, but the Rutenberg contract contains the most astounding concessions I have ever read or seen in my life. The contract gives over the development of the whole country to Mr. Rutenberg."

Mr. Pinhas Rutenberg, into whose hands the Holy Land was thus deposited, was a Russian Jew, an adherent of the Social Revolutionary group, who had been an official of Kerensky's Government.

After Kerensky's fall, Rutenberg went to Odessa and there "rendered good service in securing the escape from Odessa of large numbers of persons who were committed to the anti-Bolshevik cause." There is nothing against him personally. Those who have met him speak of him as a home-spun, companionable, exuberant person, who enjoyed the prosperity which came to him with the simplicity of a bear enjoying a pot of jam.

Mr. Rutenberg himself, however, is not important. Active as he was, he was merely an agent of the Zionist bodies and their sympathizers. It is his Company's concessions that are important, and proved to be of unexampled comprehensiveness when they were first announced in 1921.

His principal concession, the Jordan concession, was granted for seventy years. It could be bought in by the High Commissioner after 37, 47, 57, or 67 years, but otherwise was renewable under its original conditions after the seventy years had elapsed. The outstanding trait of the concession was the summary manner in which it dealt with any other firms or persons who might think of applying for concessions which ran athwart it. It dealt quite as summarily with any who ventured to possess any such concessions already.

So long as Rutenberg's existed, no similar concessions were to be granted to other bodies or persons within its area, which meant within Palestine. As for existing concessions, they were allowed compensation: that was all. Those which the Rutenberg Company desired to have annulled were to be annulled. Those which the Rutenberg Company desired to expropriate were to be expropriated. Towards any compensation which it might have to pay the Company was to be allowed to increase its rate of charges to consumers. Also "any land, property, buildings, or easement" which the Company might desire to have expropriated, either for use as building sites or communication-routes or in general for the mere "conveniences of the Concessions" were duly to be expropriated too.

Throughout its area no other body was to be permitted to distribute or to sell electric energy, or to construct

> canals, dams, reservoirs, watercourses, pumping-stations and other works of whatever kind for the generation of electric energy from water-power, or to construct or equip or install or operate overhead lines and underground cables or to install electric lighting in streets, dwellings and buildings of whatever kind or to supply electrical energy for consumption by docks, wharves, railways, plantations, mills, factories, workshops, laboratories, offices, houses and by all agricultural, industrial, commercial and public or private establishments and undertakings of whatever kind unless in each instance the Concession shall have first been offered to the Company upon similar terms, which shall be fair and reasonable, and such offer shall not have been accepted in writing by the Company within six months.

So the clauses went on, breathlessly, with inexorable monopoly gabbling like a goose.

Privileges were piled on exemptions for the Company till they become farcical in the end. The great water-power Concession was to have

> liberty during the said period (of 70 years) to produce supply and distribute electrical energy within the concession area by any other means than water-power. [And the] High Commissioner may from time to time delegate to any other person or persons any of the powers and discretions vested in him under or by virtue of this Concession.

There was no bar of nationality or of status. The High Commissioner could install in his place the staff of Swan and Edgar's or the President of Peru, or the Brandeis regime.

Lord Brentford in his speech quoted a letter he had received from Jaffa from a Christian Arab of standing, married to an Englishwoman, in which his correspondent recounted how on his return the previous October from England he had been summoned by a District Governor and threatened by him, "as he threatened all the other notables and landowners where Rutenberg's works have to be erected, that 'if you do not agree to Rutenberg's scheme you will be acting contrary to the British Government's policy. The Government is determined to enforce it, and those who oppose it will be very sorry and will be liable to deportation.'" The writer added that he was ready to come to England and give full evidence of this charge before a Committee of the House. Mr. Churchill in reply could only say that no such orders had been given by the Governments of either Britain or Palestine. I fancy that the word "deportation" should have read "expropriation." Either way, the charge provided a valuable side light on the aims of the Concession.

What indeed was this Concession? What did it represent? It in fact represented nothing else than the carrying into effect, after five years' endeavour, of a cardinal item of the "October Programme" laid in 1916 before the Cabinet by the Zionist Organization. Under this Programme (cf. Chapter 8) "in the event of Palestine coming under the control of England and of France" a Jewish Company was to be empowered "to acquire for its own use all or any concessions which may at any time be granted by the suzerain Government or Governments."

No one had studied the matter enough to make this confrontation in 1921. But by then Members of Parliament had grown rather more aware and suspicious of what was happening in Palestine, or the clearer sighted of them had. So when Mr. Amery made his statement that applications for concessions now would be entertained, some members guessed that this meant a scheme for granting them to Zionists only. The failure of non-Zionists to obtain any had come to the knowledge of Lord Brentford, Sir John Butcher and others. Consequently, after Mr. Amery had spoken, the following dialogue ensued on the rebound, pro-Zionist Commander Kenworthy (as he was then) excitedly putting through his own goal.

> Commander Kenworthy: "May we take it that there will be no preference given to any special nationality in granting these Concessions? Is that perfectly clear?"
>
> Mr. Amery: "Yes, I think so."
>
> Lord Winterton: "In view of the most critical situation as regards land rights between Jews and Arabs, will my honourable and gallant friend

give an undertaking that these Concessions will be given, if they are to be granted at all, to anyone applying for them, and not necessarily to one race?"

Mr. Amery: "No, sir, I do not understand that there is any question of confining concessions to any one section of the community."

Mr. Amery at the time was Parliamentary Secretary to the Admiralty; the question which had elicited his original statement had been addressed to the Under-Secretary for Foreign Affairs; and it was on behalf of the Secretary for the Colonies that he replied. This system of delegating answers from Ministry to Ministry has the advantage that it gives several opportunities for innocence to creep into a reply and for responsibility to creep out of it. It seems to have been screened from Mr. Amery, busy between decks at the Admiralty, that the Government had every intention of confining concessions to "one section of the community" in Palestine. It is unnecessary to say which was that section.

This was how the business worked out. After the Under-Secretary's April statement all was left in abeyance till July. Then Mr. Churchill, "not until July," as he put it himself, directed the High Commissioner to make the general announcement that applications for concessions would be entertained. No tenders were invited for specific purposes, none especially for the specific purpose of harnessing the water power of Palestine. No public mention was made that the harnessing of the water power was contemplated, or that plans for harnessing it had been drawn up, or that these plans had been in the possession of the Government since 1919.

They *had* been in Government possession since then. Mr. Churchill was to testify to this in the debate of next year, when, contrasting the merits of the Rutenberg plans with the demerits of non-Zionist applications which also had been submitted in 1919 (and earlier), he said, "At the same time Mr. Rutenberg put in, in the utmost detail, and with considerable backing, his important scheme.

Nothing of all this, then, was breathed; no tenders were invited; and in September, after a mere two months' delay to maintain appearances, the Rutenberg contracts were signed. It was another appalling blow for the Arabs, who as usual had been given no say whatsoever in a matter of first importance, in the disposal of a principal natural power-supply of their country. It was vain for them to try and obtain any such say.

The municipality of Jaffa, Arab of course, actually had applied (I quote Lord Brentford) "for a concession for the use of the Auja river, which is part of the Rutenberg Concession, for the electric lighting of their own town and district [the Auja is close to Jaffa], and that was again turned down by the Government."

The Bicknall applications had also covered a section of the Rutenberg project. After his second application and his second refusal, in May 1920, Mr. Bicknall went again, said Lord Brentford, "to the Overseas Department, and he was told that all his papers had been sent out to Palestine. He then went to the Zionist Organization [it became the regular practice afterwards, especially at the Colonial Office, to bid suppliants or dissatisfied persons "go and see the Jews"] and he was astonished to find that the Zionists knew all about the scheme and all about his plans. He has had no reply at all from the Government of Palestine as to this scheme [of his], part of which is now embodied in the Rutenberg contract."

Very edifying. When Mr. Churchill replied to Lord Brentford, or rather spoke after Lord Brentford, he could not deny these facts and so he held his peace concerning them. Both cases are flagrant examples of discrimination against non-Zionists. There is something else, though, to be observed about them. The Jaffa Municipality and Mr. Bicknall had made their applications for what were to prove no more than portions of the entire Rutenberg Concession. If that entire concession had been thrown open to public tender in July of 1921, there was small likelihood of any non-Zionist persons or engineering firm submitting a tender for all of it.

At first sight this may seem to exculpate the Colonial Office, but the reason for it puts the nature of the Rutenberg Concession and the acts of the implicated Department in a different and a clearer light, which only enhances the guilt of those in the Department who were responsible.

The reason that none but the political Zionists, through Mr. Rutenberg, were likely to submit a scheme on such a scale was that the project for obtaining control of the water-power of Palestine was not a commercial project at the bottom. It was a commercial project in the sense that it went into the business of selling electric current, but it was not at all commercial in the sense that men of business themselves use. When they talk of an enterprise being commercial, they mean that it is one launched to make money and having proper prospects of making money. That is the end which it subserves, and any other results it happens to achieve are incidental. Even if it does a great deal of good, by providing households for example with some article which diminishes women's toil, it is not launched to do good and to relieve womankind, but to make money through helping the women.

The Rutenberg Concession, though it dealt in electric power, was not a commercial project, because in its case the money-making was the incidental item. Selling this power was the occupation of the Company and it would do its best to sell at a steady profit, but this was not the final aim of the Concession.

However, it had the form of a commercial project, so this form had to be preserved, and accordingly the necessary contract was drafted as though dividends were its sole object. None the less, as a commercial undertaking it was so uncommercial that in addition to those already noted the most singular provisions had been inserted in the contract in order that these dividends might be secured. During the first ten years of occupation it was to be relieved of the common dues levied on business enterprises. During this period any of its profits which were scheduled as devoted to capital-amortization, or as put to reserve, or as set against depreciation of assets, were "to be deemed as expenses and not profits," not only in respect of any existing taxation, but in respect of any future taxation which the Palestine Administration conceivably might impose

Besides this, the Company was to be freed for an indefinite period from the payment of Customs dues upon material which it imported. These dues nominally were payable, but:

> "… the actual payment thereof shall if the Company so request be deferred until the profits of the Company, after writing off Amortization, Depreciation and Reserve, are first sufficient to enable the Company to pay a dividend of at least eight per centum per annum tax free."

Lord Brentford might well say he had never heard of such a contract. At a superficial view enterprising firms of engineers should have leapt at it. They knew, as important firms have a way of knowing, that an electric-power contract in Palestine was to be granted. In the course of the July 1922 debate Lord Eustace Percy, always a maladroit defender of Zionism, trying to disengage the Concession from the charge of clandestinity, had declared, "The Rutenberg Concession has been a matter of common knowledge among all engineering firms for the last three years at least. I discussed it with the representative of one of the greatest British engineering firms in the East at least fifteen months ago. Every one knew it was coming along." "Everyone," therefore knew it was coming along in (fifteen months from July 1922) the very month of April 1921 when Mr. Amery announced that the idea of granting concessions had just come into the mind of the Government as a new policy.

If the great British engineering firms, who are not blind to chances, did not leap at this contract which they knew was "coming along," this was for a good reason. Without the unbelievably advantageous conditions specially arranged for the Zionists, the contract had no commercial appeal.

Sir John Norton-Griffiths, when Mr. Churchill pleaded in the July debate that no other application save Rutenberg's had been made to the Government, stood up and said, "I purposely refrained from intervening in the Debate solely because I myself and my firm had the very concessions offered twice. It was hawked all over London, and refused by house after house. I have the documents on my file. I would not give a bob for it now."

Mr. Churchill, continuing his speech after this very informative interruption, himself acknowledged that the Rutenberg scheme was of no ordinary character. He came to the remarkable conclusion that it was quasi-religious. He said that Mr. Rutenberg, as evidence of his financial backing, had put in letters to him from Baron Edmond de Rothschild (the founder of the pre-War colonies) offering to place at his disposal from £100,000 to £200,000, on "absolutely non-commercial terms, for long periods," for the development of his scheme.

> "Mr. Rutenberg [continued the Colonial Secretary] asserted, and his assertion has been justified, that he had behind him all the principal Zionist societies in Europe and America, who would support his plans on a non-commercial basis.
>
> As a matter of fact, this concession has fallen extremely flat outside the circles of the Zionist followers. Nearly all the money got up to the present time has come from associations of a Jewish character, which are almost entirely on a non-profit-making basis. I have no doubt whatever—and after all let us not be too ready to doubt people's ideals—that profit-making, in the ordinary sense, has played no part at all in the driving force on which we must rely to carry through this irrigation-scheme in Palestine.
>
> I do not believe that it has been so with Mr. Rutenberg, nor do I believe that this concession would secure the necessary funds were it not supported by sentimental and quasi-religious emotions."

Mr. Churchill tackled the description of the emotions which launched the Rutenberg Concession as best he was able. It is just these emotions, these motives which are so important. Desirable as was the attention which in 1922 went to the shady details of the Government's signature of the Concession, it would have been better fixed upon the "sentimental and quasi-religious" ends which the Zionists had in applying for the Concession, and upon the ends which the Government had in granting it, to say nothing of incubating it almost to the degree of motherhood.

The Concession had been engendered by the Zionists though. No Chief Administrator of Palestine during the O.E.T.A. period had looked over the country on arrival and cried, "The Jordan calls imperatively for damming. The electric current must be obtained for want of which the land is perishing." The land could have done with electric current in Haifa, Jerusalem, Jaffa and, say, Nablus, but it could have done without it just as well. Probably of Tel-Aviv alone might it be said that there was real need for more light upon it. In general there was no noticeable public outcry for electric current, though some Arabs had it in mind. They would have provided it more suitably for most towns by local powerhouse schemes. Nazareth and Tiberias were lit already by such local schemes, and the principal buildings in Jerusalem had their own plants.

It was the Zionists who had nourished this other grandiose scheme in their heads and had set about preparing it when the Armistice came, indeed before. For it to have been ready down to the last detail in 1919, preparation *must* have begun months before. At the right time the Zionist leaders had gone to the Government and had said, "This is what we propose to do in Palestine," and the Government had seen what was afoot and had acquiesced and coalesced with the greatest pleasure. The Colonial Office and the Zionist representatives had worked resultant details out between them. The blundering Lord Eustace Percy had disclosed this too. "It is common knowledge," said he, "that this concession was negotiated and granted by a British Department in Whitehall and not by the British Administration [in Palestine].

But why? Why had the Government involved itself in this queer affair? Why had the Zionists gone to such infinite trouble? Why had the Rutenberg Company been promoted with "an authorized capital of not less than a million pounds," and why was the Jordan to be harnessed with elaborate works—when the only apparent scope for all this was to light a few streets and such houses as might desire it, in four small towns where most of the inhabitants retired to bed with the dark?

In 1922 critics went astray and bothered themselves about Mr. Rutenberg's past and upon whether his plans were scientifically satisfactory. This was beside the point. The point was why should all this water power be extracted—24,000 h.p. had been proclaimed as the first instalment—just to supply a little public current at twopence farthing, and three or four hours' private current to a few Europeanized families at sevenpence halfpenny per kilowatt-hour? The game was so obviously not worth the candle power, that it should have set those who felt that there was something strange inquiring what did he behind it all. But in the July debate the point was not raised, though for a fleeting moment it looked as though it were going to be.

This was when Lord Brentford said that the real scheme for Palestine should have been an agricultural one, and revealed that two eminent British engineers had put in a large agricultural scheme, which would have irrigated 1,200,000 acres of land in Palestine. This scheme, need it be said, had not been entertained. After making this disclosure, however, Lord Brentford passed on to another subject.

Under the Rutenberg plans some use would be made of the current for irrigation works, but a use in nowise approaching the scale of the rejected British scheme, which was wholly agricultural. Significantly, Mr. Churchill, when he came to speak, kept referring to the Rutenberg Concession as "this irrigation scheme," as though he knew in his heart that it ought to have been an agricultural scheme and had best appear as such. But it was not an agricultural scheme. In the twenty-three pages of the contract the word "irrigation" occurred but once, in a subsection of the nineteenth clause, where the price for "street lighting, water supply, irrigation and industrial purposes" was fixed at a uniform rate.

On the other hand, clause 18 ensured that besides the right to build such "factories, works and undertakings" as might be required for producing material or machinery needed for purposes of the Concession, the Company was also to be entitled to "build, set up, establish and carry on such factories, works and undertakings as may be able to utilize large quantities of electrical energy."

And in the next clause it was specified that "for large consumers of energy the rates shall be fixed by special agreement between the Company and the consumers," a clause which, when considered alongside the previous one, held the most fetching prospects for the rates which the Company would be entitled to fix, as distributor, for the Company, as consumer.

In these clauses though, the aim of the Rutenberg scheme was made manifest. To provide current to "factories, works and undertakings," to "set up and carry on factories, works and undertakings"—that was the goal of the scheme. Its devisers meant to make of Palestine a land of industrialism, linked with the centres of industrialism about the globe.

It is true that this seems in flagrant contradiction with their most advertised intention, that of restoring the Jewish people to contact with the soil, by agricultural work. But agricultural work has never appealed to more than a small minority of the Zionist public. Most of that public has never had the faintest intention of taking to the cultivation of the soil, were Palestine as fertile as the Ukraine and as empty as the Sahara.

The Zionist bodies and the Zionist press agents, of course, have always seen to it that newspapers everywhere have been supplied with attractive pictures of sunburnt young Jewish haymakers, and the Zionist orators have always supplied equally attractive word-pictures of the same haymakers to countless meetings and discussions. But the real emblem of the National Home should be a clerical worker or a shopkeeper at his Tel-Aviv counter. More than three-quarters of the Jewish population is, and always has been, as far from the land as Tom Moore's heroine. It congregates in towns and in urban areas which are becoming yearly more distended. The Zionists nominally fled from cities and towns, but once in Palestine they started to build them with every sign of glee.

Behind the Rutenberg scheme, therefore, lay the firm intent of urbanizing and of industrializing the land. The "white coal" of Palestine was acquired because in an industrialized country the control of main natural resources meant political power. To great engineering firms the industrialization of a small place such as Palestine, and the mastery of Palestine's resources, presented no attraction, for they gave no prospect of high dividends within a reasonable period. But they meant everything to the Zionists, whose aim at this stage was to master Palestine, whether it paid or not, to turn it into a business-land, whether the business were good or not.

In the previous chapter the effect upon Jewish life in Palestine of the new immigrants with their Western affiliations was shown. The Rutenberg scheme was an absolute pendant to the new immigrants. In its fashion it was an immigrant too. It was the first immigrant of Zionist Capital, as they were the first immigrants and instalments of Zionist Labour. Between Zionist Capital and Zionist Labour, even though they had their internecine disputes, Palestine was to be given an office complexion, anything but sunburnt. The most fervent landworkers amidst the Chalutzim contributed to the establishment of the Zionist industrial policy. In short, Zionist workers and Zionist company-promoters together brought, and took pride in bringing, the Industrial Revolution to the Holy Land.

It was a new style of Industrial Revolution, since it was installed by politicians and pioneers suffused with "sentimental and quasi-religious emotions" and not by industrialists. With these types of men industrialism was only a means to an end. Their business community was to have a strong scientific tinge. Probably Manchester was always in Dr. Weizmann's mind, without his even being awake to it, a denicotinized sort of Manchester with the fundamental money-making motive eliminated— though money might be made. Palestine would be shaped to the model of Manchester, modified by orange-groves. Thanks to its geographical situation between Europe and Asia it might become the mart of the Levant and of the Middle East, with connections extending even to India. That would mean great wealth, and wealth, though not sought for its own sake, meant power and a Jewish State worth having, a Jewish State the equal of any other State. "It is not only in Palestine we are interested," one of the Zionist Commission said to me in Jerusalem that year, "we are interested in the whole Orient. We have a safe production of intellectual forces."

Such views were held and were divulged, though not very often, by Zionist leaders or by those who were interested in Zionism. The words of

Mr. Horace Samuel may be quoted. Speaking of the Zionist agricultural settlements, he concluded:

> "But under any circumstances the agricultural settlements will be on too small a scale to constitute the economic basis of the country, unless it resigns itself to these minimal dimensions.
>
> It follows that the one hope of a Jewish Palestine is the building up of an intensive industrial civilization. This hope is focused on the success of the Rutenberg scheme, which, with its promise of the provision of practically unlimited power at a cheap rate, represents the economic equivalent of coal."

After saying then that power, though, was only the first stage and after computing various of the difficulties which must beset the industrial project, Mr. Samuel continues:

> "The whole thing is in the nature of an experiment and an adventure, albeit an adventure to which the Jewish communities of the world are willy-nilly committed. It would obviously be far too great a stultification for Jewry in general for the enterprise to be allowed to be a failure."

In the High Commissioner's Report on the Administration of Palestine from 1920 to 1925 it is stated too that:

> "... the practical interest in Palestine that is now being taken by Jews throughout the world, and especially the tendency of a number of industrialists in Poland and in Russia to invest their capital and to employ their experience in establishing factories and workshops here, are rapidly changing the situation. If this movement continues at its present rate, in a single generation Jaffa and Haifa will have become the principal manufacturing centres of the Middle East."

This particular passage is quoted in a Report issued in 1930 by the Executive Committee of the World-Union of Zionist-Revisionists which itself adds:

> "This is a matter of great importance to the development of the Jewish National Home, inasmuch as it may be possible through an introduction of industries to extend the absorptive capacity of the country far beyond that which can ever be made possible by agriculture alone, [i.e., far more Zionist immigrants could be brought into an industrialized Palestine than into an agricultural.]"

The Report, after speaking of the industrial possibilities arising from Haifa harbour and from the oil pipelines to Irak, goes on:

> "There are also the chemical industries and ancillary trades that will grow up around the exploitation of the Dead Sea deposits [of potash, etc.]. In addition the progressive electrification of the country should make possible a speedy development of the new industries whose growth has hitherto been retarded by the absence of cheap power."

These quotations provide interesting disclosures of Zionist policy, but it is important to understand that the Zionist industrial schemes for Palestine were not bound up with the success of their most ambitious developments. The feeling amidst those who nurtured these schemes in 1921 was that the future might make a success of an industrialized Holy Land, but that the business of the present was to get the Holy Land industrialized and urbanized as much and as soon as possible, without consideration of success. Even if the greater success, even if becoming the principal manufacturing centre of the Middle East, were not attained, none the less the smaller but more vital success for Zionism of mastering the country would be obtained. In an industrialized Palestine the Zionists would be at the head of things. "*Nous aurons le pays économiquement*," a French-using spokesman had said to me in a frank moment.

The public programme naturally was not worded in his candid terms. It figured as the introduction of higher conditions of living in Palestine, as the development of civilization there, as the opening of a new era of prosperity for the Arabs. "It was inevitable," declared Mr. Churchill, "that by creating these new sources of wealth, and bringing this new money into the country, they [the Zionists] would not only benefit themselves, but benefit and enrich the entire country among all classes and races of its population."

The groundless assumption that riches meant benefit to the Arabs introduces the chief point of this matter, the effect upon the Arabs of the Rutenberg scheme and of all the kindred activities of the Zionists. What was the Arab Palestine upon which the industrial cornucopia was to open? It was an agricultural country of the Eastern type, absolutely non-industrial, exporting the best oranges in a rather gentlemanly way, as a duke sells his prize livestock. It had a trading community in its coastal towns, but though these traders were competent men of business, they worked in a quiet style, and were not pushing. Outside Syria, in Egypt and South America and the many other lands which they frequented, Syrian traders were sharp and assiduous dealers. But on their native soil they preferred, even those who had returned from successful high-speed commerce abroad, to let the rhythm of life be slower.

It was to be expected that as the acute penury provoked by the War and the lesser penury due to Turkish methods of rule worked themselves out under a better Mandatory control, the state of the farmers would improve.

It would improve though in the way of the country. The tillers of the soil would become increasingly free of debt, but Palestine would remain what it had always been in essence, a land of people who did not live to make profits, but to keep themselves. The desire of the Arabs to lead this sort of life should always have been borne in mind, and indeed should have been the guiding principle of any Western State called to assist them in the government of their country. The Western State had no business whatsoever to try and force upon them the Western style of existence, which roughly is the making of profits in order to spend them upon alleviations of life. The Eastern idea, that ingrained in Palestine, is the making of a subsistence ensuring life itself.

Merely to keep himself sounds a doleful lot for a man in the West, and perhaps it is, since in the West nearly all relaxations and interests have to be provided for the population and therefore must be bought. For three-quarters of the year within their homes the British people have to pay the coal-merchant and the gas company and the electric company for their very climate.

But in a country like Palestine, with its short winter and abundant sun, all that the population asks as a whole is to be freed of debt, and then to work, gossip and savour the warmth peacefully.

Under a properly conceived system of government Palestine would have conformed to the simple ideas of its people, with a reasonable modicum of development. The population would have grown, since the youth of the country would have escaped the murderous Turkish military service which every year had destroyed them in their thousands. The seaward pressure of migration, too, would have brought in numbers escaping from the desert to become cultivators. Malaria and other such diseases would have been extirpated: medical progress, a necessity in a world wherein we keep our health but share our illnesses, would have been constant and welcomed by the population. More land would have been reclaimed, and irrigation would have made more of it cultivable.

The obvious destiny of Palestine was to become a nest of smallholdings, of which the smallish external wants would be supplied by the coastal towns.

This was a simple and thoroughly native prospect. It connoted a Palestine suited to the feelings and the customs of the population. It connoted, too—this being a point never enough raised—a Palestine in complete accordance with its other, transcendental self, the Holy Land.

The first sanctuary in the world would stay a sanctuary. Arable and pastoral Palestine would encompass Jerusalem and Bethlehem and Nazareth. The deep passages and the high-walled streets of a still Holy City would girdle the Sepulchre of Christ, and for this true God's acre ensure at least as much peace as the cloisters of Europe ensured for their derivative God's acres and the churches and cathedrals which rose beside them.

Such a retention of the ancient character of the Holy Land was indeed the right of its own people and also the due of Christendom. To Moslems, because of their own holy places, and to faithful Jews it would be equally gratifying. No doubt it would have been accompanied by a legitimate amount of material progress. Material progress in general is not to be confused, however, with such special and recommendable items of it as the medical progress just mentioned. There would have been no worshipping of material progress for its own sake.

It must not be forgotten that material progress has to justify itself in every case. It is not enough to show that such and such an undertaking is a piece of this progress, for the beginning of work upon it to be at once licensed. Material progress is but the conveniencing of life, a third-rate issue. The real issue was never better put than by Brunetière, who said that civilization did not lie in gas or in steam [or in electricity or in the petrol-engine]. "*Elle est dans la diminution du péché originel.*" Civilization lies in the reduction of original sin.

The fact that the Rutenberg Concessions were progressive was only a plea in their favour: it was far from being a sufficient cause for their being granted. If the people of Palestine wanted to advance in the Rutenberg manner, well and good: but if they did not, then away with Rutenberg.

Chapter 26

Governmental apologia for the grant of the Rutenberg Concessions.
A plot against the Arabs.
Balfour's negotiations in the United States reveal this.
His suppressed paragraphs.
He cajoles the Secretary of State in Washington.
The Perfidy of the Government.

The grant of the Rutenberg Concessions, the manner of which was detailed in the preceding chapter, introduced into the Palestine Question the primary consideration earlier mentioned. So that the Zionists might master the country, an accomplice British Government improperly set Palestine upon the track of industrialism. The natural right of the Arabs to preserve their country as an agricultural one was profaned. The people were forbidden, by the mother of democracy, any chance of expressing their wishes in the matter. Mr. Churchill boasted even that the deal was carried through without their adherence. "Left to themselves, the Arabs of Palestine would not in a thousand years have taken effective steps towards the irrigation and electrification of Palestine. They would have been quite content to dwell—a handful of philosophic people [an admission]—in the wasted sun-scorched plains, letting the waters of the Jordan continue to flow unbridled and unharnessed into the Dead Sea."

As, in point of fact, the waters of over 90 percent of rivers in British territory, sun-scorched or rain-washed, flow into their seas. How adroitly the Colonial Secretary spoke to his brief, and how thoroughly he misrepresented the situation. How neatly he mixed up needful improvements and excessive development. The useful irrigation, upon which every Arab peasant, as far as he can, labours all his life through, was partnered by Mr. Churchill with the superfluous electrification for the benefit of "factories, works and undertakings," with which Arabs would have nothing to do, as though the two were inseparables. "Not in a thousand years," he said, "would the Arabs take effective steps towards 'irrigation and electrification,'" that is, towards the full Rutenberg plan.

No doubt the Arabs would not. Why should they? It was unnecessary;

the Arabs did not want factories. But the Arabs had done all that lay in their power to take "effective steps" towards proper irrigation, the irrigation of their land, their agricultural holdings. By saying that they would not take wholesale steps towards the kind of "irrigation" which meant water power for factories and what not, the Right Honourable Gentleman concealed that the Arabs and their British friends had taken or had tried to take eminently suitable retail steps, so to put it. They *had* applied for local electrifications: they *had* asked for concessions based on agriculture. The obstacle they had encountered had been the Right Honourable Gentleman himself, for he was responsible for his Colonial Office which, through the fictitious Jerusalem Administration, had disallowed or prevented these agricultural emprises. The Colonial Secretary spoke scornfully of the Arabs for their never attempting what he, as head of his Department, never allowed them to try.

That this policy of preventing Arab and non-Zionist effort was deliberate there is no trace of doubt. During the 1922 debate Mr. Churchill could' not give one single denial to the instances which Lord Brentford gave of non-Zionist applications having been refused or blocked. The best he could do was to throw a pailful of muddy cold water over two applications which he mentioned. He complained that these were not detailed, that they furnished no full estimates, that the applicants only "indicated that if there were any concessions going they would very much like to have them." The British application to provide electric power for Jerusalem, made in 1919, would, he said, have been at double the rates of the Rutenberg scheme. He tried to make a great deal of the clause in the Rutenberg scheme by which all profits over 10 percent were to be divided with the Palestine Government, all profits over 15 percent to go wholly to that Government, and the right of purchase of the entire business was secured to the Government at ten-year intervals, after the passage of thirty-seven years.

We are still awaiting today a dividend of 10 percent from the Palestine Electric Corporation. It did not begin to declare dividends till 1933, though in 1932 it gave a 10 percent capital bonus. In 1933 it declared a 5 percent dividend on a net profit of close on £81,000. From then on profits increased. Next year there was a net profit of £140,000 and a dividend of 7 ½ percent was reached. There dividends stopped though profits increased. Despite assiduous efforts, as the increasing profit shows, it seems to have proved impossible to reach the 8 percent dividend which would have entailed grateful payment to the Palestine State of accumulated customs dues. "The little less and what worlds away," as Browning has said. The dividend of 7 ½ percent declared on the £140,000 of 1934 was also declared on the £178,000 of 1935 and on the £217,000 of 1936. I confidently prophesy the same dividend for the profits of 1937.

[Author's note: A dividend of *7 ½* was declared on a net profit of £235,566 for this financial year. The company now has a general reserve of a quarter of a million pounds.]

As regards the nobly consented reversion after thirty-seven years to the Palestine State, the feeling rises insistently that the public-spirited altruists who drafted the Concession expected that after thirty-seven years there would be a Jewish State in Palestine.

To Lord Brentford's main charges that the Bicknall applications had been cast aside, that the applications of the Jaffa Municipality had been cast aside, that the Arif el Namani application had been cast aside, the Colonial Secretary had no word of answer to give. (Arif el Namani was a well-to-do Arab with British trade connections, who formed a syndicate to drain swamps.)

Lord Brentford, if he had known them, could have brought various other unassailable charges. Here are a few of which I learned myself when in Palestine. A number of prominent Arabs of Haifa had wished to install an electric-lighting system for their town. There was nothing fantastic about it: it was a plain power-house scheme, such as some English towns find sufficient for their needs. Permission was refused to them. They were told they must go to the Rutenberg Company. From this alien board they might buy the privilege of lighting their own town. Another case: in the autumn of 1922 the Township of Tul-Keram, a Moslem one not far from the seacoast, wished to install a lighting scheme of its own. The Municipal Council applied to the Governor. The Governor told the Council "You must apply to Rutenberg." Very properly they refused to do so, and decided to abide as long as they could by the oil-lamps of their fathers.

In 1920, a former Governor of Nablus, Captain Ross, an ex-gunner, who was anxious to settle in Palestine, formed an Anglo-Arab group to reclaim malarial marshes at Ghor el Fara and to introduce cultivation thereon afterwards. The spot was in the Jericho district, by Beisan. He was refused, on the grounds that no concessions could be given till the Mandate was ratified. The next he heard was that the Rutenberg Concessions had been granted, the Mandate still being unratified, and indeed not in existence at all. A number of Australian soldiers and officers who wished to settle were served in much the same way.

The excuse adopted, when the Government bothered to adopt an excuse, was that given by Mr. Churchill, that the non-Zionist applications were undetailed and so forth. In some cases this was not true. In other cases the persons and firms involved had not prepared specifications just because they had been told that their applications could not be entertained while the Mandate was unratified. They imagined that when the Mandate was ratified, then tenders would be invited and due time be given them for sending in specifications. They expected to be informed of this likelihood: the aim of their applications was to receive this information. But it was never given them. They were suddenly confronted after two months with the Rutenberg *fait accompli,* which blocked all other projects. The expected appeal for tenders on a scale within their reach never was made.

As for Mr. Churchill's contention that the British proposal to install electric power in Jerusalem was at double the rates of the Rutenberg scheme, of course the charges were double. It was a genuine commercial bid. The men who made it, if they had been permitted to carry it out, would not have had their profits "deemed as expenses and not profits"; they would not have had taxation remitted them for ten years; they would not have been able to adjourn the payment of customs dues till they were making at least 8 percent on their capital. If they in 1919 were only asking double of what the Rutenberg Company, with these eccentric subventions, was asking in 1921, Mr. Churchill's hearers might well have demanded to know why Rutenberg dared to charge what he did.

Perhaps the best commentary upon these Governmental excuses was to be found, or seen, in Palestine itself, on the banks of the Auja. Even though the Jaffa municipality did not propose to let the not too copious waters of this river run sun-scorched to the sea, but to harness them and to light their town from the resultant current, it was not permitted to do so. The Jaffa men were told, as usual, to go to the Rutenberg Company.

I remember standing in the winter of 1922 beside what Mr. Ormsby-Gore and other Zionist partisans celebrated in the corridors of the House of Commons as the Auja works. The only missing thing at this scene of activity was the Auja waters. Instead of them there were two Diesel engines which Mr. Rutenberg or some of his associates had bought in Germany. These reposed under tarpaulins, and when various stagings upon which the workmen were engaged had been finished, Jaffa was to be lit by them. This was getting on for two years after the Auja contracts had been signed!

None the less, the Arabs were not allowed to proceed with their own water-power scheme, but were driven to apply for current drawn from the Zionist river Diesel.

Such excuses as Mr. Churchill offered bore their own refutation. If there was one thing which an honest Mandatory should have done it was to have shunned commitments on the Rutenberg scale and with the Rutenberg aims, and to have encouraged any least initiative which the Arabs showed. If Arab applications, or Anglo-Arab applications were on a small scale, or their plans were not fully detailed, that was not a drawback. It was a recommendation, an opportunity. What else was the Mandatory there for, the

Mandatory real or supposititious, but to welcome small schemes, and to decline those which exceeded the degree of industrial enterprise fit for an agricultural land? Its duty was precisely to help municipalities to provide their own electricity, and to put lesser Anglo-Arab reclamation and minor irrigation schemes on their feet.

What the Covenant bade the Mandatory in Palestine to exercise was "tutelage": the Mandatory was to "render administrative advice and assistance until such time as they [the mandated population] can stand alone." The Mandatory Power therefore was bound in honour, supposing it to have honourable intentions towards the Covenant, not to exceed the limits of tutelage. Whatever it did should bear the stamp of this particular quality, which implied that the capacities of his wards should be observed by the Mandatory-Tutor, whose care it would be to cultivate those particular capacities.

The duty of the Mandatory in Palestine was to develop at all costs farming of the most widespread and simplest nature, and to see that the educated Arabs had opportunities for leading the country to its bent. Nor was this the British Government's duty merely: these were its absolute orders under the Covenant. As for industrial progress, that would have to go to the devil, which after all would not be as bad a fate as it sounded, since he was accustomed to giving it a helping hand.

Yet, instead of carrying out its duty, the first thing the Government did in 1921-2 by way of fulfilling the Covenant was to establish an industrial monopoly. Anything more remote from the tutelage of a people than the imposition on it of an industrial monopoly in the hands of externs is hardly to be conceived. In the interests of this monopoly the Government stifled the small but well-directed attempts at self-betterment—and even a larger attempt or two—of the Arabs and their British friends. The Government as good as said to the Arabs, "Don't pester me with your individual production and your home-made plants. Go and buy your electricity and your irrigation and whatever else you want, or don't want, from the Zionists. Buy it in tins from the mass-production factories they are going to establish. You'll get nothing else, so you'd better be sensible and buy what they offer you."

"Don't you come to me," said the Government to the Arabs, "with vague requests for concessions as soon as concessions are going. Bring schemes to me. Bring me great, thoroughly itemized, costly schemes. Bring me for preference schemes in which I've had a share myself." That was the policy fixed in the early twenties, and pursued ever since.

It has been to foster industrialism, to favour undertakings which are on the largest scale, to slide farming itself on to co-operative and corporate and intensive and all those least individual bases which substitute profit for subsistence. Thus money has always told and technical accomplishments have always told, and office experience has always told, and every hook which is to bind Palestine together has slid easiest into a Zionist eye.

The excuse which has covered this policy has been conform, easy to make, and deceptive to the ignorant. The Zionists have never been favoured, it is protested: efficiency has been the watchword. If the prosperity of the country has grown more and more involved with Zionist prosperity, if its activities seem to be in Zionist hands, that is because when there is a big job to do it is only the Zionists who can do it. Only Zionists have the ability and the backing. Zionists have connections with world markets: Zionists can reclaim land on the proper scale.

So the apologia runs, and it is sound enough in this respect, that if undertakings are kept on large and highly developed scales, then of course only those who have important reserves or connections or backing can cope with them. But should they be kept upon a large scale? Great Britain is in Palestine as a Mandatory. She has not been set there in order to rationalize the country in the most up-to-date way, as though Palestine were a legacy it had fallen to her to exploit. She went to Palestine, let it be repeated, to help the native people to stand upon their own feet and then to take the road which they chose, which at all times has been that leading to the most ancient and honourable of all callings, peasant cultivation.

Large-scale efficiency, therefore, and industrial competence, and other such qualities are beside the mark in Palestine and can enter no claims to be compelling factors in the administration of the country. As excuses for the policy pursued there they will not do at all. As an explanation of that policy therefore we come back to the British Government setting Palestine for political purposes upon the track of industrialism and of as-big-as-possible business.

This means of course that there was a plot against the Arabs. So there was. But it was a plot of a kind. I do not suggest that it began with one of those old-fashioned gatherings at which men sat round a table and exchanged pure deceit behind drawn curtains. I do not suggest that Zionists and Cabinet Ministers met and arranged deliberately with each other that the social and economic level of Palestine should be raised to a height beyond the Arabs' reach, so that the country must fall, or rather must soar, into the Zionists' grasp.

But I do suggest that Government personages met Zionist personages and that they talked together of the economic development of Palestine and about the introduction of prosperity there and about the utilization of the country's untapped resources, and of all the good which this would do for the Arabs as for the Jews. I suggest that the Zionists on their part were conscious that the control of this particular kind of development and prosperity and goodness must in the course of nature, or in the course of art, accrue to themselves. I suggest that the Zionists felt, without a word being spoken, through the imperceptibilities of contact with politicians, that the Government personages, on their part, were even more shrewdly aware than they were that this must happen. Upon this common perception of the future, and upon the knowledge that it *was* common to all their minds, they parted happily to draw up their plans, and that was the plot.

When these plans were drawn up, they continued to be called plans for the "development of Palestine" and the amelioration of the Arabs. But the Arab people were no more asked how they wished to ameliorate themselves than if they had been Arab horses running at Longchamps or Auteuil, where the race-cards insist that the races are gatherings only held *"pour l'amélioration de la race chevaline."*

As will be seen, there happened to be an Arab delegation in London at the time. The moment the delegates heard of the Rutenberg contract, they protested at the Colonial Office. What, will it be imagined, was the reply that they received? The Colonial Office declined all responsibility, said the concessions were the affair of the Palestine Administration. In Palestine the Administration met protests with the truth that the concessions were the affair of the Colonial Office. That the Arab delegation might telegraph the reply it had received to Palestine apparently troubled nobody in Whitehall.

The refusal to consider non-Zionist applications also, of course, revealed that there was real plotting afoot. This generally took the form just detailed, statements of inability to entertain applications coupled with forgetfulness of those already made when applications *were* entertained. After the Mandate came into force, the technique was to dally with unwanted applications, London playing off Jerusalem and Jerusalem London, till commercial backers lost all patience and only Zionists were left in the field.

In the early 'twenties, as afterwards, any such discrimination was denied of course, as Mr. Amery had denied it in the House of Commons. But Government denials were only statements for the consumption of the public and of Members of Parliament. A very different tale was told in private life, or in those negotiations of diplomacy which it was not expected would be disclosed.

Fortunately, though, some of them have been disclosed, though only in another country. The United States is to be thanked again for the publication of the necessary documents in its too little known Buff Book of 1927, reprinted in 1931. (I do not think the phrase "Buff Book" is used in the United States, but that is the colour of the binding of the official publication, and the name is convenient.)

In Chapter 21, I quoted the dispatch of Mr. Bainbridge Colby, the Secretary of State of the Washington Cabinet. In this he said that he believed he discerned departures in a note of Lord Curzon's from the underlying principles of a Mandate, as it should be applied by the Allied and Associated Powers to the territories brought under their temporary dominion.

> "This dominion [had concluded Mr. Colby] will be wholly misconceived, not to say abused, if there is even the slightest deviation from the spirit and the exclusive purpose of a trusteeship as strict as it is comprehensive."

The date of Mr. Colby's dispatch was the 20th of November, 1920. He followed it up in February with an extremely sharp note to the League of Nations, declaring that the United States would not be bound by any decisions on Mandates taken without their consultation, and requesting that any decisions already taken should be re-opened. The Council of the League replied in March in a letter of almost tearful willingness to oblige, but correctly pointed out that it had been powerless to prevent the Powers from distributing the Mandates to themselves absolutely as they pleased. The Council's letter used more circumlocutory terms than these, but that was what it said.

The next step of interest was taken by the United States Government, which, through its Ambassador in London, presented to the British Government a full-length memorandum formulating the American position upon Mandates. What was still more important, the memorandum went on to specify those changes in, or additions to, the terms of the Palestine Mandate which the American Government desired should be made.

In regard to Palestine, the memorandum first requested that in framing the Mandate provision should be made for the maintenance of the capitulatory rights of foreigners, which had existed under Turkish rule. These should be continued till adequate courts had been established. Provision should also be made for the revival of capitulatory rights in the event of the termination of the Mandatory regime. The memorandum then went on to the subject of concessions. I quote from Clause 5 (b):

> "It is desired that there should also be provision against discrimination in concessions. The British "B" Mandate for East Africa, Article 7, provides as follows: 'Concessions for the development of natural resources of the territory shall be granted by the Mandatory without distinction on grounds of nationality between the nationals of all States members of the League of Nations, but on such conditions as will maintain intact the authority of the local Government.'

> Similar provision should be inserted in "A" Mandates and broadened to embrace the United States.
>
> There should also be appropriate provision against the granting of monopolistic concessions or the monopolizing of natural resources by the Mandatory itself."

This memorandum must have come with the chill of an iceberg to Whitehall. The Government was on the point of signing away to the Rutenberg Company (even before Mr. Rutenberg had formed that company) the first of a pair of the very monopolistic concessions which the Americans now declined to admit.

Heaven knows what followed on its receipt. During the next four or five weeks enough strings of personal influence must have been pulled in London and in Washington to have set up a ropemaker in frayed yarn. But the Government had a final string to pull, proof against any strain. Lord Balfour sailed for the United States. The main cause of his journey was the Washington Disarmament Conference, but it can be assumed correctly that it was not the only object of his journey. He embarked in early November, equally equipped to achieve an able and meritorious settlement in the naval field, and in the Palestine field to cajole and to beguile, and to play-act the extremes of injustice into an apparent discharge of duty.

On the 29th of December, he being in Washington, the official British answer to the American memorandum of August was handed to the United States' Ambassador in London. It said that with regard to capitulatory rights in Palestine there would be a proviso inserted in the coming Mandate by which in any but trifling cases foreign nationals should only be tried by a bench containing a majority of British judges. A rather misty arrangement was suggested for the safeguard of American capitulatory rights in case of termination of the Mandate.

Then the Foreign Office dispatch—it was signed by the Permanent Under-Secretary for Foreign Affairs, Sir Eyre Crowe—came to the crucial point, the American demand for alterations in the draft Palestine Mandate, to prevent the creation of monopolies and discrimination in concessions. His Majesty's Government, said Sir Eyre Crowe, regretted that it could not see its way to adopt the American demand (or suggestions as the dispatch preferred to call them), which appeared "to overlook the peculiar conditions existing in Palestine." So far as Palestine was concerned, explained the writer:

> "Article 11 of the Mandate expressly provides that the Administration may arrange with the Jewish Agency, mentioned in Article 4, to develop any of the natural resources of the country, in so far as these matters are not directly undertaken by the Administration."

This reply must count as one of the coolest ever ventured. The American Secretary of State complained that monopolies were being created, and to this Sir Eyre Crowe or whoever was the author of the Foreign Office dispatch rejoined that in the draft Mandate the British Government was making arrangements for monopolies to be created. That passed as an excuse!

In December of 1921 there was no Mandate in existence, as the Foreign Office well knew. There was only a proposed text. Articles 4 and 11, and others quoted by Sir Eyre Crowe as though they were binding clauses in a Constitution, were nothing but the momentary forms of a supposititious project, and could not "expressly provide" for anything in the world. The Jewish Agency itself was not in being. All these Articles and Agencies and what-not were a year and nine months away from coming to life, even supposing them to be legitimate in themselves. Yet they were put forward as authorities. To quote future events as the source and the warrant of present events, to justify 1921, in 1921, by 1923 was, indeed, not merely cool. It was incredible; it was fantastic. It was to make a harlequinade of diplomacy.

But thereon the unknown impresario of the Foreign Office reply proceeded to give a reason for his reason. A remarkable one too.

> The reason for this is that, in order that the policy of establishing in Palestine a national home for the Jewish people should be successfully carried out, it is impracticable to guarantee that equal facilities for developing the resources of the country should be granted to persons or bodies who may be actuated by other motives.

There, anyhow, was the naked truth, in all its seriousness. To grant equal facilities to all comers for developing Palestine's resources was "impracticable"—superb pseudonym for "not intended." It was not intended to give concessions to those not actuated by Zionist motives. Only Zionists need apply.

To the United States the truth had to be exposed. To the House of Commons the Government, per Mr. Amery, had said that there was no question of confining concessions to any section of the community. Per Mr. Churchill it was to say that "at the time the Rutenberg Concession was granted, no other application was before us," and to let it be believed that if there had been one it would have been considered.

I add no more comment. The major disclosures of the Palestine Question speak for themselves.

Yet this particular matter does not stop here. Lord Balfour naturally had known that the Eyre Crowe note was to be presented. It had been marked "Urgent," and without doubt was timed to dovetail into his own lobbying in the American capital.

But there were delays: Washington was occupied with the Naval Treaty. So a fortnight after the delivery of the Eyre Crowe note, we find Balfour writing to the Secretary of State, who was no longer Mr. Colby, but Mr. Charles Hughes. His letter is dated the 13th of January, 1922. He spoke in it of his "great anxiety to get the agreements in regard to the Mandate for Palestine advanced a stage" so that the League of Nations might "give it their blessing" at the meeting then going on in Geneva. He had, he said, hoped to discuss the situation with Mr. Hughes, but "we have all been so busy that you have not been able to find a moment." Lord Balfour therefore, as the matter was pressing, now brought it again to Mr. Hughes's notice.

In this letter Lord Balfour began by mentioning the proposal he had always enjoyed putting forward, that the United States should have undertaken the Palestine Mandate, though he recognized now that this would not have commended itself to the American people:

> "However that may be [he went on] the duty has devolved *[sic]* upon Great Britain, and I hope the American Government will do what it can to lighten the load. Your Ambassador in London will have forwarded you the official note upon the subject. Let me add to what Lord Curzon has said [the attribution of the note is interesting] one or two further remarks."

The pity of it is that these one or two further remarks, which it is clear depicted the reality of the situation in Palestine and the intentions and hopes of the Government there, are hidden from us. The United States Government has chosen to excise them from the text of its Buff Book. It has judged no doubt that they were too plain for publication. When the Buff Book was being prepared possibly there was an appeal that this much at least should be kept secret. In the place of Lord Balfour's remarks, therefore, is a blank space peppered with seven dots.

After the dots is printed the final paragraph of his letter, which links up with the censored portions as follows:

> "If such a situation is to be dealt with successfully by the civilian Government, the position of that Government must not only be secure, but must seem secure in the eyes of the populations concerned."

The rest of the missive is not notable. Lord Balfour ended by begging the special attention of Mr. Hughes to the problem before his Government. This attention he succeeded in winning. There was a little more delay, but on the 26th of January he was able to have with Mr. Hughes the discussion of the situation which he had sought.

It proved to be all important. On its morrow Mr. Hughes wrote to Lord Balfour, recalling, in order to prevent misunderstandings, what had passed between them at their meeting. He referred to the meeting as an "informal conversation," but evidently in the course of it the British statesman had secured the alteration of United States policy concerning concessions. For of these Mr. Hughes wrote:

> "In view of the paucity of the resources of Palestine, and particularly in view of the special conditions there prevailing, to which reference is made in the British note of December 29th, it is not my intention to insist on the proposals put forth in the American memorandum of August last for the inclusion of appropriate provisions against the granting of monopolistic concessions."

Balfour had gained a great victory. He had talked Hughes round, and the American embargo, which in one vital subject might have done so much to keep Palestine in the grasp of its own people, was withdrawn. In the month of April an official dispatch from the United States Government to the Foreign Secretary confirmed the Hughes-Balfour arrangement. In this dispatch Mr. Hughes's original phrasing was maintained in part. It ran:

> "It is not the intention of my Government to insist on the inclusion of a provision in this Mandate against the granting of monopolistic concessions, as it is recognized that these may be justified to a certain extent for appropriate local development."

There is a sad little hint of pricking conscience in the words "to a certain extent," added to the Hughes text. The State Department did not seem able when examining justifications to attain that accomplished vagueness of perception which came so easily to its distinguished visitor and mesmerist.

Even with Balfour's victory however, this affair does not end. In Mr. Hughes's letter to him there occurs a passage which, though it has no bearing on the concessions issue, has a very considerable bearing on the general issue of the Palestine Question. It also has a bearing on the sealed portion of Lord Balfour's own communication to Mr. Hughes, his undisclosed "one or two further remarks."

As Balfour's letter shows, his principal anxiety was to convey the said remarks to Mr. Hughes. Not having been able to convey them by word of mouth, at first he wrote the substance of them to Hughes. But thereon he obtained the desired interview, the "informal conversation" of the 26th. It stands to reason that they became the burden of this conversation. Next day Mr. Hughes, in his turn, wrote a résumé of the same conversation. From his résumé, therefore, printed in full, it is possible to get a glimpse of a part of the Balfour *non legenda*. "The paucity of the resources of Palestine." Who but Balfour would have suggested or, as Mr. Hughes's compatriots say, could have "put across" the American Secretary that because there was so little in Palestine it should all be given to the Zionists.

But the noteworthy passage deals with the intricate subject of Capitulations. On this subject Balfour did not win a victory. I imagine that he did not press for it so as to gain his other essential point. Mr. Hughes was satisfied with the proposal that foreign subjects in Palestine should only be tried by a bench with a majority of British judges or magistrates. But he was not satisfied with the indeterminate proposal (in the original Crowe note of the 29th of December) that if the Mandate was ended Great Britain would arrange with the League of Nations for the safeguarding of American legal rights. He insisted that American capitulatory rights should be revived automatically if and when the Mandate was terminated. The American Government would then take its own decisions about what was to become of these rights. It is the terms in which Mr. Hughes framed this insistence that are so notable:

> "It will be necessary [he said] to provide for the revival of our original rights in that respect, upon the termination of the Mandate regime. *Even in case a Jewish State should survive,* it would still be necessary for the United States to reach a decision for itself on the question at that time."

The italics here are mine, but in a way I imagine they will also be the reader's. The irrepressible truth breaks out again, this time through the involuntary agency of Lord Balfour, for quite obviously it is to his contentions that Mr. Hughes is replying. Hughes sums up the case as Balfour put it. In the December note there had been no mention of the Jewish State nor any word about conditions in Palestine if the Mandate were terminated. Balfour in the conversation, however, had come to facts—he may have done so in the missing passage of his letter too—and had asseverated that the Mandate would only be brought to an end when the Zionists were ready to establish a State. Hughes might have confidence in a Jewish bench under Jewish rule.

But Hughes was dissatisfied. Even if Balfour's assurances were justified, "even if a Jewish State did survive," he thought that America ought to be able to make her own bargain with that State.

His qualms do not concern us. What does concern us is the discussion which took place between the two statesmen upon the assumption that a Jewish State was to be the successor of the British. Like a messenger-boy at the head of a theatre-queue, Britain was only to occupy the chair till Zion was ready to sit down on it.

As the reader is learning over and over, this had always been intended. But it is satisfactory to have one more undeniable proof of it, and thereby to have the fraudulence of the professions made to the Arabs once more demonstrated. Balfour and other Cabinet Ministers spoke to the Arabs and to the British public about a Palestine in which "Arab and Jew would unite in the service of their common fatherland" or words to that effect. There were no longer to be either Arabs or Jews, but "Palestinians." All this jargon was dropped, though, when discussion occurred with knowledgeable persons in private, and negotiations were put on the real basis of the eventual Jewish State.

Chapter 27

"Sie hat mir Treu' versprochen,
Gab mir ein'n Ring dabei.
Sie hat die Treu' gebrochen,
Mein Ringlein sprang entzwei;
Sie hat die Treu' gebrochen,
Mein Ringlein sprang entzwei."
—Old German song.

When the would-be Mandatory Government was installed and Palestine passed from the control of the Foreign to the Colonial Office, within a year, in February 1921, Mr. Winston Churchill was appointed Colonial Secretary. This appointment led the Arabs into some false but understandable hopes. Their new immediate ruler was a man who, by all accounts would not accept any line of conduct from a predecessor or from his permanent officials. He had the reputation of examining afresh even questions which had been long sunk in routine, and of reassessing their merits. There seemed at least a fair chance that when confronted with the Palestine Question he might reconsider it from its beginning, perceive where the truth lay and inaugurate a new policy.

Almost his first action on taking office encouraged these hopes. Faced with an altogether unsettled Near and Middle East and alive to Great Britain's responsibilities, he abandoned the usual procedure of trying to arrange everything from Westminster. He sailed for Egypt, and in Cairo held a short and decisive conference, a magnificent affair in its way, a species of Privy Council with himself as monarch and pro-consuls, chiefs, and bearers of great names giving him the light of their opinions. Allenby, Lawrence, Cox of Mesopotamia and others such were present. Feisal and Abdullah stood by. Determinations came upon a fitting scale and speedily, and with in a fortnight all was finished. There and then Transjordan was erected into a principality and the future of Irak was fixed. The two sons of Hussein, Abdullah and Feisal, were given these realms, though in the case of Irak there had yet to be a referendum (of which the conclusion was foregone) before Feisal would mount his throne.

Arab delegates from Palestine hurried to Cairo, hoping to see the vigorous Churchill and to discuss the fate of their country with him in an atmosphere which promised so well. But they returned almost at once. It seemed that the affairs of Palestine had been put to one side, because the Colonial Secretary meant to go there and to investigate, and presumably to come to a decision upon the spot.

On the 24th of March he arrived and stayed a week, soon showing that for him, as for so many, his behaviour elsewhere gave no key to his behaviour in Palestine. He investigated Jewish colonies far more thoroughly than he investigated British policy. He did nothing new, and even more remarkably he had nothing new to say. His active spirit went into an odd mental retreat: he seemed tired of his own abilities, and when he spoke found relief from them by mingling stock arguments with blind insistence upon the very points which were worst in his case.

He talked impatiently to Arab deputations, as though his hearers were boys or minors who understood nothing and were being tiresome and perverse, and must have what was for their good told to them sharply. Only in one instance, and that not of the happiest, was there a true glint of his individuality in these harangues. Perhaps a record was set up for aggressive bluff when Mr. Churchill on the eve of his departure informed a Moslem deputation that they were "partisans." To call inhabitants who were defending their right to their native soil "partisans" was far beyond the range of the average politician.

There were other lesser touches of arrogance in this discourse, introduced at intervals like cordials for the speaker's own heartening:

> "You ask me [he said] to repudiate the Balfour Declaration and to stop immigration. This is not in my power, and it is not my wish… Moreover it is manifestly right that the scattered Jews should have a national centre and a national home in which they may be reunited, and where else but in Palestine, with which for three thousand years the Jews have been intimately and profoundly associated. We think it is good for the world, good for the Jews, good for the British Empire; and it is also good for the Arabs dwelling in Palestine, and we intend it to be so. They will not be supplanted nor will they suffer, but they will share in the benefits and the progress of Zionism.
>
> I draw your attention to the second part of the Balfour Declaration, the sacredness of your civil and religious rights. I am sorry you regard it as valueless. It is vital to you and you should hold and claim it firmly. If one promise stands, so does the other. We shall faithfully fulfil both. Examine Mr. Balfour's careful words, Palestine to be "a national home" not "the national home," a great difference in meaning.
>
> The establishment of a national home does not mean a Jewish

> Government to dominate the Arabs… You need not be alarmed for the future: Great Britain has promised a fair chance to the Zionist movement, but the latter will succeed only on its merits…. We cannot tolerate the expropriation of one set of people by another. The present form of Government will continue for many years. Step by step we shall develop representative institutions leading to full self-government, but our children's children will have passed away before that is accomplished."

The Arabs are a people who understand the value of words and the niceties of language. Their own is full of a thousand shades. So to be treated thus to rough mis-statements and to flimsy assurances, as though anything were good enough to say to them, was more than ordinarily wounding. When a statesman of Mr. Churchill's calibre, as a supposed assuagement of their distress, told them that something like a century must pass before self-government (and what sort of self-government?) came to Palestine, and invited them to admire the malignant quibbles of the very document which disfranchised them, was it surprising that resentment mounted in their hearts?

In his speech open contempt was shown by Mr. Churchill for the Covenant of the League as much as for the Arabs. The Covenant said that the existence of the Palestine people as an independent nation could be recognized provisionally because they had attained a sufficient stage of development. It did not say this was to occur *when* they had attained it, or was to occur by and by or eventually or at any future stage. It said of the ex-Turkish communities, as it called them, that they "*have* reached this stage of development." They were immediately fit for this independence. In fact of which the Colonial Secretary ventured to tell his hearers that their children's children must pass away before self-government could be theirs. He would not be bothered even to yield momentary lip-service to the Covenant. However, there was honesty of a sort in that.

But there was hypocrisy in his invitation to the Arabs to "hold and claim firmly" their civil and religious rights. Civil rights were undefined, unstated, uncodified, valueless as guarantees, and a long way from being offered as a panacea to the least of the Zionists. Yet he told the Arabs to look upon them as "sacred." His adjective should have gone into the French language.

The Colonial Secretary's oration, losing nothing of aggravation as mouth-to-mouth versions of it spread amidst the Arabs, certainly contributed to the growth amid them of the more desperate temper which a month later ended in bloodshed. If the Churchill of Cairo had diminished so strikingly British responsibilities, the Churchill of Jerusalem had increased them heavily.

This much good, however, came out of the evil, that the leaders of the Arabs saw how useless was any action on their part at home. A special National Congress was summoned—they had held three since 1919—and decided to send an official delegation to England, which would also visit Geneva and other centres of the Continent of Europe.

The delegation was a joint Moslem-Christian one. Its President, Musa Kazim Pasha al Husseini, was the head of one of the chief families or clans of the country, and had been Governor of the administrative district of Jaffa under the Turks. In this position he had shown himself helpful and kindly to the Jews who came under his control, and had assisted the establishment of their colonies of the old school. He had been Mayor of Jerusalem in 1918, but in 1920 had been compelled to resign because he would not comply with Governmental orders to employ Hebrew as an official tongue in his department. He was very much respected by his fellow-Arabs.

The change which had come to his situation is one upon which to ponder. As an Arab he could no longer govern Jaffa nor hold any ruling position over and among those of his race. What a cynical distortion it was of a Mandate which professed to prepare men for ruling positions, when it was employed to oust from such positions men who actually had had experience in ruling.

The secretary of the Delegation was Mr. Shibly Jamal, a Christian business-man, the head of a firm of tourists' agents and shippers. The other members were Hadj Tewfik Hammad, Ameen Bey Tamimi, Moueen Bey el Madi and Mr. Ibrahim Shammas, all men of ability. Haj Tewfik Effendi Hammad was a notable farmer. He had inherited a small estate near Nablus, and by steady work during eighteen years had brought it from being of no worth to yield him a substantial income. He bred cattle and carried off most of the prizes at the shows instituted by the Government. From the day of his arrival in England he consecrated all his leisure to technical study of the methods of the Board of Agriculture, to visits to the Wisley gardens and other such occupations.

Delegates of this character moved of course at ease in English circles. It is almost silly to have to say this of them, but the name "Arab" with its purely Bedouin associations in England, has been so disadvantageous to its owners and so useful to their opponents, that it was a great gain in 1921 for Members of Parliament and such others as met the delegates to discover themselves in the presence of equals. Some of these meetings indeed were disconcerting, because it was found that not only were the Arab delegates obviously fit to stand by themselves and to cope with the modern world and its "strenuous conditions," but had long entered the modern world, had lived in it, had estimated its value and did not desire its intrusion into

Palestine save in the most homeopathic doses, and with the "strenuous conditions" left far away where they belonged.

For this and for other evident reasons the presence of the Delegation was not at all welcomed by the Government when in August its members reached London and settled in the Hotel Cecil. They opened operations by demanding a Commission of Inquiry with terms of reference which would have entailed the exposure of the transactions which form some of the subject-matter of this book. They demanded the revocation of the Balfour Declaration, and supported this demand with reasoned state.

The following month they went to Geneva for the meeting of the League Assembly, and here, as in London, their very presence and demeanour proved most awkward and annoying for the Government delegates. Balfour himself had gone to Geneva. During a five-weeks' stay the Arab delegates made many attempts to see him, but time and again were rebuffed with the insolent message, "if it is anything to do with Palestine, Mr. Balfour has already seen Dr. Weizmann." The delegates preserved their tempers, which cannot have been easy, and continued to demand an interview, and to make known in the League corridors that they were determined upon one, till further refusal would have degenerated into a scandal. So Balfour finally received them. But he sat wrapped in absence of mind and incomprehension and evasiveness, and all they could get from him concerning Palestine was a repeated, "It is an experiment," and the injunction to go and see Dr. Weizmann.

That interview was the only time the Arabs met their evil genius. They returned to London and concentrated on the resentful Colonial Office. It was a new era. Hitherto the Arabs had been passed off as inconsequential tribesmen. They had only been noticed when they rioted. Now they appeared as a nation in the person of their representatives, who were either very distinguished-looking or very indistinguishable from the average European citizen. It was hard to say which of the two presentments was the more displeasing to the Government and to its Zionist friends. The delegates, also, insisted on communicating with the Colonial Office as the envoys of the people of Palestine, on a par with any other people's plenipotentiaries.

It proved impossible to shake them off, though some of the Colonial Office officials tried their hardest, descending to rudeness. "Why are you back here?" Ameen Bey Tamimi was angrily greeted by a Mr. Young, when he called one day at the Office. "Haven't you been told to go to the Jews?" But the delegates stuck to their guns and laid siege to the Colonial Office. They stayed very nearly a year, and they succeeded in forcing the issue between them and the Government to the front, and drove Mr. Churchill to produce such arguments as he had.

The first important event in the long negotiations was that in February of 1922, proposals for a Constitution for Palestine were submitted to them, for such observations upon these as they might feel called to make. It was an advance. Till then, as we have seen, in anything of importance the Arabs of Palestine had been ignored. Seven Arabs, it is true, had been nominated by the High Commissioner to an "Advisory Council" which had been created by decree in the October following the establishment of the "Mandatory" regime. But as three Jews had also been nominated—out of all proportion to their numbers—and ten official members of the Administration, the Arabs formed a permanent minority. Besides this, the Council, as its name showed, was purely consultative, and enjoyed no say in matters of organic policy, such as immigration.

It was now proposed by the Colonial Secretary, supposedly as a step forward, that a Legislative Council should replace the Advisory one. The draft scheme communicated to the Arab delegates allowed for a Council of 26 members, besides the High Commissioner. Eleven of these were to be official, 15 non-official; these latter being divided into 12 elected by the Turkish electoral-college system and 3 nominated. The representation would have worked out at 9 Moslem Arabs, 3 Christian Arabs, and 3 Jews.

That such was its purpose would, no doubt, have been disclaimed, but this classification of electors by creeds did have the effect of dividing the Arab *bloc*. It enabled the Jews also to have more members than was their democratic desert. Since the Arab Christians received 3 seats, the Jews, who on the voting-lists would be about 4 to 3 as compared with the Christians, seemed generously reasonable in being satisfied with a like number. The Government itself appeared if anything, over-careful of Arab rights in conceding the Jews no more.

But the truth was that if the Arabs had been considered as a whole, then the Jews would only have been entitled to one seat. The specious little juggle adopted to pack the Council gave 17,000 (in round numbers) Jewish voters 3 seats, but to 150,000 Arab voters only 12. In just proportion the Arabs should have received 26, and the Council have been enlarged, or in a smaller Council these proportions should have been maintained.

Also, the whole mass of Zionists were classified with the traditional Jews as a religious entity. This was in absolute contradiction with their own tenets, but they shut their eyes to it because it was a means of winning more electoral power. Though they claimed Palestine as a race and not as a religion, they were willing to be called a religious community for the sake of three seats in a Council. At one moment they repudiated a religious basis, at another they accepted it gratefully.

In itself the draft Legislative scheme—in which alterations of no radical importance were proposed afterwards—would not be worth consideration now but that it is well to show the gerrymandering which accompanied every stage of the development of Palestine as conceived by the Government and the Zionists. This Legislative Council never came into being, owing to the general abstention of the Arabs from the elections, when eventually these were held.

The results because of this abstention were so unrepresentative, out of 663 secondary electors only 97 being named, and the Arabs chosen resigning punctually, that the elections were nullified.

The gerrymandering reached extravagant proportions for these elections. On the 1st of September Sir Herbert Samuel published an "Electoral Order-in-Council" under which any person of other than Ottoman nationality habitually resident in Palestine who desires to apply for Palestinian citizenship shall make a declaration before the Governor of the District in which he resides, in the following terms:

> "I, A——— B———,hereby apply for Palestinian citizenship and declare that I intend to reside permanently in Palestine. And I agree to hand over any foreign passport which I now possess and to renounce my claims to any foreign nationality."

The application had to be made within two months from the 1st of September and to be supported by evidence of the applicant's *bona fides.* These regulations having been carried out, the applicant received a certificate, and if over twenty-five years of age was then entitled to vote as a primary elector.

The High Commissioner's proclamation was issued of course as the means of extending the vote to the Zionist immigrants. About 20,000 of the pre-War colonists had assumed Ottoman nationality, but the great majority of Jews of voting age were alien subjects.

Poor Sir Herbert Samuel's demand that these men should now surrender their passports and give up their foreign nationality will have appeared to him no doubt as an essential step. So it would appear to any reasonable person. But Zionist pressure was at once brought to bear, and on the 6th of October the Electoral Order was rescinded as below:

> The formal declaration to be made by the applicant has been amended to read as follows:
>
> "I, A——— B———, hereby declare that I intend to apply for Palestinian citizenship and to reside permanently in Palestine."
>
> All declarations made in accordance with the form contained in the proclamation published on the 1st of September shall be read as if they

> had been made in the amended form herein. This notice does not apply to Ottoman subjects.

The removal of the passport clause meant that the Zionist immigrants could remain foreign subjects, keep their foreign rights, yet vote and stand for election as though they were natives. In addition, they did not even have to apply for Palestine citizenship. All they need do was to say that they intended to apply for it. There was no time-limit. Any year in the elusive future would do. The only trouble was to know upon what this wonderful franchise rested; it was difficult to find for it a local habitation and a name. But presently a name was found, a name beyond all guessing. The immigrants were described as "Candidates for Prospective Palestinianism" and as such were placed on an absolute electoral level with Arab families of immemorial habitation.

So, when the time for exercising this franchise came, what happened was that Ottomans, and Candidates for Prospective Palestinianism clutching foreign passports, were invited to the booths by an illegal Government to vote in an illegitimate election for members who could not legislate in a Chamber of a nationality which did not exist.

These elections took place in the spring of 1923, so that a year was to pass between that climax and the submission of the first draft for the Legislative Assembly to the Arab delegates in London. The document as they had it was a section of the general scheme for the Constitution, which the delegates soon rejected, declaring in their reply to the Colonial Secretary:

> "If the British Government would revise their present policy in Palestine, end the Zionist condominium, put a stop to all alien immigration and grant the people of Palestine—who by right and by experience are the best judges of what is good and bad for their country—executive and legislative powers, the terms of a Constitution could be discussed in a different atmosphere. If today the people of Palestine assented to any constitution which fell short of giving them full control of their own affairs they would be in the position of agreeing to an instrument of government which might, and probably would, be used to smother their national life under a flood of alien immigration."

The facts were well put. Under the proposed Constitution Arab members would have been no better able in the Legislative Council than they were in the Advisory Council to bring Zionist immigration to a halt. The balance of numbers would have kept them in a minority to the official and Jewish members together, and powers were secured to the High Commissioner and beyond him to the Home Government by which no measures passed by the Legislative Council would be valid without one or the other's assent. The Council therefore, as stated a few paragraphs ago, could not legislate. It could propose legislation but could not pass it. It was only another advisory Council under an alias, and if the Arabs joined in it they would form part of machinery which could be used to advance Zionism. The quorum of attendance had been fixed carefully by Mr. Churchill at ten members, so that Arab abstention would not affect the validity of a sitting.

For rejecting this sufficiently obvious trap the Arabs gave eight detailed reasons, the chief being that Great Britain was not carrying out Article 22 of the Covenant, though ostensibly acting as Mandatory under this very Article. Under the circumstances, they declared, using with no little humour one of the phrases dear to the Colonial Office, that "no useful purpose would be served in entering into a detailed discussion" of the draft Constitution. They proposed instead that a Constitution should be elaborated which would:

1. Safeguard the civil, political and economic interests of the people.
2. Provide for the creation of a national independent Government in accordance with the spirit of Article 22 of the Covenant.
3. Safeguard the legal rights of foreigners.
4. Guarantee religious equality to all peoples.
5. Guarantee the rights of minorities.
6. Guarantee the rights of the Assisting Power.

It will be evident from their communications, and particularly from this last one, so sober and reasonable, that the Arabs, if unable to stand by themselves, were exceedingly well able to write by themselves.

Of Mr. Churchill's reply, sent on the 1st of March (by Sir John Shuckburgh on the Colonial Secretary's behalf), all that can be said is that he had his self-stability to console him.

His main points were:

1. The Colonial Secretary was anxious to discuss informally his proposals for a Constitution with recognized representatives of the inhabitants of Palestine, but could not negotiate officially with the Delegation, or any other body claiming to represent the whole or part of the people of Palestine, as there was no official machinery for such representation. It was "with the object of providing the people of Palestine with a constitutional channel for the expression of their opinions and wishes that the draft Constitution had been framed."

This very point had been put to the Arab delegates at one of their interviews with Mr. Churchill himself. They seem to have met it, irritatingly but fully, with smiles. If they had wished, they could have gone on to ask the Colonial Secretary how it was that the Government had never found any difficulty in negotiating officially with the Zionist Organization. They might have asked him how a constitutional channel possibly could be provided in the frame of Palestine's then unconstitutional Government.

2. The Colonial Secretary could not discuss the future of Palestine on any other basis than the letter commonly known as the "Balfour Declaration." The Government could not repudiate its obligations towards the Jewish people.

The Arabs reminded Mr. Churchill that there were earlier obligations to the Arab people which had to be fulfilled before any others could have been justly assumed. (This important question will recur shortly.)

3. As regards the non-fulfilment of the Covenant, Mr. Churchill said that "the position is that His Majesty's Government are bound by a pledge which is antecedent to the Covenant of the League of Nations, and they cannot allow a constitutional position to develop in a country, for which they have accepted responsibility to the Principal Allied Powers, which may make it impracticable to carry into effect a solemn undertaking given by themselves and their Allies."

The passage may be Mr. Churchill's own, but it looks as though in this matter he had let his correspondence be drawn up for him by those permanent officials in the Colonial Office who had charge of Palestine. They were well practised in sonorous bathos and could write down without perturbation such cant as the above description of the Balfour Declaration. The "responsibility to the Principal Allied Powers" was another piece of cant, and meant nothing but the scrubby deal at San Remo.

Such a defence invoked the crushing response it received. The members of the Arab delegation on the 16th of March reminded Mr. Churchill of Article 20 of the Covenant:

> "The Members of this League severally agree that this Covenant is accepted as abrogating all obligations or understandings inter se which are inconsistent with the terms thereof, and solemnly undertake that they will not hereafter enter into any engagements inconsistent with the terms thereof. In case any Member of the League shall, before becoming a Member of the League, have undertaken any obligations inconsistent with the terms of this Covenant, it shall be the duty of such Member to take immediate steps to procure its release from such obligations."

The first paragraph of Article 20 put paid to San Remo. The second paragraph put paid to the Balfour Declaration, which was flagrantly inconsistent with the terms of the Covenant. In fact to say that the Balfour Declaration was inconsistent with the Covenant is an understatement. It was an anti-Covenant. It substituted, for the independence of Palestine, foreseen under Article 22, the erection in it of the "National Home."

It substituted, for a native Government receiving advice from the Mandatory according to Article 22, an autocratic Government ruling by edicts, over which the people had no control. Violation of the Covenant could not have been more patent, and so, in faithfulness to Article 20, the Government should have taken "immediate steps to release itself" from the Balfour entanglement.

In his note of the 1st of March, indeed, the Colonial Secretary had not attempted to deny that the Declaration contravened the Covenant. He could not deny it. He followed, as later Colonial Secretaries and Governments were to follow, the blustering policy of proclaiming as loudly as possible the necessity for being faithful to this "solemn obligation," which was neither solemn nor an obligation.

This policy, followed then by Mr. Churchill, this policy of, as it were, vindication by hullabaloo may have had the immediate advantage he sought in it, which was the distraction of attention from the real issue. But as we examine it now, it is not to be hidden that the only point he could make on behalf of the Balfour Declaration was that it preceded the Covenant. But to maintain a prior obligation of this type was equally against that Charter. So that Mr. Churchill's reply came to this that when he defended himself, or the Government, from breaking Article 22, he did so by breaking Article 20.

What follows from that is very grave indeed. Neither by himself nor by any Minister or Government since, in seventeen years, has an answer to the charge of breaking Article 20 been made. In the particular correspondence the Colonial Secretary, in the next note sent to the Arab delegates, on the 11th of April, for the most part indulged in wide generalities. His letter was sprinkled with those "regrets that the Delegation had not shown a more responsible attitude" and those invitations to be "practical" and "not to adopt a purely negative action" which, in all controversies of this kind, are the certain signals of moral defeat. But to the accusation that the Government had broken Article 20 no reply at all was ventured.

It is noteworthy, while we are on this point, that in the summary of the Churchill-Arab-Delegation correspondence given in the Peel Report, which may be taken as the present-day version of the Palestine Question offered to the public, there is not any reference to this failure of Mr.Churchill to find an essential reply, nor is there any reference to the Arab accusation nor to Article 20 in whatsoever fashion. The Peel Report's account of this vital business cannot therefore be accepted as satisfactory.

Still, the members of a Royal Commission have no onus upon them of mentioning everything. It is their affair if they omit something which takes away from the quality of their Report, but they are under no obligation to include it, unless it is specifically in their terms of reference.

It is very different for a Government, and that is why the failure of the 1922 Government to reply to the Arab charge was so grave. A Government must take notice of a charge against it that an action which it proposes is contrary to a treaty or to some other pledge which it has sworn.

If the action, the proposed policy, be dropped, the Government may be excused from disavowing itself perhaps in so many words, but if it intends to go on with the policy it must disprove the charge. If it does not do so, such a Government leaves the highroad for the morasses of bad faith and shames itself and the nation over which it rules.

This unfortunately now occurred to Mr. Lloyd George's Administration in the spring of 1922. In the affairs of Palestine, the dishonesty and perfidy of that Government have cumbered the British people ever since.

Further discussion of the correspondence between Mr. Churchill and the Arab Delegation may appear after that as the pursuit of an anticlimax, but it is not so, for in the further exchange of notes two more primary questions were raised by the Arab delegates. In their note of the 16th of March, following upon Mr. Churchill's of the 1st, they pointed out:

1. That the measures taken for the furtherance of Jewish immigration into Palestine and various other actions taken by the Palestine Government in pursuance of its general policy were illegal under the Hague articles to which Great Britain had sworn adherence.
2. That in 1915, before the Balfour Declaration was published, His Majesty's Government made a pledge to the Arabs in which it undertook to recognize the independence of those Arab States which formerly had belonged to Turkey. "Palestine is one of these States, as is clearly shown by reference to King Hussein's letter dated the 14th July, in which the western boundary is denoted as 'the Red Sea and the Mediterranean.' There can be no question but that Palestine comes within these boundaries."

To reinforce the second claim, the Delegates quoted again part of the Anglo-French Proclamation of the 9th of November, 1918, by which the two Powers declared their aim in the countries liberated from the Turks to be "the establishment of Governments and Administrations deriving their authority from the initiative and the free choice of the native populations." (They were not aware of the preamble of this Declaration, which would have been still more telling to quote.)

To the first of these claims, which struck at the root of everything since it invalidated most of the legislation of the Palestine Government and inferentially invalidated that Government itself, what answer did Mr. Churchill give? He gave none. Once more he had absolutely nothing to say in his defence, but the Prime Minister and he held to the course which they could not deny to be in violation of law. Therefore on this other count, one involving the respectability of its own administration, the British Government again had defaulted from pledged engagements.

To the second claim Mr. Churchill did attempt some answer. It is not so easy to place the importance of this answer. It was upon a primary matter, but so were those other matters, to which no answer had been vouchsafed. Possibly there is no particular call to establish a scale of precedence between betrayals. Enough to make clear that to the charge of betraying The Hague the Government had no defence to offer. To the charge of betraying the Covenant the Government made a preliminary reply but when the charge was pressed home had no defence to offer. To the charge of betraying its word to the Arabs a reply was now attempted.

"This promise," said Mr. Churchill, "to recognize the independence of the Arabs was given subject to a reservation made in the same letter, which excluded from its scope the country lying to the west of the Vilayat of Damascus."

So the great matter of our pledges to the Arabs through King Hussein was thus brought to the front again. In Chapter 6, in which the text of the McMahon-Hussein papers was given, I said that I should not go then at any length into the details of our pledges under this pact (which, by the acknowledgement of Mr. Lloyd George, had the quality of a treaty) since I should have to return to it when a British statesman endeavoured to escape from them. The occasion has come, and the reader must forgive me for some repetition now upon the subject of these pledges. Though the Balfour Declaration is completely discounted on other grounds too, yet under the McMahon pact the British obligation to make an independent Arab country of Palestine is so undeniable, and therefore the subsequent making of the Declaration is so illicit, that the relevant facts deserve more than single mention.

In the second place, the deplorable endeavours of the Government to escape from the McMahon pledge merit full scrutiny.

In the third place the opportunity of driving anything home by repetition, with a reasonable chance of its being read, is one rare and precious beyond belief to the Arabs and to their defenders.

Mr. Churchill, then, in his note continued by explaining the reason for the exclusion of Palestine from the area covered by the pledge of independence. But before giving his explanations, it will make for clarity if I repeat the essential clauses of the McMahon-Hussein papers, italicizing the more important words. In his letter of the 25th of October, 1915, Sir Henry McMahon had written:

> I communicate to you on behalf of the Government of Great Britain the following statement.
>
> The districts of Mersina and Alexandretta and *portions of Syria tying to the west of the districts of Damascus. Homs, Hama, and Aleppo cannot be said to be purely Arab and therefore should be excluded* from the desired boundaries.
>
> *Subject to the above modifications,* and without prejudice to certain treaties enacted between ourselves and some Arabian chiefs, *we accept these boundaries.*
>
> And as regards those portions of the territories therein in which Great Britain is free to act without detriment to the interests of her ally, France, I am empowered in the name of the Government of Great Britain to enter into the following covenant and reply to your letter as under:
>
> "Subject to the above modifications. Great Britain is prepared *to recognize and support the independence of the Arabs within the territories included in the limits and boundaries proposed by the Shereef of Mecca.*"

The boundaries proposed by the Shereef had been stated by him in his letter to Sir Henry McMahon of the 14th of July previously, in the following clause:

> "England to acknowledge the independence of the Arab countries, bounded on the north by Mersina-Adana up to the 37th degree of latitude, on which degree fall Birijik, Urfa, Mardin, Midiat, Amadia Island, up to the border of Persia: on the east by the borders of Persia up to the Gulf of Basra: on the south by the Indian Ocean, with the exception of the position of Aden, to remain as it is: *on the west by the Red Sea and the Mediterranean Sea up to Mersina.*"

That is to say, the Arabs had demanded the independence of all Syria, including naturally the southern half of it, Palestine. A frontier formed by the Mediterranean coastline from the Red Sea to Mersina meant a frontier of every mile from Egypt to Asia Minor, as a glance at the map shows immediately. Sir Henry McMahon had demurred to one section of this frontier, saying that the territory to the west of Damascus, Homs, Hama and Aleppo was not purely Arab.

The four towns are almost straight one above the other: they are like ships lying off the land at regular intervals. A line drawn through them runs nearly direct north from Damascus to Aleppo, and the country to the west of them is precisely the northern half of Syria, coinciding to all intents with the later French Mandated area.

The Shereef, in his letter of the 25th of November, renounced the Mersina and Alexandretta claim. But, maintained he, "the provinces of Aleppo and Beyrout and their sea-coasts are purely Arab provinces." Sir Henry McMahon took note of this contention of the Shereef's, but repeated that French interests were involved in these vilayats or provinces. To which the Shereef, on the 1st of January, 1916, responded by accepting the provisional exclusion of the provinces till the War was over. "Then," he said, "we shall ask you for what we now leave to France in Beyrout and its coasts." This solution was found satisfactory by Great Britain, and after correspondence upon war-supplies the Pact was sealed by a letter from Sir Henry McMahon dispatched on the 10th of March.

The situation is plain. The "French area" would be left in French hands for the present. The Arabs did not drop their claim to it, but they would not compromise the alliance by insisting upon it then. They were satisfied to conclude the Pact on the present basis of the independence secured to Mesopotamia, to Arabia proper, and to the remaining territory of Syria, to that part of it which was comprised of the four towns and the land east of them, and to that part of it which lay south of them, to wit, Palestine.

How did Mr. Churchill in 1922 try to slip these bonds? With the most extraordinary carelessness, as though treaties were nonsense which he could not be troubled to scan. It is impossible to say of course what his actual part was in the composition of the note to the Arabs which contained the plea he now put, but he endorsed it and must bear the responsibility for it. He said that the reason for including Palestine in the reserved area was that the Vilayat of Damascus contained the whole of Transjordania (as it was then called). Transjordania stretched right down from the borders of the French area to south of the Red Sea, and Palestine lay parallel to it and west of it all the way.

Therefore, argued he, since the portions lying to the west of the Vilayat of Damascus were excluded, and Palestine lay west of Transjordania which was part of this Vilayat, Palestine was one of those portions and was excluded. Thus put, the exclusion of Palestine had the certainty and the fatality of a proposition of Euclid about it.

But, as the reader must have perceived, in order to present his proofs in this overwhelming fashion Mr. Churchill had done something very unusual for a Cabinet Minister. He had altered the text of the document under consideration. The text spoke of the portions of Syria lying to the west of the four towns. The Colonial Secretary had suppressed the four towns—which went north—as towns. In their place he had substituted, or reintroduced, one of them, Damascus, no longer as a town at the base of a line which went north, but as a vilayat, or province, which according to him stretched south. Mr. Churchill altered "the portions of Syria lying to the west of Damascus, Homs, Hama and Aleppo" to: "the country lying to the west of the Vilayat of Damascus."

Startling enough: but that did not end the tale. On reading of this vilayat the Arabs hastened to the Colonial Office, where they were received by Sir Herbert Samuel, who had come to England for the negotiations, and by one of the chief Permanent Officials, Sir John Shuckburgh I think. This was on the 1st of June. To them the delegates pointed out that not alone was there no mention of the Vilayat of Damascus in the text of the treaty, but that there was no such thing in existence, nor ever had been, as a Vilayat of Damascus. The Vilayat which turned tail and ran south was a fabrication of Mr. Churchill's, or of his advisers.

The Turkish dominions between Asia Minor and Egypt had contained three vilayats, those of Beyrout, Suriya and Aleppo. These provinces were subdivided into lesser divisions called sanjaks, and there were three sanjaks—Lebanon, Jerusalem and Zor—which were independent of the vilayats and communicated directly with Constantinople. That was the political construction of the country, which could have been learned instantly from any geography or guide book. But apparently so little was thought of Britain's pledge to the Arab people that in preparing to brush it aside no pains had been taken. No map nor work of reference had been consulted, but the name of a town and the name of a division had been seized and strung together, and half a sentence of reply had been vamped out of them.

What is to be said of this? How is such action by His Majesty's Secretary of State for the Colonies to be qualified? At least it should be exposed to the four quarters of the earth, for it was through these tamperings with texts that what really *was* a solemn engagement of this country to a war-ally was evaded.

The sequel is unimaginable. Mr. Churchill was preparing the issue of a White Paper, summarizing the whole correspondence between him and the Arab delegates and on the basis of that making a declaration of Governmental policy in Palestine. It was in a draft of this White Paper sent to the Arabs the day before, the 31st of May, that the south-bound "Vilayat of Damascus" had figured prominently. Next day in consequence they had gone, as we have seen, to the Colonial Office and had exposed it.

They had to wait some three weeks to learn the result. On the 23rd of June, the expected communication from the Colonial Office arrived, the White Paper in its proposed form for publication, with enclosures, among which was their own correspondence.

On the subject of the false Vilayat, with all its consequences, this was the response:

> "The comments you were good enough to offer were carefully considered by the Secretary of State who, after consulting the authorities concerned with the early correspondence between Sir Henry McMahon and the King of the Hedjaz, *decided to make a modification in the draft on a point of fact.* [My italics.]"

The phrase is one which ranks with the celebrated "terminological inexactitude." There is a gracious air of concession about making the modification. Who would suppose that this "modification" in the draft-text was imposed because a vital truth had been suppressed and a vital falsehood had been suggested?

What, however, *was* the modification? The Arabs searched the enclosed White Paper with the eagerness which can be imagined and here was what they found:

> It is not the case, as has been represented by the Arab Delegation, that during the War His Majesty's Government gave an undertaking that an independent national government should be at once established in Palestine.
>
> This representation mainly rests upon a letter, dated the 24th of October, 1915, from Sir Henry McMahon, then His Majesty's High Commissioner in Egypt, to the Shereef of Mecca, now King Hussein of the Kingdom of the Hedjaz. That letter is quoted as conveying the promise to the Shereef of Mecca to recognize and support the independence of the Arabs within the territories proposed by him. But this promise was given subject to a reservation made in the same letter, which *excluded from its scope, among other territories, the portions of Syria lying to the west of the district of Damascus. This reservation has always been regarded by His Majesty's Government as covering the Vilayat of Beyrout and the independent Sanjak of Jerusalem.* The whole of Palestine west of the Jordan was thus excluded from Sir Henry McMahon's pledge.

Once more the same tamperings with texts, the same cool indifference to facts, the same slipshod, yawning duplicity. It is hard to contain one's temper on reading this effusion, knowing that its authors were to escape with it, for the time at least, and in practice were to carry their point. They knew only too well, though, what they were about. Their version of the reservation might not stand an instant's analysis, but who was going to analyse it? To where was there any appeal from it?

It would be printed as a White Paper, and it was only in White Papers, in official documents that a full record of what had been written by the Arab delegates and by the Colonial Office in reply would be found. When Mr. Churchill himself had ordered copies of the Arab letter of the 21st of February and of his reply of the 1st of March to be sent to the Press, a summary of Mr. Churchill's reply had appeared in some papers, but the Arab letter had been left unprinted.

As for White Papers, they were read only by interested parties and by a few dilettantes of foreign politics.

Would the British Press, would the American Press, which had not published the Arab notes to Mr. Churchill, publish the still longer McMahon-Hussein correspondence? Neither Press was really aware of the McMahon-Hussein papers, and if they had wished to publish them they did not possess them. The papers were coyly secluded in Whitehall safes.

If the newspapers *had* known all about them and *had* possessed copies of them, were the British and the American Press going to print all this long apparent labyrinth of words? Were they going to find space for the detailed explanations which were necessary to show that there might be many words but there was no true labyrinth? Europe and America were overcrowded with incident, and the affairs of nations and of men fought for mere inches in the daily Press.

What space, at this crucial moment, the Arabs did receive actually for expounding their case is indeed well worth some further consideration. The delegation whose fortunes we have been following had the most important role of any that came to England. It arrived when the future of Palestine, with good will, was relatively open to settlement, and when the Government was about to draw up a scheme of policy for that purpose, which included a Constitution. The Arab delegates had a share in the negotiations which dealt with this, and they came to England as bearers of their compatriots' instructions and expounders of their compatriots' attitude in a matter which concerned them and concerned Britain vitally. So that the amount of publicity they received is very important indeed.

The Delegation remained in England for eleven months. During those eleven months there were, in *The Times*, only ten references to it. And *The Times* was the paper with the "*officieux*" character, which gave more space to foreign affairs than any other, to which readers concerned with high politics were most likely to turn, upon which readers of this class largely were dependent for what they knew.

Most of these ten references were of a few lines. The delegates arrived in August 1921, but did not obtain a headline and three-quarters of a column till the 5th of May, 1922, when there was an account of a lunch at which they were the guests, and some phrases from the speeches. When Mr. Churchill's White Paper was published, on the 3rd of July, two columns were given to a summary of the White Paper and of his correspondence with the delegates. But the Arabs' letters were reduced to a few lines again, and while readers were informed that the Delegation had advanced reasons for considering Palestine included in the McMahon-Hussein pledges, not a word was consecrated to what these reasons were. Nor did Mr. Churchill's "Vilayat of Damascus" win mention.

On the eve of their departure from London the Arab delegates were granted their first and only column. It was a good column and contained an interview with Musa Kazin Pasha and the text of a telegram sent from Palestine by Christians and Moslems rejecting any Mandate based on the Balfour Declaration and demanding the fulfilment of the McMahon pledges. Musa Kazin Pasha also gave his interviewer a manifesto to the British people. About half of this was published, but the important dissection of the Governmental defence of its Palestine policy, made in the recent Commons debate, was omitted altogether. "After criticizing the defence of the Government's policy, the manifesto goes on to say..." were the terms employed.

Nothing ever appeared therefore even approaching an exposition of the Arab case. On the 25th of February, 1922, the delegates were given twenty lines for a summary of their opinions. This again was a good summary, but all that this or any other opportunity which they received gave them was an opportunity to outline their opinions. They never were able to support these with detailed argument or close reasoning, and this was in the chief newspaper of the kingdom, which gave more space than any other to the Delegation.

So, as we have just seen, only dilettantes of foreign politics who read the White Papers would have any chance of grasping the Arab case, and they were either interested parties who did not wish to grasp it or were persons who could be ignored.

So it did not matter then what went into the White Paper. Today, however, what we have to remember is that what did go into the White Paper is the only effort of a British Government to clear itself from the charge of disloyalty to its pledged word. So it must be examined. It is a pitiful business, but it has to be done.

The White Paper was published on the 30th of June. Annexed to it were the Arab Delegation's letters of the 21st of February and the 16th of March, and Mr. Churchill's of the 1st of March and the 11th of April, as well as correspondence between the Colonial Office and the Zionist Organization. There was no change in the text of the White Paper from that submitted last to the Arabs, on the 23rd of June, so that all Mr. Churchill and his advisers did was to ring the changes on the false Vilayat. They did not withdraw their assumption based upon this fiction, but substituted for "Vilayat of Damascus" a "district of Damascus."

It is to be noted that in the Arabic text, that actually sent to King Hussein by the High Commissioner, the word "district" is not found.

ان "مرسين" و"اسكندرونه" وبعض الاقسام
السورية الواقعة في غربي دمشق ،
وحمص ، وحماه ، وحلب ، لا يمكن ان
يقال عنها انها عربية محضة

The Arabic text is [in English]:

> "… indeed Mersina and Alexandretta and some of the Syrian parts (or "divisions") lying to the west of Damascus and Homs and Hama and Aleppo, it is not possible that it can be said of them that they are Arab pure… "

Since, however, the word "districts" is found in the official English text, at a pinch it may be retained, though its sudden appearance is very suspicious. It may be accepted or condoned since its presence makes no real difference in the Arabic, the word used, "*moukataa*" when the English version was Arabized, being equivalent to a town and its immediate adjacencies, in this case the urban district of Damascus, or "Damascus and its suburbs" would be nearest.

So, to return to the White Paper plea, the Government, by the mouth of Mr. Churchill, declared that the portions of Syria lying to the west of this newly introduced district of Damascus were excluded from the scope of the promise made to King Hussein, because "this reservation has always been regarded by His Majesty's Government as covering the Vilayat of Beyrout and the independent Sanjak of Jerusalem." These latter divisions between them contained all Palestine west of the Jordan, which accordingly, the plea indicated, was excluded from Sir Henry McMahon's pledge.

The use of "always" here was particularly good, considering that the claim had just been trumped up and evidently the Vilayat of Beyrout and the independent Sanjak of Jerusalem had only now been discovered in a hurry by the Colonial Office. But it will be best to deal with the White Paper plea point by point:

1. There is the point of bad faith. The Government might have a worthless case, but so long as it was argued upon the facts, the valueless-ness of it would have to be proved by any opponents and the Government would at least have the air of believing in its own case. But when the precedent of the "Vilayat of Damascus" was followed, as it was followed, and in order to make a case the Government maltreated the texts which it presented, then its opponents need hardly argue.

The text of the McMahon document produced in the White Paper was not the text of the McMahon document. In the White Paper no quotation marks were used: direct quotation from the text was evaded, and a supposed summary was used instead which in fact misrepresented the true text. Instead of quoting within inverted commas, in which event the Government would have had to acknowledge that the portions of Syria to be excluded were those "lying to the west of the districts of Damascus, Homs, Hama and Aleppo," the Government by the pen of Mr. Churchill said that what was excluded, among other territories (Mersina and Alexandretta), was the portions of Syria lying to the west of the district of *Damascus only.* The Colonial Secretary again got rid of Homs, Hama and Aleppo from the text.

Let me transfer the pledge to British soil, so that what was done may be clear as the day. A similar pledge would be to grant independence except to the "portions of Britain lying west of Salisbury, Birmingham, Sheffield and Berwick." A similar way of trying to dishonour this pledge would be if the Government made the plea that Poole and Weymouth and Dorchester were excluded from independence because the portions of England lying "to the west of Salisbury" were excluded.

The fraud in the Government reply would be to drop Birmingham, Sheffield and Berwick from the text of their pledge. To drop anything material from the text would be fraudulent, but here it would be outstandingly fraudulent since if these three cities were properly included it would be clear at once that the line of exclusion only began at Salisbury and went steadily upward from there. So that it was impossible for any places below Salisbury to lie off the line of exclusion and to be covered by it. On the other hand, the use of the single city Salisbury automatically created a certain vagueness, and gave a possible impression that places southwest and south-south-west of Salisbury perhaps might be included.

Just as in this supposititious case Birmingham, Sheffield and Berwick were suppressed, so in the real case, in the actual endeavour to evade its obligations to the Arabs, the Government suppressed the towns of Homs, Hama and Aleppo. The excision of these essential towns was entirely dishonest. In the Arabic text of the British pledge to King Hussein the whole four towns were linked by the conjunction "and," to make their situation as a unit more evident. The excluded territory lay to the west of "Damascus *and* Homs *and* Hama *and* Aleppo." "*Dimishk wa Hims wa Hamá wa Halab.*" If these towns had been properly quoted, it would have been impossible, of course, to utter the plea in the White Paper with the faintest showing of sense. Picture Jerusalem excluded by Hama, two hundred and fifty miles above it, or Gaza, on the threshold of Egypt, excluded by Homs, in the latitude of Cyprus and of Crete.

2. But this suppression of evidence by the Government drove it to something worse. To something that appears worse at least, for in reality there is nothing to choose between suppression of part of a text and the changing of the part which is left unsuppressed.

As the English text lay, the plural of the word "districts" was an obstacle to the Government plea. "The portions of Syria lying to the west of the districts of Damascus" would have made anyone prick his ears and ask, "What are these districts of Damascus?" So the plural had to go. The Government, like the steward in the Bible, took up its pen and wrote down "district," or scored through the letters.

This deed is not going to be explained now by saying that the White Paper text is only a summary, any more than the suppression of the three towns is explained by it. The accusation is that the summary does not contain the three towns and the missing S, and that without them it is a fraudulent summary, and that the Government uttered it knowing it to be so.

3. Now we come to the automatic consequence of tampering with texts without concern for their sense or intention. The Government in the White Paper gave to the district of Damascus the same territorial extent which it had given to the imaginary Vilayat in the draft. This was unavoidable, since for the purposes of the Government's plea the district *had to cover* the real Sanjak and Vilayat wherein Palestine was contained. Whatever excluded Palestine had to outflank it from top to toe.

But what did this entail? It entailed that, to fulfil the Government's argument, Damascus and its suburbs (in the Arabic text Damascus alone) stretched southward all along the flank of the excluded territory, down to Akaba at the head of the Red Sea. Even supposing that the prehensile city only went as far south as the edge of the Dead Sea, so as to get Gaza and Beersheba to the west of it in this political deer-stalking, it would still have to be about 175 miles in length. There would of course be as much more of the city going north to above Latakia, where was the end of the Vilayat of Beyrout with which Mr. Churchill said it was conterminous. That meant another 170 or so miles of streets and mosques and gardens, and 345 miles of length in all.

Is it a lunatic who asserts that Damascus is some three hundred and forty miles long? Is it a comedian who is responsible for this tomfoolery? Not at all. It is, upon analysis, revealed as an integral part of the excuse put forward by a British Government for not carrying out its word to an ally.

4. Let us leave the Government's tampering with texts, and return to its mere absurdities. The boundaries of the Arab countries to receive their independence as set out by King Hussein, ran normally north, south, east and west. The boundary on the west was thus stated: "On the west by the Red Sea and the Mediterranean Sea up to Mersina." This was formally accepted by Sir Henry McMahon on behalf of the British Government, with the "modification" we know. The French area, Northern Syria, the north part of the Mediterranean frontier was excluded, temporarily.

No one denies this exclusion. But if the plea of the White Paper be accepted, and Palestine also be excluded, then the whole Mediterranean frontier disappears. The entire Arab structure caves at the bottom on the west, and since nothing is anywhere mentioned as substituting the lost Palestine boundary, the Arabian State is left with no frontiers at all from Damascus to the Red Sea. This passes as a "modification" and is accepted without a word by King Hussein and the Syrians at his elbow! On our part, we British promise that limits which we do not fix shall be those which we shall support and recognize. What sense is there in this?

5. From the earliest stages of the War the British Government used, as we know, the word "Syria" to designate the French area only. The French themselves most often, up to the Mandatory period, employed "Syria" in the sense of the whole country, French and British areas together, which is the right sense.

But this was never official British practice in the war-time, and apologists of Zionism indeed have employed this fact to try and explain away the joint Anglo-French Proclamation of the 9th of November, 1918. The Proclamation—without the Preamble, I suppose—was cabled to General

Wingate in its French text. He sent it to Lord Allenby, who published throughout Palestine a translation in English and Arabic in which the promise to set up native governments in Mesopotamia and Syria was given.

Mr. Philip Graves, who takes the official view, has explained that "the proclamation was not addressed to the Palestinians but to the peoples of Syria and Irak." Shortly after, in the chapter of his *Land of Three Faiths* whence these words are taken, he refers to an article of my own in the *Daily Mail* (January 1923) and criticizes my "rather singular premise, Syria=Palestine"— that is, includes Palestine. Other writers beside Mr. Graves take the same view. There is no need to quote any one of them, since all are alike. Only the Arabs and their defenders have used "Syria" in the sense of integral Syria including Palestine.

But in the text of the McMahon-Hussein papers, the reserved area is "the portions of Syria lying to the west of Damascus, Homs, Hama and Aleppo." The reserved area is altogether in Syria, in which British documents not only did not include Palestine but refused—or the compilers of them did—to include Palestine.

Therefore on the face of it it is useless to pretend that any part of the reserved area, wholly in Syria, contained Palestine. Our adversaries dare not assert now that it did. To assert, when a treaty was being drawn up, when everything depended upon the terms of a pledge, that official practice, that the universal phraseology of British official documents, was all at once and without notice changed over and that the word "Syria" was for this one occasion given a sense the British Government never used nor acknowledged then nor since—that would be too much to ask the most gullible to swallow.

So, upon this count, as upon others, it is beyond denial that the only reservation made was in the French zone, and that the independence of Palestine was guaranteed along with that of the other Arab lands.

6. On the 5th of November, 1919, the French Government published a statement in the *Temps*, its usual vehicle for pronouncements, the aim of which was to distinguish between the parts of Syria it acknowledged to be "*purement arabes*" and those which it did not, and over which in consequence it maintained the familiar pretensions. British attitude was quoted to support the distinction. At the time the Emir Feisal was in violent disfavour with the French, and they added to this statement a rider pointing out that neither France nor Britain had pledged themselves to establish the Emir's personal authority even in the "*purement arabes*" regions.

This particular point dealing with Feisal is of no consequence, since it was personal, but what is of consequence is that in making the point, and the previous one, the French Government automatically defined which were the purely Arab regions where the much-quoted "reservation" from Arab rule did not apply. Here is the text:

> "1. La Grande Bretagne a toujours exclu des régions dites purement arabes non seulement le Liban mais toute la région cotière syrienne située á l'ouest des quatre villes, c'est à dire précisément la zone blanche où doit s'opérer la rélève des troupes britanniques par les troupes françaises.
> 2. Ni la Grande Bretagne ni la France ne se sont engagées à imposer aux régions dites arabes l'autorité personnelle de l'émir Feiçal, fils du roi Hussein, qu'il s'agit des quatre villes ou de la Palestine ou de tout autre pays de langue arabe."
>
> 1. Great Britain always has excluded from the regions styled purely Arab not only the Lebanon but the whole coastal region of Syria to the west of the four towns, that is to say precisely the "white zone" wherein French troops are to relieve British troops.
> 2. Neither Great Britain nor France have bound themselves to impose upon the regions styled Arab the personal authority of the Emir Feisal, son of King Hussein, whether in the case *of the four towns or of Palestine or of any other Arabic territory.*

It is quite plainly stated here that the regions not acknowledged as purely Arab, where independence consequently was not predicated, were precisely the northern parts of Syria where, at that date, by the arrangement between Mr. Lloyd George and M. Clemenceau, French troops were to replace British. Not one French soldier replaced a British soldier in Palestine, nor was arrangement made for such relief.

It is equally plainly stated that the officially styled Arab regions, where Arab independence was guaranteed, comprised the four towns (Damascus, Homs, Hama and Aleppo) and Palestine.

With this the section of the White Paper of 1922 dealing with the pledge to King Hussein may be dismissed. It added false witness to perfidy, and it did so in a defiant fashion. The Arabs, need it be added, rejected these falsities, returned to the charge, repeated their case, and have been repeating it ever since.

Chapter 28

Other endeavours to justify the Government's broken faith to the Arabs.
Their refutation from official sources.
Great Britain absolutely pledged to establish Arab government in Palestine.

Though that stream of Arab protest has been left generally to flow unheeded, yet this much of it has, as it were, leaked through to public consciousness—that the Government's arguments, based on whatever papers there were, were not too strong, that they did not hold together over well.

That is a very watered version of the truth, but it has led, even so, to the production of another kind of defence, or of excuse for evading fulfilment of the Pact. This excuse comes into play rather after the fashion of the successive defences which law students practise, I think, at the debates which they stage amongst each other. An imaginary accused is put up, and those who argue for his acquittal accumulate defences for him after the manner of a trench-system facing in all directions. As soon as each trench is made untenable they vacate it for another enfilading it or outflanking it.

Their pleadings are something like this: (a) The accused did not commit the act; (b) if he did commit an act, it was not an offence; (c) if he did commit an act and it was an offence, he was not responsible at the time. This may be a layman's version and legally fantastic, but it represents substantially the style of performance.

Amidst lawyers no doubt it is an entrancing performance. But it is surely not a method of argument which they prefer to employ in court (if they ever employ it) on behalf of clients when a jury is sitting. Everyone knows how unhappy even is the effect of a change of plea from "Guilty" to "Not Guilty." If the average juror were informed as a defence that the man in the dock had not committed the crime with which he was charged, but that if he had committed it he did not mean to commit it, then the average juror would be convinced that the man in the dock had committed the act and knew what he was doing. With some common sense, the juror would feel that innocence does not spring from alternative reasons.

It is this defence of "innocence from alternative reasons" which has been adopted in the last resort to justify the Government's default from its pledge to the Arabs. The defence changes from "the Government gave no pledge" to "the Government gave no pledge, and if the Government gave a pledge it did not mean to give it." There was a flavour of accident about the adoption of this final defence, as it happened. Sir Henry McMahon in July of 1937 wrote a letter to *The Times,* and this letter was at once seized and, as it were, manned by Governmental and Zionist supporters at their wits' end for a line of resistance.

For a public letter Sir Henry McMahon's was a rather belated one, coming as it did twenty-three years after the event. But as far as the writer was concerned there were sufficient reasons for this, and indeed his role in the matter calls for no criticism. The Government and its defenders took advantage of his letter, but there is no suggestion that he wrote it to please them or as part of a combined arrangement. He wrote it to make his own position clear. In the summer of 1937, because of the recrudescence of the Palestine troubles, and so of the Palestine Question, the validity of the pact bearing his name was either being asseverated or being denied all over again. Under the circumstances, as he wrote in his opening paragraph, "silence on the part of the giver of the pledge might be misinterpreted."

No doubt it was being misinterpreted, since some of those who followed the affair were saying that "McMahon himself has never attempted to deny the pledge," or words to that effect. Such conclusions of course should never have been drawn. In the first place there is an established practice by which retired civil servants generally do not speak of the confidential details of their official life. Therefore silence in their case does not mean assent or dissent to any assumptions about what they did or did not do when they were in office. It means discipline. So it was unfair to assume from Sir Henry McMahon's disciplined silence that he agreed to the charges against the Government.

In the second place, what Sir Henry McMahon might or might not say about the pledge was of no consequence. There was the pledge, with as self-evident a meaning as anything could have. He could not strengthen it by saying he meant it nor weaken it by saying he did not mean it, any more than Mr. Lloyd George can affect the Treaty of Versailles today by his writing any account of his thoughts in 1919.

But Sir Henry McMahon undoubtedly was placed in a very invidious position by the talk which circulated, and it will be agreed, I think, that he was justified in writing his letter. The precedent of Civil Service silence has not been absolutely observed, and in his case there was less reason to observe it since, fourteen years before, in 1923, he had already written a letter upon this very subject. It was not a public letter, however, as it was addressed to the Colonial Office, but the Colonial Office, as probably it would have put it, had facilitated the publication of an abstract of the letter in a book. This was Mr. Philip Graves's just quoted *Land of Three Faiths.* In that abstract it is stated, by Sir Henry McMahon of course, that it was his intention in his letter to King Hussein of the 25th of October, 1915 (in which he detailed the excluded area) to exclude Palestine from the independent Arab territories. As this contention, however, was renewed in his letter to *The Times,* it will be enough to give the more recent and public of the two letters, which can be quoted textually.

In his letter to *The Times*, then, after saying, as above, that continued silence on his part might be misunderstood, Sir Henry McMahon continued:

> "I feel, therefore, called upon to make some statement on the subject, but I will confine myself in doing so to the point now at issue—that is whether that portion of Syria now known as Palestine was or was not intended to be included in the territories in which the independence of the Arabs was guaranteed in my pledge.
>
> I feel it my duty to state, and I do so definitely and emphatically, that it was not intended by me in giving this pledge to King Hussein to include Palestine in the area in which Arab independence was promised.
>
> I also had every reason to believe at the time that the fact that Palestine was not included in my pledge was well understood by King Hussein."

This is well stated. The writer confines himself rigidly to certifying what he is in a position to certify, that is, the nature of his own intentions. He does not say that the pledge of independence for Palestine was not given to the Arabs; all he says is that he did not mean to give it. Very rightly, too, in the same measure in which he is categoric about himself he refuses to be categoric about King Hussein. He can speak for himself, but concerning Hussein, whom he was not meeting, though he was exchanging documents with him, he was dependent upon the reports of other parties. So he is careful not to put any rumours into Hussein's mouth nor to father upon him unprovable attitudes.

He avoids the error, which would have been easily made, of speaking as though his own acquaintance with Hussein's attitude was first hand. He himself did not know what King Hussein's sentiments were. He had "every reason to believe" that they were what he states, but most punctiliously he does not exaggerate this into knowledge. In the same way he does not suggest that King Hussein ever took any step which would confirm him in these beliefs of his. No, he merely puts forward as his personal opinion that King Hussein well understood that Palestine was to be excluded from the freed area. He had in *his own* mind this assumption of what Hussein had in *his* mind, and gives it for what it is worth. But since it is all a business of states of mind and understandings and beliefs, he keeps his account conscientiously upon that plane, where nothing is established, and does not attempt to present anything as a fact.

The same is the case with the naming of Palestine as a portion of Syria, in his first paragraph. He meant at the time to include Palestine in Syria, as he meant to exclude Palestine from independence. He does not say that the Government so included it. He would not say so, because the Government's speeches and texts are to the contrary. There is no official passage of 1915-16, in the course of correspondence with the Arabs, speaking, as he speaks, of "that portion of Syria now known as Palestine." By that date the British Government had ceased to include Palestine in Syria. But he himself had the sounder and older opinion of Syria's geographic extent, which governed his use of the word, and he is entitled to clarify this point now, all the more since it was not clarified by him twenty-three years ago.

Accordingly, no one championing the Arab cause can complain of Sir Henry McMahon's letter to *The Times*, though it is evident that he was misled by such information as reached him concerning Hussein, and has not perceived what stands out from his own documents.

High Commissioners are human, and it is legitimate to add, their memory is not necessarily perfect. *The Times* letter rather gives the impression between the lines of a Britain master of the situation in the Near East, picking the Arabs at leisure as her allies, and rewarding them with what seemed good to her out of her bounty. Whereas we were desperately anxious to obtain the Arabs as allies, and it was not at all reservations from them, but concessions to them which filled the Imperial mind. In Chapter 6 the reader has seen already that if King Hussein had pressed for it, Sir Henry McMahon had received instructions to waive British control over Basra and Baghdad themselves. He has seen that not long before the crucial letter of the 25th of October was sent to King Hussein, Aubrey Herbert, fresh from meeting Sir Henry McMahon and others in authority in Egypt, had written that it was considered "of almost supreme importance to get the Arabs in with us."

Seven months before even, in late March of 1915, before our plight at the Dardanelles had changed high advisability into stringent necessity, the Near Eastern anxiety of the Government had been shown in a passage of a note sent by it to the Russian Government:

> "His Majesty's Government considers it essential, the moment the expected disappearance of the Turks from Constantinople occurs, to establish in some other place an independent Moslem Power as a

> political centre of Islam. The existence of such a Power, which must have a completely Moslem if not an absolutely Turkish character, is absolutely necessary, and the [Moslem] Holy Places must naturally form the centre. It is likewise absolutely necessary to answer the question whether any other territory in Asia Minor is to be included in its composition, and if the answer is in the affirmative, which territory."

So there was no atmosphere of aloof benevolence in the Foreign Office, it may be confidently asserted, when King Hussein received his pledges in return for his alliance. *The Times'* letter, therefore, hardly reproduces the stress of the period, but, of course, it was not concerned to do so. To explain what were his own ideas at the time is what Sir Henry McMahon's communication sets out to do, and nothing more, and, as I have said, on this score there is no complaint or criticism to be made of it.

But when it comes to other parties, in or out of the Government, seizing this essentially private explanation of Sir Henry McMahon's purely about himself, and trying to use it as a public document, as an alternative line of defence for Government conduct, then indeed we have every complaint to make. This is a question in which there can be no alternative defences. We are dealing with the fate of nations, not with oratorical jousts between law students. The place and time irretrievably chosen by the Government to exonerate itself from the charge of perfidy was in the White Paper of 1922. It had to decide then either to plead that there was no pledge, or that there *was* a pledge which however it had given without meaning to give it. The Government chose to plead that there was no pledge, with the results we have observed. The spokesmen of the Government cannot now, seventeen years later—and could not even one year later—turn round and say that the Government did not mean to give the pledge, after pleading previously, with all the force in them, that no pledge existed.

If, twenty-three years ago, they had, however, chosen the other line of defence and had argued that they did not mean to give the pledge, the White Paper would have been just as valueless. What any signatory of a treaty thinks or intends or imagines at the time it is signed is not of the slightest consequence. It is what the signatory signs that matters, and that alone. Imagine Great Britain demanding of other Powers that they should keep the treaties made with her, if in a White Book she declared that she herself was loosed from a treaty because her envoy at the time did not intend to write what he wrote.

If engagements are to be abrogated by retrospective inattention or forgetfulness or failure to express oneself, then there is no longer any safety in texts, there is no longer any reason for texts at all, nor for treaties, nor for faith amidst peoples.

Therefore it is depressing to find Lord Samuel, generally so careful, using this plea of non-intention, and marring with it his speech in the Lords on the Peel Report. His particular non-intentionist is not Sir Henry McMahon but Sir Gilbert Clayton. Sir Gilbert Clayton, at the time Major Clayton and Soudan agent in Cairo, had been (in the words of a note addressed by him in 1923 to Sir Herbert Samuel) "in daily touch with Sir Henry McMahon throughout the negotiations with King Hussein and made the preliminary drafts of all the letters." Presumably this refers to the English text, since the Persian intelligence agent Ruhi and Sir Ronald Storrs, as best they could and Storrs "without deputy, staff or office" and "often under high pressure," respectively wrote and checked the Arabic text. Relating this, Sir Ronald Storrs adds that when he was away on mission his work of checking "was carried on (perhaps better) by others, but the continuity was lost."

The glimpse of the conditions obtaining is significant. However, Major Clayton—in his note to Sir Herbert Samuel when the latter was High Commissioner—went on to say that "it was never the intention that Palestine should be included in the general pledge."

Similar testimony was produced during the Peel Debate in the Commons by Mr. Ormsby-Gore, who also was upon, or I am inclined to say of course was upon Sir Henry McMahon's staff in 1916. He assured the House that it was "never in the mind of anyone on that staff" to include Palestine west of the Jordan in the Arab pledge.

With what an inhibited, tongue-tied staff Sir Henry McMahon was blessed in Cairo in 1915-16. There they were, these men of ability and of education, all desirous of excluding Palestine from the Pact which was being drawn up, but not one of them able for the life of him to find the words in which to do it. Even born supernumeraries, such as Mr. Ormsby-Gore, who had no obligation to draft it, were vainly intent upon it, trying by mental processes and by thought-transference to aid their comrades in the toil of exclusion. It is indeed likely that all these minds in the air may have helped to cloud the High Commissioner's. Cairo throbbed with the pulsating brains of men aching to make it quite clear to King Hussein that Palestine was not to be independent, but unable to find a formula. They wanted to say to him, "Palestine is to be excluded from the terms of this covenant," but how were they to get that into plain English?

I do not treat this business a whit more seriously than it deserves.

Are Britain's representatives to be absolved from their word because of self-confessed incompetence? There is no reason in all this, let alone justice. Into what a situation the adoption of the plea leads its adopters may be seen from a further passage in the speech of Lord Samuel. He declared that he had been "much disturbed," when High Commissioner in Palestine, by the words of Lord Grey in 1923. Lord Grey (cf. Chapter 7) in the House of Lords debate on the McMahon pledges had "implied that the Arabs had a legitimate grievance." Whereon Sir Herbert Samuel, as he then was, talked to Sir Gilbert Clayton, told him he intended to write to Lord Grey, and received for the purpose the note from Clayton already quoted.

Now what did this sending, or quoting, of Clayton's note to Lord Grey mean? I do not suppose the sender envisaged this, but it was equivalent to telling Lord Grey that the views of a subordinate in Cairo determined his own policy. The crux was considered to be, not what Grey said or Grey signed, but what Clayton intended. How Sir Herbert Samuel phrased his letter to the Foreign Secretary we do not know, but it can only have amounted to this, "My dear Grey, Here is evidence from Major Clayton that in making the McMahon Pact there was no intention amidst the responsible parties of conferring independence upon Palestine."

In the name of Heaven, who were the responsible parties? The Soudan Agent in Cairo or His Majesty's Secretary of State for Foreign Affairs? Whatever his faults of commission or of omission in 1915-16, Grey did show compunction in 1923 and spoke in the House of Lords of "the pledges undoubtedly given to the Arabs" and of how they were "conflicting with the Balfour Declaration." Whereon he is given to understand that he has missed the point, that whatever pledges *he* may have given the Arabs, various subordinates in Cairo had not in their minds to give these pledges. *Their* intentions were the governing factor.

That is to say that the responsibility of policy is transferred from Westminster to the Savoy Hotel in Cairo and the Foreign Minister is told what he is to do and even what he is to intend by a group of gentlemen in Egypt, who acknowledge at the same time that they are unable to express their own intentions!

Let us get on. Mr. Ormsby-Gore, in his speech on the Government's behalf which opened the Peel Report debate in the Commons on the 21st of July, 1937, leaving these intentions of his and of his friends for more perceptible things, turned for an argument to France. "The then British Government," said he, "was not in the position, even if it had had the wish, to promise the Shereef of Mecca that Palestine would be included in the Arab territories, because at that moment it was clearly bound to France, and France had reserved, and told the British Government so, the future of Palestine, and aspired to the hope that it would be French."

So France is brought in too, with the verisimilitude of a Dumas novel, "*vingt ans aprés*," twenty and more years after, to try and win a case irretrievably lost upon the facts. From the Government's point of view it was a blunder to bring in France, but Mr. Ormsby-Gore can always be relied upon for blunders. They were the relief of his career at the Colonial Office, as far as Palestine is concerned.

The exact position of France towards Palestine at the time we made the McMahon commitments can be ascertained, from French official statements and from the documents in the Russian archives published after the fall of that Empire. The status of Palestine was the subject of, or allusions were made to it in, a series of diplomatic notes which passed between the Ambassadors and Foreign Ministers of Great Britain, France and Russia.

On the 14th of March, 1915, the French Ambassador in Petrograd told the Russian Government that France, "after discussing the peace-terms which are to be dictated to Turkey, proposes to annex Syria." He asked for the agreement of the Tsar to this, so it was evident already that the Government of the Republic claimed no existing proprietorial rights in Syria.

About the same time, on the 20th of March, the British note to Russia, of which I have just quoted one half upon page 506-7, ended:

> "His Majesty's Government considers it would be precipitate to discuss the question of the possible division of Mesopotamia, Syria and Palestine or of the neighbouring territories between the Powers, provided the question of the [creation of the] aforesaid Moslem State is not lost from sight."

So that whether the French had claimed proprietorial rights or not, Great Britain was not conceding them. Furthermore, the establishment of the Moslem State, into which "Arabia will probably enter," as the first part of the note had said, was in British eyes the conditioning factor. The Moslem State was the thing to be remembered: the division of "Syria and Palestine" between Britain and France and Russia could wait. The essential precedence of things is set forth beyond ambiguity, and it is not the precedence which Mr. Ormsby-Gore pretends existed.

The Russians had nothing contrary to say to this. To the French note of the 14th they replied inquiring whether Syria in the French view included Palestine. The French Ambassador answered that he thought it did. The Russians asked him to be so good as to find out, because, while they were willing to consent to "fulfil in a large measure the desires of France concerning Syria and Cilicia," Palestine raised a fundamental issue and the question "would have to undergo a more careful discussion with regard to the Holy Places."

The Russian Ambassador in Paris meanwhile put a query to M. Delcassé, the French Foreign Minister, upon the French attitude to Palestine. Delcassé did not claim Palestine. He said the French Government "probably would insist on the possession" of (unscheduled) parts of it, but agreed that the Holy Places must be the subject of 'a special and more careful discussion." There the question lay, for nine months, till the end of the year, all the while that King Hussein and Sir Henry McMahon were corresponding.

The French were told of the Pact which was being prepared with King Hussein. It has been seen that when M. Picot came to London to begin the conversations which were to end in the Sykes-Picot Treaty he was instructed about the negotiations with the Arabs by Sir Arthur Nicolson, the Permanent Under-Secretary of the Foreign Office, on the 23rd of November, 1915. The Arab negotiations were practically concluded then, for it had been on the 25th of October that Sir Henry McMahon had agreed to Hussein's boundaries with the reservation for French interests in "Syria," not, be it noted, for French interests in Palestine.

When Sir Henry McMahon had sent to the Foreign Office the letter of King Hussein to which this one of his, of the 25th of October, had been an answer, he had enclosed a note from King Hussein's representative in Cairo. The latter declared on Hussein's behalf, that as far as French interests in Syria went the Arabs would resist French occupation of Damascus, Homs, Hama and Aleppo by force of arms, but would consent to modifications of the "north-western frontiers."

This was communicated to M. Picot and (to repeat the point) he came back on the 21st of December to the Foreign Office to tell Sir Arthur Nicholson that France accepted Arab administration in the four towns, but insisted upon the coast-areas parallel with them.

On the 30th of December the Russian Ambassador in London was informed of the progress of things. He was told that "the Arabs had approached Great Britain with the request for the setting-up of an independent Arab State, of which Arabia and the Holy Places would form part." The British Government had agreed, "in so far as it was affected," on condition that the Arabs declared war on Turkey and that "Syria be excluded from the new State, in view of the obligations which have already been undertaken towards France."

In February 1916, M. Cambon, French Ambassador in London, told the Russian Ambassador in Paris that, in the matter of the independent Arab State, France's demands in Syria and Cilicia were based on her agreement with Russia (of the 18th of March, 1915) concerning Constantinople and the Straits. The significance of this is that when the Russian Empire fell and all its agreements were abrogated by the succeeding Government, the basis of any French claims disappeared.

Through March the French and Russians exchanged notes on Palestine. These are very much to the point because they make evident that France had not yet got in Palestine the fixed status that Mr. Ormsby-Gore for his good reasons has ascribed to her. On the 26th of March the French Ambassador in Petrograd, M. Patéologue, sent to M. Sasonoff, the Russian Foreign Minister, an *aide-mémoire*, one of those letters which diplomatists commonly write to avoid dispute about the substance of conversations in which they have just engaged. He said:

> "During the conversation which you were good enough to hold with me this afternoon you were pleased to state, in response to my inquiry, that if the Government of the Republic were to receive the agreement of the British Government to the inclusion of Palestine in French Syria, the Imperial Government would have no objection to it."

If the British Government and *if* the Russian Government were to agree, then Palestine *would be* included in French Syria. This was written on the 26th of March, sixteen days after the Pact giving independence to the Arabs within an area including Palestine had been concluded. That settles the matter. France was no more than making diplomatic eyes at Palestine when it had already been conceded to the Arabs. As a matter of interest, the Russian Foreign Minister did not at all agree to the version of their interview which M. Patéologue sent him, and answered in a note of the 28th in which he only spoke of the "probable agreement of the Russian Government to the inclusion of Palestine in French Syria," and went on:

> While confirming this statement I nevertheless consider it my duty to add that it naturally does not refer to the Holy Places and territories where there are religious Orthodox institutions. The aforesaid towns and places must receive an international administration with the assurance of free [customs] entry into Mediterranean harbours. For reasons which are not unknown to you, the Russian Government would not consider it possible in this matter to recognize the exclusive sovereign rights of any Power.

An international administration, in the sense of some form of internationalization, of the Shrines of Christendom, it is to be noted, is not to be considered as antagonistic to Arab independence for Palestine. Feisal had bruited the possibility of some such arrangement at the Peace Conference.

However, what concerns us in this is that Palestine was anything but pledged to France in those last days of March 1916. Lord Grey's dispatch to Russia of the 13th of March (discussed at length in Chapter 7), in addition to that of the 20th of the preceding March, shows too that France was not considered as having any paramount situation in Palestine or lien upon it, for despite Lord Grey's fundamental proposal of giving to the Jews "the administration of the internal affairs" of this region, as he styled it, there is no word of France in the dispatch. If it had really been France's situation in Palestine which was preponderant and she had, in Mr. Ormsby-Gore's words, "reserved the future of Palestine," this dispatch would have been an intolerable trespass upon the rights of the Republic.

It is obvious too that if Lord Grey felt himself able to dispose of the future of Palestine for the benefit of the Jews, he was equally entitled, putting it mildly, to dispose of its future for the benefit of its inhabitants, the Arabs. If he could envisage a "transaction securing Jewish support" he could envisage one securing Arab support, having obtained, as was obtained, the agreement of the Allies to it. Nor did he invest the proposal for internationalization with any sacredness. Had this been fixed in principle between the Powers as the essential status of Palestine, whatever regime was settled for that country would have had to conform to it. Whatever plans were mooted would have been acceptable in their degree if they were not barred by internationalization. But in Lord Grey's dispatch the position was reversed. He cited the "opposition of influential Jewish circles" as an impediment or bar to an international protectorate.

Therefore, as the spring of 1916 came in, the real situation of Palestine with the rest of the Turkish Levant merely was that the three Powers were jockeying for what they might lay hand upon. The Sykes-Picot Treaty of March provided a condensation of these ambitions but, as the Patéologue-Sasonoff notes show, it was unsatisfactory to Russia, and this treaty never became valid. Two years later parts of it, red and blue and brown zones and the like, were taken out of it and were inserted, like parts from a crashed aeroplane, into the Anglo-French territorial concordat.

In any event, it was recognized at the meeting of the Supreme Council on the 20th of March, 1919, that the Arab pact was prior and superior to the Sykes-Picot Pact.

Under these conditions, there was nothing to prevent the McMahon–Hussein Covenant from being concluded. An intention in abeyance between three Powers to parcel up Syria somehow, if and when they all could come to an agreement about it, cannot be presented, dare not be presented as an impediment. That is, it dare not be presented even were secret treaties or arrangements making or made between the three Powers to be considered lawful, when the effect of them was to divide territory which did not belong to these Powers and was inhabited by allies in the war which they were waging.

De jure such a division was not lawful, and *de facto* the secret treaties had evaporated. What made the McMahon-Hussein Pact so different from them and from the various arrangements made later was that it had a legitimate national basis. It was concluded with the representative of the

Arab people, the age-long owners of the soil with which it dealt.

Only one more item in this long tale now remains to be mentioned, the supposed acquiescence of King Hussein in the supposed exclusion of Palestine from this pact. It is not mentioned by Sir Henry McMahon indeed as anything but a mere supposition which he entertained, but his supposition, when recounted by others, easily becomes an affirmation, so the attitude of the King had best be considered.

How can King Hussein possibly have intended to exclude Palestine? He was speaking on behalf of all the Arabs, with Syrian advisers at his elbow. His very text was based on a programme drawn up by Syrian exiles in France twenty years before, a programme which included all Syria in the independent Arab State and made the Mediterranean its western boundary. He had demanded the autonomy of all Syria from the Turks, before the British offer came to him, and when the Turks would not grant it, he would take nothing less and broke off parleys with them. The status of Syria as an independent Arab State, which the Turks would not give him, was the goal he set himself to reach through Great Britain.

In what fashion and when is he supposed to have acquiesced in the exclusion of half of this essential desideratum? Certainly not before he began negotiations with Cairo, for if he had acquiesced in the exclusion of Palestine at the outset, he would not have written down immediately thereafter a demand for boundaries including Palestine.

Did he then acquiesce during the course of negotiations? If he did it was a change of the first importance, an abandonment of a primary postulate. How then was this signified? How was Palestine excluded? How did King Hussein show that he understood that half of his western boundary was to vanish? The Government thesis is that all concerned in the Pact knew all they were doing and that half the western boundary was intentionally rejected by all in concert and Palestine thus was intentionally excluded. But there is no mention of Palestine in the text of the Pact. Therefore the exclusion can only have been accomplished by the High Commissioner intentionally not mentioning the matter and by King Hussein intentionally saying nothing about it in return. The highest affairs are incorporated in treaties by no reference to them being made. Once more the Government's case ends in "Alice in Wonderland," if not in Hanwell.

There is a most important rider to this question of King Hussein's attitude. To avoid complications when discussing another issue, I have said, as it is generally said, that he abandoned his claim to the coastal areas west of the four towns, to the coasts of Syria above Palestine. But in fact he only abandoned it temporarily. He never yielded purely Arab land to non-Arab rule, he yielded only semi-Turkish, semi-Arab Mersina and Alexandretta and their hinterlands. He agreed to let the Arab claim to the coastal plains below lie dormant till after the War, but announced that he would resume the claim then.

So he did resume it, and pressed it till he lost his throne. Those in whose name he had spoken, the Arabs everywhere, all after the War revendicated the right to independence of the area under the French. The French went through a period of revolt, and suffocated it, but the political agitation continued and grew. In the end it was met in a statesmanlike way by the Blum Cabinet. A treaty of alliance between France and the self-governing States into which French-held territory had been divided, by which France recognized their independence, was signed in 1937 and is to be ratified before 1940 [The present French Government unhappily shows signs of evading ratification of the Treaty. Considerable pressure from London has been brought to bear on Paris to this end.].

Therefore the argument that King Hussein agreed to the reservation of Palestine from the area of Arab independence, based on interpretation of the restrictive clause of his covenant with Sir Henry McMahon, falls to the ground, and falls heavily. "The promise to the Shereef of Mecca to recognize and support the independence of the Arabs," says the 1923 White Paper, "was given subject to a reservation which excluded among other territories the portions of Syria lying to the west of the District of Damascus. This reservation has always been regarded by His Majesty's Government as covering the Vilayat of Beyrout and the independent Sanjak of Jerusalem. The whole of Palestine west of the Jordan was thus excluded."

We have seen what this contention is worth in itself. But supposing that there had been any truth in it, accepting momentarily, nonsensical as it is, the claim of the Colonial Secretary that this reservation did include Palestine, what then? It was only a reservation for the years of the War. King Hussein only postponed the Arab demand for this area (including, on the Government's own insistence, Palestine), till a day which turned out to be the 11th of November, 1918. Upon that date all the whole provisional reservation, whether it was of north or of south Syria, of Palestine or of the Lebanon coasts or of the whole Levant, of the deserts or of the seas, came to a sharp end.

To the finish of the correspondence with the High Commissioner King Hussein maintained his point that whatever reservation he made was provisional, and to this standpoint no objection was raised. It was with the knowledge that the Arabs would resume their claims to the reserved areas, whatever they were, upon the day of victory, that Great Britain concluded her treaty with them. Therefore, even if the reservation cited by Mr.

Churchill were to be regarded, through perversions of text and fantastic interpretations of language, as applicable to Palestine, that reservation ceased upon Armistice Day.

The reservation had been made, as Sir Henry McMahon had declared, solely in the interests of France. Two days before Armistice Day in the Joint Anglo-French Proclamation the French Government had declared that its only aim was to free the peoples between the Taurus and the Persian Gulf and to enable them to establish throughout this territory national governments of their own choice, drawing their authority from these peoples themselves

Let us have done therefore with any more of this dishonourable pretence, upon any of the grounds traversed, that we are not firmly bound to carry out the provisions of Hussein's treaty with us. We are thrice pledged to grant the Arab people of Palestine that independence. We are pledged to grant it to them by our own bond, by the Covenant of the League of Nations, and by respect for the simple principles of human freedom, unless respect for Covenant and for freedom is merely something to preach to other nations, but amongst ourselves to disregard.

Chapter 29

The achievement of the Arab delegates in 1921-22. Subterfuges of the "White Paper."—Lord Northcliffe in Palestine. The House of Lords censures the Cabinet's infidelity. The Treaty of Lausanne. The Mandate comes into force at last.

The Arab Delegation of 1921-2 did not at the time seem, in the eyes of careless observers, to have accomplished anything. The political situation of their compatriots in Palestine was not bettered, and that of the Zionists was slightly improved, as a result of the declarations of the White Paper which sprang from the delegates' visit to England.

That, at least, was the ostensible result of their stay. It was, however, only ostensible, and a closer view shows that the Delegation really accomplished a great deal. They could not gain justice, because there was no intention of doing justice to them. But they could get on record that justice had not been done.

They worked for posterity when they drove the Colonial Secretary to put on to paper the Government's excuses for breaking its word. The section of the White Paper containing them was the equivalent of a signed confession of dishonesty, and though at the time few read it or bothered themselves with it in any way, it remains as evidence for a later court and for a more conscientious generation.

The other section of the White Paper sprang equally from the Arab Delegation's work, and was bound to be equally valuable in the long run to their cause. In this section Mr. Churchill "defined" the policy of the Government in Palestine. He did not and could not define it in any true sense of that word, because the essence of it was that it should be an undefinable means of passing from an Arab Palestine via Palestinianism to a Jewish Palestine. But he was forced to draw some contours of the Government's cloudy intentions, and after a few years had passed this too became evidence.

The salient passages of Mr. Churchill's statement of policy, and of the way in which the Government, publicly, envisaged the future of the Holy Land came at three points in the White Paper. At the beginning reference was made to the "Balfour Declaration."

> Unauthorized statements have been made [said the White Paper] to the effect that the purpose in view is to create a wholly Jewish Palestine. Phrases have been used such as that Palestine is to become "as Jewish as England is English." His Majesty's Government regard any such expectation as impracticable and have no such aim in view. Nor have they at any time contemplated, as appears to be feared by the Arab Delegation, the disappearance or the subordination of the Arabic population, language or culture in Palestine. They would draw attention to the fact that the terms of the declaration referred to do not contemplate that Palestine as a whole should be converted in a Jewish National Home, but that such a Home should be founded in Palestine.

Later on it was declared that:

> It is contemplated that the status of all citizens of Palestine shall be Palestinian, and it has never been intended that they, or any section of them, should possess any other juridical status

and, a few lines after, the Balfour Declaration was reaffirmed, in deference to the apprehensions of "some of the Jewish population of Palestine."

> That Declaration, reaffirmed by the Conference of the Supreme Allied Powers of San Remo, and again in the Treaty of Sèvres, is not susceptible of change.

Then came the most often quoted passage of all:

> When it is asked what is meant by the development of the Jewish National Home in Palestine, it may be answered that it is not the imposition of a Jewish nationality upon the inhabitants of Palestine as a whole, but the further development of the existing Jewish community, with the assistance of Jews in other parts of the world, in order that it may become a centre in which the Jewish people as a whole may take, on grounds of religion and race, an interest and a pride. But in order that this community should have the best prospect of free development and provide a full opportunity for the Jewish people to display its capacities, it is essential that it should know that it is in Palestine as of right and not on sufferance. That is the reason why it is necessary that the existence of a Jewish National Home in Palestine should be internationally guaranteed, and that it should be formally recognized to rest upon ancient historical connection.

This, then, is the interpretation which His Majesty's Government places upon the Declaration of 1917, and so understood, the Secretary of State is of opinion that it does not contain or imply anything which need cause either alarm to the Arab population of Palestine or disappointment to the Jews.

Under the policy interpreted in these passages of the White Paper of 1922 Palestine has been ruled ever since, the only country in history to have been ruled under an explanation.

How worthless this explanation was as an explanation, to say nothing of its being made to serve as a charter, the shortest analysis of its phrases will disclose. In the first paragraph cited comes the denial that it is the Government's purpose "to create a wholly Jewish Palestine," and the disowning of the Zionist slogan "a Palestine as Jewish as England is English."

Necessity was never louder proclaimed as a virtue. The Government could not create a solely Jewish Palestine. It could not exile more than a few Arabs, nor suppress a fertile population, much as the existence of that population was an impediment to its plans. The Government could not say, as had been said of another country, that "man had long been a nuisance and population a drug on the market," however much those were its feelings. Therefore, since the Arabs could not be removed, or notably removed, Palestine obviously never could be "wholly Jewish." But Palestine could become a Jewish State, and to that the Government did look forward.

The very Peel Report recognizes this. "Though the phraseology (of his White Paper) was clearly intended to conciliate, as far as might be, Arab antagonism to the National Home, there is nothing in it to prohibit the ultimate establishment of a Jewish State, and Mr. Churchill has told us himself in evidence that no such prohibition was intended. This view was naturally shared by the Zionist Organization."

The Peel Commissioners are, as is to be expected, careful in their language. But one can put crudely what they so decorously convey. "Though the phraseology of the White Paper was clearly intended, as far as might be, to wheedle the Arabs along, of course the aim all the time was a Jewish State, and this was what Mr. Churchill himself had in mind." In a bolder passage, the Peel Report acknowledges that at various dates Mr. Winston Churchill, Sir Herbert Samuel, and Lord (Robert) Cecil "spoke or wrote in terms that could only mean that they contemplated the eventual establishment of a Jewish State." Sir Herbert Samuel was open about this: he never hid it. He is credited with a large share in the compilation of the White Paper, which is declared in its first sentences to have been compiled "in consultation with the High Commissioner." But I cannot believe that he was responsible for its quibbles and tongue-in-the-cheek definitions.

For example, what a description of the injection of more and more thousands of Zionist immigrants into Palestine is the phrase "the further development of the existence of the existing Jewish community, with the assistance of Jews in other parts of the world."

In the third paragraph is to be found the disclaimer of the intended imposition of Jewish nationality upon Palestine and the celebrated password by which Zionist immigrants entered Palestine, "of right and not on sufferance."

Here was the major quibble, the matrix-quibble, from which copies might have been cast as gramophone-records and played over to ambitious young equivocators, to form their style. The White Paper said that the inhabitants of Palestine were not to be made Jewish subjects, but it was silent about the way in which they were to be made subject to the Jews. It was silent about the way in which the power and the connections and the modern aptitudes of the Zionists inevitably must put into their hands the mastery of a so-called Arab-Jewish State. It was silent about the way in which Palestine was being organized so that the Zionists might achieve this as easily and as soon as possible.

The White Paper said that Jewish nationality was not to be imposed upon Palestine, but it did not say a word about how Arab nationality was being abstracted from Palestine. It said that attention should be paid by the Arabs to the fact that by the Balfour Declaration the Government did not contemplate that Palestine as a whole should be converted into a Jewish National Home, but that such a Home should be founded in Palestine. That was put forward as a great distinction, but the difference between the two conditions was negligible. The Government might as well have said in a White Paper to butter-merchants that it did not contemplate converting the warehouses where they stored their butter as a whole into blast-furnaces, but only contemplated founding blast-furnaces in the midst of their butter-kegs.

As for the immigrants' password into Palestine "of right and not on sufferance," upon which was scaffolded the whole edifice of prospective Palestinianism and of Jews returning to the lands of the Philistines, that "right" was one which not one line in one code of law in the entire universe justified. "Sufferance," too, so ingeniously employed, with its suggestions of suffering and of contemptuous treatment, was in reality the common lot of any man going to settle in a country which was not the place of his birth.

Legions of Britons have gone to establish themselves in the Argentine or the United States, or in the British Dominions themselves, upon sufferance, and have treated it as a natural condition. Innumerable colonists have made their homes in lands overseas, and some in time have qualified as citizens or have become naturalized, but most of them lived their lives out on sufferance and are prosperous and envied in that state.

"Of right and not on sufferance" was nothing but a phrase concocted to permit aliens to disembark at Jaffa or Haifa as natives, a clever, delusive phrase. What are called "inner circles" in Jerusalem talked of its origin, said that it had been invented neither by Mr. Churchill nor by Sir Herbert Samuel, but by an accomplished, disabused officer of the Administration, when he was working up the case. He had devised it one day at home at his writing-desk, recalling perhaps a line from *The Merchant of Venice*, and had, as it were, tossed it across the room to his wife, who was reclining on a couch, reading a novel. " How quite too cynical, dear," she had said, and gone on with her book. The phrase was embalmed at once, and was taken to England for insertion in the dead matter of the White Paper.

I do not guarantee this story, but the sources of it were good, and it is perhaps as near to the truth as anything ever has been in Mandatory Palestine.

To proceed, one or two events deserve mention as well as Mr. Churchill's insincerities. Relations had grown strained in 1921–2 between Whitehall and Mecca. King Hussein had resolutely refused to recognize the Treaty of Versailles, because of the interpretation given to Article 22 of the Covenant.

He was very angry with his son, Feisal, for having signed it, and would not ratify it. "If they had obeyed me," he said to the Arab author Ameen Rihani, to whom he opened himself, "there would have been no vacillation and no compromise at the Peace Conference." Rihani adds that when Feisal returned to the Hedjaz after he had been to Europe for the third time, because of his discontent, "his royal father did not come down as usual from Mecca to meet him in Jeddah. Nor did he send him an automobile. The famous Feisal went to Mecca as the Emir Feisal of pre-War days, riding like a local Arab on a camel."

Churchill tried to win Hussein over by sending Lawrence himself to the Hedjaz in this autumn of 1921, to persuade Hussein to sign a treaty with Great Britain and to accept Versailles. "The English," writes Captain H.C. Armstrong in his *Lord of Arabia*, "sent Lawrence to reason with the old man, to persuade him to compromise. They offered, provided he signed the Treaty of Versailles and so agreed to their adjustment of the Arab countries, to make a pact with him guaranteeing him protection against all aggressors—including Ibn Saud." The stern and powerful Ibn Saud by now was a close peril to Hussein's kingdom.

But Hussein would not barter the integrity of his own realm for recognition of the status of Palestine and of French Syria. He "simply would not consent to the exclusion of Syria and Palestine from the area of independence. Argument and persuasion were fruitless." (Kenneth Williams.) Lawrence spent a month in Jeddah and gained absolutely nothing.

Even before the Great War had ended Hussein had shown his determination in the matter. Three months before the Armistice he had threatened to abdicate, unless the pledge to him was honoured in full.

"The lowest of the Bedu," he had said to Rihani, "will not break a pledge," and again, "I say we are steadfast in our purpose, unchanging in our service to the nation, no matter how the complications develop and the difficulties multiply. We only desire the good of Arabia, and the Syrians are of the heart of Arabia," meaning of course by Arabia here the whole Arab demesne. He sent messages of goodwill and of solidarity to the Arab delegates in London in 1922, and repeated these to later delegations.

While the same Arab delegates were conferring in London, an event occurred in Palestine, which in its way was to have an effect upon the future. Lord Northcliffe, who was making his last great world tour, arrived in mid-February. He brought to Palestine what the Colonial Secretary so conspicuously had failed to bring, an objective mind. He learned the facts on the spot and formed from them his judgment of the situation, instead of trying like Churchill to force the foot of fate into the boot of circumstance.

He was accessible. The news spread that here was a great Englishman who listened, and during his stay two hundred visitors waited upon him. Petitions were drawn up and presented to him not only by the Arabs but also by the maltreated Jewish bodies, those Zionists who had committed the ultimate mistake of demonstrating by their presence that "rights" and exemption from "sufferance" were superfluous for Jews who came in faith to Palestine.

The Rutenberg monopoly was made clear to him, and the fiction that Palestine was a Jewish country faded as he used his ever-open eyes.

His general judgment went straight to the truth. "This country," he said in the words used to open this book, "runs the risk of becoming a second Ireland." The prophecy was only too accurate. Balfour, not satisfied with his achievement of one embittered Ireland, had arranged for us a second one.

The great consequence of Lord Northcliffe's visit was that the Arabs henceforth obtained in his newspapers some space for the presentation of their wrongs. His last illness came, alas! on his return home, and in August he was dead, England losing more than has ever yet been realized, a purely candid mind. But his impetus in the Palestine affair stayed, and was given a fresh impulse by his brother and successor, Lord Rothermere. It was the means of my returning to that country. I was dispatched there in the autumn of 1922 by Mr. Thomas Marlowe, the editor of the *Daily Mail*, with general instructions to go fully into the question.

In Chapter 19, this journey has been mentioned already, but in regard only to the specific point of the legality of the Palestine Government, which was raised after the disclosures I made on my return, and "settled" by Mr. Ormsby-Gore explaining that this Government was "carrying on in the spirit of the Draft Mandate."

But while I was in the Near East, where I spent several months in my investigation, I procured my copy of the McMahon papers, and besides drawing attention when I returned to the absence of any Mandate, I published the salient portions of these in the *Daily Mail* during the months of January and February 1923. So far the only knowledge of the McMahon texts had come from the single-line excerpt made by the Arab Delegates the previous year and from Mr. Churchill's brief quotation in reply, if indeed this can be described as a quotation from the text.

Their fuller publication caused some stir, and led to the House of Lords' debate on the 27th of March, which must be recalled, as it was the only occasion upon which one of the Houses of Parliament passed a direct vote upon the legitimacy of the Mandate as framed and exercised by Great Britain. Lord Islington moved, in fact, that:

> "The Mandate for Palestine in its present form is unacceptable to this House because it directly violates the pledges made by His Majesty's Government to the people of Palestine in the declaration of October 1915 [in the McMahon] papers and again in the Declaration of 1918 and is, as at present framed, opposed to the sentiments and to the wishes of the great majority of the people of Palestine: that therefore its acceptance by the League of Nations should be postponed until such modifications have been effected therein as will comply with the pledges given by His Majesty's Government."

By this time there was a change of government. Mr. Lloyd George had gone in the previous autumn. The Bonar Law Ministry had succeeded, and there was a new Colonial Minister, the Duke of Devonshire, who in the business of Palestine lived in a state of being prompted continually by permanent officials. The defence of the Government in the Lords rested really with the new-made Earl of Balfour.

The debate, admirably introduced by Lord Islington, furnished the already quoted and several times mentioned speech of Lord Grey. Balfour came into the House late, with clear expectations of conquest. It was his first speech, I think, in the Lords, and probably his worst:

> "I ask my noble friend [he said] who takes up the cause of the Arabs, and who seems to think that their material well-being is going to be diminished [this had in nowise been his noble friend's thesis] how he thinks that the existing population of Palestine is going to be effective unless and until you get capitalists to invest their money in developing the resources of this small country."

He made a too usual display of affected ignorance, expressing surprise that the question at issue, if it meant so much to his opponents, "had never been raised in the House," whereas, as Lord Sydenham answered, it had been raised many times.

He trifled with the amusing texture of truth, turning it in his fingers as it were and playing with it and saying, "I cannot imagine any political interests exercised under greater safeguards than the political interests of the Arab population of Palestine." This from the man who had abolished the Arabs' political rights! He ended on his favourite note, "This is a great adventure. Are we never to have adventures?"

As for the McMahon pledges, he slid past them. Lord Grey, who had been responsible for their being given, made his pathetic statement of unacquaintance with their details. The most striking speech came from Lord Buckmaster, who had been Lord Chancellor. Referring to the McMahon-Hussein papers he said:

> "If these documents are accurate—and I am bound to say that upon the face of it they appear to me to be perfectly sound—they show unmistakably that there has not been, as the noble viscount, Lord Grey, suggested, something in the nature of casual inconsistency between different announcements at different times, but that a deliberate pledge has been given on the one hand and has been abandoned upon the other."

From a man who had been the first lawyer in the realm, this was crushing testimony. On a rather full division the ministerial case was defeated by fifty votes to twenty-nine, and Lord Islington's motion that the Government had violated its pledges was passed. That day was about the high-water mark of the poor Arab cause. The Arab delegates, who had left England in the previous July and returned (reduced in number to the President, the Secretary and Ameen Bey Tamimi) on the 29th of December, cabled the news to Palestine, where hopes rose.

But the Government resisted by paying no attention to anything and by doing nothing. Internal politics became pressing and ousted other affairs: Mr. Bonar Law's health was failing and in six weeks there was a new Cabinet under Mr. Baldwin. Some Members of Parliament put questions in Parliament concerning Palestine to Ministers who had no adequate replies to give, but in truth Ministers and other pro-Zionists were not greatly disturbed, for their principal danger was passing. The Lausanne Peace Conference had opened in November, three days after the last of the Sultans had fled Constantinople. A settlement was in sight in the spring, and peace with Turkey was signed at last on the 24th of July. On the 29th of September the Mandate came into force. When the Palestine Government woke on the morning of that day it was an honest legislator, with a birth certificate under its woolsack or whatever corresponded.

The Treaty of Lausanne was a very different kind of document from the stillborn Treaty of Sèvres. The effort to enshrine the Palestine plot within a treaty and in this way to give it some form of legal sanction, which had marked the Sèvres text, was abandoned. The Lausanne document was a pretty simple one, and the future of the Arab countries was not determined in any of the forty-five clauses which made up the political half of it. Under clause 16 Turkey simply registered the cession of the Arab territories as follows:

> "Turkey declares her renunciation of all rights and titles whatsoever over or concerning the territories situated beyond the frontiers anticipated by the present treaty and over the islands other than those over which her sovereignty has been recognized by the said treaty, the destiny of these territories and islands being settled or yet to be settled by those concerned."

In the original French:

> "La Turquie déclare renoncer a tous droits et titres de quelque nature que ce soit, sur ou concernant les territoires situés au delà des frontières prévues par le présent Traité et sur les îles autres que celles sur lesquelles la souverainté lui est reconnue par ledit Traité, le sort de ces territoires et îles étant réglé ou à régler par les intéressés."

No terms could have been more open. The destiny of Turkey's former Asiatic possessions was to be determined by "those concerned." A clause for the protection of minorities was part of the Treaty too, and under Article 44 any member of the Council of the League of Nations could draw the attention of the Council to any infraction or danger of infraction of any of the obligations entered into by the contracting parties under this clause, on which the Council could "act and give such instructions as may seem suited and efficacious under the circumstances." The Council, that is, was given power to preach political sermons to those who might maltreat minorities. Nothing was said of the maltreatment of majorities, so that the Arabs could not benefit by this disposition.

The following States signed the Treaty: France, Great Britain, Italy, Japan, Greece, Roumania and Jugoslavia.

Upon Palestine and its people, therefore, the Treaty of Lausanne had the main effect of detaching them from Turkey. In the so-called "Palestine Question" the result of the Treaty was to bring the Mandate into being, and the entry into being of the Mandate provides the proper occasion here for passing under review the origins and birth of that charter.

The importance of knowing how the Mandate was composed and came into existence cannot be overstressed. It is the flooring of the Government platform. But before coming to the Mandate itself it is necessary to deal first with the Covenant. The Mandate sprang of the Covenant. It was the embodiment for Palestine of Article 22 of the Covenant. So the first step in tracing its descent is to trace the descent of Article 22, which means in some degree recurring to the origins of the whole Covenant.

Chapter 30

The drafting of the Covenant.—The shifts of General Smuts. Article 22 drafted so as to evade its own ends. The fate of the Vesnitch amendment.

If "pascua" and "rura," "pastures and country places" may be taken, not unreasonably, as the equivalent of peace, then Vergil's celebrated epitaph upon himself may be applied with some fitness to the Covenant, especially to Article 22:

> *Mantua me genuit: Calabri rapuere: tenet nunc*
> *Parthenope. Cecini pascua, rura, duces.*

That is, thus construed, "Mantua bore me: the Calabrians carried me off: Parthenope holds me now. I sang peace and rulers." President Wilson was the Mantua that bore the Covenant: we, the British, were the Calabrians who carried it off: the Parthenope, or Naples, which now shelters it is Geneva. The end of the distich is particularly appropriate, for the great handicap of the Covenant was that it had, at one and the same time, to sing peace and to sing rulers such as Mr. Lloyd George, Lord Balfour and some others.

This is not to say that Britain has no large and enviable claim to the good that is in the Covenant, nor any primary share in its creation. As upon many of the greatest inventions, many minds were busy upon it before it appeared. It was, or passed as being, an amalgam of British war-aims and of President Wilson's celebrated Fourteen Points. The earliest steps to it, though, were taken in England by the Phillimore Committee. This committee was a Foreign Office creation, known by the name of its President, Lord Phillimore. Its other members were Professor Pollard, Sir Julian Corbett, Mr. Holland Rose, Sir Eyre Crowe, Sir William Tyrrell, and Mr. Cecil Hurst.

Since early in 1916 the idea of grouping the peoples of the world together with an international code for the maintenance of concord had been under examination in one way or another. In the end this Committee was appointed to consider the question of what form such an international body might take. It held its first meeting on the 30th of January, 1918, and nine other meetings between then and the date of its interim Report, which was issued on the 20th of March. In June its full Report was published. This dealt with the formation of a League and did not enter into details upon such subjects as the type of government for countries which might come under British or other Allied influence as a result of the War. Copies of the July Report were sent at once to President Wilson.

Six months before, on the 10th of January, the President had issued his famous Fourteen Points, of which the Preamble and the Twelfth may be repeated:

> "It will be our wish and purpose that the processes of peace, when they are begun, shall be absolutely open, and that they shall involve and permit henceforth no secret understanding of any kind. They days of conquest and of aggrandisement are gone by.
>
> XIIth Point. The Turkish portions of the present Ottoman Empire should be assured secure sovereignty, but the other nationalities which are now under Turkish rule should be assured an undoubted security of life and an absolutely unmolested opportunity of autonomous development."

Mr. Lloyd George in his War-Aims Declaration of the 5th of March had declared already that "the consent of the governed must be the basis of any territorial settlement in this war." He accepted the Fourteen Points enthusiastically on behalf of Great Britain. They were spread through the Turkish dominions, and through other enemy States, as the principles which would govern the Peace, and they were a great factor in disintegrating resistance and in bringing victory. Copies of the Twelfth Point and kindred matter were broadcast over the Arab countries by our aeroplanes.

In the Phillimore text President Wilson before coming to Europe found something on which to work, either to frame his own ideas on it, or to adjust its ideas to his. He talked things over with his friend and adviser, Colonel House, who made a draft-scheme, which owed much to the Phillimore Report. From this the President himself typed out his First Draft for the Covenant.

The War came to an end. Austria and Turkey sued for peace, and then Germany, upon terms governed by the Fourteen Points. Meanwhile the discussion of a League had progressed in England. A group of writers and others who had given much thought to the matter found a centre in the well-known *Round Table Review*, and was called the " Round Table" group. The editor of the Review was Mr. Lionel Curtis, and members of the group were the present Lord Lothian (then Mr. Philip Kerr, long while secretary to Mr. Lloyd George), Mr. J. A. Hobson, Mr. G. L. Beer, and Mr. H. N. Brailsford. General Smuts was in close touch with them. In December of 1918 an article upon the characteristics and aims which a League might have, entitled "*Windows of Freedom*," appeared in it, written anonymously, after the custom of the Review, but attributed to Mr. Curtis. It was a development of conversations on the subject with Mr. Kerr and one or two more of the group. This was read by General Smuts, and had the effect of leading him to take the formation of a League and a Covenant a step forward.

He wrote a pamphlet, *The League of Nations: A Practical Suggestion*, which was published on the 16th of December. It was a species of Constitution for a League, with twenty-one articles, the first nine of them upon Mandates. Of this Mr. Lloyd George said, according to Lord Riddell, that "Smuts had written a memorandum on the League of Nations which he thought the ablest State-paper he had seen during the War." Smuts himself disclaimed for his pamphlet any quality as an official or semi-official project, saying that it was only meant "to awaken interest and stimulate discussion." But by now he had been appointed one of the two British members on an inter-allied Commission to consider the formation of a League, and, as will be seen, his "Suggestion" became one of the documents out of which the Covenant was evolved, and its author one of the Covenant's chief makers.

This therefore gives his pamphlet considerable importance. Few writings of equal importance have had some parts of their text more quoted and others less quoted, and in the present case it is very necessary to reproduce the latter, the unquoted sections. I give the relevant passages, italicizing where it is desirable:

> As a programme for the Peace Conference I would begin by making two recommendations ....
>
> 2. That as far as the peoples and territories formerly belonging to Russia, Austria-Hungary and Turkey are concerned the League of Nations should be considered as Reversionary in the most general sense and as clothed with the right of ultimate disposal in accordance with certain fundamental principles.
>
> These principles are, firstly, that there shall be *no annexation of any of these territories to any of the victorious States*, that in the future government of these territories and peoples the rule of self-determination or *the consent of the governed to their government* shall be fairly and reasonably applied.

General Smuts went on to say that conditions for self-government would vary very considerably.

> ... there will be found cases where, owing chiefly to the *heterogeneous character of the population* and their incapacity for administrative co-operation, autonomy in any real sense would be out of the question, and the administration would have to be undertaken to a very large

> extent by some external authority. *This would be the case, at any rate for some time to come, in Palestine, where the administrative co-operation of the Jewish minority and of the Arab majority would not be forthcoming…* In all the above and similar cases this external authority should be the League of Nations in accordance with the second proposition above.
>
> No State should make use of the helpless or weak condition of any of these territories in order to exploit them for its own purposes or to acquire rights over them in the manner which has hitherto been a fruitful source of trouble and of war. This may be summed up in the following recommendation: That any authority, control or administration which may be necessary in respect of these territories and peoples, other than their own self-determined autonomy, shall be the exclusive function of, and shall be vested in, the League of Nations, and be exercised by or on behalf of it.

Clauses numbered 5 and 6 stated that:

> Wherever possible the agent or Mandatory of the League of Nations shall be nominated or approved by the autonomous people or territory.
>
> Complete right of ultimate control and supervision to be vested in the League, as well as right of appeal against any gross breach of the Mandate.

But:

> "There will, however, be cases, such as *Palestine* and Armenia, where for reasons above referred to, *an autonomous regime cannot be adopted at the start, and where the consultation of the country on the question of its Mandatory State is, therefore, not formally possible. Even in such cases the League will, as far as possible, follow the trend of popular opinion…*
>
> The League should in a proper case assert its authority to the full, even to the extent of removing the Mandate and entrusting it to some other State if necessary. No pegging-out of claims under the guise of the Mandate should be allowed."

These quotations from his plan are highly valuable and show too the mood in which Smuts approached his task. It is a pity that his action must be criticized now. Smuts was a beacon in our darkest days. But there it is, he has his frailties. What he has written he has written, and his acts come up for judgment like those of lesser men.

In his pamphlet were preparations for the Calabrian rape of the Covenant. The principles of the Peace of which the Covenant was to be the charter, the principles of the Fourteen Points, had been universal of application. They set aside conquest everywhere, they predicated freedom everywhere, and in the particular case of the ex-Turkish dominions specified that these were to have "unmolested opportunity of autonomous development."

Smuts's plan came on this with a great rush of noble sentiments, which of course were thoroughly noble and genuine as far as they went, but were of that secondary form of nobility, the baronetage of idealism, which consists in proposing unselfish schemes for other people. Where the political foibles which came home to Smuts and to the Prime Minister and to their friends entered into play, immediately there was a slipping away, a departure from the Fourteen Points, and from nobility.

In Palestine there was to be no "unmolested opportunity of autonomous development," no self-determination, no "consent of the governed to their government." These fundamental changes were brought in with the air of being mere postscripts, ensuring the better working of the principles which in reality they displaced. General Smuts was thoroughly involved in the policy of the Balfour Declaration, and now, instead of sinking that exceedingly particular arrangement to make way for the universal scheme of the League of Nations, he began by fitting the universal scheme to the Whitehall bargain, in the Churchill manner.

Fitting the universe to a bargain must result in strange distortions of fact, and there they were in his text. On his own authority, on the mere strength of his own views and desires, he doled out rights to countries or took them away. He said that "the heterogeneous character of the population" of Palestine made autonomy, as promised by Wilson, out of question for that country in any real sense. This was false, false, false.

The population of Palestine was not heterogeneous. Palestine was more homogeneous, more uniform than the United States or Canada, far more homogeneous than Smuts's own South Africa. He and others who were of his way of thought and were in positions of power were doing their utmost to make Palestine heterogeneous, but that was an altogether different story. General Smuts wanted Palestine to be heterogeneous, he was determined it should yet be heterogeneous, but it was not heterogeneous. As he wrote; 90 to 91 percent of the population was Arab. It was a country (if it has to be repeated ad nauseam) of Arabs amongst whom lived a small and recent Jewish colony.

The next excuse was on a parallel with the plea of heterogeneity, sharing with it the same dubious recourse to lengthy, pseudo-technical phraseology where plain English would have been embarrassing. The second quality of the Arabs which, in General Smuts's opinion, debarred them from independence was their "incapacity for administrative co-operation." What this "incapacity for administrative co-operation" of the Arab majority in Palestine with the Jewish minority meant really was that the Arabs could not and would not give to a handful of Zionists a power over Palestine equal to that of all its native inhabitants. "Incapacity" was a way of putting this indeed. Under the Fourteen Points governing the future Covenant the true question to be put should have been whether the Arab majority in Palestine would give the members of the Jewish colony their full rights as citizens.

This the Arabs were perfectly willing to do, and had affirmed it. They therefore were ready to co-operate administratively with the Jewish minority. The trouble was that, not so much the true Jewish minority, as those Zionists who had been and were being planted by General Smuts and his friends in the Holy Land were not willing to "co-operate administratively." They were the non-co-operators. They wanted everything which normal administration forbade, rights to which their birth did not entitle them and political power so beyond that due to their numbers that it was a form of dictatorship.

The subterfuges of General Smuts's plan, which thus reversed realities, were notable in the later clause upon the consultation of countries before their Mandatory was appointed. In Palestine this was "not formally possible." Why "formally"? What was that word doing? What did it mean in the case? Nothing at all. It was inserted to give an air of complication to what was in fact an easy process, which was to be carried out by the Crane-King Commission very quickly with a small personnel.

The last straw was the phrase, "No pegging-out of claims under the guise of the Mandate should be allowed." If General Smuts had tried to describe better than this the method and aims of the Balfour Declaration, as inserted afterwards in the Mandate, he could not have done so.

However this text of his, this scheme of his in which the right hand manumitted and the left hand enslaved, because of his vast prestige, won much notice, and in its turn, was studied by President Wilson, who received a copy of it before leaving for Europe and the Peace Conference.

The President was influenced by it, but not so much as all that. He copied out General Smuts's twenty-one articles, but he was not subjugated by them. When he came to make his Second Draft for the Covenant, in Paris now, early in the second week of January 1919, though phrases of Smuts's appeared in this draft, none the less there were marked differences from Smuts's Wilberforce-Legree proposals. Passages which concerned the Palestine issue are as follows:

> Clause I
>
> In respect of peoples and territories which formerly belonged to Austria-Hungary and to Turkey, and in respect of the colonies formerly under the dominion of the German Empire, the League of Nations shall be regarded as the residuary trustee with sovereign right of ultimate disposal or of continued administration in accordance with certain

> fundamental principles hereinafter set forth, and this reversion and control shall exclude all rights and privileges of annexation on the part of any Power.
>
> These principles are that there shall in no case be any annexation of any of these territories by any State either within the League or outside of it, and that in the future government of these peoples and territories the right of self-determination, or the consent of the governed to the form of government, shall be fairly and reasonably applied and all policies of administration or economic development be based primarily upon the well-considered interests of the people themselves.
>
> Clause II
>
> All authority "other than their own self-determined and self-organized autonomy" shall be vested in the League in respect of these peoples or territories…. Wherever possible or feasible the agent or Mandatory appointed by the League shall be nominated or approved by the autonomous people or territory.
>
> Clause III
>
> Such peoples are to have the right of appeal for the redress of a Mandate or the correction of any breach of it or for the substitution of some other State as Mandatory.

President Wilson, therefore, despite his sympathy with Zionism, showed here that spirit which a little later was to take shape in the dispatch of the Crane-King Commission to Syria. He refused to follow Smuts by constituting himself as an authority self-empowered to concede or to refuse rights to the ex-Turkish peoples. His Clause I held no arbitrary exceptions to the right of self-development. Smuts's phrase that "the consent of the governed to the form of government should be fairly and reasonably applied" had been taken over by him. But Smuts's heterogeneous shifts for excluding Palestine from the operation of his own precept had not been taken over.

Then Smuts had said that the consultation of Palestine upon the Power which was to receive the Mandate was "not formally possible." In his Clause II ,Wilson removed the gloss, "formally," and retained the principle of consultation for all peoples who were concerned.

His Clause III gave them the right of appeal against the terms of a Mandate as well as against a breach of the Mandate. Smuts only allowed appeal against the Mandatory when the Mandatory broke the rules which the Mandatory himself had fixed. Wilson's clause allowed appeal for the redress of the Mandate, that is appeal against the Mandatory's scheme for the Mandate. Smuts's clause was only an alleviation of subjection: Wilson's was liberty.

So that the position now was that the Covenant, after swinging away from the principles of the Fourteen Points in Smuts's plan, had been drawn back to them in the President's Second Draft. Meanwhile, though, another draft had been prepared in another quarter. Lord Cecil (then Lord Robert Cecil), who was chief of the League of Nations section of the British Peace Conference delegation, had drawn up one of his own.

Lord Cecil had the British side of negotiations very much in his charge. Mr. Charles Seymour, one of the United States legal delegates to the Conference, in his book written in collaboration with Colonel House, *What Really Happened in Paris*, says: "How and what attention Lloyd George paid to the League of Nations question I do not quite know. It always seemed to me that Lord Robert Cecil, though not a member of the British Government, had authority to go ahead on his own."

Lord Cecil's plan amounted to the perpetuation of the war-alliance as a peace-alliance. The chiefs of Government of the Allies were to be a ruling council at the head of the League. There were to be meetings of this every year, to be attended by the Prime Ministers and Foreign Secretaries of the British Empire, the United States, France, Italy, Japan and "of any other States recognized by them as Great Powers." The lesser States were to be given an occasional share in deliberations, as there were to be special Conferences every four years for all the States included in the League. The composition of the League was to be determined at the Peace Conference.

It is interesting today to know that Lord Cecil's intention was to exclude Russia. "Definitely untrustworthy and hostile States, for example Russia, should the Bolshevik Government remain in power," were to be excluded. "Otherwise it is desirable not to be too rigid in scrutinizing qualifications (for membership of the League), *since the small Powers will in any case not exercise any considerable influence.*" (My italics.)

Lord Cecil, says Seymour and House, "felt that the Great Powers would have to be the directors of the League for it to be a success." This plan encountered a good deal of opposition amidst the Americans. They had no Premier, which would place an American delegation at a tactical disadvantage, and in any event they were opposed to the regular intermixture of United States ministers in a European Council.

Also they saw that the whole structure of Lord Cecil's plan depended upon the altruism which he predicated in the Prime Ministers and Foreign Secretaries of the Allies. Mr. Lansing, the United States' Secretary of States, was uncompromising in his opposition. In his *The Peace Negotiation: A Personal Narrative*, he said of the Cecil scheme:

> There was nothing idealistic in the plan of Lord Robert Cecil, although he was reported to be an idealist favouring a new international

> order. An examination of his plan shows it to be a revival of the old and discredited ideas of a century ago.
>
> He proposed the formation of a Quintuple Alliance which would constitute itself Primate over all nations and the arbiter of world-affairs—a scheme of organization very similar to the one chosen by General Smuts. Lord Robert Cecil made no attempt to disguise the purpose of this plan. It was intended to place in the hands of the Five Powers the control of international relations and the direction in large measure of the foreign policies of all nations. It seemed to provide for a rebirth of the Congress of Vienna which should be clothed in the modern garb of democracy. Its adoption would mean that the destiny of the world would be in the hands of a powerful international oligarchy possessed of dictatorial powers.

Mr. Lansing was somewhat unjust to Lord Cecil in saying that he was "reported to be an idealist" but in reality wished to revive the Holy Alliance system of a century back. Lord Cecil believed genuinely and fervently in a new international order, and had nothing in common with Metternich. But the complexities of his idealism, which were beyond the American who only understood men as all of a piece, are not our immediate interest. In the present issue the interest lies in his plan for the League. Therein is to be seen converging upon Palestine the settlement of its destiny by that "powerful international oligarchy possessed of dictatorial powers," of which Mr. Lansing had such fears. What he feared was exactly what did come to pass in the Holy Land.

The oligarchy was not established quite as Lord Cecil intended. But it was established just as effectively by the creation of a League which had to accept Mandates in the form which the oligarchs chose for the Mandates.

The development of this situation proceeded apace in the first months of 1919 in Paris. President Wilson and Mr. Lansing did not approve of the cast of Lord Cecil's proposals because they were not as sure as he was of the character of the actors for whom he had destined the principal roles. But Mr. Wilson perceived the good intent of the proposals, and as it were took the good intent out of them and transferred that much that was Cecil's into his own forthcoming draft. Some phrases he transported directly, as he had transported phrases of Smuts's.

The President however was now isolated in Europe and under continual assault by all those whose standards for the League, whether they realized it or not, were, in Lansing's words, "political expediency tinctured with morality." Under their influence, as a consequence of conversations in which the need for finding a "practical framework" for the League was stressed, expediency slipped or was slipped into his drafts. He held to some of his doctrines, but gave way upon the question of effective power being exercised over the League by the Five Founder-States. Lord Cecil's idealist oligarchy was winning its position. There is a comment of Mr. Ray Stannard Baker, the friend and biographer of the President, upon this stage of the Conference, which is profoundly significant. He says, "Smuts, Labour and the Jews accounted for all the alterations," in the President's Second Draft. This is a solitary reference, but shows how the forces of Zionism, omnipresent in Paris then, already were using their vast private power to deflect the Covenant to their ends.

Mr. Wilson now prepared a Third Draft, which was circulated, but did not hold the field long. His personal share in the work of drafting was ebbing, and with it—despite the accommodations he had been led to make—was passing the reign of pure principle. Through Colonel House, however, Lord Cecil and Mr. Hunter Miller were brought together to consider the various texts and at a later meeting, where the President, General Smuts and Colonel House joined these two, the drawing-up of a new and definite draft was confided to Mr. Miller and Mr. Cecil Hurst, the legal representatives of the United States and of Great Britain. Time pressed, but by working together all through the night of the 1st to 2nd of February, they produced a compromise moderately satisfactory to both of them.

While this drafting was going on, the Peace Conference proper, during these first days of its deliberations, had kept its eye upon the question of the League, this being the particular business of the Council of Ten. The terms of reference of the Council were really to settle which matters should be reserved for the Plenary Conference, but it solved that problem by keeping everything of importance in its own hands. "This (the Council of Ten) was the real Peace Conference till mid-March, when the Council of Four was substituted for it." (Temperley.) It was an extension of the Supreme War Council, composed of the heads of the Governments and the Foreign Ministers of the United States, Great Britain, France and Italy together with two Japanese representatives; very much, in fact, the group of men to whom in his draft Lord Cecil had entrusted the League and the world

Sittings of the Council had begun suavely, but grew more animated when opposing ideas between the American and European delegates showed forth, as soon as the Mandates question passed from theory to possible practice. Mr. Gerig, a detached American commentator, says of the sitting of the 30th, "The immediate stakes were taken to be manoeuvring for favourable positions in territorial distribution, and it would be folly to presume that the Mandatory principle and its implications were as yet regarded seriously...Lloyd George made a skilful compromise resolution."

Previously on the 23rd Mr. Lloyd George had brought up the matter with proposals for ex-enemy territory which the Americans qualified as equal to annexation. Mr. Lloyd George's idea was, to serve oneself of his own well-worn phrase, that this was the annexation to end annexation. Mr. Wilson broke out, "The world will say that the Great Powers first parcelled out the helpless parts of the world, and then formed a League of Nations." He repeated his own different views, but says Professor Quincy Wright, "it required all his strategy to prevent the Mandatory idea being negatived in detail." The President later on was to sum up Mr. Lloyd George's tactics at the Conference as "acceptance in principle combined with negation in detail," the same gambit as that used by Smuts in the Palestine part of his plan.

Differences were patched up, and on the 25th a British resolution was passed establishing the League of Nations as an integral part of the Peace Treaty. A Commission of the Conference was to work out the details of its constitution and functions. It was here that Wilson, with a stroke of generalship, for once outwitted Lloyd George. The Premier had automatically appointed his trusty team, Cecil and Smuts, to this Commission. He expected the President would name some of his own counsellors. But Wilson nominated himself. Mr. Lloyd George could not now follow suit, having already chosen Smuts and Cecil.

On the 27th, Wilson said that "if the process of annexation went on the League of Nations would be discredited from the beginning." Next day Balfour, when the discussion was running high, intervened with his elsewhere quoted statement that he himself was "strongly in favour of the principle of Mandates," and that as far as the British Empire was concerned, the only difficulty lay in the areas conquered by the self-governing Dominions.

At the important sitting on the 30th the matter came to a head. The representatives of the Dominions brought this about through their insistence upon *de jure* recognitions of their de facto possession of German South West Africa, New Guinea, Nauru, Samoa and so forth. The Japanese supported kindred claims, and the Americans opposed with vigour. Feeling crept, or leapt, into the discussion. It was Mr. Lloyd George who saved the situation in the end, proposing the "skilful Resolution" which was accepted.

This salving resolution was no impromptu adaptation. Mr. Lloyd George's salvage-gear was in readiness, just round the comer, for the stormy meeting which was expected. The lifeboatman had an understanding with the tempest. The divergencies between the Dominion representatives and the United States' delegates were not appearing for the first time, and the formula which the Prime Minister put forward had been sketched out by Smuts. Mr. Lloyd George now took the opportunity of the differences about the German colonies to gain some vantage-ground for his Palestine schemes. He employed his favourite method of winning on practical grounds a situation which was unattainable ethically.

Keeping all Great Britain's troops of occupation in the Near East was, he said, too expensive. "The financial responsibility of his Government towards Parliament requires an immediate determination of the status of occupying troops in German East Africa and the Arab countries. If British troops are kept there until we make peace with Turkey and until the League of Nations has been constituted and has started business and until it is able to dispose of the situation, then the expenses will be something enormous, and really we cannot face it. Especially since we have not the slightest idea of being Mandatory of a considerable number of territories we now occupy, such as Syria and parts of Armenia."

The excuse was adroit, but it was only an adroit excuse. The expenses, of which Mr. Lloyd George made so much, easily could have been lessened by lessening the numbers of the occupying forces. Certainly, if it had not been for Zionism, the troops could have been reduced to a skeleton force in Palestine, where the people were friendly to the army, and there was no longer any trace of an enemy whom it was necessary to overawe. If larger occupying forces had to be maintained in Palestine and large expenses had to be incurred, this was solely due to the Prime Minister's own policy. The long and short of his "National Home" was that, as it progressed, more and more thousands of Zionist immigrants would swell its size, and would require consequently the expenditure of more and more thousands of British pounds upon the maintenance of those military forces which gave these immigrants police protection. Without the presence of the forces they would never have been able to enter the country. Mr. Lloyd George, however, spoke of the expense of keeping the soldiers who protected the "National Home" as though this expense was one which sprang from the mere delays of peace-making.

President Wilson suggested that the military advisers of the Powers might consult together and find means of sharing and economizing upon the burden of occupation. Mr. Lloyd George assented to this: it did not matter much to him. Assent made the passing of his Resolution easier: and in this way he achieved what he had set out to do, to establish a tacit agreement that, whatever the Conference settled about Mandates now, in or out of Covenant drafts, must be settled quickly in order to avoid the supposedly inherent piling-up of enormous occupation costs.

Thus this clever man had recovered from the setback of a month before. The certainty now was that the completion of the Covenant would be hastened. There would have to be a quick compromise upon its text, and, as a beginning, in regard to the cardinal article upon Mandates, Lloyd George was ready immediately with his generalized formula, the work of Smuts (with the assistance of Philip Kerr).

This formula, this Resolution, had been submitted to Wilson the day before it was produced in the general Conference. As we have seen, it was produced there on the 30th of January. Smuts's draft of it was sent to the President on the morning of the 29th, while it was being discussed amongst themselves by the members of the British Delegation. "Lloyd George and the Colonials," wrote Colonel House in a covering note to the President, "are meeting at eleven-thirty, and this is a draft of a Resolution which Smuts hopes to get passed. He wants to know whether it is satisfactory to you. It seems to me a fair compromise."

So it would have seemed to House, who either did not perceive the skilful defects in it or was sufficiently in the power-policy camp of the intending Mandatories to be indifferent to these defects.

President Wilson agreed to the Resolution (of which the terms will appear shortly in their final setting), intending in his own mind to employ it as a basis for a text more satisfactory to himself. He agreed to it because it settled the acrimonious dispute between the British Dominions and the Japanese on one side and the Americans on the other. The Turkish part of it slipped through as a mere codicil to the section dealing with the former German colonies in Africa and the Pacific. M. Tardieu, interrogated by the French Press on this point, had made that clear, saying on the 30th that the Resolution so far (this was after its acceptance, in the evening of the 30th) "had only been discussed in regard to Germany."

But Wilson at once set to work on the Resolution, in order to emend it by enunciating definitely both the subordination of Mandatories to the League of Nations and the rights of the mandated peoples, points which in the Smuts Resolution somehow had lost clarity of definition. He now used the Resolution and his own previous drafts and out of this combination drew up his Fourth and last Draft of the Covenant. His emendation of the Resolution took the form of a couple of paragraphs which he attached to it. In these he stipulated as before that the future League was to have the right of trusteeship of the mandated countries vested in it. The Mandatory was to be the League's nominee, and the League might even nominate not an individual nation but an "organized agency," a ruling panel (such as the Tangier Administration), as Mandatory. The League was to have the right of supervision and of "intimate control" and could receive petitions directly from the Mandated populations.

The "object of all such tutelary oversight and administration" by the League was "to build up in as short a time as possible out of the people or territory under its guardianship a political unit which can take charge of its own affairs, determine its own connections and choose its own policies.

This Fourth Draft was dated the 2nd of February; on that date therefore the prospect of freedom still existed for Palestine. The Mandatories were still to be the nominees of the League, not of themselves. The prospective Mandatory populations still had the right of appeal against the terms of the Mandate as it might be constituted. The order to the Mandatory to establish independence in as short a time as possible for these populations was categoric.

But this prospect was not to last. All discussion of the Covenant terms had been transferred to the Commission which had been created at the Council of Ten meeting of the 25th of January. This Commission consisted at first of ten members representing the P.A.P. and five representing the smaller States. But four more members of the latter group were added presently, which gave the Commission quite an international aspect, no doubt, but still left the Five Powers in a majority of one over the other countries.

Between the 3rd and the 13th of February the Covenant of the League of Nations was drawn up by this Commission in the course of ten sessions. But when the members met to begin their work, it was not President Wilson's Fourth Draft which was put before them. The President's Draft lasted only for a day, and disappeared.

The historians are laconic about this strange disappearance. Quincy Wright says of the Fourth Draft simply that "it was not used." How much lies behind those four words, what play of manoeuvring forces: and, in the sequel, what hopes of peoples vanished with that draft. But how did it disappear? It does not seem reasonable to assume, after the effort which the President had made to produce it, and after his placing within it essential stipulations which he had found lacking in the Smuts Resolution, that he suddenly threw away or tore up his work. Most probably he intended to sit upon it a little more and then to reintroduce it.

This seems likely because the Hurst-Miller draft was placed before the Commission in its place. That was the draft over which the American and British legal Delegates had laboured intensively through the night, two days before. The Hurst-Miller draft will have presented, therefore, a text to his liking, but more legally phrased and so more accurate than his own over the general ground of League formation. On the other hand, it did not enter really into the specific Mandate question. "It contained a brief article on Mandates," says Quincy Wright, "evidently with the thought of supplementing it with an annexed convention."

The reasonable conclusion is that President Wilson intended his Fourth Draft to become that annexed convention. It would have been of advantage to him to let the Commission deal with the numerous other matters involved in a League Covenant while he reconsidered what concerned him most, the Mandates, and polished his all-important supplement.

Whatever were his intentions, whatever reasons guided or restrained his actions then, a different climax came, at the first session of the Commission on the 8th. It was the day of the Calabrians. They arrived with conquering impetuosity, and the President offered no resistance. It was as though the struggle had gone on too long behind the scenes, so that the chief combatant was tiring unknown to himself, and when he stood in the comparative open of that Commission meeting, he felt suddenly spent and was worsted with a stroke or two, and let his child be carried away.

No immediate welding of drafts was undertaken, nor was any suggestion put forward of waiting for a convention to be attached to the short Hurst-Miller article. General Smuts arose and moved that the Hurst-Miller article on Mandates should be substituted altogether by a text he now produced. This text to all intents was the Resolution of the 30th of January all over again, the so-called compromise. "The text actually adopted," says Professor Quincy Wright, "was introduced in the League of Nations Commission on February 8th by Smuts as a substitute for the brief Hurst-Miller article. It included almost verbatim the resolutions of the Council of Ten on January 30th. The latter had been introduced by Lloyd George, and was actually drafted in the main by Smuts. *Thus both the original proposal and the final form of Article 22 were largely the work of Smuts.*" Since Mr. Philip Kerr collaborated with General Smuts it may be said that the "Round Table" plan had won through in the form to which the Commission without much ado now agreed.

So that instead of all the President's and other drafts for the Constitution of the Mandatory System and for its definition in the Covenant, General Smuts's text, patronized by Mr. Lloyd George, was adopted, and was enshrined in the Covenant as Article 22.

"The carefully drafted compromise which appears bodily as Article 22," Lansing calls it. Its final text may well be repeated here:

1. To those colonies and territories which as a consequence of the late War have ceased to be under the sovereignty of the States which formerly governed them and which are inhabited by peoples not yet able to stand by themselves under the strenuous conditions of the modern world, there should be applied the principle that the well-being and the development of such peoples form a sacred trust of civilization and that securities for the performance of this trust should be embodied in this Covenant.
2. The best method of giving practical effect to this principle is that the tutelage of such peoples should be entrusted to

advanced nations who by reason of their resources, their experience or their geographical position can best undertake this responsibility, and who are willing to accept it, and that this tutelage should be exercised by them as Mandatories on behalf of the League.

3. The character of the Mandate must differ according to the stage in the development of the people, the geographical situation of the territory, its economic conditions, and other similar circumstances.
4. Certain communities formerly belonging to the Turkish Empire have reached a stage of development where their existence as independent nations can be provisionally recognized subject to the rendering of administrative advice and assistance by a Mandatory until such time as they are able to stand alone. The wishes of these communities must be a principal consideration in the selection of the Mandatory.

5 and 6 dealt with the African and Pacific Mandates.

7. In every case of Mandate, the Mandatory shall render to the Council an annual report in reference to the territory committed to its charge.
8. The degree of authority, control, or administration to be exercised by the Mandatory shall, if not previously agreed upon by the Members of the League, be explicitly defined in each case by the Council.
9. A permanent Commission shall be constituted to receive and examine the annual reports of the Mandatories and to advise the Council on all matters relating to the observance of the Mandates.

There is no difference that matters between the text of the 30th of January and the final text accepted by the Commission as Article 22. But before the final text was passed there was a noteworthy incident. At the meeting of the 8th of February, M. Vesnitch of Serbia, after talking with colleagues of the smaller States, put forward an amendment, in French, to the proposed Article. It was a codicil, as follows:

La Commission Mandataire pourra aussi, quand elle jugera le moment venu, suggérer que l'indépendance d'un peuple, quel qu'il soit puisse être proclamée et reconnue en vue de son admission éventuelle comme Membre de la Société des Nations.

The Mandatory Commission shall have power also, when it shall judge the moment for this to have arrived, to propose that the independence of any given people shall be proclaimed and be recognized with a view to its eventual admission as a Member of the League of Nations.

This amendment would have secured any Mandated people—if the League of Nations Commission did its duty—from the fate which actually has overtaken the people of Palestine, since it would be open for such a people at any time to ask the League of Nations Commission to proclaim its independence. If the amendment had been passed it would have prevented any Mandatory from adjourning *sine die*, on such pleas as he cared to make, the establishment of this national independence. The Mandatory would no longer have been sole judge of when the mandated people was "ripe" for it.

This amendment therefore was of the first importance, and would have regained for the mandated peoples much of the ground lost by the Smuts resolution. This latter had with some ingenuity turned the obligation to establish independence into the mere power to establish independence, by introducing the word "can." The existence of the ex-Turkish nations "can be provisionally recognized," ran the Smuts clause, not "shall be recognized."

Ingenious as it was, this trick did not stand examination, since the avowed and proclaimed aim of the Covenant was to grant independence when the requisite stage of development had been reached, and the same paragraph recognized that the ex-Turkish countries had reached this stage. So that to make the grant only permissive was in contradiction with the spirit and text of the Covenant, and was indeed in its substitution of "can" for "shall," a sort of forgery.

M. Vesnitch's amendment would have swept away all this falsification. Its author asked Mr. Miller to translate it into English for him, which he did. It came up at the next meeting of the Commission, the Seventh Session, on the 10th of February. But it was never put to the vote.

Lord Cecil stood up and besought M. Vesnitch to withdraw his amendment "for reasons of expediency." This was all that was said. No word of explanation or of justification was uttered, and the very terms of M. Vesnitch's amendment were not inserted in the English text of the meetings of the Commission. One has to turn to the French text and to the watchful Mr. Hunter Miller, in his account of the drafting of the Covenant, to learn what occurred. Yet another damning disappearance of awkward texts.

Lord Cecil's white-hot plea for expediency, coming from the representative of Great Britain, seems to have been enough. M. Vesnitch dutifully withdrew his amendment—an indication of the position of the smaller States in framing this part of the Covenant.

The justice of Mr. Lansing's phrase—"political expediency tinged with morality"—was made manifest then out of our best-known moralist's own mouth. It is clear enough that what Lord Cecil found inexpedient was the guarantee of the emancipation of all ex-Turkish subjects. It was not the admission of South Sea Islanders or African tribes to the League which perturbed him by its dangerous proximity. Into that short phrase of his therefore were condensed years of lobbying and of intrigue, volumes of false evidence, and the whole plan for subjugating the Arabs in Palestine. It is not to the point that Lord Cecil, that temple of twisted pillars, himself probably imagined that he was securing the future of Palestine or of other lands.

A Drafting Sub-Committee now was named to make a final Covenant text. When it came to the Mandates article it achieved a small alleviation in principle of the Mandated peoples' lots. In practice this change of text introduced by the Drafting Commission made no difference. But in itself it is very interesting because of the light thrown on the Resolution of the 8th of February. In its pristine form of the 30th of January this had spoken of the "peoples not yet able to stand by themselves." General Smuts seems to have found the "yet" therein dangerous, presumably because it held out hopes of the said peoples standing alone some day. In his text of the 8th of February the word was removed, and the peoples who were to be the beneficiaries of civilization's sacred trust were described as "not able to stand by themselves"—a permanent condition. The Drafting Committee restored the "yet."

With or without "yet" this text, when adopted as the twenty-second Article of the Covenant, was to prove fatal to the independence of Arab Palestine. The text did not venture to remove the promise of independence, but made it possible for the Mandatory to juggle with the promise. A foreign statesman has well expressed the form of action chosen, explaining that agreements can be "so worded that under certain circumstances they allow of a certain elasticity of interpretation."

In Wilson's draft the fate of Palestine and other Mandated countries had been put in the hands of the League. How far this might have saved the Arabs is a moot point. All would have depended upon how the League was constituted. The Assembly might have established its primacy better and have listened to the Arabs.

It was a tiny chance but it was a chance. If a League had been created with more effective power coming to the small countries than Lord Cecil had anticipated, then such a League, in Wilson's plan, would have been in authority over the Mandatory, have been able to appoint or dismiss him. It would have fixed the terms of the Mandate and thereby have fixed the limits of the Mandatory's power. The Arabs would have had the right of appeal against the terms, and might have had their existence recognized by the Assembly.

But in the Smuts Resolution all safeguards had been witched away. No longer merely manning the League, but superseding the League, stood the

P.A.P., the Principal Allied Powers. No longer could the League appoint or dismiss a Mandatory. No longer could the League fix the terms of a Mandate. By the Resolution the role of the League was reduced to what it has been ever since in Palestine, that of a gas-inspector who is not allowed upon the premises, but receives the record of such ohms or therms as the Mandatory chooses to send him from such meters as the Mandatory chooses to install.

The League was not ousted and the P.A.P. were not inserted by direct statement in the Resolution, which would have betrayed too much of its intent. The change-over was achieved by vagueness of definition. The definite statements of Wilson were replaced by what Professor Quincy Wright calls with truth "the orotund circumlocutions of Smuts and Kerr." As the acute American historian observes:

> "The well-phrased second paragraph of Article 22 left it uncertain where the ultimate or sovereign authority rested, by whom or how the Mandatory should be selected, or how much control the League should exercise… The final text of Article 22 did not mention appeal nor did it specify whether the League or the interested Mandatory Power should have the right to decide when the people of the Mandated territory had become "able to stand alone."

In fact, the methods of the smoke-screen were employed by Smuts and Kerr, as they had been employed in the Balfour Declaration. Clouds of magnanimity and of disinterestedness gushed forth from their preamble and hid the lineaments, such as they were, of the succeeding paragraphs of Article 22. A later acknowledgement of Balfour's, sprung of one of those moments when he was bored with placating opinion, that "an undoubted vagueness—probably intentionally—was introduced into the Covenant," is worth keeping in mind. At the time the usual pleas were used on behalf of this vagueness. Those who made them said that the essential thing was to get the League started and that it was very inadvisable to delay this by trying to create a perfect League there and then. Here is a characteristic utterance of the period: "If ultimate perfection be aimed at before the foundation-stones are laid, the most powerful lever for putting the world on a basis of peace may be put out of gear."

There is some truth, of course, in the danger of trying to perfect an experiment before launching it, if it would be very valuable immediately in an imperfect state. But in the matter of Mandates the Smuts Resolution did anything but leave the Covenant free for future development. The whole aim of the Smuts Resolution was to fix the position. It took the power of conferring and of drawing-up Mandates which Wilson had given to the League, and transferred it to the Principal Allied Powers. It fixed the system firmly at the start, under the mask of not fixing the system too soon. There was no accident about all this either. Only last June, 1938, Mr. Lloyd George broadcast to us all:

> The Covenant of the League of Nations was in the main the work of a great Dominion statesman—General Smuts—and the whole of his proposals were sifted and examined by the Imperial Cabinet before they were submitted to the Allied Committee that drafted the Covenant.

That the system was fixed through vagueness of statement carries in it no contradiction. The most definite aims can be reached through a little neat obscurity.

The best example of that quality in Article 22 is paragraph 8. It has the air of confiding the composition and the allocation of Mandates to all members of the League. But we shall see presently what happened in the working-out of this paragraph, how the Council, without the leave of the Assembly and therefore of the vast majority of League members, defined that all the "members of the League" meant itself alone. That was a year later, in 1920. In 1919 it was not certain still whether the Council of the League would consist of the P.A.P. (according to the Cecil plan), or of the representatives of the P.A.P. diluted with some small-State delegates. But of whichever it consisted the result would be the same. The Council of the League would be composed of the original P.A.P. or it would be a proxy for the P.A.P.

So that far from leaving the issue open, as was the pretext, the P.A.P. by the Lloyd George-Smuts Article 22 displaced the League and made themselves the makers and donors of Mandates. The limitation of the Mandatories' authority therefore now could only proceed from the Mandatories themselves. It did so proceed quickly enough, the position being incarnated in a grotesque letter written by the President of the Council of the League to the Principal Allied Powers to inquire "what degree of authority, administration or control they suggest that the Council should confer upon the Mandatory Powers under the term of paragraphs 4 and 5 of Article 22." Whereon the Principal Allied Powers were so good as to write back and to offer their "suggestions" for the power they were to enjoy.

Letters like this belong to the realm of comic opera. If Sir Arthur Sullivan had been alive he might have set them to music.

The way in which the Mandatory scheme came into being and was comprised in the Covenant now has, I think, been shown sufficiently. Little or nothing of this, it must be explained, was publicly known in 1919. The best correspondents of the world, gathered in the enormous palace of M. Dufayel in the Champs Elysées, ran about like a multitude of prize chicks in a golden incubator, pecking, jostling, and raising a continuous uncertain murmur. But they could send home no regular definite news of the development of the peace-making. They were only admitted to the plenary sessions of the Conference, where none of the events mentioned took place. They did what they could with leakages of news here and leakages there, followed by complaints and *démentis* and counter-*démentis*. But the meetings of the Council of Ten, were, as its members insisted, on a parity with Cabinet meetings, and its proceedings were not made public.

The connected records of the historians, particularly of the American historians, which have appeared since then have only been read by a molecule of our public. The result is a common belief that "the League of Nations wrote the Covenant," and that the Covenant is in every line an exposition of disinterestedness.

Whereas, whatever the origin and the merits of most of it, the cardinal Article 22, out of which the Mandatory system proceeded, was the work of an interested man, or pair of men, and of a Government determined to phrase it as far as possible to suit its ulterior purposes.

That is not to say that the Covenant is unworthy of respect, or that Article 22 itself is to be disregarded. It is necessary to distinguish between the great principles behind Article 22 and the form given to it. Its ultimate drafters themselves were in their degree actually imbued by these principles, though where these principles conflicted with their own pet theories they suddenly lost for them their quality as great principles. They phrased the Article therefore so that plausibly they might avoid carrying them out where this conflict arose.

In the record of events the Mandate now, in 1919, was to be attached to the false superstructure which General Smuts and Mr. Lloyd George had erected over the Article of the Covenant which ought to have provided a genuine basis for it.

Chapter 31

The manoeuvre of "fidelity to the Mandate." The Mandate really written by Zionists in collaboration with the Government. The League of Nations deliberately prevented from fixing its terms.

The Mandate for Palestine has been the subject of a good deal of comment for a good many years, but what is surely the most striking thing about it does not appear to have been noticed at all. This is the Mandate's own reticence about itself. Any person coming fresh to the subject—which is to say pretty well everybody—will see on reading the text of it, given later in this chapter, that therein there is not the slightest clue to where the Mandate was composed nor to how it was composed nor to when it was composed nor to the identity of those who composed it.

The nearest approach in the document to a mention of its origin is to be found in the fifth sentence or paragraph of the preamble:

> "Whereas the Mandate in respect of Palestine has been formulated in the following terms and submitted to the Council of the League for approval... "

It will be agreed that this approach does not bring us very near. Who "formulated it in the following terms"? Who even submitted it to the Council of the League of Nations? There is no indication.

This mystery goes hand in hand, or glove in glove, with the most reverential attitude towards the Mandate on the part of those who have occasion to speak of it. In an unmindful House of Commons and upon innocent public platforms such respect is paid to it that one might imagine that it had been revealed from some holy source. In Parliament particularly, this devotion has become almost a criterion of debate.

"We must be faithful to the Mandate"; "Duty to the Mandate demands this of us"; "Duty to the Mandate will not permit that to us"; "Loyalty to the Mandate must inspire our action"; "If we are to fulfil the obligations we have accepted under the Mandate"; phrases of the sort fill most of the discourses delivered at Westminster upon the Palestine Question.

Mr. Lloyd George, Lord Balfour, Mr. Churchill, Lord Melchett, Sir Archibald Sinclair, Lord Reading, Colonel Wedgwood, Lord Strabolgi, Mr. Amery, Mr. de Rothschild, and Heaven knows how many more past or present leaders or companions of opinion have implored us publicly never to swerve from our fealty to this Magna Charta of the Holy Land. As for the summonses to the nation to be true to the Mandate issued by Mr. Ormsby-Gore, while he was in charge of the Colonial Office, he used or borrowed every instrument in the Governmental orchestra to issue them, from the trumpet and the bassoon to his own masterly triangle.

His appeal when opening the Commons debate on the Royal Commission's Report of last year may be quoted:

> "The truth which I want to bring home to the House [he said] is that the Mandate is a very different thing from the Balfour Declaration. Because the Balfour Declaration is in the preamble of the Mandate, people think that it begins and ends there, but the Mandate is a written Constitution of twenty-eight Articles which governs the action of the British Government in the administration of Palestine, and the action of this House too, and we are unable to violate it."

The tone is that of one speaking of a set of twenty-eight Commandments which even the Government is unable to violate. Such a constraint in regard to Palestine is suspicious, and the suspicion is but too well founded.

The construction of the Mandate began before the Peace Conference had been held or the War had come to a close. The ultimate sources of it mainly are to be found, not in the archives of Geneva, nor in those of Whitehall itself but in the various Zionist documents which led up to the Balfour Declaration. They have been cited in earlier chapters, and are the same documents from which sprang most statements of Zionist policy, or of policy in which the Zionists had any share. They were assembled in the formal Zionist pronouncement made to the Peace Conference on the 27th of February, 1919. This pronouncement (cf. Chapter 16) made after much consultation with British officials, represented the Zionist view of how the Balfour Declaration should be put into force in Palestine and the National Home be established. It followed the insertion, just about three weeks before, of Article 22 into the Covenant, and without doubt had the advantageous drafting of this article by General Smuts well in mind.

There is a very significant reference based on this February statement in the Peel Report:

> "On the 27th February [says the Report] its leaders [that is the Zionist Organization's leaders] appeared before the Supreme Council and explained the scheme. A more detailed plan, dated the 28th March, was

> drafted by Mr. Felix Frankfurter, an eminent American Zionist. From these and other documents and records it is clear that the Zionist project had already in those early days assumed something like the shape of the Mandate as we know it."

The Peel Report is conspicuous for saying things which have not been said, officially, before, but also for saying them generally in such softened tones that they are hardly heard and are not recognizable for themselves. The third sentence in the above quotation is an example of the Report's delicate alleviations of fact. It speaks of the Zionist project assuming the shape of the Mandate. One might as truly speak of a father assuming the shape of his son. It was not the Zionist project which grew like the Mandate, but the Mandate which took the image of the Zionist Project, of which it was the natural child.

For the Mandate followed the precedent of the Balfour Declaration. It was drafted in quiet between the Government and the Zionists, mostly by the Zionists, and then was issued under cover of the League of Nations, as though it were the result of the collected debates of the world's lawgivers. Just two or three brief acknowledgements of the Government's part in its origin were made rapidly in Parliament. There was no breath in them of the Zionist leaders' preponderant share in the business, and misleading as these acknowledgements were, they were soon forgotten, and have remained forgotten ever since. In a few cases forgetfulness has been wilful.

No one waited for the League of Nations to prepare the Palestine Mandate, or any other Mandate, in 1919. The P.A.P., with the diluted Article 22 behind them, which left unlocated the power of composing Mandates, got to work in the early summer before the League could do so. "A few months after Article 22 was drafted and before the Treaty of Versailles was ratified there was a meeting in London of the colonial experts of the P.A.P. to draw up drafts of the different categories of Mandates." These are the words of M. Hymans, the Belgian statesman, at the meeting of the Council of the League at San Sebastian in 1920.

The League, being constituted as part of the Treaty of Versailles itself could not begin its functions till that Treaty was concluded. Ratification of the Treaty took place on the 10th of January, 1920, so the "colonial experts" of the P.A.P. had had half a year's start. These "colonial experts" were, more formally, a Commission appointed by the Supreme Council, representing the Principal Allied and Associated Powers, with British, French, Italian, Japanese and United States representatives, under the presidency of Lord Milner. It first met on the 28th of June, 1919.

The precedent of the Balfour Declaration was followed very faithfully. Lord Milner, a notable ally of Zionism, had been one of the chief

British drafters of that Declaration. It was he who gave its final cast to the Declaration after the Brandeis regime had sent back from New York the revised American draft. He was accustomed to work with the Zionists upon parallel lines, which were drawn down to meet at frequent intervals. This system of preparation of the Balfour document, was resumed now.

The Zionist Organization did not keep its part in these negotiations for drafting the Mandate any more secret from its own people than it had done for the Balfour Declaration drafting, so that the course of events can be followed from this source. The *Zionist Organization Report* containing the account was not much circulated beyond Zionist adherents and, in a lesser degree, the Jewish community, and is very rare now. Quotations, unless otherwise attributed, will, in the description of the Mandate-making, be from this Report.

> In the spring of 1919 the experts of the British Delegation to the Peace Conference in Paris opened informal discussions with representatives of the Zionist Organization on the draft of a Mandate for Palestine.

The Zionists got the matter on to a steady basis by appointing special committees for the purpose—the Balfour Declaration system once more. Dr. Weizmann and M. Sokolov and the American Zionist Delegation took a share in preparation of plans, but both of the two leaders were a good deal away, Dr. Weizmann in Palestine, during that year.

> The work was carried on for some time by a temporary political committee, of which the Right Hon. Sir Herbert [then Mr.] Samuel, Dr. Jacobson, Dr. Feiwel, Mr. Sacher [of the *Manchester Guardian*], Mr. Landman, and Mr. Ben Cohen were the first members.

Professor Frankfurter—the Frankfurter of the Feisal letter—seems to have been the chief drafter, along with Mr. Gans. They prepared drafts for the leaders, and no doubt the Frankfurter "detailed plan of the 28th March," of which the Peel Report speaks, was one of these, probably by its date the first of them.

It is to be noted that the Peel Report mentions this document as though it were a sort of second part of the official Zionist Statement of the 27th of February before the Peace Conference. But since that Statement was over and done with by the end of February, what purpose did a second part serve? The Peel Report is understandingly mute upon this. But the Zionist Report recognizes that the American Zionist professor was writing "drafts for the Mandate."

It goes on to say of them: "After consultation with various members of the 'Actions Committee' and Palestinian [Zionist] delegates in Paris, these proposals were handed to the British delegation, and were largely embodied in the first tentative draft, dated 15th July. In form it was then contemplated as part of the proposed Turkish Treaty."

The last sentence is not very specific: the reference is to the first British official draft, though the writer may be excused for barely distinguishing between British and Zionist drafts.

The drafting was not kept within the bosom of the Milner Commission, for the Report attributes some of it to Balfour—yet again a similarity with the Balfour Declaration. It says of the draft that it "recognized the historical connection of the Jews with Palestine (the wording is believed to be that of Mr. Balfour himself) and the claim which this gives them to find a national home in that country."

Other clauses in it:

1. Made Great Britain responsible for "placing Palestine under such political, administrative, and economic conditions as will secure the establishment there of the Jewish National Home."
2. Stated that the "ultimate aim of the Mandate was the creation in Palestine of a self-governing Commonwealth."
3. Referred to a Provisional Jewish Council, later to be Permanent, "representing Jewish opinion both in Palestine and in the world generally" which was to advise the Palestine Government upon all questions "touching the welfare" of the Jewish population, and "was to have very wide powers of carrying out public works."
4. Granted "preferential consideration to this Council in regard to concessions."
5. Outlined a system of Government, consisting of a Governor appointed by the Mandatory, an Executive Council in which the Palestinian population and the Jewish Council were to be represented, and a Representative Assembly "of an advisory character," which was "to be transformed gradually and given wider powers as the Palestinian nation progressed towards full self-government."
6. Jewish immigration and colonization were to be facilitated by the British Government.
7. Hebrew was to be an official language.

Despite all it gave them or they gave themselves in it, the members of the Zionist Organization were dissatisfied with this draft. Having obtained so much, no doubt they were avid for more. The draft, when sent to their "Actions Committee" for consideration, was considerably altered by them. The words "historical connection" were not thought satisfactory, and were substituted by "historical title." A text for the Preamble was submitted, which explicitly stated the recognition of the historic title of the Jews to Palestine and of the "right of Jews to reconstitute it as their National Home. *It was clearly explained that the Jewish National Home is not limited to a part of Palestine but is co-extensive with the whole of Palestine*" (My italics.) A number of suggestions were made besides this. The chief of several was that the development of Palestine into a self-governing Jewish Commonwealth was to be mentioned in the Mandate. The formation of a Jewish Agency instead of a Jewish Council was a further suggestion.

It does not appear that all these and other suggestions were sent as a whole and at once to the Drafting Commission or to the Government, so time was consumed. The failure to negotiate a treaty with Turkey also slowed, and then stopped the work of the Commission. Thereon the business was kept up in a desultory way by the Government, by Balfour and others, under the rubric of "exchange of views." The P.A.P. Commission had never been much more than a nom-de-plume for the Government. In the candid Zionist account of the Mandate-making no parties but themselves and the Government are mentioned.

Months passed in this "exchange of views," and the second Draft of the Mandate was not ready till towards the close of 1919. This draft "showed clearly that very serious consideration had been given to the Zionist suggestions." The Zionists did not get their "historical title," but the preamble of the first Draft was altered to include recognition of "the historical connection with Palestine and the claim which this gives them to *reconstitute Palestine as their National Home (Erez Israel).*"

The draft also conceded the demand for a Jewish Agency and the recognition of the Zionist Organization as that Agency—thereby placing the native Jews of Palestine in the hands of the Zionist immigrant body. Preferential rights were granted to the Agency in public works (it will be remembered perhaps that in 1919 the Rutenberg scheme had been confided to the Government and had been stowed in the Government's arcana).

But in late 1919 and early 1920 the Cabinet, and Mr. Lloyd George in particular, were more occupied with the preparations of the Turkish Treaty and of the San Remo Conference than with the actual Mandate drafting. The immediate preoccupation became not the making of the Mandate, but the taking of it, and the insertion of the Balfour Declaration in the prospective Treaty.

In the spring drafting was resumed again, however. But a measure of opposition arose. Perhaps it was felt in Whitehall that the insertion of the Balfour Declaration in the Treaty had to be offset by a less obvious compilation of the Mandatory document from Zionist matter. Perhaps a change in Foreign Office outlook sprang from Lord Curzon having obtained more control of his ministry from Balfour as 1919 ended. For whichever reason, "various fundamental changes made their appearance" in the draft-Mandate. "These were finally embodied in the draft of June 10th, which may be considered the first official draft."

These changes were not to Zionist taste. The reference to "historical connection," let alone "title," had been expunged from their preamble, the "right of the Jewish Agency to be consulted in regard to concessions which it does not itself take up" had been removed also, and the clause making the whole organization of Palestine openly subserve the creation of the National Home had gone with it.

In reality the insertion of the Balfour Declaration in the draft-Treaty made up for these disappearances in the draft-Mandate, and though "immediate steps were taken to convey to the Government our serious objection to the proposed change" it is doubtful if the Zionists were not better off than they realized, or cared to realize. Their real perturbation probably was that most of their eggs were being transferred from the Mandate basket to the Treaty basket, and the future of the Treaty was now beginning to look doubtful. The first three months of 1920, it will be recalled, were a period of Zionist depression. Feisal had been proclaimed King of Syria and Palestine, and the Zionist leaders had grown nervous. American Zionists had thought it necessary to recall to Great Britain the "arrangement by which the Zionists should get Palestine under something tantamount to a British protectorate."

By June, too, more attention was being focused upon the Mandate-making, in Parliament at least. Some information about it was vouchsafed. Lord Curzon, speaking for the Government said, "We are making it." Lord Balfour, with habitual organized uncertainty, "thought that the terms of the Mandate were to be determined by the Peace Conference." Mr. Lloyd George contented himself with saying that the terms would be submitted to the League. Lord Curzon then topped the situation by saying, "If you look at Article 22 of the Covenant of the League, reference (of the terms) to the League of Nations is not obligatory." The Smuts formula for Article 22 was bearing its first interest.

Lord Curzon added that the matter might be determined by agreement amongst the members of the League, "which meant not the Assembly, but the Council." "The Government," he said, "has decided to go at once and unhesitatingly to the Council." The Mandate was to be drawn up by the Government, was then to be approved by the Great Powers, and lastly was to be submitted by them, but only voluntarily submitted, to the Council.

This reply was aimed at Lord Cecil, who had become disturbed at the turn of events and had attacked the Government. It is even harder than usual to understand Lord Cecil's mind then. The P.A.P. had grasped control of the League, but there was nothing in that to distress him surely, since he had been the author of a project for placing the P.A.P. in control. He too had obtained the withdrawal of the Vesnitch motion for the complete emancipation of the Mandated peoples, and it is not to be denied that he had taken a full share in securing that the terms of the Palestine Mandate should be fixed without any consultation of its inhabitants, and indeed in opposition to their known desires.

But now, because under the Smuts Article 22, to which he had never objected, the League was to be treated by the P.A.P. as he himself had treated the people of Palestine, that is to say, because the League was to be unconsulted when the terms of the Mandate were being fixed—now Lord Cecil was intensely exercised. On the 30th June he put his feelings into a letter to *The Times*, which most certainly is to be quoted for the admirable presentation of the truth in it however much it leaves one in a quandary concerning the writer's mentality.

After complaining of Lord Curzon's pronouncement and citing other statements by Lord Balfour and by the Prime Minister, he said:

> Lord Curzon, stating the collated view of the Government, denies the right of the League to settle the terms of the Mandate. This really, though the Government do not see it, is a vital matter. Unless the League controls the terms of the Mandates, the whole Mandatory system becomes little better than a sham. If each Mandatory, with the assistance of a few selected "members of the League," can determine the conditions of his trust, he can, and will, so draw the Mandate as to give himself such liberty of action as he may desire. It is not easy, with due regard to international comity, to point out what this may mean, but anyone with any knowledge of the subject will agree that the Government doctrine, if persisted in is a death-blow to all our hopes for a new era in colonial government and for the abolition of one of the chief incentives to predatory wars.
>
> To me, this is a test case. Do the Government really mean to stand by the Covenant, or do they mean to whittle it away whenever its provisions are inconvenient to them?

These words cannot be praised too highly. Nothing more applicable to the Palestine Mandate ever has been said. But that when he wrote this letter

Lord Cecil had the sham Palestine Mandate in his mind, unfortunately is not to be imagined. It looks as though when he spoke of a Mandatory drawing up his Mandate to his own pleasure, what was worrying him most was not so much that our Government was making a sham of its Mandate, but that our Government in its guilelessness was giving other less righteous Governments the opportunity to make a sham of their Mandates. His disinclination to dot his "i's," because of regard for international comity, seems to point to this, and still more does the ingenuous sentence, "This really, though the Government do not see it, is a vital matter." As if the Government did not see it! Nothing has ever been more clearly seen. A congress of the world's oculists might have been gathered to admire the crystalline focus of Mr. Lloyd George's gaze, as he watched the realization of his plans.

None the less, Lord Cecil did speak of his own Government as "whittling away the provisions of the Covenant when they were inconvenient," and it is something to have his views put on record. Within a month his fears that the right of the League was to be denied were justified.

The League Council met on the 31st July at San Sebastian, its first summer meeting since its inauguration in January. Naturally at first questions of procedure and the apportionment of responsibility were discussed by the delegates, who represented France, Italy, Japan, Belgium, Brazil, Spain, Greece and the British Empire, Lord Balfour being the representative of the Empire. Thus the Allied and Associated Powers held seven of the eight seats and with all respect to Señor Quinones de Leon, the Spanish delegate, the Council was an embodiment of the Allied Countries, quite under the sway of the P.A.P., whose envoy was Lord Balfour, with French, Italian and Japanese attachés, as it were, attendant upon him.

M. Hymans of Belgium had been charged, as *rapporteur* (secretary and foreman in one) of the Council-in-Committee, with the duty of clarifying the obligations of the League under the Covenant. He came to the evident conclusion that, in the matter of Mandates, the League's obligations were stated in the eighth paragraph of the familiar Article 22. This said: "The degree of authority, control or administration to be exercised by the Mandatory shall, *if not previously agreed upon by Members of the League*, be explicitly defined in each case by *the Council*."

M. Hymans, whether he had seen it or not, had an opinion of Lord Cecil's to help him in elucidating this paragraph. The first part of Lord Cecil's letter of the 1st July had dealt with it. He had said:

> Although Lord Curzon declares that it is quite wrong to say that the "members of the League" means the Assembly, he does not say what it does mean. By Article 3 the Assembly consists of the representatives of the members of the League. One would naturally think, therefore, that

> an agreement by "members of the League" meant an agreement by the Assembly, just as a vote by the Lords would mean a vote by the House of Lords. I venture to ask Lord Curzon what there is in the context of Article 22 to alter the plain grammatical meaning of the words.

There was nothing to alter the plain meaning, of course. What there was though in Article 22 was phraseology which permitted escape from application of anything plain which it enjoined. Article 22 should have been a sort of prison of honour, but those who had made such show of constructing it with that aim had provided themselves with a key of egress from the detention of its provisions. Lord Cecil could not or would not perceive the duplicity of his colleagues, but it is possible that M. Hymans did, though he was circumspect in his remarks.

He began by saying that if the relevant phrases were to be "taken in their literal sense, it points to the Assembly as the body to determine the conditions of the Mandate, since the Assembly alone brings all the members of the League together." "However," he concluded, "those who drew up Article 22 would have cited the Assembly if they had meant it."

This could not be controverted. To cite the Assembly would have been obvious routine under the circumstances. In fact the parties concerned had to go out of their way not to cite the Assembly. In the Second Article of the Covenant "those who drew up Article 22" were stared in the eye by their own instruction that "the action of the League under the Covenant shall be effected through the instrumentality of an Assembly and a Council, with a permanent Secretariat." The word "shall" was used. It was an imperative upon them to arrange any action they intended through these named groups, Assembly and Council.

There was M. Hymans's dilemma. The drafters (to use the plural) of Article 22 in the eighth paragraph of their Article had to propose an "action of the League under the Covenant." Very well. If they were sincere in their adherence to the terms of the Covenant, why had they not proposed that the said action, which was the definition of the "degree of the Mandatory's authority, control or administration," should be carried out by the Assembly? Why did they not write in the eighth paragraph that "the degree of authority to be exercised by the Mandatory shall, *if not previously agreed upon by the Assembly*, be defined by the Council"? Why did they write instead "the degree of authority to be exercised by the Mandatory shall, *if not previously agreed upon by the Members of the League*, be defined by *the Council*"? Why did they carefully leave out the name of the Assembly, through which the action of the League had to take place, and introduce in its lieu, the indeterminate and unstatutory words "the Members of the League"?

Why indeed? We may say frankly that they had left it out because the professions of the P.A.P. were bogus, and because the P.A.P. had no intention of giving the Assembly or any body but themselves any chance of action. The way in which M. Hymans, with real or unintended satire, put the reality was, "Probably the Principal Allied Powers thought that on the day of the League's foundation they would be its only members." Just so.

From these considerations the Rapporteur turned to the practical problem. He thought that since no arrangement, such as was implied by the Covenant, actually had been made in Article 22 to consult all the members, therefore the Council itself had a contingent right to regulate the Mandatory's authority. "The right appears theoretically incontestable," he said, but then, under the eye of Balfour, added, "it is one which it would not be opportune to exercise." It was the Vesnitch situation once more. Lord Balfour does not seem to have said that for the Council to exercise its right would be inexpedient as Lord Cecil had said that the Vesnitch motion was inexpedient, but Balfour was there in the Council chamber, blandly radiating prepotence. "We must bear in mind," ended M. Hymans, with a sort of verbal bow to him, "that in the A Mandates the degree of authority must vary according to the population of the mandated territories and according to who is the Mandatory Power."

As for the Assembly, M. Hymans, who had already pronounced it "too numerous for the delicate task," came to the conclusion that the Council must replace it as the body entitled (in principle, as distinguished from practice) to define how much authority the Mandatories were to have in their mandatory areas. This conclusion was adopted with the rest of his report by the Council. Lord Balfour expressed a gracious and flippant approval, making his already quoted remark that an "undoubted vagueness probably intentionally—had been introduced into the Covenant." As for the situation between Council and Assembly, "to try and formulate the relations of Council and Assembly," he said, "would throw undue emphasis on this."

On the hothouse proceedings a gush of breathable air came from the Italian delegate, Tittoni, of the old Roman school, who detested hypocrisy. "Mandates," he said gruffly, "are regarded as convenient fictions of a temporary character." But Italy herself then appeared to be among the coming winners in the Sèvres prize-distribution, only three weeks ahead, and Signor Tittoni went no further. The Hymans Report "was unanimously adopted by the Council, and it expresses," declared the final resolution, "the Council's understanding as to how it should carry out the mission entrusted to it by the Covenant."

So, when the Treaty of Sèvres missed fire that August, the position was that the Zionists and the Government were drawing up the Mandate in concert, emending each other's versions of the basic Zionist draft; the Council of the League had pronounced that the terms of this document were not the concern of the Assembly but of itself, adding though that "it was opportune" to let its rights in the matter be taken over by the P.A.P.; and the P.A.P. had benignly accepted the opportune homage. In its own glorious phrase our Government had "decided to go at once and unhesitatingly to the Council," and not to be outdone, the Council had decided to go at once and unhesitatingly to our Government. Altogether August 1920 was a month with a very high content of chicanery.

Before it was over the constant Zionist drafters registered a success, for the intermittent British drafters at their instances restored the "historic connection" clause to the preamble. Meanwhile, too, the Mandatory-sans-Mandate Government had been set up in Jerusalem. But on the other side of the ledger, the American State Department had begun to show its inconvenient interest in the terms of Mandates. For this or for another reason in October the "historic connection of the Jews with Palestine" vanished again from the up-to-date preamble. The sincerity of the business, and the extent of the belief of the Government in this "historic connection" plea, can be gauged from the fashion in which the phrase appeared in one draft as the basis of everything, and in the next was removed as superfluous.

But the Zionist drafters reacted. It will have been about this time that the Organization put the work into the hands of a permanent sub-committee, "formed specially for the Mandate and frontier questions," consisting of Messrs. Sacher, Stein and Ben Cohen. The date of their appointment is not given; the "later stage of the drafting negotiations" is the period mentioned.

Early in November Dr. Weizmann had two interviews with Mr. Balfour, with whom he had been in correspondence on the subject of the Mandate during October, and who had been familiarized with the principal features of the current draft which appeared from the Zionist point of view to require modification. The Prime Minister was also approached, both directly and indirectly [my italics] and the situation fully explained to several leading members of the Cabinet, including Lord Milner and Sir Alfred Mond. Sir Herbert Samuel also supported our representations in his capacity as High Commissioner. Recognition is due to the valuable services rendered at this period, as on many previous occasions, by Major James de Rothschild.

The point at issue was also brought to the notice of Lord Robert Cecil and to the Parliamentary group for Palestinian affairs, of which he is the Chairman. The Group met on the 9th November, 1920, at the House of Commons and passed the following resolution:

> "That His Majesty's Government be urged to include in the terms of the Palestine Mandate definite recognition of the historic connection

> of the Jewish people with Palestine, and of the status of the Zionist Organization, and of the policy of the development of Palestine into a Palestinian self-governing Commonwealth."

About the same time the Zionist Organization of America approached the British Ambassador at Washington and made representations in the same sense.

The sub-committee brought, therefore, much the same spell-binding organization into play as had been used for appeals and addresses at the opening of the San Remo Conference, and as it was using at this moment for the frontier negotiations. In fact, Lord Cecil and Mr. Ormsby-Gore's resolution of the 9th was double-barrelled, "supporting the Jewish standpoint" both in regard to the Mandate and the frontiers. *The Times* and the *Manchester Guardian* also "supported the same view in leading articles."

There must have been some leakage of news about the share that the Zionist Organization was taking in the drafting work about then, for questions were put in the House of Commons by Sir Philip Magnus and Sir John Rees. "Will the Mandate be prepared by the British Government, by the Foreign Office?" asked the latter, unsatisfied with Lord Curzon's earlier assurance that, " We are drawing it up." "It is being prepared by His Majesty's Government," was the reticent official answer. Then came one of the too rare, deadly supplementary questions. "Will the League of Nations have anything to say to these terms? Can they disregard them after they are decided by the Government?" "I must have notice of that," replied the Under-Secretary. But notice does not seem to have been given, and the question never reappeared.

Sir Philip Magnus asked whether the Mandate would be submitted to the House and was told that that was "rather a matter for the Leader of the House."

These questions were put on the 24th of November, and indicate a period during which the Government walked warily. The result of all the approaches, direct and indirect, to the Prime Minister and to others did not meet with the overwhelming success which their organizers had hoped. None the less the Zionists achieved their principal point. The "historic connection" clause, rather frayed by now with wear and tear, was inserted or reinserted for the fourth time in the preamble of the draft.

On the other hand "it became apparent that no substantial concessions would be obtainable in respect of the economic clauses of the Mandate." The reason for this was, without any doubt, a stiff dispatch which had reached the Foreign Office from the United States. It was penned by Mr. Bainbridge Colby, and followed a reply by Lord Curzon to the American notes upon the economic conditions of the Mandates which have been quoted in an earlier chapter:

> The United States Government [said Mr. Colby] is unable to concur in the view that the terms of the Mandates can properly be discussed only by the Council of the League of Nations and by the signatories of the Covenant...As a participant in the war the United States, and indeed all the belligerent nations had a right to be consulted in the discussions which had followed upon it...This Government notes with interest that the draft-Mandates for Mesopotamia and for Palestine will, when approved by the interested Allied Powers, be communicated to the Council of the League of Nations.
>
> [But] the United States is undoubtedly one of the Powers directly interested in the terms of the Mandates and I therefore request that the draft-Mandate forms be communicated to this Government before their submission to the Council of the League. The establishment of the Mandate principle would seem to require the frankest discussion from all pertinent points of view. It would seem essential that suitable publicity should be given to the drafts of Mandates which it is the intention to submit to the Council, in order that the fullest opportunity may be afforded to consider their terms in relation to the obligations assumed by the Mandatory Power and the respective interests of all Governments which are or deem themselves concerned or affected.

The American dispatch then turned to the discussion of the oil-question in Mesopotamia. In its last paragraph it came back to the principal issue, in the most decided tones.

> But it is not these aspects of oil production and supply, in so far as they are of domestic interest to the United States, with which I am concerned in this discussion. I have alluded to them in order to correct confusing inferences, liable to arise from *certain departures which I believe I discern in Your Lordship's communication, from the underlying principles of a Mandate*, as evolved and sought to be applied by the Allied and Associated Powers to the territories brought under their temporary dominion by their joint struggle and common victory. This dominion will be wholly misconceived, not to say abused, if there is even the slightest deviation from the spirit and the exclusive purpose of a trusteeship as strict as it is comprehensive. [My italics.]

It is not easy to appraise this note. So much depended upon how Mr. Colby would have followed it up, and without knowledge of his opinions this cannot be surmised. He went out of office with the coming of the Harding Administration. His note at least seems to provide evidence that in America the State Department, as in England the Foreign Office, held men—diplomatists proper—who were not happy about what was occurring in Palestine.

If Mr. Colby had stayed longer in office, it is possible that further United States action true to his note might have emerged, but with the Brandeis regime hovering about the President it cannot be considered too likely. In any event, his successors made a mere facade of his note, departing altogether from its underlying principles. The end it was to serve, as the situation developed, was only the maintenance of United States trading opportunities and privileges of status. Mr. Colby had said that the "Mandate principle would seem to require the frankest discussion from all pertinent points of view." The most pertinent of all points of view, however, was that of the Mandated population, and to the wishes and hopes of the Mandated population United States Governments, then and since, have remained as deaf and blind as British.

But at the time it was written, the American note, though it did not stop the growth of the Zionist Organization's mortmain over Palestine, changed its appearance. The delivery of the country's resources into Zionist hands was no longer crudely proposed in the Mandate. It became a matter of covert understanding between the Zionists and their allies in the Cabinet and in other high places. The prospective arrangement is described perfectly in the Zionist Organization's Report:

> There could be no doubt that Zionist co-operation in the economic development of Palestine would, in practice, be welcomed, and the Zionists would have every opportunity of participating in it to the full extent of their resources. On the other hand, the concession in terms of far-reaching privileges, while in itself adding little of practical value, would excite opposition which there was no advantage in gratuitously challenging, and might even be plausibly represented as inconsistent with the Covenant of the League of Nations.

The concluding words might have been penned by Balfour. Perhaps they were. The sense of the passage, of course, is "You shall have all you want, but don't say anything about it. The Americans will make trouble if it is put into words."

A couple of months passed before Washington received a British reply to Mr. Colby's "plausible representations." It is a pity that this reply, dated the 28th of February, 1921, is not printed in the United States Buff Book. Was it, like parts of Balfour's letter of eleven months later, rather too awkward to reproduce perhaps, because of the nature of the references in it to Palestine?

While it was being examined, in any case, the Prime Minister characteristically got ahead with his policy. The draft-Mandate, with the "historic connection" clause now well gummed in, was considered by the Cabinet and was passed. On the 6th of December Lord Balfour sent it with a covering letter to the Secretary-General of the League of Nations.

It is worth considering for a moment what was the status of this letter. Its sender acted on behalf of the British Government which acted on behalf of the Supreme Council of the Allied Powers. Letters passing from the Supreme Allied Council to the Council of the League of Nations had the air of passing from one international body to another international body, the twain being aloof, disinterested and unrelated to each other. But in reality they were intertwined. M. Matsui of Japan belonged to both. It is unnecessary to enlarge upon Balfour's presence in the League Council and his close connection with the Supreme Council.

The League Council in the affairs of Palestine was an orchestra which he conducted. The Supreme Council in the affairs of Palestine, once the French had been placated concerning the frontiers of their mandatory area, was nothing but an alias of Mr. Lloyd George's, and he in Palestine affairs was one with Lord Balfour.

So in truth there is scarcely an exaggeration in saying that when His Majesty's Government, acting on behalf of the Supreme Council of the Allied Powers, pompously was proclaimed as submitting the draft-Mandates for Palestine and for Mesopotamia to the Council of the League of Nations, little more occurred than that Lord Balfour sent the draft-Mandates for approval to Lord Balfour.

Balfour dispatched the Mandate from his desk, pursued it, caught it up in the Council Chamber, and surpassed any farce on the stage by having its contents laid before him, and in a covering letter "venturing to hope" that what he had drawn up "would satisfy" himself.

It is somewhat fitting that there is no League document to mention the proceedings which followed the arrival of this singular missive. The minutes of the Council meeting during which it came to hand are *omitted from the records of the Council.* Here, however, are the terms of Balfour's letter to the Chairman of the Council:

> "In accordance with instructions received from my Government, I have the honour to transmit herewith copies of the texts of the Mandates for Mesopotamia and Palestine as drawn up by His Majesty's Government, and to request that you will be so good as to lay them before the Council of the League of Nations.
>
> His Majesty's Government have prepared the terms of these Mandates in conformity with the spirit of Article 22 of the Covenant of the League of Nations, and have throughout been in consultation with the French Government, with whom they are in complete agreement on the subject.
>
> His Majesty's Government venture to hope that an examination of these documents will satisfy the Council that they are in compliance with Article 22 of the Pact, and that the Council will be prepared to approve them.

I should add that, in the interests of the native inhabitants of Mesopotamia arid Palestine and with the object of conferring upon them with the least possible delay the benefits of a system based on the stipulations of the pact, His Majesty's Government desire to draw the attention of the Council to the advisability of bringing to an early close the temporary arrangements at present in force."

Tartuffe would have cleared his throat and hesitated before reading that last paragraph.

Of the draft-Mandate which was enclosed with Lord Balfour's letter the whole text need not be reproduced here, because the final text of the Mandate will be given shortly. But the Preamble deserves quotation, because of a difference between it and that of the final text. It was drawn up as though it actually had been drafted by the Council of the League. Not so much as a comma was left to the Council's initiative: the document was sent ready for issue, with blanks only for the date and place of publication and for the necessary signatures on the dotted line:

"The Council of the League of Nations

Whereas by Article 132 of the Treaty of Peace signed at Sèvres on the tenth day of August 1920, Turkey renounced in favour of the Principal Allied Powers all rights and title over Palestine: and

Whereas by Article 95 of the said Treaty the High Contracting Parties agreed to entrust, by application of the provisions of Article 22, the administration of Palestine, within such boundaries as might be determined by the said Powers: and

Whereas by the same Article the High Contracting Parties further agreed that the Mandatory should be responsible for putting into effect the declaration originally made on November 2nd 1917, by the Government of His Britannic Majesty, and adopted by the other Allied Powers, in favour of the establishment in Palestine of a national home for the Jewish people, it being clearly understood that nothing should be done which might prejudice the civil and religious rights and political status enjoyed by Jews in any other country: and

Whereas recognition has thereby been given to the historical connection of the Jewish people with Palestine and to the grounds for reconstituting their national home in that country: and

Whereas the Principal Allied Powers have selected His Britannic Majesty as the Mandatory for Palestine: and

Whereas the terms of the Mandate in respect of Palestine have been formulated in the following terms and submitted to the Council of the League for approval: and

Whereas His Britannic Majesty has accepted the Mandate in respect of Palestine and undertaken to exercise it on behalf of the League of

Nations in conformity with the following provisions:

HEREBY approves the terms of the said Mandate as follows:

(Whereon followed the 27 then drafted Articles.)"

Comment upon the general principles of the Preamble will come with the discussion of the final text. In that text the references to the defunct Treaty of Sèvres of course disappear. But the point of difference to be mentioned now occurs in the third paragraph. The Draft of December 1920, while introducing the Balfour Declaration into this third paragraph, only introduced those "safeguards" in it which applied to the Jews. The full "safeguard sentence" in the Balfour Declaration ran " … it being clearly understood that nothing shall be done which may prejudice the civil and religious rights of existing non-Jewish communities in Palestine or the rights and political status enjoyed by Jews in any other country."

The sentence in the draft-Mandate was "… that nothing should be done which might prejudice the civil and religious rights and political status enjoyed by Jews in any other country."

Therefore in the 1920 preamble of the draft, prepared by the Government and the Zionists, even the illusory guarantees to the Arabs were suppressed. Not even one hollow word was wasted upon them, though perhaps this was preferable to insincerity.

There was bitter humour of a kind in the consequence of their act, for by it the Jews were invested automatically with the miserable, meaningless "civil rights" which had been specially prepared, like a cheap "sale-line" in a store, for the consumption of the Arab herd.

Though not specified in the Council minutes the departure from Lord Balfour's residence and arrival at the Palais des Nations of the draft-Mandate was fairly common knowledge. In the Commons there were requests for publication of the document, but on the 16th of December the Prime Minister stated that "there will be no publication of the Mandate till it is known what action the Council of the League intends to take in the matter." Whereon Mr. Ormsby-Gore, in an uninformed mood, asked had the Mandate been shown to any other Government, or had it been prepared by the British Government and sent direct by them to the League. "I think," said Mr. Lloyd George, not so sure about it as Lord Balfour had been in his letter to the League, "I think that there was consultation at least with the French Government."

There is no evidence that the French Government, which had no better intentions now towards its Arabs than our Government had towards our Arabs, played any part in the drafting of the Mandate for Palestine, in so far as the issue between Arabs and Zionists was concerned. The consultations with Paris were for the purpose of "having a general agreement in terms" with the French Mandate preparing for "Syria."

Upon this Great Britain similarly was "consulted." Consultation was one of the many "do ut des" arrangements, and appears to have been carried out in such careless ecstasy of reciprocity that texts were not well scrutinized. The American Buff Book contains a footnote to say that the "French text" of the draft had the same preamble as the ultimate Mandate. Whether this means the text in French submitted to Geneva or the text prepared by the French Government is not clear. In either case, this French text included so the "guarantee" to the Arabs removed from the English or British text.

The variation between the texts may have represented one of the many little intrigues going on, but is more probably to be ascribed to pure carelessness or indifference. It would have been very like Lord Balfour, however, to have given the Council two different texts, for the subtle amusement to be extracted from the Council's complaisance therewith. But in a document with the Mandate's antecedents the existence of a couple of preambles is nothing out of the way, and need not detain us.

In Geneva the arrival of the draft brought about one entirely satisfactory result. The Assembly of the League reacted against the conjuring tricks by which its right to decide upon the terms of Mandates had been abstracted from it. The Assembly met that December and requested the Council to communicate to it the draft-Mandates which the Council had received from Lord Balfour. The Council, now thoroughly at home in its new role, refused.

The Assembly, in the expectation that it would obtain the Mesopotamia and Palestine drafts at once, had appointed its Sixth Committee, of which M. Branting was chairman, to deal with them. The intention had been that the Committee should study at length the terms of the Mandates. In the League way, the Sixth Committee charged a sub-committee with the task, thinking that it would be best for a sub-committee to make this prolonged study of the Mandate's terms its sole work. Because of the importance of the matter, the famous Dr. Nansen was made chairman of the sub-committee, and it was he who applied for the text of the drafts to the Council and was refused. Without them the sub-committee could accomplish nothing, and Nansen made a second appeal. Despite his great standing, all that he could achieve was that the texts would be sent to him "confidentially." His committee-members might read the drafts, but the drafts must not be laid before them in an official manner permitting comment. Still less would alteration of them be permitted.

In consequence the sub-committee could but issue an empty report. The time spent by Nansen in endeavouring to obtain the drafts for it made this report very late, and the Sixth Commission had no opportunity to examine it, and had to submit it as it was to the Assembly. The Assembly in its turn could not make walls without bricks, and was only able to send general recommendations concerning the Mandates to the Council. The chief of these were that:

> (a) An organic law should be drawn up as soon as possible for the Mandated territories, and should be laid before the League of Nations ere it came into force.
>
> (b) In general in the future draft-Mandates should be made public before the Council of the League enacted them.

Lord Curzon, it will be remembered, had presupposed the creation of such an Organic Law. Yet no such law was ever even mooted.

These recommendations, a well-deserved rebuke to the Council, were accompanied by a still more condemnatory Resolution which began:

> "The Assembly of the League regrets that the Council should have refused to publish draft-Mandates before they came into force."

The publication of the oil-deal with France in Mesopotamia, and the news of the intended exploitation of Palestine in the interests of Zionist dominion, which had leaked through from the United States, drew the Assembly to add:

> "... a Mandatory must not be allowed to use its power under the Mandate in order to exploit for itself or its friends the natural resources of a Mandated territory."

Before the adoption of this Resolution, too, there occurred a most unpleasant episode for those who were responsible for the draft-Mandate and for the trickery attendant upon its presentation to the League. It should have served as an admonition to them. The Sixth Committee received the Report of the sub-committee at a meeting on the 18th of December. Dr. Nansen expressed his feelings shortly on this occasion, and Lord Cecil expressed his at length. They had the advantage of speaking in the presence of M. Hymans, who had to attend as President and representative of the Council.

But it was when the Canadian delegate spoke that M. Hymans heard some disagreeable home-truths:

> I feel strongly [declared he] that there is occasion to express a feeling of disappointment which certainly the Delegation of my own country has felt, which also I believe to be largely shared in this Assembly and moreover to a very considerable share outside this Assembly, over the fact

that there have been inadequate opportunities for the nations assembled here to consider this most important subject of the Mandates to be given over the territories which have ceased to belong to our defeated enemies. When it was first made known to the world that in the Peace Treaty we were to have a new departure—in that territories passing out of the hands of the defeated nations were not to be treated as the acquired property of the victors, but that their administration, when it was necessary, was to be provided for by a system that would have for its end and purpose the best interests of the populations of the territory in question—when this became known to the world, there was a general feeling of satisfaction, a general rejoicing that a new and better era was dawning. For the justification of that pledge the world has been waiting.

It seeks to find that justification in the manner in which the terms of these Mandates are settled, and still more in the manner in which, having been settled, they will be lived up to. There will be no more effective test of the sincerity which inspired the provisions for the bringing into existence of these Mandates, and of the sincerity of this League itself, than will be found in the execution of the provisions with regard to these Mandates and in the faithful fulfilment of the trusts they carry with them. And just because that is so, this matter of Mandates was perhaps as important a subject as the nations here gathered together could have sat down to study, and, as I have said, I am satisfied that there will be a feeling of disappointment that the opportunity of that study has been inadequate.

The Canadian delegate went on to say that the responsibility for the terms of the Mandates, as things were, rested with the Council now, and that "with regard to all these Mandates, of whatever class they be, the great and important thing is that their terms should bring out the fiduciary nature of the holding of the territories confided to them [the Mandatories] by the Mandators." (The speaker did not realize that Mandators and Mandatories had been one and the same.)

Lord Balfour, after this and after the already quoted resolutions had been proposed, made an interminable apologia for the Powers and their Council. It did not impress. In his turn, before a final vote was taken, the Australian delegate declared:

Might I be allowed to say, in explanation of the vote I shall feel obliged to give, that whilst I agree with the spirit underlying many of these recommendations, I think that sufficient time has not been afforded the Sixth Committee, of which I am a member, of discussing them with the thoroughness they deserve. Therefore I feel obliged to vote against all of them.

It was a serious event when the representatives of Canada and of Australia, knowing that it was the influence of the British Government which was keeping the draft-Mandates from proper consideration by the Assembly, spoke and voted in this manner. Neither of them though was aware of the full extent to which they and their colleagues of the Assembly were being manipulated. If they had been, there would have been a resounding scandal. As it was, their temperate protests roused no attention, for all their importance, and such is the general ignorance of the facts of the whole question that perhaps not fifty people in the United Kingdom today are aware that Canada and Australia even raised their voices.

Their complaints and the Resolutions of the Assembly were assisted into oblivion by the Council, which took no heed at all of them. It began the routine of mandatory administration by the appointment of a Commission which would act as the permanent representative of the Council in its relations with Mandatories. On the Commission a majority of subjects of non-Mandatory States was ensured. The Marchese Theodoli, of Italy, was named Chairman. Great Britain was represented by Lord Lugard, who had retired after a distinguished career in the Colonial Service. No one actually in the service of a Mandatory could sit on the Commission.

In February, Mr. Colby sent a strong note to the Council demanding that draft-Mandates should be forwarded for examination and approval to the United States before being accepted by the League. The Mesopotamia and Palestine drafts accordingly were sent to America, and the United States Government was invited to discuss them at the summer meeting of the League. But to this invitation Washington returned no reply. The State Department seemed unhurried, and in August Lord Curzon, like a man asking for a heavy bill in order to get his trouble over, begged that the "statement of criticisms and objections" to the Mandate draft for which the Foreign Office was waiting should be sent as soon as possible. He received it at the end of the month.

He may well have been anxious for it, because by now the text of the draft had been six months published. Quite appropriately this publication was the work, not of the Government, but of the Zionists. They were too proud of their Mandate not to proclaim its terms. It was so often their characteristic that when they reached or were placed in a commanding situation, as now, they would not be satisfied with private fruition of their influence, but in an overweening way must have the world know of it. Such friction as there ever was between them and their Governmental associates derived from this.

On the 5th of February *The Times* published the text of the draft-Mandate, but this was a text which it had submissively extracted from the current issue of the *Jewish Chronicle*—or the latter journal may have gratified *The Times* with a copy. The text was duly credited in *The Times* to the *Jewish Chronicle*. The situation between the two organs was a perfect counterpart of the situation between Zionists and Government, between Zionist Mandate-drafters and British Mandate-drafters.

The text was not tabled for Parliament till August. The House of Commons had been so supine, with the few marked exceptions amidst Members which we know, that it deserved this serving-up to it of an old and well-gnawed bone. It is to be observed that there was still no question of the Commons and Lords being permitted to debate the Mandate terms clause by clause: these were only "tabled," that is to say laid before members for their information, for the information of such of them as had not read *The Times* or the *Jewish Chronicle* half a year before.

This extinguished role of Parliament—to which reference has been made already—needs to be dinned in. The Mandate, in so far as it was a British creation, was only a Governmental creation. Parliament never examined and passed the terms of the Mandate as it examines and passes legislation. The House of Lords, owing to its more elastic procedure and its greater independence, was able to register its disapproval of the terms next year. The terms, though, were never presented to the Lords for acceptance or rejection, and as far as the Lords' vote was concerned, the Government simply ignored it as the Council of the League had ignored the Assembly.

The Commons were in even worse case. They could have rejected the Mandate as a whole, but only (as we have seen) at the price of rejecting peace with Turkey. If Members of Parliament wanted peace with Turkey, which of course they and the whole country behind them wanted, then they had to take the Mandate holus bolus, just as it was penned, in order to have that peace. The two things had to be taken or dropped together, as in those miscellaneous auction-lots which a bidder can only secure in bulk. With the tables and chairs of the Turkish Treaty Parliament had to take the Mandate what-not.

In its Report of the situation the Zionist Organization summed up the position thus:

> "When the Council has given its approval the Mandate may still have to be formally presented to the House of Commons for acceptance by Parliament, but it is believed that according to the present intention of the Government, no further discussion of the terms will take place."

Obviously assurances had been given by Parliament's leaders that Parliament would not be permitted any opportunity of interfering with the chosen text of the Mandate, though even the Zionist Organization does not seem to have expected that the Commons would have been as openly flouted as they were.

This draft of August 1921 was described hopefully by the Government as a "Final Draft," though it was not to prove so. Two things chiefly distinguished it from the 1920 or Balfour draft. Firstly, in the 1921 preamble the P.A.P. now were described as selecting Great Britain for Mandatory over Palestine in virtue of the Treaty of Sèvres and of Article 22. In the Balfour draft (q.v.) the selection of Great Britain had been uncomplicated by credentials, had been in what is called the free style.

Secondly, doubts had evidently overtaken some drafter or drafters, and the "guarantee" passage from the Balfour Declaration in favour of non-Jewish Communities had been reinstated, in the third paragraph of the preamble. Therefore "civil rights" were restored to the Arabs. The Zionists had been surcharged with them for but eight months, and then only theoretically and along with "political status," so that their situation in other countries really had not been impaired.

The Draft as it now stood, this "Final Draft" of 1921, was to all intents a Zionist draft, with some British modifications. Only the collapse of the Sèvres Treaty and the American demand for clauses in the Mandate text establishing more clearly the economic and judicial rights of United States citizens prevented it from being put into force. Nor in substance was it changed afterwards, certainly not in any way which weakened the position attained in it by the Zionists.

Chapter 32

The text of the Mandate. Its important Articles all of Zionist origin.

When the summer of 1921 passed without the Turkish Treaty being concluded, the rest of the year was spent in desultory negotiations between Great Britain and the United States upon the American claims. As the year closed the Government and its friends grew impatient. On the 29th of December Lord Curzon, in a letter, part quoted in Chapter 23, informed the United States that it was the British intention to "invite" the Council of the League to express formal approval of the Mandate as it stood, at the Council's forthcoming meeting beginning on the 10th of January, 1922.

This was putting on a somewhat bold face to express feelings which cannot have been so certain. With the United States Government's very specific remarks in their minds the members of the Council could not yet dare to give approval to the Mandate, and the Foreign Secretary must have been aware of this. The 10th of January came and went without any event to mark it, and on the 13th Balfour in Washington wrote his before quoted letter to Mr. Hughes, now Secretary of State:

> "You will remember that some days ago I mentioned my great anxiety to get the agreements in regard to the Mandate for Palestine advanced a stage in order that the Council of the League might give it their blessing at the meeting which is now, I think, going on at Geneva."

The "I think" is a museum-piece amidst Balfouriana. As we know, Mr. Hughes yielded to his correspondent's persuasions, and the formal capitulation of the United States in the matter of the Palestine Mandate followed in the spring.

So, though nothing was accomplished during the January session, in June the Council announced its official satisfaction with the terms of the Mandate. This session was a long one and at its beginning, in mid-May, Lord Balfour, back from the United States, delivered in Geneva a memorable speech. Though he spoke to the Council as one of the Council, in the course of this speech Balfour the spokesman of the P.A.P. put Balfour the Council member very much into his subordinate station.

> "Mandates [he said] are not our creation. The Mandates are neither made by the League nor can they in substance be altered by the League. Our duties are of two kinds. It is our duty in the first place to see that the specific and detailed terms of the Mandates are in accordance with the decisions come to by the Allied and Associated Powers in Article 22 of the Treaty of Versailles. It is our duty in the second place to see that in carrying out these Mandates the Mandatory Powers shall be under the supervision—not the control, but the supervision—of the League of Nations, which possesses an admirable organization through which it can obtain the fullest information as to the method in which each Mandatory Power fulfils the duties which are entrusted to it.
>
> Remember that a Mandate is a self-imposed limitation by the conquerors of the sovereignty which they obtained over conquered territories. It is imposed by the Allied and Associated Powers in the interests of what they conceive the general welfare of mankind, and they have asked the League of Nations to assist them in seeing that this policy should be carried into effect. But the League of Nations is not the author of the policy but its instrument. It is not they who invented the system of the Mandates: it is not they who have laid down the general lines on which the three classes [of Mandates] are formed."

He concluded by saying:

> "Whatever is done in Palestine at this moment, or in the future, is done in the full light of day. The machinery of the Mandates Commission, of the Council and of the Assembly of the League is so contrived as to make it quite impossible for any transaction of general interest to take place except in the full glare of the noonday sun of public opinion."

A conclusion so utterly detached from truth that it can scarcely be considered the mere converse of it, a falsehood. There was no genuine deception in it, for all listening, including the speaker, knew that it had nothing to do with reality, and everyone was aware that everyone else knew this, and that the speaker knew that they knew that he knew, and so on inextricably. The statement was one more complex artificiality through which Balfour entertained himself and sported with his environment.

But his earlier paragraphs, leading off with the incomparably derisive "Mandates are not our creation," fulfilled a certain purpose. In them the orator made a major move in the Palestine manoeuvres, no less than a change of front. So far Balfour had held with requisite devotion the "no annexation" front. The time for that he, and his friends no doubt, now judged to have come to an end. So before the Council of the League he executed a right-about-turn to the "sovereignty" front.

He spoke of the "conquerors' self-imposed limitation of the sovereignty they had obtained over conquered territories." The new suggestion was that instant sovereignty over enemy territories had accrued from victory, and that this remained the fundamental status of the said territories, which status the victors had not abrogated but only limited in practice by the institution of the Mandate. It was a superfine distinction, such as Balfour could produce, and was something to say where probably no one else could have found anything to say.

But it was altogether a perversion of the facts, and had even been contradicted by Balfour's own previous declaration in Paris at the Council of Ten meeting. President Wilson had laid down then that "no conquest" was both prelude and basis of the Mandatory scheme, to which Balfour had agreed. Lloyd George and a variety of Government spokesmen too had rejected annexation, in direct terms which could not now be denied.

The real situation therefore was quite clear. No conquerors' sovereignty existed in Palestine (or Irak) at all. Even had there been intent of sovereignty, this could not have fructified till the treaty with Turkey was concluded. But this treaty was not yet signed, and was to be made on the principle of no annexation, so that the intent of sovereignty itself (supposing it ever to have existed) had not fructified. Still less had the practice of sovereignty ever come into being.

However, when Balfour was speaking with Palestine in view, facts were but so much thoughtlessness. The Council of the League listened dutifully to the twisted dictums of its monitor and placed its cross against the terms of the Mandate.

Thereafter, in correspondence with the United States, Lord Curzon and others spoke of this League visa as though it were equivalent to final authorization. But the Americans passed that claim by in silence, and they were right. The Council's approval, however formally expressed, could not be effective till there was peace with Turkey. Other obstacles indeed began to accumulate for this very reason: Italy would not confirm any Mandate till the title to it had been cleared by the conclusion of the Treaty.

The Holy See too, through the Cardinal Secretary of State, had expressed its disquietude with the terms of the Mandate, which of course deeply concerned it because of the Holy Places. As a result some small changes were made in the terms, and these, with the usual verbiage to excuse the treatment of the Arabs, were enshrined in a rather dingy little White Paper, in the Ormsby-Gore manner.

More of a novelty was the lovers' tiff which arose between the Colonial Office and the Zionist Organization, ere the League had passed the Mandate. The Zionists, as various witnesses testify, had been made to understand that they must approve the Churchill Statement of Policy of the 30th of June.

If they did not, the Government intimated that it might not see its way to asking for League approval, and so issue of the Mandate would be blocked. But the Zionists knew that the Government was as anxious as themselves for the League to pass the document. They were so little perturbed that their Organization addressed a memorandum of its own to the League, demanding on its own authority the acceptance of the draft-Mandate by the Council.

> What the Zionists demand and have demanded from the outset is not a matter of toleration but a matter of right. To this is added, as a corollary the demand that the establishment in Palestine of the Jewish National Home should be recognized as an undertaking in which the Jewish people as a whole has a legitimate interest and an unquestionable status.

Thus a too brief quotation from this memorandum given by Mr. de Haas. The tiff between the Colonial Office and the Zionists ended in due season, but a good deal of correspondence between the British and the United States Governments, and between the French and the Italian Governments touching rights in the French area of Syria, dragged through the year. A special convention had to be drawn up between Great Britain and the United States to enshrine their Palestine arrangements. In October Lord Curzon begged that this convention should contain a "specific allusion to the National Home Policy."

The Americans later in the month said it was better to leave conclusion of the Anglo-American Convention till the end of the Lausanne Conference should have brought at long last the Turkish Treaty. This, as we have seen, was signed on the 24th of July, 1923. The French and Italians reached an agreement upon the matters in dispute between them just over a month later, and the Mandate came into force, though the Anglo-American Convention was not signed till the 3rd of December, 1924, and ratified exactly a year later.

The following is the text of the Palestine Mandate thus, rightly or wrongly, brought into being by the Council Resolution of the 29th of September, 1923:

The Council of the League of Nations

> Whereas the Principal Allied Powers have agreed, for the purpose of giving effect to the provisions of Article 22 of the Covenant of the League of Nations, to entrust to a Mandatory selected by the said Powers, the administration of the territory of Palestine, which formerly belonged to the Turkish Empire, within such boundaries as may be fixed by them; and
>
> Whereas the Principal Allied Powers have also agreed that the Mandatory should be responsible for putting into effect the declaration originally made on November 2nd, 1917, by the Government of His Britannic Majesty, and adopted by the said Powers, in favour of the

establishment in Palestine of a national home for the Jewish people, it being clearly understood that nothing should be done which might prejudice the civil and religious rights of existing non-Jewish communities in Palestine, or the rights and political status enjoyed by Jews in any other country; and

Whereas recognition has thereby been given to the historical connection of the Jewish people with Palestine and to the grounds for reconstituting their national home in that country; and

Whereas the Principal Allied Powers have selected His Britannic Majesty as the Mandatory for Palestine; and

Whereas the mandate in respect of Palestine has been formulated in the following terms and submitted to the Council of the League for approval; and

Whereas His Britannic Majesty has accepted the mandate in respect of Palestine and undertaken to exercise it on behalf of the League of Nations in conformity with the following provisions; and

Whereas by the aforementioned Article 22 (paragraph 8) it is provided that the degree of authority, control or administration to be exercised by the Mandatory, not having been previously agreed upon by the Members of the League, shall be explicitly defined by the Council of the League of Nations;

Confirming the said mandate, defines its terms as follows:

Article 1

The Mandatory shall have full powers of legislation and of administration, save as they may be limited by the terms of this mandate.

Article 2

The Mandatory shall be responsible for placing the country under such political, administrative and economic conditions as will secure the establishment of the Jewish national home, as laid down in the preamble, and the development of self-governing institutions, and also for safeguarding the civil and religious rights of all the inhabitants of Palestine, irrespective of race and religion.

Article 3

The Mandatory shall, so far as circumstances permit, encourage local autonomy.

Article 4

An appropriate Jewish agency shall be recognized as a public body for the purpose of advising and co-operating with the Administration of Palestine in such economic, social and other matters as may affect the establishment of the Jewish national home and the interests of the Jewish population in Palestine, and, subject always to the control of the Administration, to assist and take part in the development of the country.

The Zionist organization, so long as its organization and constitution are in the opinion of the Mandatory appropriate, shall be recognized as such agency. It shall take steps in consultation with His Britannic Majesty's Government to secure the co-operation of all Jews who are willing to assist in the establishment of the Jewish national home.

Article 5

The Mandatory shall be responsible for seeing that no Palestine territory shall be ceded or leased to, or in any way placed under the control of, the Government of any foreign Power.

Article 6

The Administration of Palestine, while ensuring that the rights and position of other sections of the population are not prejudiced, shall facilitate Jewish immigration under suitable conditions and shall encourage, in co-operation with the Jewish agency referred to in Article 4, close settlement by Jews on the land, including State lands and waste lands not required for public purposes.

Article 7

The Administration of Palestine shall be responsible for enacting a nationality law. There shall be included in this law provisions framed so as to facilitate the acquisition of Palestinian citizenship by Jews who take up their permanent residence in Palestine.

Article 8

The privileges and immunities of foreigners, including the benefits of consular jurisdiction and protection as formerly enjoyed by Capitulation or usage in the Ottoman Empire, shall not be applicable in Palestine.

Unless the Powers whose nationals enjoyed the aforementioned privileges and immunities on August 1st, 1914, shall have previously renounced the right to their re-establishment, or shall have agreed to their nonapplication for a specified period, these privileges and immunities shall, at the expiration of the Mandate, be immediately re-established in their entirety or with such modifications as may have been agreed upon between the Powers concerned.

Article 9

The Mandatory shall be responsible for seeing that the judicial system established in Palestine shall assure to foreigners, as well as to natives, a complete guarantee of their rights.

Respect for the personal status of the various peoples and communities and for their religious interests shall be fully guaranteed. In particular, the control and administration of Wakfs shall be exercised in accordance with religious law and the dispositions of the founders.

Article 10

Pending the making of special extradition agreements relating to

Palestine, the extradition treaties in force between the Mandatory and other foreign Powers shall apply to Palestine.

Article 11

The Administration of Palestine shall take all necessary measures to safeguard the interests of the community in connection with the development of the country, and, subject to any international obligations accepted by the Mandatory, shall have full power to provide for public ownership or control of any of the natural resources of the country or of the public works, services and utilities established or to be established therein. It shall introduce a land system appropriate to the needs of the country, having regard, among other things, to the desirability of promoting the close settlement and intensive cultivation of the land.

The Administration may arrange with the Jewish agency mentioned in Article 4 to construct or operate, upon fair and equitable terms, any public works, services and utilities, and to develop any of the natural resources of the country, in so far as these matters are not directly undertaken by the Administration. Any such arrangements shall provide that no profits distributed by such agency, directly or indirectly, shall exceed a reasonable rate of interest on the capital, and any further profits shall be utilized by it for the benefit of the country in a manner approved by the Administration.

Article 12

The Mandatory shall be entrusted with the control of the foreign relations of Palestine and the right to issue exequaturs to consuls appointed by foreign Powers. He shall also be entitled to afford diplomatic and consular protection to citizens of Palestine when outside its territorial limits.

Article 13

All responsibility in connection with the Holy Places and religious buildings or sites in Palestine, including that of preserving existing rights and of securing free access to the Holy Places, religious buildings and sites and the free exercise of worship, while ensuring the requirements of public order and decorum, is assumed by the Mandatory, who shall be responsible solely to the League of Nations in all matters concerned herewith, provided that nothing in this article shall prevent the Mandatory from entering into such arrangements as he may deem reasonable with the Administration for the purpose of carrying the provisions of this article into effect: and provided also that nothing in this Mandate shall be construed as conferring upon the Mandatory authority to interfere with the fabric or the management of purely Moslem sacred shrines, the immunities of which are guaranteed.

Article 14

A special Commission shall be appointed by the Mandatory to study, define and determine the rights and claims in connection with the Holy Places and the rights and claims relating to the different religious communities in Palestine. The method of nomination, the composition and the functions of this Commission shall be submitted to the Council of the League for its approval, and the Commission shall not be appointed or enter upon its functions without the approval of the Council.

Article 15

The Mandatory shall see that complete freedom of conscience and the free exercise of all forms of worship, subject only to the maintenance of public order and morals, are ensured to all. No discrimination of any kind shall be made between the inhabitants of Palestine on the ground of race, religion or language. No person shall be excluded from Palestine on the sole ground of his religious belief.

The right of each community to maintain its own schools for the education of its own members in its own language, while conforming to such educational requirements of a general nature as the Administration may impose, shall not be denied or impaired.

Article 16

The Mandatory shall be responsible for exercising such supervision over religious or eleemosynary bodies of all faiths in Palestine as may be required for the maintenance of public order and good government. Subject to such supervision, no measures shall be taken in Palestine to obstruct or interfere with the enterprise of such bodies or to discriminate against any representative or member of them on the ground of his religion or nationality.

Article 17

The Administration of Palestine may organize on a voluntary basis the forces necessary for the preservation of peace and order, and also for the defence of the country, subject, however, to the supervision of the Mandatory, but shall not use them for purposes other than those above specified save with the consent of the Mandatory. Except for such purposes, no military, naval or air forces shall be raised or maintained by the Administration of Palestine.

Nothing in this article shall preclude the Administration of Palestine from contributing to the cost of the maintenance of the forces of the Mandatory in Palestine.

The Mandatory shall be entitled at all times to use the roads, railways and ports of Palestine for the movement of armed forces and the carriage of fuel and supplies.

Article 18

The Mandatory shall see that there is no discrimination in Palestine against the nationals of any State Member of the League of Nations (including companies incorporated under its laws) as compared with those of the Mandatory of any foreign State in matters concerning taxation, commerce or navigation, the exercise of industries or professions, or in the treatment of merchant vessels or civil aircraft. Similarly, there shall be no discrimination in Palestine against goods originating in or destined for any of the said States, and there shall be freedom of transit under equitable conditions across the mandated area.

Subject as aforesaid and to the other provisions of this mandate, the Administration of Palestine may, on the advice of the Mandatory, impose such taxes and Customs duties as it may consider necessary, and take such steps as it may think best to promote the development of the natural resources of the country and to safeguard the interests of the population. It may also, on the advice of the Mandatory, conclude a special Customs agreement with any State the territory of which in 1914 was wholly included in Asiatic Turkey or Arabia.

Article 19

The Mandatory shall adhere on behalf of the Administration of Palestine to any general international conventions already existing, or which may be concluded hereafter with the approval of the League of Nations, respecting the slave traffic, the traffic in arms and ammunition, or the traffic in drugs, or relating to commercial quality, freedom of transit and navigation, aerial navigation and postal, telegraphic and wireless communication or literary, artistic or industrial property.

[Article 20 deals with co-operation with League measures for the prevention of disease, and Article 21 with the protection of antiquities, which was to proceed "by encouragement rather than by threat."]

Article 22

English, Arabic and Hebrew shall be the official languages of Palestine. Any statement or inscription in Arabic on stamps or money in Palestine shall be repeated in Hebrew and any statement or inscription in Hebrew shall be repeated in Arabic.

Article 23

The Administration of Palestine shall recognize the holy days of the respective communities in Palestine as legal days of rest for the members of such communities.

Article 24

The Mandatory shall make to the Council of the League of Nations an annual report to the satisfaction of the Council as to the measures taken during the year to carry out the provisions of the Mandate. Copies of all laws and regulations promulgated or issued during the year shall be communicated with the report.

Article 25

In the territories lying between the Jordan and the eastern boundary of Palestine as ultimately determined, the Mandatory shall be entitled, with the consent of the Council of the League of Nations, to postpone or to withhold application of such provisions of this Mandate as he may consider inapplicable to the existing local conditions, and to make such provision for the administration of the territories as he may consider suitable to those conditions, provided that no action shall be taken which is inconsistent with the provisions of Articles 15, 16 and 18.

Article 26

The Mandatory agrees that if any dispute whatever should arise between the Mandatory and another Member of the League of Nations relating to the interpretation or the application of the provisions of the Mandate, such dispute, if it cannot be settled by negotiation, shall be submitted to the Permanent Court of International Justice provided for by Article 14 of the Covenant of the League of Nations.

Article 27

The consent of the Council of the League of Nations is required for any modification of the terms of this Mandate.

Article 28

In the event of the termination of the Mandate hereby conferred upon the Mandatory, the Council of the League of Nations shall make such arrangements as may be deemed necessary for safeguarding in perpetuity, under guarantee of the League, the rights secured in Articles 13 and 14 and shall use its influence for securing, under the guarantee of the League, that the Government of Palestine will fully honour the financial obligations legitimately incurred by the Administration of Palestine during the period of the Mandate, including the rights of public servants to pensions or gratuities.

The present instrument shall be deposited in original in the archives of the League of Nations and certified copies shall be forwarded by the Secretary-General of the League of Nations to all Members of the League. Done at London the twenty-fourth day of July, one thousand nine hundred and twenty-two.

Such, then, is the Mandate for Palestine, with which one British Government after another has had such a medley of relations, now grasping it and now consenting to receive it, now its author and now its executant, now enslaved to it and now interpreting it, but in every relation and in every mood "feeding it with soft dedication all day long."

With its complete text before me, I am reminded of a story of boyhood which, though at first sight it may appear irrelevant, is really most germane to the analysis of that text. The story is of a school where at dead of night there was an illicit gathering of boys who should have been in their beds.

By accident their headmaster dropped upon them, just as a young ringleader whispered, peering through the dark, "I think we're all here now." "Yes," said the headmaster, as he turned the lights up, "and since we're all here now, let's see who we are."

In this spirit, since all the Articles of the Mandate are here now, exposed to the light, let us see who they are, and whence they came. The reader indeed knows by now whence they came, and must forgive an occasional repetition, made to press the matter home. It is not till the Mandate is taken item by item, that its origin can be as nakedly exposed as is necessary.

Here, then, are the chief Articles, either their whole or their essential parts, printed in parallel columns with the original Zionist texts of which, it will be seen, the Mandate Articles are never anything but a slightly varied resetting, and are often an unruffled reproduction. In general I confine myself to the mere identification and confrontation of the texts, leaving comment to follow upon this. The Mandate text is given, followed by the Zionist original, its source in brackets.

Preamble

[For the preamble there is no need, however, to use this method, since the way in which it was compiled has already been made especially clear. Paragraph 2 of the Preamble repeats the Balfour Declaration, itself largely composed by Zionists, both European and American. The kernel of this Declaration, it has been seen, is to be found in a "Joint Manifesto" of a number of American Zionist societies, dated the 2nd of February, 1916. Paragraph 3 contains the "historical connection" phrase on which the Zionist Organization set such store.]

Article 2

Mandate Text:

The Mandatory shall be responsible for placing the country under such political, administrative, and economic conditions as will secure the establishment of the Jewish national home ... and the development of self-governing institutions, and also for safeguarding the civil and religious rights of all the inhabitants of Palestine...

Zionist Text:

Palestine shall be placed under such political, administrative and economic conditions as will secure the establishment there of the Jewish National Home, and ultimately render possible the creation of an autonomous Commonwealth, it being clearly understood ... etc. as in the Balfour Declaration.

(Paragraph 5, Sub-section I of the Zionist Statement of Views to the Peace Conference, 3rd February, 1919. For convenience this will be abbreviated to Z.S.P.C. henceforth.)

Article 3

Mandate Text:

The Mandatory shall, so far as circumstances permit, encourage local autonomy. (Final text.)

The Mandatory shall encourage the whole measure of self-government for localities consistent with the prevailing conditions. (1920 Draft.)

Zionist Text:

The Mandatory shall encourage the widest measure of self-government for localities practicable in the conditions of the country.

(Z.S.P.C. Paragraph 5, Subsection III.)

Article 4:

Mandate Text

An appropriate Jewish agency shall be recognized as a public body for the purpose of advising and co-operating with the Administration of Palestine in such … matters as may affect the Jewish national home and the interests of the Jewish population in Palestine…

Zionist Text:

The Jewish Council shall be recognized as a legal entity and shall have power to co-operate and consult with and to assist the Government of Palestine in any and all matters affecting the Jewish people in Palestine.

(Z.S.P.C. "Proposals for the Jewish Council for Palestine.")

Article 6

Mandate Text:

The Administration of Palestine, while ensuring that the rights and position of other sections of the population are not prejudiced, shall facilitate Jewish immigration … and shall encourage close settlement by Jews on the land…

Zionist Text:

The Mandatory Power shall, inter alia, promote Jewish immigration and close settlement on the land, the established rights of the present non-Jewish population being equitably safeguarded.

(Z.S.P.C. Paragraph 5, Subsection IIa.)

Article 7

The story of the source of Article 7 is best taken from the Zionist Organization Report:

> The clause facilitating the acquisition of Palestinian nationality in this draft (December 1919) is noteworthy for the fact that at this time it was proposed to make the acquisition of Palestinian nationality compulsory upon all Jews who became permanently resident in Palestine, and that penalties were contemplated upon such Jews as were unwilling to comply with this provision without adequate reason. This clause was modified in consequence of our objections, and later withdrawn in favour of a more general wording, the details to be settled when the Government of Palestine proceeded to draft its Law of Nationality.

How the Nationality Laws of the Government of Palestine themselves were to be "modified" in consequence of more objections from the same source the reader has seen.

Article 11

Mandate Text:

The Administration of Palestine shall… have full power to provide for public ownership or control of any of the natural resources of the country or of the public works, services and utilities established or to be established therein.

Zionist Text:

Provision to be made for public ownership or effective public control of the land and natural resources of Palestine and of public utilities, with a view to prevention of exploitation for excessive profits.

(No. 3 of a group of nine "alterations in and additions to the July 1919 draft" suggested by members of the "Inner Actions Committee" and other leading Zionists.)

The Zionist demand for public ownership or control of the land and natural resources of Palestine was not conceded in 1919 but the Zionist drafters insisted, and it was accepted as in Article 11 above.

Mandate Text:

It shall introduce a land system appropriate to the needs of the country, having regard, among other things, to the desirability of promoting the close settlement and intensive cultivation of the land.

Zionist Text:

The Mandatory Power shall appoint a Commission with power… to propose measures for the taxation and the tenure of land and in general any progressive measures in harmony with the policy of making the land available for close settlement and intensive cultivation.

(Z.S.P.C. Proposals for a Land Commission (e). Throughout these Proposals which range from (a) to (g) the phrase transferred to the Mandate "close settlement and intensive cultivation" recurs.)

Mandate Text:

The Administration may arrange with the Jewish Agency mentioned in Article 4 to construct or operate… any public works … in so far as these matters are not undertaken by the Administration. Any such arrangement shall provide that no profits … shall exceed a reasonable rate of interest… and any further profits shall be utilized for the benefit of the country…

Zionist Text:

The draft of 1919 concedes all the demands in regard to the Jewish Agency…. It gives a preferential right to the Agency in public works etc., provided the rate of interest is limited and excess profits are utilized for the benefit of the country as a whole.

(Z.O. Report to Xllth Zionist Congress, p. 29, detailing Zionist items in the 1919 draft. For this Article the 1919 terms were maintained in the 1920, 1921 and final drafts.)

Article 15

Mandate Text:

No discrimination of any kind shall be made between the inhabitants of Palestine on the ground of race, religion or language.

Zionist Text:

There shall be no discrimination among the inhabitants with regard to citizenship and civil rights on the grounds of religion or of race.

(Z.S.P.C., Paragraph 5, Subsection IV.)

Article 22

Mandate text:

English, Arabic and Hebrew shall be the official languages of Palestine. Any statement or inscription in Arabic on stamps or money in Palestine shall be repeated in Hebrew and any statement in Hebrew shall be repeated in Arabic.

Zionist Text:

Hebrew shall be one of the official languages of Palestine and shall be employed in all documents, decrees and announcements, and on all stamps, coins and notes issued by the Government.

(Z.S.P.C., "Proposals to the Mandatory Power," Paragraph 5.)

Article 23

Mandate Text:

The Administration of Palestine shall recognize the holy days of the respective communities in Palestine as legal days of rest for the members of such communities.

Zionist Text:

The Jewish Sabbath and Holy Days shall be recognized as legal days of rest.

(Z.S.P.C., "Proposals to the Mandatory Power," Paragraph 6. The two Articles, it should be noted, follow in order the two Z.S.P.C. paragraphs.)

That completes the confrontation of texts, but something remains to be said concerning the particular Articles which figure in it. With the Preamble, they make ten of the twenty-nine sections of the Mandate. It should be realized that these ten sections, in the question between Arabs and Zionists and ourselves in Palestine, are the sections which matter. Of the remaining nineteen (as the reader can verify) half deal with formal, non-political, and religious affairs, with the affairs of foreigners living in the Mandated area, with such matters as consular representation, adherence to international health conventions, rights of access to the Holy Places, antiquities and so forth.

Four Articles, 8, 9,18 and 28 were mostly drafted to meet the American objections concerning the situation of United States subjects in various conjunctures, and Article 25 served to exclude Transjordan from the Palestine orbit.

This leaves five Articles, 1, 5,24,26 and 27. So out of the entire Mandate there are only these five Articles really affecting in any way the political position of Palestine which are not perceived at first sight to have been compiled by the Zionists or adapted from Zionist texts, though this does not exclude that they may have been so compiled or adopted. Furthermore, of these five articles all but Article 1 treat of what did not occupy the Zionists much, the external relations of the country. They were content probably to leave these Articles to be written by the Mandatory whose credentials and policy, within Palestine, they had drawn up.

Article 24, 26 and 27 covered the relations of their Mandatory with the League of Nations. These relations were such as they desired, and the Articles enshrining them they had read in draft and found satisfactory. The phrasing of these Articles too they could leave to the Government, which indeed, in so far as the Zionists had expressed opinions upon the point, had only departed from their opinion in one instance.

In its Statement to the Peace Conference the Zionist Organization had petitioned for sovereign possession of Palestine to be vested in the League of Nations, prior to the creation of "an autonomous Commonwealth." This request met with no response. No doubt it appeared injudicious to the Government that the League of Nations should start an era of moral suasion by annexing a country outright, and also of course such an annexation would have made a sovereign Power of the League itself. Nor was ownership of Palestine by the League as sure a preliminary to the "autonomous Commonwealth" as were the Government's own arrangements to that end. It also might have interfered with those military plans which the Government liked to keep covert.

As for Article 1 it also served Zionist aims, since it only restricted the powers of the Mandatory by "restrictions" which he and the Zionists had agreed upon together. Article 1 is indeed merely an enabling clause for the benefit of the subsequent Zionist-drafted Articles.

These latter and the equally Zionist Preamble controlled everything in Palestine. The Preamble contained the authorization and the title-deeds of the Mandatory. The nine Zionist Articles governed immigration, the establishment of the National Home, the installation of the Jewish Agency as a public body, local government, the land system, the laws of citizenship, the use of natural resources, the programme of education and the official mediums of speech. The political structure, the development, the whole of Palestine's national life was under their sway.

No other party of drafters interfered with the hegemony thus instituted. The Americans did not in the alterations made by them or at their request, and these are the only changes in the later drafts of any consequence, except for one. This, though it is a very notable change, cannot be traced to any particular source upon the available evidence. The Americans of course may have been responsible for it, but they do not mention it. The original "Balfour" draft of 1920 declared, in Article 10, that "the extradition treaties in force between the Mandatory and foreign Powers shall apply to Palestine." In the next, the 1921, draft this was altered to "the extradition treaties between the Mandatory and other foreign Powers shall apply to Palestine," and these terms were maintained in the final version. There is no clue to how this change came to be made, but it is important since it defines the situation of Great Britain in Palestine as that of a foreign Power, and there will be occasion to recur to it. It is probable that the Zionists did not trouble about it at the time: it seemed destined to be of no moment. But the course of events may give it consequence.

It is not however germane to the immediate issue which is, to resume, that the Mandate for Palestine in all its effective parts was composed by the Zionists or adapted from their texts. They themselves, with more caution than usual, state that their primary drafts, by Messrs. Frankfurter and Gans, "were handed to the British Delegation and were largely embodied in the first tentative draft of July 15th, 1919." But from the evidence laid before the reader it is clear that this statement is one after the manner of the Peel Commissioners, and that the Zionist drafts were more than "embodied" in the first official draft. The official draft was an embodiment of them.

The Frankfurter-Gans manuscripts were the basis of the Mandate, which the governmental drafters merely emended here and there and toned down as circumstances demanded. When circumstances were not so pressing, the Frankfurter-Gans version was emended back again, and at intervals was reinforced by revised versions of Preamble or Articles from the pens of the members of the Zionist Organization's specially appointed "Mandates Sub-Committee." The mere appointment of a committee for Mandate-drafting was a piece of effrontery on the part of the Zionist Organization, but in practice was proof manifest of the favourite's licence given to that body by the Government.

Such being the origin of the Mandate it is not strange that it was a document which broke every law and principle which it was supposed to safeguard. But though the Zionists had drafted it a hundred times over, it is not upon them that the supreme censure for this must fall. They were drugged by a delusion, and they were pretty frank about what they were doing. It is the Government of the day, the Government of Mr. Lloyd George which, to say nothing of its betrayal of national pledges, must bear once more the responsibility for deliberate violation in Palestine, through the imposition of such a Mandate, of the Covenant of the League which elsewhere it professed so glibly.

The Government's true duties under the Covenant, despite the game played with the text of the Mandate Article, were unmistakable. As Mandatory it was under bond to establish Palestine as an independent nation, not ultimately nor in the long run nor some time, but provisionally at once. The Covenant was explicit upon this. "Certain communities," it said, "formerly belonging to the Turkish Empire have reached a stage of development where their existence as independent nations can be provisionally recognized subject to the rendering of administrative advice and assistance by a Mandatory, until such time as they are able to stand alone." The tense of the word "reached" is to be noted. Not "will reach" nor "may reach," but "have reached." Palestine had reached the required stage of development—the Covenant acknowledged it.

The Covenant was explicit too about the role of the Mandatory. The latter was to give nothing but administrative advice and assistance "until such time as they [the said communities or independent nations] are able to stand alone."

But the Mandatory could not give administrative advice and assistance unless there were administrations, formed by the nations indicated, to which the two gifts could be proffered. Advice and assistance cannot be given to an Administration which is not there. Under this obligation alone, therefore, the creation in Palestine of a national government was predicated and presumed by the Covenant.

The obligation, however, was resolutely evaded by the Lloyd George Government, unless indeed the Prime Minister suggested that his Administration was carrying out the Covenant by giving advice and assistance to itself, in the form of Sir Herbert Samuel and some Civil Service officials. But that perhaps would have been too preposterous even for 10 Downing Street to sustain to 11 Downing Street in those years of grace.

Nor could the Cabinet wriggle out of its Covenant obligations by saying that there had to be a space of time while Palestine was learning to stand alone, and that the regime established in Jerusalem was part of the preparation for independence. The Covenant did foresee a preparatory or interim period during which Palestine would be engaged in learning the technique of government, but it also laid down unmistakably that during this period the Mandatory was only to offer assistance and advice.

No such thing as preparatory or interim government by the Mandatory was conceived. Even were the thesis of successive British Governments accepted, that during the last sixteen years the people of Palestine has remained unripe for independence, even accepting this assumption, then during these sixteen years the duty of the Mandatory under the Covenant has been merely to continue tendering them assistance and advice. No unpreparedness nor unripeness of the Arabs has justified or could justify the foundation of government by the Mandatory, with full powers of administration.

The action of the League Council in condoning this infringement of the Covenant by the Mandatory altered nothing. The Council's action was of no consequence, in the sense that it had no legitimizing value. The Council was not above the League. It was only (after a fashion) the custodian of its statutes. If it permitted the statutes of which it had the custody to be broken, all the Council did was to commit moral suicide.

This was bad for the Council, but did not affect the Covenant. When the guardians of the law assist in its violation, it is not the law which is abrogated, but the number of the culprits and the extent of the guilt which are increased.

So whether the servile Council of 1922 approved or not of any or of all the false Mandate Articles does not alter a whit the character of that Mandate's terms, which violate the Covenant. The laws of the Covenant not merely never conceived government by the Mandatory in Palestine, but precluded it. The paragraph of Article 22 of the Covenant next in order to that recently quoted is irrefutable upon this point. The "ex-Turkish" paragraph having laid down that the Mandatory shall give administrative assistance and advice to the ex-Turkish peoples, this succeeding paragraph begins:

> "Other peoples, especially those of Central Africa, are at such a stage that the Mandatory must be responsible for the administration of the territory."

These "other peoples" were the B mandate peoples, and in the next paragraph the same principle was applied to the C mandate peoples.

That is to say, the Covenant laid down that any other Mandated peoples except the ex-Turkish, any other Mandated peoples except those under A mandates, any other Mandated peoples except those of Palestine and "Syria" and Mesopotamia, were to be placed under the administration of their Mandatory. These other peoples were to be ruled by their Mandatory. Palestine, "Syria" and Mesopotamia were not. The combined equivocations of Mr. Lloyd George, General Smuts and the Zionist Organization cannot alter or disguise that.

But instead of being faithful to the Covenant and securing a Mandate in agreement with it, the Government of Mr. Lloyd George took various Zionist pronouncements and the Zionist-inspired and Zionist co-drafted Balfour Declaration, and out of them, with the connivance of the unworthy Council of the League of Nations, forged a false Mandate.

The government and the organization of all Palestine were made to subserve the erection and the sustenance of the National Home, an institution which had no place in the Covenant and was in flagrant opposition with the Covenant from which alone the Mandate honourably and legally could proceed. Under the terms of Article 2 the land and the resources of Palestine were used by the Mandatory for a Zionist speculation instead of being kept in trust for its lawful owners, the native population of the country. That was fraudulent trusteeship at its worst. But it is unusual for the trustee and his associates in this particular type of venture to put their arrangements upon paper as in this case they had done in Article 2. One result of this was that a dispute arose between some of the parties when these arrangements came to be worked out.

Chapter 33

The stage-fight between Government and Zionists.
The theory of two primary "obligations."
The Council of the League plays traitor.
The responsibility of the League in the Palestine affair.

The dispute which arose eventually between the Government and the Zionists sprang from the wording of Article 2, from the clause:

> "The Mandatory shall be responsible for placing the country under such political, administrative and economic conditions as will secure the establishment of the Jewish national home... and the development of self-governing institutions."

This was one of the clauses of Zionist origin. Till mid-1920 the Government had adopted the Zionist original version, by which the National Home was to have been developed into a "self-governing Commonwealth." Later the Article (Article 3 in that draft) was altered by changing "self-governing Commonwealth" to "self-governing institutions," which became the prospect of Palestine at large rather than of the National Home.

The Zionists found this altogether unpleasing and reacted as has been described in Chapter 31. The events therein mentioned followed, and the Mandate was published containing Article 2 as above.

The difference of opinion between the drafting bodies did not correspond to anything real in the working out of the Mandate. The Zionists chafed at the concession to the Arabs apparently involved in the promise of development of self-governing institutions. But since nothing was ever done to develop self-governing institutions, but only proposals made for Councils which were not to be allowed to trench upon the realm of self-government, the Zionists might have spared their tempers.

The sequence of events will now take us out of the chronological order, from the immediate morrow of the Mandate to seven years later. This leap is necessary because it was not till 1930, when Mr. Ramsay MacDonald's Labour Cabinet was in power, that the dispute between Zionists and the British Government upon Article 2 came to a head.

It was an empty dispute, a stage-conflict, though a few of the contestants fought in the dark and thought it was genuine. The Government of Mr. Ramsay MacDonald, like its predecessors, had at bottom the same outlook as the Zionists had. It too intended to establish the National Home and to make of it the basis of every administrative, social or economic ordinance or act in Palestine. But it did not feel like saying this openly, very much because it suffered singularly from self-delusion, and imagined that it could couple this programme with the fair treatment of the Arabs.

Such an attitude of mind, of course, could only be preserved by the Government's never examining below the surface of its deeds. But it avoided the examination in question, and perhaps in order to preserve its own self-esteem, it entered upon this stage-conflict with the Zionists. The Zionists engaged in it maintained that by Article 2 the primary obligation of the Mandatory was to establish the National Home, and that any other obligations which might appear in the Mandate, that is the obligation to promote self-governing institutions, were subsidiary.

What did the Government retort to this? It declared—despite the meaning of words—that in Palestine it had, not one, but two primary obligations, the development of the National Home and the development of self-governing institutions. The pair were incompatible, of course, but never mind: they held together as long as the Government carried out the first and did not carry out the second, which was the Governmental way of carrying out both.

Sometimes the second "primary obligation" was declared to be the safeguarding of our old friend the "civil and religious rights" of the Arabs.

But in whichever fashion this second "primary obligation" was framed, the Government now affirmed that it was co-equal, co-existent, collateral, concurrent, confederated or what you will with the first "primary obligation" to establish the National Home.

Some of the Zionist leaders, who were men of insight, can hardly have been disturbed by this affirmation. As the promise with which it dealt had not been and never would be carried out, what did the affirmation of it matter? But many Zionists, particularly those of the United States, who were always slow to seize the simplest of subtleties, cried out that they had been betrayed. They believed this.

Though the Government of the time would never have admitted this to itself, nothing could have suited it better. Zionist cries of betrayal coming from the wings lent verisimilitude to the stage-management.

It is necessary to give an outline of this supposed difference of opinion, because it has been exploited sedulously on the Governmental side, not alone by the Labour Government, but by all the Coalition Governments which have succeeded.

A typical Governmental statement may be given, to begin with, in this case the product of the Labour Cabinet of 1930, part of a speech in the House of Commons of Mr. Ramsay MacDonald.

> His Majesty's Government [said he] will continue to administer Palestine in accordance with the terms of the Mandate as approved by the Council of the League of Nations. That is an international obligation from which there can be no question of receding.

He then cited the terms of the Balfour Declaration, as coming under the obligation, and went on:

> "A double undertaking is involved, to the Jewish people on the one hand, and to the non-Jewish population of Palestine on the other; and it is the firm resolve of His Majesty's Government to give effect, in equal measure, to both parts of the declaration, and to do equal justice to all sections of the population in Palestine. That is a duty from which they will not shrink, and to the discharge of which they will apply all the resources at their command."

In a later White Paper issued by the same Cabinet it was stated that:

> Attempts have been made to argue in support of Zionist claims that the principal feature of the Mandate is the passage regarding the Jewish National Home and that the passages destined to safeguard the rights of the non-Jewish community [sic] are merely secondary considerations qualifying to some extent what is claimed to be the primary object for which the Mandate has been framed.
>
> This is a conception which His Majesty's Government has always regarded as erroneous... His Majesty's Government will not be moved by any pressure or threats from the path laid down in the Mandate.

These phrases lie uneasily upon the stomach, but will the reader bear with them for information's sake. They were repeated in Geneva, where the farce of Government disinterestedness was played to an applauding house. There between Government and Council the last trace of anything genuine vanished. Those Zionists who demanded their interpretation of what after all was their Mandate at least had given a display of honest aggression. But at Geneva the Council, and particularly the Mandates Commission of the Council, surpassed the Government in mincing pretence.

What generally went on in Geneva in the late 'twenties and early 'thirties, and has gone on ever since, was a factitious searching of consciences in public. The Government (whichever it happened to be), possibly when presenting its annual report, would say that it viewed "its mission" in Palestine in such and such a fashion. Did the Mandates Commission, it would ask, feel that this point of view conformed with the obligations laid upon the Government as Mandatory by the League? The Mandates Commission would anxiously ponder the point and, after a paper-deep criticism or so, would propound that the Mandatory was carrying out his obligations most satisfactorily.

Proceedings always ended in exchanges of compliments, after a preliminary exhibition of virtue fearful of itself, during which Government spokesmen and members of the Mandates Commission:

> … like mountebanks did wound
> And stab themselves with doubts profound.

The principal outpouring of the Mandatory conscience on these lines took place at an Extraordinary Session of the Mandates Commission in June of 1930, when a Report of the Commission to the Council upon the Palestine Mandate was presented, and official "Comments of the Mandatory Power" were registered. Dr. Drummond Shiels, then Undersecretary of State for the Colonies, went to Geneva to represent the Government. The session sprang from another outbreak of violence in Palestine, which had begun with a dispute upon rights at the Wailing Wall of Jerusalem. Dr. Shiels portrayed the Government's motives in the accepted way, with a minor personal variation:

> "Our task in Palestine as laid upon us by the Mandate is, as is well known, a twofold one. We are committed not only to the establishment in Palestine of a National Home for the Jewish people but also, to the preservation of the civil and religious rights of the non-Jewish communities in the country. It is sometimes said that the two parts of this obligation are irreconcilable. We believe that they can be reconciled and must be reconciled. We believe that the National Home can be established without detriment to non-Jewish interests, and indeed that it can and will confer lasting benefits upon the country, in which all sections of the population will share."

After having completed his depositions before the Commission Mr. Shiels concluded as follows:

> "The British Government would welcome the frank opinion of the Commission on the questions which are before it. I should not like to think that any considerations of delicacy or of the difficulties with which we have to contend should cause any reservation in the expression of the views of the members of the Mandates Commission. We feel confident in the motive and the spirit with which we have tried to carry out our task

and in the substantial measure of our achievement, and we do not fear the impartial verdict of the members of the Mandates Commission."

There was indeed not the least fear of the impartial verdict of the members of the Mandates Commission. Their summing-up deserves to be pilloried:

Two assertions [of the British Government] emerge which should be emphasized:

1. That the obligations laid down by the Mandate in regard to the two sections of the population are of equal weight.
2. That the two obligations imposed on the Mandatory are in no sense irreconcilable.

The Mandates Commission has no objection to raise to these two assertions, which in its view accurately express what it conceives to be the essence of the Mandate for Palestine and ensures its future. Commission is, however, of opinion that in the interest of the restoration of a peaceful atmosphere in Palestine, the time has come to define the legal foundations of the first of these assertions. In the Commission's view, interpretations of the Palestine Mandate have too often confused two quite separate matters, namely:

1. The objects of the Mandate.
2. The immediate obligations of the Mandate.

Considering only those clauses of the Mandate which form virtually the whole subject of the controversy, the objects of the Mandate are:

(a) The establishment of the Jewish National Home.
(b) The establishment of self-governing institutions.

The Mandate fixes no time-limit for the accomplishment of these objects, which is only common sense, because the event will depend on numerous circumstances over which the Mandatory has no control. Even the most energetic action and the employment of immense financial resources cannot alone achieve the establishment of the Jewish National Home, which is dependent upon economic factors; and no political guidance, however effective, can develop except in process of time that political maturity without which the winning of complete de jure independence is a complete illusion.

The immediate obligation of the Mandate is defined in the Mandate in the following terms:

1. Placing the country under such conditions as will secure the establishment of the Jewish National Home.
2. [Placing the country under such conditions as will secure] the development of self-governing institutions.

Between the two terms of this obligation the Mandate recognizes no

> primacy in order of importance and no priority in order of execution.
>
> It would be unfair to make it a complaint against the Mandatory that eight years after the entry into force of the Mandate, Palestine has not yet been granted a regime of self-government; and it would be equally unfair to reproach the Mandatory because the Jewish National Home has not yet reached its full development. Those are the objects of the Mandate, and it is not one of the Mandatory's obligations to bring them to immediate completion. *The Mandatory's immediate obligation is solely to create and maintain in Palestine general conditions favourable to the gradual accomplishment of the two objects of the Mandate.*

This pernicious rigmarole abounds in circumlocutions, presented on a platter, as it were, to the Government, with which to describe those items of its policy in Palestine which most tax description. "No political guidance, however effective, can develop except in process of time that political maturity without which the winning of complete de jure independence is a complete illusion," i.e., whatever the Government did to tip the scales, it would have to wait some years for that Zionist majority without which there was no thought of conferring independence on Palestine. However, the general falsity of the document is so glaring that it is not worth while analysing it at length. I have italicized, though, the last sentence.

Such utter flummery as this sentence deserves a meed of attention. In practice all obligations, good or bad, were removed by it from the Mandatory's shoulders and relegated to the Greek Kalends. The particular triumph of the Mandates Commission was to accomplish this without saying so. The method employed was that of splitting the atom. The Mandatory's obligations were split into an "immediate obligation," capable of remaining indefinitely in the foreground, and eventual obligations of a contingent kind, remaining as indefinitely in the background. So it did not matter what the latter were, for they never came to the front. As for the "immediate obligation" itself, the more one reads it over, as defined by the Mandates Commission, the more it merits derision.

It is lamentable to think what an opportunity was lost by the League in its earliest days, when, rightly considered, the arrival of the Palestine question before it was a true godsend. Through this question the League might have cleared itself of an imputation which has always lain heavily upon it, the imputation that it was the creature of its creators and in particular of Great Britain.

In those days of the early twenties, when it was trying to justify its name as a League of all Nations, its Secretariat might almost have prayed for Great Britain to engage in some misdeed, so that an opportunity might be given for the League to show its independence by castigating the illegalities of its too possessive patron. As it happened the opportunity came without prayer and came speedily. But it was never seized. The Council of the League of Nations had no thought of playing Thomas H. Becket to Mr. Lloyd George's Henry II.

It is true, of course, that, as the Prime Minister and his companions had contrived things, the Council was not permitted to draw up the terms of the Mandates. But the Council need never have approved those terms: it could have declared that the Mandate presented to it was not faithful to the Covenant.

It could have demanded, for example, from the British Government how it came to present a Mandate containing an "obligation" to establish the National Home, when Mr. Lloyd George and the other Allied Ministers had officially agreed that the administration of Mandates was to be in the spirit of the Anglo-French Proclamation of the 9th of November, 1918. This they had done (cf. Chapter 14) when instructing the International Commission of Inquiry in the spring of 1919. They even had quoted their Proclamation ("Far from wishing to impose any particular institutions on the populations of these regions, their [France's and Britain's] only care is to assure by their support and efficacious assistance the normal workings of the Governments which these populations freely shall have given themselves") and announced that it had been "formally presented to the President of the United States on behalf of the Governments of France and Great Britain."

If the League authorities, in this or in another fashion, had confronted its Mandatory and required from him an explanation for the character of Mandate he now ventured to present, their own lack of power would not have mattered. The very weakness which the P.A.P. had imposed upon the League would have been its strength. A courageous protest against what it had not the power to impede would have given to its action that species of spiritual authority which it has so long sought in vain.

Had the Council done its duty in 1922, or begun doing it in 1920 when Balfour laid the first draft of the counterfeit Mandate before it, the history of Europe might have been different. But the Council chose to be complaisant and to fawn upon Balfour, and when the great stresses arose it was the sycophant in Palestine which preached integrity in Manchuria and in Abyssinia.

During the years which followed, whenever the Arabs appealed to it the League glanced away. It even evolved a stereotyped procedure for glancing away. By a regulation of its own, petitions from the mandated populations to the League had to be forwarded by the Mandatory to the Mandates Commission. If the petitions were of a secondary character, if they were only complaints that the Mandatory had not kept the terms of the Mandate (as he and the Zionists had fixed them together) then the Commission made an investigation. The depth of these investigations may be gauged from some words of M. van Rees, Vice-President of the Commission, who in October 1924 said that the "Administration in Palestine had departed from the terms of the Mandate in administering the country" but went on equably to add that this was "for reasons which doubtless would be forthcoming." They never were forthcoming, of course.

On another occasion, four years later, M. Rappard, acting as rapporteur for the session of a Palestine Report and faced with the customary Arab protest, declared that the:

> "Mandate absolutely excluded parliamentary democratic government of Palestine by its inhabitants, because it conferred certain powers on the Mandatory, in regard of that territory, which were incompatible with the sovereignty of a free Government. If a free and democratic Government were installed, the powers of the Mandatory would disappear and there would be a breach of the terms of the Mandate."

This statement was a little too much even for the Mandates Commission, and M. Rappard was asked to withdraw from his findings a sentence enshrining this dictum of his, on the grounds that it "would be capable of different interpretations." The truth was that it was too plain.

However, the more important point is that when petitions to it were not of secondary, but of primary character, when they touched upon essentials and protested against the terms themselves of the Mandate, the Commission declared itself incompetent to consider such petitions. When the Report of the Commission containing this declaration of its incompetence was presented to the Council, the Council declared its approval of the Commission's resolution of incompetence, and the matter ended.

The procedure may be studied in the Reports of the Commission and of the Council, issued in July and December of 1924:

> The permanent Mandates Commission, having taken note of the "Report on the state of Palestine during the four years of Civil Administration, submitted to the Mandates Commission of the League of Nations through H.E. the High Commissioner for Palestine by the Executive Committee of the Palestine Arab Congress" transmitted by the British Government on October 24th, 1924:
>
> 1. Notes that it contains two kinds of complaints, which the Commission thinks it necessary to separate clearly from one another:
>
> (a) First the petitioners (the Executive Committee of the Palestine Arab Congress) allege a large number of facts which, if found to be accurate, should be regarded as administrative abuses; and
>
> (b) Secondly, the petitioners protest against the terms of the Mandate itself, as established by the Council of the League of Nations on July 24th, 1922.

> 2. With regard to the facts in the first category the Commission makes recommendations [which do not concern the issue].
>
> 3. As regards the protests of the petitioners against the terms of the Mandate itself, and more especially as regards the desire for the establishment in Palestine of a fundamentally different regime from that of the Mandate at present in force, the Commission, considering that its task is confined to supervising the execution of the Mandate in the terms prescribed by the Council, is of opinion that it is not competent to discuss the matter.

This Report was duly forwarded to the Council, which met and reported on the 10th of December as follows:

> The Council of the League of Nations, having taken cognizance of the report of the Permanent Mandates Commission …
>
> Expresses itself once again satisfied that the Mandated territories, the administration of which forms the subject of the report of the Permanent Mandates Commission, are in general administered in accordance with the spirit and letter of Article 22 of the Covenant and of the terms of the Mandates;
>
> Desires to repeat to the Permanent Mandates Commission its sincere thanks for the great competence and zeal which it has shown in the execution of its mission; and decides:
>
> (a) To forward the observations of the Commission to the Governments of the Mandatory Powers concerned…
>
> (b) To approve the conclusions of the Commission with regard to the petition of the Executive Committee of the Palestine Arab Congress, and to instruct the Secretary General to bring them to the knowledge of the Petitioner and of the Mandatory Power.

In this way, between the labyrinthine phrases of clause 3 of the Commission's Report, and of sub-section (b) of the Council's Report on the Commission's Report, the Arabs' appeal for justice was made to disappear unanswered, and unconsidered even. The Commission declared that it was incompetent to discuss the character of the Mandate, the Council approved of the Commission's incompetence, and that was the end of it. The conscience of the League was buried under captions, and nobody cared.

Thus was the "sacred trust of civilization" interpreted by its guardians. Thus were transactions which meant everything to Palestine carried out, according to Lord Balfour, "in the full glare of the noonday sun of public opinion." The Arabs, in fine, were not allowed to appeal upon anything fundamental: they were like innocent prisoners forbidden to appeal against their sentence, only permitted to complain if their treatment in prison transgressed regulations.

It is a sorry story, this share of the League in the Mandate conspiracy, and there is little relief to it. Since 1922 the personnel of the Council has undergone changes, of course, and members have spoken at times as though they were not altogether happy about Palestine, but there has been no revocation of the work of 1922 and of the years immediately ensuing. On one special occasion, when the abject M. Rappard made his pronouncement against free institutions, a single member of the Mandates Commission did utter a protest. He was a German, Herr Kastl, the first German appointed to the Mandates Commission. Europe has changed since then. Herr Kastl declared that in his opinion democratic government, far from being excluded, was enjoined under the Mandate in Palestine.

If there are no more official Germans speaking, as he did, of democratic rule as a right and a privilege, the Council of the League in the 'twenties, and its successors, have a full share of the responsibility for this. It is not realized in Britain how the democratic principle has been discredited by the way in which our own Governments, one after another, have cast it off in Palestine, and the League has connived at this.

Another Mandates Commission member, though, whose words deserve favourable record is Lord Lugard (then Sir Frederick Lugard), who in 1922, after listening to a statement upon the administration of Palestine made by Sir Herbert Samuel, observed that "the principle of government by the majority of the population and the policy of the scheme for a Jewish National Home are at present difficult to reconcile." Like Lord Wakehurst on another issue, Lord Lugard weakened his statement by qualifying it, with the words "at present." But the intimation was there.

In this matter the guilt of successive League Councils is of the type which cries out to heaven for vengeance, and indeed the League seems to have been visited with it. Whether the present Council will recognize facts, and seek to work out its salvation anew, if indefensible proposals for Palestine, under any form, come before it again, is a question it had best take very deep to its conscience.

There is a postscript to be added to the story of the scene staged at Geneva between the Council and the Mandatory. We have seen, some pages back, that the Zionists and their Whitehall accessories differed in that the Zionists desired the common inner intentions of the two parties to be exposed outwardly as the aims of policy in Palestine, while the Government did not want, if this could be helped, to make its intentions public. At Geneva therefore it kept quiet about them.

But sometimes it could not help disclosures elsewhere. There were some occasions upon which the Government was obliged to expose its intentions. In 1922 Mr. Churchill had been driven to expose them by the

Arab delegates in London.

Eight years later, in October of 1930, the MacDonald Government also was forced by the circumstances of the time into an official " Statement of Policy." "It is equally useless," ran its operative passage, "for Arab leaders to maintain their demands for a form of Constitution which would render it impossible for His Majesty's Government to carry out, in the fullest sense, the double undertaking already referred to." The double undertaking, of course, was the familiar one of promoting the National Home *pari passu* with the maintenance of the "civil and religious rights" of the Arabs.

So on both these occasions (and others might be cited) British Governments had to acknowledge that they made the creation of free institutions in Palestine subservient to the creation of the National Home. All the recitative which has been intoned since from the Treasury bench upon the reconcilability of Arab rights and of the Zionist establishment, all the chanting of the faithfulness with which these dual obligations were being honoured, have only been strophe and antistrophe in an endless psalmody of pretence.

It is high time that this was confessed. Confession will do us no harm: we fortunately have our great makeweights. We have contributed less than others to the State-tyranny and to the bondage of public opinion by which certain countries in recent years have lowered the standards of civilization. What we have contributed of this nature has been confined to Palestine. Elsewhere we have done our genuine best with vigour and devotion to keep the old standards high. All the same, let there be no self-deception: do not let us imagine that we are untainted champions of lofty principle, nor even austere and incorrupt witnesses of the world's decline.

We too have assisted in the collapse of the moral order by our behaviour in Palestine, in some degree by the arbitrariness of our regime, but much more by its falseness. For nearly two decades now we have given there perhaps the most sustained exhibition of hypocrisy that has ever been seen. Our cant about the Mandate is unsurpassable. In another era the pretext that the Mandate was anything but a flimsy document constructed and used at a given moment to advance given plans would long ago have been dropped, out of sheer weariness of playing a part. But our chorus of voices vowing unselfish devotion to it still rises in faultless unison, and the well-adjusted reverences and hieratic bowings of our Ministers whenever its "obligations" are mentioned have provided fleeting Masquerade with a permanent Court and a ceremonial.

How odious are these bows and reverences when the object upon which they are lavished is considered, when what the Mandate is is set against what the Mandate purports to be.

It purports to be a code for the emancipatory government of Palestine drawn up by the conscience of the world, though, for the best of reasons, how this was accomplished has never been explained.

It purports to have been laid by this same world-conscience upon the shoulders of Great Britain, and by Great Britain to have been accepted manfully and administered impartially.

It purports to be a charter containing provisions in favour of the Zionists, but also provisions in favour of the Arabs, and these two sets of provisions are supposed to have sprung each from an independent and disinterested source, and to be as valuable the one set as the other. To the Arabs in particular the Mandate has been represented by a succession of British Governments as something within the terms of which these Governments are confined by duty.

Whereas in honest reality not one of these things is true of the Mandate. Supposing that the League of Nations represents the conscience of the world, which is a large supposition, even so every precaution was taken by the Mandatories that the conscience of the world should not draw up their Mandates.

The Mandate was not laid upon the shoulders of Mr. Lloyd George, but was grabbed by him with the clutch of an eagle short of prey. Its provisions in favour of the Arabs are worth exactly nothing. Its wrongfully inserted provisions in favour of the Zionists condition it from end to end.

Worst of all, the Mandate represented by British Ministers to the Arab people as a behest sacredly received and dutifully observed by them was in all that mattered written by the Zionists and for the rest written by themselves.

Chapter 34

The years from before 1923 are those which matter in the Palestine Question.
Irrelevance and insincerity of the argument that Zionism means prosperity.
Abdication of King Hussein. The Mavrommatis case.
The Government impeached at last and found guilty.

The Mandate for Palestine slunk into force—no other phrase describes so fitly its way of appearance—fifteen years ago. Since then in the Holy Land a great many things have occurred, including about two years of insurrection. If here all these events, from 1923 to the publication of the Peel Report in 1937, are confined to final chapters, this is not done for any enforced reason, but because the affairs of Palestine are not seen in their proper perspective if the foreground is filled with the happenings of those years from 1923 to 1937.

Some of these happenings, Heaven knows, were important enough in themselves, and with some the world rang, though, as usual, not with those which mattered most of all. None the less they were never anything but the mere consequences of what had been schemed and accomplished by the political Zionists and by our own Governments during, roughly, the decade before. And in Palestine it is not consequences but causes which cry out for examination. The causes, which have been kept concealed or as far out of sight as possible, all are to be sought within the period from the War to 1923.

Therefore it is upon this period and not upon the ensuing fifteen years that attention should be concentrated.

It is a significant thing that Governmental and political-Zionist spokesmen have always done everything in their power to remove discussion of the whole Palestine affair from the primary pre-Mandate era to the subsidiary post-Mandate era. There have been only two post-Mandate events upon which they have kept silence, and these of course were the two occasions upon which a post-Mandate event has called for as much attention as anything which occurred in the preliminary stage.

With this exception, they have written and talked themselves dry upon the events of the later years, upon such topics as the effect of the growth of the National Home during 1923-38 upon Arab prosperity—as though the real doubt which the world had to solve was whether or no the National Home put money into Arab pockets. To pretend in this way that the issue in Palestine is an economic one has suited the Zionists very well indeed. It has suited still better various British ministers to presuppose the same thing, and to assure Parliament with false sincerity that immigration into the Holy Land would be determined inflexibly by what they have called the "economic absorptive capacity" of that hapless country.

In the same vein there has been the endless argumentation upon the degree of British fidelity to the Mandate.

Now to let discussion turn upon these subjects is to derail all genuine consideration of the subject at all. There is neither sense nor morality in inquiring whether Great Britain executed faithfully a Mandate which was fraudulently composed.

As for the other main subject of general discussion, the precious "economic benefits," "material prosperity," "raising of the standard of living" and other paraphrases for such cash as may or may not have accrued during the same epoch to Arabs from the presence of the Zionists in Palestine, these gifts correspond perfectly to the gold proffered more immediately and more copiously to the Belgian peasants by the van of the invading German cavalry in 1914.

Standards of living and material prosperity could have been raised pretty considerably for awhile on the hither side of the Meuse if the local Belgians, civil and military, had all pocketed the glittering twenty-mark pieces. But the Belgians saw from the start without difficulty that the issue before them was not whether Belgium was to be enriched either by specie or by the establishment in their midst of a national home of German civilization, but was whether Belgium should be invaded by the Germans.

The situation in Palestine is, and always has been, identical. The political Zionist invaders may have ridden in upon economic stirrups. They declare that they have done so. Even if this were true, however, it would be of no real account. What matters is that they entered Palestine, and stay in Palestine, by the brute force of British arms. If their stirrups had been of diamonds and their housings of gold, which, as they cavalcaded along, they removed and scattered amidst the inhabitants, that never made any difference to the subjugation they brought with them by abstracting from the Arabs the sole possession and control of the Arabs' native land. No one who understands the position will ever let this point be lost from sight, nor let himself be drawn for a moment into intricate discussions upon the economic benefits (if any) of an invasion, as though the presence or absence of such benefits were the question at issue between invaders and invaded.

Even when in the upshot the trend of economic events has proved altogether to the advantage of the Arab case, still it would be an error to dream of founding the Arab case upon it. Argument on such premises provides a means of escape for those against whom it is directed.

Land questions; the size of the "*lot viable*" (the amount of land needed by an Arab family to make a living); the uselessness of mere cash compensation to such a family when dispossessed; the sum needed to resettle the dispossessed upon land elsewhere: these and kindred points require to be set out in detail, with accompanying calculations.

The Zionists have many able controversialists at their service, who can prolong and complicate discussion upon these matters till it is altogether involved in technicalities. Plausible pleading flows from their pens that Arab impoverization is exaggerated or that it is not imputable to the National Home.

The instant counter to their pleading would be to take those who hear or read it to the outskirts of Jaffa or Haifa and other such spots to see for themselves the condition of the Arabs there. But that is not practicable, and countering argument with argument far away in England takes time and space. As pleading and counter-pleading go on and on, the phenomenon just indicated occurs. The political question is subtly transferred to economic ground. It does not matter at bottom what the Zionist controversialists say: the important thing for them is that the origins of the business are lost from sight. Their arguments appear to spring from the mouths of long-settled denizens of the country, debating with their fellow-citizens a vexed internal question, and not from the ranks of the foe and the invader.

So though the major events between 1923 and today must naturally be recapitulated, there is anything but occasion to give to them, save to a couple of them, the prominence of the momentous earlier happenings. They will present to us not the sources but the symptoms of the Palestine question. Even the hamstringing of the Passfield White Paper in 1930, about which so much has been written, was only an aggravation of long-existent ills and a sequel to long-existent ill-doing. It was not till the Peel Commission's Report was published in 1937, and the scheme for partition of Palestine was adopted in theory by the Government, that a new cause of the Palestine Question was created and a fresh acceleration to the initial velocity of revolt in that country was applied.

The last remnants of the special pre-Mandate intrigues trailed into the period when the Mandate was being established, and into that following. Up to 1924 hopes lingered of securing the recognition of the National Home from an Arab prince over the heads of the Arab people. The Colonial

Office's approach to the malleable Emir Abdullah has been chronicled already. The crown of Palestine and Transjordan was dangled before him on condition that he accepted the National Home. He may have found the offer alluring, but he found the combination more dangerous.

Negotiations for a Treaty of Friendship were resumed with King Hussein, but the old stalwart would never succumb to any of the temptations whispered to him, at the price of Palestine. Even when Lord Curzon dropped diplomatic methods, in a mood of annoyance, and dispatched a letter in which the King was summoned peremptorily to accept the Balfour Declaration, Hussein remained unstirred. He retorted in kind by proposing a constitutional Government in Jerusalem.

Sir Herbert Samuel previously had conferred with him in January, and Amman. Two days of almost continuous conversation yielded nothing beyond the proof that Hussein's goodwill to Britain was joined to unswerving principles where Arab independence was concerned.

He had everything to lose then from his fortitude, for the Wahabis were advancing into his kingdom, and his only chance of preserving this would have been by bartering acceptance of the situation in Syria against a British guarantee of his frontiers. But as he said that February, "My honour is at stake." He stood his ground, believing till the last that Britain would fulfil her engagements to him. This was not to be.

The Wahabis under the Emir Ibn Saud pursued their conquering course and took Mecca. King Hussein was forced to abdicate and retired to Cyprus, where he died in 1928, an exile but enthroned in Arab memories. The new Wahabi Kingdom of the Hedjaz signed the Treaty of Jeddah with Great Britain in 1927, a regional one, leaving the larger Arab issues significantly untouched. With Ibn Saud the rights of the Arabs of Palestine are as safe as with King Hussein.

An important feature of the early post-Mandate days was that in England the affairs of Palestine began to fall more and more into departmental hands. Under the Lloyd George-Balfour regime, the Prime Minister and his companion had known only too much about them.There now began a period in which Foreign Secretaries and, even more, Prime Ministers knew too little about them. Heads of the Government came to depend increasingly upon the Colonial Office for their information, and for their policy. Of Colonial Ministers, Mr. Churchill's doings have been described. Mr. Amery, in the Baldwin Cabinet of 1924, had the strongest Zionist affiliations. His version of the Mandate-making deserves to be reproduced in the Palestine anthology:

> "It has been suggested [said Mr. Amery (Under-Secretary then)] that each Power invented its own Mandate and then put it before the League

> of Nations. That was not the process. The process had been *one of evolution from the clause of the Covenant by negotiation and discussion.*"

Mr. Ormsby-Gore himself never tended a fairer flower of speech, the glowing calyx of which I italicize.

It was after Mr. Amery that the same Mr. Ormsby-Gore reigned as Under-Secretary, from 1922 to January 1924, and from November 1924 to 1929. He, as the reader has seen, was Zion itself. His appointment as holder of the scales, nominally poised as they were, between Arabs and Zionists, when he was promoted by Mr. Baldwin in 1936 to the Colonial Secretaryship, showed in itself how little Mr. Baldwin understood the Palestine Question.

Short of appointing Dr. Weizmann, he could have done nothing more exasperating to the Arabs. The news of the appointment seemed incredible when first it was announced: it was such sheer lunatic trailing of the tail of the Zionist coat.

When Mr. J. H. Thomas was made Colonial Secretary in the first MacDonald Cabinet, as in the case of the late Duke of Devonshire, certain permanent officials of the Colonial Office became masters of the situation. Mr. Thomas announced in Parliament that the Government had taken over Palestine as "a going concern," but whither it was going he was either innocent enough never to know or careful enough never to say. The one Colonial Secretary who showed signs of emancipation from Zionist influence was Lord Passfield. He was put quickly into his place.

As time passed, too, and Houses of Commons changed, the number of members of Parliament who had had contact with Palestine or had knowledge of it, never large, decreased correspondingly. There were always a few valiant defenders of the Arabs, but they were lost amidst the Zionistic and the uninformed, like the architects of today amidst builders and joiners.

No doubt most Members, though Arab delegations came regularly to England to try and open their eyes, really were deceived by the "communities" story and thought that there always had been in Palestine mere clumps of Arabs dotting a basic carpet of Jews. Other Members counted the population of Palestine in England, so to speak. "I have been asked by a Member," says Sir Ronald Storrs in *Orientations*, "as guest at a party-luncheon in the House of Commons, whether the Palestine Government was advancing as swiftly as possible with the National Home, 'for,' said he, 'I have in my constituency some thousands of Jews who are continually inquiring, whereas,' he added with engaging candour, 'I have no Arabs.'" Thus may empires be endangered so that constituencies may be saved.

But there were, as I have said, always some valiant defenders of the Arabs' rights, and men like Colonel Howard Bury and Sir Frank Sanderson prevented the body of private Members of the House of Commons from sinking quite to the level of the Governments of these dark years. Otherwise the Zionists had everything their own way. Successive Cabinets justified Mr. J. H. Thomas's dictum by accepting the Palestine situation as a legacy from their predecessors. I remember writing in bitterness on some occasion after elections, when Palestine policy was being transferred like a canary in a cage from the drawing-room of one Government to the bedroom of another, that "the Palestine Question appears to have become the traditional mascot of British Prime Ministers."

Much earlier than that I had written, "For months the Palestine Question has been drifting, drifting, drifting. The Lords alone seem to perceive that there is any danger there. The Commons ask desultory questions, listen unmoved to outrageous replies from the Colonial Office, and get back as quickly as they can to domestic politics. The one thing which is certain is that concentration at Westminster upon domestic politics alone means that some fine day all the domestic talk will peter out suddenly in the discussion of blood and bayonets in Palestine." That appeared in the *Daily Mail*, in June 1923, and may be quoted perhaps as a discharge of a journalist's responsibility.

That same year a proposal was put before the Arabs, which was described by its originators as "a great concession to Arab sentiment." Nominally it was the late Duke of Devonshire, then Colonial Secretary, who made it, but the poor Duke at the Colonial Office, where Palestine was concerned at least, was but a species of publisher issuing without hope of gain the works of his permanent officials. It is upon these latter that must lie the onus of proposing to the Arabs, with airs of largesse, an offer equivalent to an offer to the British people of a "British Agency" in Great Britain. The Arabs were offered in fact an "Arab Agency" in Palestine. What is more, the offer was commended to them upon the grounds that it would give them a position exactly analogous to that accorded to the existing Jewish Agency.

To this offer the Arabs gave the reception which we should give to an offer of a "British Agency" in Britain. They dismissed it without thanks. Whereon they were lectured with infinite smugness upon their refusal to accept the opportunity of having official representation when it was given to them. But it is to be noted that when in the autumn of the succeeding year, on behalf of the Government, Sir Herbert Samuel submitted at Geneva to the Mandates Commission of the League a statement on Palestine, this particular proposal drew remark. Bad as is the record of the Mandates Commission for its subservience to the Mandatory in Palestine, on this occasion one member of the Commission at least was found to express his opinion of the proposal with a measure of frankness. This was Senhor

Freire d'Andrade. "The High Commissioner," said he, "was proposing to organize a Jewish and an Arab Agency with equal rights. In my opinion the Arabs will find it difficult to accept such an organization, for the role of the Jewish Agency is defined in Article 4 of the Mandate, which contemplates that it shall assist in the administration of the country, though only to a certain extent, according to the terms of the Article. The Arabs, however, who are in their own country, must feel that they have the right to exercise more influence in administrative affairs than newcomers. In this I cannot say that they are wrong."

Sir Herbert Samuel's only reply was that he recognized that the Arab Agency "could not altogether satisfy the claims of the Arabs," which was no reply. He evaded the cardinal issue, raised guardedly by Senhor d'Andrade, that the supposed concession to the Arabs was a patent trick to place a small minority of newcomers upon a complete level of representation with the vast majority of immemorially established Arabs.

As this plan was rejected by the Arabs along with the plan for a packed Legislative Assembly, both projects had to be abandoned. Therefore 1924 saw the continuation of government in Palestine by the High Commissioner with an advisory council of officials.

The Abdication of King Hussein took place in October and was very satisfactory news to the Zionists. The most noteworthy Zionist comment on it appeared in Germany. In those days a good deal of Zionist comment was published in Germany which was much more open than anything which appeared in England. The Jerusalem correspondent of the *Vossische Zeitung*, Dr. von Weisl, said without further ado in his message on Hussein's abdication what most political Zionists were thinking.

> King Hussein's fall is of decisive importance [wrote he]. As King of the Hedjaz he could not but combat the efforts which are being made to form a real new Palestine, a Palestine, that is to say, which will exclude his Arab State from the open sea. As the champion of the Pan-Arab Federation King Hussein feared the growing Zionist immigration which is driving the wedge of a foreign race into the homogeneous population of the Peninsula.

Dr. von Weisl was honest about it. General Smuts should have received a cutting from that article of the *Vossische*. Ziono-Governmental policy could not have been better defined than in this "driving the wedge of a foreign race into the homogeneous population of the Peninsula."

In December the United States signed the Convention by which the Government of the American Union consented to British administration of Palestine. But the outstanding event of that year 1924 was one of which the British general public knows nothing, one of the hidden events mentioned at the start of this chapter. This was the delivery of the first judgment in the Mavrommatis case.

The very name "Mavrommatis case" will be without significance to most people. M. Euripides Mavrommatis was a Greek engineer and contractor who before the War had obtained from the Turkish Government certain concessions in Palestine. In consequence of the outbreak of the War he could not carry them out, but his right to take them over at the close of hostilities was ensured by the Treaty of Peace. A special codicil to this laid down, as indeed in common justice had to be laid down, that concessions granted by the Ottoman Government to Allied or neutral subjects remained good under the Mandatory regime.

M. Mavrommatis claimed concessions for irrigation works and general agricultural development in the Jordan valley; for irrigation works and for the supply of water and of electric light and current, drawn from the Auja river, at Jaffa; for the establishment of a water-supply and a tramway system in Jerusalem, as well as for electric light and power there also. The three groups of concessions were not quite on the same footing. They were on the same footing as far as feasibility went, and M. Mavrommatis had been preparing to begin work upon all of them when the War supervened. But the unbusiness-like Turkish authorities, sufficiently tired with the effort of discussing and conceding them, for concede them they undoubtedly did, had been dilatory about signing, and the War had supervened. The Jerusalem concessions had been signed before that happened, but the trouble with the Jordan and Jaffa concessions was that signatures had been appended just after the War began. On the other hand there was written evidence that the Turks ere then had regarded them as granted and had expected them to be started any day. Also when the War did come, the Turkish authorities had written consenting to their postponement, which was a proof that they acknowledged them as existing already. Still, these points were arguable, when technical rather than moral validity came to be examined.

The pre-eminent interest of the Mavrommatis concessions was that all or any of them ran athwart the monopoly planned in complicity by the Zionists and the Colonial Office for the Rutenberg scheme. If Mavrommatis were allowed to take up his concessions, as he proposed to do, it was good-bye to the Zionist domination of the natural resources of Palestine and also to the hopes of turning Palestine into a modernized industrial country in which the Arabs would be extinguished. Mavrommatis had no grandiose schemes of the Zionist kind.

The importance of Mavrommatis is evident. As soon as the Civil Government, or what passed as a Government, was set up in Jerusalem, he had obtained from his backers, the French Banque Périer, full guarantees of funds. The Banque Périer had offered him a large sum before the War with which to set about operations. By the spring of 1921 he had the necessary assurances from the bank that it would again credit him with the advances he required to carry out his undertakings, provided his claims were ratified by the new Government in Palestine. He thereon made formal application to that Government to be allowed to take up his concessions, and submitted the papers which dealt with them.

Only a fortnight before this Mr. Amery had made the announcement in the House of Commons—on the 4th of April—that the Government now proposed to entertain applications for concessions. Till then (cf. Chapter 23) it had refused to consider them, though it had had the bulk of the Rutenberg plans in its pigeon-holes for at least two years. In July Mr. Amery's promise was fulfilled by a proclamation of the High Commissioner of Palestine inviting applications for concessions.

M. Mavrommatis's papers were referred in May from Jerusalem to the Colonial Office, which found them entirely detestable, since that Office had negotiated the Rutenberg plans itself and had no other aim in life but to install Rutenberg. But the officials thought at once that they had found a flaw in Mavrommatis's papers. In one of the documents granting his concessions he had been described as an Ottoman subject.

This was a Turkish fiction, so that the Porte might not have the air of granting concessions to foreigners, as in practice it did. Concessionaires were not expected to notice the error. Mavrommatis was in fact a Greek. If he had been an Ottoman subject, he would have been an enemy subject, and his Concessions would have lapsed. But when the Colonial Office ferreted out this flaw, as it thought, in his claims, M. Mavrommatis explained that he was a Greek subject and that he would set about procuring formal papers to prove this. These papers were received on the 1st of September by the Colonial Office.

The date is important because it shows the contumaciousness of that Ministry. It had been aware for months of the claims of M. Mavrommatis, who, indeed, was to tell me himself later that, through the Palestine Administration, official circles in England must have been cognizant of them long before that Spring of 1921. He, however, had found it useless, as the various British and Arab post-War tenderers had found it useless, to enter his claims till after the April announcement of Mr. Amery. M. Mavrommatis, of course, was in a different position from the hapless Mr. Bicknell and other post-War applicants for concessions. He appeared, not as an applicant but as a holder, and when the obstacle of nationality had been raised he without delay, as we have seen, declared that he would have no difficulty in proving his Greek citizenship.

The Colonial Office, therefore, knew perfectly well that all their plans were imperilled, for if Mavrommatis could produce his nationality papers and otherwise establish any of his claims, then the proposed Rutenberg monopoly would infringe his existing rights. When the citizenship papers came to hand on the 1st of September, the Mavrommatis affair became of paramount importance. The first thing that should have been done in Whitehall then, the only thing to be done, was to examine his claims thoroughly at once, since so long as there was a possibility of any of them being well-founded, obviously it would be dishonest to deliver over to the Zionists what might prove to be the legally secured property of Mavrommatis. That issue had to be settled in honour before another step towards granting concessions could be taken.

Yet, with its eyes wide open, not to say intermittently constricted in the corners, the Colonial Office instead of adjourning the Rutenberg transaction, eleven days later, on the 12th, and again on the 21st of the month, made official Agreements with M. Rutenberg. By these, if and when he formed a Company within a given date, concessions centring on the Jordan and the Auja would be granted his company, equivalent to the monopoly of electric generation and supply throughout Palestine.

The Agreements were signed by the Crown Agents on behalf of the High Commissioner for Palestine, but these parties were but the technical agents of the Colonial Office and the Home Government. By the terms of the intended concessions not only was Mavrommatis's field of action handed over to Rutenberg, but the Rutenberg Company could obtain at once, by mere request in writing, the annulment of any valid prior claim, such as his, provided that it paid agreed or arbitrated compensation. (The reader may refer back to the text of the Concession in Chapter 25). More than this, the Agreements themselves, from the moment of signature, debarred the High Commissioner from granting any concession which might conflict with the Rutenberg concessions, even though the Rutenberg Company were not yet formed and its concessions therefore not yet granted. This guarantee that everything should be kept at a standstill in Palestine till Rutenberg was able to begin his industrialization scheme was, if necessary, to last for two years.

So the position was that Mavrommatis was prevented from starting his works while the Company which was to jump them was not ready, and as soon as this Company was ready it could demand the annulment of his right to start them. Such were the practices of the Government in the early 'twenties. The morality of it all was not appreciably mitigated by the compulsory compensation, and was still less mitigated by the statements of official spokesmen afterward. Foremost of these statements was that of Mr. Winston Churchill, made in the House of Commons by him as Colonial

Secretary during the debate on the vote for his Ministry in July of 1922. This speech has been dealt with already in Chapter 26, but not with reference to the Mavrommatis matter, as unfortunately this was not mentioned in the debate and I have thought it better to keep it, because of its gravity, as a separate issue.

In this debate Mr. Churchill said:

> At the time the Rutenberg concession was granted, no other application was before us.... It was not until July 1921 that, seeing the long delay in getting any move on in the country, and the urgent need of making things self-supporting, I directed the High Commissioner to say that we would entertain applications for concessions in regard to certain public services. That declaration was publicly made by the High Commissioner. A considerable interval elapsed. No other application was received except the scheme of Mr. Rutenberg.

This was a fine statement to give to the House of Commons at a time when, at the lowest computation, M. Mavrommatis's schemes had been a full year deposited with Mr. Churchill's own Ministry. Mr. Churchill's officials had been in correspondence with Mavrommatis during the whole of this interval, and within a month of the speech recognized to Mr. Mavrommatis, through a third party, that at least his Jerusalem concessions, as they chose to put it, "endowed him with certain rights."

Is it to be understood that, in order to make his statement that there were no other applications, the Colonial Minister made use of the fact that Mavrommatis had made not "applications" but "claims" for concessions? Or was the other subterfuge, that at the time the Rutenberg application was granted no other application had been made, based on the plea that the Rutenberg and Mavrommatis "applications" did not cover the same field? Whether the first piece of chicanery was within the procedure of Mr. Churchill, I hesitate to pronounce. In other matters than those of Palestine it would not have been. It certainly was within the procedure of the Colonial Office at the time. It is just possible, as an alternative, that the Mavrommatis documents had not been brought properly to the Colonial Secretary's knowledge, though not to have had important papers communicated to him was never surely in Mr. Churchill's way of life.

As for the second subterfuge, that the Rutenberg and Mavrommatis documents did not cover the same field, it is impossible to sustain. They so much covered the same field that Rutenberg had been given by clauses 13 and 14 of his Jordan and Auja concessions, the right to expropriate them. Whether his Company later either exercised or did not exercise it (which remains unsolved), the concession certainly declared that the Company had this right of expropriation.

What stands out, in any event, is that when Mr. Churchill said there had been no applications save those of M. Rutenberg, M. Mavrommatis had demanded leave to begin electric, transport, water supply and irrigation works at Jaffa, at Jerusalem and in the Jordan valley. Furthermore he had declared that he was ready to adapt his existing concessions to the altered conditions which the War had brought to the country, and he had outlined his emendations of his original plans. He had also submitted proof that an influential banking company was ready to advance him all the funds he needed the moment his concessions were ratified

Therefore, even supposing that his plans, as existing concessions, were not valid, as applications they were superfine, conforming to every requirement of authority and to the needs of the country. If the population of Palestine had had any say in their lives under British rule they would have chosen Mavrommatis by an overwhelming majority to undertake such development as they wanted. Yet not merely was he rejected, either as established concessionaire or as applicant, in order that a Zionist monopoly might be set on foot, but his very name was kept secret by the Colonial Secretary from the Commons and from the nation. That this was no chance, but deliberate policy in the interests of the Zionist monopoly, the happily disclosed intrigues of Lord Balfour in the United States make evident.

It remains to be added only, on a point of fact, that in one case Mavrommatis would have been unable perforce to carry out a concession. In 1918, Sir Ronald Storrs, as Military Governor, had given Jerusalem, with the aid of the Royal Engineers, the water-supply which it by then sorely needed. This was a military act, and since, however necessary, it supplanted Mavrommatis it gave him in the result right to compensation for his vanished opportunity.

What was the first sequel to Mavrommatis's presentation of his claims? One which probably was no surprise to the Colonial Office. When Mr. Churchill, uttering nothing of Mavrommatis, had pleaded on behalf of Rutenberg, he had vaunted, it will be remembered, that M. Edmond de Rothschild had offered to finance the latter to the tune of £100,000 to £200,000. Strange, but £200,000 (five million francs at the then rate of exchange) was the very sum which the Banque Périer had guaranteed to Mavrommatis before the War. Mr. Churchill went on to say that he did not believe that "this (Palestine) concession would secure the necessary funds were it not supported by sentimental and quasi-religious motives," that is by Zionist and extremely-quasi religious motives.

But in this last statement of Mr. Churchill's there was an approach to reality, though no disclosure of real facts. Faced with the sudden announcement of the Rutenberg concessions by the Palestine Government, with the British Government behind it, the French bank had written to M. Mavrommatis, in the previous December (1921), to say that it could no longer undertake to finance him. The bankers stated that it was because of the granting of the Rutenberg concessions that they must withdraw their promise of funds. So that Mavrommatis was not merely prevented from carrying out any valid concession which he held. The funds too with which he counted on carrying them out were suddenly withdrawn from, him because of the vanity of trying to compete with the company-promotion of the Colonial Office. The climax was to have Mr. Churchill unctuously declaring that non-Zionist contractors would in his belief never get advances for works in Palestine because of their lack of semireligious motives. All the time it was the action of his own Ministry which stood between such a contractor and his funds. A miserable episode.

When the Colonial Office saw that M. Mavrommatis was indeed a Greek citizen, none the less, as we have just observed, it pursued undeterred the plans which it had concerted with the Zionists. It became necessary, though, to draw Mavrommatis into these plans, though nothing was said of him. Much as it might be desired to oust him or non-suit him, there would have been a risk in taking no account of him at all, for even after the French bank had withdrawn its support he maintained his claims. He was in Jerusalem at the time and there he was given to understand, with much bluffing and pooh-poohing on behalf of London, that his prospects were not bright and that the best thing he could do would be to "go to Rutenberg."

M. Mavrommatis had no particular political relationships, was unconcerned with politics, and anxious at all costs not to lose his rights, so he followed this advice. The event, and its sequel, are described with a delicate choice of words in the judgment of the Court of International Justice which was delivered four years later, in the course of the process which was to supervene at The Hague:

> "It has been alleged by the claimant—and the respondent has not disputed the contention—that during the negotiations which took place at Jerusalem, M. Mavrommatis was recommended, on behalf of the Palestine Government, to come to an understanding with a certain M. Rutenberg, with a view to collaborating in the carrying out of the works contemplated in the agreements under which M. Mavrommatis was the beneficiary. M. Rutenberg, for his part, however, seems to have thought that any understanding would be premature, pending recognition by the local authorities of the validity of the concessions."

So when 1922 came in Mavrommatis appeared to have been sidetracked rather successfully. All the proceedings, it should be added, which had brought him to that position, were entirely illegal. They were carried out under and by virtue of the forged Mandate of 1920-23. "Moreover," ran the dry judgment of the Court of The Hague, when appraising the situation, "moreover, at the time in question the document entitled 'Mandate for Palestine' was not yet in force."

But Mavrommatis was not so easily side-tracked as Whitehall had hoped. He was determined to fight his case, either to obtain his concessions or to be compensated for them. He fought for seven years against his mighty opponents. During those years, especially during the earlier half of them, every resource of official dilatoriness was brought into play against him. Now he was told that his valid rights would be "respected," now that his schemes were impossible of operation. At due intervals he was bidden to "go to Rutenberg." This was, of course, a most improper invitation. If Mavrommatis had rights (which was the only possible reason for his being sent to Rutenberg) it was the Rutenberg Company which should have been ordered to go to him and to throw itself upon *his* mercy.

One moment the Colonial Office was bidding Mavrommatis produce a scheme for water-supply for Jerusalem, on top of or underneath or alongside or heaven knows where in relation to the military water-works. Then just afterwards the presence of the military works was flourished at him as a system which "appeared to have deprived his concession of any value."

He spent his time either applying for compensation which was always in the offing but never came into port, or else begging, quite in vain, to be permitted to exploit his concessions. He had to supply the Colonial Office with relays of documents, and negotiated at length with Zionists. The choicest feature of his endless correspondence with the Colonial Office, though, was that every now and then, at a loss for other means of delay, that Ministry was seized with compunction about the validity of Mavrommatis's rights while the Turkish Treaty remained unsigned. No such compunction had seized a soul in that Office concerning the works which the Rutenberg Company had been allowed to start near Jaffa.

The Colonial Office also, through the Crown Agents, during the same treaty-less period had handed over to the Palestine Administration considerable advances upon a still unfloated and unsecured loan, which were used largely to tide over the unemployment amidst the Zionist immigrants forced on the country. The same advances, along with half a million due to the bondholders of the Ottoman Public Debt, figured presently amidst the assets of the Palestine budget. Thus an unfloated loan and a standing debt contributed to the revenue of an illegitimate Government.

On their part, the Zionists could hardly attain the achievements of their Colonial Office comrades. However, in the middle of 1924, after three years, the Rutenberg Company declared that it would not expropriate M.

Mavrommatis's Jerusalem concessions, because the £125,000 compensation he asked "would prove an extremely heavy and unproductive burden on the comparatively poor Jerusalem population in the form of excessively high rates for electricity." It was not the Company therefore, but the Jerusalem population which was envisaged as paying Mavrommatis his compensation, via the excessively high rates for electricity which the Company, on its own showing, would have felt itself obliged to levy, under stress no doubt of quasi-religious motives.

This statement occurred in a letter of the 1st of May to the Colonial Office in which the Company said that it had been prepared to pay reasonable compensation to M. Mavrommatis "whilst not admitting the validity of the above-mentioned concession, previously annulled by His Majesty's Government." That declaration led to an interesting dispute between the two parties, the Government maintaining, in order to save its face, that it never had annulled Mavrommatis's concession. After which the situation developed. The next step was that the Government demanded that the Zionist Company should corroborate the Government version, but apparently this demand was to no purpose, for eight months later, in January of 1925, the Colonial Office officials were repeating the demand, this time by cable.

But all they got out of the Company was (1) a statement that it had never objected to Mavrommatis's carrying out his water-supply concession, which was no wonder, since the Army had forestalled him, and the Zionists would never have objected to Mavrommatis doing what was already done. And (2) a reiteration of the Company's statement of the previous May that it did not now propose to call for the annulment of the tram and electric-power concession. This statement dealt, therefore, with the future only, and the Government was still without its corroboration.

There matters stayed, very singularly. No effort seems to have been made to get to the bottom of them. Yet it should have been very easy to do so. If the Mavrommatis concession had been annulled by the Government this would or should have been as a result of a request in writing by the Rutenberg Company, according to the terms of its concession. In May the Company said that the concession had been annulled so it must have had prominently in its mind the letter which it had sent to the Palestine Government to obtain this annulment, unless indeed the Palestine or British Governments had annulled without bothering about a letter.

Why was no search made amidst the documents of the Palestine Government for this letter, or for that Government's acknowledgement of it? The Court of The Hague does not seem to have pressed the point. Its reference to it in the judgment of March 1925 is as follows:

> "It is true that in its letter of May 1st, 1924, the Palestine Electric

> Corporation Ltd. said that M. Mavrommatis's concessions had already been annulled. The British Government, however, denied the accuracy of the statement, and, as has already been said, there is nothing to show that such annulment had really taken place."

But there was nothing either to show that it had not taken place. The total evidence in the official account is a statement by the Government and the absence of a confirmatory statement by the Rutenberg Company. This in spite of an imperative request by cable for confirmation. Why then was the matter not settled for good by a demand from London that the Company should either (1) produce the letter, in consequence of which the alleged annulment had taken place, or (2) should declare upon what foundation its statement of the 1st of May rested? Why not indeed?

The position was important enough surely to have this point cleared up. In fact it was essential that it should be cleared up, since if the Government, as the 1st of May statement alleged, had annulled the concession, it would have made a great deal of difference to Mavrommatis, who would thereby have had a claim for damages against the Government for a definite act. But in the judgment delivered by the Court the matter is left unsolved, or solved by an asseveration of the Colonial Office, which is about the same.

It is all unsatisfactory. Even today there would seem to be call for a search amidst the archives of the Palestine Government to see whether in its contention the Government really was "accurate," as the Hague judges rather malignly phrased it. The only difficulty is that in Palestine the touch of time seems to be heavy and rapid upon documents. A request of my own for the text of the important proclamation of 1921 by which tenders for concessions were invited by the High Commissioner has proved fruitless, though addressed to the proper authorities. They are courteously sorry, but have no trace of it.

But let all that be for the moment. M. Mavrommatis journeyed to England in the autumn of 1921 to prosecute his case, and I made his acquaintance. He read my articles in the *Daily Mail* on other aspects of the "*Palestine Deception,*" which was their general heading, and wrote to me. I saw a good deal of him in the end: he was living in Linden Gardens, in Bayswater, and he put his correspondence and other of his papers into my hands. I took his case up and was able to give him some publicity, which was very good for him and very bad for his opponents, even though I could not manage much of it.

My particular advice to him—though I do not suggest that I was the only one who gave it—was that he should have recourse to his Government and sue through that Government at The Hague. I was satisfied enough to help him, of course, because "he had his quarrel just," but far more because I saw in his case—and this is the great ultimate importance of it—an unhoped opportunity for unveiling a corner, if no more than a corner, of the whole facade of dishonesty and falsehood in Palestine. The difficulty had always been to find a locale for the unveiling.

The terrible handicap of the Arabs was, and is, that not being a constituted Government nor the subjects of a constituted Government they have never been able, because of the regulations of the League, to summon our Government before the Hague Court, or indeed before any Court, upon any of the numerous accusations which should have been brought against it, such as the violation of Articles 20 and 22 of the Covenant. History is not likely to record a more iniquitous contrivance than that by which through being prevented by the Mandatory from governing their country they are unable to plead against the Mandatory for not allowing them to govern it.

Fortunately Mavrommatis was a subject of an established State, and so on his behalf the Greek Government could summon the British Government before the Court of The Hague and could accuse it, under one set of terms or another, of using a Mandatory situation (even when it had not got one) to set aside Mavrommatis's rights.

Before the case came on the Greek Government decided to drop the Jordan claim, and to base its application to the Court on the Jaffa and Jerusalem concessions. The Greek lawyers considered that the technical hitch in the Jordan papers very probably would lead to a decision against them on this claim. They were not confident about Jaffa, but on Jerusalem they felt certain of success.

The principal Mavrommatis cases, thus amended, came before The Hague Court in 1924 and 1925. Their final stage was not reached quickly. Mavrommatis tried to obtain compensation for his Jerusalem concessions through his Legation, after the failure of his own efforts. But the Foreign Office, which had always disliked having responsibility thrust upon it for the offences of the Colonial Office, evaded the move and returned the Greek Legation and M. Mavrommatis to the Colonial limbo. M. Mavrommatis's lawyers had already proposed arbitration, but this had been refused by the Colonial Office. The Greek Government, to which Mavrommatis had now had recourse, proposed again to the British Government to accept the award of any judge of the High Court, but the Government refused to place the issue before one of our own judges even.

What followed deserves emphasis. All our Governments since the Palestine Question began, secure in their inviolability from judicial investigation into their actions, have behaved as though their declarations upon the Question were as good as proof. If the British Government said something, then it was true.

If, however, statements of the British Government were thought so convincing in themselves that they were equivalent to proof, in the present instance the Government had a miraculous opportunity for presenting before the Court of The Hague one of these statements and of winning its case out of hand. Since the Government of Mr. Lloyd George, deep in the vitals of its truth-telling conscience, felt the Rutenberg concessions to be an example of its fidelity to the Mandate, here was a chance such as it would not have again to make this clear before the most desirable of all audiences, the Court of International Justice.

But did the Government seize this heaven-sent opportunity? Not on its life. It recoiled from it like a sinner from punishment and proceeded to do what everyone does who has a bad case and a worse conscience. It tried to impugn the jurisdiction of the Court. The Greek accusation was that "His Majesty's Government has wrongfully refused to recognize to their full extent the rights acquired by M. Mavrommatis." On which the Government put in Sir Douglas Hogg and other forensic talent to contend that the Hague Court was not competent to judge the issue. The Colonial Office, which manipulated the Government, knew in its heart of hearts, or in some inmost den where it computed what was what, that a verdict of the Court upon some of its actions in Palestine was not to be evaded. So it did its best to stop the trial, and its objections to being tried formed the subject-matter of the sessions of the Court in July 1924.

The words with which M. Politis, an eminent lawyer who had been M. Venizelos's Minister of Foreign Affairs, opened the Greek pleadings are worth quoting. "This is," he said, "a highly instructive spectacle, and one full of promise for the future, to see an arch-powerful Empire being summoned before your bench by a little country, which calls upon that Empire to render account to you of certain of its acts, stigmatized as illegal under the laws of the world [in the original French '*taxés d'illégalité internationale*']." He went on, when opening the details of his case, to say that in the British plea M. Mavrommatis had been called "a concession-hunter." "I feel obliged to the British counsel," said M. Politis, "for his not having confounded M. Mavrommatis with the 'concession-poachers' found at times even on the very banks of the Auja river."

Very stinging was the manner in which he described some of the methods of the Colonial Office, which amongst other things had done its best to oust Mavrommatis through the unratified Treaty of Sèvres. M. Politis was able to point out that while the text of that treaty had been employed by the Colonial officials to reject certain rights of Mavrommatis, at the same time the non-ratification of the treaty had been employed as an excuse by them for not acknowledging others.

The counter-pleas of the Government were all fugitive, based on technicalities. For example it was claimed that the suit could not be brought because it was not between the Greek Government and the British Government, but between the British Government and the Greek Government taking the place of an individual Greek. The Colonial Office had tried, as we know, to oust Mavrommatis on the plea that he was not a neutral or allied subject but was an Ottoman. It now, through the counsel representing it tried to oust him because he was not an Ottoman, but had been described as one. Such pleas had their own moral repercussion upon the party presenting them.

However, technical pleas were so far successful that the Court judged that the Jaffa concessions did not fall under Article 11 of the Mandate, and therefore escaped from its jurisdiction. To Mavrommatis himself this of course was a misfortune, but it was no real gain to his adversaries, for the Court dismissed the contentions of the British Government in respect of the Jerusalem concessions. It reserved this part of the suit for "judgment upon its merits" (or in the French, *"pour statuer au fond,"* "to enact upon the real basis"), at a later session.

This second session was held at The Hague in March 1925. There were twelve judges, of whom one was Lord Finlay, who had been successively Solicitor General, Attorney General and Lord Chancellor. So after all, by a rebound of fate, the decision of a British judge, and the highest of British judges, though out of office now, was not to be escaped by the Government.

Judgment was delivered on the 26th of March. The Court held that it had three points to decide. One was a technical point.

Had M. Mavrommatis been caused loss justifying his claim for compensation? This point went against Mavrommatis for a curious, indeed a remarkable reason. He had retained an intrepid feeling that if he could only secure his concessions, then he would obtain the funds he needed to carry them out. He had never ceased to demand the concessions therefore. Legally this meant that his adversaries had not forced him to abandon them, and so he had incurred no "loss" justifying compensation.

This decision was hard on Mavrommatis, but the law was the law, and it was not a point, moreover, which touched the political issue. Nor did the second point upon which the Court gave its verdict, though a cardinal point, deal with the political issue. This point was: Were M. Mavrommatis's Jerusalem concessions valid? The Court found that they were.

But the third question upon which the Court issued a verdict was of the greatest political importance, since it dealt with the alleged unfaithfulness of the British Government to its obligations in Palestine. Not, be it marked, to its own, to its habitual, version of its obligations, the version composed by itself and passing muster in Parliament, in most of the Press, in official documents of the day—and to pass muster in the future in the Peel Report. It was not with the Government's faithfulness to these cooked obligations that the verdict dealt, but with its faithfulness or lack of faith to Great Britain's real obligations, under the Covenant and the Peace Treaty properly interpreted.

This crucial question, in the words of the judgment, was "whether by giving M. Rutenberg the right to claim the annulment of previous concessions covering the whole or any part of the concession promised to him, the Palestine Administration failed to observe the international obligations accepted by the Mandatory." Upon this the Court returned a unanimous verdict, as follows:

> The existence, for a certain space of time, of a right on the part of M. Rutenberg to require the annulment of the aforesaid concessions of M. Mavrommatis was not in conformity with the international obligations accepted by the Mandatory for Palestine.

So if only on that single occasion in many years the truth came forth. The British Government had violated its obligations. It had violated the Treaty of Peace. The monopoly it had granted to the Zionists in Palestine was illegal. Every judge of the International Court agreed upon this.

It is to be noted that just as Mr. Churchill when defending this monopoly never mentioned that there were anterior legal claims which challenged it, so Lord Balfour also procured the adherence of the United States to it without informing the American Secretary of State of these claims. Unless indeed they were mentioned in the portions of his letter to Mr. Hughes which have been kept from public knowledge. From the tenor of Mr. Hughes's subsequent documents in reply to Lord Balfour and to the Foreign Office this appears in the highest degree unlikely. There seems, however, to be a strong case for publishing the missing section of the letter in question, so that Mr. Hughes may be cleared from the suspicion of abetting Balfour in the wilful establishment of the Treaty-and-Covenant-breaking monopoly.

There was, it remains to be added, a third session of the Court of The Hague devoted to the Mavrommatis affair. This was held two years later, in October 1927. After the judgment of 1925 Mavrommatis was entitled to proceed with his Jerusalem claims, and tried to do so. He now sought and obtained British backing, not Ziono-British, but purely British. This, of course, was what was wrong with it from the point of view of the Colonial Office, more than ever determined to install the Zionists, in the teeth of Covenant or Treaty or Court of International Justice. M. Mavrommatis, fondly believing that if he gained this British backing he would no longer be opposed, turned to the City firm of Birch, Crisp and Co., and from them he received the assurance of the necessary advances to carry out his Jerusalem works.

He was undeceived soon enough. The Colonial Office, safe in public ignorance of the whole affair, repeated its tactics of 1921 to 1925. This time it could not impede Mavrommatis in quite the same way, but the style was identical. It quarrelled with his plans and methods of adaptation to the post-War conditions in Palestine, and again successfully dillied and dallied for the two years within which Mavrommatis was to form his company. Once more these tactics were successful. The British firm withdrew as the French bank had withdrawn.

Mr. Crisp made the reason of his withdrawal perfectly clear in a letter to M. Mavrommatis's lawyers, dated the 18th of January, 1927. He said:

> I confirm what I told you in the autumn. Any firm considered this good business, but obviously we could not undertake to finance these concessions owing to delay in the approval of the plans, inadequate time, and the uncertainty of the attitude of the authorities.

The firm therefore was quite satisfied with the plans. It was the delays in Governmental approval which forced them to withdraw. A genial stroke of Colonial Office tactics was to grant a useless extension of time to Mavrommatis (till February 1927) to form his Company, having previously made it quite impossible for him to form it. The whole thing was so beyond bearing that the Greek Government, despite the cost and its dislike of offending Great Britain, again took up the case on behalf of its subject.

Again our Government gave proof of the state of its conscience. It did not attempt to contest the facts by accepting trial upon the facts. The Greek Government had accused the British of "making it materially and morally impossible for M. Mavrommatis to obtain the financial assistance indispensable for the formation of a company to operate his concessions, through the delays above-mentioned and the hostility displayed towards him by certain British authorities." For this £217,000 compensation now was claimed. But this issue was not tried. The Government side-stepped as in 1924, and pleaded that the Court of The Hague was not competent to pronounce a judgment upon it.

The Greek lawyers had some telling points to place before the Court, notably Mr. Churchill's speech of 1922. The Government conscience functioned at its best in the reply made by Sir Douglas Hogg, who endeavoured to have this speech ruled out of the evidence upon the grounds that *a statement made by a Member of the House of Commons who happens to be a member of the Government did not constitute evidence against the Government of which he may be a member.* "Happens" and "may be" are particularly good. Another blossom for the Palestine anthology.

Alas, however, the case was lost on such technical grounds, the Court concurring with the thesis that once Mavrommatis had his concessions recognized, any dispute dealing with them was an internal affair of Palestine, which could only be pleaded in the Palestine courts.

That was the end of Mavrommatis. He compounded with the Colonial Office for a lump sum of £60,000, of which little enough must have come to him after he had paid his years of expenses. The Colonial Office did not call it compounding, though, it declared that the £60,000 were given by an act of grace on its part, Whether "grace" was the word for the occasion the reader will judge for himself.

The Hague Court verdict of 1927, it should be clearly understood, was no acquittal for our Government. It was merely a finding by The Hague Court that it could not hear the evidence for and against the guilt of our Government. The 1924 verdict on the Jaffa count had been of a kindred type.

Therefore the one real trial, on the rights and wrongs of the case, was that of 1925, and at that trial, the Court of International Justice of The Hague unanimously declared that the British Government had violated its obligations in Palestine by the creation of the monopoly which it had granted to the Zionists. Without any doubt this is the chief happening of the post-Mandate period. Due mention of it is never to be found in the writings and references of Zionist and Governmental commentators. I find no word of it in the Peel Report.

Yet, to repeat finally what has been so little repeated at all, it was the one occasion in which the Government of Mr. Lloyd George, the primarily responsible Government which had granted the Zionist monopoly, and the later Governments which had become accessory to this, were dragged by the hand of justice from the hiding-places where they lay screened by false Mandates, false vows, false Administrations and the debris of the Covenant of the League. On the 26th of March, 1925, one truth about Palestine was proclaimed officially to an inattentive world. Since then such a chance has never come again.

Who can doubt that if it were possible to cite the incriminated series of Governments for the rest of their deeds in Palestine, as for this one, before the same tribunal, a like verdict would be attained. I draw attention again to the quiet statement of the Hague Court, interpolated in its solitary judgment, that in 1921 "the document entitled 'Mandate for Palestine' was not yet in force." What caustic appreciation lies in that term "The document entitled 'Mandate for Palestine.'" It was under the document entitled "Mandate for Palestine" that between 1920 and 1923 the expropriation of the Arabs, like so many Mavrommatises, from the proprietorial rights granted to them by nature and by contract was thoroughly begun.

Chapter 35

Balfour's journey to Syria.
More granting of Concessions.
The outbreak of 1929.
Another Commission.
The Labour Party and Palestine.

In the March of 1925 Lord Balfour journeyed to Jerusalem to open the Jewish University. Under other circumstances the opening of a university in Jerusalem might have been attended by all the leaders of the people of Palestine. Even as it is that University has not failed from the character of such institutions, since while it has served a mixture of aims, yet it is from there that more than one Jewish voice has been raised against the unspiritual doctrines and the overbearing methods of political Zionism in Palestine.

But in 1925 its opening was a mere display of power-politics, as the presence of Lord Balfour indicated more than anything else. His presence was a taunt to the Arabs, because, whatever might be pretended, it was not for the sake of his attainments that Balfour came to preside over this festival. It was as the Strongbow of Palestine he arrived, a Strongbow who had never had the invitation of a single Dermot, an absentee Strongbow who came to inspect the expeditionary force which he had not accompanied hitherto, and to consecrate its occupation.

The festival of the opening of the University was not very successful as it happened, though there were official corteges and a wealth of fluttering robes and Zionist crowds, and hawkers (with unsuspecting symbolism) sold quantities of "Balfour gingerbread" to the thirsty. The first Zionist orator welcomed in an impassioned zeugma the visitor and the future of the National Home, at such length that pullings at his garments and the uprising of other dignitaries had to be employed in the effort to stop him, with no success, and this anti-climax dominated the ceremony.

The judgment of The Hague Court, too, delivered just before the opening of the University (which was the 1st of April of all days) and quickly noised about in a country where it was headline-news, had the effect of a ground-frost on the buds of enthusiasm. Icier still was the douche of the three days' mourning proclaimed by the Chief Rabbi of the Orthodox Jews, the true Zionists, the Jews not in Palestine but of Palestine. The Arabs, on their part, shut their shops and filled the streets with black flags. Lord Balfour himself met with various rebuffs. It had been arranged that he should read a Lesson during the service in St. George's Cathedral on the eve of the opening, a Sunday, in order to dissipate the belief current amidst the Arab Christians that he was really a Jew. Whether he was aware of the motive of his reading I cannot say, but in any event the reading did not come to pass. There was a real climax this time: the choir of the Cathedral threatened to strike if he were allowed to take any share in the service. In fear of disorder the Bishop cancelled the arrangements.

The chief rebuke to the undesired visitor, however, was the closing to him of the precincts of the Dome of the Rock, or Mosque of Omar as it is traditionally called. The mufti and other authorities refused him admittance, granted as a rule without question to all comers. Sir Ronald Storrs, greatly distressed, told them they were affronting a most distinguished man. There is no record of the terms of their reply, but the sense of Arab sentiment was that in Palestine Lord Balfour was anything but a distinguished man, whatever he was in Europe. His reward for being barred from the Mosque of Omar was a visit to Tel-Aviv, where Saint Saens's *Samson and Delilah* was performed for him. The visit seems a just recompense.

Why Lord Balfour should have expressed a desire to visit the Arab Mosque at all, since he was understood to be fitfully unaware of the presence of Arabs in Palestine, is something of a puzzle. He continued to be unaware of them after his arrival in their country. At the end of a small dinner in his honour, at which a few British personages were the other guests, he strolled to the window and looking out on the passers in the street below, asked, "Who are those men in petticoats?" The men in petticoats, of course, were Arabs, which Balfour knew well, but he displayed his best museum-interest in the specimens after he had been informed solemnly who they were.

He progressed from one Zionist settlement to another, making airy speeches upon his Declaration; upon the place it had given to Zionism in Palestine: upon the League's, or Europe's, or the world's, or the universe's, or the cosmos's deliberate decision to install the National Home; upon Britain's fidelity to the Mandate, and upon other residue subjects. But when he left the British zone to visit Damascus, there very nearly was a disaster.

The French had not taken the needful intense precautions to guard him—in Palestine he had been guarded like a State prisoner—and in Damascus an Arab mob gathered round his hotel. The city filled with turmoil. The booths and warehouses of "The Street that is called Straight" and the other bazaars had been shut. The mob, yelling, "Palestine is Arab! surged up to the bolted doors of the hotel. Coming on to the balcony with a few companions, Balfour faced the rioters very bravely, but provocatively. He never even missed a cue, asking for the reasons of this obscure riot, and watching with lengthening surprise while cavalry charged the crowd. Next appeared a group of armoured cars. The people resisted and soon there was a desperate melée. There were hand-to-hand struggles; rifle-butts, the flats of sabres, and whips rose and fell, while to add to the uproar and confusion aeroplanes came dipping down and dropped smoke-bombs.

General Sarrail himself, the French High Commissioner, stood in protection at the main door of the hotel, till the reluctant Balfour was smuggled out by a side-entrance, to save him from an infuriated populace which knew no better than to offer violence to a man who should have been treated with disdain. He was rushed to Beyrout, taken on board the Messageries liner *Sphinx* anchored in the harbour, and in her, the only safe retreat for him, he had to remain. "Is all this really because of my Declaration?" he inquired. He was three days on board till she sailed and took him off with his undoubted courage, but also his spiritual footlights and rhetorical asides, on the first stage of his return to England.

Meanwhile, behind the academic joy on Mount Scopus, an ingenious plan of six years before was being revived, largely through the efforts of a very unacademic person, a Mr. Rosenblatt, American member of the Finance Committee of the World Zionist Organization. Its object was to hasten the process of securing Palestine for the Zionists. The scheme was called "The League of Autonomous Municipalities." Zionist immigrants were to be gathered into townships as far as possible. As most of them had gone to the towns this presented no great difficulty, but wider areas dotted with close settlement would have to be declared, "townships."

Then, with the agreement of the eternal accomplice, the Colonial Office, and of the marionette Palestine Administration, each of these townships would be declared a "self-governing Jewish Municipality"—on the lines of Tel-Aviv. It would have power to raise taxes, to hold courts, to maintain police. The next step was that the "autonomous municipality" would be granted power to extend itself, by the inclusion of such territory, no longer necessarily urban, as could be considered "economically dependent" upon it. The third step, which as it were reached the landing, was that all these Municipalities were to be joined together into the "Municipal League of the Land of Israel," a very ingenious title which introduced Zionist nationality much as the first bars of a theme steal into a concerto.

The whole body of settlements in this way would coalesce into a large self-governing unit spread through the Holy Land, and over it the population of the country would have no control of any kind. This "League's" next requirement would be a governing body of some kind. Accordingly plans were being prepared for a "General Council" to which the various autonomous municipalities would send delegates. So there would have been your Zionist Parliament ruling over your Zionist State, but disguised, for as long as was thought necessary, as the "League of Autonomous Municipalities of the Land of Israel."

As far as I remember, it was through the self-satisfaction of the Brandeis regime that news of this scheme leaked out a little in the United States. From there it came to the ever-vigilant ears of Miss Broadhurst and Miss Farquharson (cf. Introduction), and they told me. A little inquiry and examination showed the implications of the affair, showed how the municipal seeds were meant to grow into a State and the share the Government would have in fostering its growth. The Palestine Government indeed had already given permission for the first autonomous formations to be created, though in Palestine the Arabs do not seem to have learned what was afoot.

Fortunately, there seemed still a chance to take counter-steps. I was in London then, and provided some publicity explaining what the scheme meant. This was followed by pertinent questions in Parliament from the small band of active sympathizers with the Arabs. The Arabs themselves, enlightened from Europe, broke into general complaint in their Press. The Arab Executive announced that it would petition the League of Nations against the permission granted by the Administration. It was not so much the proposed petition as the announcement of it that was valuable.

This exposure was successful. There was some screening of retreat, and cloudy phrases about "Arab misapprehensions" were puffed forth to cover it, but the "League of Autonomous Municipalities" faded from sight. It was a signal and rare little victory against the usual enormous odds. We were just in time to seize the passes before the enemy came up.

In October Sir Herbert Samuel's term as High Commissioner ended. He had been sent to Palestine to serve as an example of Zionism to the Arabs, but had ended by proving himself an exception. It is of interest that his guiding dictum, "Before you do anything, you must first consider its effect upon the political situation," has been cast up against him. Really, it showed that he understood the position of things in Palestine, where the status of the Administration itself was not such that it could lay down the codes of a Cato.

"Why worry?" a Chief Justice once had said benignly on a fatiguing day in Jerusalem to a counsel trying at great length to have some evidence ruled out as inadmissible and illegal. "Why worry? Everything is illegal here." That Sir Herbert Samuel would have admitted as much as this is highly improbable, but it is not so improbable that chill doubts not altogether remote from the judge's words sailed the occasional east winds of his mind.

He was succeeded by a very different sort of man, Lord Plumer. This soldier was not the type of successor the younger van of Zionists wanted, any more than they had come to want Sir Herbert Samuel. The Government did want Lord Plumer, though, because Lord Plumer was exactly the sort of pillar behind which the Government could conceal itself. But the very Zionist *Palestine Weekly*, when his appointment was announced, declared, "The Holy Land or the Jewish Homeland, whichever you will, are both objects of deep study calling for the highest attributes, intellectual and spiritual, in an official and an administrator. In this respect Lord Plumer is only an average resident of the country [England, presumably], the type of law-abiding, God-fearing, church-going, perfect old gentleman." "We stressed some time ago," said the *Palestine Weekly* annoyedly, "the necessity of having an intellectual government."

The unintellectual victor of Flanders unperturbedly proceeded to Palestine and calmly did sentry-go for the Government for three years. His not to reason why, nor to do anything but keep Palestine orderly.

In this he was perfectly successful, but was helped by general conditions. The years 1926 and 1927 were years of slump, while 1928 was well advanced ere signs of improvement showed. That had a marked effect on Zionist immigration, which dried up, and that again had its effect upon the Arabs' demeanour.

Between 1920 and 1925 some 80,000 Zionist immigrants had entered Palestine, immigrants accounted for, that is to say. There will have been some thousands of so-called "clandestine immigrants" too; the only difference between the two groups really being that the scaling-ladders of the 80,000 were officially stamped before use, and that the clandestine used their own implements. In 1925 the influx began to grow alarming for the Arabs, because the rate of entry had more than doubled that of the previous year, and probably not far short of 35,000 recruits came to swell the forces of the National Home.

However, with the advent of the general monetary slump of 1926, immigrant entries fell by half, and what is more, large numbers of immigrants began to leave Palestine and to seek their fortunes elsewhere. So in 1926 the actual increase of Zionist population was but 5,700. Thirteen thousand came in, but 7,000 went out. By mid-1926 there were more Jews leaving Palestine than entering it. The Zionist population had dropped about three thousand by the beginning of 1927, and since the July of the previous year there had been a steady monthly deficit of entries compared with departures. This looked then like continuing indefinitely, and the Arabs began to believe that the National Home was on the way to disintegration. They were content to watch this develop, and something of the peace which attends upon natural processes unwontedly covered the land.

As a result the Mandates Commission of the League, at the close of the session of June 1928, recorded in tones of mingled relief and triumph that for the first time since the Mandate had been established the Arabs had not entered a complaint against the form of Mandatory rule imposed upon them. The attitude of Geneva was that it was at last freed of a tiresome buzzing noise in its ears.

When the slump was ebbing out, Lord Plumer's term was ending too. During his reign, however, though the Zionist many had lost ground, the Zionist few had bettered their situation in various ways. M. Rutenberg's Jordan Concessions were recast and affirmed in a grant signed by the High Commissioner, on the 5th of March, 1926. The clause of the 1921 agreement was maintained, by which any existing undertakings could be expropriated by the Rutenberg Company, under the same conditions as before. But the judgment of The Hague Court hovered in the background apparently, for the new clause read that the High Commissioner was to expropriate at the Company's request "so far as he lawfully can."

By a new clause fresh privileges arose. The use became unlawful of:

> "such waters of the Jordan, its basin, including the Yarmook and all other affluents of the Jordan and its basin, as may be now or shall hereafter be brought into the Concession area, in such a manner as to reduce the quality of water available to the Company below the quantity required for the generation of electrical energy by the Company's works from time to time affirmed by the High Commissioner, Provided no owner of land is deprived of water for drinking and other domestic purposes and for his animals and for the irrigation of any land which he has irrigated and planted with trees or other permanent plantations at the date hereof."

This raised a poor prospect for any Arab landholder who after 1926 in any of the riverine basins of Palestine desired to extend his holding by irrigation and plantation.

Also, the great potash concessions of the Dead Sea, where vast quantities of minerals lay—potassium chloride, magnesium bromide and other chemicals—were indented to a semi-Zionist syndicate. Probably it was the richest deposit of potash in the world. A British syndicate, known as the Homer group from the name of the chief chemist who had conducted investigations, had been on the ground since occupation by the Army had begun, had investigated thoroughly and had drawn up a fully worked-out scheme for the exploitation of the concessions. But its prompt application had met with no success, and the concessions had been awarded by the Government, through the Palestine administration, to the Tulloch-Novomeyski syndicate. M. Novomeyski was an early Palestinian, Major Tulloch a Scot.

There were a number of questions put in Parliament concerning this syndicate and its affiliations. Sir Alfred Mond denied that it was a child of his Imperial Chemical Industries Company. He said however "that he was prepared to explore the situation and to form an opinion of the commercial value" of the Concession, if terms of a satisfactory nature could be arranged. There was only road transport available, and this would be too costly for a large output. It would be a long time, he said, before the Dead Sea would be able to dominate the potash markets of the world, as French, Germans and Spaniards all produced potash at low prices.

The point of importance was that the Homer group—Dr. Homer had done much research work for the country during the War—which had no Zionist connections nor any wish for them, did not get the concessions, even though they had none of Sir Alfred Mond's misgivings concerning the future of these. Some substantial American bids met with a like failure, and a certain amount of comment followed upon this in the technical journals of the United States. The Americans, like the Homer group, did not seem as impressed with the great difficulty caused by transport problems and by world competition as the diffident Sir Alfred Mond had been. They were rather headstrong in wanting to obtain some share in concessions, and were peevish when the Tulloch-Novomeyski syndicate carried everything off.

The plans of this syndicate, however, found greater favour than any others with the Palestine Government and the Colonial Office. [Author's note: The Novomeyski concessions (Major Tulloch is dead) are challenged in their entirety by a pre-War Turkish concession in British hands. There are many points of resemblance between Mavrommatis claim and that of the British claimant, Mr. Maitland Edwards. I abstain from further reference because this claim has not been fought yet in all available courts.] M. Novomeyski was understood to be a satisfactory engineer, with special experience of evaporating, which would suit the concessions. Evaporation was the most likely method of separating the mineral salts of the Dead Sea deposits.

Sir John Chancellor, who succeeded Lord Plumer, had less good fortune than the latter. His arrival in office coincided with a restoration of general financial conditions and so with a recrudescence of Zionist immigration into Palestine, though it was five years before the 34,000 figure of 1925 was approached again. It became clear to the Arabs though that British policy had no part in the 1926-7 setback of the National Home. They perceived that they had nothing but a progressive development of immigration to look forward to, and they became correspondingly disturbed and angered.

References made in Britain to Palestine, cabled out and reproduced in the Arabic Press, gave at irregular intervals a fillip to their anger. Mr. Ormsby-Gore and others for a long while past had developed a standard way of descanting on the situation in Palestine, which had been retained automatically by the spokesmen of all Governments.

This was to assume that Arab discontent and opposition arose from "Arab fears," which fears, as they went on to show, were "groundless." To be told regularly that their fears were groundless was in itself bad enough for the Arabs, but what made the practice unbearable was that the orators in question always gave their own definition of "Arab fears" in terms which bore no relation at all to anything in the mind of any Arab.

"Arab fears," as formulated in the Ormsby-Gore manner, were fears that the Zionists would be allowed by Great Britain to deprive the Arabs of their half-share in Palestine, or of their part in the common inheritance, of the two races—or some such phrase. Now this was not the Arabs' fear at all. It was what Mr. Ormsby-Gore and his friends wished the Arabs to fear. The true Arab fear could scarcely be termed a fear by 1929, for it was by then swiftly changing from apprehension to certainty. It was that, by way of a start, the Zionists were being given by Great Britain this half-share in Palestine, to which they had no right whatsoever.

Despite their full acquaintance with facts, those who played the Ormsby-Gore gambit represented the Arabs as contented so long as the Zionists merely took over Palestine along with them, but as breaking into a sweat of fear if the Zionists looked like exaggerating their "share in the common inheritance." The next move in the gambit was to sweep away this "fear" in clouds of verbiage, under cover of which the false premise was established that the Arabs would be voluntary partners under what are called "fifty-fifty" terms with the Jews. An ingenious stratagem in its way, but extremely inflaming to those whose national sentiments were traduced repeatedly.

Palestine began to simmer and boil again. In September a couple of incidents occurred, petty things, the second of them sprung from the unauthorized bringing of a screen to the Wailing Wall by some of the Jewish worshippers.

As a result of these incidents feelings mounted gradually higher during nine months, supported by all manner of paper and verbal incitements, and ended unsurprisingly in an outbreak (after a preliminary affray on the 17th during which a Jewish boy was stabbed) at Jerusalem on the 23rd of August, 1929. It spread soon to various provincial towns. A hundred and thirty-three Jews were killed and eighty-seven Arabs, a number of the latter from the fire of the armed forces restoring order.

At the time the High Commissioner, Sir John Chancellor, was out of the country. He was at home, on leave but conferring with the Government on the question of the appeal for a Representative Assembly, which the Arab Executive, the leaders of the people, had made with renewed force upon his entry into office. He of course returned at once to Palestine and the first result of the outbreak was that he announced on arrival that he had broken off his discussions with the Government "in view of recent events." He emphasized in his proclamation the savagery of the attacks on the Jews, particularly in Hebron, where indeed only the bravery of a British police officer, Mr. Cafferata, had prevented a massacre. It was a worse outbreak than that of 1921. Several Jewish synagogues were desecrated and a hospital sacked, while for the first time there was Zionist retaliation, in Jerusalem, upon a mosque, which also was sacked and desecrated.

Next month came the inevitable sequel. A Commission was appointed to inquire into the disturbances and to report to the Colonial Secretary, who was Lord Passfield. The appointment of a Commission of Enquiry was of course a superfluity, if inquiry were to mean a search for the fundamental causes of the outbreak. The labours of a Commission were not needed to discover these: everyone of the age of reason in the population knew what they were. Any four intelligent Britons could have been gathered in England, and without leaving its shores, if a true summary of past history had been put into their hands, could have formed a Commission and within a week have reported that "The fundamental cause of the outbreak in Palestine is the policy which has been pursued there by His Majesty's Government and its predecessors."

The Arabs had the hope though that the Commission might register what was self-evident, and with the local experience it would have gained might register it with such emphasis that the Government might be guided by the Report. The Arabs had begun to indulge in hopes when that Government had come into office, based upon a Labour Government's presumably emancipatory doctrines. The Labour Government, too, was free of responsibilities for the creation of the Palestine Question, though the Foreign Secretary, Mr. Arthur Henderson, was a sort of creative remnant left in it from the Lloyd George days.

Time passed however without any fulfilment of the Arabs' expectations. There were enough Zionistic elements in the Labour Party to prevent any change of policy. The very nature of its own creed impeded that Party from making such a change. Its long and honourable struggle in Britain had been to obtain for the workers good conditions of life, to free them from poverty, from bad food, from bad housing, from all the too familiar concomitants of their lot. No political body could carry on such a struggle for so many years without becoming penetrated with this single purpose. Always striving to obtain material benefit, the Labour Party would not have been human if it had not slipped into regarding material benefit as the supreme good. Also, as it was in every core of its being an internal Party, concentrating essentially on the conditions of the United Kingdom (whereas the Conservatives were an external Party on the whole), it thought in terms of the British Isles, had little knowledge of foreign ideas—none at all of Islamic—and only saw in Palestine another Hartlepool. The Zionists' declared aim was to raise the conditions of life and to Westernize a poor, backward land. "What more could the Arabs ask?" was the average Labour feeling. That the Arabs' desires were only for a degree of material betterment which would leave their country still poor and backward compared with Becontree and Ruskin College was (and remains) a conception untranslatable into any language Labour folk apparently could or can understand.

Mr. Ramsay MacDonald himself had the usual Zionist connections of his Party, though it must be said of him that he had strivings of mind, and would drift away from these connections at times. Lord Passfield from the Zionist viewpoint was the sole permanently uncertain factor in the Cabinet, and it was he who had been made Colonial Secretary. Above all things he was of an investigatory temper.

He probably did hope for enlightenment through the Commission he now appointed. But he was out-manoeuvred from the start by the wirepullers of Zionism. The last thing they wanted was that the fundamental causes of the outbreak should be investigated. The terms of reference drawn up for the Commission showed their influence. They were "to inquire into the immediate causes which led to the recent outbreak in Palestine and to make recommendations as to the steps necessary to avoid a recurrence."

In these terms of reference the operative word was meant to be the adjective "immediate." The Commission was to inquire into immediate causes; not into ultimate responsibilities. It was not to inquire into the genesis of the National Home, but into the traditional rights and usages pertaining to the Wailing Wall; not into the immigration-edicts of the Government, but into the recriminations of Arabs and of Zionists; not into policy but into police-measures.

It was as though a coroner's court were told to exert its utmost energies to discover whether a traffic victim had succumbed through too sharp a blow from a car's bonnet or too heavy a pressure from its wheels, but were not given powers to inquire what agency was responsible for the mortal blow or the deadly pressure.

Chapter 36

The Shaw Commission.
Its Report a blow for the Government.
Endeavours to destroy the effect of the Report.
Sir John Hope Simpson sent to Palestine.
His Report no better for the Government.
Lord Passfield's White Paper.

There seems small doubt that the intention to circumscribe to this nonsensical degree the field of inquiry of the newly appointed Commission sprang from the lesson which had been received from the Haycraft Report of 1921. The Haycraft Commissioners (cf. Chapter 24) were given terms of reference to inquire into the riots of 1920 in Jaffa, which bade them simply "to inquire into the disturbances and to report thereon." They very properly therefore did not restrict themselves to the details in Jaffa, but passed to the general causes of the outbreak, as the reader has seen.

It was determined in London, therefore, that this mishap should not recur, and so the new Commission was bridled—it was thought—by the specific order to inquire into the immediate causes of the fresh outbreak. The Commissioners to whose activities this restricted scope was offered were Sir Walter Shaw, Sir Henry Betterton, Mr. R. H. Morris and Mr. H. Snell, the three last being Members of Parliament. The Chairman, Sir Walter Shaw, had had a long judicial career in the Colonial Service, in the West Indies, in Ceylon and in the Straits Settlements, of which he had been Chief Justice. Sir Henry Betterton had been Parliamentary Secretary to the Ministry of Labour, and both he and Mr. Morris had practised at the Bar. They journeyed to Palestine, stayed there three months, heard a hundred and thirty witnesses, returned and presented their Report in March 1930.

Then it was seen that everything had gone wrong. In a minor degree the Commission had accepted Government premises. But the Commissioners had not turned out at all docile in the matter of the general causes of the outbreak. The Shaw Report proved to be anything but the species of Dunmow Flitch trial of supposedly conjugal Arabs and Zionists, betrayed into difference by unfortunate and locally remediable circumstances, on which the Government had counted.

One member of the Commission, indeed, Lord Snell (as he has become since) did sign a minority-codicil on these lines. He could not believe that, when the Arabs became conscious of the "material benefits" and the like which Zionism would bring them, they would not happily work with the Zionists for a united future. He developed for them the "lucre, not liberty" doctrine so amazingly put forward by the Labour wing of pro-Zionists. That the Orient had a precious civilization of its own which Zionist "prosperity" must destroy was a thought that did not occur to him evidently. He also blamed the Mufti for provoking the disorders, but had nothing to say on the failure of the Government to heed anything but disorder.

The other members of the Commission, while reviewing at length as was expected of them, the local symptoms of the outbreak, went on like conscientious physicians to seek for its origins in the history of the ailing country for which they had been called in to prescribe. Nor did Lord Snell enter any objection to this prosecution of the inquiry.

"We consider," the Report ran, "that the political and economic grievances of the Arabs, as explained to us in evidence, must be regarded as having been immediate causes of the disturbances of August last." The introduction of "immediate" here was neat: the drafters of the terms of reference were knocked over with a swing of the very curtain which they had meant should exclude the light. The Commissioners' next words completed official discomfiture.

> But even if this were not our view [they added] we should have been bound to examine those grievances in the light of the second part of our task, since it is clear that recommendations, even when most carefully considered and most thoroughly applied, could not, unless they went to the root of the matter, succeed in avoiding a recurrence of the recent unfortunate disturbances.

This statement of the Commissioners was in the sixth chapter of their Report, where they turned to the question of preventing such recurrences. They proceeded to examine, under the three headings of immigration, land, and "constitutional development," whether Governmental policy was responsible for the outbreaks of the previous year. The position was not put as crudely as that, of course; the Commissioners used various circumlocutions. It was to this, however, that their examination amounted. I do not say that they examined right back to first principles. They did not ask, for example, whether the Government had any right to impose immigrants upon the people of Palestine against their will.

But they stated the grounds upon which the Government had instituted immigration, without comment upon their character, and then found that:

1. Even on the Government's own basis and own grounds too many Zionist immigrants were being brought into the country.
2. These immigrants were displacing the Arabs and that "the one period when immigration was heavy was followed by severe unemployment and economic disturbance."
3. Arab opposition to Jewish immigration was "well-founded in that it has its origin in the known results of excessive immigration in the past and that, given other and more immediate causes for disturbance, that feeling undoubtedly would be a factor which would contribute to an outbreak."

They quoted with great effect Zionist evidence before them upon the Zionist attitude to immigration. They did not emphasize the point, but from their mere quotations it stood out that "excessive immigration," i.e., large-scale immigration, was essential for the Zionist schemes.

Three years before that the Zionist Organization, with Jewish-American help, had appointed a Survey Commission of experts to give them the equivalent of "second opinions," upon the general question of colonization in Palestine which then was in the throes of the slump. The chief of these outside experts was Sir John Campbell, a League of Nations authority on the settlement of refugees and transference of populations.

From his Report the Shaw Commissioners cited one or two telling passages:

> The idea [he wrote of Zionist colonization] was firmly established that over-expenditure was necessary for propaganda purposes; the Jewish psychology was such that funds could not be obtained, in adequate amounts, unless the Palestine Organization could point to new colonies "established," to additional lands "acquired," to steady and large increases in the number of immigrants.

From Sir John Campbell's Report the Commissioners extracted too the judgment that it was the Jewish Federation of Labour—(of all bodies the most determined to de-Arabize Palestine)—which really controlled the volume of immigration. The then Government (by the mouth of Mr. Churchill in 1922) might have proclaimed that the whole policy of immigration was subject to the most careful study and that the character and qualifications of the immigrants were "subject to the most rigid scrutiny under the control of the Government." But it was clear, said the Commissioners, that:

> this in no way represents the practice which obtains under the arrangements in force at the present time for the control of immigration into Palestine. [Quite bluntly they concluded] We are of opinion that what is practically the delegation of responsibility by the Palestine Government to a body whose members comprise less than 3 percent of the population of that country cannot be defended.

The Commissioners followed up this rebuke by saying that the Government should "at an early date issue a clear and definite declaration of the policy which they intend to be pursued in regard to the regulation and control of Jewish immigration into Palestine"; that until "some form of representative government is established in Palestine" what they described as "non-Jewish-interests" should be consulted upon immigration, and that the Government should "aim" at carrying out the scrutiny of immigrants which in 1922 it had declared it always carried out. That was the sense of the Report, though the pill of this last recommendation was perfunctorily gilded.

Coming to land questions, the Commissioners examined the question of the dispossession of the Arabs from the lands acquired by the incoming Zionists. Their conclusions may be quoted:

> We are only concerned with the land-problem in so far as an examination of it was necessary to enable us to estimate the extent to which the difficulties involved in it were either a contributory cause to the recent disturbances or are likely to be a cause of disturbance in the future. But for this purpose such an examination was clearly essential. We think that a continuation, or still more an acceleration, of a process which results in the creation of a large discontented and landless class is fraught with serious danger to the country. If it be accepted that the conversion of large sections of those who are now cultivators of the soil into a landless class be, as we think, not only undesirable in itself, but also a potential source of disturbance, it is clear that further protection of the present cultivators' position and some restriction on the alienation of land are inevitable. The "Protection of Cultivators" Ordinance of 1929 does nothing to check the tendency to which we have referred. The mere provision of compensation in money may even encourage it.

This gradual creation of landless and homeless Arabs through the extension of the National Home called for legislation, in the opinion of the Commissioners. They agreed that the solution of the land problem was "obviously a difficult and delicate task," because Article 6 of the Mandate on the one hand called for close settlement of the Jews on the land, and on the other hand declared that the rights and position of other sections of the population should not be prejudiced. "Some solution however," said the Report, "is essential."

The Shaw Commission was obliged to take the Mandate at its face value and to visualize the Government as confronted in it with contradictory obligations. It could not inquire into who wrote the Mandate, who arranged the "obligations," and for what reason the contradictions were placed in it. But, debarred from this primary exposure, the Shaw Report exposed as much of the Mandate as it could upon the secondary plane of its execution in practice. The Commissioners had heard and had recorded in their Report much Zionist evidence that the National Home did not produce landlessness and homelessness amid the Arabs.

But the just-quoted terms of their conclusion show that they did not give credence to this evidence, since they spoke with alarm of the "continuation of a process which results in the creation of a large discontented and landless class." Here again they refrained from dotting their i's, but the process in question could be no other than the continuous development of the National Home by immigration, under the aegis of the British Government.

This therefore was a second severe rebuke to Government policy, and a second finding that Government policy was the source of "disturbances" in Palestine.

The third heading under which the members of the Commission examined Government responsibility was that of "constitutional development." There was a pretty acerbity about the use of these words, for the burden of this particular section of their Report was that in the matter of constitutional development in Palestine the Government had provided no constitutional development at all.

The Commissioners first enumerated the Arabs' grounds of grievance on this score, describing them as four in number: the Government's failure to honour its pledge of independence given to the Arabs through King Hussein; the Government's alienation from them of the right of self-determination; the Government's refusing to them the representative system which it had conceded to neighbouring Arab lands on the same plane of political ability; the Government's violation of Article 22 of the Covenant.

Again the Commissioners were not in a situation to consider the absolute foundation of charges against the Government, but they were not quite content to set these down with no least hint of their opinion on the subject.

With regard to the McMahon pledges they quoted in full the proclamations showered from British aeroplanes in 1917 upon the soil of Palestine, by which King Hussein called on all Arabs to leave the Turks and join the national movement for independence. To examine and comment upon the McMahon Correspondence itself clearly did not, they said, fall within the scope of their inquiry. They summed the matter up thus, though,

> The Arabs argue that if these proclamations and appeals did not constitute a pledge, then they were a deception practised in the moment of her need by a great nation upon the credulity of a trusting and confiding people. They aver that if they had suspected that the policy of Great Britain was, or would be, to create a National Home for those whom they regard as an alien race in the country in which they have lived for thirteen hundred years, they would not have taken the action they did or have incurred the risks inseparable from it.

This was indeed a mere summary by the Commissioners of an Arab argument. Yet it is not possible to read it without drawing from it the same lesson which the members of a jury draw from the mere summary by a judge of the convincing arguments of a party to a case before him. The Commissioners, too, were quick to add:

> That this argument has not been evolved long after the event in order to justify a political demand is shown by the following passage taken from the Report of the Military Court appointed to inquire into the disturbances which occurred in Jerusalem in 1920.

Then they quoted from the unpublished Palin Report (cf. Chapter 19) some paragraphs, of which the last sentences may be included here:

> As late as June 1918 active recruiting was carried out in Palestine for the Shereefian army, our allies, the recruits being given to understand that they were fighting in a national cause and to liberate their country from the Turks. These men, it is believed, actually took part in the offensive against the Turks. The tendency of the evidence is to show that in spite of the fact that nothing had been said about Palestine being included in the Hedjaz Empire and the fact that the Balfour Declaration had been published in 1917, the real impression left upon the Arabs generally was that the British were going to set up an independent Arab State which would include Palestine.

It is to be observed, in comment upon this extract, that in saying Palestine was not included in the "Hedjaz Empire" the Palin Report spoke loosely. Palestine may not have been mentioned by name, but it was very much included within the detailed boundaries of the Arab territories.

Mesopotamia, and the Hedjaz itself, also were not mentioned by name but solely through their inclusion within the same itemized boundaries, this being the necessary method employed in treaties and kindred doctrines to ensure exactitude. No Arab territory was mentioned by its name, but the boundaries were given within which all territory was Arab.

To return to the Shaw Report, the fact that the Commissioners published these extracts, that from the Palin Report being a revelation and a most damning one for the Government, was a reasonable indication of their own opinion.

With the second and third Arab charges the Report dealt more briefly, giving the official as well as the Arab arguments in the matter of withheld self-government.

Upon the charge that the Covenant had been violated (by Mr. Lloyd George's Government), the manner in which the Commissioners gave the Arab case is decidedly to be noted.

> What Paragraph 4 of Article 22 of the Treaty of Versailles purported to do, they [the Arabs] say, was to impose on Palestine an "A" Mandate with all the implications of such a Mandate. What in fact emerged after the Conference of San Remo, at which the Arabs of Palestine were not directly represented, was a Mandate with conditions and limitations and provisions for the establishment of a National Home for another race—provisions which they fear not only make the burden of the Mandate in effect perpetual but which definitely deprive the people of Palestine of the legitimate expectations which are inherent in an "A" Mandate. On this point it is interesting to note that Mr. Sacher, the Chairman of the Palestine Zionist Executive, when asked whether he thought that the Mandate should go on forever, replied, "Certainly."

"What emerged after the Conference of San Remo"—the situation is restrainedly stated, but within the limits of restraint no more suspicious inflection could have been applied to any account of the San Remo proceedings.

After the summary of the Arab case there followed paragraphs which must be quoted at a little length. For some reason, possibly etiquette, the Commissioners in penning them do not remark that the ground which they cover (the part of the whole population in the national movement of Palestine) had been traversed nine years before by the Haycraft Commissioners. Sir Walter Shaw and his colleagues could have pointed out that they were obliged to repeat, at greater length, what their predecessors had stated long ago, because no notice had been taken of the words of the previous Commission.

Out of evil, though, good may come sometimes, and there is a great advantage in a declaration by another Commission, which after a lapse of some time confirms absolutely upon the evidence before it the finding of its predecessor-Commission. These two declarations of the Haycraft and the Shaw Commissions are especially to be read and pondered today when the members of the Palestine Arab Executive have been confined in prison-islands or driven into exile, on the pretext of their baneful influence upon their humbler compatriots.

> "It has been argued before us [runs the Shaw Report then] that the Arab fellah takes no personal interest in politics and that the present state of popular feeling, which in every village and in most country districts finds its expression in such cries as "Down with the Balfour Declaration" and in demands for a national government, is the result of propaganda promoted artificially and for personal ends by men who wish to exploit what may be, as far as they are concerned, quite genuine grievances.
>
> The contention that the fellah takes no personal interest in politics is not supported by our experience in Palestine. No one who has been about the country as we have been and has listened to the applause which greeted many passages in the addresses read to us by village heads and sheikhs could doubt that villagers and peasants alike are taking a very real and personal interest both in the effect of the policy of establishing a National Home and in the question of the development of self-governing institutions in Palestine. No less than fourteen Arabic newspapers are published in Palestine, and in almost every village there is someone who reads from the papers to gatherings of those villagers who are illiterate.
>
> During the long season of the year when the soil cannot be tilled the villagers, having no alternative occupation, discuss politics, and it is not unusual for part of the address in the mosques on Friday to be devoted to political affairs. *The Arab fellaheen and villagers are therefore probably more politically minded than many of the people of Europe.* [My italics].
>
> We are not prepared to say that there is no truth in the argument that the increased interest which the fellaheen of today are unquestionably taking in political and constitutional issues is the result of propaganda. Opposition to the present policy is the very foundation of the political creed of the Palestine Arab Executive: the members of that body have made no secret of their beliefs and it would not be unnatural were they to seek to convince fellow-countrymen of their own race that the present policy is inimical to Arab interests. We have no reason to doubt that in the prosecution of their demand for self-government the Arab leaders, as a whole, have been inspired by a genuine feeling of patriotism: some few may desire a return to the days of a corrupt regime, but of that there is no evidence. We are therefore unable to accept the contention that propaganda on the constitutional issue has been fostered by the leading Arab politicians with the motive of gratifying personal ambitions or of attaining personal ends.
>
> The position today is that the Arab people of Palestine are united in demanding some measure of self-government."

From this dismissal of what is still a favourite official calumny, the Shaw Report turned to a special chapter covering what it called "Difficulties Inherent in the Mandate." As before the Commissioners did not (and could not) inquire into the making of the Mandate. They had to take it as it was. But within these limits they did what the Navy calls "a good job of work." They analysed the Balfour Declaration and showed that this oracle could be construed (as we know) in any desired way. "It follows therefore," they said, "that were the Balfour Declaration the only instrument of guidance to the administrator in Palestine, he could by reference to that document justify any of the large number of varying lines of policy."

If the administrator in search for guidance turned from the Balfour Declaration to the Mandate, he got no further. "Here again," ran the Report, "we find in close conjunction both aspects of the policy. Here again a wide variety of interpretations are possible." Nor, taking the dilemma a step further, did the Administrator find any guidance in the "definition" both of the Balfour Declaration and of British policy which had been issued in 1922 by Mr. Churchill, supposedly to supply the clarity and guidance missing from Declaration and from Mandate.

> "It is not possible by summary [said the Report] or by quotation to indicate either the purport of the statement or the extent to which Mr. Churchill defined the meaning of the Balfour Declaration. We therefore reproduce his statement in Appendix V to this Report.
>
> Within its limits the statement is clear and explicit but, as we read it, it was designed as a corrective to the aspirations entertained among certain sections of Jewry rather than as a definition of the rights of the non-Jewish sections of the community in Palestine.
>
> In our view it would be of great advantage if His Majesty's Government were to issue some more positive declaration of the meaning which they attach to the second part of the Balfour Declaration, and to those provisions in the Mandate which, being based upon that part of the Declaration, provide for the safeguarding of the rights of the non-Jewish communities in Palestine.
>
> We should further urge that in the interests alike of all sections of the people of Palestine and of the local Administration, His Majesty's Government should define with unequivocal clearness the meaning which they attach to the Balfour Declaration as a whole, and should state with equal clarity the course of policy which they intend to be pursued in that country in the future."

It cannot of course be asserted, but it is hard not to think that in these statements and recommendations the Shaw Commissioners gave an exhibition of admirable satire. Men of their intelligence, of their status, and of their calling, after studying the Palestine Question for some months, were not likely to be the dupes of any thesis of Government irresponsibility.

It is true that in their comments and recommendations they presented, implicitly, everything which they found unsatisfactory as unsatisfactory by accident, by concatenation of events. They never suggested that the Government had wished for these unsatisfactory things, still less, had contrived them. But if they employed satire, herein lay their skill.

They spoke of the "difficulties inherent in the Mandate." Were they unaware that Mr. Lloyd George's Government and the Zionists had carefully written "the difficulties" in the Mandate? It is not very probable.

Was it mere coincidence which led them to recommend that His Majesty's Government should state with unequivocal clearness the meaning of the Balfour Declaration, when the whole intention of the Government which had issued that Declaration was that it should be equivocal?

Did they proclaim themselves unable to divine to what purpose Mr. Churchill had issued his 1920 White Paper or to comprehend what his definitions in the White Paper even meant—only because of innocent bewilderment?

Was the fact that Mr. Churchill, while asserting that Arab rights would be preserved, had taken care not to explain what those rights were—was this so very indefinitely insinuated in the Report? Let the reader peruse the relevant sentence again.

Did the Commissioners, finally, ask the existing Government to state clearly its future policy in Palestine without another thought in their heads than that a statement of this kind was an essential step to peace or to the next best thing in Palestine, a clear issue?

Maybe, but maybe again they knew well that the essence of the policy which the MacDonald Government had inherited was that policy should not be clearly stated, that nothing at all ever should be defined in terms which should prevent anything at all from being done. The first stage of the policy had been to put Palestine into a muddle, to create the "Palestine Question," and the pursuance of the policy was to keep Palestine in a muddle. Afterwards one Government or the other might talk retrospectively perhaps of "muddling through," with a deprecatory mien and with the air of contemplating a series of plain statesmen, its predecessors, for whom an intricate situation had proved too much, who had been rather admirable in their simplicity and in their inability to cope with all the conflicting requirements of Palestine. Ormsby-Gore, overwhelmed and struggling with duty! Balfour plodding about, adrift, misunderstood and misunderstanding! Lloyd George in his yeoman's gaiters dragging himself by force of character through slimy, un-British morasses to his native highroad. That indeed proved to be the sort of picture which was painted by and by.

However, to return to the Report, whether any section of it was written in seriousness or in satire, there was the Government confronted with its text, with the chapters devoted to the local causes of the outbreak quite blanketed by those devoted to its fundamental clauses.

> "There can be no doubt [was its general summing-up] that racial animosity on the part of the Arabs, consequent upon the disappointment of their political and national aspirations and fear for their economic future, was the fundamental cause of the outbreak of August last."

In addition to its recommendations for a clear statement of policy by the Government and for a definition of what exactly were the rights which were said to be safeguarded for the Arabs (a devilish recommendation), the Commission in its final summary called for the change, already mentioned, in the methods of immigration. It also suggested that an expert inquiry should be made into Palestine, with a co-ordinated land policy, and that it should be reaffirmed that the Zionist Organization was not entitled by reason of its position under the Mandate to share in the Government of Palestine in any degree.

These recommendations and judgments had surpassed the Government's fears. I have said earlier that when the Report was presented it was seen that everything had gone wrong. But the character of the Report was not a complete surprise: if only something had gone wrong and not everything, the Government would have been in a degree prepared for it. Towards the close of 1929 the impression had spread amidst knowledgeable persons in Palestine, and had of course been sent to England, that the Shaw Commissioners would issue findings much more far-reaching than had been expected of them.

So that by December there already was much disquiet in Whitehall and in the circles linking Government, the elder group of Zionistic statesmen, and Zionist leaders together. The outcome was a letter published in *The Times* of the 20th, a week before the last sitting of the Commission in Palestine, signed by Lord Balfour, Mr. Lloyd George and General Smuts. They declared that as members of the War Cabinet which had been responsible for the Balfour Declaration and for the policy of the National Home they:

> "...viewed with deep anxiety" the situation in Palestine. They would not comment upon the events of last August, since the Commission in Palestine was inquiring into them, but whatever the findings of that inquiry might be, it was clear that the "work to which Britain had set her hand at the close of the War was not proceeding satisfactorily."
>
> "Causes which are still obscure," they wrote, "have impeded the task of administration and consequently the full carrying out of the policy"

> to which Britain was pledged. Therefore they urged the Government to appoint an authoritative Commission "to investigate the whole working of the Mandate. The Commission at present in Palestine was appointed with limited terms of reference to inquire into specific matters. The Commission, in our view, must, as soon as it has reported, be supplemented by a searching inquiry into the major questions of policy and of administration."

This was an ingenious counter-move. Under cover of giving vent to the strain of their feelings the signatories warned the Palestine Commission—the letter of course would be cabled to Palestine—to keep to their "limited terms of reference." In the event that this warning had no effect, which was probable, they moved for the creation of a super-Commission which would supersede the Shaw Commission. If a super-Commission, authoritatively composed—and it can be guessed what the signatories considered authoritative composition—was appointed and sent out to Palestine, probably crossing the Shaw body on the way, it would most effectively side-track, not to say hide from view, the latter's Report.

Any unwanted recommendations upon major policy by the Shaw Commission would be whelmed in the recommendations of its successor.

This proposal, however, was not adopted. Mr. MacDonald, for one thing, had genuine scruples about appointing one Commission to supersede another, and however ingeniously phrased, it was to this that the proposal amounted. Nor did the idea commend itself to Lord Passfield. The fingers of the 1920-Cabinet-Zionist-Organization group played upon the Labour Government already, but as yet it was not quite under their thumbs.

So the Shaw Commission ran its course and its recommendations held the stage. When they were first read in Whitehall there was consternation. Before the Report was published, while it was still in the Cabinet's hands and only being shown to Dr. Weizmann and a few friends, there was much questioning of what was to be done next. It went to the printers, and was due to appear on the 31st of March, a Monday. The previous Friday a very intimate and important meeting for consultation on future action took place between the Prime Minister, the Colonial Secretary and Lords Reading and Melchett, Dr. Weizmann, and Mr. Felix Warburg, the millionaire Chairman of the Administrative Committee of the Jewish Agency in the United States. Mr. MacDonald was very worried.

He said that the members of the Commission had gone far beyond their terms of reference. He said, and the visitors agreed, that the Commission had taken under consideration questions of major policy from which they had been specifically excluded. (There was a sort of echo of the Balfour-Lloyd-George-Smuts letter in his remarks.) They had, in his opinion, made recommendations or statements on insufficient evidence.

Though the triune letter had failed in its immediate end, there was again a sort of echo of it in the suggestion for the next step, which took form now at the meeting. Not a Commission, but an individual, not an authoritative little group, but one man of outstanding importance, should be sent to Palestine. His terms-of-reference, too, would be to see what administrative machinery should be installed to secure proper execution of the Mandate, or some formula akin to this and equally absorptive of the Shaw recommendations. Though it is probable that the facts were not put as crudely as that by those who proposed his dispatch.

The man of outstanding importance suggested for the mission, not very astonishingly, was General Smuts. The Prime Minister said that he had had him in mind, but so had the Zionist leaders: his name seems to have issued simultaneously from all available minds. It was proposed that he should spend from a month to two months in Palestine, if he could manage it, for he had gone back to South Africa and had his duties and difficulties there.

Meanwhile Mr. MacDonald promised that he would make a statement in the House of Commons during the coming week declaring the determination of the Government to maintain the National Home policy. So he did, on the 3rd of April, making the familiar declaration that under the terms of the Mandate the Government was responsible for promoting the National Home in the terms of the Balfour Declaration. Of the Shaw Report he said cautiously that in endeavouring to carry out faithfully its terms-of-reference the Commission must have found it difficult to draw lines very rigidly.

The Government was studying the Report and "was in active consultation with all the parties concerned, both those in Palestine and those available for conference here."

There the matter rested for a short while. But General Smuts did not go to Palestine. Whether he was prevented by his home duties or whether it was recognized by the Government that he was too committed to be given the position, is not clear. It seems as though Mr. MacDonald presently enjoyed one of his escapes from Zionist leading-strings. The policy at least finally adopted by Mr. MacDonald and Lord Passfield was to send an uncommitted expert to Palestine, who would present a purely technical report on the questions of "immigration, land settlement, and development." This would be honouring the recommendations of the Shaw Commission in its own way.

As for the constitutional observations in the Report, they were met by opening consultations, upon constitutional points amidst others, with one of the succession of Arab delegations, which had reached London the day before the Shaw Report was published. It was composed of Musa Kazim Pasha, who though eighty-two years of age and always ill at ease in London, returned to the ungrateful task of negotiation in which he had been engaged so vainly for years. With him was the Grand Mufti, now (1938) in flight from Palestine, Ragheb Bey Nashashibi, the Mayor of Jerusalem, Alfred Effendi Roch, Jemal Bey Husseini and Auni Bey Abdel Hadi.

The chosen expert was Sir John Hope Simpson, who had had much experience in the Indian Civil Service. He also had been Vice-President of the Refugee Commission in Athens which had accomplished the great task of transferring those Greeks from Turkey and Turks from Greece who had had to leave these countries under the treaty which had ended the Graeco-Turkish War. He had also been Member of Parliament for Taunton for two years. It was generally acknowledged, when the nomination was made, that it was a good one and that Sir John Hope Simpson was an entirely neutral-minded man.

He reached Palestine on the 20th of May, and at once began a most exhaustive inquiry in which, as he testified, all parties helped him as fully as possible. Before he reached his destination, the conversations in London between the Arab delegates and the Government had come to an end, abruptly.

It is to be noted that the Arabs had not been summoned to London. Arabs never were summoned to London: it was not done. They had come upon their own initiative, because the publication of the Shaw Report was, or should have been, an important stage in the struggle for their rights. They had confidence in the case which had been presented by them in Palestine to the Commissioners, and the willingness of the Commissioners to listen to the whole case and not to stop dead at the Mandate, as though they stood at the door of a harem, gave them the conviction that the Report might introduce a new era. Obviously therefore London was the place for them, despite the fate of previous Delegations.

Since they were in London, the Government took up conversations with them. It was a means of dealing temporarily with the Shaw political suggestions, and it gave Mr. MacDonald opportunity during his escapes of conscience to confer with the Arab leaders. Lord Passfield conferred with them also. The Arab delegates on reading the Report were fairly satisfied. The Commission, after months of inquiry, had reported that the outbreak in Palestine sprang fundamentally from the policy pursued there by His Majesty's Government. That was the sense of the Report.

But on arrival in London they discovered that this made no difference worth mentioning. They were told indeed that the Government contemplated introducing some constitutional changes. Behind this lay the good intentions of Lord Passfield, and the interim feelings of Mr. MacDonald that "something ought to be done." But whatever the changes were to be they would not mean democratic government in Palestine; that stood out.

The Arab delegates had evidence of the force of the powers arrayed against them on the morrow of their arrival and of the Report's publication, when there was another letter in *The Times* signed by Sir Archibald Sinclair, Mr. Malcolm MacDonald (the present Colonial Secretary), Mr. John Buchan (as he then was) and the odd, eternal, inexplicable, hallucinatory Lord Cecil. The over-Government outside the Government, the ruling conflux which Mr. Belloc first diagnosed and brought to public notice (though making it perhaps more self-consciously conspiratory than it is), had manifested itself. Its vehicle of utterance was its accustomed one: "A Plea for Non-Party Treatment" was *The Times*' heading to the letter. The non-partisan signatories, after compliments, as they say in India, announced that the Shaw Commissioners had gone beyond their terms-of-reference, that matters of major policy were the concern of the Government (and apparently of the out-of-office signatories). They "urged," an absolutely classic word always employed on these occasions, that the Government should reaffirm the adherence of Britain to the letter and the spirit of the Mandate and should take "full and responsible advice" upon the methods by which its terms could best be fulfilled.

In fine, the letter was the perfection of self-deceit. In it the reader recognizes doubtless the variations upon a uniform theme which were repeated at the meeting between the Prime Minister and the Zionist leaders, in the triune letter of the preceding December, and in the declaration of Mr. Ramsay MacDonald in the House of Commons. Needless to say, such a reproduction of authoritative and minatory opinion was not made in vain. The Arab delegation's demands for the stoppage of immigration into Palestine, for the legal inalienability of Arab lands to be declared, and for the establishment in Palestine of a national Government elected by normal adult suffrage, were rejected.

The Colonial Office issued a communique on the 13th of May declaring that the conversations with the delegates were at an end, and that the sweeping constitutional changes demanded by them were wholly unacceptable since they would have rendered it impossible for His Majesty's Government to carry out its obligations under the Mandate. The Government stood fast at the door of the harem.

For all that, it was not happy as it guarded the familiar threshold. The breaking off of negotiations had been the Arabs' work. They had said that if their demands remained unheard they would return home, and this return after only a fortnight, with the Shaw Report barely published, made a sensation. The Arabs had counted upon this: there was no reason why they should not use strategy as well as their opponents, and the strategy was good. A strike was declared in Palestine, mass meetings were held demanding the fulfilment of the Covenant and of Great Britain's personal pledge of independence.

What was still more unpleasant for the Government, the Moslem world outside Palestine began to raise its voice. An all-India Moslem Conference for Palestine was held in Bombay and passed a resolution that the Holy Land of Palestine was the trust of the whole Moslem world and not of the Moslems of Palestine alone. It demanded the abolition of the Balfour Declaration, the termination of the Mandate and the establishment of self-government there. It decided to celebrate a "Palestine Day" throughout India, Burma and Ceylon, on Friday the 16th, to begin after prayers at the mosques.

This was held as arranged, and in Bombay particularly was on an impressive scale. Long processions paraded through the Moslem quarters, waving banners inscribed "Down with the Balfour Declaration!" and Reuter cabled that a meeting in the evening was attended by 100,000 persons.

No doubt in these resolutions and demonstrations there will have been admixture of the elements in India and in the other countries hostile to British rule, who took advantage of this opportunity to further their own aims. But it was a magnificent opportunity, one such as never previously had been granted to them, and no one had provided them with it save Mr. Lloyd George and his friends.

With this news coming from India, and with Palestine fermenting again, the Government came back to the "something must be done" attitude, and something was done. The Palestine Administration had recently, in the ordinary way of business, granted certificates for the entry of two thousand three hundred new Zionist immigrants during the coming half-year. These were cancelled.

Cries of anger at once arose from every Zionist cenacle. The *Manchester Guardian* hinted at the resignation of Dr. Weizmann from the Zionist Organization as a form of protest. *The Times'* correspondent in Jerusalem telegraphed that "the appointment of Sir John Hope Simpson to report on land settlement, immigration and development, *which is resented here* [my italics], is considered comparatively tolerable in comparison with this action of the Government's, which is interpreted as pre-judging Sir John's problem under Arab pressure and as striking at the foundation and object of the Mandate." The Government, returning glumly from its excursion to the mat where it stood by this same Mandate, was conscious of shrill objurgatory voices from beyond the *purdah* screen.

Sir John Hope Simpson, though, went briskly on with his work in

Palestine and completed it. The Government received his Report in the fourth week of August, during the Parliamentary recess. Publication of it was postponed till the 20th of October, the eve of the new session. This gave time for preparing a White Paper, which the Government had decided to issue simultaneously with the Report. The White Paper was to enounce the course of its future policy in Palestine, based upon, or as a sequel to, the recommendations both of the Shaw and the Hope Simpson Reports.

It cannot have been a very easy task which the Government set itself between August and October, for Sir John Hope Simpson's Report on the whole bore out Arab contentions as thoroughly in detail as the Shaw Report had favoured them in general trend. It may be summarized more rapidly than the Shaw Report however, because of its very nature it did not deal with primary questions. The point made at the beginning of the last chapter applies particularly to it. It deals with the effects of Zionist immigration, and it is the primary illegitimacy of Zionist immigration by force of arms which matters, not the secondary effects of it when established.

The Hope Simpson Report was most damaging to the National Home, but in the sense only that it showed that the results of establishing the National Home were nearly as unsatisfactory as the credentials for establishing it.

It showed that while the Arabs had benefited unquestionably from the old true Jewish colonies, which admitted Arab labour, the new political-Zionist colonies were steadily creating a landless Arab class. Undoubtedly the Zionist purchasing bodies brought money into the country and paid compensation to tenants whose holdings were bought over their heads, and sometimes even paid a good deal of money which legally they were not called upon to pay. But monetary compensation was of no permanent value to peasants who did not understand it, from whose hands it vanished. What the peasant needed when he lost land was to be given more land. The Report quoted the results of Zionist purchases in the Valley of Esdraelon, where out of 688 Arab agricultural families "three hundred and nine had joined the landless classes," entailing by official estimate a displacement from the soil of 1,270 small farmers, and of at least some 5,000 persons in all.

The Report animadverted on the practice (still obtaining) by which under the leases issued by the land-acquiring Zionist societies all land was to be inalienably Jewish. The land was extraterritorialized.

> It ceases to be land from which the Arab can gain any advantage either now or at any time in the future. Nor can anyone help him by purchasing the land and restoring it to common use. The land is in mortmain and inalienable. It is for this reason that Arabs discount the professions of friendship and goodwill on the part of the Zionists, in view of the policy which the Zionist Organization deliberately adopted.

With this attitude of the Arabs the Report itself as good as concurred. It quoted some of the "lofty sentiments ventilated at public meetings and in Zionist propaganda," and said of them "the provisions included in legal documents binding on every settler in a Zionist colony are not compatible with the sentiments publicly expressed.."

The Report emphasized the over-taxation of the poor Arab peasant, whose crops were only too frequently seized to pay the taxes of a State which left him "in a condition little if at all superior to what it was under the Turkish regime." It also emphasized the lack of any endeavour to deal with the grazing claims of the Bedouin, whose numbers had been estimated at 100,000 but were not really known. Their rights would have to be recorded scrupulously and be considered as a factor, if there was to be more development of the land, upon which the Bedouin by immemorial custom had rights of seasonal squatting and of pasture for their herds.

A notable portion of the Report treated of industry in Palestine. Perhaps it was the most notable portion, for by quoting a memorandum submitted to him by the Jewish Agency, Sir John Hope Simpson cast accurate light on the character of the industrial aims of the Zionists. It has been pointed out in an earlier chapter that it was through the industrialization of Palestine that Zionism hoped (and still hopes) to de-Arabize the country and establish its own supremacy. The Jewish Agency memorandum, in a spasm of petulance, betrayed these aims.

> From the point of view of industry [it ran] the whole talk of the absorptive capacity of the country is out of place and should be disposed of once and for all. [The aim of Jewish industry is not] to cater for the wants of 600,000 Arabs, three-quarters of whom are poor peasants. It is to the Jewish community itself and to export that Jewish industry looks in the first place. It is quite incorrect to believe that Jewish immigration is dependent on a market being already available: it is above all things Jewish immigration that creates the home market and conquers the foreign market.

Sir John Hope Simpson was content to let these quotations have their own effect on the readers of his report without adding comment. It may be asked, though, could there be clearer proof than this of the Zionist intention that Palestine should be used entirely for the ends of the National Home, and that the "600,000 Arabs, mostly poor peasants," were thought of as mere livestock in the fields?

The Zionists demanded more immigrants in order that they might create more markets, and so might need more industries to supply these markets, and so might need more immigrants to man these industries, and thus on indefinitely. "It would be a bad, and might prove a fatal policy," rejoined the Report, "to attract large capital in order to start doubtful industries in Palestine, with the object of justifying an increase in the number of immigrants."

After acknowledging that there was considerable and growing Arab unemployment and that the policy of the Jewish Labour Federation was successful in preventing Arab employment in Jewish colonies and enterprises, so that "no relief was to be anticipated from an extension of Jewish enterprise," Sir John Hope Simpson reached his final conclusion, that the only way in which the contradictory provisions of the Mandate—he also being obliged of course to take the Mandate at face value and to assume that the contradictions were accidental—could be carried out was by the intensive development of rural Palestine. He had already pointed out that the Arab peasant was "neither lazy nor unintelligent, but a competent and capable agriculturist," who would rapidly improve his position if he had a chance to learn better methods. Not that his own methods were bad: Sir John Hope Simpson quoted the testimony of an expert that the Arab plough "performed, very slowly, it is true, but very thoroughly, all the functions for which a combination of modern machines is required—a plough, a roller and a harrow."

But he had calculated that even if, under present conditions, all the cultivable land in the country not already in Jewish occupation had been divided up amidst Arab husbandmen, yet there would not be enough plots to maintain them and their families in a decent standard of life. In the Beersheba area there was indeed "an inexhaustible supply of cultivable land," if it were irrigable. (This was an enormous "if." The Beersheba area, about half of the whole area of Palestine—six-thirteenths—was the home of the Bedouin. They at least encamped upon it and in very rainy seasons might raise a scant crop here and there. It was their reserve, over which their rights could no more be set aside than those of the Arab husbandman in the more settled areas. The existence of subterranean water-supplies was an imaginative supposition.) As things were therefore, with immigrants pouring in, only "intensive development" could save the situation. With such development there would, in his belief, be room for another 20,000 families of settlers from outside in addition to the present population.

These were his conclusions. It was not his business to say how the Arabs were to be turned into "intensive cultivators," which meant learning a very scientific, expensive, professorial method of cultivation, as distinguished from practising very good cultivation by improvement of existing and traditional methods. Like a doctor, Sir John Hope Simpson had to prescribe ideally. The Arabs might well ask, as later they did, whether they were all to be turned into Western agricultural experts in order that 20,000 more "families from outside" should enter Palestine to destroy its Arab character.

Otherwise they were grateful for his Report.

But Sir John Hope Simpson's Report was necessarily overshadowed by the White Paper, which not only contained the gist of the Report but also the very important Governmental statement of what Great Britain's policy in Palestine now was to be. The White Paper was a twenty-three page document, which took up the various issues raised by the Shaw and Simpson reports one by one.

Experience, it said, had proved that "certain administrative defects" had made their appearance in Palestine, but none the less the Churchill White Paper of 1922, "issued after prolonged and careful consideration," still provided the foundation of future British policy in that country.

Then Lord Passfield, the issuer of the statement as Colonial Secretary, turned to a major question—immigration. The decision upon this was that "immigration cannot be so great in volume as to exceed whatever may be the economic capacity of the country at the time to absorb new arrivals." In estimating this absorptive capacity, the Government would have to consider the state of Arab unemployment as well as of Jewish unemployment, and "it is the intention of His Majesty's Government to ensure a more exact application of these principles in the future."

Next, after declaring that machinery must be devised for closer co-operation both of the Jewish Agency and of the "non-Jewish sections of the community" with the Administration, the White Paper took up the question of the obligations under the Mandate. It was on old ground here, and repeated the familiar formula that the Mandatory obligations to Zionists and to Arabs were of equal weight, and that neither was to be subordinated to the other. It quoted with satisfaction the declaration of the Mandates Commission of the League of Nations—the sham-fight declaration of that June—that the two obligations "were in no sense irreconcilable."

There was a passage about Public Security, and then came the chief question of all—that of "Constitutional Development." The White Paper spoke in impressive accents:

> It is the considered opinion of His Majesty's Government that the time has now come when the important question of the establishment of a measure of self-government in Palestine must, in the interests of the community as a whole, be taken in hand without further delay.

The Government, to this end, intended to set up a Legislative Council "generally on the lines indicated by Mr. Churchill in 1922." It was to consist of the High Commissioner and twenty-two members, ten official and twelve unofficial. But the Government was not merely going to propose such a Council; it would insist upon its formation. If the deadlock of 1923 recurred (that is if the Arabs refused to vote because of their insufficient representation in the Council and of the purely nominal part it gave them in legislation), then:

> ...steps will be devised to ensure the appointment of the requisite number of unofficial members to the Council, in the event of one or more members failing to be elected on account of the non-co-operation of any section of the population, or for any other reason.

Coming to the land question, the White Paper reproduced and endorsed Sir John Hope Simpson's facts and deductions concerning the area of land available for cultivation and the condition of Arab husbandmen. It quoted his statement that of the 87,000 or so rural Arab families in the villages; more than 29 percent were landless.

The Government was satisfied that under the circumstances a "more methodical agricultural development was called for," which however would take years to study and to put into practice. While this was going on, "fortunately the Jewish organizations are in possession of a large reserve of land not yet settled or developed."

> During this period, however, the control of all the disposition of land must of necessity rest with the authority in charge of the development. Transfers of land will be permitted only in so far as they do not interfere with the plans of that authority. Having regard to the responsibilities of the Mandatory Power, it is clear that this authority must be the Palestine Administration.

In other words, there was to be, at the best, a marked slowing-down of Zionist immigration, and the Government would only allow newcomers into the country under schedules which would be governed by new principles. These principles would be based upon the economic capacity of the country.

> Clearly, if immigration of Jews results in preventing the Arab population from obtaining the work necessary for its maintenance, or if Jewish unemployment unfavourably affects the general labour position, it is the duty of the Mandatory Power under the Mandate to reduce, or if necessary, to suspend such immigration until the unemployed portion of the "other sections" [of the population: that is Arab] is in a position to obtain work.

Such, in general summary, were the proposals of the Government for the future rule of Palestine. The moment they appeared they were greeted with a clamorous farewell.

Chapter 37

The White Paper of 1930.
Mr. Ramsay MacDonald surrenders to Dr. Weizmann.
The "Black Letter."
The Report of Mr. French.
The growing peril of the Arab peasant being dispossessed for ever.

To throw a proper light upon what now occurred, it will be best to resume what the White Paper of 1930 proposed to do, and what it did not propose to do. It proposed:

1. To reduce or even to suspend Zionist immigration into Palestine;
2. To stop Zionist acquisition of land without special leave from the Government;

...so long as, in both cases, economic conditions rendered these steps necessary. Immigration henceforth was to be anchored for good to the "economic absorptive capacity" of the country, and the acquisition of land was to depend on the advance or the retardation of a new agricultural system which might take many years to install. These two proposals were the outcome of the economic recommendations of the Shaw and Hope Simpson Reports, and were a change of policy, in theory at least.

What the White Paper did not propose to do was to pay any real attention to the constitutional, that is to say, to the political, recommendations or observations of the Shaw Commission. Strictly speaking the Shaw Commissioners had not offered "recommendations," and even had disclaimed the intention of offering them, but like Mark Antony they succeeded in saying what they had to say in the field of constitutional politics. They had pointed out that the continued failure of the Government to grant any measure of self-rule, to Palestine was a cause of the outbreak into which they had to inquire. They had also detailed the political grievances of the Arabs so meaningly that this was a plain invitation to the Government to give open consideration to these grievances.

To these recommendations, or observations, the only sequel vouchsafed by the Government was the reintroduction, all over again, of the so-called Legislative Council of eight years before. There was no change of policy here therefore, no willingness to adopt a new constitutional system more favourable to the Arabs. This *non possumus,* or rather *non volumus* attitude of the Government was even more clearly shown in its neglect of the most striking passages of the Shaw Report.

The Report had begged that the Government should define with unequivocal clearness the meaning attached to the Balfour Declaration. The White Paper passed this over in silence. The Shaw Report had emphasized the need of defining the Arab rights which had been "safeguarded" since 1920 without it ever having been stated what they were. The White Paper passed this over too.

The Shaw Commissioners had declared that the ostensible definition and clarification of the Balfour Declaration by Mr. Churchill in 1922 was upon essential points so far from clarifying and defining it that they themselves could not attempt to offer a summary of Mr. Churchill's meaning. Despite this the White Paper not alone left Mr. Churchill's explanation unexplained, but said that it was the foundation of future British policy in Palestine.

As for the menacing catalogue of Arab grievances, no mention was made of inquiry into the broken treaty with Hussein or of the violation of the Covenant by the Lloyd George Government. The harem remained sacred.

It is very necessary to establish these points, because it was shortly to be claimed, by the usual groups, that the White Paper conceded everything to the Arabs. It did nothing of the sort. What it did give to the Arabs was, in prospect, a practical concession, a brake upon immigration and upon the sale of land. But of course the absolute value of it would depend upon the extent to which the brake was applied.

At first sight it appeared as though this concession or pair of concessions covered two out of the three demands made to the Premier by the Arab Delegation.

But when it was analysed, it shed a great deal of its benevolence and of its real value. The right of the Arabs to arrest Zionist immigration because it was undermining their possession of Palestine (not in the mere sense of tenancy of land, but of possession as Englishmen possess England) was nowhere conceded. Immigration would only be halted or reduced in volume in so far as it led to economic straits. Political straits were of no account. If there were enough abatement of unemployment and so forth, the political supersession of the Arabs could begin merrily again at once. Also it would be left entirely to the members of the Palestine and Home Governments, to decide how soon the stage of adequate employment and bettered financial conditions in Palestine necessary for resuming immigration had been reached. The Arabs themselves would not be an inch nearer having any control over the Zionist influx, because this was a reserved subject with which their representatives in the so-called "Legislative Council" would not be permitted to deal.

Whatever alleviation, too, the new concession might bring, it sprang of an insufferable theory. This theory—that "economic absorptive capacity" should govern immigration—was not only false, it was immoral and un-Christian. It deprived the people of Palestine of the exercise of free will. For they would be turned from being men into being counters, voiceless, inert economic units placed or displaced, increased or reduced by the lingers of officials pushing them about on maps. "Economic absorptive capacity" was, in fact one of those evil, heavy, pseudo-scientific phrases under which the humanity was crushed of those upon whom it was laid. Where it had originally come from was not clear, but it had gained currency in the Papers and the Reports of Palestine. An odious phrase for an odious system, it might justifiably be used to describe the limits reached by Treasury clerks in their cups, if they have any, and that would be the extent of its usefulness.

What was true of immigration was true of land-purchase also. It was for stoppage of this in principle that the Arab delegates had asked. What they got in the White Paper was stoppage or reduction in practice, and they and theirs were to have no voice either in imposing this or in preventing its withdrawal. As for the constitutional concession, it contained the threat of a packed Council, where the Government would nominate its own men-of-straw against the desires of the people, and yet present them as the first instalment of self-government, which is government by the people's choice. One of the most extravagant propositions ever made, even for Palestine.

Therefore the White Paper of 1930 boiled down only to this, that the Government, through the Palestine Administration, would keep its hand on Zionist immigration and land-purchase and would prevent the increase of either throwing the country into economic disorder.

Yet the uproar which greeted the White Paper was volcanic. The protests of May against the cancellation of the immigration-certificates was in comparison the humming of a top. The White Paper was but two days published, when General Smuts cabled to the Prime Minister his "deep perturbation" at this "retreat from the Balfour Declaration." He urged ("urged" again) that the Declaration should be reaffirmed and the Government's new Palestine policy recast.

Dr. Weizmann no longer threatened to resign, but instantly did resign his presidency of the Zionist Organization. In the United States Mr. Warburg resigned a kindred chairmanship. Lord Melchett resigned from the Zionist Organization and from the Jewish Agency. Everybody in sight resigned from everything possible except, as fate would have it, Messrs. Novomeysky and Rutenberg. There were violent demonstrations by a mob of prospective-Palestinians in front of the British Embassy in Warsaw. Protests rained in from Roumania. The "*Union de la Jeunesse Sioniste*" convened a public meeting of protest in Paris. Of course in London, in Manchester, and all over the British Isles similar meetings effervesced.

But it was in the United States that the volcano spouted highest and most flamboyantly. Great mass-meetings of Zionists were held. At one which filled Madison Square Gardens some tens of thousands indoors were matched by fifteen thousand in the streets, whom squads of police kept in order with difficulty. Orators addressed them from all points in the hall and outside. Wild cheering greeted denunciations of British policy. Mr. Warburg said he had invested a million dollars in Palestine on the strength of what Lord Passfield had told him and vociferated that he had been misled. Mr. Frankfurter, the celebrated epistolarian, presided and announced that the White Paper was "less a statement of the policy of His Majesty's Government than a revelation of the prejudice of one man, Lord Passfield." Dr. Wise, the liaison-agent between everybody and everything at Versailles, cried that "Lord Passfield's statement has dishonoured Great Britain."

At another meeting in the (of all places) Mecca Temple, another gathering of thousands, under the auspices of the Zionist Organization, booed and hissed every reference to the British Government. One speaker called on the Zionists of Palestine to make common cause with the Arabs against "the alien Empire which misrules and exploits both peoples."

Amidst all this volatile protestation and abuse, the one man who kept his head was the President of the American Jewish Congress, Mr. Bernard Deutsch, who "expressed his faith that the decision announced in the recent White Paper would soon be reversed." Mr. Deutsch was a knowledgeable man.

The only place to which the White Paper brought quiet was Palestine. About a week after its publication, when the anniversary of the issue of the Balfour Declaration came round, for the first time in memory Jerusalem was peaceful. The usual celebrations and counter-celebrations were not held. The Zionists of the Holy City had all resigned from celebrations, and the Arabs, poor men, thought there was no occasion to express their feelings now.

Meanwhile in London the inevitable letter to *The Times* had been taken out of storage and had been sent on the 22nd to Printing House Square, on the same day that Smuts's cable had come. Dr. Weizmann's resignation caused the writers "deep concern." They pointed out that he had suggested in vain to the Government that a Round Table Conference should be summoned between Jews and Arabs, at which the Government should undertake the part of "honest broker" between the two parties.

The writers were "profoundly conscious of the twofold obligation of the Mandate," which had been the basis of every Government's policy in turn. Now the Government of Mr. MacDonald appeared to have abandoned that policy. It had ignored Dr. Weizmann's proposals. (It had not as a matter of fact. The Arabs would have nothing to do with the Round Table Conference when the Government proposed it to them, as it was one of the series of Zionist moves for winning acceptance of equal status for Zionists with Arabs.)

Without giving either Jewish or Arab opinion time to manifest itself, went on the letter, or giving Parliament an opportunity to speak, the Government had laid down a negative policy which conflicted with the desires of the Council of the League, with the spirit of the Balfour Declaration, and with the statements made by successive Governments for twelve years past. The letter ended, "It is only too evident that the effect of the White Paper upon public opinion in American Jewry and elsewhere is to create a feeling of distrust in that British good faith which is the most precious asset of our foreign Imperial policy."

The signatories on this occasion were Mr. Baldwin and Sir Austen Chamberlain, who were at sea about it all, and Mr. Amery who by this time was not at sea, but on ground he knew. Mr. Churchill, in a note to Mr. Nathan Laski, published by the *Manchester Guardian*, declared that he was in full agreement with the other Conservative leaders. He also wrote a long letter upon British policy in Palestine, in which he referred to his own Statement of 1922 as one of a set of "milestones" of that policy, and called Lord Passfield an "aged minister worn with a lifetime of literary and sociological labours, who has, as is well known, long been anxious to seek repose. It may well be that he has not given that intense personal attention and original effort to the White Paper that controversial delicacy and importance of subject required." Certainly there were no intensely personal vilayets and very original texts in Lord Passfield's White Paper.

Mr. Lloyd too declared that the White Paper was in substance a revocation of a good part of a solemn pledge given at a most solemn moment.

Sir John Simon and Lord Hailsham wrote to *The Times* a letter in more measured style. They might have been a Commission of Inquiry, for they did not inquire into the genesis, or the Geneva exodus, of the Mandate. But they suggested that the Council of the League should be "induced" to obtain from the Hague Court an advisory opinion. This would not have been upon whether the Mandate was in accordance with the Covenant, unfortunately, but upon whether the White Paper was in accord with the Mandate, which they doubted.

Every gun, in fine, of the great battle-fleet of the Government-beyond-the-Government was trained upon the Prime Minister and Lord Passfield. The latter hoisted a flag-of-truce in *The Times* by a letter in which he removed the "misconception" that every Arab had to be in employment ere Zionist immigration could be resumed, and that such land as might yet be reclaimed by the Palestine Government was only to be used for settling disposed Arabs. Of the nine categories of immigrants into Palestine, but one, said he, that of the "wage-earners," was so much as mentioned in his White Paper.

This apologetic letter was a prelude to submission. On the 14th of November, the following official announcement was made:

> "Doubts having been expressed as to the compatibility of some passages of the White Paper of October 21st with certain Articles of the Palestine Mandate, and other passages having proved liable to misunderstanding, His Majesty's Government have invited representatives of the Jewish Agency to confer with them in these matters.
>
> As the parties to the Mandate are strongly desirous of securing its correct interpretation and impartial administration, it is hoped that agreement will be reached on any points of difference, when a further statement on these issues will be made."

Plain enough: the Government would comply with the demands, or orders, of its masters. But it has never been observed that in the haste and in the heat of this compliance the Downing Street communique actually blurted out that the Mandate was the common production and property of Government and Zionists. It referred to the representatives of the Jewish Agency and His Majesty's Government as "the parties to the Mandate," hoping that agreement would be reached since these parties had the same feelings about it.

The Arabs were not mentioned in the communique, and of course none of them were to be summoned in consequence of it. They were not considered parties to the Mandate in any form at all, which, of course, was the true situation but one which hitherto had been concealed. Now the truth had foamed up, out of the sparkling wine of excitement.

After this the recantation of the White Paper was a mere matter of time and of arrangement between, the "parties to the Mandate." While this was going on, there was a supererogatory debate in the House of Commons on the 18th of November, during which Mr. Lloyd George reached the peak of supererogation by declaring that he certainly had never been consulted about the terms of the White Paper. He said that he doubted whether the Prime Minister had been consulted. So, by a slight alteration of fleet-tactics all guns now were trained on Lord Passfield alone. His letter had not availed him. He was made out to be the sole author of, and responsible person for, the White Paper.

When Mr. MacDonald rose to speak he paid no overt attention to Mr. Lloyd George's gibe that he had not been consulted. But he made it evident that he had been a partner in the White Paper. He told the House that when the recent Arab delegation had come to London he had himself several times conferred with the delegates and as he put it was "thoroughly seized of their case." Evidently it had made some impression upon him, and these conversations had influenced the proposals of the short-lived White Paper.

But most of his speech was a further preparation for submission to the will of the Zionist caucus. "There is nothing in the White Paper," he said, "which justifies the conclusion that the Government wishes to stop immigration or that it wishes to curtail immigration merely on the figures of unemployed Arabs." This was a further descent from Lord Passfield's "every Arab."

Mr. MacDonald, however, at the outset of his speech said one thing, and said it with some fire, which deserves to live. It was his last shot before he surrendered, and it was about the best phrase that he ever delivered in his career. Rounding on Mr. Lloyd George, who had talked fustian about the need for the Government to show fidelity to the word of England, in continuation of the fidelity of his own Government to it, the Prime Minister said, "It was not a word we inherited. We inherited words—and they are not always consistent."

Mr. Hopkin Morris, the Shaw Commissioner, made a good speech, but the real truth was heard, too briefly, from Mr. Somers Cocks, who went to the sources of things and spoke of the humbug of the Mandate. His words underwent the accustomed boycott, outside Hansard.

The final act of surrender was not accomplished till three months after this debate. It was very ignominious in the end, for it took the form of an apologetic letter from the Prime Minister to Dr. Weizmann, dispatched on the 13th of February, 1931, which began:

> "Dear Dr. Weizmann,
>
> In order to remove certain misconceptions and misunderstandings which have arisen as to the policy of His Majesty's Government with regard to Palestine, as set forth in the White Paper of October 1930, and which were the subject of a debate in the House of Commons on the 17th of November, and also to meet certain criticisms put forward by the Jewish Agency, I have pleasure in forwarding you the following statement of our position, which will fall to be read as the authoritative interpretation of the White Paper on the matters with which this letter deals."

The effect of this was very much as though His Majesty's Government were sending in its accounts to be audited and passed by Dr. Weizmann.

and indeed, substituting national policy for national accounts, this was what it was doing. The Prime Minister's letter was a long one, under eighteen heads, and some 2,700 words in length, and was to all intents another State Paper. It was to become known amongst the Arabs as the "Black Paper" or "Black Letter."

Mr. MacDonald himself was very anxious though that it should not be published as another State Paper, since if this had been done it would have been impossible to sustain the theory that it was not a substitution of the 1930 White Paper but a mere elucidation or explanation of it.

So by arrangement, on a selected date, Lieutenant-Commander Kenworthy, *ami de cour*, put a leading question to Mr. MacDonald, and in replying to it the latter gave the text of his letter. Thus it appeared automatically in Hansard amidst the "Written Answers" of the day. The expedient was a poor one, which only emphasized what it had been desired to avoid.

The salient passages in the letter declared (numbering and classification are mine):

1. That while under Article 2 of the Mandate the Mandatory had to safeguard the civil rights of all inhabitants of Palestine, this was not to be interpreted as meaning that the civil rights which existed at the beginning of the Mandate were to remain unaltered throughout its duration. To take this view would be to prevent all legislation. This had been the opinion expressed by the Privy Council in a case which had come before it.
2. Under Article 6 of the Mandate the "rights and positions of other sections of the population were not to be prejudiced," i.e., impaired or made worse. But to facilitate Zionist immigration and to encourage close settlement by the Zionists could be fulfilled without prejudice to the rights and position of the Arabs.
3. As for limiting the acquisition of land by the Zionists because of Arabs being landless, this "in nowise detracted from the larger purposes of development which His Majesty's Government regards as the most effectual means of furthering the establishment of a National Home for the Jews." An inquiry would be instituted to inquire what "State and other lands are, or properly can be made, available for close settlement by the Jews under Article 6."
4. While this inquiry was going on there really had to be some centralized control of "transactions relating to the transfer and acquisition of land" [*a thin evasion of the crude word "sales"*], but only for a reasonable period, and "the power contemplated is regulative and not prohibitory, although it does involve a power to prevent transactions which are inconsistent with the

tenor of thc scheme."

5. The White Paper did not imply a prohibition of acquisition of additional land by Jews. It contained no such prohibition, nor was any such intended. What it contemplated was "such temporary control of land-disposition and transfers as may be necessary not to impair the harmony and the effectiveness of the scheme of land settlement to be undertaken."
6. Immigration always had been controlled by the Government. It was an error to suggest that His Majesty's Government now meant to "permit no further immigration of Jews so long as it might prevent any Arab from obtaining employment." The sole intention of the Government was to apply the absorptive capacity principle. "The considerations relevant to the limits of absorptive capacity are purely economic considerations."
7. His Majesty's Government "did not contemplate any stoppage or prohibition of Jewish immigration in any of its categories." The practice, however, of sanctioning a Labour Schedule of wage-earning immigrants would continue. In each case under this schedule consideration would be given to "anticipated labour requirements" for works which being Zionist or mainly Zionist would not have been or would not be undertaken without a supply of Zionist labour. "Immigrants with prospects of employment other than employment of a purely ephemeral character will not be excluded on the sole ground that the employment cannot be guaranteed to be of unlimited duration."

And, after asserting that "To the tasks imposed by the Mandate His Majesty's Government have set their hand, and they will not withdraw it," the Prime Minister subscribed himself, "Yours very sincerely, my dear Dr. Weizmann, J. Ramsay MacDonald."

Such venture as there had been in the White Paper to curb Zionist immigration and Zionist acquisition of land was abandoned in this letter of Mr. MacDonald's. The White Paper's proposals were not definitely abrogated or withdrawn, of course, but disappeared in a mass of diffuse explanation, some of the sentences in which this was achieved being examples of circumlocutory verbiage which are never likely to be surpassed.

In the White Paper Lord Passfield had said pretty plainly that the Government through the Palestine Administration intended to be the sole authority in charge of land-disposition. Sale of land would only be permitted in so far as it did not interfere with the plans of that authority. Now in the Black Letter it was stated that "the power contemplated is regulative and not prohibitory, though it does involve a power to prevent transactions which are inconsistent with the tenor of the scheme." A will-of-the-wisp standard called "the tenor of the scheme" was thus set up—also called "the larger purposes of development"—and any Zionist acquisition of territory easily could pass muster now as being generally consonant with a tenor or with a larger purpose.

In the White Paper Lord Passfield had said, again pretty plainly, that it was the duty of the Mandatory Power under the Mandate to reduce, or if necessary, to suspend Zionist immigration until the unemployed portion of the other sections of the population was in a position to obtain work. In the Black Letter it was "an error to suggest that His Majesty's Government meant to permit no further immigration of Jews so long as it might prevent any Arab from obtaining employment." Arab unemployment, or Zionist unemployment itself (of which there had been plenty), would be replaced as a determining factor by "consideration for anticipated labour requirements," that is immigrant workers would be admitted if someone hoped that they were likely to be employed, even though there was no employment ready for them.

The last sentence (quoted as Clause 7) was absolute abracadabra. "Immigrants with prospects of employment other than employment of a purely ephemeral character will not be excluded on the sole ground that the employment cannot be guaranteed to be of unlimited duration." Which might be justly paraphrased: "Unless immigrants have only come to Palestine for a couple of weeks' work or so, the fact that they have no prospect of steady labour is not to bar their entry."

As for the recommendations or observations of the Shaw Commission that the political grievances of the Arabs should be considered, these vanished entirely in the Black Letter. It did not spend a comma on the danger of Arab subordination of which the Commission had treated, and Dr. Weizmann was assured in it that when the limits of Zionist immigration were to be determined none but economic considerations would be allowed to enter the mind of the Government. (Five years, in fact, were to elapse before "a measure of self-government was taken in hand without delay," by another Government, and that under the usual pressure of bloodshed.)

Altogether therefore the Black Letter was indeed an abandonment of the position which the Labour Cabinet had assumed momentarily. It is a melancholy document, in which the process of relinquishing under pressure a project in which the better emotions had enjoyed play is cloaked in a threadbare apologia.

But in justice to its co-authors it should not be forgotten that however they veered about, or recanted later, they were the only Prime Minister and Colonial Secretary of Great Britain during two decades who ever showed any passing sign of having listened to the Arabs' fundamental grievances, or of having felt a moment's compunction for the Arabs' treatment or a moment's desire to amend it.

Naturally, the result of the letter was disastrous in Palestine. The Arabs, who had been taught by direful experience, had not indeed based great hopes on the White Paper, the more so, since the manoeuvres to supplant it, or alter it out of knowledge, had begun as soon as it had been published. The Arab Executive refrained from expressing an opinion upon it, and in mid-December explained that it was no good commenting upon the document till the Anglo-Zionist tractations in London had ended. From experience, they opined that what might be left of the White Paper by that time would not be "worth the waste of ink and paper" in reply.

None the less, Lord Passfield's document had made an impression in Palestine. When the Black Letter was published in Palestine, whither it had been sent as an official instruction to the High Commissioner, the reaction was violent. The chief Arab newspaper, *Falastin*, declared that the Arabs had been swindled. The President of the Arab Executive wrote to the High Commissioner to declare that the letter constituted a new policy adopted by His Majesty's Government which was completely inconsistent with the White Paper.

The Peel Commissioners themselves acknowledge in their Report the evil consequences of the Black Letter, though they endeavour to sustain with silkworm's threads the enormous platform that the striking difference between it and the White Paper was not "in statements of opinion or of policy but in tone."

> In Arab eyes [says the Report] the substitution of the Black Letter for the White Paper was plain proof of the power which world Jewry could exact in London, and such confidence as they might previously have had in British determination to do at least what justice could be done under what they have always regarded as an unjust Mandate was seriously shaken.

Why the substitution should be called plain proof only in Arab eyes of the power of the Zionists in London is hard to appreciate, since every eye in Europe perceived it. However, Arab feelings were correctly recorded.

So that Palestine in 1931, outside the Zionist centres, became more resentful and hopeless than ever. To the country in this state yet another Commission was now dispatched. Nominally it was not a Commission, it was another one-man inquiry, but it was of Commission status, and indeed had administrative action attached to it also. The new envoy was Mr. Lewis French, another able and experienced man. All the Governments which sent Commissioners of any kind to Palestine—and which did not—seem to have modelled themselves upon Mrs. Beeton in her celebrated (and perhaps apocryphal) recipe that as a first step in cookery the pudding-basin should be filled with the best brandy, which then should be thrown away. They filled their basins with the best Commissioners and then threw them away.

Mr. French had done a great deal of work in India which qualified him in a high degree for the position he was now given. He was made "Director of Development" in Palestine. That is to say, he was sent out to report on the initial steps to be taken in order to put into effect the recommendation that the whole agricultural policy of Palestine must be remodelled by the introduction of intensive development throughout its rural areas. This had survived in some attenuated fashion from the Hope Simpson Report, after passage through the Black Letter sieve.

He was, with the help of the staff appointed to him, to make a register of Arabs who had been displaced by Zionist occupation and had not obtained satisfactory holdings for themselves afterwards. He was to draw up a scheme for the resettlement of these displaced Arab families, with as close an estimate of cost as possible, was to ascertain what State or other lands could be made available for close settlement by Jews, was to make proposals for irrigating, draining and generally reclaiming uncultivated land, was to inquire whether it were feasible to provide credits for Arab and Jew cultivators and if it were how best this could be done.

He was in fact to examine every facet of the question of intensive development and of the questions allied to it. It was clear that his findings would be arch-important for the following reasons. The Shaw Commission had pointed out that a process was under way in Palestine which was creating a large landless (and discontented) class. What this meant was that the extension of Zionist holdings was by degrees driving the Arabs out of possession of the land. The Hope Simpson Report examined into this situation and reached the same conclusions, but having studied the situation more closely was even more alarmed, and declared that unless there was intensive development of rural Palestine, the "contradictory provisions of the Mandate" could no longer be carried out. What this meant was that it would be impossible to go on allowing the entry of Zionists, since, if the present agricultural regime continued unaltered (in the words of Sir John Hope Simpson) "there is no room for a single additional settler if the standard of life of the fellaheen is to remain at its present level."

That is to say that the artificial cramming of Palestine with immigrants, what may be called the *foie gras* policy of the British Government, the National Home policy, could not go on unless the new proposed intensive agricultural settlement should prove feasible. It was upon this feasibility that Mr. French had to report. Upon his report, therefore, obviously everything in Palestine depended—if there was any sincerity in the Government's adherence to the entire structure of Reports and White Papers.

Behind the dispatch of Mr. French to Palestine lay the sincerity of Lord Passfield. There lay too the sentiments of Mr. Ramsay MacDonald, sincere in his way, since it is possible that he was self-deceived about his Black Letter and thought most often that it was a restatement and not a revocation of the White Paper. To send out Mr. French was to ease such inklings of doubt as must have assailed a man of his temperament. Through Mr. French's investigation the accumulated recommendations of the various Reports and Papers of the last two years would receive a meed of official honouring. Indeed two and a half million pounds were ear-marked as an allocation of funds for the prospective scheme (as French would draw it up) by Lord Passfield.

All this, however, was upon the principle that an effective scheme would be found feasible. But suppose that it were not found feasible, suppose that Mr. French had to report that what Sir John Hope Simpson had called "the only way" was an impassable way through obstacles, or an impossible way because of its own defective nature, what happened? The test for the Government came then. Would it recognize that there was no way out, that its policy could not continue? Would it stop Zionist immigration? The future would show, but, to judge from the happenings which had ended in the Black Letter, the response to these test-questions would be found in the celebrated words of Mr. George Bernard Shaw in his play *Pygmalion.*

In any event, the "Black Letter" itself was soon, after a fashion, to be superseded. Mr. French got his instructions in June: in August the Labour Cabinet resigned. The French investigation was now at the mercy of the new Coalition Cabinet, wherein, though Mr. MacDonald remained nominally at its head, the conduct of Palestine's affairs passed either directly into the hands, or indirectly into the overseership, of those who wrote letters to *The Times* about the sanctity of the Mandate

However, Mr. French, like the Shaw Commissioners and Sir John Hope Simpson, went on with his work uninfluenced by political events at home. He soon found that the new Cabinet's level of interest in his investigation was low. His work would involve expensive surveys and experimental inquiries, for which a credit up to £50,000 was to have been placed at his disposition. He never got the full sum. He was to have been provided with Arab and Jewish assessors. The Arabs refused to appoint anyone if the investigation was based on the Black Letter, as it was based.

The Zionists took no steps to appoint anyone. The Investigator had recourse to private advice thereon, and he gained by this, for he received the best in the country. His own Indian experience was of the greatest use. He had prevented the severance from the land of the best peasant elements in the Punjab, who were (much as in Palestine) having their lands sold over their heads, and had been without resources to meet this crisis because of their indebtedness to moneylenders.

The French Report was rendered to the new Government in two sections, the first on the 23rd of December, 1931, the second on the 20th of April, 1932. Between the first and the second Reports the prospect of the two and a half millions promised to finance the proposed great scheme had vanished. In January the Colonial Secretary, Sir Herbert Cunliffe-Lister, informed Mr. French and the new High Commissioner (Sir Arthur Wauchope had succeeded Sir John Chancellor) that conditions had changed very much in England and that "it could not now be assumed that it would be found practicable to make two and a half millions available for development purposes." All he could do was to "hope to take early action to give effect to a limited scheme of development."

This meant that a feasible scheme—if there was one—was cancelled in advance. The whole sense of the scheme was that it should be upon an unlimited scale. It was not a question of doing a modicum of good here and there in Palestine by restricted arrangements. It was a question of finding a universal solution for conditions in Palestine which either must be mended everywhere through this solution or else must be ended everywhere. Either Palestine must be developed according to the prospective French proposals, or the development of Palestine on its present lines must cease.

It is possible that from perusal of the first of the French Reports the Home Government had perceived that, upon the facts submitted, there could not even be a pretence of accomplishing this saving development of the country, which was the only alternative to stopping immigration. The sole escape it now saw open to it was to evade the desperate issue. But the trouble, of course, was that Mr. French could hardly be recalled, for to recall him would have meant that even the nominal effort to comply with the surviving recommendation of the White Paper had been dropped.

There was no way out of this quandary. Mr. French and his staff therefore continued their minute and painstaking labours. His December Report had been devastating. His April Report was but to confirm and deepen the conclusions of the previous one. The two may be taken together here for convenience of summary.

He found that, supposing a scheme could be devised in theory, the mere preparation of it was going to demand not weeks or months, but "must be reckoned in years," while in the interim the process of Arab dispossession would continue unabated.

Before a scheme could be considered in its details, various things were essential which in themselves would take an enormous time. The land of Palestine would have to be surveyed in full. The ownership of village and rural lands would have to be established and codified, and this, owing to the incredibly involved conditions of Arab or Moslem inheritance and ownership, was a prodigious task. A Land Administration Agency would have to be established. The Government of Palestine would have to take over control of any areas coming under development, and not of the land only, but of all water supplies, existing or supposititious.

The determination of water was of the first importance. It would have to be sought everywhere by boring for underground supplies, and only when there was complete tabulation of all supplies could an estimate of the possible cultivability of yet unoccupied land be attempted.

It was hopeless, too, to talk of creating a settlement-scheme unless the survey of the country kept far ahead of it. At present after three years of active work the land of only 30 villages out of 1,039 had been surveyed.

Individual ownership of land in great part not merely would have to be discovered with terrible difficulty, it would have to be created. Village lands, that is to say rural Palestine in general, would have to be partitioned amidst the individuals who now held them under fantastic common tenures. Under one form of title every male, from the babe in arms to the centenarian, alive in the village upon the day of partition was entitled to his share in the land, and that too according to complicated ratios which were never even constant. It was hard for the Englishman, said the Report, to understand the complications but "if he could imagine a village where every year every farmer was compelled to pass on his lands and buildings to a neighbour and receive some other farm in exchange he would get some inkling of the difficulties in Palestine." Men had minute shares in land which, in a Western way, would have to be expressed in several places of decimals.

Hardly anyone had any papers attesting his rights, his boundaries or any of his claims. When the Administration asked for papers on some matter relating to a village the village headman employed "any chance literate person there may be in the village." "Local records of transactions in land, or of crops, or of rights and changes therein do not exist. Nor are there any registers to show the relations of tenants to their landlords." In order to write down everything now, where before nothing ever had been written, village registration staffs would have to be created, and trained, and that would take a long time. Land-partition alone would take years, if indeed the exorbitance of Government fees, on the Western scale, did not nullify everything. The needful registrations involved payments for certificates of succession, up to 5 percent of the market-value of the land to establish the claim, beside survey charges running into pounds, registration fees, and prospective doubling of land-tax at the end of it all. Were Arab peasants going to pay all this? Could they?

There was another factor, a complementary factor, tending to utter confusion. These unenscribed rights existed everywhere. "I incline to the belief that little or no land of any cultural worth in any State Domain is now likely to be discovered which is not subject already to hereditary or to analogous tenancy rights," wrote Mr. French. For every inch of the soil, therefore, there were claimants; and if soil had to be secured for dispossessed tenants it could only be secured by dispossessing further tenants who thus would go out at one door of the scheme only to come in at the other.

The finishing chaotic touch was supplied by the water question. The aridity of so much of Palestine made water very precious. In fact it was the prime factor generally in deciding whether land was cultivable or not, though this had never been considered properly in the land agreements of the Palestine Administration. Amongst the Arabs water was sold or bartered like land and was "inherited as complexly as land." A share might be "a fifteen-minutes supply to be used at intervals of six weeks," time and not volume being the standard of disposal. "A cultivator may sell half his area of land but only a quarter of the water-rights going with it." "Water may be leased for a crop, a season, a year or a period of years. It may be pawned."

Yet all these immense difficulties were but the preparatory difficulties of "intensive development of rural Palestine." Imagining them to have been straightened out, there came the question of resettling the Arab families who had been displaced by the growth of the National Home. The Zionists had "contended consistently that there were very few Arabs who could be brought legitimately within the definition of landless," that is made landless through Zionist occupation. But already three thousand seven hundred claims "had survived to his [Mr. French's] office." Some might be untenable but all would have to be investigated. In every case the Zionists wished to express their views. In every case an Arab claim had to "pass through five hands or stages, one being the Jewish Agency, for submission of views."

The amount of time which would be spent in this way was no space "of a few short weeks," and when a claim ultimately was allowed, the laws and ordinances dealing with it were too complicated. One hundred clauses dealt with settlement operations. The result was that "even after three and a half years, settlement legislation was becoming too intricate for the comprehension of the plain man."

In three months 72 Arab claims had been accepted finally and 80 provisionally. Some 650 had been rejected, but "probably between 1,000 and 2,000 claims will have to be provided for out of the 3,700 preferred." "I have only to add," continued the Report, "that the process of converting Arab cultivators into landless Arabs does not necessarily cease with the receipt of claims already put in."

Next came the major questions. Where were the landless Arabs to be settled? How much land were they to be given? What would the cost be?

The general conclusion of the Report was that the land for settlement simply was not there. "The current belief that the Government has command of large areas is a delusion." "There are no vast virgin lands. Every suitable dunam (the local measurement standard, about a quarter of an acre) is already subject to proprietary right or tenancy, and will have to be expropriated in some way or another. There is no escape," said the Report plainly, "from this difficulty."

There were the "possibilities of the Beersheba area," but these depended upon water being found, and the time taken in irrigation and other development would be scarcely calculable. (The size of the Beersheba area was estimated by Sir John Hope Simpson as 800,000 acres, of which 370,000 might be cultivable, "but figures were pure guesswork".) It had taken ten years merely to demarcate and partition the 97,000 acres in the Beisan area: for this minor area "it had been opined by a Jewish scientist, if pessimistically, that a development policy worth the name would take thirty years." In the dry tracts "cultivated by semi-nomadic Bedouin more than one good harvest in five years cannot be counted upon." If their crops failed the Bedouin "moved elsewhere to get some scanty pasture for their flocks, but the fellaheen if placed there would starve unless they threw themselves on the Government."

Thus the Report disposed of the Beersheba area as bringing a solution of the problem upon any adequate scale or within rational limits of time. (In the eight years which have passed since the Report was issued all endeavours to find water for irrigation in the Beersheba area have been fruitless. Deep borings have only brought up minor deposits impregnated with salt.)

Nor was the parcelling out of land anywhere a mere matter of arithmetical division, if so be as there was land to parcel out. "People cannot be put down anywhere. Bedouin cannot be put amidst fellaheen." "Another great delay would lie in the preparation of allotments," and a very important point was that displaced Arabs were not likely to have retained their cattle, of which the mortality had been high in Palestine. "As regards State Domains there are no lands at all available therein in existing conditions either for resettlement or for colonization." The Zionist organizations had "tracts of land in reserve, which cannot be less and may be more than 10,000 acres, still awaiting development." "For landless Arabs there is practically no land … so far only some 4,000 acres of cereal or dry-farming land, which, providing they fulfil all other conditions, may possibly be suitable for purchase."

The next difficulty registered by the Report in its unique collection of difficulties and impossibilities was one concerning the quantity of land which would have to be provided (always if it were available) to sustain the average Arab family—the *lot viable*, the convenient Gallic phrase calls it. Into this most complicated question Mr. French's Report went at length. The situation was, it pointed out, that the declared policy of the Government was "closer settlement." This meant "higher farming." This meant that the Arab fellah must abandon his custom of growing his own foodstuffs for himself and his family, because these were of low monetary value. He would have to replace these by citrus fruit, dairy farming, stock-raising, poultry and egg dealing.

Seven and a half acres were, on calculation, about the minimum and average *lot viable* which the Arab ought to receive. "The aims were admirable," said Mr. French, adding with, I think, a little cynicism, "but idealism should not blind us to the very grave risks of devoting a third of this" (the area likely to be used) "to the above marketable crops and stock." It remained to be seen whether oranges could be grown outside the coastal area. The question of markets being always available for oranges was a serious one. It was assumed (by the Zionists, though the Report did not say so) that oranges and grapefruit could be produced in indefinite degree and that the more fruit was grown, the more markets would arise for it. "To my mind," said Mr. French, "this concept errs in putting the cart before the horse."

Besides, the Arab's *lot viable* under a country-wide intensive-farming scheme, would have to be bored or made irrigable and stocked with trees. The owner would have to wait five or six years till the trees reached bearing. How was he to support himself in the meanwhile, since his subsistence crops could no longer be grown? He would have to be supported out of a fund. This raised a perspective of vast cost. It was indeed impossible to begin estimating the total cost of a comprehensive scheme for all possible present or future landless at the present stage, with every factor more or less imponderable.

But it was likely that the cost of resettling one dispossessed Arab family on ordinary dry-farming land with a *lot viable* of about 75 acres would be from £350 to £400. On land irrigated and prepared for citrus or other intensive farming, with a smaller *lot viable*, it would be round about £800. Intensive farming, "close settlement" as it was called, was the policy of the Government. "Therefore every 1,000 dunams (250 acres) purchased by

Jews involving displacement of ten existing Arab families meant a prospective outlay of £8,000 by the Government. The Arab population was increasing at the rate of 18,000 a year, and there was the further factor in causing yet greater increase that with the end of the Turkish regime military service had been abolished. The Report pointed out that Turkish military service took 10,000 to 20,000 young Arabs out of their country every year, "the majority of whom never returned to their homes." Now the young Arabs were no longer being annihilated, but were growing up and increasing the numbers in every homestead. Thus the former average of five persons to every *lot viable* was being far exceeded.

A further factor developed in the Report was the impoverishment of the peasants, who were in no situation to find a farthing themselves towards any scheme. Just after the War they had bought animals and implements to replace their destroyed stock, at the high prices of the time. Prices then had collapsed, and the peasants, in receipt of these collapsed prices, in so far as they dealt in cash at all, were saddled with debts which were not scaled down by their creditors. Mr. French, who at no point sought to make a case against the Zionists, described how Arab capitalists and money-lenders bore the primary responsibility here. He told of one moneylender in a sub-district who had twenty-six mounted debt-collectors working for him, reported that in another in the hills nearly a third of the land had passed through foreclosure into the hands of native creditors, and prophesied the inevitable absorption, at this rate, of the Arab peasant by the Arab landlord.

In reference to which, it may be interpolated, that there has never been any intention in this book to suggest that Palestine is a country without its own intrinsic defects and plagues. It would have been the first duty of an Arab Government to deal with them, and as, under a system of responsible rule, pretty well all the electorate would have been concerned in remedying these abuses, there would have been no delay about tackling them. An Arab Government, if it wished to stay in office, would have had to ruin the moneylenders pretty ruthlessly, which would have been no particular harm. The Mandatory Government, imbued with western ideas about the rights of property, would never proceed to such necessary extremes.

The Zionist apologists, of course, have tried to cover themselves under this plea of Arab extortion. "There is no tendency on our part to oust Arab farmers from their holdings. The few cases where Arab tenants were displaced by Jewish purchases are negligible in comparison with the much bigger number of Arab farmers who have become landless by foreclosure of their holdings owing to debts to Arab creditors" (the Zionist agricultural expert Dr. Ruppin, in evidence to the Peel Commissioners). As though the Zionists could have acquired—as they had at that date—some 90,000 acres of Palestine, in addition to 160,000 acres bought by the Jewish Colonies before the War, without displacing quantities of Arabs, there being virtually no cultivable land which was unowned.

The position induced by these huge acquisitions was that in a country which without them would have had a difficult agricultural situation the agricultural situation had been rendered insoluble. The development of the National Home was not so much, under the circumstances, the last straw as the haystack hoisted on to the camel's back.

To return to the French Report, it was not surprising, after all the crushing figures and observations contained in it, that the Report summed up the practical prospects of Arab resettlement as follows:

> Taking all factors into consideration I do not think that within the next twelve to eighteen months it will be possible to resettle, or begin the resettlement of, more than 100 to 200 landless Arabs, as an initial proceeding. I am quite sure it will not be wise to attempt more than this.

The homestead area of a cultivator, the Report recommended, should be made inalienable.

> If the process of dispossession continues, in another three or four decades the Arab peasant-proprietor will have become extinct.

To this warning, the gravest that could be given, some general observations upon the consequences for Palestine of a continuation of the existing modernizing policy added force.

Palestine has a great scarcity of natural pasture, and with the reclamation of marshlands and the extension of the fruit-growing area these are shrinking.

The provision of water for the individual Arab husbandman on his small plot was the most fundamental need of the country, yet it was being diverted for projects of another kind. No doubt, said the Report, the diversion of water for Haifa harbour was essential, yet "if this is taken from the springs which are available this supply must interfere with domestic uses."

> It is quite uncertain whether water is not being dried up in the coastal plains through the great expansion of cultivation there. Experts say that the question has never been thoroughly examined. In California, with a climate like Palestine, large orange and other fruit-areas had been thrown out of cultivation owing to the fall in the water-table in this way. It is vital that no such disaster should overtake the citrus groves of the coastal plain, where at present these are being extended without any regard to their possible ultimate effects on subterranean water-supplies.

> Under existing legislation the fellah, an extensive cultivator, is being squeezed out steadily, as the ownership of water is tending to go into the hands of the capitalist…

…and repeating the warning given just above:

> The chief and ever-present risk is that the progress of comparatively large growers backed by plentiful financial resources, which weight the scale so heavily against the independent small Arab proprietor, will mean the entire and permanent displacement of the latter from the soil.

Amidst all the suppression of undesired facts and unwelcome truths which has characterized the Palestine Question, nothing is more notable than the obscurity in which the damning French Report has been kept. The references in it to Arab capitalists or native money-lenders have enjoyed indeed a certain circulation, but the rest of it has remained unpublicized. Yet there is an intimate connection between its disclosures and the sudden discovery by the Peel Commissioners that Palestine must be partitioned. The regime of the false Mandate was breaking down. The establishment of some other sort of regime was essential unless the whole burden of the coming collapse, and the whole responsibility for it, were to lie upon the Government which had insisted upon the guilty regime. If two States *could* be set up in Palestine, an air of starting all over again would be achieved, and the cause of the collapse would be found in the inevitable dissensions between them.

I do not assert that the Peel Commissioners thought the future out in this somewhat Machiavellian way. It is rare for our Royal Commissioners or diplomatists or even statesmen to think things out in a Machiavellian way, and I say this quite seriously, without a grain of irony. But they have a trick of acting by instinct, as women act in private life, and of doing or proposing something through synthetic leaps of thought, with no analysis of motives or methods and with no absolute disclosure to themselves of their aim, but with a curious surety of reaching somewhere. What they thus propose always turns out to be what the diplomatists and so forth of other nations could only have achieved after much Machiavellian excogitation from point to point. The said nations, who do not understand the British mind, refuse to believe in the sequel that some British act overreaching them was not the result of their own sort of plodding cunning.

This for the exoneration of the Peel Commissioners. One point of the French Report deserves a final couple of paragraphs. Mr. French's register of landless Arabs was confined to principal tenants whose land had been sold over their heads directly to Zionists. The sons, dependants and labourers of these men, who worked for or with them, were not classified as "landless" though they were severed from the land. Also if a man sold land to an intermediary—every country has its quantum of venal intermediaries—who then resold at a profit to the Zionists, then again the original holder was not classified as landless through the sale to Zionists. Nor did a man who, after his plot had been sold, was established briefly on some hide of soil till the poverty of the holding made him abandon it, count among the landless. The tenant again of two separate plots, who sold one of them, was not included amidst the landless, though it might be obvious that the second plot would prove insufficient to support him.

Admittedly, the points thus raised were difficult and complex. But second-hand sales; transient establishment of individuals on insufficient plots after leaving their real ones, so that only the second plot counted officially as vacated; the kindred situation resulting from selling half a man's land—these were so many loopholes which would make any legislation based on the register nugatory. There were other loopholes too, and more than anything else they all showed that as long as Zionist acquisition of the land was permitted to continue, codes introduced to counter it while at the same time maintaining it, would prove hopelessly artificial and useless. In the present case the number of "landless Arabs" on the register was but a section of the landless Arabs not on the register. Calculations based on the register total were altogether false and misleading, as the Peel Report itself has pointed out since.

Chapter 38

Increase of Zionist immigration.
The pretext of refuge from the German persecution.
How the Legislative Council was rejected.
The Great Strike of 1936.
The Arab Officials' Memorial—Resignation of the Chief Justice.
The Peel Commission's Report and project of Partition.
Private arrangements of Mr. Ormsby-Gore and Dr. Weizmann.

The period within which Mr. French's inquiry took place, 1931 and 1932, is generally described as moderately quiet, as a period during which nothing much was said or done in Palestine, and public order was not too disturbed. But for the Arabs these years were a repetition of the old story. For them they formed yet another case of: "the all-endured this nothing-done costs me."

In practice Zionist encroachment continued, and theoretically no sign appeared that the Arabs were to receive that proper status for which they had been so long and so vainly appealing. Distant promises were made. A Local Government Ordinance was held out as a concession for the following year. But any development of purely local government always meant enabling Zionist colonies and bodies to dig themselves in with local powers shading (as in the Rosenblatt plan) into autonomy. So that for the Arabs increasing municipal rule was never anything but a yielding of their situation under the customary guise of receiving some grant.

After the very doubtful gift of local government, there were proposals for the elusive reward of self-government at last, "next year perhaps." That was 1933.

But in 1932 Zionist immigration, public and assisted Zionist immigration, had begun to mount again dangerously, to say nothing of (so to speak) Zionist autonomous immigration. It was within a few hundreds of 10,000. The recommendations of the various Commissions, the declarations of the White Paper, all were being disregarded very quickly. Even the mechanical "economic absorptive capacity" functioned like a turnstile out of order, whirling round and round as the immigrants went through and giving them a pleasant sense of being superior to obstacles.

The Arabs protested violently, as violently as they could in the official vacuum in which they had to live. The first warnings now came that Arab national feeling was turning from considering the Zionists as the principal foe to placing the Government in this situation. After all, the Government was the essentially responsible party, since it had installed the National Home, under the colour of obligations which it had composed itself, in company with the Zionists. An unhappy, and desperate turn. But was it unnatural? Under kindred circumstances would the British people have waited so many years to discover what was so patent?

A national manifesto (quoted by the Peel Commissioners) was published by the Arab Executive Committee in March 1933, declaring that the "Government will be looked upon as the true enemy whom they (the Arab people) must get rid of through every legal means." But here lay the crux of the whole situation. Where were the legal means? What legal means existed for a Mandated population, not necessarily to get rid of a Mandatory, but even to charge him with tampering with his title-deeds and misusing his Mandate? None.

The League of Nations which should have been the Court of Appeal, refused to hear an appeal against the character of the Mandate. The Court of The Hague was inaccessible. There was no legal means in the wide world provided for the Arabs. Yet presently, when they resorted in despair to strikes and to insurrection, their conduct was greeted with cries of "Illegality!" "Violence!" "Lawlessness!" and all the rest.

From 1933 onwards things began to take a fatal air. In August the Zionist Congress in Prague demanded that the National Home must be "built as speedily as possible and on the largest scale." Musa Kazem Pasha, the President of the Arab Executive, retorted with a public demand to the High Commissioner that Zionist immigration should be stopped immediately. Instead of this, the total of Zionist immigrants admitted in 1933 rose to 30,000.

This increase was ascribed to the inflow of fugitives from anti-Semitic persecution in Germany, or the assumption that this was the cause of it was spread by the usual apologists. At the same time the same apologists introduced the plea of pity, which Herr Hitler had put into their hands so conveniently. Were the new Jewish exiles from Germany, so often men of worth and high attainments, to find no home? The political Zionists had never had so powerful a plea to produce before, as the Nazi Government indeed had been brutal, while the ejected or banished Jews were frequently persons of considerable merit and were always worthy objects of sympathy.

But a moment's thought, that special momentary thought which never seems to be taken, would have shown that to cure tyrannous and enforced expulsion of thousands from Germany by tyrannous and enforced impulsion of thousands into Palestine was only to double the wrong and to extend the sphere of moral disorder. The voices which were raised then to demand the lowering of all immigration barriers in Palestine in order to cope with the exiles of Berlin, were not raised then to demand the lowering of all immigration barriers throughout the vast Empire of Britain and of the Dominions.

It was, where the question arose at all, pleaded that the unemployment situation in Great Britain and in the Dominions did not permit the introduction of immigrants save in small numbers. This argument, quite reasonable for Great Britain, but not so reasonable for all other British areas, was, however, not found applicable to Palestine. Yet Palestine was tinier than Britain, Palestine was in such a situation of unemployment and of dispossession that a series of Commissions and inquiries had made the gravest reports about it. Palestine, too, was not British property. This did not prevent the Government from turning to the poor fugitives of Berlin and welcoming them effusively to the soil of another people.

More than this, amidst the 30,000 immigrants of 1933 only some 5,000 came from Germany. The remainder came from the regular Eastern European sources, from Galicia, the Ukraine and Bessarabia, from those swarming Zionist lands Economica, Absorptivia and Capacitas. The figures meant, leaving the German exiles out of consideration, a leap in numbers of the usual immigrants to 25,000.

"From that time onwards," says the Peel Report, "the Arab Press, already virulent enough, became steadily more inflammatory." Was it surprising, it must be asked again? Had not immigration, already virulent enough, become steadily more inflammatory?

In 1934 it rose with another leap to 42,000. In the previous October the Arabs, whose petitions seemed only to be heeded when they were written in blood, had rioted again, and there had been a strike for a period. Twenty-six persons were killed and 187 injured by police-fire: the police lost a constable and 56 injured. The area of affray was wide, at Jaffa, Haifa and Nablus. The new factor in these riots, as the Peel Commissioners point out, was that they were directed against the forces of the Government. "In 1920, 1921 and 1929 the Arabs had attacked the Jews. In 1933 they attacked the Government. The idea that the British authorities in London or Jerusalem were trying to hold the balance even, between Jew and Arab, was now openly scouted."

In the autumn the Arab Executive tried one more effort within the narrow legal limits open to it. It submitted another formal protest to the

High Commissioner, in the strongest terms, against continued immigration and land-acquisition by the Zionists. Sir Arthur Wauchope, impotent in the hands of the Home Government, had only the lame answer to make that the number of immigrants had not exceeded the economic absorptive capacity of the country and that he was "doing what he could" to protect the Arab husbandman and to increase the productivity of the soil. But nothing worth mentioning, in proportion to what needed to be done, was done. There was not the money, there was not the staff, there was not the impulse nor even the wish from London.

The innate complexities were too great, if there had been. A protective Ordinance issued in 1933, to try and defend the Arab peasant a little more, had failed. In 1934 it was amended and another one introduced throwing on overburdened District Commissioners the charge of deciding land rights, water rights, grazing rights, hereditament rights, and every other kind of rights at his own Court, or as it must turn out, his own succession of Courts of Inquiry, if the dispute over rights threatened to cause a breach of the peace. So the time passed.

The year 1935 came; *annus terribilis.* Sixty-one thousand Zionist immigrants poured into Palestine. Another Zionist Congress, at Lucerne this time, declared that it was "the only country at present open to Jewish immigration on a large scale" and demanded that "immigration and settlement should proceed far more rapidly than hitherto." "The Zionist Organization would focus the energies of the Jewish people on the extension and acceleration of its resettlement of Palestine."

With such words in their ears and watching the thronged gangways of the immigrant ships, the Arabs meanwhile saw their own people sinking into the degradation of a workless industrial proletariat. It was no good for displaced peasants to ask for land: there was none for them. At the end of 1935, four years after the register of landless Arabs had been begun by Mr. French, the claims of 660 only had been admitted. Land had been bought for them at a cost of £72,000 by the Administration, but they had not yet been installed.

This was all that had been achieved for the Arab race, while 61,000 Zionist immigrants were allowed to enter. At the time in Haifa alone there were some 11,000 landless Arabs living in huts made of rusty petrol-tins. The petrol-tin hut had become their national home and, as a count of the huts had revealed, there were about 2,500 of these national Arab homes. This meant more than four Arabs to the hut. They were employed, those who *were* employed, in the harbour-works, in navvying and in the kindred jobs of the port and the town. The Government had been pressed by the Arab Workers Society to find land for housing them, but replied regretting that it had none which could be allotted for the purpose.

In Jaffa, as Mr. Mansur, the secretary of the Arab Federation of Labour records, in that autumn there were a thousand of its members unemployed and another four thousand Arabs without work in the city. Of the Zionist immigrants, in the workers' schedule, only about a half was absorbed in the colonies. "Of those who remained in the towns," the Report of the Zionist Executive to the next Zionist Congress said, "some were engaged in various industrial branches, port-labour, porterage at railway stations and the like, and some found no employment whatsoever... During the entire period covered by this Report (1935-7) the position obliged the Executive of the Jewish Agency and the Labour Department to take all possible measures to prevent the outbreak of a disastrous and destructive crisis and the growth of unemployment to catastrophic proportions."

There were 5,000 Zionist unemployed in Palestine at the close of 1935. This did not prevent the Jewish Agency for applying for 10,900 permits for Zionist workers, and the Administration from granting over 3,000. Unemployment increased amidst the Arabs, the pressure brought to bear on the Administration to find jobs for the continuously arriving Zionists contributing to swell it. For example, the contract for building three Government schools for Arabs in the purely Arab town of Jaffa was given to a Zionist contractor employing Zionist labour. The Arab unemployed came on the scene and, after disorder, obtained that at least half of the workers on the schools should be Arabs.

From all this the general situation in the country can be realized. The only thing which prevented an outbreak in the winter probably was that at long last, towards the end of December, the High Commissioner submitted to the Arab Executive a scheme for a Legislative Council. This, without deserving that name, was an advance on previous offers as far as representation upon the Council was concerned. Any step towards a proper political settlement was a step towards the subsidiary economic settlement.

In this Council out of twenty-eight members only five would be officials. Of the twenty-three remaining eleven would be Moslems, three Christians, seven Jews; and two would be representatives of commercial interests, a sort of recognition of the true faith of the mandatory world. The President was to be "an impartial person unconnected with Palestine."

The Council would not be allowed to meddle with primary matters, for by order it was not to question the validity of the Mandate. The High Commissioner, too, could govern by proclamation if needs be, without the consent of the Council, and control of immigration would be kept in his hands. But as a great advance towards liberty, the Council was to be allowed to discuss (only to "discuss," not to fix) the labour schedule of immigrant admissions.

This scheme contained no fraction of self-government, yet was far too evocative of it in the opinion of the Zionists and of their friends. Knowing that it was under way, most probably having perused drafts of it, the chiefs of the Zionist Congress at Lucerne in the summer had rejected it in advance. They passed a remarkable Resolution declaring the establishment of a Legislative Council to be "a step contrary to the spirit of the Mandate" and one to which they must reaffirm the opposition of the Congress "in the present stage of the development of Palestine."

A remarkable Resolution, indeed, when the inner meaning of the "development of Palestine" is considered, and when it is remembered how when they were still few in numbers and most of their immigrants were becoming emigrants, in 1922-3, the Zionists had affirmed enthusiastic adherence to the then proposed Legislative Council. They protested loudly then against the Government's condonation of the Arab boycott of the elections. "The Jewish Press was indignant at the 'weakness' of the Government and asked, 'Now that elections have been ordered by an Order in Council and that it was proclaimed that any one interfering with the elections would be prosecuted, why was this not carried out? Why was not the poisonous agitation stopped?'" (Storrs.)

However all this was put out of sight, the Zionist Congress reaffirmed blithely the reverse of what had been affirmed before, and Dr. Weizmann and his colleagues "accordingly informed the High Commissioner that they rejected the scheme and had resolved to take no part in its operation." (Peel Report.)

The Arabs, despite the intrinsic worthlessness of the proposed Council, were disposed to accept it without enthusiasm as a first instalment towards a first instalment of justice. In Mr. Churchill's "Legislative Council" they would not have been allowed to speak of immigration. In the new "Legislative Council" they at least would be allowed to speak of it, though no heed would be paid to what they would say. The Peel Commissioners attribute what they style the Arab acquiescence in the Council scheme to the vehemence with which the Zionists opposed it. This certainly was an advisory pointer for the Arabs; but possibly their acquiescence sprang chiefly from the fresh outlook in the Council scheme. For the first time they were recognized as men who had to be allowed to open their mouths, however vainly, upon the fate of their country. Hitherto they had been treated as the impedimenta of Palestine, left like stock and crops in the hands of engineers and economists under "absorptive capacity" and such schemes. Now they were to be left, still helpless it is true, but in the hands of the High Commissioner, who presided over men. It was, as I say, an advance for the Arabs, an advance of genus to human dignity, if no more.

That after their experience of the past fifteen years or so, the Arabs should have shown a disposition to accept this promotion as an earnest of future freedom, shows how long-suffering this people was and shows for how many years they clung to the idea of winning their rights, some day or other, from Great Britain. They saw too that a sort of test-case had arisen through the proposed Council, the Home Government having been placed for once, through it, in a situation which could not be evaded. The White Paper—and this the Black Letter had not altered—had declared in as many words that the Government would stand no nonsense from "Palestinians" who refused to elect representatives to the Legislative Council. If the Palestinians would not vote, then the Government would name occupants for the empty seats.

Now a Legislative Council in pursuance of the White Paper was to be set up, and Dr. Weizmann and other Palestinians had refused to elect representatives. So unless the previous threat had been merely a piece of coercion meant for Arabs only, the Government now would stand no nonsense from Dr. Weizmann and would name representatives for the Legislative Council in place of the unselected nominees of the men of Lucerne. The Arabs had never had a chance to sit back and watch the development of a situation like this one, so they took a waiting posture.

It was rather simple of them. What happened is best told in the words of the Peel Report:

> Its [the Legislative Council scheme's] fate was soon determined outside Palestine. On the 26th February, 1936, it was debated in the House of Lords and on the 24th March in the House of Commons. On the former occasion Lords Snell, Lytton, Lothian, Jessel, Elibank, Mansfield, Melchett, Marley and Cecil, representing all parties in the House, were agreed in urging that the scheme should either be abandoned for the present or suspended while a Royal Commission inquired into the question on the spot. The Government spokesman, Lord Plymouth, was its only supporter. In the House of Commons the result was much the same. Twelve members asked for the suspension or drastic modification of the scheme; and the Secretary of State [Mr. J. H. Thomas] whose speech was constantly interrupted, had only two supporters.

That was the end of the Legislative Council. There were a few new names in the list of peers, but the familiar ones were there, and the dozen Commoners were of the old stock. The Macedonian phalanx of professional idealists, with Lord Cecil at their head, had come clashing on to the scene and assumed charge. In the House of Commons Mr. Churchill led the attack.

The general burden of Commons speeches was that the Commons should have been consulted before such a "momentous step" was taken. But the step was not momentous at all, save for the Arabs in that their humanity was acknowledged. Sir Ronald Storrs describes things well when he says, "In the subsequent debate in both Houses, the Arab case may be said, without exaggeration, to have gone by default… Mr. Winston Churchill, Public Orator of the British Empire, adroitly shifting his ground to the German treatment of Jews, shouted aloud, 'Vile tyranny!' and shook his fist at the ceiling. Not a soul could disagree with him; yet the Germans admitted [that is German-Jew exiles admitted to Palestine] amidst the record entry of 61,849 amounted to less than 16 percent (say 9,500)."

The Peel Report apologia for this exhibition deserves as much as Mr. Churchill to be cited:

> Re-reading the debates [say the Commissioners] in the light of our experience in Palestine, we have been impressed by the fairness of most of the speeches. If the case against the scheme was partly based on the likelihood that it would operate to the disadvantage of the Jewish National Home, it was also based on such general considerations as the desirability of allowing more time to elapse for training in local government, or the unwisdom of committing Palestine to a form of Constitution which would naturally lead, and had elsewhere led, to Responsible Government. And on this last point it should be remembered that for several years past Parliament had been discussing the difficulty of introducing Responsible Government in a country so deeply divided by communal differences as India.

If it were not for the final sentence, one would almost think that in this comment the Peel Commissioners were being sarcastic. The identity of "more time for training in local government" with "more time for the increase of the Zionist population" forces itself upon the reader with much emphasis. In respect of the last sentence, it scarcely needs to be observed that in India Great Britain is a free agent. The affairs of that Dominion are affairs between herself and the people of India. In Palestine she was not a free agent. She was there as Mandatory to carry out the Covenant, and it was the business of her legislators not to gain time by displays of canting doubt concerning the wisdom of Responsible Government, but to do their duty and install Responsible Government.

The Peel Report, after this little display of sciolism, recognized, however, after its usual compensatory fashion, that it was "unfortunate that the Jewish side of the case was so much more fully stated than the Arab," and that the Debate was "a striking illustration of the disadvantage which the Arabs suffer whenever the field of controversy shifts from Palestine to the United Kingdom."

The Arabs though were coming to the end of their extraordinary patience. The debates in the two Houses and the instant capitulation of the Government in sequel to them were too much to stand. An added irritation was a request from the Colonial Office to send yet another delegation to London. There had been five so far, "five peaceful and unsuccessful delegations to Whitehall" (Storrs) besides the Palin, Haycraft, Shaw, Hope Simpson and French inquiries, to say nothing of one or two subsidiary emissaries.

The hapless Sir Arthur Wauchope was just preparing an Ordinance forbidding the sale of land wherever the occupant would lose his subsistence thereby. But what was the good of it now, years overdue? In April what may be called Outbreak V occurred, the pyre being lit through a crime of a thieving and murderous Bedouin, but the cause being the same as disturbances I, II, III and IV, previously mentioned, with the addition of the sickness of the nation's heart from long-deferred hope once more indefinitely adjourned.

Assassinations, and assaults on both sides, culminated in the great general strike of that year 1936. It began on the 21st of April by the uniform decision of the Arab public and of the leaders of all Arab parties. All parties met to form a representative national council, which was entitled the Arab Higher Committee. The Mufti of Jerusalem, Haj Ameen Al Husseini, was nominated President, and amongst its members were Auni Bey Abdel-Hadi, Ragheb Bey Nashashibi, the Mayor of Jerusalem, the Manager of the Arab Bank, and two Christian members, Yakoub Effendi Farraj and Alfred Effendi Roch.

The Higher Committee formally demanded:

1. The stoppage of all Zionist immigration.
2. The prohibition of transfer of any more Arab land to Zionists.
3. The establishment of a National Government responsible to a representative Council elected by democratic suffrage.

The strike developed into general "civil disobedience" upon Indian lines, refusal to pay taxes and so forth. The life of the country came to a standstill practically, outside the Zionist quarters and colonies. Rioting developed and damage was done to Zionist property and lands all over the country.

Gradually the disorder hardened into a small war, with attacks on railways and police-stations and widespread sniping. Bands formed in the hills. On the other hand heavy reinforcements of troops were sent to patrol the country and protect communications, and towards the close of May the

Irish parallel was made complete by the arrest of sixty Arabs for incitement to disturbance and the setting-up of a Concentration Camp at Surafend, where presently Auni Bey Abdel-Hadi and other leaders were interned.

Meanwhile there had been the announcement in the House of Commons of the intention to send to Palestine a sixth Commission, a Royal Commission this time, and the disastrous appointment of Mr. Ormsby-Gore as Colonial Secretary. His declarations of impartiality were received with derision in Palestine. The announcement of the Government concerning the Commission was that it would advise the King, "after order had been restored, to appoint a Royal Commission which, without bringing into question the terms of the Mandate, will investigate causes of unrest and alleged grievances either of Arabs or of Jews." The old familiar terms of reference therefore reappeared, with the usual proviso that the bona tides of the Mandate was not to be a subject of inquiry, though there was a touch of panic this time in the way in which the proviso was at once plastered in.

After the arrests and establishment of the Concentration Camp, a striking event occurred. A memorandum was handed to the High Commissioner in the name of 137 senior Arab officials in the Civil Service.

It "was signed or afterwards endorsed by all the senior Arab officials, including highly placed officers in the political as well as the technical departments of the Administration (police officers being the only exception) and—still more remarkable—by all the Arab judges," says the Peel Report, adding, "It seems to us to throw a sharp light on the state of affairs in Palestine that a British Government should ever have been confronted with such a situation."

The Arab officials of the Second Division of the Civil Service followed suit later with a memorandum or petition bearing 1,200 signatures.

The memorandum of the senior officials began by a statement that besides their general duties as Civil Servants a particular duty in their opinion lay upon them of acting as a link between the Government and the Arab population, and that in view of the absence of representative institution this duty was of essential importance. In pursuance of this conception of their role they ventured, they said, with all respect, to submit the following:

> The underlying cause of the present discontent is that the Arab population of all classes, creeds and occupations is animated by a profound sense of the injustice done to them. They feel that insufficient regard has been paid in the past to their legitimate grievances, even though those grievances had been inquired into by qualified and impartial official investigators, and to a large extent vindicated by those inquiries. As a result the Arabs have been driven into a state verging on despair, and the present unrest is no more than an expression of that despair.

This was the opening clause. The signatories went on to say that this despair was due to the Arabs' lack of faith in the value of official assurances for the future, instancing the abandonment under Zionist pressure of the White Paper and of the scheme for the Legislative Council. "We should," they said, "be doing a disservice to the Government and an injury to our consciences if we were to conceal our belief that the Arab complaint on this head is substantially justified."

They had tried to quiet the population by citing the appointment of the Royal Commission, but with no result save that of earning for themselves odium and suspicion. They assured the High Commissioner that the present feeling of the people "was not to be crushed by force." The insurrection could be stamped out by the military resources of the Government, but never the national feeling. "The only way in which it can be removed is by removing the causes which have brought it about."

The announcement of the Royal Commission had not allayed the situation because of the general loss of confidence in the Government. The only thing which could allay it and end the deadlock was to stop immigration pending the arrival of the Commission. This had been done under similar circumstances twice before, in 1921 and in 1929, so there was a good precedent. Only a provisional stoppage was asked, till the Commission had reported, and the request was the more reasonable since the Commission would have to report on this very question of immigration.

> In other words, the choice between an immediate return to normal conditions and an indefinite continuation of the present disorders and bloodshed depends, not on a matter of policy or principle, but solely on a matter of provisional regulation, that of whether or not immigration is to be stopped.

The signatories said they knew that it might be argued that to stop immigration now would be to yield to violence and to put the Government's prestige at stake.

> We yield to no one in upholding order and authority as the foundation of all good government. But authority implies justice all round, and when justice is denied or when confidence in its impartiality is shaken, then authority becomes undermined, and it shows a mistaken notion of prestige to suppose that it can be restored by the use of force. In this case, the prestige and authority of Government would not only not lose but would gain by a timely act of conciliation.

There is no need to commend this document, however unusual was the act of its presentation. Desperate situations demanded action such as the signatories took. To read the memorandum carries the mind back to the Damascus Resolutions of the Syrian Congress, seventeen years before. It has the same quiet reasonableness. The same thought must come to the mind upon reading it as upon reading the Damascus Resolutions—how could men who wrote like this be treated as illiterate tribesmen unable to govern themselves.

In addition to this memorandum, the Home Government received private advices from the highest quarters amidst the British officials of the country advising the suspension of Zionist immigration pending the arrival of the Commission, as the only means to secure a stoppage of the strike and of the bloodshed.

But neither to private British advice nor to the memorandum of the Arab Civil Service was any attention paid. The Labour schedule granted to the Zionist leaders during the previous month was left in force. This admitted 4,500 immigrants. Though that was a lessening of volume compared with 1935, yet in this year of 1936 with warfare alight throughout the land, 30,000 Zionist immigrants were brought into Palestine. This in addition certainly to 10,000 so-called "clandestine" entries during these two years.

We have now reached pretty recent days, and I do not propose to recount at length the course of well-recorded events. In June there was an event though which was not so well recorded. A considerable section of the older buildings of Jaffa was blown up by military engineers. It was a quarter of ancient dwellings, difficult to penetrate. Shots had been fired from it, though as generally occurs in this sort of strife, most of the people inhabiting therein had taken no part in the business. Its real defect, from the point of view of the maintenance of peace and order, was that it was labyrinthine, that insurgents could disappear through it and above all that it impeded the manoeuvring of troops.

Under an Order in Council of 1931 the High Commissioner could empower the military authorities to destroy any buildings for the purpose of the country's defence. But what distinguished the destruction in Jaffa was that before it took place no such powers were obtained, nor even were ever sought. Some official, whose name has remained shielded, not desiring to have to state a case, issued on his own authority what passed as a Government pronouncement. No signature nor legalization of any kind was attached to it, but it bore a footnote saying that it had been printed at the Government printing-press. The pronouncement declared that:

> "The Government was about to initiate a scheme for opening up and improving the Old City of Jaffa by the construction of two roads,"

and that:

> "The first steps necessary will be the demolition and clearance of

> certain existing buildings which are congested and insanitary, and advantage is being taken of the presence in Palestine of Royal Engineers to begin these operations."

Inhabitants of the buildings were "duly warned to evacuate them" by the distribution of the "Government" pronouncement by hand and from aeroplanes, and by reproduction of it in the local papers. Two days' notice was given.

The conditions caused by the general strike, with the curfew imposed upon this, made it all but impossible for the inhabitants of the doomed houses to get even their simple household belongings and food-stores away in the time provided. An Arab resident of the quarter, all its residents of course being Arab, applied at once for a rule *nisi* against the order for destruction. After it had been granted, the question of its being made absolute (that is changed from a temporary to a permanent rule) was considered at a sitting of the High Court, the Chief Justice and the Senior Puisne Judge being on the Bench and, because of the importance of the case, they both delivered judgments.

They delivered similar judgments, both discharging the rule *nisi* and therefore permitting the destruction, but they did so only upon a point of law, namely, that the acts of the Civil Authorities of the Administration, who had employed the military forces, and consequently had been cited, were not subject to the 1931 Order in Council.

> The Petitioner, however [continued the judgment of the Chief Justice] has done a public service in exposing what I am bound to call the singularly disingenuous lack of moral courage displayed by the Administration in the whole matter. I am not surprised in the circumstances to find that no responsible officer of the Government would affix his signature to the notices under review. As to their origin, the Junior Government Advocate claims to have been kept in a state of ignorance which is as remarkable as it is profound; and as to their distribution he declines to say with certainty who is responsible therefore.
>
> It would have been more creditable if the Government, instead of endeavouring to throw dust in people's eyes by professing to be inspired with aesthetic or other quasi-philanthropic motives, such as town-planning or public health, in the demolition which was contemplated, had said frankly and truthfully that it was primarily for defensive purposes, which one may assume means enabling the forces of the military or the police an easier means of access in the congested quarters of the town in question.
>
> If this had been done, this High Court, when presided over by my learned brother, would not have issued a rule *nisi*, and the bona fides of the Government, which cannot escape responsibility by hiding behind the anonymity of the notices, would not have suffered.

> It would be a negation of justice if, in a glaring case of evasiveness such as that before us, this High Court did not speak its mind freely.

The Senior Puisne Judge concurred with the Chief Justice and the Bench, while discharging the rule *nisi* "marked, their disapproval by doing so without costs."

The Jaffa houses were blown up, amidst the cheers of Zionists congregated on the beach at Tel-Aviv. This demolition was more symbolic than anyone in Palestine then realized. In the early part of the War, when the Turks still held the country, Djemaal Pasha, infuriated by Arab action amidst his own forces and by the betrayal by Arabs of military information to the Allies, cried out in a passion one evening, "The Jaffa people are all British. I shall blow up Jaffa stone from stone." The Jaffa people were indeed "all British" then. But it had remained for the British to blow up Jaffa stone from stone.

Within a few months of delivering the judgment which so well sustained the traditions of the judiciary never to be the creature of the State, the Chief Justice, Sir Michael McDonnell, resigned. It was widely asserted, not alone in Palestine, that he had been forced to resign because of the action of the Bench in the Jaffa case. A question was put in the House of Commons. Mr. Ormsby-Gore in reply repeated the formal terms in which the Chief Justice had said good-bye to the Palestine Bar at his last sitting, which by inference deprecated any suggestion of an enforced retirement. In these matters, though, much depends upon the exact meaning given to the word "force." Not a soul in Palestine believed that the Colonial Secretary was a complete stranger to the Chief Justice's retirement, nor will Mr. Ormsby-Gore today dare for one moment to say that he had no share of any kind in it. Another cherished British principle had gone by the board in the service of political Zionism.

The insurrection continued unabated through the summer of 1936, the Arab bands gaining something of the semblance of organized forces through the leadership of an ex-Turkish officer, Fauzi el Kauwakjee, an able man who had served in the French Intelligence Service in the northern zone, been military adviser to King Ibn Saud and then passed into the Irak regular army. Martial law was proclaimed, and in the autumn reinforcements had brought the number of British troops in Palestine to some 20,000, as the Peel Report states. This was about one soldier in every six out of the military strength of Great Britain, and must have left the country dangerously free of defence.

These large reinforcements and an appeal addressed through the High Committee by the Kings of the Hedjaz and Irak and the Emir of Transjordan, which begged the Arabs to "resolve for peace," led to a subsidence of the fighting, and after six months the strike also was brought to an end. The Arab monarchs had declared that they relied on the good intentions of their friend, Great Britain, who had promised that she would do justice. So once more the Arabs set their hopes upon a Commission, and in November the Peel Commissioners arrived.

The Commission remained in Palestine till the middle of January 1937. At first the Arab leaders boycotted it because of the refusal of the Home Government to suspend Zionist immigration, but they were induced in the end by the Kings of Hedjaz and of Irak to present the Arab case before Lord Peel and his colleagues. This they did during the final ten days of the Commission's stay.

On their return to London the Peel Commissioners heard some witnesses there. Eight persons "who had held official positions or high offices of State" were examined during private sessions. In July the Commissioners rendered their Report. They declared that "the Mandate had proved unworkable" as constituted. They recommended that Palestine should be split into three sections. One of these, to which Transjordan would be annexed, would become an Arab State. The second would be a Jewish State. In both of these areas the Mandate would cease, treaties would be made by Great Britain with the new Governments, and Great Britain would patronize the requests of either of them to be enrolled as members of the League of Nations.

The Holy Places, defined as an enclave containing Jerusalem and Bethlehem, with Nazareth and the waters and shores of the Sea of Galilee, were to be separated from the above areas and for them Great Britain was to obtain a permanent Mandate, only terminable by the common desire of the League of Nations and of the United States of America. The inhabitants of this Mandated area would be Mandated subjects and English would be the only official language.

In addition to this dispersed mandatory district, of which the Jerusalem-Bethlehem enclave would be joined to the Mediterranean by a corridor, terminating at Jaffa, but not including that town, the creation of temporary British-Mandatory spots was recommended. These were the towns of Acre, Haifa, Safed and Tiberias. Yet another Mandated enclave was recommended, to be set up on the north-west coast of the gulf of Akaba.

As for the boundaries of the two new States, the Jewish State, with a marked exception, would be formed mainly of land in Jewish occupation already. It would embrace the maritime belt from a point about twenty miles below Jaffa to the frontier about twelve miles above Acre, to which would be added nearly all the plain of Esdraelon. But it would also be swelled enormously on the north by the addition of Galilee, where some six hundred square miles of the highlands into which the Zionists had not penetrated would be included in their State. It was in the centre of these highlands that lay El-Bukerah, the remote hamlet where the only Jewish families lived which were believed to have survived upon the soil since the time of Christ. The few Jews to be found in this quadrilateral of mountain-land had never been political Zionists, whom of course they ante-dated.

The Arab State would be composed of the hill-country, with Jaffa and a fag-end of Esdraelon between Megiddo and Jenin. The Arabs, in fact, after the Jewish State and the inland archipelago of British mandated areas had been determined to satisfaction, would get whatever was left over.

These frontiers, however, were only proposed by the Peel Commissioners as those which they would suggest upon first consideration. They did not attach finality to them, and they added as a principal recommendation of their Report that a further technical Commission should be appointed to proceed to Palestine and to delimit definitely the frontiers of the States and Mandated areas they proposed.

Such were the main recommendations. But in the case that Partition should not be accepted and that the present Mandatory system should be retained for any period, certain other recommendations were included in the Report. They were attached in response to an itemized catalogue of seven Arab and ten Jewish principal grievances or demands, which arose out of the Mandatory system as it had been put into practice. The chief of these subsidiary recommendations was that for the next five years the high-level of Zionist immigration should be fixed at 12,000. "Immigration should be reviewed and decided upon political, social and psychological as well as economic considerations," said the Report.

Thus they proposed that "economic absorptive" capacity should no longer form the standard of immigration. Apart from fixing this point, the recommendation was in the best Sibylline style, for it could be interpreted in either of two ways. It might mean that there were limits to Zionist immigration, even should the country be considered physically capable of holding more. On the other hand it might mean that Zionists would be allowed to enter Palestine if they were thought to be "socially necessary" for its well-being and that the Arabs might have to submit to the further and horrifying prospect of "psychological immigrants."

This recommendation was one of nine made to satisfy Jewish grievances, so that only one Jewish grievance was not entertained. This was the complaint that Transjordan had not been opened to their immigration.

By the contrast now familiar, only one of the Arabs' grievances or demands was entertained. This solitary accepted Arab grievance was that insufficient money was being consecrated to Arab education. The Commissioners said that they would welcome more expenditure on Arab education, especially on village agricultural schools.

All the remaining Arab grievances were declared to be illegitimate under the terms of the Mandate, and no response to them was offered. It was stated specifically that the "attitude of Arab officials" precluded their employment, as requested, in the higher posts of the Administration. The Report went on: "In the peculiar circumstances of Palestine under the Mandate self-governing institutions cannot be developed," and in the 404 pages which the Peel Commissioners wrote the adjective "peculiar" in the above sentence was perhaps the happiest achievement of their pens.

After the Report had been published, the Government issued with the least possible delay a White Paper declaring itself to be "in general agreement with the arguments and the conclusions of the Commission." Full-dress debates in both Houses of Parliament followed. Mr. Ormsby-Gore asked the Commons straight away to "approve the policy of His Majesty's Government relating to Palestine, as set out in the White Paper." But the disconcerted Ormsby-Gore had even a worse time than, as he afterwards told Dr. Weizmann, he expected. The House refused to be rushed by him or by the Government.

The gist of the debate was that the question was too important for Parliament, without any delay or any time for consideration, to endorse the Cabinet policy of Partition. A mixed amendment of Mr. Churchill's and Mr. Lloyd George's was proposed and carried. On the Government's behalf Mr. Ormsby-Gore, putting himself into reverse with extraordinary speed, swiftly accepted the amendment.

By this amendment, the Government's White Paper proposals should

> be brought before the League of Nations with a view to enabling His Majesty's Government, after adequate inquiry, to present to Parliament a definite scheme taking into full account all the recommendations of the Command Paper.

In short, the Partition proposal was remanded. A speech in the Lords by Sir Herbert (now Viscount) Samuel had served considerably to discredit the details of the Peel proposals.

> This Commission [he said] seems to have gone to the Versailles Treaty and to have picked out all the most difficult and awkward provisions it contained. They have put a Saar, a Polish corridor, and half a dozen Danzigs and Memels into a country the size of Wales.

He added that:

> under the Partition scheme only 258,000 of the 400,000 Jews in Palestine would be in the Jewish State, and in that State there would also be 225,000 Arabs.

A statement which was correct, yet did not put the position as between Arabs and Jews correctly. Of the 142,000 Jews who would not be in the Jewish State, hardly any—only 1,200 or so—would pass under Arab rule, if the proposed frontiers were adopted. Their lot would be to pass under British Mandatory administration. The situation of the Arabs would be something very different. Two hundred and twenty thousand of them would be placed under Jewish rule, or be forced to leave their native places. The Peel Report had recommended too that in the last resort what it euphemistically called "exchange of population" should be compulsory. If the people earmarked for exchange refused to abandon their homes, they were to be carried away forcibly from them.

This generous project, with the rest of the Report, had been debated and criticized in Parliament on the 21st of July. In pursuance of the amendment there passed, Mr. Ormsby-Gore proceeded to Geneva in the first week of August, and expounded the Partition proposals to the Mandates Commission of the League of Nations. He was cross-questioned there for the better part of a week by the members of the Permanent Mandates Commission upon the customary false issues dear to that Commission. Such as it was, the cross-examination was carried out with a severity which he deserved thoroughly, but the Permanent Mandates Commission's members had not a shred of the necessary moral status to justify them in employing. On this occasion, as upon all since it had been created, the Commission gave no sign—save possibly upon one point— of trying to do its duty, or of insisting that an opportunity of doing its duty should be granted to it instead of the artificial functions in which it had spent its useless days.

The one point in discussion of which the Commission showed an inclination to quit its habitual attitude was that which concerned the removal of the Arabs in the prospective Jewish State. But it demurred, not so much to the morality as to the practical difficulty of transporting the 225,000 from Galilee. As it happened, reflection in the interval had shown to Mr. Ormsby-Gore and to his Cabinet colleagues, again not so much the inhumanity as the embarrassment of tearing such a multitude of persons from their homes, and he now informed the Chairman of the Mandates Commission that the Government had decided not to enforce this recommendation.

He was asked then how the Government did expect to get the Arabs out of Galilee, or, in the deceptive phraseology accepted by the Commission, how the "transfer would be effected." "It was quite possible," came his inconceivable reply, "that the Arabs will trek voluntarily." Even the Chairman of the Mandates Commission could not push complacency to the point of accepting such an answer. "I am an old man," he said, "but never in my life have I heard of people, especially of peasants, voluntarily emigrating from the richest part of their country to the poorest parts."

The Mandates Commission, after examining the Colonial Secretary, passed a resolution by which it agreed in principle to Partition, but declared that it was opposed to the immediate creation of two new independent States in Palestine. It suggested a prolongation of the period of what it called "political apprenticeship" under the Mandate, and its discussions faded out with talk of whether "provisional cantonization" or a pair of new Mandates, one for an Arab area and another for a Jewish area, might not be desirable.

But while the phylacteries fluttered on the nodding foreheads of the Permanent Mandates Commission, not so far away, in Zurich, the Twentieth Zionist Congress was being held. It was a stormy affair, where a good deal of opposition was displayed to the Partition scheme and to Dr. Weizmann as the man responsible, apparently, for having committed the Zionist body to support of it in advance. The opposition came from the zealots, the obtuse and all the various categories of the Zionist cult who demanded Palestine served up to them without an instant's delay. Opposition was led by men like Ussischkin and Wise who never grasped that the new Zionist State was meant as a beginning and not as an end, and would not see with Weizmann that the gift of a bud was the gift of a flower. But what was highly interesting now was less this ingenuousness and these inner disputes than the information which broke on the world through the ventilation of them during a secret session of the Congress.

There never had been a secret session of a Zionist Congress before, but on the present occasion the Zionist Executive, no doubt very wisely from its own point of view, decided to hold the main political debate, on the Partition scheme, in camera. This debate began on Thursday the 5th of August, the only stranger present being Mrs. Dugdale, Lord Balfour's niece and biographer. There was a second and then a third secret session, the latter on the 7th, which went on till after midnight, and produced the revelation.

This was not made public, however, till the 13th, when in London the *Jewish Chronicle* published a pretty full account from its special correspondent in Zurich of all the proceedings at the sessions in camera. The outstanding item was the reproduction of the text of a document which Mr. Meir Grossman, a member of the important "Actions Committee" of the Zionist Organization, had read out to the assembly. According to the speaker it was a record made by Dr. Weizmann of the substance of a conversation which he had had with Mr. Ormsby-Gore and the Under-Secretary for the Colonies, was initialed "Ch. W." and was dated the 19th of July, two days, that is, before Mr. Ormsby-Gore had introduced the Partition proposals in the House of Commons.

Mr. Grossman's interest in the account of the interview between Dr. Weizmann and Mr. Ormsby-Gore lay in the evidence it held that, in his opinion, Dr. Weizmann was precommitting the Zionist body to the policy of Partition, before the Congress had examined the Government's project and had taken its own decisions concerning if. This, of course, is not our interest in his disclosure, which is attracted by something else, the evidence which it supplies of the familiar collusion between the Government and the Zionist leaders. It displays Mr. Ormsby-Gore, before the Partition plan had been presented to Parliament, jettisoning in it whatever Dr. Weizmann found displeasing.

Dr. Weizmann had been given a copy of the Peel Report in advance: it was to have his opinion upon it that the interview took place.

> "Mr. Ormsby-Gore [began the summary of the interview] asked me what was my attitude towards the Royal Commission's proposals now that I had read the Report. I said that I had come to see him in order to clarify a number of points. The Jews were perplexed and a great number of them were against the scheme for Partition. It would be my duty to explain my attitude in due course before Congress.
>
> 1. Sovereignty:
>
> a. I pointed out that this must be a genuine affair if this scheme were to be considered at all. I referred to the recommendation for the establishment of a joint port between Jaffa and Tel-Aviv, under British direction. Mr. Ormsby-Gore replied that it was unthinkable that this recommendation should stand. It was even inconsistent with the Commission's own views.
>
> b. I then took up the question of the temporary Mandates over the four towns in the Jewish State. Mr. Ormsby-Gore agreed that these should be liquidated as soon as possible. He thought that the only difficulty with regard to these would be the case of Acre, which for historical reasons was specially bound to England. He thought that Acre would be the last of the towns to be released. Mr. Ormsby-Gore went on to say that the Admirals had been after him with regard to Haifa. I replied that the Admiralty had unfortunately woken up four years too late. Ten years ago we had foreseen and had tried to impress upon them the future value of Haifa. I went on to say that the Admiralty could get all they wanted from us by direct agreement, but not through the Government itself. If they tried to collar Haifa we should make things extremely unpleasant for them in Geneva.
>
> c. I then raised the question of the collection of Customs duties and of the annual tribute which it was proposed the Jewish

State should pay the Arabs. I said that it was conceivable that we might, for a consideration, enter into an agreement with the Arab State, but that this could not be imposed upon us by the Government. Mr. Ormsby-Gore agreed.

2. I then raised the question of the inclusion of the new Jewish Jerusalem quarters in the Jewish State. Mr. Ormsby-Gore said that he did not see any difficulty in such inclusion, and that it seemed to him a reasonable claim.

3. Transfer of the Arab Population: I said that the whole success of the scheme depended upon whether the Government genuinely did or did not wish to carry out this recommendation. The transfer could only be carried out by the British Government and not by the Jews. I explained the reason why we considered the proposal of such importance. Mr. Ormsby-Gore said that he was proposing to set up a Committee for the twofold purpose

a. of finding land for the transferees—they hoped to find land in Transjordan, and possibly also in the Negev (the region bordering Egypt, south of the Beersheba-Gaza line), and
b. of arranging the actual terms of the transfer. He mentioned the name of Sir John Campbell, who had had much experience in connection with transfers of population between Greece and Turkey, and who knew all about the matter. He agreed that once Galilee was given to the Jews and not the Negev, the position would be very difficult without transfer.

4. I referred to the statement in the Official Summary of the Commission's Report that approximately one-third of Palestine was to be allotted to the Jewish State. I suggested that either this statement should be corrected, or alternatively, we were owed 4,000,000 dunams (1,000,000 acres). Mr. Ormsby-Gore said that this showed that there was room for concessions. I remarked that the Jews were a logical people who would follow with the closest attention every action and statement of the Government. It would be the greatest mistake to insult the intelligence of the Jews.

5. I referred to the exclusion of the Potash Works and the Rutenberg Electric Power Station from the Jewish State. Mr. Ormsby-Gore said that Lord Lytton and Mr. Rutenberg had been sitting on him for the last ten days. He added that the matter would have to be adjusted.

6. Transition Period. Mr. Ormsby-Gore gave some idea of the Government's time-table. They would go to the Mandates Commission and to the Council at Geneva, and were hopeful of getting release from the Mandate, possibly by the beginning of October. Their first step thereafter would be the appointment of a Boundary Commission, which would in all probability be an international body. Next they would appoint a

> Finance Commission, these in addition to the Transfer Commission mentioned above. The Government would then undertake the negotiation of the treaties with the Arabs and the Jews. It would probably take about two years before these were concluded, and their conclusion would be followed by the immediate appointment of provisional Jewish and Arab Governments for the respective States. Mr. Ormsby-Gore said that his statement in the House of Commons would be vague, and he expected he would have rather a bad time.
>
> At the conclusion of the interview, Mr. Ormsby-Gore turned to me and asked me what my own personal opinion was. I replied that if the points which I had raised in the interview were settled to our satisfaction, I personally would look with favour on the scheme. I added that what I had told Mr. Ormsby-Gore and what he had told me I should repeat, naturally in confidence, to my closest friends in Zurich, and also to every member of the Permanent Mandates Commission."

This document is one of those which are best left to provide their own comment upon themselves. There are a number of them in the story of Palestine, documents so self-condemnatory that they cannot survive a reading. There will be reference presently to the "admirals" on the Colonial Secretary's traces, however.

With that we may pass on, though before doing so the responses of Mr. Ormsby-Gore to Dr. Weizmann in the course of their interview merit collection.

> Mr. Ormsby-Gore replied that it was unthinkable this recommendation should stand. Mr. Ormsby-Gore agreed. Mr. Ormsby-Gore agreed. Mr. Ormsby-Gore agreed the position would be very difficult. Mr. Ormsby-Gore said that he did not see any difficulty. Mr. Ormsby-Gore said that this showed there was room for concessions. Mr. Ormsby-Gore added that the matter would have to be adjusted. Mr. Ormsby-Gore said that his statement in the House of Commons would be vague.

These answers of the dutiful Minister to the Zionist leader with the rest of the account of their interview were republished in the British Press with a full appreciation of their import. In journalistic lingo, "the story was splashed," given a position of first importance with big headlines. The newspapers sought to obtain a statement on the matter from the Colonial Secretary, but he refused to say anything. Parliament had risen, so there was no opportunity for questions being put concerning it. Searching questions were promised indeed when the House should assemble again, but somehow they never eventuated. Perhaps this was because Mr. Grossman's document was authentic. In a later speech during the Congress Dr. Weizmann did not deny it, and next spring he was to speak of the propositions in it which he put to Mr. Ormsby-Gore as forming a basis of negotiation between him and the Colonial Secretary from which he could not retreat.

Nor had Mr. Grossman obtained the memorandum in any underhand way. It had been sent to him in a closed envelope, possibly because of his position as a member of the General Council of Zionism. After some while he was summoned before a "Court of Honour" appointed by the Zionist Congress, which Court sat in Jerusalem, and was indicted for using the summary of the interview during a closed Session of the Congress, and for publishing it. In punishment he was suspended for two years from all his posts in the Zionist movement.

Various prominent Zionists took up his defence in public after this sentence, and from what they wrote there was every indication that he had right on his side. But no doubt his disclosure of the relations between Mr. Ormsby-Gore and Dr. Weizmann was unforgivable from the point of view of the Zionist Organization. A member of the Political Department of that body, Mr. Lourie, in a letter to the *Jewish Chronicle,* sustained the sentence of suspension upon Mr. Grossman, declaring that "the implications of a publication of this nature as regards the relations between the Zionist leaders and members of the Government are clearly not matters which lend themselves to public discussion." Mr. Lourie put the position most accurately.

Dr. Weizmann had his way with the Zionist Congress in the end, and it passed a resolution empowering the Executive to keep in negotiation with His Majesty's Government, in order to discover what would be the precise terms under which the proposed Jewish State would be established. The scheme as put forward by the Peel Commission was declared unacceptable. In its future negotiations with the Government the Zionist Executive was ordered not to commit itself or the Organization to any definite plan which might emerge for a Jewish State. Any such scheme must be considered by a Congress specially elected and specially convened for the purpose.

Chapter 39

League "neutrality" in the Palestine question.
The Palestine Government dissolves the Arab Higher Committee and exiles leaders.
The Mufti escapes to the Lebanon.
The Technical Commission leaves for Palestine.
Mr. Malcolm MacDonald succeeds Mr. Ormsby-Gore.
Foreign interference in Palestine.
The Galilee-Sanjak of Alexandretta campaign.
Awaiting the Woodhead Report.

A month passed and the scene moved to Geneva again, where the Council of the League was sitting. Mr. Ormsby-Gore had been shelved, and it was Mr. Eden, the Foreign Secretary, who appeared for Great Britain and asked formally for the Council's authority to permit the Government to study and to work out in detail a Partition scheme. In the meantime Jewish immigration into Palestine would be reduced to 8,000 entrants during a period of eight months. Mr. Eden repeated that the Mandate was now seen to be "unworkable." The Council took its *congé d'élire* from him and agreed to the "Government of the United Kingdom carrying out the aforesaid study and taking such steps as it may entail."

The position of the Council of the League had developed by now from that of earlier days when it was merely subservient in the affairs of Palestine. Several States belonging to it—and also several in the Assembly—had become voluntary adherents of Zionism in an odd fashion of their own. This gave a particular character to proceedings of the Council which was not at all perceived.

For example, after Mr. Eden had addressed its members the Council appointed what it dubbed a "Neutral Committee" composed of the Foreign Ministers of Latvia, Sweden and Roumania, to submit a Report on the Palestine affair as presented to it. But of these States, Latvia had a lesser and Roumania a very big Jewish population and problem.

The chief wish of Roumania, which had to cope with aggressive Fascism and anti-semitism threatening her whole stability, was to get rid of as many of her multitude of Jews as possible. In the eyes of Roumania, the Arabs were but an annoying impediment to great numbers of them vanishing into Palestine. Latvia was not in as difficult a situation, and was more liberally minded, but was by no means averse to losing five or six or even as much as eleven hundred Jews or so a year. Only Sweden was really neutral, and it was a misnomer to call the Committee a "Neutral Committee."

When it came to the other members of the Council, who had to pass judgment on any sub-committee's Reports, and also would have to pass judgment upon the British Government's proposals for Palestine eventually, their kind of "neutrality" was more marked still. There was Poland, for example. Poland's attitude has changed since 1919. She has a threatening internal situation: her population is increasing enormously with no outlet: she has asked for colonies, which has been thought rather a joke by uninformed people in the West, but is a genuine demand and under the circumstances reasonable. Her immense Jewish population is a terrible problem because of the continual conflicts between it and various peasant and other groups. Disorder has become endemic in the country because of it.

In 1934 she had managed to dispossess herself of 18,000 Jews to Palestine, in 1935 of 30,000. No wonder that M. Beck in the debate which followed Mr. Eden's speech to the Council had said that his country was "keenly interested in the Palestine problem," and had ended his discourse by declaring that "Poland will endeavour to secure for Palestine maximum possibilities of absorption. The provisional restrictions on Jewish emigration to Palestine are at present a handicap to the Polish Government's policy." They certainly had been. In 1936 only 11,000 Jews left Poland, a drop of 19,000 from 1935.

Other Central European States shared the Polish attitude. At the debate of the Political Commission of the Council upon the question the Jugoslav delegate made a declaration on behalf of the entire Little Entente (Roumania, Czechoslovakia and Jugoslavia). "The Little Entente," he said, "hopes that a solution will be found which will ensure a large Jewish immigration into Palestine in the future."

The reality of the League debates, therefore, is that a number of States which in the eyes of the ordinary man pass as independent and unconcerned and well fitted to consider the Palestine situation impartially, are anything but independent and unconcerned. They have every interest in the triumph of the Zionists in Palestine, since that means relieving themselves of some of those unhappy Jewish subjects whom they find an incubus. They may make profession of being swayed by the arguments of Zionism, but they do not in their hearts give two farthings for Zionism and its arguments. They act entirely according to what they deem their own interests, and it is not Arab protests which are going to move them.

France too, for another set of reasons, always has been and always may be counted upon when votes are cast, to fall in with British policy in Palestine. She has conducted all her own policy, perforce, as a three-legged race which she runs across the world with Britain as her partner. This has been the only wise policy to employ for her own sake and for the general sake of peace, but it has entailed accepting the British official thesis about Palestine.

It will be seen that Dr. Weizmann, a consummate practitioner of the art of lobbying, had admirable opportunities for it that autumn in Geneva, as indeed he still has, since the position there has not changed. The Arabs on the other hand have little or no chance of just consideration of their cause, as at Geneva an enormous bias against them amid apparently independent countries must exist. To the adverse Central European bloc and to France must be added, unfortunately, the bulk of the smaller democratic States, Switzerland, Holland, the Scandinavians, Belgium, which know nothing whatsoever of the facts of the Palestine Question, and in a general way follow the leadership of the great democratic countries. They take them like bridegrooms for better, for worse, adopting their manias and meannesses for the sake of their general merits.

Portugal is half-bound by her ancient alliance. Russia and Turkey are silent, their possible sentiments more or less having paired with their certain interests. In America, from Cape Horn to the Arctic Ocean, where independence of view might be thought lodged, there is not much of it. In the United States Zionist writers and speakers have created a grotesque picture of Palestine for the United States people. In South America official British influence is not inconsiderable, and amidst South American delegates in Europe, particularly at Geneva, it is considerable.

On the other hand all that the Arabs can count upon is the tiny band of Islamic countries. Only one of these, Persia (or Iran) is upon the League Council. It is Islamic too after a special fashion, and if blood is thicker than water, so is oil. Irak and Egypt spoke up for their Arab brothers and kinsmen during the autumn debates of 1937, and that was the sum of genuine support.

The lesson of those League sessions, with their inconclusive Resolutions, is not to be lost. Still more, it is not to be misunderstood. There was never any examination in 1937 or 1938 by a detached League of the Governmental proposals for Partition. There was what is called a "line-up" of the adherents of the two attitudes, pro-Arab and pro-Zionist, with the pro-Arabs in a hopeless minority. These conditions continue and it is under them that any new Governmental proposals most likely will be considered.

While the League meetings were going on, the tumult in Palestine had increased, and in the last week of September the District-Commissioner of Galilee, Mr. L. Y. Andrews, and Police-Constable McEwen, who was acting as his guard, were shot as they were leaving church in Nazareth. Officers and men of the R.I.C. had been shot in this very same way, in Ireland, as they were leaving church, and the cycle of resemblance to the Irish rising was now complete with this crime.

During the climax of that rising a false and detestable theory had prevailed amidst a certain group that, since a genuine military insurrection was impossible against the armed might of Great Britain, what was termed individual or one-man warfare against individuals could take its place legitimately. In other words assassination was war, the defencelessness of the person or persons attacked being sophistically assimilated to a surprise or ambush in true warfare. The theory had not been invented in Ireland, of course. In many revolutions and risings elsewhere in earlier days insurgents of various races, ungrounded in moral principles, had succumbed to its plausibility. They were not able to love their God and their honour more than their country. Several countries themselves with no better outlook have made national heroes, or something very close to it, of well-intentioned assassins. Men like Princip and Oberdan have been raised to secular altars.

In fine, the murder of Mr. Andrews was one of too long a series in too many lands. What followed on it also belonged to a series. Throughout history deeds like it have been succeeded most often by the severest repression, and governments have found in them excuses for measures not merely against the criminals but against the whole nation which has confronted them. If they could not find and sentence the guilty parties, they could take capital action against the national movement, making its mariners responsible for its pirates. In Palestine this opportunity was seized now.

The Administration, under the conduct of the Office Administering, in the absence on leave of the High Commissioner, took its opportunity to strike at the whole native cause. On the 1st of October the Arab Higher Committee was dissolved. All national Committees throughout Palestine were dissolved too. The Mufti of Jerusalem, generally termed the Grand Mufti, the President of the Higher Committee, was deprived of his offices. Orders for arrest of other members were issued. The grounds given for this action was that the Arab leaders were "morally responsible for these events" and that their "activities had been prejudicial to the maintenance of public security."

This proclamation was perfectly true to precedent, and might have been translated from the archives of any given absolute government of the past, or from the preambles to orders of confinement issued by the totalitarian autocrats of today. It was followed a fortnight later by a second order forbidding four other Arab leaders who were abroad—two had been attending the League of Nations sittings—from re-entering their country. Amongst the persons arrested or exiled were the bearers of the familiar names of Jemal Husseini, Alfred Roch and Auni Bey Abdel Hadi. Mr. Jemal Husseini had evaded arrest under the first warrant and had fled into French Syria, where he was followed before long by his kinsman the Grand Mufti, who had taken refuge in the Mosque of Omar and later escaped to the coast and thence to Beyrout. The other two had been in Geneva and were proscribed. Auni Bey Abdel Hadi even was refused a visa for England, not quite the bourne which would have been chosen by a man with an uneasy conscience.

The victims of the Administration's *lettre de cachet* were the Mayor of Jerusalem; the director of the Arabs' bank where lay or were supposed to lie the funds of the High Committee; a Moslem mufti of prominence, Rashid Haj Ibrahim; and Mr. Saba, the other Christian member of the High Committee with Mr. Roch. They were seized in their homes, and were deported to the Seychelles Isles in the Indian Ocean. There they have been confined ever since, for more than a year at the time of writing, without knowledge of any offence, without a charge having been brought against them, without the production of a single proof of their part in any misdemeanour, and without any prospect of trial. [Author's note: They now have been released to take part in the choosing of Arab delegates to the forthcoming Conference in London.]

The orders of arrest were carried out under an Order in Council. The novel order of proscription was made under a regulation devised for the purpose and put into force upon the day it was published.

The sole result however of the Administration's coup has been to show the emptiness of the old pretence that if the chief "effendis," the people's leaders, were but out of the way, the movement of opposition to the National Home would fall to pieces, and that the Arab fellaheen would hold out their hands to the Zionists who were bringing them prosperity, and so forth. Far from diminishing, the outbreak in Palestine strengthened, spread, and became a thoroughgoing insurrection. The only men who could at least have tried to control it were imprisoned or exiled.

To explain away the failure of the coup of the 1st of October, the entire development of the insurrection now was ascribed to the Mufti and his friends, working from the safety of Lebanese and French-Syrian soil.

Much always had been made of the Mufti's influence: while he was still in Jerusalem he had been called the soul of the revolt. Presently letters of his were published, sent by him to Arab nationalist leaders in the French African dominions, which called for union between all Arabs against European imperialism.

There seems little doubt that the Mufti is a man of conspiratorial temperament, and that he may have come to have a hand in the propagation of armed resistance on the soil of Palestine is pretty likely. But the point to be put concerning the Mufti is this. What attitude exactly, and what action, was to be expected of him when it had grown absolutely plain that years upon years of pacific request and remonstration had not succeeded in winning discussion of the charges brought by him and other Arab leaders against the Mandate and its makers, much less the rebuttal of these charges?

If he did take to intrigue after years of non-suited appeals and disallowed petitions, and if no reasoned arguments of his had obtained even consideration of the subject of appeal, then who is to judge him? Certainly not men in the high places of Governments or Leagues with twenty solid years of intrigue with the Zionists behind them.

The chief of the other exiled or proscribed Arabs had actually themselves been long engaged in these peaceful appeals, which had brought them nothing but disconsideration. Their political lives had been spent on the triangle Jerusalem, London, Geneva.

Their so-called "moral responsibility" for the disorders of Palestine simply consisted in repeating their open programme of demands, in repeating in Jerusalem the reputable claims they had put forward time and again in London and Geneva. There was nothing anti-British in these claims, nothing illegal. The sole fault indeed they had (in official eyes) was that they were legal, that they could not be controverted, and were based on the Covenant.

With the stimulus to public security thus given by the Administration Palestine continued on its miserable way through autumn and winter. In the first week of 1938 the Government issued a White Paper containing the terms-of-reference of the Technical Commission which was to go to Palestine to study and draw up a new and full scheme for Partition. That this scheme would be a close development of the Peel Commission's scheme seemed less certain by now. Opposition to the Peel project had stiffened amidst some of the Zionists, who found it unpalatable that the smallest Arab Statelet should be created.

Zionist demands for room to settle vast numbers of immigrants did not abate. Mr. Jabotinsky brought forth a Ten Year Plan of land development, and spoke of introducing two, three, four, five, six or more million Jews eventually. The Government, veering about under various strains, though still clinging to the general idea of Partition, produced lengthy terms-of-reference for the prospective Commission. It was to "take into account" the Peel plan for Partition, but was "given full liberty to suggest modifications of that plan, including variations of the areas recommended for retention under British Mandate."

The Technical Commissioners were also to report, under no less than ten counts, upon various economic and financial questions involved in Partition, such as the apportionment of the (enormously increasing) public debt and the "treatment of industrial and other concessions."

If as a result of their investigations, "which would undoubtedly occupy many months," the Commissioners evolved a "scheme of Partition regarded as equitable and practicable by His Majesty's Government, then this would be referred to the Council of the League

> If the scheme is approved by the League Council, a further period will be required for the establishment of new systems of government under Mandate in the areas concerned and, if the necessary consent is forthcoming, for the negotiation of treaties with a view to the eventual establishment of independent States. It may also be necessary, in the light of the Commission's report, for His Majesty's Government to give further consideration to the suggestion of the Permanent Mandates Commission that the Arab and Jewish areas should be administered temporarily under a system of "cantonization" or under separate Mandates. It is obvious, therefore, that for some time to come any action taken will be only of an exploratory nature.

This last paragraph of the terms-of-reference left everything open. Any solution really might be adopted now, with or without Partition, incorporating Mandates of all styles, numbers and durations.

Dr. Weizmann left Palestine for England to consult with the Government. Before departure he made a speech, on the 23rd of January, in the course of which he remarked pregnantly that the Jewish people could accept a Jewish State in a part of Palestine "without forgoing in any respect its great hopes for the future."

The members of the Technical Commission were appointed at the close of February. During February and March Dr. Weizmann, just as in the old days, talked strenuously in London to Cabinet Ministers and other men of influence. A summary of his doings was given by him to the Actions Committee, that is the main council, the Assembly as it were of the Zionist Organization, at its meeting in London in later March. The official Report of his speech ran:

> Dr. Weizmann told the British Government that the Peel Partition scheme was unacceptable, but would form a basis for negotiations, and that any retreat from his letter to Mr. Ormsby-Gore in July last [the Grossman document) was to him unacceptable.

In another part of his speech he explained that the Peel Report must be modified and improved "rather from a moral than a territorial standpoint," whatever that meant.

The Technical Commission, whose president was Sir John Woodhead, left England in April for Palestine, and Dr. Weizmann returned there also. He was one of the first witnesses heard by the Commission, and asked that his evidence should be taken in camera. Mr. Rutenberg made the same request. Some public sessions of the Commission also were held, but its activities were quite overshadowed by the widespread increase of the revolt and the revolt's growingly desperate character.'

More than twenty battalions of troops were drafted to Palestine. For a length of about fifty miles a wire entanglement or fence, guarded by strong posts at intervals, was built along the northern frontier, to prevent the entry into Palestine of reinforcements or supplies for the Arab insurgents. "Tegart's Wall," as it was named after its deviser, is twenty feet high. It was constructed by nearly a thousand Zionist workmen, and a Zionist firm contracted for it, at a cost which is believed to have exceeded £100,000.

But all the resources of military, police and armament lavished upon Palestine have not suffocated the revolt. It has taken on all the worst traits of civil strife; kidnappings, murders, waylaying, arson, bomb outrages. It is Ireland before the Treaty of 1921 all over again.

However, as some account of the conditions of Palestine, though but a tepid one, has been reaching the public through the Press and the wireless, I shall not enlarge upon the state of things in that country. My object is to show who and what have been responsible for them.

In early August the Woodhead Commission returned to England, where it held some sessions to hear evidence. Ere this Mr. Ormsby-Gore, who had succeeded to a barony, had resigned the Colonial Secretaryship and in mid-May Mr. Malcolm MacDonald had been appointed in his place. Though never involved with Zionism after the fashion of his predecessor, Mr. MacDonald had signed one of the communications to *The Times* which invoked the "Black Letter" from his father, then Prime Minister.

When he was appointed the *Jewish Chronicle* wrote:

> About eight years ago Mr. MacDonald declared his sympathy with the Zionist Movement. He was a member of the Palestine Mandate Committee, which worked unofficially "to mould public opinion in favour of the Balfour pledge and the upbuilding of the Jewish National

Homeland." He did helpful work during the negotiations which succeeded the publication of the Passfield White Paper.

So that while his arrival in the Colonial Office was an amelioration, once more the Cabinet Minister entrusted with the affairs of Palestine was one who had taken a position upon the side of one of the parties to the issue and, particularly, had defended the indefensible Balfour Declaration.

Mr. MacDonald had not been three months in office when he paid, literally, a flying visit to Jerusalem to consult with the High Commissioner, Sir Harold MacMichael, and General Haining, in command of the troops in Palestine. There was no immediate sequel in Palestine to the journey.

But on his return to England Mr. MacDonald broadcast a message to the public, in which several of the familiar governmental commonplaces were repeated. He spoke of the "peaceful invasion of a great host of Jewish immigrants," though it was only the presence of British arms which had made the invasion peaceful or even possible at all. He spoke of the "solemn obligation" of the Balfour Declaration, and repeated its terms. He spoke of "exiled Jews returning to their home of centuries ago,' when the only exiles in sight were in the Seychelles, and most of the Jews were returning to homes which had been for ever Arab.

"The British Government," he said, "will administer its trust on a basis of justice between the Jews who are building at long last their National Home and the Arabs whose title in the land of their birth is indisputable." Mr. MacDonald did not mention that the title of a majority in the land of their birth is to the land of their birth.

His statement was in an over-familiar groove. It was followed however by the issue of the Woodhead Report (to which it is only possible here to interpolate the briefest reference), practically revoking the Peel Report. [Author's note: The report showed the absurdity and the iniquity of the Partition scheme].

Since then Mr. MacDonald has given evidence that a Colonial Minister at last is appreciative in some degree of the Arabs' rights. The Arabs however are prevented by experience from being optimistic concerning the Arab-race-British-Government Conference which he has proposed for the New Year, 1939. This Conference at present holds the field, and it appears that its terms-of-reference may not circumscribe it in the way in which its predecessors were cabined. But here this narrative reaches present day and its own conclusion.

Two matters, though, which did not fit well into the chronological sequence, call for attention at this stage. The first of these is the immixture of foreign Powers with the Arab movement. In early 1938 much capital was made of the Bari broadcasts from Italy and of the provision of funds from

Italian political sources for the Arab cause. The Bari broadcasts now have shed any obnoxious character, and as for the distribution of funds, there has been much exaggeration of what occurred.

This obviously is not a question concerning which precise figures can be provided, but from reliable sources I have learned that at the time complaint was rampant among pro-Zionists the amount which had found its way into Palestine from Italy was about £35,000 in English value.

Nearly all this was in a single sum, which two persons in Palestine mainly were responsible for obtaining. A good part of it went into the pocket of one of them, a Syrian who professed a fictitious zeal for the popular movement. What was spent was spent on little more than the customary "boosting" of Italian national stock amidst the Arabs—a pursuit upon which most nations waste funds among other nations.

The young Italian functionary involved, however, undoubtedly insisted too much in the course of his activities upon the demerits of the occupying Power as compared with his own. Diplomatic complaint against him was accompanied by Arab exposure in Italy of the dishonest intermediary, and the episode ended with the recall of the erring functionary and his departure for South America.

What has to be remembered when complaints are made against recent official Italian displays of sympathy with Islam, made with an eye to the Moslems in Palestine, is that any effectiveness these may have—and their effectiveness is most doubtful—springs from our own behaviour to the Arabs. If we had not denied the Arabs their rights for so long, there would have been no discontent among them. Without that discontent there would have been no broadcasts and no approaches to them from other Powers. It is absolute pharisaism for ourselves to look upon Arabs who listen to appeals of this kind as departing from civic virtue, considering that we have steadily refused to listen to *their* appeals for these twenty years.

In reality, the Arabs have no particular trust in any of our competitive Western Powers today, and have a poor estimate of all their blandishments. It seems unlikely, but beneath everything probably the strongest current of feeling among their most intelligent leaders—even among those exiled—still flows towards this country. They still distinguish between perjured governments and an honest people, and in the individual Briton perceive a sincerer friend than they are likely to find elsewhere.The paradox is a strange one, but it is in the individual Englishman that they hope still to find protection from England.

I have vividly before me conversations I had in Paris last autumn with Auni Bey Abdel Hadi. There he was, proscribed from his country, separated from his family, his own affairs in chaos, forbidden even to come to England to counteract with a single interview the enormous Zionist propaganda, and yet he spoke without a trace of rancour. He recalled all the personal kindnesses to himself of various persons in Palestine, how willingly the High Commissioner visited him when he was interned, and how this official or the other had spoken friendly words to him. He said that if there were two sets of interests in the world which coincided it was those of the Arab peoples and of Great Britain, and that if only the Arabs were granted their prescriptive and promised rights, these interests would adhere into a strong and natural affiance. "I ask for nothing better than such an alliance," he said.

If any Arab leaders, or any sections of the people, have cultivated any kind of relations with Powers who are hostile to ourselves or are rivals to ourselves, it has not really been zealous cultivation, but enforced acceptance of the only relations they have been able to obtain. If any insurgents have turned to German gun-runners to obtain rifles, it is because since 1919 no Arab in Palestine has seen anything else (morally always and physically sometimes) but the barrels of our rifles and the immigrant ships coming up from the sea behind them.

The danger of an Arab-German coalition is one which is growing, though a reasonable and honest policy in Palestine would even now dissipate it soon enough. The Italian danger is all froth: our own discord with Italy is artificial. Anglo-German good relations may be more difficult to establish. To discuss them is not the scope of this book. But in so far as we have enemies in Germany we have done our best to push the Arabs into their arms.

It is not the occasional German gun-runners and their rifles that are disturbing, but such institutions as the "Panislamic Bureau" in Munich. Very possibly the Panislamic Bureau in 1939 is preparing new von Stotzingens for a task amid the Arabs which the Arabs prevented von Stotzingen from accomplishing in 1916. Preparations to this end have been going on for some years certainly. Last January the *Manchester Guardian* published the text of a letter sent in May of 1935 by the Ministry of Propaganda in Berlin to the Ministry of Foreign Affairs. Its authenticity has not been denied. Here is an extract:

> We thank the Herr Reich-Minister for the kind help given with regard to colonial propaganda, and we are conscious of being in agreement with the aims that are being pursued in this respect. The directives of the Herr Reich-Minister of Propaganda were made known to the representatives of the Foreign Ministry at the meeting on May 8th, 1935, and [when?] he expressed complete approval. Our agents have received instructions and orders for their task, and we have informed our Consular representatives

> in Haifa, Jaffa, Algiers, Agadir and Rabat. We have also informed our agents and influential natives. We, too, are of the absolute opinion that success can only be achieved if the most intense propaganda effort is concentrated on the natives.

The Diplomatic Correspondent of the *Manchester Guardian*, who communicated this document, added on his own authority that three groups of six "German propaganda-agents" arrived before the close of that year in Haifa, Jerusalem and Jaffa in order "to conduct anti-Jewish propaganda on a Panislamic basis and to stir up the population against British rule." The eighteen gentlemen must have been in the good books of the Propaganda Ministry to have received such sinecures.

How far propaganda work of this type has developed may be judged from the report that at the fateful Nuremberg Congress of last year when European war nearly was precipitated, amidst those present to listen to Herr Hitler were a hundred young Arab guests from Palestine. It is possible that their numbers were exaggerated, but certainly there was a large deputation, transported at German expense.

The question we have to put to ourselves, however, is again—who at the bottom is responsible for these propaganda-missions finding fruitful soil, and for these young Arabs sailing to Hamburg? We do not know who paid for the youths' tickets and maintenance, though it may be assumed it was the German Ministry of Propaganda, but the responsibility for these invitations and these departures ultimately lies with Mr. Lloyd George and Lord Balfour, and with those who have maintained their policy since then in the Holy Land.

The second matter which requires attention, and a good deal of it, is the proposal of the Peel Commissioners to partition Palestine and to include Galilee in the intended Jewish State. The importance of this is unaffected by the abandonment of the project, for when they proposed Partition the Peel Commissioners left the sphere of comment unfortunately for the sphere of action, and added no mere Report but a new cause and factor to the Palestine Question.

Their proposals were taken over by the Government. What is more, they did not come out of the sky to the Commissioners, who completed their Report in London, and both in London and in Palestine had been subject to the filtrations of Governmental opinion. The point about these proposals is that if they were a thousand times abandoned, none the less the Government in 1937 treated them as morally acceptable. They were abandoned, not for moral, but for practical reasons.

Till then British Governments had assured the Arabs and the world that they had no intention of establishing a Jewish State in Palestine. The Arabs did not credit this, believing that all British Governments would deny that intention till the time came for a particular Government to put it into effect.

When, therefore, the Peel Report proposed the Jewish State, the Arabs saw that their beliefs were justified and that the Government which was to carry the business through was in office. A part of their country was to pass for ever from their control. It was the best part too, but any part removed at all was a mortal amputation. On its side, the British Government had committed itself irretrievably to the doctrine that the Arabs had no right to Palestine, since it had meant to offer the Zionists sovereignty in a part of it without the Arabs' consent. All was lost therefore for the Arabs, and they took recourse to arms with fresh despair.

To the Peel Report therefore must be ascribed the new virulence of the insurrection, and as a cause of the insurrection its findings must be considered, even though they stayed upon paper. Since the proposal for the Jewish State reached instantly the limit of aggravation, it is impossible to say that one detail in it more than another went beyond bearing, but the plan to include Galilee in the new State was peculiarly indefensible and embittering.

This plan, as we have seen at first envisaged the compulsory transportation of the Arab population out of Galilee. The dropping of compulsory transportation, while removing the supreme arbitrariness did not diminish the general injustice and arbitrariness of the whole proposal, when the character of the population of Galilee is considered. Galilee is sub-divided into the districts of Acre, Tiberias, Nazareth and Safad, with a population at the last census in 1931 of 140,422, of whom in round figures, 15,000 were Jews and 125,000 Arabs. The passage of seven years will only have served to increase the disproportion between the two races, and the vast excess of Arabs.

But the excess of Arabs over Jews becomes more notable still when the town-dwellers are separated from the rural population. In the four towns giving their names to the sub-districts some 9,000 of the Jews are congregated, and some 26,000 Arabs. The Arab rural population of Galilee may be taken to be about 100,000, the Jewish 6,000. This is the population which matters in the present instance, as all the four towns of Galilee by the Peel plan were to be placed, Safad, Acre and Tiberias for an unstated period and Nazareth permanently, under British Mandate.

The smallness of the Jewish population which this arrangement left in unmandated Galilee will be appreciated when a map, such as that of the Jewish settlements in the Peel Report itself, is studied. Galilee proper is blank of Zionist settlements. The Zionists, pursuing the policy to which allusion was made at the beginning of this book, disdained the great bulk of Galilee, settling only in the rich coast belt between Haifa and Acre. They established other new settlements round Safad and on the shores of Lake

Tiberias and at Metulla, at the tip of the northern prong of Palestine. That is to say, they established an area of settlement on the rims of Galilee. But all Galilee proper, the mass of Galilee between the rims, from the sea to the Jordan west and east, and from the French frontier to (roughly) the Haifa-Tiberias line north and south, is in Arab occupation. Ninety-four percent of its people is Arab, and the scattered 6 percent of Jews is made up of Jews of the old order, biblical, not political and Zionist.

So that what the Peel proposal for Galilee amounted to was to hand over to the Zionist State the whole solid intact square of Arab Galilee, to give to the Zionist State an Arab fastness. The excuse of the Peel Commissioners for this proposal was that it was the part of Palestine where the Jews had maintained a foothold since the days of the Diaspora, "had retained a foothold almost," they said, "if not entirely without a break." They said nothing however of the character or size of the foothold, and then proceeded to adjudge the mountains of Galilee to the owners of a foothold instead of to the owners of the mountains themselves.

The excuse hardly held together, and a very different complexion was put upon the award of Galilee to the Zionists by a statement of Dr. Weizmann's. This statement was another thing made known through the chance of the publication of the proceedings at the Secret Sessions of the Zurich-Congress. It did not gain outside attention, the letter to Mr. Ormsby-Gore having secured all this. It was at a meeting of the Political Committee of the Congress that Dr. Weizmann spoke of Galilee.

There had been demands amidst his opponents at the Congress to know why he had dropped, to all seeming, the claim to have the Negev included in the Jewish State (the Negev being a triangular waste area of land in the extreme south).

Mr. Ormsby-Gore had alluded to this in one of his answers to Dr. Weizmann on the 19th of July, saying that "once Galilee was given to the Jews, and not the Negev, the position would be very difficult without transfer."

Mr. Grossman, after reading the Weizmann-Ormsby-Gore memorandum, had gone on to say that there had been a time when Dr. Weizmann had thought the Negev of great importance, but now he said it was a speculative proposal. Why was this?

The answer was "Galilee." It had indeed peeped forth in Mr. Ormsby-Gore's remark to the Zionist leader. But Dr. Weizmann, in his unnoticed statement—made next day—put the situation quite plainly. To quote the *Jewish Chronicle*'s account, he said that he:

> had not insisted upon the inclusion of the Negev area in the projected Jewish State because it was a question of the Negev or Galilee. Although

> the Arabs were prepared to give up the Negev in place of Galilee, it was, he said, felt "in certain high circles" that the Jewish frontiers should run parallel with those of Christian Lebanon.

Here we have Dr. Weizmann engaged once more in the unwarranted pursuit of speaking for the Arabs. They never had said they were prepared to give up the Negev. But what mattered in Dr. Weizmann's statement was the revelation in it of the real reason for which it was proposed that the Jewish State should be given Galilee, and the revelation of those who desired that the Jewish State should be given Galilee. It was not only the Zionists, but "certain high circles," that is to say, the British Government or the British Ministers involved, who had felt that 100,000 Arabs and some 400 square miles of Arab land should be handed over to the prospective Zionist State. This scheme was a Government scheme and the Colonial Secretary avowed that it was going to be difficult to carry out unless the Arab population went away or was removed. The reasons for the scheme were not at all the crippled theories of Jewish continuity but the desire of the "persons in high circles" that the Jewish State should have a common frontier with the Christian Lebanon.

It might be supposed that the desire of the persons in high circles, being Christian persons in the high circles of a Christian country, was to give to their co-religionists of the Lebanon neighbours, in the rabbinical persons of Dr. Weizmann, Mr. Rutenberg and the *halutzim*, who perhaps would be more religiously sociable than a multitude of Moslems would be. But this was not their aim, since, as it happens, in Galilee there are more Arab Christians than there are Jews. If it was religious sociability the high-placed persons wanted, they had a perfect opportunity of putting Christians next to Christians.

But Christianity did not enter into their calculations. What the persons in high circles wanted was not so much the proximity of Jews and Christians as that the Arab State should be deprived of a common frontier with the Lebanon. The aim was to separate the Lebanese from their fellows in the Arab State, to prevent the Lebanon Christians at all costs from coalescing with the Christians of Palestine.

Signs of such a scheme had appeared during the September-October meeting of the League of Nations Council. It had become current knowledge in the corridors of the Palais des Nations that the French Government favoured a common frontier between the Lebanon and the Jewish State. As a matter of fact, France at large was divided about policy in Syria, but the existing Cabinet, or those in it who were interested at all, had lent their ear to Zionist suggestions that the Lebanon, under suasion from Paris, should adopt the National Home policy and invite Zionists to settle in its territory.

When M. Blum was in office Zionist emissaries had brought all their powers of persuasion to bear upon the Maronite Patriarch in the Lebanon, Mgr. Moubarak, and upon other accessible elements in the little republic, to this end. The Patriarch and the President of the Lebanon had been specially invited then to Paris, whither Dr. Weizmann also had gone, and conferences were held there. The errand of the Patriarch was so well known that before he embarked a special reception was held for him by the Jewish community in Beyrout, or by those of them who sympathized with the political ideal of Zionism. The Patriarch made an indiscreet speech, which together with his action in general, led to much recrimination and dissension amidst his fellow Lebanese. In Beyrout, where there are many Moslems, the majority of the population favours a federal union between the Lebanon and the rest of Syria, and will have nothing to do with Zionism.

The policy of the Zionists has been to prevent the federal union at any cost, and to insinuate themselves into the Lebanon by flattering the separatist elements there, by trying to divide the Christian Lebanese from the Palestine Christians, and by making the usual promises of wealth and development. The Lebanon, it is to be noted, has the two chief ports of the littoral, Beyrout and Tripoli, in its ownership. The "Syrian" State has to be content with Latakia, a port with a narrow entrance and poor connections.

To make the Zionists masters of Galilee and to give them a contiguous frontier with the Lebanon, then, was the aim of "certain high circles." The Zionists themselves had greater ambitions still, and hoped that the whole Arab State of Syria might yet be crushed between a Zionized Lebanon and the Turks moving down from Alexandretta. In the middle of 1938 the League of Nations' scheme for a plebiscite in that Sanjak was fraying away, through complicated conditions of disturbance which had been most suspiciously engendered there. The League officials charged with the plebiscite expostulated to no purpose. It had been generally assumed that there was a Turkish majority in the Alexandretta Sanjak, but the League preparations for the plebiscite, which had involved preparing voters' lists, had raised doubts on this point.

Eventually the League elections were abandoned, and a compromise was arranged between the French forces of occupation and the Turkish authorities, by which Turkish troops entered the Sanjak and a duplicate Franco-Turk occupation was begun. Recently this has embraced some mysterious elections and the establishment of a small local republic, the Republic of Hatay, which is of Turkish temperament though the Arabs, Armenians and other races have large representations in the prospective Assembly. At the time of writing the situation there is not at all clarified.

To return to the middle of 1938, about then the Zionist Press began to develop a singular interest in the lot of the Turks in the Sanjak. Turkey's attitude towards Zionism had been till then generally inimical. She had been for so long on close terms with the Soviet that she had imbibed the outlook of Moscow in some degree towards the National Home. She had even been upon the point of legislation of anti-Zionist type, but this trend was stemmed through British influence. Gradually the relations between Turkey and Great Britain became more intimate, and ended in the British loan of £16,000,000 to Turkey, mostly for armaments.

This loan was a triumph for Sir Percy Lorraine, Ambassador to Angora, who had had a preponderating part in the complete restoration of Anglo-Turkish friendship.

It is quite evident, however, that the active political Zionists thought that their influence at home could turn the new Anglo-Turk relations to their advantage, and indeed believed, with their characteristic overweening touch, that Turkey could now be brought to round on the Arabs and to crush them from the north. Their Press began to couple remarks about undetailed "injustice done to the Turks" by the Arabs of the Sanjak with complaints against those French authorities there who kept a regard for Arab interests. This again was coupled with still stronger complaints that the Mufti of Jerusalem and other Arab leaders who had taken refuge in the Lebanon or in "Syria" had not been expelled.

The French authorities who suffered this Zionist displeasure belonged to the Lyautey school in colonial affairs. This school aims at developing the French overseas dominions into self-governing bodies on the lines of British intentions for India, judging very rightly that the days of "possession" of Algeria, Tunis and Morocco, in the form of protectorates, have passed away. The Lyautey school, born of the precepts of the great Marshal, wishes to make of France's overseas lands areas which their constituent peoples will control in union and amity with France, on principles of equality, the two partners, France and her Arab peoples, supporting and being essential to each other. It reasons that the one thoroughly sound and reliable defence of the African dominions lies in giving to them institutions in which the population will take pride.

French officers and French officials belonging to this school of thought have been numerous enough in the Syrian Mandated area and have their representatives in the ministries of Paris. The last thing they have wished to do is to alienate the Arabs of North Africa by a hostile attitude to Arab independence in Syria. On the other hand the Zionists have had their allies in the French Government.

How the Zionists in mid-1938 dealt with the Lyautey school, what was the action of their own friends in Paris, and what was the general Syrian situation is well shown in some quotations from the *Jewish Chronicle*. On the 10th of June its Diplomatic Correspondent wrote:

> As I anticipated in last week's issue, M. Daladier has intervened personally, with characteristic energy and thoroughness, in the Alexandretta Sanjak *affaire*, and with prompt and serious consequences for the officials who had shown over-much complacency towards the local Arabs. The civilian Acting Governor has been recalled and replaced by a French General, whose appointment and known record should inspire respect for law and order amidst Syrians and Turks alike. The French Government have also undertaken to stand by their pledge to Turkey that the large Turkish element within the Alexandretta and Antioch regions, which if not actually a majority, constitutes by far the largest racial element there, shall enjoy in the local Parliament and Government the predominance due to these circumstances.

This came well from the writer, fortunately unmindful of the treatment meted out to the "largest racial element" in Palestine. He went on:

> At any rate, the Turkish element, if it does not exceed or actually reach the 50 percent quota, *should certainly exceed it in collaboration with the Jewish element*, which has complaints almost as bitter as the Turks to make about its treatment by Arab officials and by French officials with Arab sympathies. It is considered probable that the changes of personnel in the civilian administration and the police in the Sanjak will be followed by a corresponding purge in Syria and the Lebanon, where the strengthening of the powers of the French military would be equally expedient, having regard to the prevailing lawlessness, one of the ugliest features of which is the hitherto unimpeded passage of armed bands across the border into Palestine. I have no doubt that the French Prime Minister will presently give his attention to that aspect and will take the necessary steps, through the Quai d'Orsay, to bring this shocking scandal to an end.
>
> *London's representations on the subject*, though discreetly worded, were bound to make an impression on a French statesman like M. Daladier, who realizes perhaps better than any other the need of a whole-hearted and comprehensive Anglo-French collaboration on all the "fronts," and in all the danger-zones. I understand that the question of requiring the Mufti of Jerusalem to leave French Mandated territory, and that of his future residence, are now under consideration by the French Government. [My italics.]

The reader will notice the resemblance of the position of the French administrators in the Sanjak and "Syria" who had dared to "show complacency to the local Arabs" to the situation of the British officers and administrators who had dared to show similar "complacency" towards the local Arabs eighteen years before in Palestine. The same sort of persons in Paris as in London, with the same sort of entry into Ministerial circles, made the same sort of representations, and at once the same prompt and serious consequences occurred for the French officials as for the British. The Acting-Governor was recalled just as though his name had been Gabriel or Waters-Taylor or Bols.

However, in "Syria" and the Sanjak the same clean sweep of opposition was not achieved as in Palestine. A fortnight later in the *Jewish Chronicle* the well-informed writer was obliged to speak his mind about it:

> "It is unfortunately true that some French officials have what are commonly described as 'reactionary tendencies.' In the Metropolis Ministers as a rule are able to check them, but this is not always the case with their representatives abroad, or in the colonies and mandated areas."

Here again is the perfect repetition between Paris and Syria, only more soberly described, of the 1919 contrast between London and Palestine, when the Zionist report said it was "impossible to reconcile the melancholy reports from Palestine with the cloudless benevolence pervading every Government office in London." Continuing,

> "The Alexandretta Sanjak and Syria are a case in point—a case which is almost incredible, yet well authenticated. I hear that the persistence with which the French civil and military authorities, more particularly the former, are daily flouting M. Bonnet's instructions, with the remark that "in Paris they don't understand the local situation in the Levant," is astonishing."
>
> Thus the Quai d'Orsay was able, on a Monday, to assure the Turkish Ambassador that it had ordered its subordinates in the Sanjak to do justice to the local Turks: but on the Tuesday Angora learned with amazement and indignation that the orders from Paris were being wholly disregarded by the "men on the spot." Even the French and the Turkish generals are constantly at loggerheads. The same influences, and not the French Government itself, account for the fact that the Mufti has not yet been deported to Madagascar, nor have the arsenals of the Arab bands which infest the Syro-Palestinian border been closed down.
>
> Lord Halifax might find it expedient to draw the French Government's attention to this aspect of the Palestine problem. But some of the officials of the Eastern Department of the Foreign Office are not free from a pro-Arab and anti-Jewish bias, resembling their French opposite numbers in this respect."

Despite these discouragements hopes for Turkish action against the Arabs stayed high. Mysterious messages appeared out of the blue in several European newspapers about developments of the "Turco-Syrian Question," though the origin of these messages was itself far more of a question. Geneva was the place of dispatch of one at any rate, published on the 27th of June in the *Daily Telegraph*, which no doubt saw no more in it than interesting news. Dealing with the subject of the Alexandretta Sanjak, this pointed out that the International Commission (the League of Nations Elections Board) had power to function only till the 15th of July, after which date its power of holding elections ceased.

> With this main obstructive point of difference between France and Turkey removed, the road would be clear to discuss some other form of mutual agreement, as France fully recognizes Turkish rights in the Sanjak.
>
> Actually, as the Mandatory Power, France is bound to resist any territorial aggression in her mandated countries, and, while there is no question of force in the present instance, it is interesting to note that the French Mandate for Syria, including the Sanjak of Alexandretta, expires at the end of 1939.
>
> Indications are that these territories are *almost certain to become an integral part of Turkey again*, but of a modernized Turkey, governed with vision and intelligence, incomparable with the old Ottoman Empire, and which will *develop the rich oil-resources* of the Djezereih, in north-east Syria, and also the deposits in the Sanjak of Alexandretta. [My italics.]

From whatever sources this information sprang, in it were to be seen chapter and verse of the expectations which ardent Zionists caressed. Syria would be invaded and become "an integral part of Turkey again." Arab independence—though a thousand times prescriptive and guaranteed by a hundred Covenants and treaties—would disappear for good in a welter of vision and intelligence and oil-resources.

In some quarters it seems to have been thought that this millennium was not far off. In later July at least Mr. J. M. Levy, a knowledgeable person, for he is the very active correspondent of the New York Times in Jerusalem, hastened northward to Angora and to Stamboul. He was able to record that negotiations for a Treaty of Friendship which were going on between Turkey and Arab "Syria" had broken down or, at least, had been adjourned till the autumn. Whether this suggested a crisis or not to him, he obtained an interview with M. Rushdy Aras on board the train between Angora and Stamboul, and his immediate query to M. Aras —unquoted in this country—was, "How soon before your troops march into Aleppo?"

The bubble of Zionist expectation was pricked by the Turkish Minister's reply. "Never, never," he insisted. "We do not want Aleppo nor any other part of Syria, even if it were made a present to us. I repeat again that we do not want to acquire any more territory. Turkey is twice the size of France and much undeveloped. We are busy repatriating Turkish citizens from the Balkans and other places. We need people, not territory."

This wise and admirable statement calmed Arab fears, which throughout Syria had been much stirred by the prospects raised by the Alexandretta situation. It did not perhaps dissipate them entirely, because the Arabs knew that in the border districts, where there were Turkish elements, there was always an opportunity for trouble-makers, since the most minor local squabbles there as in other parts of the world could always be enlarged to more than life-size. Still they no longer felt as apprehensive as they for long had been through the appearance in their Press of a great deal of disquieting matter of the type from which I have made some citations. Yet, if the Alexandretta threat had proved unsubstantial it was only because the Turks themselves were unwilling, and the Arabs remained conscious of the presence of the inimical forces which had hoped to enlist the Turks, and might most likely only consider their hopes as having suffered a set-back.

The manoeuvres, too, which centred round the Lebanon remained to disquiet them, and to fill their brethren in Palestine with indignation. The Zionist movement to obtain Galilee had been launched in the spring in London with every circumstance of importance. Dr. Weizmann and other chiefs of the Zionist Executive started the campaign with an appeal to the Zionists of the world to support an "Onto Galilee" fund. "Hitherto," it said, "the north has benefited only meagrely from the boon of Jewish creative effort."

But now strategic reasons involved a campaign for what was called "the redemption of Galilee" and produced a sudden re-evocation of Galilee's Jewish connections in the past. These strategic reasons were not concealed in the literature of the movement. "Safeguard the frontiers of Palestine," said a typical slogan amidst the announcements of the new drive for Galilee. Zionist settlements, it was made clear, were to be set down like strong-points along the frontier, so as to establish an occupation and to justify the handing-over of the province to the Zionist State. The Zionist Press gave details of the foundation of these fort-settlements in hostile territory. At Hanuta, the first of them on the northern frontier (this was in March) "the permanent buildings and *defence stockades* [my italics] at the village are rapidly being completed by the group in occupation."

"It is of paramount importance," continued the *Jewish Chronicle* when giving this information, "for a larger Jewish area to be established in Upper Galilee, where the Jewish agricultural community has been more or less static since the initiation of post-War colonization. The area of Jewish settlement will have to be taken into account by the authorities as a decisive factor in the formulation of any definite policy. Such colonization is necessary also from the point of view of the security of the existing Community."

The strategic character of Hanuta soon was endorsed by an attack upon it, in which one of its defenders was killed, and one of the assailants. Three hundred new "settlers" were sent up to this isolated position. They would have been better described as reinforcements.

On the eastern side of Galilee the drive had begun earlier, and M. Ussischkin, in London for the inaugural dinner of the "On to Galilee" fund, could state that "on the most easterly frontier of Palestine, in the Beisan district... twelve new settlements would save this area for the Jewish people when the question of boundaries came to be discussed in connection with Partition." It had been decided, he went on, by one of the soundest organizations in the Jewish world, the "Keren Kayemeth" (owning £7,000,000 of unmortgaged property and with an annual income of £400,000) "to purchase land on the northern frontier of Lebanon and Syria and to create there as soon as possible a whole series of new points of settlement."

All these new points of settlement mean another series of purchases over the heads of the Arab peasantry. The small Arab farmer, already in such dire straits for land that, by the testimony of the French Report the existence of the whole farmer class is imperilled, will perceive in North Galilee further tracts of his country being alienated for ever.

What can the Arab farmer do, or the entire Arab people of Palestine with its modest resources, when faced with great corporations disposing of incomes of £400,000 a year?

Whether the present Government will permit the establishment of these fort-settlements by these wealthy corporations, and will condone the progressive Zionization of Galilee through the coming year of 1939, we can but wait and observe.

There, at the close of 1938, the situation stands.

Chapter 40

Illegality of any solutions of the Palestine Question not granting independence to the Arabs. Impossibility and wrongfulness of any turning of Palestine into a Colony or Dominion. The question of our strategic needs in and round Palestine. The only settlement. The honour of Great Britain at stake.

The moment has arrived for summing-up, but of pure summing-up there is not much to be done. In the interests of Ministerial and politico-Zionist policy in Palestine, during the last twenty years offence upon offence against honour and against justice has been committed. But the reader has, as it were, seen the commission of them with his own eyes, and will not need any particular jogging of his memory to remind him of such vivid iniquities.

With regard to the future, with regard to Governmental proposals which may be made in the future, the situation is very simple. If they reverse the policy of the last twenty years and recognize the paramount rights of the Arabs over their native land, well and good. There will be time enough to discuss the details of Arab independent rule when it is in sight.

But if future proposals are based upon the old platform of the Balfour Declaration, of our false compacts and of the warped Mandate, then their inner details do not matter. It is of no importance what form they take, whether some species of Cantonization—which is little more than a pet-name for Partition—or any variation of the Mandate as at present conceived and carried out. Any of these will be morally wrong and based upon the premises of broken Covenant and Treaty.

What is to be avoided for the future is the attitude generally adopted by or forced upon the members of the Peel Commission. Their Report (to consider now its recommendations, not its general text) deserves to be studied a little for more than one reason. The Report, at its very beginning, on page 20, declares in reference to the Arab claims,

> We have not considered that our terms of reference required us to take the detailed and lengthy research among the documents of twenty

> years ago which would be needed for a full re-examination of this issue. We think it sufficient for the purposes of this Report to state that the British Government has never accepted the Arab case.

Now, in the first place, there could not be a re-examination of an issue which previously never had been examined at all. In the second place, since the Arab claims conditioned everything in Palestine, to pass them over was like holding a trial and leaving out the charge.

On page 107 of their Report the Commissioners themselves acknowledged that the "overriding or setting-aside of them [the Arab claims] was the main cause of the disturbances" into which they had to inquire. The Peel Report therefore was one which on purpose did not inquire into what it acknowledged was the main cause of its inquiry.

If future Governmental proposals or future Governmental Conferences, with whomsoever they may be conducted, are to be on such lines, they will be just as much failures, to use no other qualification, as the Peel Report was. If, on the contrary, they are to have any success, there will have to be a very different attitude observed in proposals or at Conferences towards the refusal of British Governments to accept the Arab case.

The situation would be different if the Governments implicated had produced any arguments against the Arab case in a neutral arena and had been held by an unbiassed and disinterested authority to have sustained these arguments. But the implicated British Governments have been extremely careful not to do anything of the sort. None of them ever has offered any evidence except to itself, and that was sixteen years ago when Mr. Churchill produced the testimony by which Damascus was three hundred and forty miles long.

From that day, British Governments have gone on and on repeating monotonously that their own opinion was the right one and prejudicating that this repetition kept the affair closed. Year after year they have offended against the first canon of fairness in human differences—that no man can be a judge in his own quarrel. Governmental behaviour has been just like that of the parrot in one of Logan Smith's adages:

> "What I say I say," I vociferate, as a parrot in the great cage of the world. I hop screeching, "What I say *is*," from perch to perch.

"What I say is," Churchill had screeched in 1922, with menacing erections of his feathers, and had given a verdict in his own favour upon his own evidence, judge, jury and witness in one.

If the Peel Commissioners found that sufficient for their Report, they may esteem their own Report as they please, but there is nothing else, nor will be, for which it is sufficient.

They also found sufficient for their Report another Governmental achievement towards which most certainly a severer attitude will have to be adopted. That was the author's manipulation of the word "can" in General Smuts's Article 22 of the Covenant. ("The ex-Turkish dominions have reached a stage of development where their existence as independent nations can be provisionally recognized.")

The Commissioners join him in making the word "can" what they call "permissive," i.e., the independence of the ex-Turkish countries may be recognized, but need not be recognized, though, admittedly, even by the terms of the perverted Article, the said countries had qualified for this recognition. The assurance to the Arabs of provisional independence as soon as they reached a stage which they had reached, could be met just as well by not giving them this independence as by giving it to them. Such is the argument.

The guarantee to the Arabs, in fact, was another of the Alice-in-Wonderland guarantees devised for them, with General Smuts this time in the role of the White Queen. "So I get independence now," said Alice to Queen Smuts. "No, dear," answered Queen Smuts, "you don't get independence. You qualify for it. You're always qualifying for it, dear, and never getting it. Isn't that a wonderful situation for a little Arab girl?"

This explanation, again, may have done for the Peel Report, but it will not do for the future of Palestine. Strangely enough, and I am glad to be able to recognize it, there are, however, some things in the Peel Report which are in contradiction to its own recommendations and to much else in the Report and serve as useful pointers for future policy.

It is by no means a meritless document, this unhappy Report. It is full of magnificently compiled information. There is little it does not tell about Palestine, some fifteen years too late. It is often splendidly written, and indeed its intolerable Partition recommendations somehow make upon the reader the impression of a hasty postscript not at all in the style of the letter to which it has been tacked on.

More than this, there are even moments when the Peel Report turns to the frankest confessions and might serve as an example not to shun, but to follow. It contains presentations of the most unpalatable realities. "The door forced open for the Jews in Palestine"; "It is the Mandate which created the antagonism between Jews and Arabs in Palestine"; "A free Palestine means an Arab State." The presence of such truths in it redeems the Report in notable degree, and leaves some wonder in the mind concerning the way in which it was compiled and, especially, was completed in London.

There are some other Reports, which in the way of guidance for the future, must be eschewed as much as unfortunately, in general trend, the Peel

Report must be. These are Reports of a kind, not official publications, but the recorded utterances of various public men whose pronouncements seem to call instinctively for a capital letter at their beginning. The burden of them is that the Palestine Question must be solved by the incorporation of Palestine as a Dominion, or even as a Crown Colony, in the Empire. Lord Snell, for example, during the Peers' debate on Partition, speaking of the prospective Jewish State, asked, "Is it to be thrust outside the British Commonwealth of Nations?" as though, save the mark, it existed and were inside.

The Dominion proposal generally mooted for all Palestine is an old one. Probably it has always figured in Zionist minds as an alternative to an independent republic, and probably it has always been a popular alternative. It gives all the advantages of independence together with all the advantages of being one of a powerful assemblage of States, and it holds the most dazzling prospects for establishing Zionism as a directing force in the councils of the Empire and of the world.

In February of last year, 1938, a deputation waited upon the Prime Minister in his private room in the House of Commons. This deputation consisted of Sir Archibald Sinclair, Mr. Herbert Morrison, Mr. Victor Cazalet and Mr. Josiah Wedgwood, the last of whom is a fiery Zionophile. He has long propagated the Zion-in-the-Empire theory in lectures and writings upon the "Seventh Dominion." The deputation expressed its concern to the Prime Minister at the trend of events in Palestine, and then came to the point of the visit. "It was impressed on the Prime Minister that, while Partition might not be the perfect solution, it would be very unwise of the Government to desert it after having supported a recommendation to this effect. At the same time the Deputation thought that the most practical solution would be the inclusion of Palestine in the British Commonwealth of Nations." (*Daily Mail.*)

It is odd that a party-leader, Sir Archibald Sinclair, and a prospective leader, Mr. Morrison, should have joined in making not alone such an unsound, but such an unfeasible proposal as this.

As for unsoundness, we all have just seen in Czechoslovakia what comes of incorporating populations in a State without inquiring as a preliminary whether they wish to be incorporated.

As for feasibility, putting aside the moral insecurity of the proposal, Palestine, it must be emphasized, could not be joined to the Empire by an act of any Government, still less by an act of our Government alone. The present control of Britain over Palestine is not a partial ownership, which could be transmuted into complete ownership by her, if she so wished.

She does not own Palestine in any way, and there are plenty of official acknowledgements and proofs of this, a number of which were quoted in earlier chapters. It will do here to recall Article 10 of the Mandate: "The extradition treaties in force between the Mandatory and other foreign Powers shall apply to Palestine." Even the Mandate defines Britain as a foreign Power in Palestine. What gives particular value to this particular definition is that the word "other" was specially inserted (cf. Chapter 32). This was one of the clauses of the Mandate which the Zionists did not draft, and I fancy it was through United States insistence that "other" was put in, to make the status of the Mandatory Power quite clear. In the first or Balfour version it had "guilelessly" been omitted.

In equity and in law Palestine belongs to its native people and to no one else, though its legal situation is curious. It was ceded by Turkey, not to Great Britain or to any one of her adversaries in the War, but to them all together, to all the Principal Allied and Associated Powers together.

The disposal of Palestine, in first resort, lay therefore in the hands of Great Britain, France, Japan, Italy and the United States. The consent of each and all of these countries always would have been necessary before Great Britain could have absorbed Palestine into her domains or Dominions. [Author's note: This stage of the situation is unaffected by the departure of Japan and Italy from the League of Nations. The cession of Palestine to the Allied Powers by Turkey was an act with which the League had not nor could have, any concern. The League only came on the scene, in respect of the Mandate, after the cession had occurred.]

But once the Mandate came into force, these Powers could not give this consent any longer. Before Turkey had ceded Palestine to them they renounced all rights of conquest and under the new regime of the Covenant established one of their number in Palestine as trustee-occupant on behalf of the inhabitants of the country.

The legal possessors of Palestine, therefore, are its people, though legally they are still in wardship. The most that the P.A.A.P. could do, were they to reassemble (and how?) their war-time combination, would be to change the trustee in Palestine, if they were unanimous upon this. The whole of them together, if they had the will, could not give Palestine to any one of them as his own possession. They would be like a group of legal trustees, if they met, administering the estate of their ward, Palestine, but quite unable to dispose of it and only enjoying temporary control of it till the ward took it over.

The implacable fact is that the Arabs own Palestine by natural right, and also by law. Nothing can surmount this. The various endeavours to surmount it, made in vain, have been recorded here. But I have not referred so far to what may be called the supreme endeavour to surmount it, the forlorn hope of all the supporters of the National Home. This is the statement made by Lord Milner in the House of Lords on the 27th of June, 1923. In this he asserted that Palestine could never be treated like other countries because it was the Holy Land. But let me give his exact words. He said (ignoring, of course, the legal position):

> If the Arabs go to the length of claiming Palestine as one of their countries in the same sense as Mesopotamia or Arabia proper is an Arab country, then I think they are flying in the face of facts, of all history, of all tradition, and of associations of the most important character—I had almost said, the most sacred character. Palestine can never be regarded as a country on the same footing as the other Arab countries. You cannot ignore all history and all tradition in this manner. You cannot ignore that this is the cradle of two of the great religions of the world. It is a sacred land to the Arab, but it is also a sacred land to the Jew and to the Christian; and the future of Palestine cannot possibly be left to be determined by the temporary impressions and feelings of the Arab majority of the present day.

It is a curious thing that some who have remained unimpressed by other Governmental pleas have seemed impressed by Lord Milner's grandiloquence. For that is all Lord Milner provides. Let us analyse what he has to say.

First of all, there are two separate things to consider:

1. The reasons for which Palestine cannot be regarded as upon the same footing as other Arab countries.
2. The way in which the special character of Palestine is honoured.

As regards the reasons which differentiate Palestine from other Arab countries, Lord Milner packed them all together, facts, history, tradition, sacred character, in an uninformative medley. But to put the situation exactly, Palestine is unlike other countries because in addition to a secular past, which every country possesses, Palestine has a sacred past such as no other country ever had or ever can have.

There is, obviously, a very vast difference between the character of these two pasts. The secular past of Palestine is a commonplace possession, since, as I have just said, every country possesses one. These secular pasts, however, vary in style and stature. The past of Denmark is not of the same kind as the past of Greece, nor that of Switzerland of the same order as that of England. In this varying range of bygone Palestine's secular past, the secular side (of the Jewish past which Milner had in mind) is one of the most trifling and least considerable that ever was. A moment's thought shows that if you abstract the writing of the Old Testament and the birth of

Christ amidst the Jews from their chronicle in Palestine, there is nothing left worth mention.

No great secular Jewish Empire ever existed in Palestine, no secular Jewish art, no secular Jewish civilization descended imperishably to mankind. In the secular order, Jewish Palestine, the tiny Jewish corners in Palestine, were never anything but the home of a few Judæan Afridis, wrangling together for their townlets. Everything that has come down to us from Jewish Palestine has been of sacred character, and its unique value springs from its sacred associations.

So that there can be no reasonable suggestion that Palestine should be treated unlike other countries because of its unique and extraordinary secular past. It had none, and even if it had had one, the possession of the greatest secular past has not invested any country in the world with a special character inhibiting in it usual political conditions.

When Lord Milner spoke of ignoring tradition and flying in the face of history, if he meant secular history and secular tradition he talked nonsense. It might well be said that all history only consists of the ignoring of history. Its whole subject-matter lies in the shift of nations and in changes of power altering traditional situations. The Normans ignored the traditions of the Saxons, the Romans scouted the facts of the Greeks, Washington flew in the face of George III.

Accordingly the only reason for which Palestine cannot be regarded as upon the same footing as other Arab countries is the reason supplied through its sacred past, through the production there of the Old Testament and through other sanctifying preludes leading to its divine insulation by the birth, life and death there of Our Lord. That being so, the question arises of how this difference of Palestine was honoured. What was the special regime with which it was invested because of this sacred past? If its sacred past demanded a special regime for Palestine, in what was this regime co-ordinated to Palestine's sacred past, as it must be, and attuned to it?

What Lord Milner proposed, and accomplished in fact, for he was a drafter of the Balfour Declaration and of the Mandate, was that the unique sanctity of Palestine received appropriate recognition through the Arabs' ownership of the land being abrogated by the introduction of the Zionists.

Could anything conceivably be more irrational, more unfit, less seemly than this? It was not a tribute but an offence to all that had been holy in Palestine. The Zionists were political Zionists, who rejected for themselves and for their institutions any religious warrant whatsoever. Whatever they made of Palestine would be as a national centre, as like as they could make it to the installations of Western nations. The marrow of their programme was that the Jews should be formed not as a religion but as a race. It was not because of their belief that they claimed the Holy Land, but because of their blood. Most of them had no belief. As one of them had said, the Bible was not their mandate, but the Mandate their bible.

Lord Milner's tribute to the character of Palestine, therefore, was to oust its inhabitants from ownership by obliging them to share their country, in the name of its holy past, with men who repudiated holy title-deeds. More than this, they even aimed at giving to the country that very self-same commonplace national political footing which he had declared to be unthinkable for it. To "determine the future" of Palestine in this way was not merely to fly in the face of its sacred character, it was to flout it with lip-homage, somewhat scandalously.

To return to the situation of today, as far as the Holy Places are concerned, the Arabs are as willing and as competent to keep them in respectful charge as anyone else. There are nearly a hundred thousand Christian Arabs, whose natural claims to be the guardians in particular of the Christian Holy Places never seem to have been considered by our politicians. There is not the faintest doubt that an Arab Government would give every possible guarantee of free access to the Holy Places and of their inviolability.

If some specialized situation were felt necessary for the holiest edifices, such as the Church of the Holy Sepulchre and the Church of the Nativity, there would not be any difficulty, I believe, in getting agreement to it. The unedifying jostling which certain Christian rivalries, particularly amid the minor sects, induce on occasions might very well be kept best in check by some tiny corps of international police, free of local affinities. Service in it might be an honour assumed at intervals by Christians of all nations.

But that the whole of towns such as Bethlehem and Nazareth should be isolated from the nation and given extraterritorial status of any kind seems really unreasonable. Faithful and believing Christians principally occupy them and cherish them. What call is there to place them in the control of any of the modern Erastian Powers, the best of whom only finds religious faith commendable and governs its own life by ethics?

The Jewish religious shrines, especially of course the Wailing Wall, would receive the same respect as the Christian, and could receive the same guarantees, under a National Government. The disturbances which have centred round the Wailing Wall have been entirely political, and once the offence of political Zionism was no longer to be feared, religious Zionism would be left at peace to carry out its age-old ceremonial. As for the Moslem Holy Places, they hardly will need protection in a predominantly Moslem land.

Next, from the religious security of Palestine, let me turn to a very different subject, its physical security. The military and naval situation of the country, at the head of the Suez Canal, is obviously of the first importance to us. This, it may be assumed, was the reason why Mr. Ormsby-Gore declared he was pursued by admirals when he was negotiating with Dr. Weizmann and was preparing to introduce the Partition proposal in Parliament in 1937.

There are signs in the findings of the Peel Report that the admirals in question caught their elusive prey. In the portion detailing the frontiers of the proposed States under Partition the Report says, on page 385,

> The use of that exit [the Red Sea] to the East might prove in course of time of great advantage to both Arab and Jewish trade and industry, and we understand that the construction of a railway down the Wadi Araba has been contemplated. Having regard to these possibilities we suggest that an enclave on the north-west coast of the Gulf of Akaba should be retained under Mandatory administration, and that the Arab Treaty should provide for the free transit of goods between the Jewish State and this enclave.

What is to be noted here is not so much the solicitude of the Peel Commissioners for trade and industry as the creation of a British mandatory enclave on the gulf of Akaba. The contemplated railway with its garrisoned terminus at Akaba presumably would carry some goods, but it would carry much more strategy. No doubt we must assume, since only commercial considerations guided the Commissioners in recommending this Akaba mandate, that its usefulness for military purposes, is just one of those fortunate coincidences which a kind Fate seems to reserve for us.

There is also a kindred prospect of which Mr. Belloc has written in his *Weekly Review*, where so much information appears which seems unable to find another outlet. On the 17th of March, 1938, he wrote therein:

> Again, all the world knows that we have been considering an alternative canal to the Suez, but nothing here, at home, has been printed on it. All that has been allowed to leak out in this country has been a vague word on the importance of Akaba. Meanwhile abroad there are detailed discussions on the whole affair and we can, from American sources, learn all about the special project of a canal starting from Haifa, following the depression between Galilee and Judæa, and then running along the sea-level contour west of the Dead Sea and so through to Akaba.

Railway project and canal project are in the same order of ideas, and there are road projects too, branching eastward over the desert to Irak and to the Persian Gulf and the waters of India. Plans for a railway from Haifa to Bagdad are docketed. In a general way it may be said that a short cut to India, less vulnerable than the narrow and too easily blocked Suez waterway, soon will be contrived, and probably not a single short cut only, in the arid lands between Palestine, Arabia and Irak. As for Haifa, besides its situation as the terminus of a future Bagdad railway and as a centre for air traffic, it is the port where the oil pipe-line from Mosul, arch-valuable for the oil-provisioning of our fleet, comes out to discharge.

The tremendous importance of Palestine and of the Palestine hinterland in quickly approaching days, if these days are not here already, is evident. It indeed has been evident for years now to those who must give their technical concern to such matters. But it has not been, to all appearance, a source of occupation to the minds of the politicians who have been in power. The policy they have pursued in Palestine has been senseless in most respects, but from the naval and military (and aerial) points of view it has been maniacal.

The primary principle of military security for vital routes, defence-points and strategical engineering works, is to have them in the midst of a contented countryside. Lord Swinton, in the course of the debate in the House of Lords upon the Peel proposals (21st of July, 1937) questioned upon the strategic side of them, answered that the advisers of the three Services found them acceptable under certain conditions, one of which was the signing of a treaty with the prospective Arab statelet. "But," he added, "they have laid stress too on this—the greatest security you can have is peace." That official avowal, however, was scarcely needed: the need of peace is self-evident. The first line of defence for defences themselves is the friendly population amidst which they are established.

We could have had absolute security of peace for our Empire defences in and around Palestine. At the close of the War we had the heaven-sent gift there of a concourse of people, the Arabs, who were our allies and were grateful to us for, as they thought, setting them free. Their interests marched identically with ours, and there was the immediate prospect of these parallel interests being drawn together into unity by a treaty. The Arabs would have asked no more of Providence than to have their forces trained by us and their ports manned and protected by us. This area of comradeship would have extended over great distances, just where it was most necessary for us, but where without goodwill penetration would have been slow and hazardous. All this we could have received for the mere asking for it, or in exchange for a simple continuation of friendship on our part and, no doubt, the provision of some necessary loans. This money would have been well spent and we should have been only too glad to provide it.

The opportunity not alone was missed by our rulers, or flung away. It was refused. The native population of the strategic areas was deliberately and progressively antagonized by the installation of the Zionists. The process could not be called anything but deliberate, since the warnings of soldiers and of administrators upon the spot were disregarded and indeed were treated as though they were a sort of contempt of court. Those who gave them were recalled home or made to resign for pointing out the danger.

There was a mad idea perhaps in the minds of those who started and continued this policy of antagonization, that the Zionists would provide a better bulwark to defend the Suez Canal and future military or semimilitary works than the native population. This idea was not current in 1919 and thereabouts; it was brought in later by way of justification for a policy which really had been adopted because of private bargains and foibles.

In fact, the supposedly superior bulwarks of the Empire, the Zionist immigrants, had no military history. They came from Eastern Europe and were of depressed, refugee stock for the most part. The younger and more active amidst them were of a turn of mind which looked unfavourably upon empires, and of Britain itself they knew nothing. No doubt we could count upon their gratitude for bringing them to Palestine, but that gratitude was tempered by their dissatisfaction when Palestine was not handed over to them lock, stock and barrel.

> The British Government, it should be remembered [says the Peel Report] is an alien Government to all but a tiny handful of the Jews in Palestine. Jews from Poland or Roumania or Germany may appreciate the difference between the British attitude to Jewry and that which they have experienced in the countries of their birth. All Jews, we were assured are grateful to Britain. But when Jews in Palestine are told that the Government's interest in the National Home is at the most half-hearted, their resentment is not softened by any sense of kinship with its British officers or any native loyalty to the British Crown.

Leaders of the get-Palestine-quick Zionist school have interpreted the governmental policy of getting Palestine for Zionism only by instalments as "half-hearted interest" to the younger ardent spirits amidst the immigrants, especially to those born in Palestine. So that the gratitude of the younger, more virile generation has been so much weakened. In a military crisis what in reality has been hoped of them was that, since no one else would support them but Britain, they would defend their holdings and a Ziono-British Palestine with the desperation of men whose only alternative to fighting was to be massacred.

Watered gratitude and prospective despair do not seem the most satisfactory animating spirit for a garrison, but that was how it has been reasoned in governmental circles. The policy of importing Zionists as defence-units, into the midst of a constantly increasing population constantly made more embittered, became the order of the day. It has persisted till now and has left us ingloriously engaged in warfare throughout Palestine.

It has also made any proper system of imperial defence at the most important strategic point of the Empire very difficult, and given to anything accomplished an underhand character which is completely odious. As a Mandatory, to repeat the point, we are not standing upon our own territory. Such defences as we may install on mandated soil honourably can only be such as the people of the Mandated area might need for their minor wants. We cannot saddle their land with the imperially-scaled defence works of our Empire, for it is quite clear that mandated peoples are not called upon to take part in the wars of their trustee. Their position may be a new one, owing to the novelty of the mandatory relationship, but there is no doubt about its character. We are foreigners in Palestine, and have not a jot of the claim there which native rulers have over their native and voluntary subjects.

Therefore to fortify Haifa and so forth, under the plea of the Mandate, but really for our own ends, is a spurious manoeuvre. It is to use once more the League of Nations as our creature, for the League, as the guardian of Mandates, has to connive at what we do. It makes a mockery of the whole Mandatory scheme; if there is anything left of the Mandatory scheme which is still unmocked.

This position is the more detestable to contemplate since if a just policy had been carried out in Palestine, none of these difficulties would have arisen nor any of these falsities have been needed. Even at this day, late as it is, a valuable and straightforward military and naval situation could be obtained with independent Arab Palestine, or Syria. An Arab Government would be satisfied still to be defended by Britain. We could take reasonable defensive measures, in Haifa and elsewhere, we could build our strategic railways and roads and fortify them, openly, by treaty with the Government of the country. I do not say that at the present moment we could expect the precious friendliness and intimate union with the Arabs which Mr. Lloyd George and Lord Balfour and the others destroyed. But we could have an understanding with them even now, and we could leave the restoration of the old comradeship to time, to that subordinate of time, the slow Briton, the Briton on the spot, and to some of those Arab leaders who at present are not permitted to re-enter their own country. They are willing enough to help, as I have heard from them myself over and over again.

The alternative, fortification and engineering works in sham Mandatory areas only means that we shall have an environing population hostile to each quay and to each girder and redoubt of a new, furtive, *sub rosa* defensive situation.

It will mean too that this hostility will spread from Palestine and the adjacent territory, first to every Arab and then to every Moslem in the

Near and the Middle and the Further East. The process has begun already, and there are interested third-parties only too anxious to hasten it. A little more of the abide-by-the-Mandate and do-our-duty-under-the-Balfour-Declaration policy, just a little more faithfulness to infidelity, and our natural-born, our ancient alliance with the Moslem world will take the road over the Moab hills and vanish in the desert.

Cries of anger and of rancour are to be expected naturally from the political Zionists in their many habitats, and from their supporters in many high places, if a policy of repentance and of understanding with the Arabs is undertaken at last. We must be prepared for this, particularly for all the influence which will be brought to bear against such a settlement by the Zionists of the United States, and even by deceived senators and other members of the Legislature and Government of that country. But as the true facts of the Palestine Question spread there this opposition will weaken and fade.

Contrary voices will rise too, supposedly on behalf of Geneva. We shall hear again about the selfless task imposed upon us in Palestine by the will of the peoples, but the invocations will not carry as they did before. The tired welkin, unable any longer to ring with hocus, will only tinkle them out.

Fifty-seven governments (or whatever the number is) were responsible for setting the political Zionists down in Palestine, were they? In what does that legitimize the Zionists' entry? By what criterion did the fifty-seven governments act? What terms of reference did they receive from the human race in this matter of Palestine? Was there one country canvassed in order to vote and to empower a representative to give his voice in favour of depriving the Arabs of their heritage? Not one. There never has been a vote in an area as wide as a hamlet, in any land, in favour of this.

If there had been such a vote, what would have been the lawfulness of taking it? What legal authority have the hamlets of Europe or the cities of America or the countries of the world over the Holy Land? Tyranny is not changed into democracy or into freedom when there are fifty-seven tyrants instead of one.

This trick of invoking the fifty-seven varieties in the League to give an air of justice to the baseness done in Palestine is one of the very worst features of the whole business. We have come to learn pretty exactly by now the role played by the smaller League nations in the mandatory plans of the Powers. At Versailles itself there was a species of mutiny amidst their representatives because they had to sign that treaty in the end before they knew really what was in it. It was a case for them of putting their signatures to the dotted line. Their copies of the text of the Treaty they received only afterwards.

In the matter of Palestine, ignorance of what they were doing was as great as at Versailles amidst the small nations, was rather worse since they joined to it indifference or complaisance. The reader has seen the behaviour of the "glass-faced flatterers" of the early Councils, at the call of Balfour, and of the still glassy personages found in the Mandates Commission ever since.

The sole effect of the League's connection with Palestine has been the discrediting of the League. This is a shame, since there are people inside the League who are more anxious than anyone for the Arabs to receive their rights. They have not prevailed against others in Geneva, who have been ready to sacrifice their own mother to please Powers who needed her good name for their purposes. But we may hope that the League will yet round on its traitors, and that the men and women in its ranks who perceive the role which has been imposed upon the League, will see that at last the Covenant is carried out genuinely in Palestine.

As far as I am concerned I have gratitude to express towards the League. The Secretariat in Geneva and the London office have tried with great patience and assiduity to satisfy various troublesome requests of mine for the purposes of this book. I am very grateful, and wish its members the reward of inscribing the first speech of a League delegate from the Arabs of Palestine upon their records.

There is not very much more to say. Perhaps it is as well to recall and to expose again the other falsetto cry which tinkles side by side with the appeal to the verdict of the Fifty-seven. "We must act impartially towards the two peoples of Palestine." Once and for all, there are not two peoples in Palestine. There is the Arab people there. The Zionists we have imported. In Palestine, when we came there, there was only an Arab population with a small Jewish colony in it. There were ninety-one Arabs for every nine Jews, and these were not political Zionists. We have imported some hundred thousand Zionists *to* Palestine, and our Zionophile politicians dishonestly speak of them as though they always had been there.

The state to which our policy has brought Palestine is hopeless for the Arabs and discreditable for us. We have encouraged the Zionists to buy up what should be Arab land, till today the Zionists hold three out of every ten acres of cultivable soil in the country, and what is still more important seven out of every ten acres of the best fertile land in the plains. All this has been acquired either over the heads of the population from absentee landlords or has been sold because the Arab vendors were in such poverty that they had no resource but to sell, in order to pay their taxes and meet their wartime debts. The Arabs are forbidden a Government of their own which would deal drastically with their indebtedness, and the taxes they have to pay are scandalously high because they are based upon a system of Administration which has to support the "National Home" and all its works. "Large industry in Palestine," says the Peel Report, "appears to depend upon manipulation of the tariff. The rest of the population is taxed in order that the proprietors of these industrial concerns may be in a position to pay the wages of their labourers and to make a profit for themselves."

The consequences of this system of high tariffs and taxes have been pointed out by Mr. Mansur, the Arab labour-leader, in an address he read before the Economic Reform Club in September last. While in French Syria the taxpayer, he showed, paid an average annual tax of £1 14s., in Iraq £1 12s., and in Egypt £2, in Palestine the taxpayer is called upon to pay £4 15s., far more than any two of the other national taxpayers pay together and not far short of the total payment of all three of them. This £4 15s. is an enormous, preposterous charge on the poverty-stricken peasants. Of the average Arab peasant family the Hope-Simpson Report states: "The balance available for personal expenditure of the whole household for a year is 18 shillings. This sum has to meet all luxury expenditure, including expenditure on the purchase of meat, and this for five or six persons."

The French Report showed that the Arab peasant-farmer—and nearly all Arabs are or wish to be peasant-farmers—was doomed, with so much of the cultivable land passed for ever out of Arab possession, unless perhaps intensive cultivation succeeded. (It was a big 'perhaps' in Mr. French's own mind.) Now this prospect of salvation, for what it was worth, depended upon the widest increase of irrigation. In Palestine there are but two rivers worth considering for irrigation, the Jordan and the Auja.

The reader has already seen that the revised charter of the Rutenberg Company reserves the water of the Jordan for that company's industrial uses, no peasant or proprietor being permitted from the date of its signature to divert this water on to his own land for irrigation or any other purpose, if thereby he reduces the quantity of water below the quantity required by the Company for its electrical works. This applies also to any affluents of the Jordan.

As for the smaller Auja, the Rutenberg Company holds the Auja concession, too. As far as irrigation goes, it "irrigates from it about 5000 dunams (1250 acres) and proposes to irrigate another 700 dunams (175 acres). It seems probable that the surplus of water remaining will be required for the water-supply of Tel-Aviv, as there is no other adequate source available." (Peel Report.)

Here therefore is the principal water-supply of Palestine, the only blood of its sapped agriculture, diverted for the industrial purposes of a Zionist company and for the supply of a swollen Zionist city. Outside the orange-districts, where there are artesian wells, boring the sub-soil has yielded nothing. In the hills, into which the Arabs are being more and more confined, there is no water to expect: "as regards land in the hill-districts, there is, unfortunately, very little chance of irrigation," said the Peel Commissioners, and thereon selected the waterless hills for their Arab national park.

That must do as an epitome of the economic condition and prospects of Palestine under our policy. It is not a side of this question into which I have entered at any length, and still less shall enter in these final pages, because even if our policy had been economically advantageous, it would have been none the less unjust and illegitimate. But it is worthwhile indicating how political dishonesty also has proved the worst economic policy. The Arabs are increasing at the rate of 24,000 a year, and what awaits them in the Palestine we have contrived

The fate of the Arab villager and the Arab pedlar, and the Arab worker at some old patient, beautiful craft which Zionist mass-production hastens to destroy, is matched by the fate of the educated man of talent. Under Ottoman rule an Arab might become a Grand Vizier: under Ziono-British rule the most he can become is a mayor. "After the partition of Syria the leading Palestine Arabs, conscious at least of some ruling capacity, found their ambitions henceforth confined to subordinate or municipal functions, with preference given to two foreign races, within a territory no larger than Wales." (Storrs.)

Political Zionism, in fact, which came to Palestine with so much talk of the great prosperity which it would confer upon the Arabs, instead of this has stopped any genuine Arab progress, by narrowing to nothing the opportunities of the higher-educated Arab to develop in his national atmosphere. Wherever an area of Palestine has passed into the ownership of one of the Zionist colonizing corporations, in that stretch of his country the Arab lawyer will never advise a client again, the Arab doctor never stand by a bedside, the Arab author will never write a book, the Arab builder never construct a house, the Arab candidate will never address his countrymen.

That is another final point to be recalled, therefore, and along with it a kindred point, the hollowness of the invitation extended by Zionist leaders to their "Arab cousins" to take common part with them in the development and progress of their common fatherland. The Arabs are welcomed to a progress, not Arabic, but alien; to a hybrid international progress, to Westernization and industrialism. It is a progress in which by his very nature the Arab cannot excel, which the Arab indeed to save his very nature must avoid. He could only succeed in it if he ceased to be an Arab and planned like a Jew, hoped like a Jew, ordered his life like a Jew, and in fact turned himself into a Jew. A Jew of the political Zionist kind, that is. The multitude of appeals to the Arabs to walk hand in hand into the future with the Zionists, under their experienced guidance, never have amounted to anything else but invitations to them to be present at their own dissolution.

A great writer who visited Jerusalem and often heard these appeals, when he came to write of his visit put them in their true light. I speak of Chesterton. Chesterton had kept in memory a typical declaration of Dr. Weizmann's that "The Arabs need us with our knowledge, our experience and our money." In his *The New Jerusalem*, addressing himself nominally to all Jews, but really to the Zionist coteries, he implored them, "Above all, I implore the Jews not to be content with assuring us again and again of their knowledge, their experience and their money. That is what people dread like a pestilence or an earthquake: their knowledge, their experience and their money... Men bar themselves in their houses when such visitors are abroad in the land."

"There is not," said Chesterton, "the slightest difficulty in stating in plain words what the Arabs fear in the Jews. They fear, in exact terms, their knowledge, their experience and their money. The Arabs fear exactly the three things which he [Dr. Weizmann] says they need."

I think that on the whole these are the truest, most enlightening, most potent and pointed words ever uttered upon the Palestine Question. They ought to be carried, emblazoned on a banner or printed a foot high upon a placard, into the House of Commons when next that Question is debated there.

Chesterton in that book of his spoke of another facet of this subject which no one dealing with it can omit. "It really seems to me," he wrote, "rather hard that the full storm of fury should have burst about the Jews at the very moment when some of them, at least, have felt the call of a far cleaner ideal (than those most often attributed to them by their enemies): and that when we have tolerated their tricks with our country, we should turn on them precisely when they seek in sincerity for their own."

This point, I think, will not be denied by any of the Zionists' critics. The Zionist idea of a return to the land and of establishing a polity wherein they will carry out all national work, from railway building to road sweeping, and so remove the reproach of parasitism which dogs them—that in itself is an idea which must arouse sympathy.

But all that was good in it was lost when it was put into execution by the political Zionists. Like everyone else returning to the land, they should have chosen a vacant plot, or chosen one which its sparse inhabitants were willing that they should occupy. Instead of this, they insisted on returning as owners to the Arabs' territory, upon the falsified plea which we know.

They refused the offer in East Africa, which was the right kind of opportunity. And in the Arabs' territory the largest crop which has sprung from their spades is Tel-Aviv.

The form which their "return to the land" has taken probably demonstrates better than anything else that the theory which inspired it, though it makes this appeal to sympathy, is after all not sound for the Jews. Those Zionists who have launched the theory so disastrously into practice have never backed it by any convincing argument. It is quite certain that the Jews as a whole cannot return to the land, nor return to a Jewish State.

There are millions too many of them to do so, even were it, which it is not, the desire of all of them. As much as they could have achieved would have been to found a sort of model of a country, a demonstration-plot of how they could till the land, a rather large agricultural exhibit.

There is no reason on earth to suppose that this would have reconciled that impenetrable antisemitism which is their bane wherever they are found. The antisemite, particularly the 10 percent antisemite who has an unsettled latent disapprobation of Jews rather than hatred of them and is the chief of their obstacles, is not the sort of man to be won round by it. The image of him turning and saying to his friends, and still more saying to himself, "Look at what the Jews have done in Palestine. It shows that it is not their fault if they do not do the same everywhere," is quite imaginary. Zionists may nourish it determinedly, and perhaps some other Jews, but they do not understand the nature of their opponents or detractors or whatever these latter are to be called.

The only people who ever would think and speak out like the suppositious converted antisemites of Zionist imagination are people who already think and speak like this. A certain number of men and women of a particular intellectual stamp are agreed in their own minds upon the effect of the Jews' disabilities and are convinced already that if the Jews had a small country of their own they would manage it as well as other nations manage theirs, better probably than some nations manage theirs. But this group is quite satisfied about the matter, and is quite willing to give the Jews credit for it, and to give them the treatment in life commensurate with this credit, without any demonstration of the Jews' capacity. No doubt most of those who think like this would wish to observe the capacity in practice, and for this reason they mostly are pro-Zionist, but the Jews would gain nothing from them by the demonstration. The intelligent persons would say to each other, at the end of it, "I told you so." The Jews, though, would not have won thereby a dozen adherents from antisemitism.

The rabid 100 percent antisemites would be moved by nothing. The 10 percent antisemites would disapprove more than before in their latent way, restive that the Jews in sight had not gone off to where other Jews were "making good." No doubt it would be nonsensical to entertain the notion of this departure, which a thought given to the size of Palestine would dispel. But the entertainment of notions in the mind without reason for them or any examination of them is the mental condition of vast numbers of people. It shows an entire absence of understanding of the Gentile public for the Jews, that is for the Zionist section of the Jews, to imagine that on the appearance of a Jewish State or enclave the public mind would be flooded with logical thought.

A Jewish State therefore, even though legitimately established, would do nothing to stem antisemitism. It would be much better if Jews and non-Jews would recognize that Jewry has another lot in the world than to create an ordinary State or any political foundation. Schopenhauer said that the fatherland of the Jews was the other Jews, and he was about right.

The condition of the "Diaspora" is treated as an unhappy accident suffered by them, but why should it not be recognized as something quite other, as their vocation? The Jews most manifestly have the quality of an essence, which requires to be distributed and disseminated. It can only be used to good purpose in solution, like some ingredient amalgamated into a thousand products of pharmacy, everywhere the same and yet everywhere different. In bulk it is overwhelming, useless and very possibly dangerous.

The Jews do not require intense localization to display the Jewish spirit: to display the Jewish soul in Palestine all they need is a tabernacle, not an administrative machine. It is to be observed that the greatest Jewish accomplishments sprang from them when they had little or no political situation at all.

> As we reach the end of the story of the Israelite monarchies [writes Professor Robinson] we must remember that in a very real sense the apparent ruin is but the beginning of her [Israel's] life, and that in the ages which followed the extinction of her political power she was the better able to give herself to the cultivation of those spiritual elements which made her in the long run the most influential nation in the ancient world.

It is a Jew himself, as it should be, Mr. Morris Jastrow, who in his *Zionism and the Future of Palestine,* best expounds the Jewish call:

> It is a fact of the utmost significance that the great contribution of the Jews to the world's spiritual treasury was made, not while the nation's life was flourishing, but while it was ebbing away. The prophets made their appearance when the southern kingdom was beginning to show symptoms of decline, and the movement reached its height after this

> kingdom had disappeared... The Hebrews disappeared. It was the Jews, as we should call the people after the Babylonian exile, who survived... The example of a people flourishing without a national background had to be furnished to the world to bring the new conception of religion to fruition, which divorced religion from nationality and made it solely the individual's expression of the individual's aspiration for the higher life and for communion with the source of all being.

At what a pole this is from the writings of the Zionists whose goal is a national hustings, crowned by the silk-hat of Dr. Weizmann as President elect. But if the Jews need no land of their own to be great and, like ever-travelling experts, to bring their special touch to this or that accomplishment of mankind the world over, Jews must have earth upon which to tread. We witness at the moment the efforts of certain nations to expel them from the soil on which they have lived so long. Europe is filled with Jewish exiles, in the real sense this time, and with Jewish refugees. They make a great problem for the remaining nations, but it is a problem for these nations within their own boundaries. It is their obvious duty to consider it at once and thoroughly, and to find place for the refugees in their territories.

It is not a problem for them to solve in Palestine. The nations concerned must not say that they cannot provide an asylum for the Jewish refugees because it would disturb their own social order, and then dispatch the refugees to Palestine to destroy the Arabs' social order. To hear, as one does at this moment, the continent of North America vociferating (though with a strong Zionist accent) that the only door open for the exiles (that is, Palestine) "must not be slammed" is to be treated to a first-class example of Pharisaism. The loud welcoming of Jewish refugees by Great Britain and by the United States to the Arabs' land cannot cease too soon.

Palestine is the Arabs' land. It is for them to decide its future. Their proposals for this have been repeated for years, in slightly varying forms, but all amounting to the same. At the time of writing they have recently been repeated by the Foreign Minister of Irak, and have incontinently been dubbed "the Irak Minister's new plan." That only shows how little attention has been paid ever to the Arabs of Palestine themselves. The Irak Minister's new plan is the Arab Higher Committee's old plan, and the plan of every Arab delegation which has visited Britain for twenty years. That plan is that:

1. Great Britain shall recognize the natural rights of the Arabs of Palestine and carry out her own treaty obligations by establishing in Palestine a national Government by universal suffrage.
2. The National Government of Palestine will make a Treaty with Great Britain upon the same lines as that made by

Irak with Great Britain. Under this treaty Palestine will guarantee to safeguard all the legitimate interests of Great Britain in her territorial area, as Egypt has done.

3. All the inhabitants of Palestine shall have equal political rights.
4. The Palestine Government will guarantee the rights of minorities.

Those are the fundamental lines of a settlement. There would be, of course, various consequences from them. Zionist immigration into Palestine would have to be subjected to the restrictions imposed by the national will. Zionists in Palestine would have to be content with what has to content all of us in the democratic countries, our rights as citizens. They would have to do what we all do, let the general policy of our country be determined by the desires of the majority. That must mean the end of industrialization in Palestine. Industrialization, with its attendant ills of unemployment, proletariatization, strikes, class-conflict and everything else which keeps the occidental world shaking in a perpetual ague of discord, cannot be scandalously and ridiculously imposed upon a country of Eastern peasants. Palestine, rid of its own physical malaria, will be even better rid of this, the moral malaria of the West.

Many matters will call for negotiation. It will be very hard for a national Government, with the country half ruined by the fight for independence, to balance its budget and to bring order at once out of the present wreck. Assistance will be needed by it, and provided that it is assistance in the strict sense Britain may expect to be called to provide it.

It is not to be expected that the settlement will be easy or swift. Twenty years of misgovernment are not to be cured in as many months. Palestine is shackled with Tel-Aviv, and what may be called Telavivery will not easily be weaned away. Most of the Zionist minority will not at all appreciate having to carry out their own nominal programme by forming part of a State devoted to agricultural small-holding. These and other such matters will give great opportunities to trouble-makers. We may expect in Jerusalem a Legislative Chamber for a while more filled with uproar than the old Austrian Reichsrath. The uproar will be still greater when Palestine is naturally absorbed into Syria, and the Chamber moves to Damascus. Minority rights will be presented as though they signified absolute autonomy, and the appeal of the Sudeten Germans will be made to the universe by Sudeten Zionists.

The difficulties of settlement in Palestine indeed are only too easily foreseen. No one in his senses would say that there was any wholly satisfactory solution to be envisaged there. That is the fault of Mr. Lloyd George and Lord Balfour and the political Zionists who between them engineered conditions beyond absolute remedy. It is said of architects sometimes that they have built for the generations, but these men ruined for the generations.

All we can do, and must do, is to see that any settlement is in accordance with the Arabs' rights. Justice, and not expediency of any kind, must guide us. We must avoid particularly false solutions based on forgiveness all round in Palestine, based on Arabs and Zionists and Britons being deemed as involved in a common misfortune and upon their all starting afresh, under some scheme which will be the old scheme disguised.

Forgiveness all round is, as a doctrine, only a label for forgiving ourselves. We are no victims of circumstances in Palestine along with the Arabs and the Jews. We made the circumstances: we, by the acts of our rulers, and we alone, are primarily responsible for the state of that country, and there must be no self-absolution proposed by us.

It was my lot in the summer of 1938 to hear Members of Parliament plead for a settlement on the principle that there had been mistakes "on all sides." There had been, they said, a tangle of conflicting pledges and the time had come to let bygones be bygones and to make a fresh start. The old gambit of the new start! On that occasion the new start was Partition, with Dr. Weizmann as starter. But it will be proposed again, no doubt, under another form and leading by some other turning back to the accustomed rut.

This sort of beginning again, like so many other things to which it has been necessary to refer, will not do. The voices which call out for the grudges and the mistakes of the past to be forgotten, and demand that bad memories shall be swept away, come, though their owners may not realize it, straight out of the dock. There is one person in the political as in the judicial forum who cannot propose a fresh start of this kind. It is the accused.

More than anything else we in Britain must keep clear in our minds today that we are the accused, and that the proofs of our guilt are only too clear. We may be pardoned—I hope and I believe that we shall be—but we cannot require pardon and we must not extend forgiveness to our victims.

This country of ours, of course, is great and powerful, and we may be able to impose for a while our will upon the Holy Land. We still are able to destroy, as it were, the whole legal situation, to bring tanks into the court, to batter down the dock in which we stand, and to emerge from it formally unconvicted. But if we do this, if we force our ownership or reimpose the old fraudulent Mandate upon this small and wronged country, we shall do ourselves as much harm as we shall do to Palestine. Not only shall we deprive the Arabs there of their birthright. We shall make away with England's own. To cover our own waste of honour we shall have foreclosed on the credit of our children and have squandered the goodwill of our fathers' names.

INDEX